DEPARTMENT OF HEALTH

PUBLIC HEALTH COMMON DATA SET
1993

INCORPORATING INDICATORS FROM

THE
HEALTH
OF THE NATION

ENGLAND

Volume II

Produced by the Institute of Public Health,
University of Surrey

Crown Copyright*

June 1994

ISBN 1852371366
ISSN 0968-9214
£48.50 net for Volumes I & II

ACKNOWLEDGEMENTS

The Public Health Common Data Set and many of *The Health of the Nation* indicators are derived from data provided by the Office of Population Censuses and Surveys (OPCS). The Department of Health and the Institute of Public Health appreciate the assistance of OPCS in making these data available.

The production of the Public Health Common Data Set and the publication of these volumes within tight deadlines present a unique challenge in terms of data analysis and presentation. The endeavour requires a multidisciplinary team of dedicated professionals working closely together. The Institute staff have developed these capabilities over the five years that we have produced the Data Set, and I would like to express my appreciation of the contribution to this national exercise of Veena Soni Raleigh and Victor Kiri, assisted by Charmaine Almond, Amanda Payne and support staff.

Professor R Balarajan
Institute of Public Health
University of Surrey

June 1994

CONTENTS

INTRODUCTION

Purpose of the 1993 National Volumes

The 1993 National Volumes provide a summary of selected indicators from the Public Health Common Data Set for 1993, including *Health of the Nation* target indicators and indicators derived from the 1991 census, made available to Regional and District Health Authorities and Family Health Services Authorities. They are intended to facilitate comparisons between Regions and Districts across England by:

- providing graphical presentations of geographic variation,
- tabulating the relative position of each area, and
- summarising local trends in mortality.

Material presented

The National Volumes for 1993 contain information drawn from the following releases of the data set:

- Public Health Common Data Set indicators for years up to 1992[1,2],
- *The Health of the Nation* target indicators[3],
- trend data for selected Public Health Common Data Set mortality indicators[4],
- trend data for *The Health of the Nation* mortality indicators[4], and
- the 1991 census supplement to the data set, containing summary indicators derived from the census[5].

The data presented here have been revised on the basis of the final population estimates rebased on the 1991 census (please see the note on Populations in the Introduction to Volume I), and these volumes provide the only hard copy version of this updated material.

There are two National Volumes for 1993. Volume I contains:
- **indicator definitions,**
- **maps** illustrating variation in the values of each indicator according to Regional and/or District Health Authority of residence,
- **maps** depicting the statistical significance of geographical variations in selected indicators,
- **scatterplots** showing District variation within each Region,
- **scatterplots** showing ratios of male:female rates for selected *Health of the Nation* mortality indicators, and
- **trend diagrams** presenting indicator values at the beginning and end of the time period examined, and the average annual rate of change.

Volume II comprises a tabular presentation of the graphical material in Volume I. Volume II also provides an indication of the relative position of each Region and District in terms of its rank orders for most indicators. In instances where more than one health authority has the same value for an indicator, all of them are assigned the same rank. For indicators where data are not available for the three Regions and ten Districts which involve cross-boundary mergers (ie abortions, and perinatal and infant mortality rates), the rank orders are based on the correspondingly reduced number of Regions/Districts.

For *The Health of the Nation* indicators Volume II includes the following for each Region and District:

- **the rate or percentage** as appropriate, the corresponding observed numbers, and the relative position of each area for most targets, and
- **trend data** for the mortality indicators (annual rates and observed numbers for each of the years 1984-92).

For Public Health Common Data Set indicators included in Volume I, the following are tabulated in Volume II for each Region and District:

- **the rate, ratio or percentage** as appropriate, the corresponding observed numbers, and the relative position of each area, and
- **trend data** for selected indicators (annual rates, ratios or percentages as appropriate and observed numbers for each of the years 1984-92).

For the 1991 census supplement indicators included in Volume I, the following are tabulated in Volume II for each Region and District:

- **the ratio or percentage** as appropriate, the corresponding observed numbers, and the relative position of each area.

The observed numbers on which rates, ratios and percentages are based should be used in interpreting the graphical material provided in Volume I, to ensure that the numbers are sufficiently large to support particular conclusions.

Data are presented for authorities on the basis of boundaries in April 1993. However, data on abortions, and perinatal and infant mortality rates (three year averages) are not available for the three Regions and ten Districts which involve cross-boundary mergers. This is indicated by hyphens in the corresponding tables. The **only** data based on boundaries in April 1992 are those relating to trends in the percent of live births in NHS hospitals (CDS - B5A), and trends in perinatal and infant mortality (CDS - C8A and CDS - C10A).

Definitions of the indicators selected for presentation in these volumes, details of the data and methods used for calculating them, a description of the graphical presentations provided, and addresses for enquiries, are given in Volume I. *The material presented in these volumes is based on final population estimates for the years 1982-92 based on the 1991 census released recently by the Office of Population Censuses and Surveys (OPCS), and hence may differ from figures released before December 1993.* For further details, please see the note on *Populations* in the Introduction to Volume I.

References

1. *Public Health Common Data Set 1993. Data definitions and user guide for computer files: Volume 1, Mortality data.* Produced by the Institute of Public Health, University of Surrey. Department of Health, July 1993.

2. *Public Health Common Data Set 1993. Data definitions and user guide for computer files: Volume 2, Demography, fertility, morbidity, and determinants of health.* Produced by the Institute of Public Health, University of Surrey. Department of Health, July 1993.

3. *Public Health Common Data Set 1993. Data definitions and user guide for computer files: Volume 5, Health of the Nation baseline and monitoring data (based on Census re-based population estimates).* Produced by OPCS. Department of Health, March 1994.

4. *Public Health Common Data Set 1993. Data definitions and user guide for computer files: Volume 4, Mortality trend data (based on census rebased population estimates).* Produced by the Institute of Public Health, University of Surrey. Department of Health, December 1993.

5. *Public Health Common Data Set 1993. Data definitions and user guide for computer files: Volume 3, 1991 Census supplement.* Produced by the Institute of Public Health, University of Surrey. Department of Health, October 1993.

THE HEALTH OF THE NATION

MONITORING DATA

HON - A1
Mortality rates from coronary heart disease (ICD 410-414) in persons under 65:
Age-standardised mortality rates per 100,000: average for the years 1990-92

		Males			Females			Persons		
		Observed	Rate	Rank	Observed	Rate	Rank	Observed	Rate	Rank
	ENGLAND AND WALES	53810	88.59		15456	24.17		69266	55.96	
O00	ENGLAND	50364	88.08		14403	23.96		64767	55.61	
A00	NORTHERN RHA	4349	113.02	14	1407	34.08	14	5756	72.81	14
B00	YORKSHIRE RHA	4303	99.11	11	1304	28.16	11	5607	62.94	11
C00	TRENT RHA	5483	95.39	10	1681	28.09	10	7164	61.45	10
D00	EAST ANGLIAN RHA	1732	69.37	3	419	15.80	2	2151	42.32	3
E00	NORTH WEST THAMES RHA	3050	76.39	6	772	19.16	5	3822	47.70	7
F00	NORTH EAST THAMES RHA	3610	84.26	8	996	22.32	8	4606	53.00	8
G00	SOUTH EAST THAMES RHA	3201	76.00	5	942	20.68	7	4143	47.65	6
H00	SOUTH WEST THAMES RHA	2424	69.36	2	575	15.41	1	2999	41.77	1
J00	WESSEX RHA	2791	75.15	4	681	17.19	4	3472	45.70	4
K00	OXFORD RHA	1961	67.34	1	462	15.94	3	2423	41.82	2
L00	SOUTH WESTERN RHA	3101	76.65	7	828	19.19	6	3929	47.32	5
M00	WEST MIDLANDS RHA	6097	94.49	9	1692	25.59	9	7789	60.00	9
N00	MERSEY RHA	3038	103.06	12	1056	33.10	13	4094	67.37	12
P00	NORTH WESTERN RHA	5224	111.29	13	1588	32.00	12	6812	71.11	13
A01	Hartlepool	125	108.45	109	47	38.35	134	172	72.86	119
A02	North Tees	251	116.64	125	83	36.12	129	334	75.99	125
A03	South Tees	409	117.19	127	140	38.23	133	549	77.35	132
A04	East Cumbria	214	90.28	83	65	26.44	84	279	57.89	83
A05	South Cumbria	192	86.54	72	56	23.89	75	248	54.50	71
A06	West Cumbria	197	111.85	118	58	31.05	108	255	70.94	114
A11	Northumberland	388	98.82	99	110	26.46	85	498	61.96	96
A12	Gateshead	325	123.10	136	110	39.56	139	435	80.72	137
A13	Newcastle	388	126.82	140	119	35.07	128	507	79.22	136
A14	North Tyneside	272	111.02	115	70	25.59	81	342	66.90	104
A15	South Tyneside	233	116.22	123	75	34.10	123	308	74.19	121
A16	Sunderland	450	124.86	138	162	41.50	141	612	82.24	139
A30	North Durham	479	116.90	126	169	38.37	135	648	77.10	129
A31	South Durham	426	120.77	133	143	37.71	132	569	78.56	134
B11	East Riding	595	94.87	92	162	23.86	74	757	58.68	87
B16	Grimsby and Scunthorpe	492	110.49	114	138	30.32	104	630	70.18	111
B21	North Yorkshire	720	80.38	51	214	21.70	64	934	50.33	56
B31	Bradford	602	116.54	124	185	33.45	120	787	74.10	120
B51	West Yorkshire	702	107.51	105	211	30.79	107	913	68.41	107
B61	Leeds	785	94.89	93	262	29.27	101	1047	61.30	94
B71	Wakefield	407	108.05	107	132	33.76	122	539	70.28	112
C01	North Derbyshire	466	98.00	97	145	29.05	99	611	63.02	97
C02	Southern Derbyshire	626	94.20	90	186	27.69	93	812	61.03	93
C03	Leicestershire	912	87.34	74	289	26.77	88	1201	57.01	80
C04	North Lincolnshire	348	96.00	94	100	26.50	86	448	60.71	92
C05	South Lincolnshire	365	88.10	76	100	22.73	69	465	55.02	73

Mortality rates from coronary heart disease (ICD 410-414) in persons under 65:
Age-standardised mortality rates per 100,000: average for the years 1990-92

		Males			Females			Persons		
		Observed	Rate	Rank	Observed	Rate	Rank	Observed	Rate	Rank
C08	Nottingham	674	91.27	84	206	27.11	91	880	58.91	88
C09	Barnsley	300	109.61	111	135	45.77	144	435	77.08	128
C10	Doncaster	318	88.17	77	121	31.37	112	439	59.33	90
C11	Rotherham	346	113.67	119	96	30.69	105	442	71.74	116
C12	Sheffield	661	108.06	108	186	28.43	96	847	67.60	105
C14	North Nottinghamshire	467	93.54	88	117	23.36	72	584	58.41	85
D01	Cambridge	165	51.73	1	37	11.48	1	202	31.57	1
D05	North West Anglia	436	87.31	73	113	21.16	61	549	53.84	66
D06	Norwich	405	65.97	15	97	14.38	10	502	39.77	14
D07	Great Yarmouth and Waveney	187	74.61	41	44	16.46	29	231	44.67	36
D09	Huntingdon	84	59.14	5	20	13.94	6	104	36.98	5
D11	Suffolk	455	67.95	20	108	15.30	18	563	41.49	21
E01	North Bedfordshire	208	71.84	34	49	17.18	37	257	44.70	37
E02	South Bedfordshire	296	91.93	86	51	16.91	34	347	55.49	75
E05	North West Hertfordshire	180	55.10	2	58	17.78	41	238	36.37	4
E06	South West Hertfordshire	202	69.19	22	51	16.31	28	253	42.44	23
E07	Barnet	255	79.03	46	67	19.30	49	322	48.19	48
E09	Hillingdon	216	79.21	47	57	20.09	54	273	49.48	52
E18	East and North Hertfordshire	407	68.08	21	100	16.29	27	507	42.07	22
E19	Brent and Harrow	415	81.72	56	115	22.44	67	530	51.88	61
E20	Ealing, Hammersmith and Hounslow	606	88.50	79	166	24.46	76	772	56.43	78
E21	Kensington, Chelsea and Westminster	265	70.52	29	58	15.50	22	323	43.23	28
F31	North Essex	732	69.82	24	210	18.92	48	942	44.18	35
F32	South Essex	665	80.94	54	173	19.72	51	838	49.81	53
F33	Barking and Havering	383	82.03	59	107	20.73	60	490	50.38	57
F34	Redbridge and Waltham Forest	407	84.10	68	127	25.20	80	534	54.22	68
F35	East London and the City	651	111.31	116	185	32.68	117	836	72.56	118
F36	New River District	414	81.39	55	128	24.82	79	542	52.92	64
F37	Camden and Islington	358	97.26	96	66	17.42	38	424	57.08	81
G04	South East Kent	212	65.55	14	65	18.10	45	277	41.35	20
G05	Canterbury and Thanet	299	85.43	69	92	22.70	68	391	52.52	63
G06	Dartford and Gravesham	230	81.96	58	55	18.66	47	285	50.10	54
G07	Maidstone	152	61.93	9	36	14.64	13	188	38.37	8
G08	Medway	320	85.60	70	101	27.06	90	421	56.43	78
G09	Tunbridge Wells	158	61.93	9	45	16.09	26	203	38.37	8
G10	Bexley	183	70.00	26	49	17.88	44	232	43.59	32
G11	Greenwich	186	83.58	63	62	26.59	87	248	54.50	71
G12	Bromley	243	66.40	17	62	14.77	14	305	39.84	15
G21	East Sussex	542	66.61	18	153	16.70	33	695	40.36	17
G26	South East London	676	94.73	91	222	29.64	102	898	61.63	95

3

HON - A1

Mortality rates from coronary heart disease (ICD 410-414) in persons under 65:
Age-standardised mortality rates per 100,000: average for the years 1990-92

		Males Observed	Rate	Rank	Females Observed	Rate	Rank	Persons Observed	Rate	Rank
H04	Mid Surrey	127	56.18	3	35	14.58	12	162	34.95	3
H05	East Surrey	173	71.14	31	39	15.15	17	212	42.90	25
H06	Chichester	133	58.56	4	35	13.73	3	168	34.80	2
H07	Mid Downs	211	62.69	11	56	15.71	24	267	38.72	10
H08	Worthing	206	71.13	30	48	14.16	9	254	41.03	18
H09	Croydon	288	79.97	50	59	15.45	21	347	47.10	43
H12	Wandsworth	182	100.40	101	51	27.28	92	233	63.60	100
H13	Merton and Sutton	286	74.42	39	58	14.07	8	344	43.39	31
H14	North West Surrey	312	63.88	13	71	14.48	11	383	39.24	13
H15	South West Surrey	177	59.79	7	48	15.39	19	225	37.13	6
H16	Kingston and Richmond	329	71.52	33	75	15.09	16	404	42.63	24
J10	Dorset	542	66.32	16	129	13.87	5	671	38.97	12
J21	Portsmouth and South East Hampshire	521	83.96	67	131	19.92	53	652	51.42	58
J22	Southampton and South West Hampshire	417	81.88	57	91	16.99	35	508	49.03	51
J23	Winchester	197	73.06	35	36	13.08	2	233	43.17	27
J24	Basingstoke and North Hampshire	319	76.74	45	73	18.47	46	392	48.09	47
J31	Salisbury	99	60.90	8	34	20.19	56	133	40.19	16
J32	Swindon	228	83.93	66	65	23.64	73	293	53.88	67
J33	Bath	343	69.98	25	89	17.00	36	432	43.13	26
J41	Isle of Wight	125	79.49	48	33	17.49	39	158	47.11	44
K11	East Berkshire	320	74.13	37	69	15.88	25	389	45.05	38
K12	West Berkshire	351	67.51	19	70	13.83	4	421	41.11	19
K24	Buckinghamshire	441	63.11	12	96	14.05	7	537	38.80	11
K31	Kettering	229	74.52	40	73	22.78	70	302	48.58	49
K32	Northampton	262	74.24	38	55	15.55	23	317	45.11	39
K41	Oxfordshire	358	59.48	6	99	16.52	30	457	38.13	7
L10	Bristol and District	817	83.63	64	205	20.10	55	1022	51.63	59
L21	Cornwall and Isles of Scilly	472	75.68	43	119	17.78	41	591	46.00	41
L35	Exeter and North Devon	403	70.23	28	111	17.87	43	514	43.24	29
L36	Plymouth and Torbay	585	83.82	65	166	21.88	65	751	51.97	62
L40	Gloucestershire	457	69.53	23	134	19.61	50	591	44.17	34
L51	Somerset	367	71.36	32	93	16.60	32	460	43.26	30
M02	Herefordshire	154	73.26	36	34	15.41	20	188	43.96	33
M04	Worcester and District	254	80.43	52	57	17.77	40	311	48.74	50
M05	Shropshire	424	83.13	62	107	20.56	58	531	51.81	60
M06	Mid Staffordshire	357	89.34	81	86	21.46	63	443	55.48	74
M07	North Staffordshire	667	113.78	120	177	28.36	95	844	70.73	113
M08	South East Staffordshire	301	93.78	89	65	20.58	59	366	57.56	82
M13	East Birmingham	251	114.42	121	78	34.52	125	329	74.79	122
M14	North Birmingham	187	90.21	82	49	22.16	66	236	55.97	76
M16	West Birmingham	295	131.56	143	70	31.22	111	365	82.29	140
M17	Coventry	308	88.03	75	103	28.82	98	411	58.11	84

HON - A1
Mortality rates from coronary heart disease (ICD 410-414) in persons under 65:
Age-standardised mortality rates per 100,000: average for the years 1990-92

		Males			Females			Persons		
		Observed	Rate	Rank	Observed	Rate	Rank	Observed	Rate	Rank
M18	Dudley	333	82.69	60	106	26.03	83	439	54.45	70
M19	Sandwell	398	108.76	110	111	29.10	100	509	68.86	109
M20	Solihull	210	79.72	49	42	15.05	15	252	46.91	42
M21	Walsall	399	117.33	128	119	34.94	127	518	76.17	126
M22	Wolverhampton	333	109.93	113	110	33.63	121	443	71.82	117
M25	South Birmingham	524	111.40	117	150	31.42	113	674	71.28	115
M26	North Worcestershire	233	70.07	27	72	21.28	62	305	45.80	40
M28	Warwickshire	469	75.63	42	156	24.54	78	625	50.14	55
N11	Chester	209	92.50	87	71	29.89	103	280	60.67	91
N12	Crewe	274	86.52	71	108	31.80	115	382	59.03	89
N13	Halton	164	98.72	98	52	30.71	106	216	64.43	101
N14	Macclesfield	184	76.20	44	49	19.87	52	233	47.74	46
N15	Warrington	218	96.78	95	83	36.63	130	301	66.80	103
N21	Liverpool	682	124.85	137	267	44.15	143	949	83.45	141
N31	St Helens and Knowsley	477	116.11	122	178	39.73	140	655	77.11	130
N41	Southport and Formby	125	80.87	53	29	16.58	31	154	47.35	45
N42	South Sefton	274	121.91	135	79	31.56	114	353	75.36	124
N51	Wirral	431	100.28	100	140	28.46	97	571	63.16	98
P01	Lancaster	158	101.15	102	50	27.96	94	208	63.53	99
P02	Blackpool,Wyre and Fylde	475	109.74	112	114	23.12	71	589	64.87	102
P03	Preston	177	118.35	129	56	37.03	131	233	77.71	133
P04	Blackburn, Hyndburn and Ribble Valley	328	105.12	104	106	32.15	116	434	68.43	108
P05	Burnley, Pendle and Rossendale	332	120.85	134	121	42.64	142	453	81.34	138
P06	West Lancashire	120	88.44	78	34	24.49	77	154	56.14	77
P07	Chorley and South Ribble	199	82.95	61	63	25.83	82	262	54.23	69
P08	Bolton	361	120.17	130	120	38.64	136	481	78.96	135
P09	Bury	252	120.21	131	67	31.21	109	319	75.08	123
P10	North Manchester	206	136.13	144	65	39.50	138	271	88.07	144
P11	Central Manchester	153	130.01	141	45	38.66	137	198	85.49	142
P12	South Manchester	218	124.97	139	65	32.89	118	283	77.12	131
P13	Oldham	301	120.65	132	90	34.22	124	391	76.99	127
P14	Rochdale	318	130.58	142	124	48.23	145	442	88.83	145
P15	Salford	374	138.54	145	100	34.87	126	474	86.01	143
P16	Stockport	315	88.64	80	78	20.41	57	393	53.83	65
P17	Tameside and Glossop	310	107.62	106	99	33.31	119	409	70.09	110
P18	Trafford	240	91.58	85	74	26.80	89	314	58.41	85
P19	Wigan	387	104.99	103	117	31.21	109	504	68.02	106

HON - A2

Mortality rates from coronary heart disease (ICD 410-414) in persons aged 65-74:
Age-standardised mortality rates per 100,000: average for the years 1990-92

		Males			Females			Persons		
		Observed	Rate	Rank	Observed	Rate	Rank	Observed	Rate	Rank
	ENGLAND AND WALES	77434	1270.04		41792	550.14		119226	872.67	
O00	ENGLAND	72108	1261.88		38983	547.61		111091	867.66	
A00	NORTHERN RHA	5979	1544.43	14	3679	760.68	14	9658	1110.47	14
B00	YORKSHIRE RHA	6265	1434.08	12	3582	658.64	11	9847	1005.68	12
C00	TRENT RHA	7919	1332.06	9	4291	605.33	10	12210	938.75	10
D00	EAST ANGLIAN RHA	2959	1095.43	3	1408	437.54	4	4367	740.36	4
E00	NORTH WEST THAMES RHA	3878	1096.55	4	1992	456.74	5	5870	745.96	6
F00	NORTH EAST THAMES RHA	5050	1213.51	8	2564	498.31	8	7614	819.75	8
G00	SOUTH EAST THAMES RHA	4914	1105.14	6	2609	457.33	6	7523	742.67	5
H00	SOUTH WEST THAMES RHA	3485	1019.51	1	1829	411.76	1	5314	677.51	1
J00	WESSEX RHA	4328	1099.06	5	2128	429.74	3	6456	729.00	3
K00	OXFORD RHA	2743	1071.85	2	1320	426.26	2	4063	720.36	2
L00	SOUTH WESTERN RHA	5085	1145.96	7	2543	457.51	7	7628	765.24	7
M00	WEST MIDLANDS RHA	8507	1350.64	10	4439	572.41	9	12946	923.02	9
N00	MERSEY RHA	3979	1428.52	11	2407	667.13	12	6386	1000.23	11
P00	NORTH WESTERN RHA	7017	1498.02	13	4192	697.25	13	11209	1050.82	13
A01	Hartlepool	169	1546.47	127	87	652.06	101	256	1051.86	113
A02	North Tees	302	1592.12	134	178	762.67	130	480	1135.30	133
A03	South Tees	500	1487.57	114	360	860.99	142	860	1143.05	134
A04	East Cumbria	341	1437.70	106	177	603.70	94	518	977.40	98
A05	South Cumbria	306	1308.35	81	167	549.57	76	473	885.99	79
A06	West Cumbria	288	1669.41	139	165	765.17	131	453	1168.72	137
A11	Northumberland	573	1390.58	97	331	678.35	110	904	1004.97	107
A12	Gateshead	467	1789.63	145	292	871.76	143	759	1278.40	145
A13	Newcastle	515	1522.97	120	300	681.91	114	815	1049.76	112
A14	North Tyneside	422	1582.80	133	228	660.78	102	650	1063.33	117
A15	South Tyneside	336	1535.79	125	231	832.81	138	567	1145.64	135
A16	Sunderland	582	1741.30	144	359	851.45	141	941	1245.29	143
A30	North Durham	621	1567.54	128	437	907.67	145	1058	1205.95	142
A31	South Durham	557	1525.99	122	367	815.56	137	924	1131.13	132
B11	East Riding	891	1403.26	100	493	620.39	96	1384	969.43	94
B16	Grimsby and Scunthorpe	667	1501.95	116	361	678.09	109	1028	1056.11	114
B21	North Yorkshire	1183	1278.84	76	629	552.70	78	1812	878.50	77
B31	Bradford	756	1476.75	112	464	729.67	124	1220	1063.31	116
B51	West Yorkshire	985	1510.37	117	628	746.33	126	1613	1081.79	122
B61	Leeds	1216	1465.59	110	662	636.43	98	1878	1007.72	108
B71	Wakefield	567	1528.93	123	345	754.53	127	912	1103.12	127
C01	North Derbyshire	653	1310.18	82	326	546.52	75	979	897.12	81
C02	Southern Derbyshire	953	1397.25	99	487	599.21	90	1440	965.85	93
C03	Leicestershire	1190	1171.61	52	619	520.31	66	1809	821.81	63
C04	North Lincolnshire	562	1386.74	95	260	549.58	77	822	938.95	86
C05	South Lincolnshire	636	1379.69	91	317	592.98	89	953	959.53	92

HON - A2
Mortality rates from coronary heart disease (ICD 410-414) in persons aged 65-74:
Age-standardised mortality rates per 100,000: average for the years 1990-92

		Males			Females			Persons		
		Observed	Rate	Rank	Observed	Rate	Rank	Observed	Rate	Rank
C08	Nottingham	939	1245.31	69	476	533.70	70	1415	860.70	73
C09	Barnsley	492	1729.25	143	299	873.96	144	791	1268.21	144
C10	Doncaster	457	1241.41	66	288	678.76	112	745	939.85	88
C11	Rotherham	456	1517.73	118	283	769.80	132	739	1107.80	128
C12	Sheffield	941	1379.51	90	600	684.29	116	1541	991.10	103
C14	North Nottinghamshire	640	1291.10	78	336	576.51	84	976	905.48	83
D01	Cambridge	315	1005.67	12	161	422.63	26	476	687.89	12
D05	North West Anglia	623	1141.94	46	294	466.14	43	917	782.26	51
D06	Norwich	766	1079.61	30	328	391.94	11	1094	710.09	20
D07	Great Yarmouth and Waveney	345	1114.32	35	191	517.12	64	536	792.76	52
D09	Huntingdon	112	916.29	4	84	581.36	85	196	733.22	32
D11	Suffolk	798	1137.80	44	350	408.67	19	1148	740.44	37
E01	North Bedfordshire	313	1200.52	62	148	484.87	51	461	816.08	60
E02	South Bedfordshire	295	1124.53	39	162	541.43	72	457	815.64	59
E05	North West Hertfordshire	296	1021.74	16	140	405.53	17	436	689.91	13
E06	South West Hertfordshire	305	1062.18	23	167	471.55	47	472	739.40	35
E07	Barnet	349	1102.11	33	162	388.99	9	511	698.80	16
E09	Hillingdon	281	1120.67	37	137	429.32	27	418	737.85	33
E18	East and North Hertfordshire	539	1023.19	17	304	480.48	50	843	728.99	29
E19	Brent and Harrow	440	1044.40	19	231	438.51	32	671	710.85	22
E20	Ealing, Hammersmith and Hounslow	766	1277.68	75	383	506.86	58	1149	852.10	69
E21	Kensington, Chelsea and Westminster	294	911.67	3	158	389.18	10	452	621.20	4
F31	North Essex	1193	1130.87	41	578	445.62	36	1771	753.79	40
F32	South Essex	979	1200.80	63	488	478.64	49	1467	802.26	53
F33	Barking and Havering	618	1263.01	71	327	540.21	71	945	863.29	74
F34	Redbridge and Waltham Forest	636	1357.73	86	310	515.41	62	946	888.54	80
F35	East London and the City	749	1371.98	88	359	569.06	83	1108	942.41	89
F36	New River District	525	1190.02	59	282	506.11	57	807	809.64	56
F37	Camden and Islington	350	1010.81	13	220	508.49	59	570	733.14	31
G04	South East Kent	394	1071.89	26	206	435.47	31	600	715.57	23
G05	Canterbury and Thanet	527	1133.83	42	279	475.30	48	806	766.06	44
G06	Dartford and Gravesham	245	1020.09	15	161	545.00	74	406	760.46	42
G07	Maidstone	224	1058.28	21	142	542.14	73	366	773.79	47
G08	Medway	396	1181.04	57	240	567.69	81	636	839.77	68
G09	Tunbridge Wells	277	1162.62	48	129	422.18	25	406	748.93	39
G10	Bexley	240	996.07	11	139	463.16	41	379	699.08	17
G11	Greenwich	292	1268.88	73	151	487.59	53	443	822.44	64
G12	Bromley	350	973.26	9	160	348.00	2	510	624.18	5
G21	East Sussex	1086	1037.19	18	506	359.02	4	1592	649.82	9
G26	South East London	883	1239.55	65	496	564.72	80	1379	869.40	75

Mortality rates from coronary heart disease (ICD 410-414) in persons aged 65-74:
Age-standardised mortality rates per 100,000: average for the years 1990-92

		Males			Females			Persons		
		Observed	Rate	Rank	Observed	Rate	Rank	Observed	Rate	Rank
H04	Mid Surrey	213	968.23	8	102	371.57	6	315	639.68	6
H05	East Surrey	238	1059.42	22	125	448.79	39	363	721.08	26
H06	Chichester	238	812.25	1	139	362.65	5	377	557.24	1
H07	Mid Downs	324	1046.12	20	166	429.51	28	490	705.85	18
H08	Worthing	419	1074.29	28	226	418.21	22	645	693.92	15
H09	Croydon	352	1138.42	45	166	419.63	23	518	732.99	30
H12	Wandsworth	193	1200.29	61	108	517.01	63	301	818.04	61
H13	Merton and Sutton	400	1116.65	36	221	464.37	42	621	745.58	38
H14	North West Surrey	391	940.75	7	201	398.68	14	592	645.22	7
H15	South West Surrey	248	898.32	2	124	348.65	3	372	590.18	2
H16	Kingston and Richmond	469	1019.78	14	251	394.30	12	720	660.39	10
J10	Dorset	1037	989.88	10	532	403.58	16	1569	665.86	11
J21	Portsmouth and South East Hampshire	721	1152.96	47	369	459.27	40	1090	764.01	43
J22	Southampton and South West Hampshire	601	1073.00	27	289	416.55	21	890	710.61	21
J23	Winchester	279	1170.85	50	144	466.63	44	423	775.66	48
J24	Basingstoke and North Hampshire	379	1163.27	49	156	385.49	8	535	738.06	34
J31	Salisbury	179	1066.75	24	85	395.37	13	264	693.73	14
J32	Swindon	328	1267.02	72	151	498.42	55	479	853.69	70
J33	Bath	551	1075.49	29	283	442.98	34	834	727.47	28
J41	Isle of Wight	253	1249.84	70	119	445.82	37	372	802.37	54
K11	East Berkshire	457	1233.01	64	229	510.53	60	686	836.73	67
K12	West Berkshire	385	922.91	5	172	330.61	1	557	599.41	3
K24	Buckinghamshire	616	1094.33	31	274	405.84	18	890	720.78	25
K31	Kettering	364	1181.64	58	186	496.55	54	550	810.34	57
K32	Northampton	406	1171.93	53	185	446.97	38	591	778.05	49
K41	Oxfordshire	515	929.09	6	274	411.49	20	789	647.73	8
L10	Bristol and District	1161	1172.64	54	651	521.95	68	1812	811.41	58
L21	Cornwall and Isles of Scilly	813	1177.86	56	374	438.66	33	1187	771.33	45
L35	Exeter and North Devon	759	1124.33	38	341	401.83	15	1100	725.47	27
L36	Plymouth and Torbay	932	1171.32	51	476	468.64	45	1408	780.62	50
L40	Gloucestershire	786	1134.29	43	382	445.01	35	1168	754.75	41
L51	Somerset	634	1069.82	25	319	433.29	30	953	717.69	24
M02	Herefordshire	255	1103.87	34	102	375.40	7	357	709.98	19
M04	Worcester and District	362	1126.27	40	168	420.78	24	530	739.56	36
M05	Shropshire	628	1284.47	77	308	510.82	61	936	858.84	72
M06	Mid Staffordshire	448	1303.91	79	244	592.84	88	692	918.44	84
M07	North Staffordshire	989	1646.96	138	449	612.08	95	1438	1077.57	120
M08	South East Staffordshire	360	1343.01	85	218	666.99	104	578	974.76	96
M13	East Birmingham	369	1462.03	108	219	671.05	106	588	1021.16	109
M14	North Birmingham	256	1318.56	83	135	532.76	69	391	871.29	76
M16	West Birmingham	326	1485.16	113	184	727.10	122	510	1077.81	121
M17	Coventry	472	1243.57	67	270	582.36	86	742	879.74	78

HON - A2
Mortality rates from coronary heart disease (ICD 410-414) in persons aged 65-74:
Age-standardised mortality rates per 100,000: average for the years 1990-92

		Males			Females			Persons		
		Observed	Rate	Rank	Observed	Rate	Rank	Observed	Rate	Rank
M18	Dudley	445	1199.26	60	226	486.40	52	671	808.00	55
M19	Sandwell	572	1497.32	115	325	667.30	105	897	1035.71	110
M20	Solihull	305	1329.09	84	133	469.36	46	438	855.38	71
M21	Walsall	491	1614.71	137	272	714.63	119	763	1113.28	130
M22	Wolverhampton	428	1358.15	87	253	672.36	107	681	985.63	100
M25	South Birmingham	701	1423.52	105	399	636.40	97	1100	985.91	101
M26	North Worcestershire	395	1304.21	80	158	431.61	29	553	824.23	65
M28	Warwickshire	705	1177.23	55	376	521.60	67	1081	821.14	62
N11	Chester	291	1382.18	92	156	599.22	91	447	947.99	91
N12	Crewe	427	1376.67	89	259	681.38	113	686	994.97	105
N13	Halton	238	1604.07	135	132	696.52	117	370	1101.22	125
N14	Macclesfield	238	1097.95	32	135	505.51	56	373	773.42	46
N15	Warrington	274	1385.83	93	169	678.65	111	443	994.88	104
N21	Liverpool	856	1581.30	132	525	728.06	123	1381	1095.04	123
N31	St Helens and Knowsley	555	1525.16	121	359	761.81	129	914	1095.68	124
N41	Southport and Formby	202	1244.22	68	114	518.18	65	316	828.05	66
N42	South Sefton	287	1423.49	104	175	645.97	100	462	974.29	95
N51	Wirral	611	1415.21	102	383	661.98	103	994	986.73	102
P01	Lancaster	254	1457.07	107	133	601.92	93	387	981.73	99
P02	Blackpool, Wyre and Fylde	694	1387.19	96	363	555.69	79	1057	922.22	85
P03	Preston	225	1530.91	124	128	674.26	108	353	1058.05	115
P04	Blackburn, Hyndburn and Ribble Valley	475	1540.76	126	270	698.93	118	745	1074.22	119
P05	Burnley, Pendle and Rossendale	459	1689.47	140	275	777.00	134	734	1174.31	138
P06	West Lancashire	161	1394.10	98	92	639.03	99	253	976.11	97
P07	Chorley and South Ribble	305	1412.33	101	152	568.23	82	457	945.87	90
P08	Bolton	457	1522.68	119	281	722.23	121	738	1073.37	118
P09	Bury	327	1691.57	141	194	783.00	135	521	1184.20	140
P10	North Manchester	289	1695.67	142	165	771.26	133	454	1188.13	141
P11	Central Manchester	181	1568.33	129	106	804.20	136	287	1156.17	136
P12	South Manchester	289	1422.79	103	187	683.08	115	476	1000.67	106
P13	Oldham	388	1610.04	136	266	846.57	140	654	1182.89	139
P14	Rochdale	365	1572.63	130	219	759.59	128	584	1122.15	131
P15	Salford	420	1464.93	109	270	722.04	120	690	1048.86	111
P16	Stockport	461	1386.36	94	252	591.31	87	713	939.69	87
P17	Tameside and Glossop	445	1579.29	131	271	730.15	125	716	1101.44	126
P18	Trafford	329	1277.29	74	191	601.27	92	520	905.33	82
P19	Wigan	493	1475.70	111	377	834.33	139	870	1111.71	129

HON - A3
Mortality rates from stroke (ICD 430-438) in persons under 65:
Age-standardised mortality rates per 100,000: average for the years 1990-92

		Males			Females			Persons		
		Observed	Rate	Rank	Observed	Rate	Rank	Observed	Rate	Rank
	ENGLAND AND WALES	8651	14.05		6637	10.49		15288	12.24	
O00	ENGLAND	8118	14.00		6194	10.39		14312	12.17	
A00	NORTHERN RHA	708	18.21	14	539	13.40	14	1247	15.74	14
B00	YORKSHIRE RHA	665	15.21	11	537	11.80	12	1202	13.46	11
C00	TRENT RHA	842	14.48	9	632	10.59	9	1474	12.51	9
D00	EAST ANGLIAN RHA	263	10.34	1	215	8.34	3	478	9.31	1
E00	NORTH WEST THAMES RHA	518	12.64	6	355	8.67	5	873	10.64	6
F00	NORTH EAST THAMES RHA	610	14.00	8	457	10.31	8	1067	12.14	8
G00	SOUTH EAST THAMES RHA	602	13.97	7	432	9.59	7	1034	11.69	7
H00	SOUTH WEST THAMES RHA	393	11.16	4	286	7.71	1	679	9.40	2
J00	WESSEX RHA	415	11.01	3	340	8.64	4	755	9.79	4
K00	OXFORD RHA	311	10.53	2	257	8.71	6	568	9.63	3
L00	SOUTH WESTERN RHA	503	12.23	5	347	8.14	2	850	10.13	5
M00	WEST MIDLANDS RHA	964	14.77	10	777	11.76	11	1741	13.26	10
N00	MERSEY RHA	467	15.67	12	366	11.75	10	833	13.68	12
P00	NORTH WESTERN RHA	857	18.07	13	654	13.39	13	1511	15.67	13
A01	Hartlepool	24	20.42	132	15	12.83	111	39	16.53	130
A02	North Tees	26	11.72	40	28	11.87	96	54	11.83	71
A03	South Tees	85	24.64	143	57	15.63	136	142	20.10	142
A04	East Cumbria	42	17.63	115	28	11.59	90	70	14.57	107
A05	South Cumbria	41	18.26	123	36	14.53	131	77	16.35	128
A06	West Cumbria	24	13.99	76	22	12.39	103	46	13.17	90
A11	Northumberland	71	18.00	119	64	16.01	139	135	17.00	133
A12	Gateshead	47	17.51	114	39	14.45	130	86	15.93	121
A13	Newcastle	59	18.90	125	46	13.94	126	105	16.28	127
A14	North Tyneside	38	14.64	84	31	12.61	106	69	13.50	93
A15	South Tyneside	34	17.00	110	23	10.29	73	57	13.58	96
A16	Sunderland	84	22.97	138	40	10.31	74	124	16.45	129
A30	North Durham	71	17.25	111	62	14.83	133	133	16.01	124
A31	South Durham	62	17.29	113	48	13.25	120	110	15.19	113
B11	East Riding	82	13.03	64	76	11.55	89	158	12.28	78
B16	Grimsby and Scunthorpe	63	14.03	77	55	12.28	101	118	13.12	88
B21	North Yorkshire	109	11.99	46	84	8.84	40	193	10.38	47
B31	Bradford	101	19.49	128	70	13.21	119	171	16.24	126
B51	West Yorkshire	117	17.82	117	99	14.29	128	216	15.99	122
B61	Leeds	134	16.10	104	100	11.32	86	234	13.67	97
B71	Wakefield	59	15.71	99	53	13.45	121	112	14.59	108
C01	North Derbyshire	61	12.81	61	45	8.87	41	106	10.82	52
C02	Southern Derbyshire	111	16.69	109	72	10.72	81	183	13.72	98
C03	Leicestershire	145	13.72	69	104	9.59	62	249	11.64	66
C04	North Lincolnshire	55	14.80	85	35	9.46	58	90	12.06	75
C05	South Lincolnshire	68	16.34	106	45	10.90	83	113	13.54	95

HON - A3
Mortality rates from stroke (ICD 430-438) in persons under 65:
Age-standardised mortality rates per 100,000: average for the years 1990-92

		Males Observed	Rate	Rank	Females Observed	Rate	Rank	Persons Observed	Rate	Rank
C08	Nottingham	107	14.48	83	87	11.39	87	194	12.92	86
C09	Barnsley	39	13.86	74	43	14.86	134	82	14.37	105
C10	Doncaster	46	12.75	60	37	9.71	66	83	11.19	55
C11	Rotherham	48	15.40	97	42	12.81	110	90	14.10	103
C12	Sheffield	97	15.46	98	56	8.46	33	153	11.87	72
C14	North Nottinghamshire	65	12.73	59	66	13.03	114	131	12.86	83
D01	Cambridge	34	10.17	24	23	7.02	14	57	8.58	17
D05	North West Anglia	59	11.79	42	46	8.96	45	105	10.36	46
D06	Norwich	51	8.03	7	51	8.03	24	102	7.99	8
D07	Great Yarmouth and Waveney	36	13.76	71	40	14.78	132	76	14.15	104
D09	Huntingdon	10	7.25	3	8	5.30	4	18	6.27	2
D11	Suffolk	73	10.92	30	47	6.95	11	120	8.92	19
E01	North Bedfordshire	26	8.83	11	34	11.70	93	60	10.23	42
E02	South Bedfordshire	41	12.31	49	35	11.61	91	76	11.97	74
E05	North West Hertfordshire	24	7.41	5	22	6.59	8	46	6.99	3
E06	South West Hertfordshire	42	14.06	78	31	9.94	70	73	11.95	73
E07	Barnet	31	9.48	20	18	5.09	1	49	7.22	5
E09	Hillingdon	39	13.75	70	25	8.69	37	64	11.21	57
E18	East and North Hertfordshire	72	11.82	44	42	7.02	14	114	9.42	27
E19	Brent and Harrow	72	13.91	75	50	9.50	59	122	11.68	67
E20	Ealing, Hammersmith and Hounslow	113	15.79	101	67	9.26	53	180	12.53	81
E21	Kensington, Chelsea and Westminster	58	14.93	90	31	8.13	27	89	11.52	65
F31	North Essex	124	11.58	38	97	9.05	48	221	10.29	43
F32	South Essex	101	11.87	45	91	10.54	80	192	11.20	56
F33	Barking and Havering	42	8.86	12	35	6.98	12	77	7.89	6
F34	Redbridge and Waltham Forest	85	17.27	112	66	13.17	118	151	15.14	112
F35	East London and the City	130	21.99	135	75	13.08	115	205	17.63	136
F36	New River District	71	13.79	72	51	9.65	64	122	11.70	68
F37	Camden and Islington	57	15.23	94	42	10.84	82	99	13.02	87
G04	South East Kent	30	8.91	13	28	7.95	23	58	8.34	13
G05	Canterbury and Thanet	57	15.95	103	47	12.31	102	104	13.85	99
G06	Dartford and Gravesham	39	13.80	73	32	11.23	85	71	12.49	80
G07	Maidstone	29	11.59	39	22	8.93	44	51	10.22	40
G08	Medway	45	11.80	43	37	9.73	67	82	10.75	51
G09	Tunbridge Wells	29	11.06	32	14	5.13	2	43	8.05	10
G10	Bexley	25	9.56	21	29	10.38	76	54	10.01	37
G11	Greenwich	40	17.67	116	26	10.46	78	66	14.01	102
G12	Bromley	40	10.83	28	33	8.26	31	73	9.52	29
G21	East Sussex	102	12.33	51	75	8.34	32	177	10.19	39
G26	South East London	166	22.45	136	89	11.73	94	255	17.01	134

11

HON - A3
Mortality rates from stroke (ICD 430-438) in persons under 65:
Age-standardised mortality rates per 100,000: average for the years 1990-92

		Males			Females			Persons		
		Observed	Rate	Rank	Observed	Rate	Rank	Observed	Rate	Rank
H04	Mid Surrey	24	10.83	28	18	7.71	20	42	9.24	23
H05	East Surrey	22	8.79	10	17	6.99	13	39	7.90	7
H06	Chichester	20	8.70	9	26	10.48	79	46	9.60	31
H07	Mid Downs	29	8.39	8	28	7.82	21	57	8.09	12
H08	Worthing	37	13.03	64	22	7.28	17	59	9.94	36
H09	Croydon	54	15.30	95	30	7.67	19	84	11.40	59
H12	Wandsworth	39	20.94	133	17	9.12	49	56	15.01	110
H13	Merton and Sutton	48	12.55	57	43	10.36	75	91	11.44	61
H14	North West Surrey	44	8.96	15	25	5.15	3	69	7.06	4
H15	South West Surrey	17	5.46	1	20	6.39	7	37	5.97	1
H16	Kingston and Richmond	59	12.54	56	40	8.20	30	99	10.30	44
J10	Dorset	85	10.35	25	80	9.18	50	165	9.69	33
J21	Portsmouth and South East Hampshire	70	11.12	33	61	9.43	55	131	10.22	40
J22	Southampton and South West Hampshire	68	12.82	62	53	9.66	65	121	11.21	57
J23	Winchester	20	7.26	4	24	8.96	45	44	8.08	11
J24	Basingstoke and North Hampshire	38	9.02	17	33	7.91	22	71	8.49	14
J31	Salisbury	24	14.85	87	15	9.45	56	39	12.08	76
J32	Swindon	27	10.00	22	24	8.59	35	51	9.32	24
J33	Bath	57	11.56	37	33	6.25	6	90	8.89	18
J41	Isle of Wight	26	16.12	105	17	9.45	56	43	12.65	82
K11	East Berkshire	46	10.53	26	38	8.57	34	84	9.54	30
K12	West Berkshire	49	9.31	18	48	9.52	60	97	9.41	26
K24	Buckinghamshire	65	9.37	19	61	8.75	39	126	9.07	20
K31	Kettering	36	11.51	35	31	9.55	61	67	10.54	49
K32	Northampton	39	10.71	27	37	10.01	71	76	10.34	45
K41	Oxfordshire	76	12.48	54	42	6.92	10	118	9.72	34
L10	Bristol and District	101	10.00	22	89	8.73	38	190	9.36	25
L21	Cornwall and Isles of Scilly	89	14.10	79	48	7.42	18	137	10.67	50
L35	Exeter and North Devon	68	11.53	36	53	8.91	43	121	10.15	38
L36	Plymouth and Torbay	88	12.32	50	67	8.87	41	155	10.52	48
L40	Gloucestershire	95	14.36	82	56	8.06	25	151	11.15	54
L51	Somerset	62	12.15	47	34	6.20	5	96	9.11	21
M02	Herefordshire	16	7.48	6	19	8.61	36	35	8.04	9
M04	Worcester and District	29	9.00	16	31	9.36	54	60	9.17	22
M05	Shropshire	66	12.66	58	53	10.12	72	119	11.40	59
M06	Mid Staffordshire	58	14.24	81	37	9.24	52	95	11.73	69
M07	North Staffordshire	88	14.92	89	96	15.89	138	184	15.35	115
M08	South East Staffordshire	40	12.50	55	33	10.41	77	73	11.48	62
M13	East Birmingham	53	24.15	140	36	16.58	141	89	20.35	143
M14	North Birmingham	26	12.34	52	14	6.66	9	40	9.46	28
M16	West Birmingham	57	24.48	141	41	18.63	145	98	21.63	145
M17	Coventry	49	14.14	80	47	12.95	113	96	13.52	94

HON - A3
Mortality rates from stroke (ICD 430-438) in persons under 65:
Age-standardised mortality rates per 100,000: average for the years 1990-92

		Males			Females			Persons		
		Observed	Rate	Rank	Observed	Rate	Rank	Observed	Rate	Rank
M18	Dudley	60	14.85	87	46	11.44	88	106	13.16	89
M19	Sandwell	88	23.53	139	52	13.82	125	140	18.64	139
M20	Solihull	23	8.94	14	23	8.15	28	46	8.56	16
M21	Walsall	52	15.16	93	59	17.20	142	111	16.18	125
M22	Wolverhampton	47	15.03	91	41	12.91	112	88	13.96	100
M25	South Birmingham	88	18.13	121	64	13.15	117	152	15.60	118
M26	North Worcestershire	42	12.39	53	25	7.10	16	67	9.75	35
M28	Warwickshire	82	13.33	66	60	9.63	63	142	11.49	63
N11	Chester	30	13.33	66	29	12.52	104	59	12.91	85
N12	Crewe	58	18.16	122	43	13.11	116	101	15.65	120
N13	Halton	20	11.24	34	14	8.11	26	34	9.63	32
N14	Macclesfield	18	7.13	2	24	9.85	69	42	8.52	15
N15	Warrington	44	19.27	126	29	12.79	109	73	15.99	122
N21	Liverpool	100	18.05	120	73	12.18	100	173	15.03	111
N31	St Helens and Knowsley	82	19.37	127	53	11.78	95	135	15.51	117
N41	Southport and Formby	19	12.93	63	14	9.23	51	33	10.99	53
N42	South Sefton	28	12.28	48	29	12.13	98	57	12.18	77
N51	Wirral	68	15.88	102	58	12.11	97	126	13.99	101
P01	Lancaster	24	15.06	92	20	12.16	99	44	13.47	91
P02	Blackpool, Wyre and Fylde	93	21.43	134	57	12.56	105	150	16.78	132
P03	Preston	23	14.82	86	16	10.92	84	39	12.86	83
P04	Blackburn, Hyndburn and Ribble Valley	51	16.48	108	46	14.25	127	97	15.40	116
P05	Burnley, Pendle and Rossendale	54	19.62	129	45	15.70	137	99	17.64	137
P06	West Lancashire	15	11.00	31	19	13.63	123	34	12.31	79
P07	Chorley and South Ribble	39	16.37	107	30	12.65	108	69	14.49	106
P08	Bolton	54	17.95	118	40	12.64	107	94	15.20	114
P09	Bury	33	15.73	100	18	8.15	28	51	11.82	70
P10	North Manchester	39	24.48	141	27	17.43	143	66	20.93	144
P11	Central Manchester	31	25.75	145	11	9.02	47	42	17.56	135
P12	South Manchester	41	22.91	137	32	16.52	140	73	19.58	141
P13	Oldham	50	19.97	131	35	13.58	122	85	16.70	131
P14	Rochdale	47	19.72	130	29	11.62	92	76	15.60	118
P15	Salford	68	24.81	144	39	13.80	124	107	19.24	140
P16	Stockport	49	13.38	68	37	9.81	68	86	11.51	64
P17	Tameside and Glossop	45	15.31	96	43	14.43	129	88	14.87	109
P18	Trafford	31	11.78	41	42	15.25	135	73	13.49	92
P19	Wigan	70	18.85	124	68	18.01	144	138	18.42	138

HON - A4
Mortality rates from stroke (ICD 430-438) in persons aged 65-74:
Age-standardised mortality rates per 100,000: average for the years 1990-92

		Males			Females			Persons		
		Observed	Rate	Rank	Observed	Rate	Rank	Observed	Rate	Rank
	ENGLAND AND WALES	18036	295.43		16830	220.26		34866	253.77	
O00	ENGLAND	16773	293.13		15689	219.07		32462	252.12	
A00	NORTHERN RHA	1437	371.46	14	1279	262.73	14	2716	311.22	14
B00	YORKSHIRE RHA	1385	317.15	10	1303	237.92	11	2688	273.35	11
C00	TRENT RHA	1808	304.56	9	1634	229.26	9	3442	263.41	9
D00	EAST ANGLIAN RHA	672	248.25	2	616	190.57	3	1288	217.14	2
E00	NORTH WEST THAMES RHA	941	265.81	6	825	188.08	1	1766	223.30	3
F00	NORTH EAST THAMES RHA	1095	263.10	5	1036	200.76	6	2131	228.56	5
G00	SOUTH EAST THAMES RHA	1225	274.64	8	1161	202.18	7	2386	234.11	8
H00	SOUTH WEST THAMES RHA	844	245.72	1	839	188.43	2	1683	213.09	1
J00	WESSEX RHA	1038	261.74	4	1009	202.62	8	2047	228.78	6
K00	OXFORD RHA	690	269.24	7	618	198.57	4	1308	230.53	7
L00	SOUTH WESTERN RHA	1127	253.34	3	1119	200.06	5	2246	223.81	4
M00	WEST MIDLANDS RHA	2016	319.89	11	1829	234.07	10	3845	272.49	10
N00	MERSEY RHA	918	329.63	12	892	245.77	12	1810	282.28	12
P00	NORTH WESTERN RHA	1577	336.55	13	1529	252.85	13	3106	289.90	13
A01	Hartlepool	50	460.69	145	37	279.34	132	87	359.86	143
A02	North Tees	71	377.61	128	70	300.44	140	141	334.67	137
A03	South Tees	137	407.09	138	102	245.98	108	239	318.67	132
A04	East Cumbria	67	283.59	69	70	235.77	98	137	256.36	79
A05	South Cumbria	69	292.64	75	69	223.66	72	138	254.68	77
A06	West Cumbria	79	456.26	144	67	302.97	141	146	370.87	145
A11	Northumberland	178	429.71	143	137	278.59	131	315	348.06	140
A12	Gateshead	99	381.28	129	84	250.19	114	183	307.52	122
A13	Newcastle	125	368.42	123	121	272.26	128	246	314.89	127
A14	North Tyneside	91	342.16	112	80	231.30	91	171	279.28	103
A15	South Tyneside	59	268.82	50	70	249.98	113	129	258.85	82
A16	Sunderland	134	399.98	133	124	293.85	137	258	340.88	139
A30	North Durham	158	400.71	134	130	267.62	125	288	327.76	136
A31	South Durham	120	330.79	101	118	257.94	120	238	290.82	112
B11	East Riding	156	246.82	30	181	225.79	77	337	234.95	52
B16	Grimsby and Scunthorpe	132	295.88	79	120	226.61	82	252	258.08	81
B21	North Yorkshire	275	295.64	77	273	236.95	103	548	263.19	92
B31	Bradford	199	391.13	131	173	271.69	127	372	324.04	133
B51	West Yorkshire	231	353.42	119	224	262.61	122	455	303.16	121
B61	Leeds	264	319.18	95	221	210.94	57	485	260.06	87
B71	Wakefield	128	346.50	117	111	241.58	106	239	288.44	111
C01	North Derbyshire	147	295.64	77	141	236.27	101	288	263.08	91
C02	Southern Derbyshire	233	342.38	113	186	226.11	78	419	279.38	104
C03	Leicestershire	276	271.53	53	253	211.49	58	529	238.84	57
C04	North Lincolnshire	140	343.69	116	97	206.23	49	237	269.39	96
C05	South Lincolnshire	104	226.64	15	115	212.01	59	219	218.93	30

HON - A4
Mortality rates from stroke (ICD 430–438) in persons aged 65–74:
Age-standardised mortality rates per 100,000: average for the years 1990-92

		Males			Females			Persons		
		Observed	Rate	Rank	Observed	Rate	Rank	Observed	Rate	Rank
C08	Nottingham	255	339.91	111	207	229.51	86	462	279.90	105
C09	Barnsley	88	310.42	91	77	225.29	76	165	263.36	94
C10	Doncaster	87	240.12	26	92	215.28	63	179	226.98	41
C11	Rotherham	103	343.63	115	97	263.52	124	200	298.74	119
C12	Sheffield	225	330.01	100	239	276.36	130	464	299.53	120
C14	North Nottinghamshire	150	303.17	84	130	221.66	70	280	258.97	84
D01	Cambridge	68	217.20	9	71	182.85	25	139	198.43	12
D05	North West Anglia	151	277.24	61	114	180.86	23	265	225.96	40
D06	Norwich	161	225.48	13	168	199.35	40	329	211.49	22
D07	Great Yarmouth and Waveney	71	228.49	16	72	194.93	34	143	210.81	21
D09	Huntingdon	23	190.74	2	23	157.85	8	46	172.96	2
D11	Suffolk	198	280.96	64	168	196.60	37	366	234.91	51
E01	North Bedfordshire	68	260.91	43	71	232.14	93	139	245.21	66
E02	South Bedfordshire	77	293.38	76	65	219.01	69	142	252.89	74
E05	North West Hertfordshire	54	185.39	1	56	160.90	9	110	173.05	3
E06	South West Hertfordshire	97	335.47	107	48	133.48	?	145	224.29	38
E07	Barnet	75	236.89	25	70	165.88	11	145	197.03	9
E09	Hillingdon	65	257.93	40	66	208.42	54	131	230.56	47
E18	East and North Hertfordshire	119	226.62	14	111	174.37	15	230	198.03	11
E19	Brent and Harrow	119	282.15	67	94	177.51	20	213	224.85	39
E20	Ealing, Hammersmith and Hounslow	183	305.60	89	171	223.92	74	354	261.43	89
E21	Kensington, Chelsea and Westminster	84	260.61	42	73	177.05	18	157	214.27	24
F31	North Essex	249	235.39	22	240	184.40	26	489	207.04	17
F32	South Essex	211	257.94	41	200	196.08	36	411	223.67	37
F33	Barking and Havering	125	256.94	37	126	207.67	52	251	229.37	43
F34	Redbridge and Waltham Forest	102	216.85	8	122	203.26	44	224	208.64	19
F35	East London and the City	183	333.94	105	151	239.05	105	334	283.70	108
F36	New River District	111	252.32	32	119	212.30	60	230	230.16	44
F37	Camden and Islington	114	330.94	102	78	178.12	21	192	245.25	67
G04	South East Kent	96	257.38	38	92	191.50	33	188	220.43	32
G05	Canterbury and Thanet	131	283.05	68	120	200.64	43	251	237.10	56
G06	Dartford and Gravesham	65	270.12	51	88	299.83	139	153	286.28	109
G07	Maidstone	54	254.34	33	48	184.47	27	102	215.01	25
G08	Medway	106	313.57	92	90	212.48	61	196	255.63	78
G09	Tunbridge Wells	63	263.91	46	69	223.72	73	132	242.17	61
G10	Bexley	57	236.35	24	57	188.80	30	114	210.35	20
G11	Greenwich	67	289.58	72	74	235.68	96	141	259.05	85
G12	Bromley	92	256.21	34	78	168.81	12	170	207.44	18
G21	East Sussex	278	265.39	47	253	177.38	19	531	215.35	26
G26	South East London	216	304.12	87	192	218.23	68	408	256.80	80

HON - A4
Mortality rates from stroke (ICD 430-438) in persons aged 65-74:
Age-standardised mortality rates per 100,000: average for the years 1990-92

		Males			Females			Persons		
		Observed	Rate	Rank	Observed	Rate	Rank	Observed	Rate	Rank
H04	Mid Surrey	52	233.69	20	41	152.24	6	93	187.99	6
H05	East Surrey	58	257.51	39	57	205.32	48	115	227.82	42
H06	Chichester	78	263.36	45	75	190.37	31	153	221.95	34
H07	Mid Downs	84	275.01	60	79	204.82	45	163	234.67	49
H08	Worthing	110	278.70	62	108	200.39	41	218	232.64	48
H09	Croydon	87	280.80	63	90	226.31	79	177	250.18	72
H12	Wandsworth	44	272.66	59	48	226.48	81	92	248.20	70
H13	Merton and Sutton	77	213.36	6	67	140.93	4	144	171.73	1
H14	North West Surrey	87	209.00	5	85	165.65	10	172	186.01	5
H15	South West Surrey	59	213.45	7	64	181.15	24	123	194.69	7
H16	Kingston and Richmond	108	232.30	19	125	198.65	38	233	212.38	23
J10	Dorset	255	240.84	27	230	173.40	14	485	203.42	15
J21	Portsmouth and South East Hampshire	178	281.33	66	189	231.53	92	367	253.12	75
J22	Southampton and South West Hampshire	163	289.09	71	134	190.65	32	297	234.75	50
J23	Winchester	71	296.86	80	42	136.12	3	113	206.15	16
J24	Basingstoke and North Hampshire	74	228.64	17	85	209.34	56	159	217.67	28
J31	Salisbury	46	270.43	52	43	199.26	39	89	230.33	46
J32	Swindon	69	267.86	49	77	252.35	117	146	258.87	83
J33	Bath	134	262.41	44	145	229.27	84	279	244.00	64
J41	Isle of Wight	48	230.78	18	64	238.66	104	112	235.19	53
K11	East Berkshire	101	271.79	55	98	215.66	64	199	240.69	58
K12	West Berkshire	107	256.42	36	77	146.47	5	184	195.10	8
K24	Buckinghamshire	168	298.79	81	140	207.64	51	308	249.08	71
K31	Kettering	69	224.92	12	92	246.68	109	161	236.98	55
K32	Northampton	106	305.17	88	86	205.09	46	192	250.74	73
K41	Oxfordshire	139	249.80	31	125	187.03	28	264	215.71	27
L10	Bristol and District	269	271.86	56	273	216.66	66	542	241.32	59
L21	Cornwall and Isles of Scilly	170	245.45	29	174	200.60	42	344	220.56	33
L35	Exeter and North Devon	191	281.03	65	148	175.17	17	339	222.15	35
L36	Plymouth and Torbay	189	235.94	23	210	205.18	47	399	218.75	29
L40	Gloucestershire	189	272.10	58	186	217.45	67	375	241.93	60
L51	Somerset	119	201.27	4	128	172.31	13	247	185.52	4
M02	Herefordshire	74	320.61	96	65	235.76	97	139	275.12	100
M04	Worcester and District	76	234.91	21	102	251.69	116	178	244.42	65
M05	Shropshire	141	289.87	73	145	236.35	102	286	260.19	88
M06	Mid Staffordshire	93	271.70	54	91	221.78	71	184	243.79	63
M07	North Staffordshire	180	300.06	82	191	256.24	118	371	276.91	102
M08	South East Staffordshire	81	303.20	85	75	229.84	87	156	263.19	92
M13	East Birmingham	78	304.00	86	73	226.37	80	151	259.52	86
M14	North Birmingham	61	314.53	93	54	208.11	53	115	254.23	76
M16	West Birmingham	71	321.37	98	60	230.82	89	131	273.53	99
M17	Coventry	162	424.83	142	107	227.54	83	269	315.93	128

HON - A4
Mortality rates from stroke (ICD 430-438) in persons aged 65-74:
Age-standardised mortality rates per 100,000: average for the years 1990-92

		Males			Females			Persons		
		Observed	Rate	Rank	Observed	Rate	Rank	Observed	Rate	Rank
M18	Dudley	151	405.21	137	108	234.06	94	259	310.74	125
M19	Sandwell	138	359.13	121	122	248.95	112	260	297.32	117
M20	Solihull	58	256.33	35	45	157.20	7	103	201.08	13
M21	Walsall	97	321.15	97	89	235.37	95	186	272.78	98
M22	Wolverhampton	113	358.31	120	102	271.18	126	215	310.00	124
M25	South Birmingham	165	334.01	106	163	256.34	119	328	291.02	113
M26	North Worcestershire	114	375.14	125	86	231.28	90	200	295.74	116
M28	Warwickshire	163	271.93	57	151	208.57	55	314	236.64	54
N11	Chester	42	199.71	3	61	236.25	100	103	220.00	31
N12	Crewe	91	291.99	74	104	274.14	129	195	282.28	106
N13	Halton	59	401.54	135	47	247.01	110	106	314.18	126
N14	Macclesfield	48	220.62	10	48	179.29	22	96	197.61	10
N15	Warrington	83	418.17	141	60	235.82	99	143	316.81	130
N21	Liverpool	208	383.39	130	207	283.63	134	415	326.55	135
N31	St Helens and Knowsley	147	407.75	139	136	289.36	136	283	339.67	138
N41	Southport and Formby	49	301.43	83	40	175.09	16	89	230.16	44
N42	South Sefton	68	338.18	109	63	229.88	88	131	276.26	101
N51	Wirral	123	284.74	70	126	216.18	65	249	245.73	68
P01	Lancaster	70	398.70	132	71	320.87	144	141	353.86	141
P02	Blackpool, Wyre and Fylde	168	337.23	108	141	215.04	62	309	268.62	95
P03	Preston	47	316.36	94	60	320.79	143	107	317.58	131
P04	Blackburn, Hyndburn and Ribble Valley	103	332.22	104	80	207.01	50	183	262.63	90
P05	Burnley, Pendle and Rossendale	90	331.90	103	93	260.54	121	183	292.87	114
P06	West Lancashire	40	346.78	118	18	124.77	1	58	223.53	36
P07	Chorley and South Ribble	57	267.29	48	60	224.54	75	117	243.11	62
P08	Bolton	92	306.81	90	113	288.67	135	205	297.56	118
P09	Bury	47	243.81	28	62	247.87	111	109	247.08	69
P10	North Manchester	63	369.13	124	43	195.68	35	106	271.25	97
P11	Central Manchester	47	403.75	136	43	328.21	145	90	363.84	144
P12	South Manchester	69	342.51	114	68	245.83	107	137	287.05	110
P13	Oldham	82	338.94	110	94	296.66	138	176	316.25	129
P14	Rochdale	87	376.70	126	66	229.28	85	153	294.35	115
P15	Salford	105	364.33	122	100	262.90	123	205	308.80	123
P16	Stockport	108	324.09	99	108	251.14	115	216	283.51	107
P17	Tameside and Glossop	107	377.43	127	106	283.48	133	213	325.22	134
P18	Trafford	58	223.09	11	60	187.88	29	118	203.36	14
P19	Wigan	137	410.76	140	143	316.73	142	280	357.59	142

HON - A5,B6

Prevalence of cigarette smoking at ages 16 and over:

General Household Survey data for the financial year 1992/93

		Males		95% CI		Females		95% CI	
		Base	Percent	Lower	Upper	Base	Percent	Lower	Upper
	ENGLAND AND WALES	7696	29	28	30	8878	27	26	28
O00	ENGLAND	7276	29	28	30	8364	27	26	28
A00	NORTHERN RHA	476	29	24	34	583	32	27	37
B00	YORKSHIRE RHA	532	28	23	33	616	28	24	32
C00	TRENT RHA	745	28	24	32	852	25	22	28
D00	EAST ANGLIAN RHA	317	30	24	36	372	25	20	30
E00	NORTH WEST THAMES RHA	407	30	25	35	497	27	22	32
F00	NORTH EAST THAMES RHA	505	28	23	33	575	24	20	28
G00	SOUTH EAST THAMES RHA	589	35	30	40	672	27	23	31
H00	SOUTH WEST THAMES RHA	474	26	21	31	556	27	23	31
J00	WESSEX RHA	440	28	23	33	529	23	19	27
K00	OXFORD RHA	530	27	22	32	571	26	22	30
L00	SOUTH WESTERN RHA	508	29	24	34	555	25	21	29
M00	WEST MIDLANDS RHA	771	28	24	32	915	25	22	28
N00	MERSEY RHA	320	29	23	35	354	28	22	34
P00	NORTH WESTERN RHA	662	29	25	33	717	31	27	35

(Not available for DHAs)

Health of the Nation	HON - A8 Average percentage of household food energy derived from saturated fatty acids: MAFF National Food Survey data for the period 1990-92	HON - A9 Average percentage of household food energy derived from total fat: MAFF National Food Survey data for the period 1990-92
Standard Regions and Greater London	Percent	Percent
ENGLAND	16.4	41.6
NORTH	16.3	41.1
YORKSHIRE AND HUMBERSIDE	16.3	41.5
NORTH WEST	16.5	41.5
EAST MIDLANDS	16.2	41.7
WEST MIDLANDS	16.3	41.4
SOUTH WEST	16.5	41.4
SOUTH EAST AND EAST ANGLIA*	16.5	41.8
GREATER LONDON	16.3	41.9

*South East and East Anglia Standard Regions have been combined, and include Greater London. Greater London is also shown separately.

HON - A10

Prevalence of alcohol consumption above sensible levels at ages 18 and over:

General Household Survey data for the financial year 1992/93

		Males		95% CI		Females		95% CI	
		Base	Percent	Lower	Upper	Base	Percent	Lower	Upper
	ENGLAND AND WALES	7677	26	25	27	8863	12	11	13
O00	ENGLAND	7257	26	25	27	8349	12	11	13
A00	NORTHERN RHA	476	32	27	37	581	13	10	16
B00	YORKSHIRE RHA	531	30	25	35	616	13	10	16
C00	TRENT RHA	741	26	22	30	847	12	9	15
D00	EAST ANGLIAN RHA	317	20	15	25	370	14	10	18
E00	NORTH WEST THAMES RHA	404	24	19	29	494	10	7	13
F00	NORTH EAST THAMES RHA	504	18	14	22	575	9	6	12
G00	SOUTH EAST THAMES RHA	589	28	24	32	671	12	9	15
H00	SOUTH WEST THAMES RHA	471	22	18	26	555	13	10	16
J00	WESSEX RHA	438	19	15	23	528	9	6	12
K00	OXFORD RHA	527	28	23	33	572	15	11	19
L00	SOUTH WESTERN RHA	509	26	21	31	557	12	9	15
M00	WEST MIDLANDS RHA	769	25	21	29	914	8	6	10
N00	MERSEY RHA	321	31	25	37	354	14	10	18
P00	NORTH WESTERN RHA	660	32	28	36	715	12	9	15

(Not available for DHAs)

		HON - B1 Mortality rates from breast cancer (ICD 174) in women aged 50-69: Age-standardised mortality rates per 100,000: average for the years 1990-92			HON - B2 Incidence of invasive cervical cancer (ICD 180): Age-standardised registration rates per 100,000: average for the years 1986-88		
		Observed	Rate	Rank	Observed	Rate	Rank
	ENGLAND AND WALES	15359	92.40		13074	16.06	
O00	ENGLAND	14460	92.63		11986	15.64	
A00	NORTHERN RHA	942	88.97	2	813	16.19	8
B00	YORKSHIRE RHA	1030	85.37	1	1166	20.39	13
C00	TRENT RHA	1475	94.02	9	1217	16.36	9
D00	EAST ANGLIAN RHA	628	90.86	5	464	13.67	5
E00	NORTH WEST THAMES RHA	924	90.11	4	693	12.58	4
F00	NORTH EAST THAMES RHA	1086	93.00	8	744	12.20	3
G00	SOUTH EAST THAMES RHA	1158	96.99	14	853	13.90	6
H00	SOUTH WEST THAMES RHA	915	94.80	10	578	11.71	1
J00	WESSEX RHA	981	94.84	11	822	16.52	10
K00	OXFORD RHA	698	95.52	12	446	11.81	2
L00	SOUTH WESTERN RHA	1050	92.15	6	845	15.81	7
M00	WEST MIDLANDS RHA	1656	95.97	13	1376	16.94	11
N00	MERSEY RHA	739	89.89	3	819	21.18	14
P00	NORTH WESTERN RHA	1178	92.38	7	1150	18.08	12
A01	Hartlepool	34	113.70	141	29	20.73	126
A02	North Tees	55	96.09	89	47	17.36	104
A03	South Tees	84	86.27	35	92	19.77	119
A04	East Cumbria	64	98.02	100	40	14.51	67
A05	South Cumbria	48	77.27	14	37	12.80	38
A06	West Cumbria	37	76.52	13	36	15.38	78
A11	Northumberland	93	86.37	36	67	13.55	54
A12	Gateshead	53	71.63	2	57	16.89	99
A13	Newcastle	87	100.63	117	75	16.41	91
A14	North Tyneside	66	93.82	74	48	13.37	49
A15	South Tyneside	47	83.53	28	34	13.93	59
A16	Sunderland	99	99.66	109	90	19.31	116
A30	North Durham	100	90.37	51	87	16.86	98
A31	South Durham	75	80.35	22	74	15.93	85
B11	East Riding	156	89.67	48	208	27.25	138
B16	Grimsby and Scunthorpe	115	97.17	97	144	25.81	136
B21	North Yorkshire	224	89.81	49	194	17.15	102
B31	Bradford	109	73.81	6	116	15.33	77
B51	West Yorkshire	133	73.87	7	175	19.61	118
B61	Leeds	180	76.48	12	212	18.65	114
B71	Wakefield	113	109.67	136	117	23.86	133
C01	North Derbyshire	126	97.13	96	85	13.92	58
C02	Southern Derbyshire	187	102.74	124	138	16.10	87
C03	Leicestershire	238	84.44	30	196	14.21	65
C04	North Lincolnshire	97	96.80	92	58	13.54	53
C05	South Lincolnshire	117	103.81	125	68	13.91	57

		HON - B1 Mortality rates from breast cancer (ICD 174) in women aged 50-69: Age-standardised mortality rates per 100,000: average for the years 1990-92			HON - B2 Incidence of invasive cervical cancer (ICD 180): Age-standardised registration rates per 100,000: average for the years 1986-88		
		Observed	Rate	Rank	Observed	Rate	Rank
C08	Nottingham	217	106.75	130	184	19.44	117
C09	Barnsley	64	85.17	31	82	23.79	132
C10	Doncaster	74	74.09	8	133	28.69	141
C11	Rotherham	70	85.46	32	62	15.71	82
C12	Sheffield	161	95.99	84	117	13.00	40
C14	North Nottinghamshire	124	93.42	71	94	14.87	70
D01	Cambridge	91	106.93	131	41	10.05	14
D05	North West Anglia	127	91.40	62	76	12.17	31
D06	Norwich	136	75.58	10	128	15.20	74
D07	Great Yarmouth and Waveney	70	91.35	60	66	18.26	110
D09	Huntingdon	36	100.05	115	30	15.06	72
D11	Suffolk	168	95.59	80	123	13.15	42
E01	North Bedfordshire	71	99.62	107	29	7.21	1
E02	South Bedfordshire	70	89.34	47	82	20.41	123
E05	North West Hertfordshire	72	86.38	37	52	12.07	28
E06	South West Hertfordshire	71	90.02	50	38	9.04	7
E07	Barnet	85	92.68	68	62	12.64	35
E09	Hillingdon	64	89.02	45	36	9.40	9
E18	East and North Hertfordshire	141	91.40	62	85	10.87	18
E19	Brent and Harrow	120	92.65	67	94	13.38	50
E20	Ealing, Hammersmith and Hounslow	156	90.90	56	139	14.02	61
E21	Kensington, Chelsea and Westminster	74	78.97	20	76	15.24	75
F31	North Essex	274	94.35	76	180	12.03	27
F32	South Essex	219	96.01	85	109	9.31	8
F33	Barking and Havering	114	82.94	26	63	9.83	11
F34	Redbridge and Waltham Forest	128	95.42	79	92	12.10	29
F35	East London and the City	142	95.26	78	140	17.92	108
F36	New River District	119	90.45	52	77	10.71	15
F37	Camden and Islington	90	92.68	68	83	15.52	79
G04	South East Kent	98	105.92	129	81	18.18	109
G05	Canterbury and Thanet	91	81.73	24	91	16.27	90
G06	Dartford and Gravesham	72	99.08	104	48	13.42	51
G07	Maidstone	54	87.05	39	41	13.61	55
G08	Medway	87	90.97	57	84	16.78	95
G09	Tunbridge Wells	68	97.73	99	30	7.83	2
G10	Bexley	78	109.01	135	32	8.52	4
G11	Greenwich	71	111.81	139	45	13.96	60
G12	Bromley	119	118.33	144	70	12.55	34
G21	East Sussex	249	96.44	90	166	13.11	41
G26	South East London	171	87.21	40	165	15.57	80

		HON - B1 Mortality rates from breast cancer (ICD 174) in women aged 50-69: Age-standardised mortality rates per 100,000: average for the years 1990-92			HON - B2 Incidence of invasive cervical cancer (ICD 180): Age-standardised registration rates per 100,000: average for the years 1986-88		
		Observed	Rate	Rank	Observed	Rate	Rank
H04	Mid Surrey	50	79.48	21	32	9.77	10
H05	East Surrey	65	103.88	126	39	12.36	33
H06	Chichester	71	100.69	118	41	13.82	56
H07	Mid Downs	99	107.30	132	55	12.71	37
H08	Worthing	72	73.76	5	60	13.27	46
H09	Croydon	93	95.77	82	63	11.43	20
H12	Wandsworth	53	115.14	142	37	13.28	47
H13	Merton and Sutton	101	93.58	73	50	8.92	6
H14	North West Surrey	107	85.78	33	65	10.76	16
H15	South West Surrey	63	81.04	23	47	11.89	24
H16	Kingston and Richmond	141	110.45	137	89	13.28	47
J10	Dorset	241	98.04	101	201	18.43	112
J21	Portsmouth and South East Hampshire	164	94.78	77	164	20.45	124
J22	Southampton and South West Hampshire	132	93.56	72	107	15.58	81
J23	Winchester	54	78.37	16	37	9.86	12
J24	Basingstoke and North Hampshire	99	98.81	103	59	10.86	17
J31	Salisbury	36	78.53	17	32	14.86	69
J32	Swindon	63	86.69	38	111	30.97	144
J33	Bath	144	107.51	133	73	11.09	19
J41	Isle of Wight	48	96.05	88	38	16.54	92
K11	East Berkshire	105	96.83	93	44	7.92	3
K12	West Berkshire	125	98.23	102	57	8.56	5
K24	Buckinghamshire	155	91.35	60	88	9.99	13
K31	Kettering	93	116.46	143	99	24.88	134
K32	Northampton	87	93.41	70	62	12.95	39
K41	Oxfordshire	133	87.65	41	96	12.02	25
L10	Bristol and District	225	85.96	34	213	16.00	86
L21	Cornwall and Isles of Scilly	152	83.49	27	135	16.84	97
L35	Exeter and North Devon	165	99.24	105	111	15.01	71
L36	Plymouth and Torbay	202	99.70	111	166	17.22	103
L40	Gloucestershire	172	95.61	81	110	13.17	44
L51	Somerset	134	90.80	55	110	16.61	94
M02	Herefordshire	54	93.89	75	31	11.58	22
M04	Worcester and District	92	107.59	134	66	16.56	93
M05	Shropshire	129	96.03	86	97	16.16	88
M06	Mid Staffordshire	98	97.35	98	56	11.49	21
M07	North Staffordshire	155	95.81	83	118	15.74	84
M08	South East Staffordshire	69	87.75	42	77	18.94	115
M13	East Birmingham	61	96.83	93	43	14.05	62
M14	North Birmingham	56	101.57	122	38	14.18	64
M16	West Birmingham	50	84.00	29	60	20.49	125
M17	Coventry	88	89.00	44	132	29.65	143

23

		HON - B1 Mortality rates from breast cancer (ICD 174) in women aged 50-69: Age-standardised mortality rates per 100,000: average for the years 1990-92			HON - B2 Incidence of invasive cervical cancer (ICD 180): Age-standardised registration rates per 100,000: average for the years 1986-88		
		Observed	Rate	Rank	Observed	Rate	Rank
M18	Dudley	108	99.67	110	76	15.73	83
M19	Sandwell	99	101.27	121	87	18.40	111
M20	Solihull	64	91.28	59	48	14.70	68
M21	Walsall	96	105.23	128	78	20.24	121
M22	Wolverhampton	84	99.77	112	56	15.26	76
M25	South Birmingham	119	92.04	65	121	17.42	106
M26	North Worcestershire	79	90.97	57	58	13.22	45
M28	Warwickshire	155	96.03	86	134	17.59	107
N11	Chester	64	101.07	120	50	17.12	101
N12	Crewe	84	99.81	113	50	12.20	32
N13	Halton	45	100.56	116	46	21.48	127
N14	Macclesfield	58	91.94	64	38	12.02	25
N15	Warrington	66	113.21	140	49	17.01	100
N21	Liverpool	147	92.11	66	204	28.37	140
N31	St Helens and Knowsley	90	77.34	15	142	27.15	137
N41	Southport and Formby	33	71.93	3	75	39.70	145
N42	South Sefton	49	78.84	19	50	18.55	113
N51	Wirral	103	81.81	25	115	17.37	105
P01	Lancaster	34	72.14	4	27	12.11	30
P02	Blackpool, Wyre and Fylde	109	87.88	43	105	16.79	96
P03	Preston	36	89.32	46	26	14.16	63
P04	Blackburn, Hyndburn and Ribble Valley	86	104.22	127	94	22.64	130
P05	Burnley, Pendle and Rossendale	56	74.11	9	76	21.75	128
P06	West Lancashire	42	120.37	145	39	22.21	129
P07	Chorley and South Ribble	60	99.99	114	50	16.24	89
P08	Bolton	63	76.11	11	81	19.92	120
P09	Bury	51	90.79	54	42	15.11	73
P10	North Manchester	44	96.86	95	54	25.41	135
P11	Central Manchester	30	99.51	106	42	27.75	139
P12	South Manchester	39	71.58	1	39	13.16	43
P13	Oldham	53	78.65	18	95	28.69	141
P14	Rochdale	66	102.06	123	63	20.25	122
P15	Salford	82	111.73	138	89	23.51	131
P16	Stockport	88	90.66	53	65	13.50	52
P17	Tameside and Glossop	77	100.93	119	57	14.26	66
P18	Trafford	71	99.64	108	42	11.58	22
P19	Wigan	91	96.73	91	64	12.64	35

HON - B3
Incidence of skin cancer (malignant melanoma, ICD 172):
Age-standardised registration rates per 100,000: average for the years 1986-88

		Males			Females			Persons		
		Observed	Rate	Rank	Observed	Rate	Rank	Observed	Rate	Rank
	ENGLAND AND WALES	3882	5.25		6673	7.96		10555	6.62	
O00	ENGLAND	3643	5.22		6301	7.98		9944	6.62	
A00	NORTHERN RHA	207	4.59	3	304	5.68	2	511	5.12	2
B00	YORKSHIRE RHA	242	4.62	4	441	7.51	8	683	6.05	7
C00	TRENT RHA	334	4.81	6	530	7.03	5	864	5.90	5
D00	EAST ANGLIAN RHA	151	4.99	9	314	9.39	11	465	7.27	10
E00	NORTH WEST THAMES RHA	271	5.45	10	405	7.03	5	676	6.29	8
F00	NORTH EAST THAMES RHA	269	4.96	8	388	6.16	3	657	5.59	4
G00	SOUTH EAST THAMES RHA	259	4.85	7	496	8.18	9	755	6.54	9
H00	SOUTH WEST THAMES RHA	254	5.65	11	482	9.36	10	736	7.56	11
J00	WESSEX RHA	347	7.63	13	583	11.26	13	930	9.49	13
K00	OXFORD RHA	195	5.66	12	379	9.76	12	574	7.72	12
L00	SOUTH WESTERN RHA	390	7.94	14	722	13.07	14	1112	10.57	14
M00	WEST MIDLANDS RHA	359	4.75	5	610	7.29	7	969	6.03	6
N00	MERSEY RHA	123	3.58	1	231	5.64	1	354	4.66	1
P00	NORTH WESTERN RHA	242	4.23	2	416	6.37	4	658	5.25	3
A01	Hartlepool	2	1.66	4	8	5.00	32	10	3.53	11
A02	North Tees	11	4.47	66	14	4.77	24	25	4.64	31
A03	South Tees	17	4.25	56	29	6.47	57	46	5.45	57
A04	East Cumbria	22	7.89	134	23	7.16	71	45	7.50	109
A05	South Cumbria	20	7.31	124	41	12.92	133	61	10.14	133
A06	West Cumbria	11	5.57	100	9	4.24	17	20	4.86	40
A11	Northumberland	27	6.19	108	37	7.27	74	64	6.49	83
A12	Gateshead	7	2.23	7	11	2.77	4	18	2.58	3
A13	Newcastle	21	5.10	85	19	3.93	13	40	4.41	26
A14	North Tyneside	11	3.87	40	39	11.02	122	50	7.73	113
A15	South Tyneside	7	3.00	17	12	4.17	16	19	3.54	12
A16	Sunderland	16	4.09	52	12	2.26	2	28	2.98	5
A30	North Durham	19	3.85	37	30	5.26	35	49	4.66	32
A31	South Durham	16	3.68	30	20	4.08	14	36	3.88	19
B11	East Riding	48	6.52	115	58	6.86	67	106	6.63	89
B16	Grimsby and Scunthorpe	14	2.89	14	34	6.31	52	48	4.51	30
B21	North Yorkshire	57	5.44	96	103	9.01	103	160	7.26	105
B31	Bradford	27	4.46	65	55	7.53	78	82	5.79	65
B51	West Yorkshire	36	4.30	60	70	7.21	73	106	5.83	66
B61	Leeds	41	4.02	47	102	8.92	102	143	6.52	85
B71	Wakefield	19	4.04	49	19	3.83	11	38	3.86	18
C01	North Derbyshire	24	4.00	45	53	8.54	94	77	6.22	76
C02	Southern Derbyshire	32	4.01	46	58	6.50	61	90	5.32	50
C03	Leicestershire	66	5.40	94	106	7.69	81	172	6.43	81
C04	North Lincolnshire	16	3.88	42	37	8.30	89	53	5.99	71
C05	South Lincolnshire	23	4.80	78	39	7.63	79	62	6.32	78

HON - B3
Incidence of skin cancer (malignant melanoma, ICD 172):
Age-standardised registration rates per 100,000: average for the years 1986-88

		Males			Females			Persons		
		Observed	Rate	Rank	Observed	Rate	Rank	Observed	Rate	Rank
C08	Nottingham	37	4.07	50	72	7.76	83	109	5.91	69
C09	Barnsley	22	6.07	107	20	5.43	38	42	5.65	61
C10	Doncaster	11	2.92	15	20	4.31	18	31	3.55	13
C11	Rotherham	19	5.28	89	34	8.58	95	53	6.97	96
C12	Sheffield	51	6.45	114	57	6.42	56	108	6.42	79
C14	North Nottinghamshire	33	5.43	95	34	5.02	33	67	5.29	49
D01	Cambridge	30	7.77	133	54	12.31	131	84	10.16	134
D05	North West Anglia	26	4.36	62	71	11.04	124	97	7.81	115
D06	Norwich	30	4.16	53	52	6.48	59	82	5.34	52
D07	Great Yarmouth and Waveney	21	6.20	109	30	8.52	93	51	7.31	106
D09	Huntingdon	6	3.76	32	22	10.79	121	28	7.63	111
D11	Suffolk	38	4.69	73	85	9.55	109	123	7.19	102
E01	North Bedfordshire	13	3.78	33	39	10.00	113	52	7.09	100
E02	South Bedfordshire	30	7.40	127	53	12.49	132	83	10.09	131
E05	North West Hertfordshire	28	6.96	122	37	8.61	96	65	7.82	116
E06	South West Hertfordshire	23	6.69	117	33	7.79	84	56	7.23	104
E07	Barnet	19	4.48	68	35	6.67	64	54	5.63	60
E09	Hillingdon	13	3.84	36	14	3.42	8	27	3.73	15
E18	East and North Hertfordshire	41	5.72	101	63	8.30	89	104	7.01	97
E19	Brent and Harrow	31	4.91	82	53	6.32	53	84	5.66	62
E20	Ealing, Hammersmith and Hounslow	46	5.26	87	48	4.37	19	94	4.83	39
E21	Kensington, Chelsea and Westminster	27	5.87	104	30	5.35	36	57	5.60	59
F31	North Essex	80	6.44	112	113	7.82	85	193	7.14	101
F32	South Essex	68	6.79	119	75	6.33	54	143	6.54	86
F33	Barking and Havering	32	5.28	89	51	7.34	75	83	6.50	84
F34	Redbridge and Waltham Forest	35	5.12	86	52	6.80	65	87	5.96	70
F35	East London and the City	12	1.55	3	28	2.84	6	40	2.27	2
F36	New River District	22	3.34	20	37	4.90	28	59	4.16	23
F37	Camden and Islington	20	4.26	57	32	5.95	48	52	5.02	43
G04	South East Kent	21	5.32	92	46	11.49	126	67	8.35	121
G05	Canterbury and Thanet	19	4.45	64	45	8.71	98	64	6.65	90
G06	Dartford and Gravesham	12	3.58	26	18	4.99	30	30	4.37	25
G07	Maidstone	15	5.00	83	21	6.48	59	36	5.68	63
G08	Medway	21	4.66	72	37	8.43	91	58	6.42	79
G09	Tunbridge Wells	10	3.42	22	16	5.07	34	26	4.27	24
G10	Bexley	20	6.24	110	33	9.05	105	53	7.80	114
G11	Greenwich	11	3.53	23	23	7.00	69	34	5.37	53
G12	Bromley	22	4.78	77	54	9.84	112	76	7.54	110
G21	East Sussex	63	5.48	97	135	10.20	116	198	7.88	117
G26	South East London	45	4.75	75	68	6.15	51	113	5.48	58

HON - B3
Incidence of skin cancer (malignant melanoma, ICD 172):
Age-standardised registration rates per 100,000: average for the years 1986-88

		Males			Females			Persons		
		Observed	Rate	Rank	Observed	Rate	Rank	Observed	Rate	Rank
H04	Mid Surrey	24	8.43	138	42	14.76	141	66	11.58	139
H05	East Surrey	26	8.77	141	50	15.81	143	76	12.45	144
H06	Chichester	15	5.26	87	58	17.92	145	73	11.98	141
H07	Mid Downs	24	6.04	105	50	11.02	122	74	8.61	122
H08	Worthing	22	5.39	93	49	9.20	107	71	7.40	108
H09	Croydon	22	4.71	74	44	8.50	92	66	6.62	88
H12	Wandsworth	10	3.86	38	19	6.37	55	29	5.24	48
H13	Merton and Sutton	20	3.56	25	42	6.54	62	62	5.10	45
H14	North West Surrey	36	6.59	116	45	7.01	70	81	6.68	91
H15	South West Surrey	27	7.42	129	27	5.88	45	54	6.71	92
H16	Kingston and Richmond	28	4.47	66	56	7.68	80	84	6.12	73
J10	Dorset	89	8.81	142	174	14.72	140	263	11.96	140
J21	Portsmouth and South East Hampshire	64	8.74	140	102	11.42	125	166	9.99	130
J22	Southampton and South West Hampshire	62	10.27	145	100	13.98	137	162	12.31	142
J23	Winchester	29	9.15	144	49	14.01	138	78	11.52	138
J24	Basingstoke and North Hampshire	24	5.09	84	41	7.18	72	65	6.21	74
J31	Salisbury	16	8.12	136	23	12.20	130	39	10.10	132
J32	Swindon	19	6.06	106	40	11.66	127	59	8.79	124
J33	Bath	30	4.88	81	40	5.88	45	70	5.42	55
J41	Isle of Wight	14	6.44	112	14	6.04	49	28	6.06	72
K11	East Berkshire	10	2.02	6	12	2.23	1	22	2.08	1
K12	West Berkshire	39	6.29	111	54	7.84	86	93	7.08	99
K24	Buckinghamshire	60	7.38	126	127	14.11	139	187	10.87	136
K31	Kettering	19	4.86	80	51	12.15	129	70	8.65	123
K32	Northampton	15	3.65	29	46	10.09	115	61	6.84	94
K41	Oxfordshire	52	7.33	125	89	10.40	120	141	8.79	124
L10	Bristol and District	93	7.54	130	162	11.80	128	255	9.66	129
L21	Cornwall and Isles of Scilly	56	7.67	131	111	13.34	135	167	10.61	135
L35	Exeter and North Devon	56	8.18	137	102	13.72	136	158	11.01	137
L36	Plymouth and Torbay	80	9.09	143	154	15.30	142	234	12.31	142
L40	Gloucestershire	53	6.86	120	83	9.25	108	136	8.14	120
L51	Somerset	52	8.67	139	110	16.05	144	162	12.47	145
M02	Herefordshire	14	5.54	99	37	13.28	134	51	9.63	128
M04	Worcester and District	28	7.73	132	42	10.21	117	70	8.90	126
M05	Shropshire	33	5.72	101	52	7.85	87	85	6.86	95
M06	Mid Staffordshire	19	4.56	70	19	4.10	15	38	4.06	21
M07	North Staffordshire	29	4.26	57	44	5.75	43	73	4.99	41
M08	South East Staffordshire	15	3.99	44	19	4.87	27	34	4.46	29
M13	East Birmingham	11	3.55	24	21	6.66	63	32	5.12	46
M14	North Birmingham	14	5.28	89	27	10.37	119	41	7.90	118
M16	West Birmingham	8	2.61	9	16	4.44	22	24	3.69	14
M17	Coventry	21	4.77	76	33	6.88	68	54	5.85	68

27

HON - B3
Incidence of skin cancer (malignant melanoma, ICD 172):
Age-standardised registration rates per 100,000: average for the years 1986-88

		Males Observed	Rate	Rank	Females Observed	Rate	Rank	Persons Observed	Rate	Rank
M18	Dudley	13	2.71	12	38	7.74	82	51	5.17	47
M19	Sandwell	14	3.27	19	18	2.78	5	32	3.23	9
M20	Solihull	15	4.83	79	35	10.00	113	50	7.63	111
M21	Walsall	12	3.60	28	29	7.49	76	41	5.42	55
M22	Wolverhampton	10	2.83	13	20	4.55	23	30	3.80	17
M25	South Birmingham	24	4.07	50	43	6.47	57	67	5.37	53
M26	North Worcestershire	31	8.11	135	43	10.22	118	74	9.15	127
M28	Warwickshire	48	6.86	120	74	9.63	110	122	8.10	119
N11	Chester	15	5.72	101	27	9.08	106	42	7.35	107
N12	Crewe	4	1.04	1	20	4.78	25	24	2.98	5
N13	Halton	3	1.49	2	8	3.79	10	11	2.76	4
N14	Macclesfield	12	4.23	55	27	9.03	104	39	6.56	87
N15	Warrington	8	3.13	18	12	4.37	19	20	3.79	16
N21	Liverpool	25	3.75	31	47	5.84	44	72	4.80	37
N31	St Helens and Knowsley	20	4.29	59	19	3.37	7	39	3.94	20
N41	Southport and Formby	8	4.33	61	13	5.61	40	21	5.04	44
N42	South Sefton	9	3.38	21	16	5.61	40	25	4.43	27
N51	Wirral	19	3.79	35	42	5.90	47	61	5.01	42
P01	Lancaster	12	7.10	123	15	6.07	50	27	6.71	92
P02	Blackpool,Wyre and Fylde	24	3.86	38	50	7.52	77	74	5.70	64
P03	Preston	8	4.42	63	14	8.17	88	22	6.21	74
P04	Blackburn, Hyndburn and Ribble Valley	12	2.99	16	27	6.83	66	39	4.81	38
P05	Burnley, Pendle and Rossendale	11	3.59	27	23	5.56	39	34	4.70	34
P06	West Lancashire	6	3.88	42	15	8.66	97	21	6.25	77
P07	Chorley and South Ribble	12	4.21	54	27	8.79	101	39	6.48	82
P08	Bolton	14	3.87	40	24	5.70	42	38	4.74	36
P09	Bury	5	1.81	5	24	8.77	99	29	5.33	51
P10	North Manchester	5	2.57	8	8	3.75	9	13	3.19	8
P11	Central Manchester	8	4.02	47	3	2.35	3	11	3.17	7
P12	South Manchester	16	6.76	118	12	3.85	12	28	4.73	35
P13	Oldham	8	2.61	9	15	4.41	21	23	3.52	10
P14	Rochdale	12	4.48	68	17	4.95	29	29	4.67	33
P15	Salford	13	3.78	33	21	4.99	30	34	4.45	28
P16	Stockport	30	7.41	128	27	4.82	26	57	5.84	67
P17	Tameside and Glossop	16	4.64	71	38	9.63	110	54	7.06	98
P18	Trafford	18	5.48	97	31	8.78	100	49	7.22	103
P19	Wigan	12	2.67	11	25	5.39	37	37	4.06	21

HON - B3 (continued)
Incidence of skin cancer (other skin cancers, ICD 173):
Age-standardised registration rates per 100,000: average for the years 1986-88

		Males			Females			Persons		
		Observed	Rate	Rank	Observed	Rate	Rank	Observed	Rate	Rank
	ENGLAND AND WALES	47313	60.84		43019	39.52		90332	48.28	
O00	ENGLAND	44619	60.90		40703	39.69		85322	48.39	
A00	NORTHERN RHA	2292	48.71	2	2363	34.66	5	4655	40.57	4
B00	YORKSHIRE RHA	3499	63.31	9	3535	45.28	9	7034	52.25	9
C00	TRENT RHA	4152	57.08	6	3806	38.68	7	7958	46.49	6
D00	EAST ANGLIAN RHA	2462	73.85	11	2052	46.85	11	4514	58.35	12
E00	NORTH WEST THAMES RHA	2618	52.56	4	2173	31.46	3	4791	40.20	3
F00	NORTH EAST THAMES RHA	2637	47.06	1	2306	29.55	1	4943	36.81	1
G00	SOUTH EAST THAMES RHA	3303	55.36	5	2850	32.42	4	6153	41.94	5
H00	SOUTH WEST THAMES RHA	2942	61.63	8	2739	38.56	6	5681	47.97	7
J00	WESSEX RHA	2590	51.44	3	2154	31.29	2	4744	39.54	2
K00	OXFORD RHA	2614	79.00	14	2165	48.49	13	4779	60.73	14
L00	SOUTH WESTERN RHA	4078	74.12	12	3477	47.24	12	7555	58.34	11
M00	WEST MIDLANDS RHA	5261	67.22	10	4874	46.42	10	10135	55.22	10
N00	MERSEY RHA	2651	74.65	13	2551	49.52	14	5202	59.64	13
P00	NORTH WESTERN RHA	3520	59.50	7	3658	41.06	8	7178	48.27	8
A01	Hartlepool	84	62.12	82	79	43.39	90	163	51.82	90
A02	North Tees	126	54.00	53	122	38.90	70	248	45.83	65
A03	South Tees	162	39.25	14	172	29.92	27	334	34.75	23
A04	East Cumbria	196	64.58	90	195	47.81	107	391	55.03	99
A05	South Cumbria	178	58.34	69	184	43.39	90	362	49.51	78
A06	West Cumbria	177	83.08	130	198	69.22	143	375	75.55	142
A11	Northumberland	260	53.26	52	281	40.77	78	541	46.05	66
A12	Gateshead	81	26.88	4	149	29.28	24	230	28.41	13
A13	Newcastle	187	42.93	21	197	25.56	16	384	32.77	17
A14	North Tyneside	113	37.98	13	110	22.03	12	223	27.97	12
A15	South Tyneside	74	28.70	5	92	24.74	15	166	26.53	10
A16	Sunderland	129	32.18	10	120	20.05	9	249	24.68	7
A30	North Durham	297	62.06	81	237	35.49	55	534	46.57	67
A31	South Durham	228	52.43	49	227	38.06	67	455	43.80	53
B11	East Riding	407	51.10	43	422	37.34	61	829	42.53	46
B16	Grimsby and Scunthorpe	446	82.74	129	443	63.28	141	889	71.35	138
B21	North Yorkshire	888	74.17	110	760	45.73	98	1648	57.02	103
B31	Bradford	393	60.84	77	486	52.36	121	879	54.80	97
B51	West Yorkshire	437	52.71	50	482	38.97	71	919	44.24	57
B61	Leeds	746	69.30	98	768	49.25	113	1514	57.08	104
B71	Wakefield	182	39.95	15	174	28.50	23	356	33.41	20
C01	North Derbyshire	387	63.51	87	367	48.91	112	754	54.62	96
C02	Southern Derbyshire	429	51.30	45	381	32.91	39	810	40.50	40
C03	Leicestershire	737	57.25	65	596	34.06	46	1333	43.97	55
C04	North Lincolnshire	362	79.60	122	301	50.57	115	663	62.33	119
C05	South Lincolnshire	287	54.46	57	235	34.87	50	522	43.51	49

HON - B3 (continued)
Incidence of skin cancer (other skin cancers, ICD 173):
Age-standardised registration rates per 100,000: average for the years 1986-88

		Males			Females			Persons		
		Observed	Rate	Rank	Observed	Rate	Rank	Observed	Rate	Rank
C08	Nottingham	413	44.02	24	429	32.63	38	842	37.72	32
C09	Barnsley	218	64.02	88	225	47.70	106	443	55.52	101
C10	Doncaster	240	56.24	61	213	36.27	57	453	44.61	59
C11	Rotherham	229	63.19	86	216	44.00	92	445	52.02	91
C12	Sheffield	557	62.84	85	589	46.61	104	1146	53.70	93
C14	North Nottinghamshire	293	48.78	36	254	31.77	34	547	39.16	34
D01	Cambridge	340	83.83	132	301	55.03	129	641	67.28	132
D05	North West Anglia	552	86.25	135	480	58.77	137	1032	70.90	137
D06	Norwich	452	50.67	41	372	31.63	33	824	39.31	35
D07	Great Yarmouth and Waveney	307	82.31	127	290	58.45	135	597	67.97	133
D09	Huntingdon	138	84.68	133	94	45.76	99	232	63.70	123
D11	Suffolk	673	76.18	114	515	44.29	94	1188	58.05	107
E01	North Bedfordshire	193	56.08	59	165	37.37	62	358	44.96	61
E02	South Bedfordshire	261	73.11	108	209	46.02	101	470	58.58	108
E05	North West Hertfordshire	271	72.95	106	219	42.69	86	490	55.08	100
E06	South West Hertfordshire	269	70.07	102	221	42.96	88	490	54.48	95
E07	Barnet	213	44.44	25	178	24.25	13	391	32.61	16
E09	Hillingdon	213	60.47	76	152	31.51	31	365	43.68	52
E18	East and North Hertfordshire	310	46.12	29	244	25.98	17	554	34.10	21
E19	Brent and Harrow	340	50.46	40	321	33.85	44	661	40.32	38
E20	Ealing, Hammersmith and Hounslow	384	42.39	20	333	26.49	18	717	33.05	19
E21	Kensington, Chelsea and Westminster	164	36.56	12	131	19.52	7	295	26.48	9
F31	North Essex	870	65.13	91	723	40.88	80	1593	51.30	87
F32	South Essex	497	48.53	35	401	26.78	20	898	35.93	26
F33	Barking and Havering	194	30.65	7	153	18.99	6	347	23.71	6
F34	Redbridge and Waltham Forest	303	43.52	22	332	32.39	36	635	36.48	27
F35	East London and the City	342	44.58	26	298	29.57	25	640	35.76	25
F36	New River District	230	33.88	11	215	21.87	11	445	26.58	11
F37	Camden and Islington	201	40.08	16	184	24.64	14	385	31.38	15
G04	South East Kent	241	51.17	44	193	27.52	21	434	36.97	30
G05	Canterbury and Thanet	325	57.12	62	234	30.10	28	559	40.65	41
G06	Dartford and Gravesham	178	57.79	66	155	35.31	53	333	45.42	62
G07	Maidstone	174	61.93	80	131	33.04	40	305	45.72	64
G08	Medway	262	58.83	70	264	41.71	82	526	49.55	80
G09	Tunbridge Wells	104	32.02	9	100	19.74	8	204	25.17	8
G10	Bexley	222	69.52	99	173	37.66	64	395	51.35	88
G11	Greenwich	190	59.50	74	142	30.13	29	332	43.00	48
G12	Bromley	225	46.16	30	200	27.98	22	425	35.48	24
G21	East Sussex	957	67.25	95	835	38.04	66	1792	49.76	82
G26	South East London	425	41.02	17	423	29.77	26	848	34.51	22

HON - B3 (continued)
Incidence of skin cancer (other skin cancers, ICD 173):
Age-standardised registration rates per 100,000: average for the years 1986-88

		Males			Females			Persons		
		Observed	Rate	Rank	Observed	Rate	Rank	Observed	Rate	Rank
H04	Mid Surrey	206	68.65	97	223	54.52	126	429	59.13	111
H05	East Surrey	194	62.64	84	188	39.87	75	382	49.51	78
H06	Chichester	364	92.44	140	338	60.52	139	702	73.59	141
H07	Mid Downs	290	72.47	105	242	42.13	83	532	54.18	94
H08	Worthing	346	68.14	96	309	34.39	48	655	47.85	75
H09	Croydon	211	47.06	32	232	35.46	54	443	39.86	37
H12	Wandsworth	108	42.15	19	90	21.46	10	198	30.21	14
H13	Merton and Sutton	220	41.76	18	210	26.74	19	430	32.85	18
H14	North West Surrey	372	65.83	92	289	36.71	58	661	49.45	77
H15	South West Surrey	308	79.77	123	273	49.75	114	581	62.88	120
H16	Kingston and Richmond	323	48.32	34	345	34.04	45	668	39.73	36
J10	Dorset	748	58.22	68	647	33.60	42	1395	44.13	56
J21	Portsmouth and South East Hampshire	752	94.44	142	638	57.23	134	1390	72.16	140
J22	Southampton and South West Hampshire	183	26.00	3	135	14.57	3	318	19.39	3
J23	Winchester	145	45.71	28	134	32.33	35	279	36.86	29
J24	Basingstoke and North Hampshire	202	45.69	27	179	30.26	30	381	36.65	28
J31	Salisbury	50	22.46	1	42	17.62	5	92	19.26	2
J32	Swindon	203	64.14	89	149	35.86	56	352	47.23	71
J33	Bath	161	23.69	2	107	11.22	1	268	15.93	1
J41	Isle of Wight	146	54.47	58	123	36.94	59	269	43.60	50
K11	East Berkshire	136	29.22	6	97	14.61	4	233	20.21	4
K12	West Berkshire	338	59.27	71	265	34.28	47	603	44.60	58
K24	Buckinghamshire	594	84.80	134	502	51.14	116	1096	63.12	121
K31	Kettering	362	93.03	141	286	53.95	123	648	70.82	136
K32	Northampton	364	86.42	136	312	54.49	125	676	68.30	134
K41	Oxfordshire	820	111.07	144	703	73.95	144	1523	89.20	144
L10	Bristol and District	885	70.06	101	827	46.67	105	1712	56.05	102
L21	Cornwall and Isles of Scilly	1008	122.12	145	879	80.96	145	1887	97.91	145
L35	Exeter and North Devon	491	59.38	73	415	38.20	68	906	47.20	70
L36	Plymouth and Torbay	664	66.00	94	532	39.92	76	1196	50.66	86
L40	Gloucestershire	446	52.28	48	373	34.41	49	819	41.87	44
L51	Somerset	584	81.63	126	451	45.99	100	1035	60.90	117
M02	Herefordshire	221	79.12	121	190	54.83	128	411	65.22	127
M04	Worcester and District	350	87.72	137	274	51.47	119	624	66.82	130
M05	Shropshire	452	74.08	109	358	44.76	95	810	57.25	105
M06	Mid Staffordshire	253	58.18	67	214	37.97	65	467	47.06	69
M07	North Staffordshire	432	60.42	75	401	41.01	81	833	48.83	76
M08	South East Staffordshire	206	61.82	79	193	42.39	85	399	50.62	85
M13	East Birmingham	205	71.96	104	191	44.27	93	396	54.95	98
M14	North Birmingham	226	88.48	138	170	48.31	109	396	65.02	125
M16	West Birmingham	172	59.35	72	186	45.68	97	358	51.54	89
M17	Coventry	390	81.12	125	356	55.87	132	746	66.97	131

HON - B3 (continued)
Incidence of skin cancer (other skin cancers, ICD 173):
Age-standardised registration rates per 100,000: average for the years 1986-88

		Males			Females			Persons		
		Observed	Rate	Rank	Observed	Rate	Rank	Observed	Rate	Rank
M18	Dudley	238	52.26	47	274	42.95	87	512	47.46	73
M19	Sandwell	233	49.17	39	243	37.19	60	476	42.37	45
M20	Solihull	227	79.95	124	232	60.78	140	459	68.73	135
M21	Walsall	184	47.20	33	192	37.45	63	376	42.57	47
M22	Wolverhampton	180	47.03	31	167	33.17	41	347	39.02	33
M25	South Birmingham	442	70.13	103	473	54.77	127	915	60.69	116
M26	North Worcestershire	290	78.02	118	269	55.72	131	559	65.15	126
M28	Warwickshire	560	74.98	113	491	51.40	118	1051	61.60	118
N11	Chester	292	110.94	143	236	65.56	142	528	84.67	143
N12	Crewe	116	30.85	8	68	13.14	2	184	20.60	5
N13	Halton	117	62.35	83	148	58.53	136	265	60.59	115
N14	Macclesfield	170	61.26	78	141	35.03	52	311	45.71	63
N15	Warrington	195	76.62	115	166	48.18	108	361	60.45	114
N21	Liverpool	563	77.56	117	584	54.28	124	1147	63.50	122
N31	St Helens and Knowsley	330	73.10	107	332	51.35	117	662	59.90	112
N41	Southport and Formby	187	91.34	139	201	59.64	138	388	71.45	139
N42	South Sefton	219	82.48	128	207	53.45	122	426	65.39	128
N51	Wirral	462	83.48	131	468	56.17	133	930	66.64	129
P01	Lancaster	179	79.00	120	161	46.54	103	340	59.07	110
P02	Blackpool,Wyre and Fylde	436	69.71	100	400	42.34	84	836	52.70	92
P03	Preston	151	78.27	119	158	55.48	130	309	64.96	124
P04	Blackburn, Hyndburn and Ribble Valley	256	65.92	93	235	39.77	73	491	49.68	81
P05	Burnley, Pendle and Rossendale	171	51.00	42	176	33.67	43	347	40.45	39
P06	West Lancashire	104	74.34	111	98	48.56	110	202	58.03	106
P07	Chorley and South Ribble	195	76.89	116	191	52.02	120	386	60.19	113
P08	Bolton	183	49.09	38	227	39.27	72	410	43.62	51
P09	Bury	141	54.44	56	176	46.37	102	317	50.26	84
P10	North Manchester	107	51.86	46	133	38.65	69	240	43.84	54
P11	Central Manchester	90	57.15	63	94	39.80	74	184	47.74	74
P12	South Manchester	192	74.49	112	198	48.86	111	390	58.90	109
P13	Oldham	181	57.18	64	204	45.25	96	385	49.78	83
P14	Rochdale	129	43.90	23	140	32.61	37	269	37.30	31
P15	Salford	206	56.16	60	217	40.51	77	423	46.91	68
P16	Stockport	233	54.23	55	206	31.54	32	439	41.04	43
P17	Tameside and Glossop	181	52.73	51	210	40.85	79	391	44.87	60
P18	Trafford	177	54.14	54	209	43.25	89	386	47.36	72
P19	Wigan	208	48.91	37	225	34.97	51	433	40.98	42

HON - B4,B5
Mortality rates from lung cancer (ICD 162) in men and women under 75:
Age-standardised mortality rates per 100,000: average for the years 1990-92

		Males			Females			Persons		
		Observed	Rate	Rank	Observed	Rate	Rank	Observed	Rate	Rank
	ENGLAND AND WALES	44029	58.19		20333	23.78		64362	39.79	
O00	ENGLAND	41363	58.24		19098	23.79		60461	39.82	
A00	NORTHERN RHA	3802	78.98	14	1950	35.93	14	5752	55.77	14
B00	YORKSHIRE RHA	3370	62.42	10	1674	27.35	11	5044	43.61	11
C00	TRENT RHA	4147	56.71	8	1843	23.16	9	5990	38.98	8
D00	EAST ANGLIAN RHA	1434	43.63	1	611	17.11	1	2045	29.62	1
E00	NORTH WEST THAMES RHA	2372	51.40	6	1163	22.63	7	3535	36.10	6
F00	NORTH EAST THAMES RHA	3091	58.84	9	1387	23.46	10	4478	40.00	9
G00	SOUTH EAST THAMES RHA	3015	55.45	7	1444	22.81	8	4459	37.73	7
H00	SOUTH WEST THAMES RHA	2019	47.05	3	965	19.21	5	2984	31.90	3
J00	WESSEX RHA	2329	48.95	5	972	17.53	2	3301	32.16	4
K00	OXFORD RHA	1623	48.53	4	699	19.17	4	2322	33.01	5
L00	SOUTH WESTERN RHA	2436	45.80	2	1076	17.71	3	3512	30.73	2
M00	WEST MIDLANDS RHA	5058	63.84	11	1946	21.96	6	7004	41.64	10
N00	MERSEY RHA	2632	74.67	13	1329	32.40	13	3961	51.85	13
P00	NORTH WESTERN RHA	4035	69.73	12	2039	30.46	12	6074	48.65	12
A01	Hartlepool	110	79.43	127	93	59.45	145	203	68.26	139
A02	North Tees	245	98.83	141	81	28.53	106	326	61.81	136
A03	South Tees	345	80.76	132	195	41.21	138	540	59.55	135
A04	East Cumbria	171	59.76	86	75	21.71	66	246	39.66	79
A05	South Cumbria	174	60.64	87	66	20.05	47	240	38.68	71
A06	West Cumbria	134	60.99	90	68	27.66	103	202	42.92	94
A11	Northumberland	317	62.96	97	168	30.90	115	485	45.93	100
A12	Gateshead	316	95.69	139	160	44.64	141	476	67.42	138
A13	Newcastle	378	93.93	138	227	47.71	142	605	68.74	140
A14	North Tyneside	261	81.58	133	141	37.05	134	402	57.20	132
A15	South Tyneside	272	102.46	143	130	44.60	140	402	71.03	143
A16	Sunderland	393	91.72	137	194	39.86	137	587	63.68	137
A30	North Durham	363	72.09	114	187	34.12	127	550	51.59	119
A31	South Durham	323	71.53	112	165	31.81	118	488	50.15	116
B11	East Riding	517	65.52	101	290	32.34	123	807	47.67	109
B16	Grimsby and Scunthorpe	348	62.75	95	143	24.12	81	491	42.30	91
B21	North Yorkshire	549	48.27	37	252	19.81	45	801	32.94	37
B31	Bradford	459	72.56	115	207	29.17	107	666	49.37	113
B51	West Yorkshire	492	61.16	92	244	26.55	98	736	42.42	92
B61	Leeds	676	66.33	102	367	30.77	114	1043	47.27	106
B71	Wakefield	329	70.60	108	171	32.26	122	500	50.13	115
C01	North Derbyshire	341	56.29	69	154	23.25	75	495	38.73	72
C02	Southern Derbyshire	461	54.89	61	188	21.04	59	649	37.01	62
C03	Leicestershire	555	43.41	14	245	17.77	28	800	29.99	20
C04	North Lincolnshire	257	52.66	51	105	19.86	46	362	35.43	50
C05	South Lincolnshire	237	43.52	17	125	21.62	65	362	32.04	29

33

HON - B4,B5
Mortality rates from lung cancer (ICD 162) in men and women under 75:
Age-standardised mortality rates per 100,000: average for the years 1990-92

		Males Observed	Rate	Rank	Females Observed	Rate	Rank	Persons Observed	Rate	Rank
C08	Nottingham	525	56.09	66	261	25.67	93	786	40.02	81
C09	Barnsley	250	71.15	109	93	24.69	86	343	46.50	102
C10	Doncaster	279	61.19	93	151	29.86	109	430	44.71	96
C11	Rotherham	254	67.66	103	103	25.40	92	357	45.06	97
C12	Sheffield	563	68.74	104	263	27.79	104	826	46.62	103
C14	North Nottinghamshire	425	68.99	105	155	23.60	79	580	45.25	98
D01	Cambridge	165	41.35	9	57	13.37	3	222	26.42	2
D05	North West Anglia	303	47.18	32	130	18.52	38	433	32.25	34
D06	Norwich	348	41.06	8	140	14.90	7	488	27.27	4
D07	Great Yarmouth and Waveney	171	47.09	31	85	21.57	63	256	33.55	38
D09	Huntingdon	98	60.74	89	43	24.96	89	141	41.89	89
D11	Suffolk	349	40.09	4	156	16.64	18	505	27.55	8
E01	North Bedfordshire	199	58.76	81	76	20.65	54	275	38.88	73
E02	South Bedfordshire	204	57.58	75	93	24.92	87	297	40.87	86
E05	North West Hertfordshire	175	46.20	27	94	23.37	78	269	33.99	44
E06	South West Hertfordshire	189	52.07	46	52	12.36	1	241	30.98	25
E07	Barnet	182	45.42	23	99	20.79	57	281	31.85	28
E09	Hillingdon	171	53.32	53	82	22.97	73	253	36.92	61
E18	East and North Hertfordshire	314	45.16	22	166	22.30	69	480	32.93	36
E19	Brent and Harrow	259	46.20	27	124	19.76	44	383	32.16	32
E20	Ealing, Hammersmith and Hounslow	441	56.36	71	230	26.07	95	671	40.23	83
E21	Kensington, Chelsea and Westminster	238	55.74	63	147	29.92	110	385	42.18	90
F31	North Essex	631	48.01	36	272	18.16	34	903	32.11	30
F32	South Essex	554	54.15	58	245	20.91	58	799	36.36	57
F33	Barking and Havering	356	59.14	82	163	24.00	80	519	40.16	82
F34	Redbridge and Waltham Forest	315	53.32	53	176	25.97	94	491	38.51	70
F35	East London and the City	592	84.86	136	237	31.86	119	829	57.60	133
F36	New River District	308	52.50	49	143	21.59	64	451	35.88	53
F37	Camden and Islington	335	75.96	122	151	30.65	113	486	51.84	120
G04	South East Kent	224	50.47	42	107	20.31	49	331	34.02	45
G05	Canterbury and Thanet	270	52.48	48	148	25.09	90	418	37.48	64
G06	Dartford and Gravesham	189	59.31	83	73	21.21	60	262	39.00	75
G07	Maidstone	128	45.91	25	60	18.17	35	188	31.40	27
G08	Medway	246	56.36	71	111	22.24	67	357	38.04	67
G09	Tunbridge Wells	138	44.51	20	55	16.21	14	193	28.91	16
G10	Bexley	181	58.32	77	92	25.31	91	273	40.79	85
G11	Greenwich	203	71.55	113	124	36.26	133	327	52.02	122
G12	Bromley	226	49.68	41	91	17.64	26	317	32.18	33
G21	East Sussex	550	46.32	29	256	17.42	23	806	30.31	21
G26	South East London	660	74.24	120	327	32.52	124	987	51.96	121

HON - B4,B5
Mortality rates from lung cancer (ICD 162) in men and women under 75:
Age-standardised mortality rates per 100,000: average for the years 1990-92

		Males			Females			Persons		
		Observed	Rate	Rank	Observed	Rate	Rank	Observed	Rate	Rank
H04	Mid Surrey	125	45.05	21	46	14.35	4	171	28.70	15
H05	East Surrey	113	39.82	3	53	16.05	12	166	27.17	3
H06	Chichester	151	46.03	26	61	15.01	8	212	28.97	18
H07	Mid Downs	190	47.22	33	82	17.24	22	272	30.96	24
H08	Worthing	164	39.60	2	91	17.71	27	255	27.49	7
H09	Croydon	199	48.86	39	98	20.73	56	297	33.56	39
H12	Wandsworth	164	78.08	125	80	32.05	120	244	53.59	127
H13	Merton and Sutton	261	56.94	73	122	23.33	76	383	38.27	69
H14	North West Surrey	245	44.05	19	120	19.59	42	365	31.03	26
H15	South West Surrey	137	38.71	1	53	13.00	2	190	24.70	1
H16	Kingston and Richmond	270	47.03	30	159	23.06	74	429	33.80	43
J10	Dorset	509	43.57	18	222	15.05	9	731	28.26	11
J21	Portsmouth and South East Hampshire	432	56.30	70	171	19.33	40	603	36.36	57
J22	Southampton and South West Hampshire	355	53.46	55	147	19.66	43	502	35.44	51
J23	Winchester	141	45.69	24	63	17.06	20	204	30.42	22
J24	Basingstoke and North Hampshire	243	54.58	60	102	20.44	51	345	36.74	60
J31	Salisbury	83	41.44	10	39	17.05	19	122	28.30	13
J32	Swindon	187	56.19	68	74	20.67	55	261	37.41	63
J33	Bath	262	41.68	11	108	14.89	6	370	27.43	6
J41	Isle of Wight	117	48.76	38	46	16.27	16	163	30.91	23
K11	East Berkshire	252	51.14	43	99	17.97	31	351	33.56	39
K12	West Berkshire	229	40.31	6	109	17.82	29	338	28.28	12
K24	Buckinghamshire	360	47.38	34	152	18.25	37	512	32.13	31
K31	Kettering	215	55.84	65	91	22.25	68	306	37.89	66
K32	Northampton	227	52.31	47	105	22.33	70	332	36.44	59
K41	Oxfordshire	340	47.97	35	143	18.56	39	483	32.50	35
L10	Bristol and District	645	52.50	49	270	19.43	41	915	34.80	47
L21	Cornwall and Isles of Scilly	359	43.41	14	146	15.42	10	505	28.42	14
L35	Exeter and North Devon	315	40.10	5	166	18.00	33	481	28.21	10
L36	Plymouth and Torbay	462	49.21	40	222	20.56	52	684	33.73	42
L40	Gloucestershire	365	43.41	14	153	16.24	15	518	28.92	17
L51	Somerset	290	41.74	12	119	14.85	5	409	27.30	5
M02	Herefordshire	120	42.24	13	51	17.63	25	171	29.06	19
M04	Worcester and District	164	40.92	7	71	16.18	13	235	27.68	9
M05	Shropshire	348	55.83	64	128	17.98	32	476	35.67	52
M06	Mid Staffordshire	271	59.53	85	102	20.62	53	373	38.99	74
M07	North Staffordshire	592	80.18	128	203	24.23	82	795	50.57	118
M08	South East Staffordshire	196	54.48	59	72	17.58	24	268	34.91	48
M13	East Birmingham	226	77.15	123	85	26.18	96	311	50.04	114
M14	North Birmingham	152	61.04	91	58	20.30	48	210	39.13	76
M16	West Birmingham	200	73.19	119	74	24.55	85	274	48.41	112
M17	Coventry	327	71.49	111	139	27.58	102	466	47.99	110

HON - B4,B5
Mortality rates from lung cancer (ICD 162) in men and women under 75:
Age-standardised mortality rates per 100,000: average for the years 1990-92

		Males			Females			Persons		
		Observed	Rate	Rank	Observed	Rate	Rank	Observed	Rate	Rank
M18	Dudley	274	57.38	74	82	15.44	11	356	35.06	49
M19	Sandwell	380	81.98	134	144	27.07	99	524	52.87	123
M20	Solihull	156	51.31	44	80	23.36	77	236	36.26	56
M21	Walsall	278	70.18	107	109	24.94	88	387	46.08	101
M22	Wolverhampton	293	74.26	121	107	24.46	84	400	47.99	110
M25	South Birmingham	429	71.28	110	183	26.31	97	612	47.31	107
M26	North Worcestershire	236	60.65	88	79	17.94	30	315	38.14	68
M28	Warwickshire	416	55.34	62	179	21.43	61	595	37.58	65
N11	Chester	157	58.36	78	69	22.68	71	226	39.28	77
N12	Crewe	220	56.18	67	78	18.18	36	298	35.98	54
N13	Halton	150	77.67	124	77	34.35	128	227	54.69	129
N14	Macclesfield	151	53.86	56	54	17.09	21	205	34.33	46
N15	Warrington	166	65.05	99	79	27.36	101	245	45.34	99
N21	Liverpool	652	96.79	140	388	49.44	143	1040	70.86	142
N31	St Helens and Knowsley	387	80.70	129	192	35.02	130	579	55.87	131
N41	Southport and Formby	115	58.60	80	72	30.12	111	187	42.71	93
N42	South Sefton	211	80.74	130	111	35.12	131	322	55.64	130
N51	Wirral	423	80.74	130	209	32.07	121	632	54.49	128
P01	Lancaster	122	57.62	76	61	24.34	83	183	39.70	80
P02	Blackpool, Wyre and Fylde	343	58.54	79	187	27.18	100	530	41.55	88
P03	Preston	131	73.04	117	73	34.75	129	204	52.89	124
P04	Blackburn, Hyndburn and Ribble Valley	240	62.56	94	102	22.89	72	342	41.51	87
P05	Burnley, Pendle and Rossendale	200	59.48	84	119	30.22	112	319	43.70	95
P06	West Lancashire	81	52.89	52	29	16.39	17	110	33.57	41
P07	Chorley and South Ribble	151	54.00	57	63	20.31	49	214	36.01	55
P08	Bolton	241	65.19	100	130	30.90	115	371	46.71	104
P09	Bury	127	51.53	45	84	29.64	108	211	39.51	78
P10	North Manchester	212	108.46	144	125	55.63	144	337	80.95	145
P11	Central Manchester	164	116.88	145	60	39.51	136	224	77.40	144
P12	South Manchester	196	83.75	135	104	37.25	135	300	58.27	134
P13	Oldham	219	72.62	116	125	36.22	132	344	52.95	125
P14	Rochdale	215	73.07	118	101	31.03	117	316	50.42	117
P15	Salford	347	100.65	142	170	42.88	139	517	69.40	141
P16	Stockport	268	62.83	96	111	21.47	62	379	40.62	84
P17	Tameside and Glossop	274	78.14	126	133	32.94	126	407	53.51	126
P18	Trafford	205	64.73	98	116	32.64	125	321	47.66	108
P19	Wigan	299	69.81	106	146	27.79	104	445	47.08	105

HON - C2
Suicide rates (ICD E950-E959, E980-E989):
Age-standardised mortality rates per 100,000: average for the years 1990-92

		Males			Females			Persons		
		Observed	Rate	Rank	Observed	Rate	Rank	Observed	Rate	Rank
	ENGLAND AND WALES	12979	16.85		4747	5.65		17726	11.14	
O00	ENGLAND	12200	16.77		4502	5.68		16702	11.12	
A00	NORTHERN RHA	751	16.24	6	297	5.95	10	1048	10.97	7
B00	YORKSHIRE RHA	944	17.30	10	353	5.97	11	1297	11.52	10
C00	TRENT RHA	1154	15.98	5	407	5.29	4	1561	10.59	5
D00	EAST ANGLIAN RHA	587	18.66	13	170	4.81	3	757	11.66	11
E00	NORTH WEST THAMES RHA	885	16.52	7	356	6.28	12	1241	11.31	9
F00	NORTH EAST THAMES RHA	893	15.62	4	359	5.71	8	1252	10.53	4
G00	SOUTH EAST THAMES RHA	1034	18.56	12	399	6.67	13	1433	12.40	13
H00	SOUTH WEST THAMES RHA	691	15.27	3	283	5.45	6	974	10.22	3
J00	WESSEX RHA	802	16.84	9	302	5.70	7	1104	11.20	8
K00	OXFORD RHA	647	16.77	8	194	4.74	2	841	10.75	6
L00	SOUTH WESTERN RHA	901	17.92	11	323	5.79	9	1224	11.74	12
M00	WEST MIDLANDS RHA	1217	15.25	1	455	5.37	5	1672	10.21	2
N00	MERSEY RHA	543	15.25	1	167	4.14	1	710	9.58	1
P00	NORTH WESTERN RHA	1151	19.40	14	437	6.72	14	1588	12.97	14
A01	Hartlepool	20	15.12	52	3	2.39	2	23	8.54	13
A02	North Tees	33	12.81	13	15	5.82	86	48	8.87	18
A03	South Tees	70	16.71	74	36	8.42	137	106	12.42	108
A04	East Cumbria	54	19.58	119	27	9.92	141	81	14.75	133
A05	South Cumbria	55	21.31	131	15	4.88	44	70	13.04	124
A06	West Cumbria	45	20.94	129	10	4.09	23	55	12.50	113
A11	Northumberland	67	14.21	40	30	6.21	99	97	10.09	57
A12	Gateshead	45	15.03	49	7	1.97	1	52	8.37	7
A13	Newcastle	89	22.05	134	36	7.99	135	125	14.76	134
A14	North Tyneside	50	17.37	87	20	5.55	76	70	11.24	84
A15	South Tyneside	31	14.06	31	16	5.92	91	47	9.90	46
A16	Sunderland	57	13.03	18	28	6.00	92	85	9.44	29
A30	North Durham	71	14.47	44	28	5.65	80	99	10.04	54
A31	South Durham	64	15.03	49	26	5.25	63	90	10.04	54
B11	East Riding	107	14.02	29	44	5.22	62	151	9.51	30
B16	Grimsby and Scunthorpe	80	15.22	56	28	5.06	56	108	10.17	59
B21	North Yorkshire	185	16.99	81	75	6.44	108	260	11.45	88
B31	Bradford	128	18.70	107	49	6.24	104	177	12.44	110
B51	West Yorkshire	173	20.28	123	60	6.30	107	233	13.11	126
B61	Leeds	196	17.64	94	77	6.97	124	273	12.35	107
B71	Wakefield	75	16.22	68	20	3.88	15	95	9.88	43
C01	North Derbyshire	98	17.19	83	32	5.01	52	130	11.03	78
C02	Southern Derbyshire	119	14.48	45	43	5.09	58	162	9.64	35
C03	Leicestershire	203	14.83	48	74	5.28	66	277	10.03	53
C04	North Lincolnshire	65	15.37	59	23	4.50	31	88	9.89	45
C05	South Lincolnshire	77	16.37	71	23	4.71	37	100	10.35	65

HON - C2
Suicide rates (ICD E950-E959, E980-E989):
Age-standardised mortality rates per 100,000: average for the years 1990-92

		Males			Females			Persons		
		Observed	Rate	Rank	Observed	Rate	Rank	Observed	Rate	Rank
C08	Nottingham	156	16.27	69	61	6.08	96	217	11.16	80
C09	Barnsley	46	13.91	26	21	5.69	82	67	9.91	47
C10	Doncaster	83	18.61	106	32	6.84	120	115	12.68	118
C11	Rotherham	65	16.80	78	20	5.40	69	85	10.93	77
C12	Sheffield	115	14.48	45	46	4.92	46	161	9.67	38
C14	North Nottinghamshire	127	20.79	126	32	4.96	49	159	12.82	120
D01	Cambridge	81	18.33	101	26	5.47	71	107	11.94	102
D05	North West Anglia	129	21.47	132	46	6.90	122	175	13.98	131
D06	Norwich	130	17.57	92	41	4.95	48	171	11.17	81
D07	Great Yarmouth and Waveney	52	17.56	91	12	3.41	9	64	10.36	66
D09	Huntingdon	35	17.18	82	7	2.89	3	42	9.93	49
D11	Suffolk	160	19.12	112	38	3.84	13	198	11.42	87
E01	North Bedfordshire	73	19.10	111	23	6.18	98	96	12.46	112
E02	South Bedfordshire	72	17.36	86	25	5.83	87	97	11.49	89
E05	North West Hertfordshire	58	14.41	43	18	3.94	18	76	9.17	26
E06	South West Hertfordshire	60	16.80	78	24	5.88	88	84	11.23	83
E07	Barnet	57	12.24	7	32	7.07	127	89	9.59	33
E09	Hillingdon	44	11.71	3	16	4.28	26	60	7.95	2
E18	East and North Hertfordshire	95	13.00	17	26	3.23	8	121	7.99	3
E19	Brent and Harrow	128	18.37	102	38	5.38	67	166	11.78	98
E20	Ealing, Hammersmith and Hounslow	191	19.25	113	79	7.35	129	270	13.19	128
E21	Kensington, Chelsea and Westminster	107	20.90	127	75	12.91	145	182	16.86	142
F31	North Essex	201	15.37	59	55	3.91	17	256	9.55	32
F32	South Essex	146	14.07	32	68	5.68	81	214	9.73	40
F33	Barking and Havering	90	16.44	72	25	3.75	12	115	9.91	47
F34	Redbridge and Waltham Forest	85	12.26	8	38	4.79	42	123	8.47	11
F35	East London and the City	151	18.05	98	57	6.22	100	208	11.95	103
F36	New River District	96	13.31	20	55	7.06	126	151	10.07	56
F37	Camden and Islington	124	22.18	135	61	10.37	143	185	15.99	141
G04	South East Kent	80	19.73	121	21	4.07	22	101	11.86	100
G05	Canterbury and Thanet	75	16.79	77	38	7.64	132	113	12.01	105
G06	Dartford and Gravesham	48	13.74	24	18	5.39	68	66	9.51	30
G07	Maidstone	46	15.15	54	15	5.03	53	61	10.00	51
G08	Medway	78	15.20	55	25	5.04	55	103	9.94	50
G09	Tunbridge Wells	41	14.12	34	18	5.27	65	59	9.64	35
G10	Bexley	40	12.66	12	14	4.35	28	54	8.05	5
G11	Greenwich	57	18.15	99	16	5.13	59	73	11.54	90
G12	Bromley	58	12.90	16	25	5.63	78	83	8.99	21
G21	East Sussex	241	22.22	136	105	7.82	133	346	14.78	135
G26	South East London	270	25.84	143	104	9.14	139	374	17.10	143

HON - C2
Suicide rates (ICD E950-E959, E980-E989):
Age-standardised mortality rates per 100,000: average for the years 1990-92

		Males			Females			Persons		
		Observed	Rate	Rank	Observed	Rate	Rank	Observed	Rate	Rank
H04	Mid Surrey	35	13.57	23	15	5.03	53	50	9.04	22
H05	East Surrey	56	19.27	114	20	6.55	112	76	12.64	117
H06	Chichester	50	20.44	125	10	3.17	7	60	11.61	93
H07	Mid Downs	75	17.37	87	29	5.89	89	104	11.57	91
H08	Worthing	71	19.45	116	31	6.01	94	102	12.52	114
H09	Croydon	56	12.11	5	26	4.69	36	82	8.45	10
H12	Wandsworth	52	19.02	110	19	7.58	131	71	13.08	125
H13	Merton and Sutton	81	15.59	62	36	6.22	100	117	10.65	70
H14	North West Surrey	77	12.87	14	36	5.25	63	113	9.04	22
H15	South West Surrey	46	12.33	10	19	4.52	33	65	8.44	9
H16	Kingston and Richmond	92	14.17	36	42	5.72	83	134	9.75	41
J10	Dorset	194	19.56	118	69	5.61	77	263	12.42	108
J21	Portsmouth and South East Hampshire	117	14.17	36	52	5.79	84	169	10.02	52
J22	Southampton and South West Hampshire	138	20.92	128	45	6.25	106	183	13.40	129
J23	Winchester	47	13.78	25	15	4.16	24	62	8.85	16
J24	Basingstoke and North Hampshire	82	14.05	30	39	6.91	123	121	10.54	68
J31	Salisbury	34	18.37	102	14	7.00	125	48	12.52	114
J32	Swindon	65	17.86	96	19	4.88	44	84	11.32	85
J33	Bath	95	15.38	61	37	5.21	61	132	10.25	63
J41	Isle of Wight	30	16.08	65	12	4.72	38	42	10.44	67
K11	East Berkshire	88	16.30	70	33	5.63	78	121	10.92	76
K12	West Berkshire	123	17.57	92	28	4.03	21	151	10.80	74
K24	Buckinghamshire	138	15.14	53	43	4.53	34	181	9.88	43
K31	Kettering	73	18.46	104	22	5.00	51	95	11.61	93
K32	Northampton	86	18.18	100	27	5.49	72	113	11.74	97
K41	Oxfordshire	139	16.93	80	41	4.39	29	180	10.67	71
L10	Bristol and District	236	18.48	105	55	3.96	19	291	11.14	79
L21	Cornwall and Isles of Scilly	117	16.18	67	81	10.26	142	198	13.12	127
L35	Exeter and North Devon	114	16.52	73	40	4.29	27	154	10.24	62
L36	Plymouth and Torbay	162	18.04	97	58	6.00	92	220	11.95	103
L40	Gloucestershire	144	17.34	85	55	6.23	103	199	11.65	96
L51	Somerset	128	20.42	124	34	4.76	40	162	12.45	111
M02	Herefordshire	40	15.05	51	14	5.91	90	54	10.14	58
M04	Worcester and District	53	14.09	33	23	5.52	74	76	9.87	42
M05	Shropshire	78	12.37	11	24	3.47	10	102	7.87	1
M06	Mid Staffordshire	76	15.65	63	26	4.98	50	102	10.17	59
M07	North Staffordshire	126	17.49	90	37	5.13	59	163	11.22	82
M08	South East Staffordshire	47	11.70	2	21	5.06	56	68	8.34	6
M13	East Birmingham	43	15.35	58	16	6.09	97	59	10.73	72
M14	North Birmingham	35	14.35	42	13	4.76	40	48	9.65	37
M16	West Birmingham	76	24.79	142	24	7.32	128	100	15.83	139
M17	Coventry	89	19.72	120	28	6.24	104	117	12.93	123

39

HON - C2
Suicide rates (ICD E950-E959, E980-E989):
Age-standardised mortality rates per 100,000: average for the years 1990-92

		Males			Females			Persons		
		Observed	Rate	Rank	Observed	Rate	Rank	Observed	Rate	Rank
M18	Dudley	66	13.92	27	21	3.89	16	87	8.77	15
M19	Sandwell	62	14.61	47	20	4.16	24	82	9.34	27
M20	Solihull	36	12.08	4	19	4.85	43	55	8.55	14
M21	Walsall	58	14.28	41	30	7.42	130	88	10.82	75
M22	Wolverhampton	71	20.07	122	25	6.56	113	96	12.77	119
M25	South Birmingham	113	17.46	89	46	6.54	111	159	11.93	101
M26	North Worcestershire	48	11.54	1	29	6.78	119	77	9.10	25
M28	Warwickshire	100	13.09	19	39	4.72	38	139	8.86	17
N11	Chester	38	14.13	35	8	3.13	6	46	8.43	8
N12	Crewe	58	15.24	57	27	6.66	116	85	10.77	73
N13	Halton	35	16.73	75	7	2.98	4	42	9.68	39
N14	Macclesfield	35	12.89	15	10	3.08	5	45	8.03	4
N15	Warrington	52	18.76	108	14	4.43	30	66	11.60	92
N21	Liverpool	110	15.86	64	29	3.86	14	139	9.59	33
N31	St Helens and Knowsley	71	14.18	38	21	3.98	20	92	8.93	20
N41	Southport and Formby	20	12.18	6	12	5.54	75	32	8.89	19
N42	South Sefton	35	13.33	21	17	4.50	31	52	9.08	24
N51	Wirral	89	17.75	95	22	3.72	11	111	10.58	69
P01	Lancaster	37	19.51	117	16	6.71	117	53	12.90	122
P02	Blackpool,Wyre and Fylde	92	18.89	109	35	6.07	95	127	12.19	106
P03	Preston	47	24.36	141	12	5.80	85	59	15.25	137
P04	Blackburn, Hyndburn and Ribble Valley	76	19.33	115	29	6.22	100	105	12.84	121
P05	Burnley, Pendle and Rossendale	79	22.35	138	37	9.49	140	116	15.94	140
P06	West Lancashire	19	12.31	9	9	5.49	72	28	8.52	12
P07	Chorley and South Ribble	49	16.11	66	22	6.84	120	71	11.38	86
P08	Bolton	82	21.01	130	20	4.92	46	102	12.56	116
P09	Bury	44	16.77	76	20	6.64	115	64	11.80	99
P10	North Manchester	63	32.13	144	20	11.17	144	83	21.43	145
P11	Central Manchester	57	34.22	145	15	8.11	136	72	21.19	144
P12	South Manchester	57	23.07	140	23	8.96	138	80	15.69	138
P13	Oldham	72	22.02	133	25	6.49	110	97	14.31	132
P14	Rochdale	68	22.30	137	25	7.88	134	93	15.01	136
P15	Salford	73	22.50	139	21	5.41	70	94	13.95	130
P16	Stockport	58	13.49	22	32	6.74	118	90	10.20	61
P17	Tameside and Glossop	53	14.20	39	20	4.65	35	73	9.36	28
P18	Trafford	44	13.95	28	24	6.58	114	68	10.32	64
P19	Wigan	81	17.19	83	32	6.46	109	113	11.64	95

HON - D3
Conception rates below age 16:
Rates per 1,000 girls aged 13-15: average for the years 1989-91

		Observed	Rate	Rank
	ENGLAND AND WALES	24844	9.6	
O00	ENGLAND	23399	9.6	
A00	NORTHERN RHA	1977	12.3	14
B00	YORKSHIRE RHA	2137	11.2	12
C00	TRENT RHA	2654	11.0	10
D00	EAST ANGLIAN RHA	866	8.2	4
E00	NORTH WEST THAMES RHA	1125	6.7	2
F00	NORTH EAST THAMES RHA	1582	8.6	6
G00	SOUTH EAST THAMES RHA	1646	9.2	8
H00	SOUTH WEST THAMES RHA	857	6.1	1
J00	WESSEX RHA	1333	8.7	7
K00	OXFORD RHA	1036	7.5	3
L00	SOUTH WESTERN RHA	1348	8.2	4
M00	WEST MIDLANDS RHA	3064	11.1	11
N00	MERSEY RHA	1236	9.7	9
P00	NORTH WESTERN RHA	2538	12.1	13
A01	Hartlepool	79	16.0	143
A02	North Tees	125	12.7	117
A03	South Tees	231	14.0	129
A04	East Cumbria	87	9.7	76
A05	South Cumbria	86	9.9	79
A06	West Cumbria	97	13.7	124
A11	Northumberland	126	7.8	41
A12	Gateshead	120	11.9	108
A13	Newcastle	189	14.3	132
A14	North Tyneside	114	11.5	104
A15	South Tyneside	94	12.3	112
A16	Sunderland	230	13.9	126
A30	North Durham	215	12.8	118
A31	South Durham	184	12.9	120
B11	East Riding	400	14.8	137
B16	Grimsby and Scunthorpe	285	14.7	136
B21	North Yorkshire	239	6.7	20
B31	Bradford	255	9.5	72
B51	West Yorkshire	337	10.8	95
B61	Leeds	399	11.2	100
B71	Wakefield	222	13.8	125
C01	North Derbyshire	189	10.2	85
C02	Southern Derbyshire	295	10.7	91
C03	Leicestershire	400	8.4	53
C04	North Lincolnshire	132	9.3	67
C05	South Lincolnshire	146	9.2	64

HON - D3
Conception rates below age 16:
Rates per 1,000 girls aged 13-15: average for the years 1989-91

		Observed	Rate	Rank
C08	Nottingham	381	12.3	112
C09	Barnsley	173	15.3	138
C10	Doncaster	241	15.7	142
C11	Rotherham	191	13.9	126
C12	Sheffield	274	11.3	101
C14	North Nottinghamshire	232	11.1	98
D01	Cambridge	85	6.0	14
D05	North West Anglia	242	11.4	102
D06	Norwich	179	7.5	36
D07	Great Yarmouth and Waveney	121	11.6	106
D09	Huntingdon	44	6.0	14
D11	Suffolk	195	6.7	20
E01	North Bedfordshire	97	7.3	32
E02	South Bedfordshire	116	7.5	36
E05	North West Hertfordshire	82	5.8	13
E06	South West Hertfordshire	70	5.6	8
E07	Barnet	70	4.9	3
E09	Hillingdon	83	7.4	33
E18	East and North Hertfordshire	156	6.2	17
E19	Brent and Harrow	144	6.4	19
E20	Ealing, Hammersmith and Hounslow	227	7.9	44
E21	Kensington, Chelsea and Westminster	80	7.5	36
F31	North Essex	298	6.8	23
F32	South Essex	315	8.7	58
F33	Barking and Havering	193	10.0	80
F34	Redbridge and Waltham Forest	144	6.7	20
F35	East London and the City	305	10.4	87
F36	New River District	204	9.2	64
F37	Camden and Islington	123	9.0	60
G04	South East Kent	139	10.1	81
G05	Canterbury and Thanet	138	9.3	67
G06	Dartford and Gravesham	94	7.9	44
G07	Maidstone	74	6.9	24
G08	Medway	174	9.5	72
G09	Tunbridge Wells	41	3.6	1
G10	Bexley	82	7.5	36
G11	Greenwich	136	12.3	112
G12	Bromley	98	6.9	24
G21	East Sussex	248	7.9	44
G26	South East London	422	13.9	126

HON - D3
Conception rates below age 16:
Rates per 1,000 girls aged 13-15: average for the years 1989-91

		Observed	Rate	Rank
H04	Mid Surrey	48	5.7	10
H05	East Surrey	48	4.9	3
H06	Chichester	50	6.0	14
H07	Mid Downs	82	5.4	6
H08	Worthing	78	7.2	29
H09	Croydon	127	8.2	50
H12	Wandsworth	61	8.5	54
H13	Merton and Sutton	115	7.6	40
H14	North West Surrey	97	5.1	5
H15	South West Surrey	56	4.4	2
H16	Kingston and Richmond	95	5.4	6
J10	Dorset	220	7.2	29
J21	Portsmouth and South East Hampshire	264	10.3	86
J22	Southampton and South West Hampshire	233	11.1	98
J23	Winchester	82	7.0	27
J24	Basingstoke and North Hampshire	112	5.7	10
J31	Salisbury	43	6.9	24
J32	Swindon	139	11.4	102
J33	Bath	172	8.3	51
J41	Isle of Wight	68	10.9	96
K11	East Berkshire	106	5.6	8
K12	West Berkshire	177	7.4	33
K24	Buckinghamshire	219	6.3	18
K31	Kettering	175	12.0	110
K32	Northampton	163	9.4	70
K41	Oxfordshire	196	7.1	28
L10	Bristol and District	352	8.5	54
L21	Cornwall and Isles of Scilly	186	7.8	41
L35	Exeter and North Devon	125	5.7	10
L36	Plymouth and Torbay	240	8.6	57
L40	Gloucestershire	276	10.1	81
L51	Somerset	169	8.0	48
M02	Herefordshire	76	9.4	70
M04	Worcester and District	118	9.0	60
M05	Shropshire	203	9.2	64
M06	Mid Staffordshire	154	9.6	75
M07	North Staffordshire	301	12.8	118
M08	South East Staffordshire	118	8.0	48
M13	East Birmingham	120	10.9	96
M14	North Birmingham	82	10.1	81
M16	West Birmingham	157	13.0	121
M17	Coventry	199	12.5	115

HON - D3
Conception rates below age 16:
Rates per 1,000 girls aged 13-15: average for the years 1989-91

		Observed	Rate	Rank
M18	Dudley	200	13.1	122
M19	Sandwell	231	15.3	138
M20	Solihull	100	9.1	62
M21	Walsall	204	14.5	135
M22	Wolverhampton	177	13.2	123
M25	South Birmingham	268	12.1	111
M26	North Worcestershire	120	7.9	44
M28	Warwickshire	236	9.3	67
N11	Chester	95	10.1	81
N12	Crewe	144	10.7	91
N13	Halton	121	14.1	130
N14	Macclesfield	67	7.4	33
N15	Warrington	93	9.5	72
N21	Liverpool	206	8.5	54
N31	St Helens and Knowsley	221	11.6	106
N41	Southport and Formby	45	7.8	41
N42	South Sefton	79	8.3	51
N51	Wirral	165	8.7	58
P01	Lancaster	67	10.6	89
P02	Blackpool,Wyre and Fylde	167	11.5	104
P03	Preston	69	9.8	78
P04	Blackburn, Hyndburn and Ribble Valley	159	10.6	89
P05	Burnley, Pendle and Rossendale	163	12.6	116
P06	West Lancashire	57	9.1	62
P07	Chorley and South Ribble	118	10.7	91
P08	Bolton	202	14.3	132
P09	Bury	111	11.9	108
P10	North Manchester	137	19.9	145
P11	Central Manchester	100	15.4	141
P12	South Manchester	139	16.5	144
P13	Oldham	129	10.7	91
P14	Rochdale	169	14.3	132
P15	Salford	178	15.3	138
P16	Stockport	142	9.7	76
P17	Tameside and Glossop	181	14.1	130
P18	Trafford	80	7.2	29
P19	Wigan	170	10.4	87

HON - E1
Mortality rates from accidents (ICD E800-E949) in children under 15:
Age-standardised mortality rates per 100,000: average for the years 1990-92

		Males			Females			Persons		
		Observed	Rate	Rank	Observed	Rate	Rank	Observed	Rate	Rank
	ENGLAND AND WALES	1176	7.89		598	4.25		1774	6.12	
O00	ENGLAND	1090	7.75		570	4.30		1660	6.07	
A00	NORTHERN RHA	86	9.54	12	50	5.79	14	136	7.71	14
B00	YORKSHIRE RHA	86	7.84	10	54	5.25	13	140	6.58	10
C00	TRENT RHA	96	7.02	7	44	3.43	4	140	5.28	4
D00	EAST ANGLIAN RHA	39	6.56	3	27	4.79	8	66	5.70	7
E00	NORTH WEST THAMES RHA	68	6.82	5	30	3.14	3	98	5.03	3
F00	NORTH EAST THAMES RHA	85	7.56	9	54	5.09	12	139	6.36	9
G00	SOUTH EAST THAMES RHA	78	7.44	8	37	3.68	5	115	5.60	6
H00	SOUTH WEST THAMES RHA	51	6.37	2	20	2.64	1	71	4.56	2
J00	WESSEX RHA	61	6.92	6	40	4.83	9	101	5.91	8
K00	OXFORD RHA	53	6.78	4	29	3.90	6	82	5.38	5
L00	SOUTH WESTERN RHA	41	4.50	1	26	3.05	2	67	3.79	1
M00	WEST MIDLANDS RHA	159	10.05	14	73	4.93	11	232	7.57	13
N00	MERSEY RHA	74	9.97	13	30	4.33	7	104	7.22	12
P00	NORTH WESTERN RHA	113	9.20	11	56	4.85	10	169	7.08	11
A01	Hartlepool	4	14.17	136	1	3.69	65	5	8.92	126
A02	North Tees	7	12.62	128	5	9.26	137	12	10.99	138
A03	South Tees	8	8.47	95	5	5.17	99	13	6.86	97
A04	East Cumbria	1	2.25	7	2	4.60	86	3	3.42	15
A05	South Cumbria	4	9.00	102	6	13.96	144	10	11.36	139
A06	West Cumbria	1	2.38	9	6	15.72	145	7	8.81	124
A11	Northumberland	6	6.91	62	2	2.46	30	8	4.73	40
A12	Gateshead	3	5.32	33	2	3.74	66	5	4.55	36
A13	Newcastle	16	20.93	144	2	2.70	40	18	12.10	141
A14	North Tyneside	6	10.67	116	1	1.76	19	7	6.32	83
A15	South Tyneside	4	9.01	103	3	6.49	118	7	7.80	114
A16	Sunderland	9	9.53	107	4	4.57	83	13	7.15	103
A30	North Durham	8	8.38	92	4	4.45	79	12	6.48	87
A31	South Durham	9	11.19	120	7	9.06	136	16	10.15	135
B11	East Riding	9	5.93	43	8	5.53	105	17	5.76	66
B16	Grimsby and Scunthorpe	9	7.94	82	6	5.66	108	15	6.84	96
B21	North Yorkshire	8	4.14	22	5	2.74	41	13	3.46	16
B31	Bradford	17	10.51	114	13	8.76	134	30	9.66	133
B51	West Yorkshire	20	11.38	122	4	2.44	28	24	7.04	100
B61	Leeds	17	8.31	91	14	7.13	123	31	7.74	113
B71	Wakefield	6	6.34	52	4	4.55	82	10	5.44	57
C01	North Derbyshire	4	3.88	20	5	5.13	97	9	4.49	35
C02	Southern Derbyshire	9	5.71	41	4	2.76	42	13	4.29	29
C03	Leicestershire	22	8.08	84	6	2.37	24	28	5.30	53
C04	North Lincolnshire	4	5.12	31	4	5.47	104	8	5.29	52
C05	South Lincolnshire	4	4.61	26	4	5.02	95	8	4.79	42

45

HON - E1
Mortality rates from accidents (ICD E800-E949) in children under 15:
Age-standardised mortality rates per 100,000: average for the years 1990-92

		Males			Females			Persons		
		Observed	Rate	Rank	Observed	Rate	Rank	Observed	Rate	Rank
C08	Nottingham	17	9.55	108	4	2.40	26	21	6.06	78
C09	Barnsley	2	2.87	12	4	6.50	119	6	4.64	38
C10	Doncaster	12	13.39	133	1	1.12	11	13	7.38	111
C11	Rotherham	5	6.44	53	3	4.19	71	8	5.33	54
C12	Sheffield	9	6.49	54	4	3.04	55	13	4.80	43
C14	North Nottinghamshire	8	6.65	57	5	4.41	76	13	5.56	62
D01	Cambridge	9	11.42	123	2	2.64	35	11	7.14	102
D05	North West Anglia	10	8.27	90	7	6.26	114	17	7.30	107
D06	Norwich	9	7.22	69	5	4.11	70	14	5.68	64
D07	Great Yarmouth and Waveney	2	3.61	18	4	7.80	126	6	5.61	63
D09	Huntingdon	1	2.17	6	1	2.48	32	2	2.37	5
D11	Suffolk	8	4.81	28	8	4.91	92	16	4.84	44
E01	North Bedfordshire	6	8.08	84	3	4.29	74	9	6.25	80
E02	South Bedfordshire	6	6.16	48	3	3.30	60	9	4.76	41
E05	North West Hertfordshire	2	2.60	11	2	2.66	36	4	2.64	8
E06	South West Hertfordshire	7	10.15	112	2	2.90	50	9	6.60	92
E07	Barnet	6	6.94	64	0	0.00	1	6	3.55	17
E09	Hillingdon	3	4.31	24	3	4.50	80	6	4.39	32
E18	East and North Hertfordshire	8	5.55	36	3	2.21	22	11	3.94	24
E19	Brent and Harrow	6	4.52	25	6	4.69	87	12	4.60	37
E20	Ealing, Hammersmith and Hounslow	18	9.90	110	5	2.90	50	23	6.49	88
E21	Kensington, Chelsea and Westminster	6	8.52	97	3	3.85	67	9	6.24	79
F31	North Essex	16	6.58	56	12	5.13	97	28	5.87	69
F32	South Essex	20	9.78	109	11	5.80	110	31	7.84	115
F33	Barking and Havering	6	5.39	34	12	11.46	142	18	8.32	119
F34	Redbridge and Waltham Forest	11	8.42	93	3	2.38	25	14	5.49	58
F35	East London and the City	14	6.56	55	9	4.41	76	23	5.52	60
F36	New River District	11	7.94	82	4	3.07	57	15	5.55	61
F37	Camden and Islington	7	8.24	89	3	3.51	63	10	5.90	71
G04	South East Kent	4	5.05	29	2	2.81	46	6	3.95	25
G05	Canterbury and Thanet	5	5.99	47	1	1.30	14	6	3.71	20
G06	Dartford and Gravesham	2	3.08	15	5	8.07	130	7	5.50	59
G07	Maidstone	10	16.67	142	2	3.47	62	12	10.27	136
G08	Medway	13	11.96	126	6	5.78	109	19	8.97	128
G09	Tunbridge Wells	4	6.93	63	3	5.86	111	7	6.38	85
G10	Bexley	4	6.22	50	1	1.68	16	5	4.01	27
G11	Greenwich	4	5.96	45	0	0.00	1	4	3.04	12
G12	Bromley	7	8.99	101	2	2.69	38	9	5.94	72
G21	East Sussex	10	5.55	36	3	1.69	17	13	3.67	18
G26	South East London	15	6.88	61	12	5.94	113	27	6.42	86

HON - E1
Mortality rates from accidents (ICD E800-E949) in children under 15:
Age-standardised mortality rates per 100,000: average for the years 1990-92

		Males			Females			Persons		
		Observed	Rate	Rank	Observed	Rate	Rank	Observed	Rate	Rank
H04	Mid Surrey	2	4.08	21	2	4.78	89	4	4.43	33
H05	East Surrey	4	7.61	74	0	0.00	1	4	3.88	22
H06	Chichester	4	9.50	106	2	5.03	96	6	7.34	108
H07	Mid Downs	7	8.57	98	0	0.00	1	7	4.43	33
H08	Worthing	5	8.20	88	2	3.42	61	7	5.85	68
H09	Croydon	5	5.45	35	1	1.10	10	6	3.33	14
H12	Wandsworth	5	11.01	119	1	2.69	38	6	6.92	98
H13	Merton and Sutton	4	4.18	23	5	5.31	101	9	4.71	39
H14	North West Surrey	6	5.67	40	3	3.02	53	9	4.37	30
H15	South West Surrey	4	5.72	42	1	1.89	21	5	3.91	23
H16	Kingston and Richmond	5	4.77	27	3	3.12	59	8	3.97	26
J10	Dorset	12	7.31	70	5	3.03	54	17	5.24	50
J21	Portsmouth and South East Hampshire	9	5.95	44	6	4.20	72	15	5.11	49
J22	Southampton and South West Hampshire	10	8.16	86	0	0.00	1	10	4.21	28
J23	Winchester	1	1.70	2	6	10.08	140	7	5.77	67
J24	Basingstoke and North Hampshire	9	7.90	79	5	4.71	88	14	6.36	84
J31	Salisbury	4	11.45	124	0	0.00	1	4	5.88	70
J32	Swindon	7	9.40	105	6	8.58	133	13	9.01	130
J33	Bath	6	5.09	30	9	8.35	132	15	6.67	94
J41	Isle of Wight	3	8.42	93	3	9.59	138	6	9.00	129
K11	East Berkshire	8	6.94	64	6	5.60	107	14	6.30	82
K12	West Berkshire	12	8.89	99	4	3.01	52	16	6.04	77
K24	Buckinghamshire	15	7.90	79	10	5.59	106	25	6.77	95
K31	Kettering	7	8.47	95	5	6.34	116	12	7.44	112
K32	Northampton	7	7.10	67	0	0.00	1	7	3.70	19
K41	Oxfordshire	4	2.55	10	4	2.58	33	8	2.56	7
L10	Bristol and District	14	5.97	46	10	4.51	81	24	5.26	51
L21	Cornwall and Isles of Scilly	8	6.19	49	3	2.47	31	11	4.38	31
L35	Exeter and North Devon	8	6.76	59	3	2.81	46	11	4.86	45
L36	Plymouth and Torbay	6	3.77	19	4	2.66	36	10	3.24	13
L40	Gloucestershire	3	1.88	4	4	2.80	44	7	2.32	3
L51	Somerset	2	1.86	3	2	1.85	20	4	1.85	2
M02	Herefordshire	6	13.14	132	5	11.63	143	11	12.42	143
M04	Worcester and District	2	2.89	13	3	4.58	84	5	3.71	20
M05	Shropshire	13	10.73	117	9	7.73	125	22	9.28	132
M06	Mid Staffordshire	15	16.15	140	1	1.19	13	16	8.91	125
M07	North Staffordshire	14	10.40	113	3	2.40	26	17	6.51	89
M08	South East Staffordshire	11	13.54	134	3	4.07	69	14	8.96	127
M13	East Birmingham	11	15.45	139	6	8.82	135	17	12.22	142
M14	North Birmingham	0	0.00	1	2	4.81	91	2	2.33	4
M16	West Birmingham	6	7.92	81	3	4.00	68	9	6.02	75
M17	Coventry	6	6.71	58	7	7.80	126	13	7.25	105

HON - E1
Mortality rates from accidents (ICD E800-E949) in children under 15:
Age-standardised mortality rates per 100,000: average for the years 1990-92

		Males Observed	Rate	Rank	Females Observed	Rate	Rank	Persons Observed	Rate	Rank
M18	Dudley	10	11.33	121	2	2.44	28	12	7.04	100
M19	Sandwell	12	13.07	131	2	2.33	23	14	7.85	116
M20	Solihull	5	8.90	100	1	1.74	18	6	5.41	56
M21	Walsall	3	3.57	17	5	6.28	115	8	4.89	46
M22	Wolverhampton	7	9.13	104	5	6.80	122	12	8.02	117
M25	South Birmingham	14	10.84	118	8	6.55	120	22	8.74	123
M26	North Worcestershire	6	7.09	66	4	4.92	93	10	6.03	76
M28	Warwickshire	18	12.96	130	4	3.10	58	22	8.18	118
N11	Chester	1	2.01	5	5	10.17	141	6	5.99	74
N12	Crewe	6	7.72	76	2	2.80	44	8	5.33	54
N13	Halton	5	10.04	111	2	4.28	73	7	7.25	105
N14	Macclesfield	4	7.73	77	2	4.78	89	6	6.29	81
N15	Warrington	3	5.18	32	0	0.00	1	3	2.67	9
N21	Liverpool	19	12.93	129	9	6.62	121	28	9.86	134
N31	St Helens and Knowsley	13	11.70	125	3	2.76	42	16	7.37	110
N41	Southport and Formby	2	6.23	51	2	8.01	129	4	7.02	99
N42	South Sefton	6	10.59	115	2	3.68	64	8	7.20	104
N51	Wirral	15	13.59	135	3	3.05	56	18	8.41	120
P01	Lancaster	1	2.92	14	1	2.86	49	2	2.91	11
P02	Blackpool,Wyre and Fylde	10	12.53	127	4	5.41	103	14	9.08	131
P03	Preston	3	7.19	68	1	2.81	46	4	5.00	48
P04	Blackburn, Hyndburn and Ribble Valley	2	2.31	8	1	1.12	11	3	1.74	1
P05	Burnley, Pendle and Rossendale	6	7.51	73	7	9.78	139	13	8.61	121
P06	West Lancashire	2	5.63	39	0	0.00	1	2	2.84	10
P07	Chorley and South Ribble	2	3.29	16	1	1.62	15	3	2.47	6
P08	Bolton	12	14.31	137	2	2.60	34	14	8.62	122
P09	Bury	4	7.35	71	3	5.89	112	7	6.63	93
P10	North Manchester	8	16.22	141	2	4.93	94	10	10.73	137
P11	Central Manchester	9	24.10	145	3	8.09	131	12	16.21	145
P12	South Manchester	8	15.17	138	4	7.71	124	12	11.54	140
P13	Oldham	5	6.76	59	3	4.59	85	8	5.71	65
P14	Rochdale	4	5.61	38	3	4.29	74	7	4.98	47
P15	Salford	12	17.61	143	5	7.81	128	17	12.84	144
P16	Stockport	7	8.16	86	5	6.41	117	12	7.34	108
P17	Tameside and Glossop	6	7.71	75	4	5.37	102	10	6.59	91
P18	Trafford	5	7.84	78	3	5.21	100	8	6.54	90
P19	Wigan	7	7.42	72	4	4.43	78	11	5.97	73

HON - E2

Mortality rates from accidents (ICD E800-E949) in young persons aged 15-24:
Age-standardised mortality rates per 100,000: average for the years 1990-92

		Males			Females			Persons		
		Observed	Rate	Rank	Observed	Rate	Rank	Observed	Rate	Rank
	ENGLAND AND WALES	3856	34.50		921	8.80		4777	21.98	
O00	ENGLAND	3625	34.30		870	8.80		4495	21.88	
A00	NORTHERN RHA	209	32.02	5	53	8.52	5	262	20.48	6
B00	YORKSHIRE RHA	317	38.43	12	68	8.66	7	385	23.93	11
C00	TRENT RHA	398	37.71	11	101	10.21	13	499	24.43	12
D00	EAST ANGLIAN RHA	201	43.91	14	40	9.68	11	241	27.54	14
E00	NORTH WEST THAMES RHA	213	27.49	1	70	9.06	9	283	18.37	1
F00	NORTH EAST THAMES RHA	257	30.32	3	67	8.55	6	324	19.60	3
G00	SOUTH EAST THAMES RHA	246	31.07	4	55	7.48	2	301	19.39	2
H00	SOUTH WEST THAMES RHA	182	29.58	2	58	10.06	12	240	19.90	5
J00	WESSEX RHA	227	33.17	7	50	8.24	3	277	21.36	8
K00	OXFORD RHA	210	35.13	9	60	10.99	14	270	23.49	10
L00	SOUTH WESTERN RHA	297	42.40	13	59	9.31	10	356	26.52	13
M00	WEST MIDLANDS RHA	382	32.22	6	98	8.99	8	480	20.96	7
N00	MERSEY RHA	194	37.63	10	42	8.37	4	236	23.23	9
P00	NORTH WESTERN RHA	292	33.31	8	49	5.81	1	341	19.85	4
A01	Hartlepool	9	48.61	128	1	4.99	36	10	27.08	106
A02	North Tees	8	23.34	27	1	2.83	10	9	13.16	17
A03	South Tees	22	34.24	71	1	1.80	7	23	18.47	51
A04	East Cumbria	16	44.77	113	5	14.85	134	21	30.16	123
A05	South Cumbria	15	42.26	107	6	17.71	139	21	30.13	122
A06	West Cumbria	16	57.52	141	5	19.75	141	21	38.97	144
A11	Northumberland	21	35.30	78	8	14.38	131	29	25.16	99
A12	Gateshead	12	27.85	46	4	10.39	97	16	19.21	59
A13	Newcastle	6	9.49	2	5	7.96	70	11	8.72	1
A14	North Tyneside	9	24.28	36	0	0.00	1	9	12.26	12
A15	South Tyneside	6	19.80	20	2	6.46	51	8	13.23	19
A16	Sunderland	19	28.66	51	3	4.30	28	22	16.55	42
A30	North Durham	27	38.09	92	7	10.34	96	34	24.49	92
A31	South Durham	23	41.26	105	5	9.26	87	28	25.35	101
B11	East Riding	39	32.74	64	7	6.32	47	46	19.93	63
B16	Grimsby and Scunthorpe	40	54.42	139	6	8.01	72	46	31.59	131
B21	North Yorkshire	74	48.40	125	17	12.19	113	91	31.03	126
B31	Bradford	40	36.52	84	4	3.95	22	44	20.64	66
B51	West Yorkshire	24	19.03	13	10	8.01	72	34	13.58	22
B61	Leeds	71	40.35	101	15	9.21	85	86	25.28	100
B71	Wakefield	29	42.53	108	9	13.12	123	38	28.06	112
C01	North Derbyshire	26	35.19	76	10	14.48	132	36	25.10	98
C02	Southern Derbyshire	53	44.29	112	13	11.25	108	66	28.34	114
C03	Leicestershire	86	40.92	102	25	12.85	121	111	27.39	109
C04	North Lincolnshire	29	51.53	135	5	9.54	91	34	31.12	128
C05	South Lincolnshire	29	47.27	123	6	10.05	93	35	29.17	119

HON - E2
Mortality rates from accidents (ICD E800-E949) in young persons aged 15-24:
Age-standardised mortality rates per 100,000: average for the years 1990-92

		Males Observed	Rate	Rank	Females Observed	Rate	Rank	Persons Observed	Rate	Rank
C08	Nottingham	49	33.07	68	11	7.49	60	60	20.73	67
C09	Barnsley	22	45.87	116	7	15.59	135	29	31.07	127
C10	Doncaster	21	33.64	69	5	8.22	74	26	21.20	73
C11	Rotherham	9	16.76	7	2	3.84	20	11	10.37	6
C12	Sheffield	25	18.55	12	6	4.69	32	31	12.03	9
C14	North Nottinghamshire	49	59.35	142	11	14.16	129	60	37.19	142
D01	Cambridge	38	49.72	132	9	14.14	128	47	33.15	135
D05	North West Anglia	43	51.11	134	7	8.59	79	50	30.43	124
D06	Norwich	55	53.17	138	7	7.59	62	62	31.41	129
D07	Great Yarmouth and Waveney	11	28.19	48	6	15.85	136	17	22.11	78
D09	Huntingdon	6	19.61	16	1	3.95	22	7	12.07	10
D11	Suffolk	48	39.03	96	10	8.96	84	58	24.74	94
E01	North Bedfordshire	17	30.82	58	8	14.74	133	25	23.12	86
E02	South Bedfordshire	30	48.43	126	3	4.37	29	33	26.61	104
E05	North West Hertfordshire	22	41.10	104	4	7.97	71	26	24.98	97
E06	South West Hertfordshire	13	26.70	41	2	4.15	26	15	15.56	34
E07	Barnet	10	14.97	4	7	11.03	104	17	12.93	16
E09	Hillingdon	12	23.00	26	5	10.95	102	17	17.22	46
E18	East and North Hertfordshire	42	40.17	99	13	13.27	125	55	27.16	108
E19	Brent and Harrow	20	18.18	11	6	6.76	53	26	12.48	14
E20	Ealing, Hammersmith and Hounslow	35	23.34	27	15	10.20	95	50	16.69	43
E21	Kensington, Chelsea and Westminster	12	19.61	16	7	7.80	67	19	13.59	23
F31	North Essex	69	37.64	89	18	11.05	105	87	24.88	96
F32	South Essex	38	25.97	40	13	9.28	88	51	17.77	47
F33	Barking and Havering	20	25.02	38	5	6.56	52	25	16.02	38
F34	Redbridge and Waltham Forest	30	29.24	53	6	6.33	48	36	17.93	49
F35	East London and the City	43	31.71	62	8	5.80	44	51	18.89	55
F36	New River District	27	23.71	32	8	7.62	65	35	15.73	36
F37	Camden and Islington	30	36.65	85	9	11.30	109	39	23.52	90
G04	South East Kent	26	47.25	122	7	13.33	126	33	30.71	125
G05	Canterbury and Thanet	25	39.68	97	4	6.82	55	29	23.50	89
G06	Dartford and Gravesham	20	40.98	103	5	11.51	110	25	26.64	105
G07	Maidstone	15	36.24	81	0	0.00	1	15	18.60	54
G08	Medway	25	32.97	66	7	10.67	100	32	22.00	77
G09	Tunbridge Wells	18	44.28	111	3	7.61	63	21	26.33	103
G10	Bexley	11	23.37	29	2	4.65	31	13	14.31	28
G11	Greenwich	10	19.70	19	6	12.32	115	16	16.01	37
G12	Bromley	14	23.51	30	3	5.14	37	17	14.50	30
G21	East Sussex	54	37.72	90	7	5.30	40	61	21.72	74
G26	South East London	28	17.17	8	11	7.88	69	39	12.43	13

HON - E2
Mortality rates from accidents (ICD E800-E949) in young persons aged 15-24:
Age-standardised mortality rates per 100,000: average for the years 1990-92

		Males			Females			Persons		
		Observed	Rate	Rank	Observed	Rate	Rank	Observed	Rate	Rank
H04	Mid Surrey	7	22.90	25	1	3.39	15	8	13.53	21
H05	East Surrey	14	38.81	95	1	2.98	12	15	21.18	72
H06	Chichester	8	24.45	37	3	9.39	90	11	16.98	45
H07	Mid Downs	25	42.05	106	8	14.36	130	33	28.40	115
H08	Worthing	20	46.38	119	4	9.98	92	24	28.74	116
H09	Croydon	19	28.63	50	8	12.48	116	27	20.60	65
H12	Wandsworth	6	8.77	1	5	10.98	103	11	9.85	4
H13	Merton and Sutton	13	18.03	10	8	12.85	121	21	15.34	33
H14	North West Surrey	20	23.81	34	4	5.27	39	24	14.71	31
H15	South West Surrey	20	36.41	82	6	11.61	112	26	24.46	91
H16	Kingston and Richmond	30	34.94	74	10	11.51	110	40	23.20	87
J10	Dorset	47	36.49	83	10	8.58	78	57	23.06	85
J21	Portsmouth and South East Hampshire	29	22.83	24	4	3.77	19	33	13.97	26
J22	Southampton and South West Hampshire	26	27.39	43	10	11.23	107	36	19.69	61
J23	Winchester	27	54.84	140	4	9.35	89	31	33.51	136
J24	Basingstoke and North Hampshire	31	33.69	70	8	10.62	99	39	23.05	84
J31	Salisbury	8	31.25	60	0	0.00	1	8	16.23	41
J32	Swindon	21	38.36	94	6	12.77	120	27	25.99	102
J33	Bath	31	35.02	75	7	8.29	75	38	22.14	79
J41	Isle of Wight	7	30.64	57	1	4.86	34	8	18.11	50
K11	East Berkshire	16	19.69	18	5	6.27	46	21	13.20	18
K12	West Berkshire	32	28.56	49	7	7.28	56	39	18.49	52
K24	Buckinghamshire	48	36.91	86	8	6.39	49	56	21.89	76
K31	Kettering	37	63.96	144	14	25.71	143	51	45.11	145
K32	Northampton	32	47.14	121	12	18.27	140	44	32.78	134
K41	Oxfordshire	45	29.75	54	14	10.80	101	59	20.93	69
L10	Bristol and District	66	34.74	73	13	7.80	67	79	21.84	75
L21	Cornwall and Isles of Scilly	43	49.21	130	11	13.14	124	54	31.58	130
L35	Exeter and North Devon	29	31.33	61	11	12.48	116	40	22.25	80
L36	Plymouth and Torbay	59	46.23	117	8	7.54	61	67	28.12	113
L40	Gloucestershire	56	49.09	129	8	7.61	63	64	28.93	117
L51	Somerset	44	52.30	137	8	10.52	98	52	32.39	133
M02	Herefordshire	16	51.05	133	5	17.15	138	21	34.71	137
M04	Worcester and District	23	45.28	114	6	12.23	114	29	29.18	120
M05	Shropshire	44	48.56	127	11	13.35	127	55	31.77	132
M06	Mid Staffordshire	30	43.60	110	17	27.50	145	47	35.96	140
M07	North Staffordshire	30	28.74	52	12	12.54	118	42	20.93	69
M08	South East Staffordshire	19	33.01	67	3	5.72	42	22	19.76	62
M13	East Birmingham	7	15.11	5	3	7.32	57	10	11.28	7
M14	North Birmingham	6	16.43	6	1	3.41	16	7	10.32	5
M16	West Birmingham	10	17.20	9	1	1.61	6	11	9.56	3
M17	Coventry	16	21.35	22	5	6.77	54	21	14.36	29

HON - E2
Mortality rates from accidents (ICD E800-E949) in young persons aged 15-24:
Age-standardised mortality rates per 100,000: average for the years 1990-92

		Males			Females			Persons		
		Observed	Rate	Rank	Observed	Rate	Rank	Observed	Rate	Rank
M18	Dudley	13	19.35	14	4	7.33	58	17	13.48	20
M19	Sandwell	22	32.95	65	3	4.97	35	25	19.11	58
M20	Solihull	15	35.77	79	4	10.13	94	19	23.37	88
M21	Walsall	16	26.74	42	3	5.17	38	19	16.16	40
M22	Wolverhampton	17	30.34	55	4	6.22	45	21	18.51	53
M25	South Birmingham	22	19.40	15	4	3.85	21	26	11.87	8
M26	North Worcestershire	29	51.73	136	4	7.33	58	33	29.87	121
M28	Warwickshire	47	45.39	115	8	8.32	76	55	27.39	109
N11	Chester	11	30.35	56	3	7.71	66	14	18.99	57
N12	Crewe	23	43.52	109	14	27.00	144	37	35.37	138
N13	Halton	15	47.34	124	2	6.41	50	17	27.14	107
N14	Macclesfield	8	23.79	33	1	3.24	13	9	13.76	24
N15	Warrington	15	38.11	93	6	16.42	137	21	27.49	111
N21	Liverpool	44	37.72	90	4	3.31	14	48	20.93	69
N31	St Helens and Knowsley	27	35.87	80	3	4.28	27	30	20.40	64
N41	Southport and Formby	7	32.60	63	1	4.79	33	8	18.96	56
N42	South Sefton	17	46.48	120	4	11.15	106	21	29.08	118
N51	Wirral	27	40.25	100	4	5.74	43	31	22.89	83
P01	Lancaster	4	14.22	3	1	4.04	25	5	9.08	2
P02	Blackpool, Wyre and Fylde	24	40.01	98	5	8.90	83	29	24.85	95
P03	Preston	16	49.38	131	7	21.25	142	23	35.43	139
P04	Blackburn, Hyndburn and Ribble Valley	12	21.20	21	5	8.80	81	17	15.08	32
P05	Burnley, Pendle and Rossendale	22	46.32	118	1	2.15	9	23	24.51	93
P06	West Lancashire	9	37.49	88	2	8.32	76	11	22.81	81
P07	Chorley and South Ribble	25	60.16	143	5	12.76	119	30	36.90	141
P08	Bolton	16	27.92	47	2	4.01	24	18	16.12	39
P09	Bury	8	22.15	23	3	8.85	82	11	15.63	35
P10	North Manchester	21	67.16	145	3	9.23	86	24	38.14	143
P11	Central Manchester	17	35.26	77	3	8.74	80	20	22.83	82
P12	South Manchester	13	27.80	45	3	5.41	41	16	16.79	44
P13	Oldham	11	24.20	35	0	0.00	1	11	12.23	11
P14	Rochdale	12	27.39	43	0	0.00	1	12	13.88	25
P15	Salford	17	31.10	59	2	3.44	17	19	17.85	48
P16	Stockport	21	37.00	87	2	3.67	18	23	20.74	68
P17	Tameside and Glossop	12	23.61	31	1	1.80	7	13	12.90	15
P18	Trafford	15	34.24	71	2	4.52	30	17	19.67	60
P19	Wigan	17	25.02	38	2	2.97	11	19	14.24	27

HON - E3
Mortality rates from accidents (ICD E800-E949) in persons aged 65 and over:
Age-standardised mortality rates per 100,000: average for the years 1990-92

		Males			Females			Persons		
		Observed	Rate	Rank	Observed	Rate	Rank	Observed	Rate	Rank
	ENGLAND AND WALES	5842	62.98		8883	49.14		14725	54.56	
O00	ENGLAND	5462	62.55		8216	48.30		13678	53.88	
A00	NORTHERN RHA	404	75.17	12	662	63.41	14	1066	68.45	14
B00	YORKSHIRE RHA	405	63.22	9	585	44.38	7	990	51.15	8
C00	TRENT RHA	549	64.30	10	789	49.40	9	1338	55.07	9
D00	EAST ANGLIAN RHA	306	70.65	11	405	53.05	11	711	60.20	11
E00	NORTH WEST THAMES RHA	349	61.26	7	460	43.75	6	809	50.31	6
F00	NORTH EAST THAMES RHA	391	61.27	8	545	42.84	4	936	50.37	7
G00	SOUTH EAST THAMES RHA	378	52.36	3	589	41.10	3	967	45.30	3
H00	SOUTH WEST THAMES RHA	303	51.55	2	437	37.26	1	740	42.95	1
J00	WESSEX RHA	310	47.96	1	524	42.97	5	834	45.40	4
K00	OXFORD RHA	232	58.61	6	390	51.90	10	622	55.22	10
L00	SOUTH WESTERN RHA	404	55.92	4	641	45.25	8	1045	49.66	5
M00	WEST MIDLANDS RHA	673	76.88	13	993	58.55	12	1666	65.32	12
N00	MERSEY RHA	234	57.00	5	305	38.02	2	539	44.76	2
P00	NORTH WESTERN RHA	524	77.03	14	891	61.84	13	1415	67.82	13
A01	Hartlepool	10	70.49	99	17	64.69	121	27	66.65	115
A02	North Tees	20	82.13	121	34	71.60	130	54	78.64	131
A03	South Tees	20	50.39	46	65	76.59	132	85	67.30	116
A04	East Cumbria	24	65.11	82	20	29.15	10	44	42.53	37
A05	South Cumbria	25	69.00	95	49	67.87	124	74	70.30	122
A06	West Cumbria	32	133.75	143	36	85.53	138	68	103.43	139
A11	Northumberland	58	102.48	137	73	66.32	123	131	79.90	133
A12	Gateshead	22	64.74	81	58	82.19	137	80	78.15	130
A13	Newcastle	32	60.60	70	52	46.86	75	84	54.98	83
A14	North Tyneside	18	47.18	28	46	64.21	119	64	59.54	95
A15	South Tyneside	28	93.38	132	31	53.83	95	59	70.41	124
A16	Sunderland	26	52.83	52	51	60.29	114	77	59.68	97
A30	North Durham	55	107.66	138	78	77.43	133	133	84.99	135
A31	South Durham	34	67.67	92	52	53.40	94	86	59.31	93
B11	East Riding	62	66.73	90	106	55.55	102	168	60.50	100
B16	Grimsby and Scunthorpe	21	30.82	4	41	35.14	32	62	34.18	11
B21	North Yorkshire	70	45.24	23	116	39.78	49	186	42.33	36
B31	Bradford	63	85.17	126	72	47.69	79	135	60.16	99
B51	West Yorkshire	72	79.83	118	107	52.47	91	179	60.56	101
B61	Leeds	92	77.38	109	110	41.72	59	202	53.85	78
B71	Wakefield	25	52.76	51	33	33.05	25	58	40.40	27
C01	North Derbyshire	74	115.36	140	142	106.51	143	216	109.02	141
C02	Southern Derbyshire	46	48.23	32	69	38.55	44	115	41.42	31
C03	Leicestershire	115	73.05	106	147	50.06	88	262	59.69	98
C04	North Lincolnshire	26	46.27	27	44	44.41	67	70	44.55	47
C05	South Lincolnshire	40	60.70	72	53	46.88	76	93	51.61	72

53

Mortality rates from accidents (ICD E800-E949) in persons aged 65 and over:
Age-standardised mortality rates per 100,000: average for the years 1990-92

		Males			Females			Persons		
		Observed	Rate	Rank	Observed	Rate	Rank	Observed	Rate	Rank
C08	Nottingham	59	52.86	53	101	47.52	78	160	50.39	65
C09	Barnsley	22	53.44	55	21	29.88	12	43	39.34	24
C10	Doncaster	28	51.78	48	39	43.83	64	67	49.05	61
C11	Rotherham	29	69.94	98	36	49.40	85	65	55.46	84
C12	Sheffield	61	56.98	64	67	33.78	28	128	42.00	33
C14	North Nottinghamshire	49	71.58	102	70	54.41	98	119	61.11	104
D01	Cambridge	52	96.64	134	81	82.11	136	133	90.19	137
D05	North West Anglia	53	69.21	96	99	71.12	129	152	69.94	121
D06	Norwich	90	73.69	107	90	44.91	70	180	56.40	89
D07	Great Yarmouth and Waveney	29	66.12	87	52	58.60	109	81	60.57	102
D09	Huntingdon	13	66.27	89	16	49.39	84	29	55.79	87
D11	Suffolk	69	60.81	73	67	33.62	27	136	44.55	47
E01	North Bedfordshire	31	77.73	110	21	30.76	15	52	46.79	55
E02	South Bedfordshire	32	79.91	119	42	62.72	117	74	68.50	119
E05	North West Hertfordshire	26	58.01	66	42	52.86	93	68	56.23	88
E06	South West Hertfordshire	28	71.74	103	45	46.48	74	73	54.47	81
E07	Barnet	20	32.95	6	53	44.58	69	73	42.93	39
E09	Hillingdon	19	46.02	25	20	28.19	7	39	35.24	14
E18	East and North Hertfordshire	47	64.14	80	64	43.99	65	111	50.84	66
E19	Brent and Harrow	40	52.99	54	40	31.35	18	80	39.08	23
E20	Ealing, Hammersmith and Hounslow	65	65.12	83	74	42.25	61	139	51.07	67
E21	Kensington, Chelsea and Westminster	41	77.81	112	59	60.56	115	100	65.95	113
F31	North Essex	77	49.18	37	134	41.59	57	211	44.84	52
F32	South Essex	50	39.36	14	82	33.32	26	132	37.18	20
F33	Barking and Havering	36	54.04	59	63	49.23	83	99	51.95	73
F34	Redbridge and Waltham Forest	61	78.98	116	93	56.43	105	154	64.69	111
F35	East London and the City	52	65.55	85	55	35.76	33	107	48.05	59
F36	New River District	63	84.18	124	66	44.43	68	129	59.59	96
F37	Camden and Islington	52	93.70	133	52	48.83	82	104	65.36	112
G04	South East Kent	49	78.83	115	88	70.52	127	137	72.94	126
G05	Canterbury and Thanet	38	51.14	47	58	38.53	43	96	43.14	41
G06	Dartford and Gravesham	18	49.43	40	18	29.29	11	36	36.72	18
G07	Maidstone	18	58.63	67	14	28.27	8	32	36.75	19
G08	Medway	17	35.69	9	40	45.69	72	57	42.08	35
G09	Tunbridge Wells	18	42.61	20	52	55.85	103	70	53.68	77
G10	Bexley	16	43.42	21	19	27.22	6	35	34.10	10
G11	Greenwich	24	78.08	113	17	24.25	2	41	40.83	30
G12	Bromley	16	29.25	2	33	31.79	20	49	29.52	3
G21	East Sussex	97	49.76	43	166	40.38	51	263	44.76	50
G26	South East London	67	62.98	79	84	41.88	60	151	49.02	60

HON - E3
Mortality rates from accidents (ICD E800-E949) in persons aged 65 and over:
Age-standardised mortality rates per 100,000: average for the years 1990-92

		Males			Females			Persons		
		Observed	Rate	Rank	Observed	Rate	Rank	Observed	Rate	Rank
H04	Mid Surrey	13	31.73	5	16	24.55	3	29	27.68	2
H05	East Surrey	18	45.34	24	27	36.30	36	45	40.36	26
H06	Chichester	26	48.70	33	46	40.92	52	72	43.86	45
H07	Mid Downs	19	37.58	12	25	25.62	5	44	31.90	4
H08	Worthing	37	48.95	35	51	34.00	29	88	38.01	21
H09	Croydon	25	53.48	56	42	43.57	63	67	47.61	57
H12	Wandsworth	15	53.52	57	23	39.36	47	38	46.39	53
H13	Merton and Sutton	32	48.91	34	54	41.65	58	86	44.77	51
H14	North West Surrey	58	86.86	128	52	38.81	46	110	57.96	92
H15	South West Surrey	16	35.78	10	44	48.77	81	60	43.31	42
H16	Kingston and Richmond	44	55.50	61	57	36.74	38	101	44.71	49
J10	Dorset	98	52.59	50	176	50.02	87	274	51.33	71
J21	Portsmouth and South East Hampshire	44	47.32	29	105	52.58	92	149	51.23	69
J22	Southampton and South West Hampshire	45	49.58	41	54	32.05	22	99	39.02	22
J23	Winchester	23	56.48	63	41	56.69	106	64	59.52	94
J24	Basingstoke and North Hampshire	36	72.50	105	43	44.32	66	79	55.64	86
J31	Salisbury	12	42.56	19	17	31.28	17	29	35.73	16
J32	Swindon	19	49.60	42	23	38.73	45	42	42.58	38
J33	Bath	26	30.61	3	50	34.17	31	76	33.78	8
J41	Isle of Wight	7	19.28	1	15	21.85	1	22	20.07	1
K11	East Berkshire	33	57.05	65	63	59.63	111	96	62.43	106
K12	West Berkshire	43	67.86	93	86	64.91	122	129	66.01	114
K24	Buckinghamshire	45	55.34	60	93	57.36	108	138	56.57	90
K31	Kettering	32	65.87	86	39	43.55	62	71	52.66	75
K32	Northampton	34	60.01	68	42	46.12	73	76	52.56	74
K41	Oxfordshire	45	50.16	45	67	39.38	48	112	43.79	44
L10	Bristol and District	74	46.26	26	86	28.33	9	160	34.80	13
L21	Cornwall and Isles of Scilly	61	56.07	62	84	41.02	53	145	46.69	54
L35	Exeter and North Devon	55	48.05	31	93	39.89	50	148	43.31	42
L36	Plymouth and Torbay	72	53.73	58	137	47.86	80	209	50.38	64
L40	Gloucestershire	72	66.25	88	119	55.25	101	191	61.70	105
L51	Somerset	70	71.01	100	122	70.56	128	192	70.81	125
M02	Herefordshire	13	34.39	8	20	31.92	21	33	32.50	6
M04	Worcester and District	35	78.64	114	38	41.04	54	73	54.40	80
M05	Shropshire	46	61.99	76	48	38.50	42	94	47.19	56
M06	Mid Staffordshire	39	87.98	130	54	63.25	118	93	69.18	120
M07	North Staffordshire	96	125.37	141	149	92.91	139	245	105.32	140
M08	South East Staffordshire	20	49.11	36	35	49.57	86	55	50.36	63
M13	East Birmingham	32	101.58	136	44	68.52	126	76	79.09	132
M14	North Birmingham	23	79.42	117	42	68.04	125	65	73.86	127
M16	West Birmingham	35	109.96	139	56	96.80	141	91	100.21	138
M17	Coventry	27	52.35	49	32	35.96	34	59	41.49	32

HON - E3

Mortality rates from accidents (ICD E800-E949) in persons aged 65 and over:
Age-standardised mortality rates per 100,000: average for the years 1990-92

		Males			Females			Persons		
		Observed	Rate	Rank	Observed	Rate	Rank	Observed	Rate	Rank
M18	Dudley	31	62.11	77	53	51.93	90	84	55.56	85
M19	Sandwell	37	71.45	101	64	61.12	116	101	64.58	110
M20	Solihull	28	92.60	131	39	64.30	120	67	74.57	128
M21	Walsall	15	40.55	15	43	57.07	107	58	51.20	68
M22	Wolverhampton	30	68.05	94	37	45.46	71	67	53.92	79
M25	South Birmingham	72	100.93	135	113	78.90	134	185	87.55	136
M26	North Worcestershire	33	84.56	125	65	74.12	131	98	77.87	129
M28	Warwickshire	61	69.39	97	61	37.09	40	122	50.08	62
N11	Chester	26	86.73	127	21	36.05	35	47	54.76	82
N12	Crewe	18	41.91	17	23	30.47	14	41	34.68	12
N13	Halton	9	47.53	30	9	25.27	4	18	32.49	5
N14	Macclesfield	17	49.30	38	24	36.91	39	41	40.78	29
N15	Warrington	12	41.33	16	23	41.37	56	35	43.13	40
N21	Liverpool	62	77.74	111	58	36.37	37	120	51.32	70
N31	St Helens and Knowsley	29	65.14	84	50	54.08	97	79	57.02	91
N41	Southport and Formby	9	33.59	7	32	51.75	89	41	44.27	46
N42	South Sefton	22	61.91	75	24	37.89	41	46	47.80	58
N51	Wirral	30	44.35	22	41	31.55	19	71	35.72	15
P01	Lancaster	25	84.13	123	38	59.75	112	63	70.37	123
P02	Blackpool,Wyre and Fylde	98	129.08	142	204	112.99	144	302	118.44	144
P03	Preston	13	67.52	91	60	129.19	145	73	110.30	142
P04	Blackburn, Hyndburn and Ribble Valley	30	61.05	74	54	59.45	110	84	60.90	103
P05	Burnley, Pendle and Rossendale	25	60.68	71	28	31.06	16	53	42.07	34
P06	West Lancashire	6	49.32	39	10	30.13	13	16	33.88	9
P07	Chorley and South Ribble	41	143.35	144	59	93.56	140	100	110.62	143
P08	Bolton	34	74.45	108	48	53.94	96	82	64.08	109
P09	Bury	18	62.21	78	35	59.79	113	53	62.59	107
P10	North Manchester	19	82.01	120	27	56.29	104	46	67.43	117
P11	Central Manchester	29	173.68	145	32	101.46	142	61	127.47	145
P12	South Manchester	21	71.94	104	52	81.69	135	73	80.00	134
P13	Oldham	23	60.01	68	34	47.12	77	57	52.66	75
P14	Rochdale	13	36.70	11	28	41.07	55	41	40.57	28
P15	Salford	35	87.29	129	49	54.67	99	84	67.64	118
P16	Stockport	22	41.92	18	32	32.98	24	54	36.10	17
P17	Tameside and Glossop	16	37.97	13	26	32.66	23	42	33.63	7
P18	Trafford	20	49.82	44	26	34.09	30	46	39.61	25
P19	Wigan	36	82.25	122	49	55.20	100	85	63.70	108

THE HEALTH OF THE NATION

MORTALITY TREND DATA

HON - A1

Mortality rates from coronary heart disease (ICD 410-414) in persons under 65:
Age-standardised mortality rates per 100,000: 1984-92
(observed numbers of deaths in parentheses)
Persons

		1984	1985	1986	1987	1988	1989	1990	1991	1992
	ENGLAND AND WALES	76.05	75.31	72.50	69.91	65.79	61.20	58.91	55.86	53.12
		(33072)	(32164)	(30471)	(29102)	(27291)	(25301)	(24318)	(23008)	(21940)
O00	ENGLAND	75.63	74.57	71.96	69.33	65.31	60.89	58.55	55.53	52.74
		(30977)	(29989)	(28481)	(27168)	(25485)	(23677)	(22739)	(21522)	(20506)
A00	NORTHERN RHA	96.68	95.63	90.03	91.23	84.86	82.40	76.75	71.85	69.84
		(2750)	(2634)	(2456)	(2455)	(2277)	(2190)	(2024)	(1890)	(1842)
B00	YORKSHIRE RHA	89.79	90.44	84.59	82.92	78.72	70.11	67.18	62.06	59.59
		(2811)	(2782)	(2542)	(2485)	(2344)	(2081)	(1997)	(1840)	(1770)
C00	TRENT RHA	80.86	80.33	79.61	73.77	71.28	66.94	64.10	62.60	57.66
		(3300)	(3231)	(3142)	(2888)	(2791)	(2614)	(2501)	(2420)	(2243)
D00	EAST ANGLIAN RHA	61.43	50.91	54.69	56.47	47.94	46.50	44.03	44.90	38.03
		(1017)	(842)	(891)	(924)	(787)	(768)	(742)	(761)	(648)
E00	NORTH WEST THAMES RHA	61.47	60.52	62.75	57.24	53.59	51.63	48.79	49.06	45.25
		(1786)	(1714)	(1743)	(1565)	(1441)	(1381)	(1302)	(1310)	(1210)
F00	NORTH EAST THAMES RHA	68.05	65.50	63.73	63.21	59.75	54.76	54.52	52.36	52.12
		(2181)	(2052)	(1958)	(1898)	(1780)	(1596)	(1590)	(1507)	(1509)
G00	SOUTH EAST THAMES RHA	62.51	64.86	56.63	61.48	53.31	48.90	52.01	47.19	43.75
		(1966)	(1993)	(1708)	(1824)	(1572)	(1422)	(1508)	(1367)	(1268)
H00	SOUTH WEST THAMES RHA	56.30	56.67	51.74	52.12	47.10	44.70	43.47	40.99	40.84
		(1454)	(1438)	(1282)	(1272)	(1137)	(1077)	(1043)	(976)	(980)
J00	WESSEX RHA	63.14	61.03	61.40	54.66	51.99	48.55	46.93	47.40	42.76
		(1611)	(1543)	(1531)	(1366)	(1297)	(1216)	(1179)	(1204)	(1089)
K00	OXFORD RHA	62.63	61.37	57.45	52.44	51.64	48.37	42.30	42.93	40.22
		(1189)	(1154)	(1080)	(981)	(971)	(912)	(809)	(828)	(786)
L00	SOUTH WESTERN RHA	67.21	63.76	66.69	58.60	56.11	51.72	50.16	47.39	44.42
		(1889)	(1765)	(1831)	(1596)	(1548)	(1427)	(1381)	(1317)	(1231)
M00	WEST MIDLANDS RHA	80.87	80.25	76.92	75.33	70.18	67.06	64.95	57.98	57.06
		(3701)	(3602)	(3402)	(3302)	(3057)	(2926)	(2815)	(2506)	(2468)
N00	MERSEY RHA	90.70	93.21	89.43	86.61	84.03	76.16	69.51	68.39	64.19
		(1926)	(1962)	(1851)	(1774)	(1706)	(1553)	(1411)	(1390)	(1293)
P00	NORTH WESTERN RHA	98.05	96.93	92.27	86.89	85.62	77.87	76.03	69.29	68.01
		(3396)	(3277)	(3064)	(2838)	(2777)	(2514)	(2437)	(2206)	(2169)
A01	Hartlepool	101.31	97.42	98.01	117.63	88.07	79.53	70.84	70.36	77.39
		(86)	(80)	(79)	(95)	(69)	(61)	(56)	(55)	(61)
A02	North Tees	79.48	85.82	85.26	88.89	75.96	74.73	64.54	83.46	79.96
		(121)	(129)	(126)	(129)	(114)	(111)	(94)	(121)	(119)
A03	South Tees	106.79	94.51	96.81	93.00	87.95	80.08	87.09	77.73	67.25
		(271)	(236)	(238)	(226)	(214)	(192)	(204)	(186)	(159)
A04	East Cumbria	85.18	75.38	84.44	69.39	71.11	74.80	66.71	48.65	58.32
		(138)	(122)	(134)	(109)	(115)	(119)	(107)	(78)	(94)
A05	South Cumbria	87.77	66.33	71.74	59.80	66.17	60.91	62.83	52.10	48.58
		(140)	(102)	(106)	(92)	(101)	(92)	(95)	(79)	(74)
A06	West Cumbria	90.11	113.39	90.13	83.02	96.14	98.15	71.13	77.61	64.09
		(119)	(139)	(112)	(102)	(114)	(117)	(86)	(92)	(77)

HON - A1
Mortality rates from coronary heart disease (ICD 410-414) in persons under 65:
Age-standardised mortality rates per 100,000: 1984-92
(observed numbers of deaths in parentheses)
Persons

		1984	1985	1986	1987	1988	1989	1990	1991	1992
A11	Northumberland	88.24 (247)	91.32 (245)	72.91 (200)	75.92 (207)	80.94 (218)	74.28 (198)	67.97 (181)	59.80 (160)	58.12 (157)
A12	Gateshead	104.67 (211)	96.60 (185)	93.70 (181)	119.66 (224)	105.00 (196)	88.95 (165)	85.07 (155)	76.88 (138)	80.20 (142)
A13	Newcastle	87.95 (212)	103.72 (249)	92.97 (217)	94.85 (217)	88.25 (198)	86.13 (191)	91.46 (197)	75.62 (160)	70.58 (150)
A14	North Tyneside	85.28 (166)	90.61 (165)	72.27 (134)	81.73 (148)	71.00 (121)	66.95 (115)	60.19 (104)	73.20 (123)	67.31 (115)
A15	South Tyneside	99.78 (158)	106.53 (165)	95.48 (145)	100.55 (150)	92.72 (135)	100.15 (142)	67.18 (92)	86.45 (121)	68.93 (95)
A16	Sunderland	112.99 (297)	107.07 (269)	99.55 (250)	101.88 (255)	86.86 (219)	92.03 (229)	79.89 (199)	84.88 (211)	81.94 (202)
A30	North Durham	106.47 (318)	104.26 (304)	103.19 (295)	97.55 (271)	85.26 (241)	90.35 (256)	87.85 (246)	68.20 (191)	75.25 (211)
A31	South Durham	102.47 (266)	95.61 (244)	95.58 (239)	94.23 (230)	91.38 (222)	83.66 (202)	85.77 (208)	73.03 (175)	76.89 (186)
B11	East Riding	87.75 (384)	85.89 (375)	70.83 (304)	76.18 (326)	74.44 (319)	67.16 (289)	60.50 (260)	54.91 (235)	60.62 (262)
B16	Grimsby and Scunthorpe	84.80 (266)	86.75 (265)	79.82 (241)	84.77 (257)	75.14 (226)	78.75 (232)	73.43 (219)	71.90 (217)	65.21 (194)
B21	North Yorkshire	70.66 (436)	71.57 (439)	71.72 (423)	72.20 (435)	63.44 (386)	54.82 (333)	55.14 (339)	50.15 (309)	45.70 (286)
B31	Bradford	106.04 (409)	119.58 (452)	104.27 (387)	98.10 (360)	101.00 (363)	71.64 (257)	82.91 (296)	73.61 (259)	65.79 (232)
B51	West Yorkshire	95.56 (463)	95.86 (453)	98.35 (451)	96.95 (439)	85.10 (382)	80.08 (358)	71.62 (321)	67.16 (297)	66.46 (295)
B61	Leeds	93.60 (584)	91.55 (554)	87.07 (516)	76.36 (445)	83.26 (482)	72.15 (414)	68.56 (392)	57.59 (328)	57.75 (327)
B71	Wakefield	99.63 (269)	91.17 (244)	83.84 (220)	85.22 (223)	73.06 (186)	76.76 (198)	66.59 (170)	75.94 (195)	68.33 (174)
C01	North Derbyshire	81.24 (275)	79.48 (268)	80.28 (263)	66.92 (218)	63.44 (204)	68.77 (225)	66.46 (217)	63.61 (204)	58.98 (190)
C02	Southern Derbyshire	83.10 (390)	84.80 (391)	77.30 (351)	79.67 (358)	67.34 (305)	70.31 (313)	64.70 (287)	58.92 (261)	59.46 (264)
C03	Leicestershire	76.10 (546)	76.79 (542)	73.05 (508)	65.84 (462)	69.19 (481)	62.00 (433)	58.26 (408)	63.36 (442)	49.43 (351)
C04	North Lincolnshire	71.14 (169)	78.33 (184)	67.89 (161)	67.11 (158)	65.80 (158)	64.90 (157)	66.50 (161)	55.15 (138)	60.47 (149)
C05	South Lincolnshire	75.04 (204)	72.05 (194)	66.84 (180)	67.35 (182)	74.04 (200)	58.16 (163)	51.37 (146)	54.59 (152)	59.09 (167)
C08	Nottingham	73.57 (390)	73.74 (386)	75.84 (391)	68.86 (350)	66.48 (339)	68.07 (341)	64.15 (325)	57.09 (283)	55.50 (272)
C09	Barnsley	94.22 (193)	88.23 (177)	98.77 (192)	92.44 (177)	84.42 (165)	99.87 (189)	81.67 (154)	75.96 (142)	73.60 (139)

59

HON - A1

Mortality rates from coronary heart disease (ICD 410-414) in persons under 65:
Age-standardised mortality rates per 100,000: 1984-92
(observed numbers of deaths in parentheses)
Persons

		1984	1985	1986	1987	1988	1989	1990	1991	1992
C10	Doncaster	81.00	76.63	82.05	79.42	71.81	57.67	62.26	61.91	53.80
		(210)	(195)	(206)	(196)	(181)	(146)	(155)	(151)	(133)
C11	Rotherham	95.99	97.87	89.56	81.79	85.98	77.02	74.32	69.12	71.79
		(209)	(216)	(191)	(172)	(182)	(162)	(153)	(141)	(148)
C12	Sheffield	88.58	84.66	96.36	86.34	80.81	66.08	71.58	69.38	61.84
		(429)	(402)	(434)	(377)	(349)	(281)	(301)	(289)	(257)
C14	North Nottinghamshire	81.65	81.29	78.53	70.31	68.24	60.76	57.57	66.07	51.61
		(285)	(276)	(265)	(238)	(227)	(204)	(194)	(217)	(173)
D01	Cambridge	52.86	43.94	46.89	52.85	50.64	35.11	29.51	32.97	32.24
		(114)	(94)	(98)	(110)	(104)	(74)	(62)	(70)	(70)
D05	North West Anglia	79.55	61.90	70.08	66.95	55.01	56.74	57.26	58.75	45.50
		(257)	(202)	(225)	(221)	(181)	(189)	(196)	(200)	(153)
D06	Norwich	51.54	52.13	49.61	47.78	40.18	41.06	40.45	43.35	35.49
		(209)	(215)	(200)	(195)	(166)	(170)	(170)	(181)	(151)
D07	Great Yarmouth and Waveney	61.56	41.70	53.16	57.13	47.97	51.78	46.07	44.34	43.61
		(111)	(74)	(91)	(100)	(81)	(91)	(80)	(76)	(75)
D09	Huntingdon	67.27	48.05	54.74	71.40	48.44	39.27	38.96	41.86	30.11
		(56)	(40)	(48)	(63)	(43)	(35)	(35)	(40)	(29)
D11	Suffolk	60.10	49.58	52.47	54.29	48.36	48.44	44.59	42.76	37.13
		(270)	(217)	(229)	(235)	(212)	(209)	(199)	(194)	(170)
E01	North Bedfordshire	62.61	54.84	65.21	54.19	52.60	46.54	38.70	51.64	43.76
		(123)	(104)	(125)	(104)	(99)	(89)	(73)	(99)	(85)
E02	South Bedfordshire	62.96	60.88	58.96	60.16	60.41	57.48	58.57	55.30	52.61
		(133)	(128)	(123)	(123)	(124)	(119)	(120)	(116)	(111)
E05	North West Hertfordshire	63.58	63.71	50.51	55.19	45.35	39.68	39.47	34.86	34.78
		(149)	(147)	(113)	(123)	(101)	(87)	(86)	(76)	(76)
E06	South West Hertfordshire	62.17	53.22	58.00	65.04	39.35	49.83	49.59	37.77	39.97
		(140)	(115)	(123)	(134)	(81)	(99)	(98)	(76)	(79)
E07	Barnet	49.04	59.11	57.55	49.30	45.09	42.36	52.37	47.93	44.28
		(123)	(143)	(138)	(117)	(101)	(95)	(117)	(108)	(97)
E09	Hillingdon	69.99	57.68	63.50	59.63	58.73	54.61	46.47	53.83	48.13
		(143)	(114)	(127)	(116)	(112)	(106)	(88)	(98)	(87)
E18	East and North Hertfordshire	53.41	58.43	61.42	52.86	53.92	51.93	40.85	41.85	43.51
		(223)	(238)	(248)	(213)	(216)	(206)	(165)	(167)	(175)
E19	Brent and Harrow	59.21	61.82	67.49	53.79	56.69	57.77	55.04	51.88	48.72
		(222)	(227)	(241)	(188)	(195)	(194)	(187)	(176)	(167)
E20	Ealing, Hammersmith and Hounslow	71.31	69.29	72.18	68.11	64.89	60.51	56.46	60.63	52.22
		(376)	(354)	(358)	(328)	(304)	(283)	(259)	(275)	(238)
E21	Kensington, Chelsea and Westminster	58.91	56.13	59.80	49.00	45.45	42.88	44.57	47.70	37.43
		(154)	(144)	(147)	(119)	(108)	(103)	(109)	(119)	(95)
F31	North Essex	58.86	58.80	60.49	51.66	52.08	45.55	44.16	44.51	43.89
		(425)	(415)	(423)	(360)	(363)	(319)	(312)	(315)	(315)
F32	South Essex	69.82	63.48	63.08	66.69	59.72	49.39	53.21	52.03	44.20
		(413)	(369)	(363)	(380)	(346)	(282)	(300)	(289)	(249)

HON - A1
Mortality rates from coronary heart disease (ICD 410-414) in persons under 65:
Age-standardised mortality rates per 100,000: 1984-92
(observed numbers of deaths in parentheses)
Persons

		1984	1985	1986	1987	1988	1989	1990	1991	1992
F33	Barking and Havering	62.83 (244)	70.37 (269)	69.26 (255)	65.37 (227)	55.31 (191)	59.22 (200)	54.93 (185)	49.67 (157)	46.55 (148)
F34	Redbridge and Waltham Forest	62.94 (239)	57.29 (215)	57.05 (206)	60.77 (217)	65.36 (222)	54.52 (182)	54.80 (183)	58.28 (190)	49.59 (161)
F35	East London and the City	86.15 (391)	79.75 (354)	78.10 (339)	78.20 (326)	77.97 (318)	65.58 (258)	74.14 (289)	67.28 (257)	76.27 (290)
F36	New River District	69.96 (271)	65.40 (243)	55.33 (200)	63.33 (224)	51.23 (179)	54.97 (185)	52.92 (180)	52.49 (178)	53.35 (184)
F37	Camden and Islington	69.74 (198)	67.56 (187)	63.17 (172)	62.77 (164)	62.77 (161)	68.85 (170)	56.66 (141)	48.78 (121)	65.80 (162)
G04	South East Kent	71.15 (165)	64.59 (146)	53.10 (118)	70.49 (156)	49.12 (110)	49.91 (110)	41.19 (92)	41.59 (93)	41.28 (92)
G05	Canterbury and Thanet	71.27 (179)	64.00 (157)	60.37 (147)	75.70 (181)	65.85 (161)	47.61 (118)	60.45 (145)	45.97 (117)	51.14 (129)
G06	Dartford and Gravesham	82.24 (158)	73.12 (137)	66.63 (127)	75.39 (142)	60.78 (115)	50.81 (95)	57.50 (109)	52.13 (98)	40.66 (78)
G07	Maidstone	65.75 (105)	62.68 (99)	52.02 (83)	62.50 (99)	57.25 (91)	41.77 (66)	47.87 (77)	36.18 (60)	31.04 (51)
G08	Medway	68.97 (175)	74.70 (189)	69.01 (170)	75.13 (185)	59.29 (145)	58.56 (147)	59.66 (148)	55.43 (139)	54.19 (134)
G09	Tunbridge Wells	52.01 (93)	49.36 (88)	55.74 (98)	46.63 (83)	37.67 (65)	38.72 (67)	40.21 (70)	36.84 (65)	38.06 (68)
G10	Bexley	60.24 (114)	53.83 (99)	49.83 (91)	60.31 (110)	42.53 (77)	54.22 (96)	49.84 (89)	40.47 (71)	40.47 (72)
G11	Greenwich	69.32 (131)	75.45 (133)	67.36 (116)	71.95 (116)	56.39 (91)	57.55 (89)	54.60 (86)	60.80 (91)	48.12 (71)
G12	Bromley	52.54 (153)	55.71 (159)	49.84 (134)	41.06 (109)	44.91 (119)	35.93 (94)	46.99 (122)	38.96 (97)	33.56 (86)
G21	East Sussex	46.52 (279)	59.39 (355)	46.50 (277)	46.41 (271)	42.84 (249)	40.66 (236)	42.28 (242)	42.89 (247)	35.91 (206)
G26	South East London	67.58 (414)	73.81 (431)	61.97 (347)	68.81 (372)	66.22 (349)	60.50 (304)	67.09 (328)	59.41 (289)	58.39 (281)
H04	Mid Surrey	56.08 (93)	55.90 (89)	38.15 (62)	45.96 (73)	34.68 (53)	42.38 (65)	32.39 (50)	40.06 (62)	32.40 (50)
H05	East Surrey	55.28 (95)	55.61 (97)	54.97 (93)	43.94 (74)	50.56 (84)	41.29 (69)	54.52 (89)	37.15 (62)	37.03 (61)
H06	Chichester	58.28 (95)	48.55 (84)	49.23 (79)	36.24 (59)	41.90 (66)	37.38 (61)	34.51 (57)	33.75 (53)	36.14 (58)
H07	Mid Downs	55.10 (130)	59.25 (137)	41.15 (95)	58.07 (134)	47.42 (110)	44.93 (104)	39.19 (89)	37.12 (86)	39.85 (92)
H08	Worthing	55.13 (117)	54.76 (115)	53.18 (111)	49.14 (104)	52.45 (106)	54.52 (117)	43.18 (90)	35.33 (73)	44.58 (91)
H09	Croydon	63.80 (174)	58.72 (155)	60.09 (155)	56.51 (142)	54.73 (134)	49.12 (121)	46.91 (115)	52.75 (129)	41.64 (103)

HON - A1

Mortality rates from coronary heart disease (ICD 410-414) in persons under 65:
Age-standardised mortality rates per 100,000: 1984-92
(observed numbers of deaths in parentheses)
Persons

		1984	1985	1986	1987	1988	1989	1990	1991	1992
H12	Wandsworth	70.65 (104)	75.98 (110)	81.40 (112)	69.12 (92)	59.97 (78)	56.61 (72)	65.19 (80)	58.41 (71)	67.19 (82)
H13	Merton and Sutton	67.26 (199)	55.04 (159)	53.54 (149)	63.86 (174)	51.81 (141)	52.28 (140)	40.35 (109)	44.94 (116)	44.88 (119)
H14	North West Surrey	44.87 (153)	48.45 (163)	44.07 (146)	47.69 (156)	33.44 (108)	37.19 (120)	40.86 (133)	40.96 (133)	35.90 (117)
H15	South West Surrey	41.47 (87)	58.62 (121)	50.02 (99)	47.30 (94)	42.55 (84)	38.26 (76)	45.58 (92)	31.95 (64)	33.85 (69)
H16	Kingston and Richmond	56.41 (207)	59.54 (208)	52.93 (181)	51.19 (170)	52.23 (173)	41.51 (132)	43.88 (139)	40.81 (127)	43.19 (138)
J10	Dorset	57.69 (336)	58.77 (341)	60.60 (345)	45.63 (259)	44.11 (256)	39.56 (226)	42.42 (242)	37.94 (221)	36.53 (208)
J21	Portsmouth and South East Hampshire	68.76 (292)	66.49 (281)	63.21 (264)	61.04 (257)	56.97 (238)	54.87 (230)	49.41 (207)	58.10 (246)	46.74 (199)
J22	Southampton and South West Hampshire	63.76 (230)	59.97 (216)	60.64 (216)	59.32 (207)	55.11 (190)	52.58 (184)	48.27 (166)	49.55 (172)	49.29 (170)
J23	Winchester	61.16 (106)	51.88 (91)	62.86 (107)	55.32 (96)	50.54 (87)	43.65 (78)	42.23 (75)	42.84 (77)	44.42 (81)
J24	Basingstoke and North Hampshire	72.52 (187)	65.06 (166)	57.06 (144)	55.59 (142)	53.05 (140)	50.43 (132)	48.98 (130)	50.25 (137)	45.04 (125)
J31	Salisbury	71.13 (78)	56.68 (61)	48.04 (50)	54.43 (58)	50.23 (53)	48.27 (51)	39.67 (44)	40.54 (44)	40.37 (45)
J32	Swindon	66.28 (123)	67.60 (123)	79.90 (147)	65.52 (117)	67.00 (119)	50.79 (90)	49.78 (89)	59.40 (108)	52.47 (96)
J33	Bath	53.27 (183)	54.67 (185)	58.14 (191)	48.25 (159)	45.19 (148)	50.67 (167)	50.22 (167)	42.85 (144)	36.33 (121)
J41	Isle of Wight	62.46 (76)	69.97 (79)	59.94 (67)	62.49 (71)	59.06 (66)	51.35 (58)	52.80 (59)	50.41 (55)	38.11 (44)
K11	East Berkshire	65.64 (198)	63.53 (187)	56.07 (165)	61.72 (176)	61.84 (175)	55.86 (159)	43.70 (125)	46.27 (134)	45.18 (130)
K12	West Berkshire	60.45 (198)	58.09 (191)	56.39 (187)	48.12 (160)	56.40 (186)	40.58 (135)	43.28 (147)	46.66 (159)	33.38 (115)
K24	Buckinghamshire	56.94 (247)	57.89 (250)	56.03 (241)	44.94 (194)	46.83 (206)	40.53 (179)	38.32 (173)	39.71 (183)	38.36 (181)
K31	Kettering	73.86 (152)	69.70 (141)	71.40 (146)	64.17 (130)	62.14 (127)	68.92 (141)	44.81 (91)	54.62 (114)	46.31 (97)
K32	Northampton	66.13 (154)	63.80 (148)	60.31 (138)	56.12 (128)	52.53 (122)	53.00 (123)	45.68 (107)	44.20 (103)	45.46 (107)
K41	Oxfordshire	60.49 (240)	60.70 (237)	52.04 (203)	49.48 (193)	39.61 (155)	45.35 (175)	41.99 (166)	33.83 (135)	38.57 (156)
L10	Bristol and District	68.30 (479)	71.66 (495)	68.27 (460)	61.00 (410)	56.84 (384)	53.11 (351)	54.66 (360)	52.72 (350)	47.51 (312)
L21	Cornwall and Isles of Scilly	66.38 (268)	65.55 (271)	69.78 (283)	56.78 (233)	57.37 (239)	53.45 (226)	48.54 (207)	40.21 (173)	49.24 (211)

HON - A1
Mortality rates from coronary heart disease (ICD 410-414) in persons under 65:
Age-standardised mortality rates per 100,000: 1984-92
(observed numbers of deaths in parentheses)
Persons

		1984	1985	1986	1987	1988	1989	1990	1991	1992
L35	Exeter and North Devon	56.80 (225)	58.02 (225)	55.72 (217)	53.84 (205)	55.12 (216)	48.34 (192)	41.69 (164)	44.32 (177)	43.70 (173)
L36	Plymouth and Torbay	80.58 (396)	70.13 (335)	78.54 (377)	72.72 (343)	61.45 (295)	56.16 (270)	51.98 (251)	54.62 (262)	49.31 (238)
L40	Gloucestershire	66.11 (305)	54.60 (247)	62.80 (280)	50.99 (225)	54.53 (241)	51.31 (228)	48.77 (215)	43.67 (196)	40.07 (180)
L51	Somerset	60.32 (216)	55.49 (192)	60.64 (214)	51.78 (180)	49.10 (173)	45.07 (160)	52.09 (184)	44.76 (159)	32.92 (117)
M02	Herefordshire	53.15 (73)	54.52 (76)	69.56 (98)	59.77 (85)	55.32 (77)	45.90 (65)	43.13 (61)	34.64 (49)	54.12 (78)
M04	Worcester and District	50.63 (108)	64.38 (133)	55.50 (117)	70.20 (145)	60.69 (127)	45.66 (96)	49.78 (105)	44.59 (94)	51.85 (112)
M05	Shropshire	73.25 (237)	76.37 (247)	69.60 (226)	70.56 (232)	69.39 (228)	60.60 (202)	57.22 (193)	47.97 (165)	50.22 (173)
M06	Mid Staffordshire	76.27 (196)	75.30 (193)	63.62 (163)	63.20 (162)	55.72 (144)	58.88 (155)	62.29 (165)	53.56 (142)	50.58 (136)
M07	North Staffordshire	102.06 (441)	96.70 (414)	91.15 (377)	91.91 (377)	86.44 (351)	80.31 (325)	78.02 (311)	66.95 (268)	67.22 (265)
M08	South East Staffordshire	73.24 (146)	85.32 (166)	74.52 (146)	70.97 (142)	67.95 (138)	72.76 (149)	66.43 (138)	63.91 (136)	42.35 (92)
M13	East Birmingham	113.25 (204)	90.84 (165)	94.94 (158)	89.42 (150)	76.65 (122)	83.64 (130)	81.92 (123)	63.18 (90)	79.27 (116)
M14	North Birmingham	68.82 (103)	83.86 (124)	66.11 (99)	65.24 (96)	44.84 (64)	58.37 (84)	67.71 (96)	51.49 (72)	48.71 (68)
M16	West Birmingham	102.98 (178)	82.80 (135)	89.99 (146)	98.92 (155)	91.92 (139)	91.03 (137)	87.97 (132)	78.15 (116)	80.74 (117)
M17	Coventry	91.55 (263)	83.54 (226)	73.71 (190)	85.06 (214)	67.96 (172)	74.23 (184)	66.49 (159)	53.33 (125)	54.51 (127)
M18	Dudley	69.99 (193)	78.61 (215)	69.28 (185)	76.96 (203)	75.41 (203)	58.33 (155)	52.27 (140)	54.40 (147)	56.69 (152)
M19	Sandwell	91.95 (264)	85.43 (236)	90.01 (242)	83.73 (219)	82.75 (215)	81.86 (207)	73.14 (183)	65.50 (162)	67.95 (164)
M20	Solihull	57.83 (105)	60.94 (108)	62.10 (112)	57.85 (105)	57.85 (103)	59.02 (106)	51.80 (93)	43.33 (78)	45.59 (81)
M21	Walsall	96.19 (230)	86.93 (204)	96.33 (224)	80.41 (186)	74.76 (172)	84.86 (196)	82.14 (188)	82.34 (186)	64.04 (144)
M22	Wolverhampton	71.24 (166)	88.41 (200)	83.61 (184)	70.91 (153)	78.18 (165)	70.24 (151)	75.29 (158)	68.15 (140)	72.01 (145)
M25	South Birmingham	93.82 (343)	95.84 (333)	86.14 (296)	87.70 (294)	80.64 (265)	72.14 (235)	78.28 (248)	70.01 (220)	65.55 (206)
M26	North Worcestershire	74.01 (157)	69.80 (150)	67.90 (143)	59.78 (128)	56.41 (121)	60.94 (134)	50.40 (112)	50.57 (111)	36.45 (82)
M28	Warwickshire	69.14 (294)	66.10 (277)	71.47 (296)	61.96 (256)	60.58 (251)	51.75 (215)	50.85 (210)	49.34 (205)	50.22 (210)

HON - A1
Mortality rates from coronary heart disease (ICD 410-414) in persons under 65:
Age-standardised mortality rates per 100,000: 1984-92
(observed numbers of deaths in parentheses)
Persons

		1984	1985	1986	1987	1988	1989	1990	1991	1992
N11	Chester	73.35 (115)	95.54 (148)	68.88 (106)	70.74 (110)	78.64 (121)	63.83 (98)	61.61 (94)	68.39 (106)	52.02 (80)
N12	Crewe	87.17 (191)	80.63 (171)	87.90 (187)	71.57 (152)	79.93 (170)	72.48 (155)	63.69 (139)	64.24 (138)	49.16 (105)
N13	Halton	108.65 (125)	107.38 (120)	87.97 (102)	103.55 (116)	82.05 (93)	63.82 (73)	68.63 (78)	70.58 (77)	54.07 (61)
N14	Macclesfield	57.26 (94)	60.38 (98)	68.21 (109)	55.80 (89)	59.14 (95)	52.12 (85)	48.80 (79)	47.42 (77)	47.00 (77)
N15	Warrington	88.73 (131)	90.53 (135)	101.21 (148)	106.00 (153)	88.85 (131)	76.26 (112)	74.14 (111)	58.60 (88)	67.66 (102)
N21	Liverpool	97.56 (421)	105.65 (450)	95.64 (392)	99.19 (402)	92.08 (361)	90.83 (358)	79.79 (304)	81.69 (313)	88.87 (332)
N31	St Helens and Knowsley	112.80 (340)	108.02 (326)	108.35 (321)	104.99 (305)	108.07 (312)	91.52 (263)	83.51 (237)	76.26 (214)	71.57 (204)
N41	Southport and Formby	76.30 (81)	75.29 (82)	79.61 (85)	66.95 (70)	71.41 (75)	62.50 (66)	53.65 (58)	47.96 (51)	40.45 (45)
N42	South Sefton	93.40 (153)	92.49 (151)	94.40 (151)	91.73 (145)	85.32 (131)	81.79 (129)	80.39 (125)	79.78 (128)	65.89 (100)
N51	Wirral	86.01 (275)	89.84 (281)	81.53 (250)	76.68 (232)	72.20 (217)	70.79 (214)	61.62 (186)	64.70 (198)	63.17 (187)
P01	Lancaster	74.44 (82)	91.72 (99)	70.12 (77)	70.82 (75)	83.12 (89)	74.09 (80)	75.77 (82)	59.23 (66)	55.58 (60)
P02	Blackpool,Wyre and Fylde	80.07 (257)	84.15 (262)	77.24 (237)	75.28 (234)	76.12 (238)	77.42 (239)	71.07 (218)	67.66 (202)	55.89 (169)
P03	Preston	80.02 (88)	83.77 (90)	115.56 (121)	90.86 (94)	83.69 (88)	55.71 (57)	83.95 (84)	68.91 (70)	80.28 (79)
P04	Blackburn, Hyndburn and Ribble Valley	106.13 (245)	98.34 (221)	80.89 (183)	97.82 (216)	90.18 (193)	84.59 (179)	74.18 (157)	70.96 (151)	60.16 (126)
P05	Burnley, Pendle and Rossendale	92.50 (185)	113.05 (218)	88.30 (169)	88.94 (168)	89.48 (164)	85.18 (161)	81.48 (151)	82.02 (152)	80.52 (150)
P06	West Lancashire	78.35 (68)	91.09 (79)	75.22 (66)	58.58 (51)	82.81 (73)	74.03 (66)	53.52 (48)	55.40 (51)	59.48 (55)
P07	Chorley and South Ribble	89.06 (140)	94.75 (148)	83.96 (133)	80.15 (125)	66.35 (104)	68.24 (107)	55.70 (90)	51.36 (83)	55.64 (89)
P08	Bolton	120.11 (261)	110.10 (243)	110.88 (232)	87.80 (183)	94.70 (198)	82.28 (167)	81.75 (167)	77.40 (156)	77.74 (158)
P09	Bury	93.51 (138)	94.29 (137)	93.51 (132)	67.88 (98)	79.06 (110)	74.28 (105)	79.84 (112)	80.76 (114)	64.63 (93)
P10	North Manchester	117.60 (151)	129.10 (153)	120.85 (141)	118.16 (135)	133.92 (145)	103.30 (108)	90.33 (96)	73.76 (74)	100.11 (101)
P11	Central Manchester	96.27 (91)	120.11 (108)	108.78 (94)	108.65 (92)	96.16 (80)	114.38 (92)	99.24 (78)	80.48 (64)	76.76 (56)
P12	South Manchester	100.90 (154)	90.31 (131)	100.56 (141)	76.95 (103)	87.19 (119)	82.76 (107)	87.22 (110)	68.40 (82)	75.73 (91)

64

HON - A1
Mortality rates from coronary heart disease (ICD 410-414) in persons under 65:
Age-standardised mortality rates per 100,000: 1984-92
(observed numbers of deaths in parentheses)
Persons

		1984	1985	1986	1987	1988	1989	1990	1991	1992
P13	Oldham	90.43	109.90	95.69	105.17	91.55	79.68	70.90	81.41	78.66
		(169)	(199)	(170)	(181)	(157)	(137)	(120)	(137)	(134)
P14	Rochdale	130.34	108.91	105.38	104.51	89.30	75.55	87.74	82.52	96.23
		(232)	(192)	(180)	(174)	(151)	(127)	(147)	(136)	(159)
P15	Salford	110.38	99.47	102.46	92.45	96.85	95.45	91.66	85.63	80.74
		(244)	(212)	(208)	(183)	(188)	(181)	(169)	(158)	(147)
P16	Stockport	83.66	82.11	81.45	67.42	71.38	59.01	59.81	50.97	50.71
		(214)	(207)	(201)	(163)	(173)	(144)	(146)	(122)	(125)
P17	Tameside and Glossop	101.86	96.97	100.86	94.04	89.70	69.54	76.32	67.56	66.39
		(217)	(198)	(205)	(188)	(178)	(137)	(148)	(131)	(130)
P18	Trafford	90.25	61.91	79.67	65.37	65.84	64.28	69.58	51.62	54.03
		(177)	(118)	(149)	(123)	(118)	(119)	(125)	(93)	(96)
P19	Wigan	110.40	104.07	91.11	103.62	85.74	82.30	76.76	66.89	60.40
		(283)	(262)	(225)	(252)	(211)	(201)	(189)	(164)	(151)

HON - A2

Mortality rates from coronary heart disease (ICD 410-414) in persons aged 65-74:
Age-standardised mortality rates per 100,000: 1984-92
(observed numbers of deaths in parentheses)
Persons

		1984	1985	1986	1987	1988	1989	1990	1991	1992
	ENGLAND AND WALES	1024.55	1029.00	997.51	975.38	953.57	924.78	895.37	880.32	842.32
		(45490)	(46559)	(45501)	(44429)	(43013)	(41264)	(40265)	(40062)	(38899)
O00	ENGLAND	1017.50	1021.90	991.33	969.36	948.02	916.66	889.41	875.15	838.42
		(42478)	(43471)	(42497)	(41477)	(40137)	(38359)	(37495)	(37315)	(36281)
A00	NORTHERN RHA	1268.13	1246.71	1205.04	1218.96	1207.58	1168.03	1113.28	1128.07	1090.06
		(3416)	(3452)	(3380)	(3432)	(3392)	(3269)	(3167)	(3271)	(3220)
B00	YORKSHIRE RHA	1194.00	1187.35	1152.84	1117.31	1128.72	1050.35	1075.29	995.07	946.69
		(3815)	(3846)	(3774)	(3633)	(3638)	(3351)	(3459)	(3239)	(3149)
C00	TRENT RHA	1078.87	1055.21	1044.17	1038.36	1038.39	993.22	960.92	943.89	911.43
		(4359)	(4370)	(4394)	(4386)	(4370)	(4164)	(4092)	(4096)	(4022)
D00	EAST ANGLIAN RHA	933.51	888.02	889.01	812.87	793.89	756.61	735.23	757.25	728.61
		(1699)	(1659)	(1687)	(1555)	(1513)	(1434)	(1415)	(1486)	(1466)
E00	NORTH WEST THAMES RHA	867.83	914.22	844.24	856.19	826.02	779.59	752.69	755.04	730.14
		(2418)	(2563)	(2368)	(2374)	(2232)	(2054)	(1970)	(1974)	(1926)
F00	NORTH EAST THAMES RHA	923.82	959.59	925.68	935.85	864.69	855.27	828.09	837.86	793.29
		(2957)	(3112)	(3000)	(3005)	(2718)	(2633)	(2549)	(2590)	(2475)
G00	SOUTH EAST THAMES RHA	894.99	889.74	882.21	826.65	783.91	747.25	760.14	746.84	721.03
		(3119)	(3157)	(3118)	(2910)	(2700)	(2518)	(2558)	(2513)	(2452)
H00	SOUTH WEST THAMES RHA	827.39	850.08	833.74	757.76	758.05	718.17	694.25	694.09	644.20
		(2284)	(2369)	(2315)	(2083)	(2031)	(1880)	(1812)	(1811)	(1691)
J00	WESSEX RHA	885.96	878.67	837.00	844.49	789.24	785.65	741.30	737.35	708.34
		(2482)	(2516)	(2446)	(2459)	(2288)	(2256)	(2154)	(2178)	(2124)
K00	OXFORD RHA	893.08	867.78	845.65	838.33	786.62	764.14	730.98	746.08	684.01
		(1571)	(1576)	(1547)	(1551)	(1448)	(1396)	(1352)	(1402)	(1309)
L00	SOUTH WESTERN RHA	925.78	907.94	888.39	877.73	827.92	797.76	782.44	777.37	735.93
		(2944)	(2943)	(2908)	(2883)	(2699)	(2583)	(2559)	(2585)	(2484)
M00	WEST MIDLANDS RHA	1066.31	1077.90	1063.88	1044.28	1003.29	1010.52	951.43	931.77	885.87
		(4635)	(4811)	(4830)	(4771)	(4576)	(4582)	(4378)	(4359)	(4209)
N00	MERSEY RHA	1174.72	1198.57	1161.32	1091.42	1110.37	1087.90	1040.54	993.17	966.98
		(2433)	(2545)	(2469)	(2326)	(2341)	(2273)	(2190)	(2114)	(2082)
P00	NORTH WESTERN RHA	1199.66	1247.83	1168.06	1138.10	1177.85	1130.45	1091.57	1041.86	1019.03
		(4346)	(4552)	(4261)	(4109)	(4191)	(3966)	(3840)	(3697)	(3672)
A01	Hartlepool	1309.02	1238.65	1135.60	1288.69	1321.05	1206.73	1091.84	1049.55	1014.19
		(95)	(93)	(86)	(98)	(100)	(91)	(86)	(85)	(85)
A02	North Tees	1090.28	1239.04	1039.66	1162.23	1110.81	1194.13	1052.06	1285.19	1068.66
		(130)	(153)	(132)	(151)	(147)	(158)	(144)	(181)	(155)
A03	South Tees	1175.21	1309.21	1121.02	1229.75	1327.96	1298.36	1182.39	1150.33	1096.42
		(261)	(300)	(262)	(292)	(318)	(313)	(289)	(289)	(282)
A04	East Cumbria	1237.34	1140.80	1107.84	1109.26	1164.41	1143.70	932.01	1033.10	967.10
		(209)	(198)	(189)	(192)	(201)	(195)	(162)	(182)	(174)
A05	South Cumbria	1089.36	1054.58	982.87	1052.40	907.62	927.30	950.38	888.11	819.49
		(194)	(190)	(179)	(191)	(163)	(164)	(169)	(157)	(147)
A06	West Cumbria	1326.74	1210.26	1208.28	1343.96	1188.37	1192.76	1251.29	1242.40	1012.47
		(155)	(146)	(148)	(167)	(148)	(149)	(159)	(161)	(133)

66

HON - A2
Mortality rates from coronary heart disease (ICD 410-414) in persons aged 65-74:
Age-standardised mortality rates per 100,000: 1984-92
(observed numbers of deaths in parentheses)
Persons

		1984	1985	1986	1987	1988	1989	1990	1991	1992
A11	Northumberland	1278.61	1227.45	1247.87	1311.40	1101.64	1096.59	979.86	1027.44	1007.62
		(359)	(347)	(360)	(377)	(316)	(316)	(287)	(309)	(308)
A12	Gateshead	1404.16	1239.83	1300.17	1238.18	1179.90	1237.09	1171.14	1406.09	1257.97
		(265)	(243)	(256)	(243)	(230)	(239)	(229)	(278)	(252)
A13	Newcastle	1313.72	1228.82	1136.63	1085.66	1113.31	1040.77	1041.45	1072.14	1035.70
		(342)	(327)	(307)	(289)	(293)	(268)	(268)	(276)	(271)
A14	North Tyneside	1348.32	1286.87	1094.90	1165.83	1214.77	1079.98	1122.99	971.47	1095.53
		(250)	(244)	(214)	(229)	(239)	(213)	(225)	(199)	(226)
A15	South Tyneside	1182.89	1161.04	1242.11	1055.24	1302.88	1157.65	1181.63	1082.06	1173.22
		(171)	(175)	(191)	(164)	(204)	(181)	(190)	(179)	(198)
A16	Sunderland	1271.87	1454.67	1279.82	1299.04	1322.81	1273.05	1317.25	1217.54	1201.07
		(296)	(346)	(309)	(315)	(320)	(307)	(324)	(305)	(312)
A30	North Durham	1278.24	1272.98	1407.39	1334.98	1368.57	1286.38	1138.52	1192.40	1286.93
		(353)	(361)	(400)	(381)	(387)	(364)	(326)	(348)	(384)
A31	South Durham	1357.09	1270.74	1327.79	1302.13	1238.86	1188.62	1154.75	1182.09	1056.54
		(336)	(329)	(347)	(343)	(326)	(311)	(309)	(322)	(293)
B11	East Riding	1074.86	1112.88	1111.97	1068.61	1008.71	1031.68	1052.36	932.97	922.97
		(498)	(523)	(528)	(503)	(472)	(479)	(492)	(442)	(450)
B16	Grimsby and Scunthorpe	1255.73	1173.62	1172.65	1209.46	1136.73	1197.71	1143.82	1020.91	1003.60
		(371)	(355)	(365)	(378)	(355)	(373)	(364)	(332)	(332)
B21	North Yorkshire	1122.00	1065.57	1024.33	1005.89	1046.10	873.88	948.09	870.65	816.76
		(746)	(717)	(695)	(680)	(704)	(583)	(641)	(597)	(574)
B31	Bradford	1187.47	1316.70	1322.48	1182.84	1226.08	1067.06	1059.87	1082.71	1047.34
		(452)	(500)	(505)	(448)	(461)	(401)	(399)	(413)	(408)
B51	West Yorkshire	1315.38	1229.83	1222.32	1236.07	1236.27	1274.93	1175.27	1080.69	989.41
		(658)	(623)	(625)	(626)	(616)	(624)	(578)	(535)	(500)
B61	Leeds	1190.33	1235.43	1117.44	1071.21	1082.03	969.68	1067.67	994.30	961.19
		(757)	(801)	(725)	(684)	(680)	(598)	(658)	(616)	(604)
B71	Wakefield	1305.65	1257.79	1243.24	1173.81	1312.59	1099.85	1206.83	1104.80	997.72
		(333)	(327)	(331)	(314)	(350)	(293)	(327)	(304)	(281)
C01	North Derbyshire	1045.29	1050.32	1057.28	959.19	1104.26	891.41	893.98	870.19	927.20
		(345)	(361)	(368)	(336)	(386)	(312)	(319)	(316)	(344)
C02	Southern Derbyshire	1167.43	1104.73	1063.62	1076.29	1000.69	1027.55	1076.73	931.57	889.26
		(545)	(527)	(518)	(523)	(486)	(497)	(527)	(464)	(449)
C03	Leicestershire	1005.92	898.34	911.72	974.64	938.19	929.63	821.83	865.49	778.11
		(692)	(630)	(651)	(699)	(669)	(659)	(591)	(634)	(584)
C04	North Lincolnshire	1064.42	1124.15	977.49	967.77	1094.12	1010.45	1090.17	902.22	824.47
		(263)	(291)	(259)	(262)	(299)	(279)	(309)	(265)	(248)
C05	South Lincolnshire	1043.25	1077.56	1001.05	1087.39	1016.09	969.66	950.64	991.33	936.63
		(308)	(327)	(308)	(336)	(317)	(304)	(306)	(329)	(318)
C08	Nottingham	1031.59	996.02	983.92	982.73	1042.97	873.11	845.49	845.68	890.92
		(534)	(529)	(530)	(527)	(556)	(463)	(455)	(463)	(497)
C09	Barnsley	1264.08	1329.27	1280.30	1336.71	1285.05	1248.72	1279.54	1291.78	1233.29
		(248)	(265)	(260)	(273)	(261)	(251)	(262)	(269)	(260)

HON - A2
Mortality rates from coronary heart disease (ICD 410-414) in persons aged 65-74:
Age-standardised mortality rates per 100,000: 1984-92
(observed numbers of deaths in parentheses)
Persons

		1984	1985	1986	1987	1988	1989	1990	1991	1992
C10	Doncaster	1006.95	924.88	931.43	805.34	912.87	836.91	847.29	915.17	1057.09
		(233)	(221)	(228)	(200)	(227)	(208)	(218)	(241)	(286)
C11	Rotherham	1230.56	1246.38	1200.03	1313.70	1213.67	1350.39	1169.78	1094.14	1059.48
		(247)	(259)	(253)	(281)	(259)	(289)	(255)	(244)	(240)
C12	Sheffield	1027.52	1095.32	1159.47	1079.10	1118.92	1073.17	970.12	1047.41	955.77
		(558)	(595)	(635)	(586)	(595)	(557)	(503)	(546)	(492)
C14	North Nottinghamshire	1188.33	1088.50	1122.39	1051.32	914.35	993.38	983.92	903.50	829.02
		(386)	(365)	(384)	(363)	(315)	(345)	(347)	(325)	(304)
D01	Cambridge	842.90	793.40	813.31	789.34	837.30	676.43	725.40	675.45	662.84
		(187)	(179)	(187)	(180)	(190)	(151)	(164)	(156)	(156)
D05	North West Anglia	1056.55	1016.22	1103.54	906.64	886.21	847.47	729.63	826.94	790.20
		(358)	(354)	(395)	(332)	(327)	(314)	(277)	(322)	(318)
D06	Norwich	917.32	816.33	801.14	769.03	731.52	677.81	705.83	716.50	707.94
		(440)	(406)	(400)	(385)	(365)	(336)	(355)	(368)	(371)
D07	Great Yarmouth and Waveney	838.49	841.82	878.78	863.96	774.89	744.22	826.34	752.72	799.21
		(180)	(180)	(193)	(191)	(171)	(163)	(183)	(169)	(184)
D09	Huntingdon	898.83	888.19	1213.52	861.17	831.96	784.38	745.42	719.84	734.40
		(71)	(74)	(103)	(74)	(71)	(67)	(65)	(64)	(67)
D11	Suffolk	951.59	931.11	807.50	770.18	768.98	803.67	730.97	789.38	700.97
		(463)	(466)	(409)	(393)	(389)	(403)	(371)	(407)	(370)
E01	North Bedfordshire	923.82	1011.66	972.51	742.92	890.83	863.98	924.09	817.63	706.51
		(160)	(180)	(177)	(138)	(164)	(158)	(171)	(154)	(136)
E02	South Bedfordshire	1018.59	977.04	907.85	966.73	985.37	787.90	793.90	808.05	844.96
		(188)	(187)	(174)	(184)	(185)	(146)	(147)	(150)	(160)
E05	North West Hertfordshire	833.77	888.38	919.19	898.51	844.30	868.73	718.74	611.34	739.63
		(164)	(178)	(189)	(186)	(174)	(177)	(149)	(128)	(159)
E06	South West Hertfordshire	860.77	897.49	775.80	829.63	904.67	779.06	723.46	813.64	681.12
		(186)	(199)	(172)	(184)	(197)	(166)	(153)	(172)	(147)
E07	Barnet	722.20	880.08	808.79	751.08	768.19	698.17	764.98	654.59	676.83
		(202)	(244)	(224)	(201)	(199)	(175)	(188)	(159)	(164)
E09	Hillingdon	963.39	902.37	802.16	949.48	644.58	775.11	740.80	710.79	761.96
		(193)	(180)	(161)	(190)	(125)	(148)	(140)	(133)	(145)
E18	East and North Hertfordshire	823.23	881.00	807.71	865.39	869.99	824.70	729.65	735.04	722.29
		(292)	(323)	(304)	(328)	(328)	(310)	(277)	(283)	(283)
E19	Brent and Harrow	939.59	955.79	810.09	837.66	816.64	718.79	746.24	684.53	701.77
		(358)	(357)	(302)	(301)	(280)	(234)	(237)	(215)	(219)
E20	Ealing, Hammersmith and Hounslow	857.66	934.09	933.13	925.99	796.19	793.96	827.86	951.36	777.06
		(451)	(493)	(477)	(463)	(385)	(367)	(376)	(426)	(347)
E21	Kensington, Chelsea and Westminster	817.62	831.79	707.97	762.95	778.99	710.18	544.49	634.06	685.04
		(224)	(222)	(188)	(199)	(195)	(173)	(132)	(154)	(166)
F31	North Essex	886.97	894.58	908.78	894.10	861.73	766.80	761.47	781.13	718.78
		(659)	(678)	(702)	(698)	(666)	(588)	(588)	(611)	(572)
F32	South Essex	923.69	941.86	867.77	917.54	842.77	882.32	831.16	824.87	750.73
		(518)	(547)	(514)	(551)	(504)	(525)	(500)	(504)	(463)

68

HON - A2
Mortality rates from coronary heart disease (ICD 410-414) in persons aged 65-74:
Age-standardised mortality rates per 100,000: 1984-92
(observed numbers of deaths in parentheses)
Persons

		1984	1985	1986	1987	1988	1989	1990	1991	1992
F33	Barking and Havering	969.45 (336)	1024.51 (366)	954.95 (345)	952.77 (346)	904.25 (326)	1063.37 (377)	882.81 (318)	847.18 (309)	859.88 (318)
F34	Redbridge and Waltham Forest	848.39 (356)	952.67 (392)	914.35 (373)	873.28 (347)	842.90 (319)	803.09 (292)	884.89 (317)	953.82 (335)	826.90 (294)
F35	East London and the City	1007.94 (454)	1038.12 (466)	1052.20 (461)	1114.02 (475)	920.04 (380)	962.22 (384)	931.64 (367)	932.78 (364)	962.82 (377)
F36	New River District	998.57 (390)	1032.33 (407)	922.98 (356)	923.47 (336)	871.88 (305)	803.65 (269)	826.20 (275)	813.46 (269)	789.27 (263)
F37	Camden and Islington	837.59 (244)	876.89 (256)	872.63 (249)	897.73 (252)	805.76 (218)	753.30 (198)	708.04 (184)	765.32 (198)	726.07 (188)
G04	South East Kent	911.05 (250)	968.91 (270)	929.59 (260)	830.62 (234)	677.49 (188)	713.05 (196)	740.09 (204)	710.08 (198)	696.53 (198)
G05	Canterbury and Thanet	973.04 (332)	842.77 (294)	973.63 (340)	890.33 (312)	859.78 (299)	713.29 (244)	743.70 (255)	811.60 (284)	742.88 (267)
G06	Dartford and Gravesham	1031.12 (172)	1100.80 (187)	1036.53 (179)	912.15 (159)	846.09 (147)	881.37 (152)	781.81 (136)	760.54 (135)	739.02 (135)
G07	Maidstone	891.95 (136)	978.28 (152)	879.49 (138)	867.42 (136)	817.43 (127)	621.87 (96)	731.93 (114)	849.07 (134)	740.37 (118)
G08	Medway	1150.71 (283)	1116.81 (280)	1109.97 (281)	921.24 (235)	953.03 (241)	815.81 (204)	942.86 (239)	758.24 (189)	818.21 (208)
G09	Tunbridge Wells	727.63 (134)	854.89 (156)	941.33 (171)	768.33 (140)	824.74 (149)	737.46 (131)	787.50 (141)	784.84 (141)	674.45 (124)
G10	Bexley	1032.19 (184)	872.83 (161)	833.47 (157)	858.50 (160)	680.87 (124)	673.15 (120)	739.00 (133)	718.91 (129)	639.32 (117)
G11	Greenwich	1060.55 (198)	956.38 (183)	929.03 (178)	985.12 (186)	840.45 (155)	929.05 (167)	842.34 (152)	772.11 (138)	852.87 (153)
G12	Bromley	818.43 (222)	848.35 (237)	813.73 (228)	790.56 (221)	837.08 (230)	790.67 (213)	675.16 (183)	592.47 (161)	604.90 (166)
G21	East Sussex	789.03 (690)	790.40 (704)	734.41 (643)	718.52 (631)	686.16 (586)	627.48 (519)	654.26 (536)	651.66 (531)	643.54 (525)
G26	South East London	849.65 (518)	860.16 (533)	895.27 (543)	838.28 (496)	800.69 (454)	875.06 (476)	871.47 (465)	897.47 (473)	839.24 (441)
H04	Mid Surrey	831.89 (144)	869.76 (148)	863.69 (148)	790.91 (133)	883.60 (146)	755.51 (123)	681.31 (111)	686.66 (112)	551.06 (92)
H05	East Surrey	837.57 (149)	848.36 (148)	881.62 (156)	750.59 (131)	701.55 (119)	760.97 (127)	808.97 (135)	710.65 (119)	643.61 (109)
H06	Chichester	772.82 (175)	787.27 (185)	813.30 (191)	618.50 (147)	603.11 (141)	697.43 (159)	618.92 (139)	513.64 (116)	539.16 (122)
H07	Mid Downs	886.49 (190)	860.19 (184)	801.65 (176)	770.94 (172)	722.26 (161)	752.17 (167)	735.59 (167)	696.47 (161)	685.48 (162)
H08	Worthing	821.00 (269)	786.40 (265)	836.31 (276)	851.40 (284)	739.49 (240)	698.09 (220)	718.86 (224)	707.41 (218)	655.50 (203)
H09	Croydon	978.84 (240)	992.59 (247)	905.61 (225)	771.38 (189)	792.34 (190)	783.96 (183)	695.61 (163)	731.55 (172)	771.82 (183)

69

HON - A2
Mortality rates from coronary heart disease (ICD 410-414) in persons aged 65-74:
Age-standardised mortality rates per 100,000: 1984-92
(observed numbers of deaths in parentheses)
Persons

		1984	1985	1986	1987	1988	1989	1990	1991	1992
H12	Wandsworth	964.62 (156)	909.66 (143)	931.35 (142)	825.74 (119)	939.84 (128)	745.25 (96)	758.49 (95)	889.93 (109)	805.68 (97)
H13	Merton and Sutton	779.01 (239)	864.38 (268)	791.83 (248)	834.81 (250)	794.09 (230)	706.79 (199)	654.97 (183)	835.97 (233)	745.79 (205)
H14	North West Surrey	764.26 (226)	763.69 (236)	848.53 (261)	695.42 (214)	724.04 (221)	721.06 (217)	732.52 (222)	633.63 (193)	569.51 (177)
H15	South West Surrey	742.56 (160)	860.43 (191)	810.18 (175)	677.18 (148)	754.34 (160)	707.03 (147)	588.21 (123)	586.86 (123)	595.45 (126)
H16	Kingston and Richmond	817.76 (336)	865.92 (354)	783.03 (317)	743.78 (296)	769.92 (295)	654.84 (242)	685.76 (250)	704.25 (255)	591.16 (215)
J10	Dorset	873.02 (672)	839.76 (658)	745.17 (596)	784.02 (621)	694.52 (543)	701.53 (541)	697.89 (542)	677.74 (533)	621.94 (494)
J21	Portsmouth and South East Hampshire	962.37 (426)	891.69 (403)	894.37 (413)	899.41 (416)	898.76 (416)	803.26 (370)	793.35 (371)	734.92 (351)	763.76 (368)
J22	Southampton and South West Hampshire	930.48 (367)	878.26 (357)	777.42 (316)	826.46 (337)	802.88 (327)	716.69 (290)	715.68 (294)	744.00 (310)	672.16 (286)
J23	Winchester	901.22 (155)	886.38 (154)	948.35 (167)	894.09 (159)	826.85 (146)	931.30 (164)	741.87 (132)	839.19 (152)	745.93 (139)
J24	Basingstoke and North Hampshire	801.66 (177)	861.15 (197)	911.46 (215)	790.29 (186)	674.75 (159)	783.64 (184)	820.88 (195)	667.22 (161)	726.08 (179)
J31	Salisbury	639.13 (78)	774.07 (94)	618.17 (78)	900.19 (111)	837.22 (104)	741.73 (91)	722.43 (90)	642.05 (81)	716.72 (93)
J32	Swindon	902.46 (147)	1012.22 (171)	1033.92 (180)	933.74 (165)	946.90 (169)	1032.69 (183)	821.64 (150)	934.11 (174)	805.33 (155)
J33	Bath	888.30 (319)	889.22 (331)	891.56 (341)	835.79 (316)	760.00 (285)	847.71 (314)	741.67 (278)	736.73 (283)	704.02 (273)
J41	Isle of Wight	898.55 (141)	972.19 (151)	875.96 (140)	929.01 (148)	882.92 (139)	768.55 (119)	660.11 (102)	859.69 (133)	887.31 (137)
K11	East Berkshire	1002.38 (256)	934.85 (251)	923.32 (246)	822.06 (222)	830.29 (222)	783.67 (210)	850.23 (229)	825.73 (226)	834.24 (231)
K12	West Berkshire	856.74 (260)	854.63 (262)	775.54 (240)	718.71 (225)	739.51 (229)	628.39 (191)	621.52 (190)	606.04 (187)	570.67 (180)
K24	Buckinghamshire	853.65 (320)	944.21 (363)	798.73 (314)	822.31 (327)	755.17 (301)	791.43 (314)	774.43 (313)	732.36 (301)	655.54 (276)
K31	Kettering	968.35 (203)	839.03 (185)	955.94 (209)	970.23 (213)	905.73 (199)	978.25 (215)	778.17 (173)	944.32 (214)	708.53 (163)
K32	Northampton	967.11 (220)	812.39 (192)	922.65 (224)	981.74 (242)	894.63 (220)	801.13 (196)	736.14 (183)	846.96 (215)	751.06 (193)
K41	Oxfordshire	801.88 (312)	809.32 (323)	786.93 (314)	799.37 (322)	693.54 (277)	685.43 (270)	661.13 (264)	639.66 (259)	642.41 (266)
L10	Bristol and District	929.40 (672)	998.28 (725)	958.39 (716)	870.85 (648)	832.91 (615)	837.59 (612)	852.72 (627)	794.72 (592)	786.80 (593)
L21	Cornwall and Isles of Scilly	985.45 (481)	982.45 (492)	926.26 (461)	894.37 (448)	852.87 (425)	845.54 (420)	775.31 (391)	794.96 (407)	743.74 (389)

HON - A2
Mortality rates from coronary heart disease (ICD 410-414) in persons aged 65-74:
Age-standardised mortality rates per 100,000: 1984-92
(observed numbers of deaths in parentheses)
Persons

		1984	1985	1986	1987	1988	1989	1990	1991	1992
L35	Exeter and North Devon	853.67 (422)	833.23 (421)	810.23 (403)	854.55 (429)	805.75 (400)	788.84 (389)	696.09 (347)	743.38 (375)	736.95 (378)
L36	Plymouth and Torbay	954.87 (567)	919.39 (561)	839.43 (515)	914.82 (562)	817.32 (493)	766.24 (457)	794.40 (473)	805.25 (487)	742.21 (448)
L40	Gloucestershire	958.79 (452)	835.09 (402)	882.04 (432)	862.94 (429)	840.26 (417)	797.99 (395)	791.24 (399)	764.93 (396)	708.07 (373)
L51	Somerset	855.64 (350)	811.60 (342)	892.30 (381)	860.63 (367)	816.05 (349)	727.86 (310)	744.00 (322)	742.67 (328)	666.41 (303)
M02	Herefordshire	937.86 (140)	904.00 (138)	829.60 (132)	895.80 (142)	759.55 (121)	764.97 (122)	729.34 (119)	744.08 (125)	656.51 (113)
M04	Worcester and District	841.88 (183)	947.77 (209)	952.65 (211)	916.35 (207)	913.29 (208)	740.47 (169)	795.07 (185)	822.30 (197)	601.31 (148)
M05	Shropshire	1029.28 (342)	1049.34 (355)	1169.51 (401)	1027.52 (355)	990.60 (344)	887.04 (308)	926.43 (329)	826.51 (300)	823.57 (307)
M06	Mid Staffordshire	1026.30 (222)	1063.72 (243)	1127.96 (261)	956.41 (226)	997.48 (237)	1027.29 (243)	1029.98 (251)	828.44 (208)	896.90 (233)
M07	North Staffordshire	1317.75 (556)	1255.31 (537)	1164.80 (504)	1182.46 (516)	1184.17 (514)	1212.01 (523)	1114.65 (488)	1099.45 (489)	1018.61 (461)
M08	South East Staffordshire	1102.18 (191)	1066.89 (190)	1132.83 (207)	1060.72 (197)	962.98 (181)	1158.10 (217)	994.43 (191)	1031.26 (204)	898.59 (183)
M13	East Birmingham	1068.05 (201)	1019.16 (198)	1135.62 (225)	991.83 (195)	1094.56 (213)	1099.54 (211)	958.22 (184)	1069.77 (206)	1035.47 (198)
M14	North Birmingham	978.47 (134)	979.36 (140)	936.86 (138)	1057.84 (156)	847.59 (125)	869.74 (128)	992.05 (147)	846.93 (127)	774.89 (117)
M16	West Birmingham	1052.71 (188)	1079.58 (191)	1062.01 (186)	1085.94 (186)	1177.05 (194)	1227.13 (195)	1000.18 (159)	1100.69 (173)	1132.55 (178)
M17	Coventry	1087.34 (297)	1103.66 (310)	1023.42 (294)	1029.81 (296)	1100.48 (313)	1027.38 (287)	974.78 (274)	848.19 (240)	816.23 (228)
M18	Dudley	995.87 (247)	1128.07 (289)	1154.45 (301)	954.99 (252)	942.41 (249)	1004.22 (268)	767.68 (208)	840.71 (233)	815.63 (230)
M19	Sandwell	1178.37 (327)	1042.36 (294)	1029.97 (295)	1170.19 (337)	1013.25 (290)	999.71 (284)	1033.68 (296)	1073.52 (311)	999.92 (290)
M20	Solihull	1100.16 (162)	935.35 (146)	913.65 (147)	927.51 (151)	753.35 (124)	773.31 (127)	885.25 (148)	822.30 (140)	858.58 (150)
M21	Walsall	1160.35 (244)	1219.46 (265)	1231.93 (272)	1186.18 (264)	1159.52 (258)	1143.67 (252)	1027.92 (231)	1184.58 (271)	1127.34 (261)
M22	Wolverhampton	899.08 (192)	1172.11 (260)	1074.82 (241)	1119.76 (253)	1011.88 (227)	1102.20 (247)	1084.50 (246)	910.57 (210)	961.83 (225)
M25	South Birmingham	1136.16 (432)	1108.02 (423)	1015.29 (393)	1117.43 (426)	902.01 (340)	1057.20 (392)	966.35 (358)	1074.24 (399)	917.13 (343)
M26	North Worcestershire	940.07 (184)	1038.26 (212)	1019.19 (215)	939.95 (201)	1083.32 (233)	992.19 (214)	907.71 (199)	720.10 (160)	844.87 (194)
M28	Warwickshire	1007.68 (393)	1018.95 (411)	986.19 (407)	982.19 (411)	962.12 (405)	940.87 (395)	850.53 (365)	833.65 (366)	779.23 (350)

71

HON - A2

Mortality rates from coronary heart disease (ICD 410-414) in persons aged 65-74:
Age-standardised mortality rates per 100,000: 1984-92
(observed numbers of deaths in parentheses)
Persons

		1984	1985	1986	1987	1988	1989	1990	1991	1992
N11	Chester	929.57 (133)	1217.49 (180)	1047.99 (157)	996.55 (151)	983.89 (149)	1037.13 (156)	896.14 (137)	1027.06 (161)	920.77 (149)
N12	Crewe	1218.22 (247)	1347.58 (288)	1258.32 (272)	1155.12 (252)	1171.37 (256)	1121.90 (247)	1130.85 (254)	937.97 (216)	916.10 (216)
N13	Halton	1173.77 (123)	1222.18 (130)	1380.26 (150)	1468.01 (161)	1185.83 (130)	1143.21 (125)	1217.88 (134)	1036.24 (116)	1049.53 (120)
N14	Macclesfield	1251.03 (189)	1015.29 (159)	746.95 (120)	832.40 (133)	892.45 (141)	795.17 (124)	845.44 (134)	718.34 (116)	756.48 (123)
N15	Warrington	1172.43 (166)	1297.28 (188)	1395.56 (202)	1221.07 (179)	1316.44 (192)	1081.75 (158)	1128.66 (166)	990.33 (148)	865.66 (129)
N21	Liverpool	1249.28 (572)	1226.31 (570)	1200.74 (548)	1191.75 (537)	1164.00 (508)	1236.16 (525)	1184.16 (499)	1008.24 (423)	1092.73 (459)
N31	St Helens and Knowsley	1303.69 (337)	1230.21 (326)	1170.00 (312)	1130.30 (304)	1285.41 (344)	1222.50 (327)	1025.32 (280)	1212.56 (337)	1049.16 (297)
N41	Southport and Formby	1123.32 (136)	1202.73 (152)	1128.63 (141)	901.82 (115)	812.10 (103)	927.23 (117)	921.27 (117)	819.96 (105)	742.92 (94)
N42	South Sefton	1144.20 (177)	1200.53 (189)	1212.15 (191)	1158.42 (184)	1217.94 (191)	1131.91 (176)	935.27 (146)	911.13 (144)	1076.45 (172)
N51	Wirral	1050.80 (353)	1064.83 (363)	1097.05 (376)	909.47 (310)	966.81 (327)	952.72 (318)	965.82 (323)	1041.35 (348)	953.03 (323)
P01	Lancaster	1008.19 (139)	1186.03 (165)	1024.68 (140)	1104.02 (149)	984.07 (131)	907.89 (118)	1144.65 (149)	895.16 (117)	905.38 (121)
P02	Blackpool,Wyre and Fylde	1122.28 (436)	1149.33 (452)	1027.35 (401)	1152.64 (444)	1148.40 (438)	1019.38 (384)	902.22 (339)	863.44 (330)	1001.00 (388)
P03	Preston	1198.97 (140)	1159.68 (135)	1230.97 (143)	998.40 (114)	1031.52 (116)	1074.74 (119)	952.65 (106)	1080.95 (121)	1140.56 (126)
P04	Blackburn, Hyndburn and Ribble Valley	1360.85 (338)	1340.05 (330)	1209.57 (296)	1141.53 (274)	1131.56 (265)	1196.79 (276)	1101.69 (253)	1044.15 (240)	1076.83 (252)
P05	Burnley, Pendle and Rossendale	1233.04 (267)	1249.10 (268)	1242.47 (261)	1128.10 (236)	1251.89 (258)	1188.77 (244)	1259.78 (260)	1170.36 (243)	1092.80 (231)
P06	West Lancashire	1071.67 (88)	1408.12 (114)	1144.09 (96)	1216.49 (103)	1296.91 (109)	1183.85 (100)	1162.79 (99)	925.99 (80)	839.54 (74)
P07	Chorley and South Ribble	1227.72 (181)	1271.76 (190)	1110.68 (169)	1096.97 (168)	1158.05 (178)	1044.50 (161)	914.52 (144)	970.05 (156)	953.05 (157)
P08	Bolton	1188.93 (267)	1316.33 (299)	1242.44 (284)	1010.85 (229)	1248.79 (282)	1095.41 (244)	1144.61 (258)	1071.71 (245)	1003.78 (235)
P09	Bury	1224.30 (188)	1281.13 (195)	1305.56 (198)	1240.89 (186)	1204.84 (178)	1250.54 (182)	1211.05 (176)	1085.65 (158)	1255.91 (187)
P10	North Manchester	1259.90 (183)	1313.64 (193)	1247.37 (180)	1361.55 (190)	1134.14 (153)	1139.55 (148)	1115.63 (143)	1239.12 (158)	1209.64 (153)
P11	Central Manchester	1281.53 (127)	1157.68 (112)	1120.61 (108)	1033.69 (96)	1080.89 (96)	1098.98 (94)	1259.26 (105)	1160.34 (95)	1048.91 (87)
P12	South Manchester	1118.83 (184)	1171.57 (198)	1012.35 (172)	1026.45 (170)	1057.59 (173)	1191.52 (190)	1011.05 (160)	1013.44 (160)	977.53 (156)

HON - A2
Mortality rates from coronary heart disease (ICD 410-414) in persons aged 65-74:
Age-standardised mortality rates per 100,000: 1984-92
(observed numbers of deaths in parentheses)
Persons

		1984	1985	1986	1987	1988	1989	1990	1991	1992
P13	Oldham	1302.88	1200.36	1162.71	1207.07	1295.43	1222.00	1222.69	1230.43	1095.53
		(257)	(231)	(224)	(230)	(242)	(224)	(224)	(226)	(204)
P14	Rochdale	1356.74	1357.33	1284.59	1306.12	1335.73	1096.73	1204.93	1058.90	1102.61
		(230)	(232)	(224)	(226)	(228)	(186)	(206)	(183)	(195)
P15	Salford	1267.71	1330.27	1310.86	1268.77	1316.40	1175.47	1157.84	1010.83	977.91
		(290)	(307)	(302)	(288)	(293)	(257)	(253)	(222)	(215)
P16	Stockport	1048.21	1099.11	1138.29	958.88	1092.45	997.23	933.13	946.89	939.06
		(258)	(278)	(285)	(241)	(272)	(245)	(232)	(239)	(242)
P17	Tameside and Glossop	1247.48	1282.92	1191.55	1162.79	1117.77	1184.29	1193.68	1150.24	960.42
		(272)	(286)	(263)	(254)	(242)	(253)	(256)	(249)	(211)
P18	Trafford	935.67	1102.75	915.53	976.94	974.02	982.37	867.73	951.23	897.03
		(178)	(213)	(177)	(189)	(185)	(184)	(164)	(182)	(174)
P19	Wigan	1298.31	1387.73	1300.61	1242.42	1373.56	1406.69	1220.28	1122.60	992.25
		(323)	(354)	(338)	(322)	(352)	(357)	(313)	(293)	(264)

HON - A3
Mortality rates from stroke (ICD 430-438) in persons under 65:
Age-standardised mortality rates per 100,000: 1984-92
(observed numbers of deaths in parentheses)
Persons

		1984	1985	1986	1987	1988	1989	1990	1991	1992
	ENGLAND AND WALES	16.34 (7173)	16.22 (6975)	15.40 (6550)	14.73 (6188)	13.61 (5699)	12.97 (5421)	12.43 (5169)	12.39 (5148)	11.89 (4971)
O00	ENGLAND	16.16 (6695)	16.03 (6490)	15.33 (6142)	14.70 (5815)	13.55 (5338)	12.89 (5067)	12.28 (4808)	12.39 (4843)	11.83 (4661)
A00	NORTHERN RHA	19.96 (575)	19.34 (543)	20.94 (580)	18.70 (510)	17.61 (476)	15.53 (413)	15.94 (423)	16.82 (442)	14.46 (382)
B00	YORKSHIRE RHA	19.04 (601)	18.28 (561)	17.06 (517)	15.83 (477)	15.89 (474)	13.89 (418)	13.97 (414)	13.80 (411)	12.63 (377)
C00	TRENT RHA	17.28 (717)	17.12 (693)	14.76 (595)	15.94 (629)	13.64 (543)	14.28 (563)	12.57 (495)	12.14 (474)	12.81 (505)
D00	EAST ANGLIAN RHA	13.60 (230)	12.17 (202)	12.02 (198)	12.34 (206)	11.16 (185)	9.35 (159)	9.15 (157)	10.39 (177)	8.39 (144)
E00	NORTH WEST THAMES RHA	13.35 (391)	13.34 (386)	13.96 (393)	12.35 (344)	12.15 (334)	11.11 (299)	10.37 (284)	11.18 (301)	10.39 (288)
F00	NORTH EAST THAMES RHA	14.10 (454)	14.72 (458)	13.88 (426)	14.40 (440)	13.18 (390)	12.69 (380)	12.57 (366)	12.69 (370)	11.15 (331)
G00	SOUTH EAST THAMES RHA	13.97 (443)	15.29 (471)	13.98 (424)	13.19 (392)	13.27 (388)	11.77 (348)	11.29 (335)	12.02 (351)	11.78 (348)
H00	SOUTH WEST THAMES RHA	12.46 (325)	12.61 (317)	11.45 (287)	11.75 (287)	9.75 (239)	9.19 (222)	9.07 (218)	9.83 (238)	9.30 (223)
J00	WESSEX RHA	12.65 (324)	13.34 (338)	12.98 (327)	11.97 (301)	10.52 (268)	10.29 (262)	9.87 (252)	9.79 (251)	9.72 (252)
K00	OXFORD RHA	13.17 (252)	12.47 (237)	11.86 (229)	11.96 (226)	11.16 (214)	10.45 (204)	8.44 (163)	10.24 (203)	10.20 (202)
L00	SOUTH WESTERN RHA	15.17 (433)	13.96 (383)	13.52 (371)	12.26 (335)	10.47 (286)	10.41 (291)	11.35 (316)	9.57 (268)	9.48 (266)
M00	WEST MIDLANDS RHA	17.33 (808)	17.48 (800)	16.92 (763)	16.23 (718)	14.36 (637)	14.88 (652)	13.58 (594)	14.06 (614)	12.15 (533)
N00	MERSEY RHA	19.49 (423)	19.08 (405)	17.32 (360)	17.23 (354)	15.11 (309)	14.99 (306)	13.32 (270)	13.13 (266)	14.61 (297)
P00	NORTH WESTERN RHA	20.71 (719)	20.46 (696)	19.90 (672)	17.96 (596)	18.20 (595)	16.82 (550)	16.17 (521)	14.86 (477)	15.98 (513)
A01	Hartlepool	22.55 (19)	14.55 (12)	23.98 (20)	19.97 (17)	22.23 (17)	14.39 (12)	14.63 (11)	21.47 (17)	13.49 (11)
A02	North Tees	13.59 (20)	18.30 (27)	20.19 (30)	21.12 (31)	15.30 (23)	14.08 (21)	12.09 (19)	13.11 (19)	10.30 (16)
A03	South Tees	22.67 (61)	24.69 (62)	19.35 (48)	22.23 (55)	18.84 (46)	10.28 (25)	19.40 (46)	22.82 (54)	18.10 (42)
A04	East Cumbria	22.84 (39)	12.94 (22)	19.89 (31)	14.76 (24)	16.04 (26)	11.19 (18)	17.77 (28)	19.32 (31)	6.61 (11)
A05	South Cumbria	14.20 (22)	12.98 (21)	21.28 (33)	11.30 (18)	13.91 (22)	12.32 (19)	13.51 (21)	22.56 (36)	12.97 (20)
A06	West Cumbria	22.02 (29)	18.21 (23)	13.06 (16)	22.40 (27)	15.47 (19)	10.52 (13)	14.08 (16)	11.21 (13)	14.22 (17)

HON - A3
Mortality rates from stroke (ICD 430-438) in persons under 65:
Age-standardised mortality rates per 100,000: 1984-92
(observed numbers of deaths in parentheses)
Persons

		1984	1985	1986	1987	1988	1989	1990	1991	1992
A11	Northumberland	21.75 (61)	19.87 (54)	24.17 (66)	14.30 (40)	19.62 (53)	13.59 (36)	19.97 (52)	14.60 (39)	16.44 (44)
A12	Gateshead	20.73 (44)	22.34 (44)	20.69 (41)	17.02 (33)	17.93 (34)	18.24 (33)	13.52 (25)	13.68 (24)	20.59 (37)
A13	Newcastle	16.47 (44)	18.37 (45)	20.05 (48)	20.97 (49)	14.81 (33)	15.30 (33)	14.88 (32)	18.02 (39)	15.95 (34)
A14	North Tyneside	14.98 (29)	20.00 (37)	19.47 (36)	20.16 (36)	16.93 (30)	15.11 (26)	15.00 (26)	12.77 (22)	12.73 (21)
A15	South Tyneside	19.51 (31)	18.10 (29)	19.90 (33)	20.47 (31)	11.80 (18)	21.94 (30)	17.81 (25)	11.49 (16)	11.42 (16)
A16	Sunderland	22.77 (59)	19.01 (50)	19.14 (49)	20.05 (51)	17.73 (45)	18.67 (47)	19.02 (49)	20.52 (51)	9.80 (24)
A30	North Durham	22.66 (67)	20.98 (62)	29.64 (85)	16.81 (47)	20.85 (58)	17.90 (51)	14.94 (42)	15.55 (42)	17.55 (49)
A31	South Durham	19.52 (50)	21.44 (55)	17.05 (44)	21.03 (51)	20.89 (52)	20.36 (49)	12.46 (31)	16.62 (39)	16.49 (40)
B11	East Riding	19.64 (87)	19.85 (84)	15.75 (66)	13.71 (60)	14.86 (63)	12.81 (55)	13.50 (57)	11.87 (52)	11.45 (49)
B16	Grimsby and Scunthorpe	25.96 (83)	13.71 (43)	16.43 (49)	13.76 (42)	14.61 (45)	9.32 (29)	15.31 (46)	13.38 (40)	10.67 (32)
B21	North Yorkshire	17.51 (104)	18.77 (113)	13.16 (80)	14.96 (88)	13.02 (78)	12.63 (79)	9.98 (61)	10.10 (62)	11.07 (70)
B31	Bradford	22.49 (86)	20.54 (77)	19.00 (71)	20.31 (76)	16.80 (62)	16.23 (58)	16.78 (58)	16.02 (57)	15.93 (56)
B51	West Yorkshire	18.91 (93)	20.18 (94)	22.20 (103)	17.50 (82)	16.92 (77)	14.49 (67)	14.66 (66)	17.49 (79)	15.82 (71)
B61	Leeds	16.94 (108)	16.98 (104)	18.38 (110)	16.19 (94)	19.08 (109)	15.02 (86)	15.55 (89)	14.90 (85)	10.56 (60)
B71	Wakefield	13.82 (40)	16.53 (46)	14.11 (38)	13.59 (35)	15.56 (40)	17.22 (44)	14.36 (37)	14.26 (36)	15.15 (39)
C01	North Derbyshire	17.44 (59)	17.15 (57)	13.64 (45)	15.56 (52)	13.89 (45)	17.00 (54)	9.66 (33)	11.72 (38)	11.07 (35)
C02	Southern Derbyshire	17.87 (87)	16.37 (75)	18.68 (87)	19.57 (88)	13.89 (62)	13.99 (63)	12.98 (57)	14.74 (66)	13.45 (60)
C03	Leicestershire	16.22 (117)	14.03 (103)	15.05 (107)	13.09 (93)	13.68 (98)	12.27 (87)	13.84 (97)	12.67 (90)	8.42 (62)
C04	North Lincolnshire	17.24 (42)	16.08 (38)	14.40 (35)	12.83 (31)	12.66 (31)	13.47 (33)	11.84 (30)	10.57 (26)	13.76 (34)
C05	South Lincolnshire	14.93 (42)	11.09 (29)	16.45 (46)	17.68 (48)	13.74 (38)	13.94 (39)	15.66 (42)	10.57 (30)	14.39 (41)
C08	Nottingham	16.84 (87)	20.20 (107)	15.76 (81)	19.09 (96)	15.10 (78)	15.27 (77)	11.67 (59)	12.49 (61)	14.58 (74)
C09	Barnsley	16.55 (35)	20.92 (40)	10.10 (20)	18.88 (36)	15.57 (30)	17.81 (34)	17.81 (34)	10.67 (20)	14.62 (28)

HON - A3
Mortality rates from stroke (ICD 430-438) in persons under 65:
Age-standardised mortality rates per 100,000: 1984-92
(observed numbers of deaths in parentheses)
Persons

		1984	1985	1986	1987	1988	1989	1990	1991	1992
C10	Doncaster	18.73 (49)	19.57 (49)	20.28 (53)	11.34 (29)	11.36 (29)	14.10 (36)	10.17 (26)	9.82 (24)	13.59 (33)
C11	Rotherham	17.84 (41)	20.70 (47)	10.48 (24)	10.75 (23)	15.22 (32)	21.53 (45)	12.98 (28)	15.99 (34)	13.33 (28)
C12	Sheffield	19.59 (99)	13.02 (63)	12.59 (59)	15.95 (71)	13.96 (63)	12.70 (55)	10.51 (46)	11.26 (48)	13.86 (59)
C14	North Nottinghamshire	16.46 (59)	24.80 (85)	11.38 (38)	18.49 (62)	10.90 (37)	11.58 (40)	12.67 (43)	11.00 (37)	14.93 (51)
D01	Cambridge	11.62 (26)	8.30 (18)	9.46 (20)	11.82 (25)	7.93 (17)	9.22 (20)	8.76 (19)	9.88 (22)	7.10 (16)
D05	North West Anglia	16.20 (52)	14.73 (48)	15.41 (51)	13.15 (44)	13.32 (45)	9.40 (32)	6.65 (22)	12.46 (42)	11.97 (41)
D06	Norwich	13.01 (55)	11.82 (49)	13.98 (55)	12.44 (51)	9.22 (38)	9.29 (41)	8.84 (37)	8.92 (39)	6.21 (26)
D07	Great Yarmouth and Waveney	11.51 (22)	12.20 (21)	11.52 (21)	16.74 (29)	15.70 (27)	10.43 (18)	13.81 (25)	17.00 (31)	11.65 (20)
D09	Huntingdon	10.02 (8)	14.76 (13)	6.87 (6)	10.86 (11)	9.33 (8)	2.68 (3)	11.72 (11)	4.25 (4)	2.85 (3)
D11	Suffolk	14.80 (67)	11.95 (53)	10.06 (45)	10.56 (46)	11.54 (50)	10.24 (45)	9.17 (43)	9.07 (39)	8.51 (38)
E01	North Bedfordshire	15.53 (30)	19.69 (39)	21.35 (40)	10.93 (21)	5.56 (11)	9.24 (18)	11.68 (23)	8.35 (16)	10.66 (21)
E02	South Bedfordshire	11.05 (24)	16.76 (37)	9.74 (21)	12.31 (26)	11.52 (25)	12.59 (26)	11.82 (25)	11.87 (25)	12.23 (26)
E05	North West Hertfordshire	12.37 (28)	11.20 (25)	12.43 (28)	9.74 (22)	11.48 (25)	9.18 (20)	6.45 (14)	6.35 (14)	8.18 (18)
E06	South West Hertfordshire	13.86 (32)	11.07 (24)	8.68 (19)	13.53 (28)	13.41 (27)	9.21 (19)	8.22 (16)	12.84 (26)	14.78 (31)
E07	Barnet	13.01 (34)	9.69 (25)	12.21 (29)	8.76 (20)	10.01 (24)	8.43 (19)	10.25 (23)	6.07 (13)	5.35 (13)
E09	Hillingdon	10.55 (22)	15.29 (32)	9.81 (20)	13.92 (27)	13.21 (26)	11.16 (21)	14.25 (27)	9.80 (19)	9.59 (18)
E18	East and North Hertfordshire	12.65 (53)	13.47 (55)	15.05 (62)	10.96 (45)	10.44 (41)	11.66 (47)	8.85 (35)	9.91 (40)	9.49 (39)
E19	Brent and Harrow	11.12 (42)	9.30 (34)	12.66 (45)	13.69 (50)	13.75 (50)	11.14 (38)	11.17 (39)	13.30 (46)	10.57 (37)
E20	Ealing, Hammersmith and Hounslow	17.09 (90)	15.28 (79)	17.34 (89)	15.20 (76)	15.19 (74)	11.38 (53)	11.78 (58)	14.22 (65)	11.57 (57)
E21	Kensington, Chelsea and Westminster	13.27 (36)	13.64 (36)	15.62 (40)	11.47 (29)	12.95 (31)	15.74 (38)	9.20 (24)	14.50 (37)	10.86 (28)
F31	North Essex	12.39 (91)	12.38 (87)	11.23 (79)	10.98 (79)	12.84 (89)	11.12 (80)	11.16 (78)	9.01 (65)	10.70 (78)
F32	South Essex	12.36 (75)	12.70 (73)	12.74 (75)	11.97 (70)	11.78 (67)	10.22 (60)	10.10 (57)	12.92 (73)	10.58 (62)

76

HON - A3
Mortality rates from stroke (ICD 430-438) in persons under 65:
Age-standardised mortality rates per 100,000: 1984-92
(observed numbers of deaths in parentheses)
Persons

		1984	1985	1986	1987	1988	1989	1990	1991	1992
F33	Barking and Havering	12.80	13.34	12.79	15.15	11.25	10.67	9.14	9.17	5.35
		(49)	(50)	(47)	(55)	(39)	(36)	(30)	(29)	(18)
F34	Redbridge and Waltham Forest	11.20	17.33	11.91	14.08	13.75	14.07	15.93	17.07	12.41
		(44)	(64)	(43)	(50)	(47)	(48)	(54)	(56)	(41)
F35	East London and the City	20.98	18.84	21.86	20.54	17.62	17.23	18.16	18.46	16.26
		(96)	(84)	(93)	(86)	(71)	(70)	(70)	(72)	(63)
F36	New River District	12.67	15.00	16.15	16.44	10.31	11.48	12.31	13.09	9.71
		(49)	(57)	(58)	(60)	(36)	(41)	(43)	(45)	(34)
F37	Camden and Islington	18.34	16.32	11.75	14.94	16.07	17.15	13.61	11.75	13.72
		(50)	(43)	(31)	(40)	(41)	(45)	(34)	(30)	(35)
G04	South East Kent	16.21	12.83	12.38	16.91	13.21	7.76	8.26	8.62	8.12
		(37)	(31)	(28)	(37)	(29)	(18)	(19)	(20)	(19)
G05	Canterbury and Thanet	15.22	15.20	16.46	12.30	17.00	14.44	15.53	15.82	10.20
		(38)	(40)	(43)	(31)	(40)	(36)	(39)	(39)	(26)
G06	Dartford and Gravesham	14.42	13.14	12.60	14.29	13.71	11.98	14.02	10.50	12.95
		(29)	(25)	(24)	(27)	(26)	(22)	(26)	(20)	(25)
G07	Maidstone	11.28	17.36	11.09	8.49	11.29	13.84	9.89	12.14	8.64
		(19)	(27)	(18)	(13)	(18)	(22)	(16)	(20)	(15)
G08	Medway	12.74	12.65	11.52	15.58	11.18	11.24	8.74	11.21	12.29
		(34)	(32)	(30)	(38)	(29)	(30)	(23)	(28)	(31)
G09	Tunbridge Wells	8.66	11.97	15.64	12.14	8.18	4.22	3.78	9.85	10.52
		(16)	(21)	(27)	(21)	(14)	(7)	(7)	(17)	(19)
G10	Bexley	11.22	18.81	11.64	9.49	7.87	11.49	8.56	10.11	11.35
		(21)	(35)	(22)	(17)	(15)	(21)	(16)	(18)	(20)
G11	Greenwich	15.12	18.25	23.75	13.86	10.49	20.45	15.93	13.69	12.41
		(27)	(33)	(42)	(23)	(17)	(33)	(25)	(22)	(19)
G12	Bromley	11.54	12.51	9.92	9.77	10.87	9.21	7.35	11.07	10.13
		(32)	(35)	(27)	(26)	(29)	(24)	(19)	(28)	(26)
G21	East Sussex	13.27	14.21	12.10	11.43	13.08	8.76	8.94	10.29	11.34
		(81)	(83)	(70)	(68)	(71)	(50)	(52)	(59)	(66)
G26	South East London	17.66	18.71	16.86	16.56	19.12	16.58	17.97	16.55	16.51
		(109)	(109)	(93)	(91)	(100)	(85)	(93)	(80)	(82)
H04	Mid Surrey	10.93	9.59	8.07	9.21	7.34	9.69	9.01	8.84	9.87
		(20)	(15)	(13)	(13)	(11)	(15)	(14)	(13)	(15)
H05	East Surrey	12.25	13.67	10.51	9.70	14.06	10.06	7.71	6.06	9.92
		(21)	(23)	(18)	(16)	(23)	(17)	(13)	(10)	(16)
H06	Chichester	10.86	11.93	16.76	11.29	7.06	7.12	7.04	11.79	9.97
		(18)	(19)	(26)	(19)	(12)	(12)	(11)	(19)	(16)
H07	Mid Downs	12.92	14.79	10.25	10.94	9.72	6.70	8.83	7.20	8.25
		(31)	(35)	(25)	(26)	(23)	(15)	(20)	(18)	(19)
H08	Worthing	12.22	12.16	15.31	9.72	7.21	10.00	8.27	9.42	12.14
		(26)	(27)	(32)	(21)	(15)	(20)	(17)	(19)	(23)
H09	Croydon	12.81	17.47	13.31	18.03	12.33	9.71	10.03	15.13	9.04
		(34)	(46)	(34)	(45)	(31)	(24)	(24)	(37)	(23)

77

HON - A3
Mortality rates from stroke (ICD 430-438) in persons under 65:
Age-standardised mortality rates per 100,000: 1984-92
(observed numbers of deaths in parentheses)
Persons

		1984	1985	1986	1987	1988	1989	1990	1991	1992
H12	Wandsworth	19.34 (29)	22.86 (33)	16.74 (23)	12.13 (17)	10.10 (13)	18.57 (24)	15.96 (20)	15.37 (19)	13.71 (17)
H13	Merton and Sutton	10.34 (31)	8.16 (23)	8.92 (26)	11.80 (33)	9.64 (27)	10.45 (28)	12.20 (32)	11.21 (30)	10.92 (29)
H14	North West Surrey	12.61 (43)	10.62 (35)	11.40 (38)	8.97 (30)	8.20 (27)	5.11 (17)	6.11 (20)	8.61 (28)	6.46 (21)
H15	South West Surrey	7.14 (15)	9.27 (19)	8.64 (17)	13.03 (25)	8.19 (16)	7.96 (16)	8.48 (17)	4.16 (9)	5.28 (11)
H16	Kingston and Richmond	15.09 (57)	12.05 (42)	10.13 (35)	12.80 (42)	11.96 (41)	10.32 (34)	9.10 (30)	11.24 (36)	10.57 (33)
J10	Dorset	13.09 (75)	13.35 (71)	14.33 (81)	12.80 (72)	10.90 (60)	9.91 (56)	10.11 (58)	7.83 (44)	11.12 (63)
J21	Portsmouth and South East Hampshire	13.27 (57)	14.47 (64)	13.54 (58)	12.79 (54)	8.68 (38)	11.21 (47)	9.82 (43)	9.01 (39)	11.85 (49)
J22	Southampton and South West Hampshire	12.46 (45)	12.81 (46)	11.36 (40)	11.21 (40)	10.16 (36)	12.16 (44)	9.49 (34)	12.57 (45)	11.56 (42)
J23	Winchester	15.40 (27)	14.30 (25)	9.20 (16)	10.00 (17)	5.05 (9)	13.22 (24)	10.23 (18)	8.10 (15)	5.92 (11)
J24	Basingstoke and North Hampshire	13.41 (36)	13.22 (34)	14.22 (37)	11.10 (29)	8.60 (23)	8.32 (23)	5.54 (15)	13.19 (36)	6.75 (20)
J31	Salisbury	10.74 (12)	15.92 (18)	8.60 (10)	14.74 (16)	10.01 (11)	9.18 (10)	11.20 (12)	13.25 (14)	11.80 (13)
J32	Swindon	17.03 (31)	13.05 (23)	13.85 (26)	13.51 (24)	11.91 (22)	8.84 (17)	11.04 (20)	8.73 (16)	8.17 (15)
J33	Bath	8.53 (30)	12.51 (43)	12.18 (40)	11.59 (38)	13.73 (47)	9.08 (30)	9.17 (30)	9.87 (33)	7.62 (27)
J41	Isle of Wight	8.97 (11)	11.89 (14)	18.38 (19)	9.60 (11)	20.72 (22)	10.75 (11)	19.60 (22)	8.10 (9)	10.25 (12)
K11	East Berkshire	13.18 (39)	13.05 (39)	6.70 (20)	13.48 (38)	12.21 (35)	12.31 (36)	7.59 (22)	10.74 (32)	10.27 (30)
K12	West Berkshire	12.95 (44)	11.61 (38)	16.10 (55)	10.14 (34)	11.00 (37)	10.20 (35)	7.39 (25)	11.10 (38)	9.74 (34)
K24	Buckinghamshire	12.01 (53)	13.38 (58)	11.13 (50)	8.70 (39)	11.76 (53)	11.07 (51)	7.64 (35)	9.27 (43)	10.30 (48)
K31	Kettering	16.52 (34)	14.39 (29)	16.08 (33)	16.37 (34)	10.30 (21)	10.42 (22)	11.83 (24)	10.11 (22)	9.67 (21)
K32	Northampton	12.56 (30)	14.20 (34)	14.42 (35)	19.54 (44)	14.41 (33)	10.48 (25)	9.71 (23)	10.47 (26)	10.84 (27)
K41	Oxfordshire	13.24 (52)	9.65 (39)	9.25 (36)	9.45 (37)	8.54 (35)	8.44 (35)	8.60 (34)	10.28 (42)	10.30 (42)
L10	Bristol and District	15.97 (115)	12.08 (85)	16.00 (109)	12.44 (84)	10.21 (71)	10.44 (71)	10.39 (71)	8.53 (58)	9.16 (61)
L21	Cornwall and Isles of Scilly	12.60 (53)	13.21 (53)	13.34 (53)	12.57 (51)	8.69 (36)	10.25 (44)	10.83 (44)	11.40 (50)	9.79 (43)

78

HON - A3
Mortality rates from stroke (ICD 430-438) in persons under 65:
Age-standardised mortality rates per 100,000: 1984-92
(observed numbers of deaths in parentheses)
Persons

		1984	1985	1986	1987	1988	1989	1990	1991	1992
L35	Exeter and North Devon	15.39 (59)	12.53 (48)	10.82 (41)	9.60 (38)	12.34 (46)	10.24 (39)	13.64 (53)	8.40 (34)	8.40 (34)
L36	Plymouth and Torbay	13.39 (66)	17.04 (80)	15.48 (74)	13.25 (62)	9.01 (42)	9.54 (47)	12.73 (63)	10.25 (50)	8.58 (42)
L40	Gloucestershire	17.12 (79)	17.85 (78)	11.69 (54)	13.42 (60)	11.77 (52)	10.26 (46)	12.32 (55)	9.70 (44)	11.44 (52)
L51	Somerset	16.45 (61)	10.82 (39)	11.42 (40)	11.73 (40)	11.59 (39)	12.21 (44)	8.24 (30)	9.44 (32)	9.63 (34)
M02	Herefordshire	15.31 (22)	9.72 (13)	16.38 (22)	11.94 (17)	9.31 (13)	11.49 (17)	9.26 (13)	8.99 (13)	5.86 (9)
M04	Worcester and District	14.19 (31)	10.16 (21)	13.85 (28)	9.17 (20)	15.03 (32)	12.66 (27)	10.35 (23)	7.49 (16)	9.68 (21)
M05	Shropshire	11.31 (36)	12.92 (43)	15.86 (54)	12.38 (41)	12.80 (42)	12.21 (42)	10.81 (37)	13.81 (48)	9.58 (34)
M06	Mid Staffordshire	18.17 (47)	16.16 (42)	13.77 (37)	16.09 (43)	11.02 (29)	11.35 (30)	11.96 (32)	13.46 (36)	9.79 (27)
M07	North Staffordshire	17.33 (78)	17.33 (75)	18.29 (81)	20.22 (82)	15.21 (63)	14.07 (58)	13.61 (53)	17.11 (70)	15.35 (61)
M08	South East Staffordshire	11.70 (23)	19.63 (41)	16.15 (33)	15.57 (32)	12.15 (25)	14.61 (30)	12.37 (26)	14.19 (30)	7.88 (17)
M13	East Birmingham	21.94 (40)	23.47 (42)	20.15 (34)	17.03 (27)	16.89 (28)	23.79 (37)	22.22 (33)	23.39 (33)	15.43 (23)
M14	North Birmingham	15.23 (24)	15.18 (22)	12.73 (20)	16.54 (23)	17.61 (26)	13.98 (20)	7.11 (10)	11.23 (16)	10.04 (14)
M16	West Birmingham	24.48 (43)	31.03 (54)	16.71 (27)	26.20 (43)	22.63 (37)	21.76 (32)	17.26 (27)	21.93 (32)	25.70 (39)
M17	Coventry	17.45 (48)	21.97 (60)	21.07 (56)	18.30 (49)	21.80 (55)	14.30 (36)	16.77 (39)	15.47 (37)	8.32 (20)
M18	Dudley	21.81 (61)	16.63 (47)	15.01 (40)	19.49 (52)	10.31 (28)	15.35 (42)	13.69 (37)	12.50 (33)	13.30 (36)
M19	Sandwell	18.96 (53)	20.65 (56)	18.23 (50)	21.72 (56)	12.40 (32)	19.05 (46)	21.53 (55)	17.40 (44)	16.99 (41)
M20	Solihull	11.20 (20)	12.85 (24)	7.24 (13)	8.56 (15)	10.86 (20)	8.58 (16)	9.01 (16)	9.97 (18)	6.69 (12)
M21	Walsall	18.30 (45)	16.35 (39)	18.34 (42)	12.43 (29)	13.51 (32)	18.96 (43)	17.72 (41)	17.92 (41)	12.88 (29)
M22	Wolverhampton	19.44 (48)	24.74 (56)	22.50 (51)	19.33 (41)	14.35 (30)	19.59 (43)	15.78 (34)	12.11 (26)	13.98 (28)
M25	South Birmingham	19.53 (78)	14.39 (56)	20.39 (73)	14.47 (50)	16.25 (55)	19.27 (62)	13.21 (43)	15.37 (50)	18.23 (59)
M26	North Worcestershire	15.27 (34)	13.17 (29)	14.49 (31)	12.24 (27)	19.19 (42)	12.21 (27)	11.60 (26)	8.12 (19)	9.53 (22)
M28	Warwickshire	17.91 (77)	19.38 (80)	16.98 (71)	17.11 (71)	11.66 (48)	10.55 (44)	11.90 (49)	12.65 (52)	9.91 (41)

HON - A3
Mortality rates from stroke (ICD 430-438) in persons under 65:
Age-standardised mortality rates per 100,000: 1984-92
(observed numbers of deaths in parentheses)
Persons

		1984	1985	1986	1987	1988	1989	1990	1991	1992
N11	Chester	17.19 (28)	10.91 (17)	14.57 (23)	17.45 (28)	10.05 (16)	9.67 (15)	13.88 (21)	12.12 (18)	12.74 (20)
N12	Crewe	14.07 (32)	14.03 (31)	12.32 (26)	15.25 (32)	14.72 (32)	11.94 (25)	13.12 (28)	15.98 (34)	17.86 (39)
N13	Halton	24.40 (28)	22.40 (26)	19.48 (22)	17.81 (20)	10.92 (13)	20.84 (24)	11.93 (14)	6.53 (8)	10.44 (12)
N14	Macclesfield	8.64 (14)	19.71 (33)	15.18 (24)	13.70 (21)	10.10 (16)	9.02 (14)	8.60 (14)	9.61 (16)	7.36 (12)
N15	Warrington	18.75 (29)	22.90 (34)	19.77 (30)	28.70 (43)	15.06 (22)	12.58 (19)	9.31 (14)	14.35 (22)	24.29 (37)
N21	Liverpool	22.82 (98)	24.00 (103)	18.92 (78)	17.59 (72)	19.57 (78)	21.91 (86)	16.73 (65)	14.32 (55)	14.05 (53)
N31	St Helens and Knowsley	27.70 (87)	21.96 (67)	19.25 (56)	20.38 (58)	17.20 (49)	17.97 (51)	16.63 (48)	13.15 (38)	16.75 (49)
N41	Southport and Formby	18.67 (20)	21.96 (23)	19.37 (22)	12.32 (13)	12.49 (13)	19.04 (20)	12.39 (13)	11.05 (11)	9.54 (9)
N42	South Sefton	18.80 (31)	20.54 (32)	16.77 (27)	13.90 (22)	19.83 (30)	12.46 (20)	7.48 (12)	14.29 (22)	14.76 (23)
N51	Wirral	17.21 (56)	12.11 (39)	16.97 (52)	14.85 (45)	12.98 (40)	10.11 (32)	13.68 (41)	14.15 (42)	14.14 (43)
P01	Lancaster	15.90 (17)	19.55 (20)	22.24 (24)	8.19 (9)	12.18 (13)	12.62 (14)	18.96 (20)	9.88 (11)	11.57 (13)
P02	Blackpool,Wyre and Fylde	16.53 (52)	19.35 (58)	22.12 (67)	16.34 (49)	18.36 (57)	16.87 (52)	21.41 (63)	11.85 (37)	17.08 (50)
P03	Preston	28.66 (33)	29.31 (30)	20.03 (21)	20.18 (21)	17.75 (19)	27.84 (28)	10.60 (11)	11.49 (12)	16.48 (16)
P04	Blackburn, Hyndburn and Ribble Valley	22.94 (54)	20.08 (46)	16.95 (38)	20.88 (47)	21.45 (46)	16.91 (36)	15.71 (33)	14.26 (30)	16.25 (34)
P05	Burnley, Pendle and Rossendale	28.24 (56)	19.58 (38)	16.38 (32)	17.55 (33)	20.24 (38)	17.26 (34)	21.00 (40)	15.00 (28)	16.92 (31)
P06	West Lancashire	14.22 (13)	18.08 (16)	18.84 (17)	12.67 (11)	10.36 (9)	13.10 (12)	11.14 (10)	14.01 (13)	11.77 (11)
P07	Chorley and South Ribble	18.19 (29)	21.40 (35)	16.19 (25)	18.53 (29)	14.26 (23)	16.64 (27)	14.08 (23)	17.70 (28)	11.68 (18)
P08	Bolton	17.23 (37)	25.41 (55)	25.00 (54)	18.76 (41)	20.88 (43)	13.59 (29)	11.81 (25)	20.05 (41)	13.73 (28)
P09	Bury	23.33 (34)	22.67 (32)	18.91 (28)	16.58 (24)	18.13 (26)	11.43 (16)	11.35 (16)	9.25 (13)	14.85 (22)
P10	North Manchester	29.99 (38)	22.14 (28)	20.99 (24)	34.93 (39)	25.80 (29)	28.78 (31)	25.03 (26)	16.88 (18)	20.89 (22)
P11	Central Manchester	27.26 (27)	24.82 (23)	31.52 (28)	24.12 (21)	16.81 (15)	17.39 (14)	18.05 (15)	18.25 (14)	16.39 (13)
P12	South Manchester	23.79 (37)	14.16 (23)	16.72 (25)	22.55 (30)	18.38 (27)	17.50 (23)	20.34 (27)	16.07 (19)	22.32 (27)

HON - A3
Mortality rates from stroke (ICD 430-438) in persons under 65:
Age-standardised mortality rates per 100,000: 1984-92
(observed numbers of deaths in parentheses)
Persons

		1984	1985	1986	1987	1988	1989	1990	1991	1992
P13	Oldham	23.04	22.52	25.94	19.93	15.57	11.74	15.33	15.54	19.24
		(43)	(43)	(48)	(36)	(27)	(20)	(26)	(26)	(33)
P14	Rochdale	12.58	19.07	17.98	18.29	21.75	16.86	15.95	12.58	18.27
		(23)	(34)	(31)	(31)	(38)	(29)	(26)	(20)	(30)
P15	Salford	25.28	25.23	20.19	13.38	21.84	18.01	19.15	17.62	20.95
		(56)	(53)	(42)	(27)	(43)	(36)	(35)	(33)	(39)
P16	Stockport	11.48	15.38	13.47	12.16	12.06	13.13	8.87	11.94	13.72
		(30)	(39)	(34)	(30)	(29)	(32)	(22)	(30)	(34)
P17	Tameside and Glossop	23.49	18.31	18.82	19.48	20.89	22.80	16.78	15.46	12.37
		(48)	(38)	(39)	(40)	(41)	(46)	(34)	(30)	(24)
P18	Trafford	18.14	12.47	18.20	11.75	14.55	14.60	14.47	12.05	13.96
		(35)	(24)	(35)	(23)	(27)	(26)	(26)	(22)	(25)
P19	Wigan	22.22	24.15	23.43	21.79	18.19	17.94	17.79	20.84	16.63
		(57)	(61)	(60)	(55)	(45)	(45)	(43)	(52)	(43)

HON - A4
Mortality rates from stroke (ICD 430-438) in persons aged 65-74:
Age-standardised mortality rates per 100,000: 1984-92
(observed numbers of deaths in parentheses)
Persons

		1984	1985	1986	1987	1988	1989	1990	1991	1992
	ENGLAND AND WALES	336.70 (15215)	319.30 (14675)	314.25 (14514)	294.80 (13550)	287.44 (12979)	275.30 (12227)	261.29 (11764)	258.41 (11830)	241.62 (11272)
O00	ENGLAND	333.43 (14166)	316.84 (13693)	312.02 (13544)	292.72 (12640)	287.24 (12174)	273.37 (11384)	259.51 (10953)	256.19 (10989)	240.65 (10520)
A00	NORTHERN RHA	423.29 (1151)	413.31 (1158)	396.33 (1120)	377.08 (1065)	351.76 (985)	337.15 (936)	314.70 (894)	312.22 (908)	306.75 (914)
B00	YORKSHIRE RHA	360.90 (1161)	341.31 (1131)	335.75 (1111)	310.47 (1020)	306.43 (988)	307.25 (974)	272.28 (876)	286.51 (937)	261.27 (875)
C00	TRENT RHA	350.28 (1441)	360.90 (1522)	335.37 (1425)	332.70 (1416)	289.21 (1216)	289.96 (1208)	261.13 (1112)	270.21 (1179)	258.88 (1151)
D00	EAST ANGLIAN RHA	316.16 (596)	283.21 (534)	287.95 (554)	262.31 (505)	257.75 (493)	233.27 (441)	224.31 (432)	224.76 (445)	202.35 (411)
E00	NORTH WEST THAMES RHA	275.31 (780)	242.44 (692)	272.84 (778)	237.49 (665)	250.38 (677)	242.84 (637)	230.38 (604)	219.34 (576)	220.18 (586)
F00	NORTH EAST THAMES RHA	309.61 (1009)	271.43 (894)	269.52 (885)	257.51 (835)	246.35 (775)	230.81 (705)	234.02 (721)	237.30 (736)	214.35 (674)
G00	SOUTH EAST THAMES RHA	288.04 (1036)	285.05 (1020)	273.08 (986)	255.46 (908)	264.69 (915)	247.21 (832)	250.96 (847)	233.89 (792)	217.48 (747)
H00	SOUTH WEST THAMES RHA	284.25 (800)	246.09 (693)	244.26 (692)	233.20 (648)	252.63 (681)	231.33 (605)	227.82 (596)	201.46 (528)	210.00 (559)
J00	WESSEX RHA	266.45 (762)	258.24 (749)	270.29 (790)	233.31 (690)	245.57 (715)	244.53 (700)	228.13 (665)	237.14 (709)	221.06 (673)
K00	OXFORD RHA	273.14 (493)	287.71 (525)	276.02 (512)	254.20 (476)	262.99 (484)	247.85 (449)	240.53 (445)	218.75 (413)	232.30 (450)
L00	SOUTH WESTERN RHA	303.34 (991)	284.87 (950)	293.35 (981)	264.27 (878)	264.25 (866)	242.17 (781)	242.31 (795)	225.86 (757)	203.26 (694)
M00	WEST MIDLANDS RHA	382.51 (1683)	357.69 (1618)	344.16 (1576)	328.22 (1507)	325.16 (1479)	300.22 (1353)	280.17 (1289)	279.27 (1317)	258.02 (1239)
N00	MERSEY RHA	375.78 (792)	348.74 (745)	335.23 (723)	326.92 (702)	315.13 (664)	306.42 (637)	291.74 (614)	289.41 (618)	265.69 (578)
P00	NORTH WESTERN RHA	401.89 (1471)	391.91 (1462)	382.80 (1411)	363.38 (1325)	346.88 (1236)	322.15 (1126)	302.07 (1063)	301.38 (1074)	266.24 (969)
A01	Hartlepool	496.30 (36)	530.94 (40)	586.93 (45)	539.90 (41)	450.04 (34)	381.59 (29)	348.29 (27)	284.66 (23)	446.62 (37)
A02	North Tees	361.40 (43)	342.98 (43)	369.08 (47)	392.57 (51)	324.78 (43)	254.27 (35)	361.41 (49)	277.37 (39)	365.22 (53)
A03	South Tees	375.65 (84)	321.52 (74)	303.03 (71)	429.63 (102)	304.41 (72)	296.96 (70)	344.36 (84)	350.72 (88)	260.93 (67)
A04	East Cumbria	410.02 (69)	394.79 (69)	407.92 (72)	377.55 (66)	330.15 (57)	313.53 (53)	281.69 (49)	258.39 (46)	229.02 (42)
A05	South Cumbria	334.65 (59)	426.32 (77)	374.93 (68)	322.47 (58)	282.19 (51)	299.88 (53)	248.29 (44)	258.47 (47)	257.29 (47)
A06	West Cumbria	402.94 (47)	562.97 (69)	404.84 (50)	464.68 (58)	377.45 (47)	269.54 (33)	377.82 (48)	331.81 (44)	402.97 (54)

82

HON - A4
Mortality rates from stroke (ICD 430-438) in persons aged 65-74:
Age-standardised mortality rates per 100,000: 1984-92
(observed numbers of deaths in parentheses)
Persons

		1984	1985	1986	1987	1988	1989	1990	1991	1992
A11	Northumberland	534.81 (150)	459.73 (134)	508.14 (149)	364.08 (105)	390.63 (112)	327.73 (93)	327.48 (96)	354.96 (107)	361.73 (112)
A12	Gateshead	347.63 (66)	385.06 (76)	330.18 (65)	270.29 (53)	401.65 (78)	333.06 (64)	287.59 (56)	359.99 (71)	274.97 (56)
A13	Newcastle	303.19 (83)	437.00 (120)	397.20 (109)	356.33 (96)	307.30 (81)	368.32 (95)	315.10 (81)	318.58 (83)	311.00 (82)
A14	North Tyneside	396.29 (74)	417.34 (81)	299.88 (58)	370.77 (73)	356.21 (70)	379.41 (74)	304.78 (61)	303.55 (62)	229.50 (48)
A15	South Tyneside	459.91 (67)	352.49 (53)	351.66 (54)	400.09 (62)	344.42 (54)	331.74 (51)	242.65 (39)	265.16 (44)	268.73 (46)
A16	Sunderland	464.30 (109)	390.17 (93)	411.04 (99)	399.77 (97)	350.83 (84)	350.74 (84)	310.22 (76)	343.61 (86)	368.81 (96)
A30	North Durham	440.28 (121)	412.11 (117)	437.01 (126)	384.93 (110)	358.86 (101)	427.99 (120)	315.00 (90)	335.42 (98)	332.86 (100)
A31	South Durham	558.46 (143)	428.05 (112)	404.81 (107)	352.30 (93)	384.16 (101)	317.82 (82)	352.08 (94)	256.05 (70)	264.34 (74)
B11	East Riding	321.57 (147)	331.42 (158)	297.63 (142)	306.37 (146)	341.89 (160)	289.69 (133)	246.09 (115)	229.09 (109)	229.66 (113)
B16	Grimsby and Scunthorpe	403.37 (121)	368.20 (114)	276.21 (87)	381.18 (120)	305.25 (95)	298.15 (92)	257.73 (82)	266.69 (87)	249.81 (83)
B21	North Yorkshire	310.63 (207)	321.89 (226)	325.44 (227)	252.62 (174)	250.15 (169)	291.86 (194)	273.28 (185)	277.83 (193)	238.46 (170)
B31	Bradford	389.27 (149)	374.52 (147)	389.76 (150)	350.45 (134)	324.49 (122)	334.96 (124)	329.66 (124)	332.92 (127)	309.53 (121)
B51	West Yorkshire	447.91 (225)	343.90 (177)	379.45 (196)	317.50 (162)	349.16 (174)	322.54 (158)	280.10 (138)	332.57 (166)	296.81 (151)
B61	Leeds	327.59 (211)	305.35 (200)	314.10 (206)	313.39 (202)	288.24 (181)	312.95 (192)	247.85 (153)	278.10 (172)	254.24 (160)
B71	Wakefield	387.90 (101)	411.54 (109)	388.18 (103)	305.88 (82)	328.18 (87)	307.51 (81)	292.67 (79)	300.41 (83)	272.24 (77)
C01	North Derbyshire	361.78 (121)	358.70 (124)	348.77 (124)	345.60 (122)	329.64 (115)	237.06 (82)	260.58 (93)	236.72 (87)	291.94 (108)
C02	Southern Derbyshire	396.11 (189)	380.63 (186)	350.25 (170)	371.19 (182)	319.76 (155)	339.03 (163)	306.38 (150)	287.30 (144)	244.45 (125)
C03	Leicestershire	314.33 (217)	337.11 (244)	328.75 (237)	305.28 (221)	246.88 (176)	275.32 (195)	236.58 (170)	216.69 (159)	263.26 (200)
C04	North Lincolnshire	393.20 (99)	355.77 (92)	293.28 (79)	275.01 (75)	223.59 (61)	274.96 (75)	257.32 (73)	244.20 (72)	306.64 (92)
C05	South Lincolnshire	360.04 (108)	342.51 (104)	301.68 (93)	354.80 (111)	285.59 (89)	250.85 (78)	214.55 (69)	230.44 (77)	211.81 (73)
C08	Nottingham	363.92 (194)	386.92 (210)	353.33 (193)	365.58 (198)	315.47 (168)	307.12 (162)	286.51 (154)	300.06 (165)	253.13 (143)
C09	Barnsley	275.59 (56)	350.88 (72)	328.92 (68)	308.47 (63)	331.32 (67)	257.65 (51)	200.77 (41)	329.74 (69)	259.56 (55)

83

HON - A4
Mortality rates from stroke (ICD 430-438) in persons aged 65-74:
Age-standardised mortality rates per 100,000: 1984-92
(observed numbers of deaths in parentheses)
Persons

		1984	1985	1986	1987	1988	1989	1990	1991	1992
C10	Doncaster	319.81 (76)	321.01 (78)	301.20 (75)	280.23 (70)	273.99 (68)	289.05 (71)	220.48 (56)	255.08 (67)	205.38 (56)
C11	Rotherham	286.32 (57)	313.10 (65)	360.97 (77)	348.62 (75)	336.63 (72)	342.68 (73)	289.34 (63)	345.22 (77)	261.66 (60)
C12	Sheffield	318.37 (175)	396.48 (221)	353.27 (194)	343.70 (187)	289.49 (154)	333.76 (173)	269.49 (140)	324.75 (170)	304.35 (154)
C14	North Nottinghamshire	445.53 (149)	368.98 (126)	335.50 (115)	323.32 (112)	264.33 (91)	247.29 (85)	292.69 (103)	253.72 (92)	230.51 (85)
D01	Cambridge	263.01 (62)	207.30 (48)	282.68 (65)	249.65 (58)	247.03 (56)	201.32 (45)	185.85 (42)	218.78 (51)	190.66 (46)
D05	North West Anglia	332.00 (116)	299.54 (106)	275.90 (101)	281.21 (103)	282.37 (104)	292.78 (108)	221.31 (84)	247.56 (97)	209.00 (84)
D06	Norwich	297.72 (147)	291.29 (144)	288.38 (146)	266.65 (135)	231.90 (116)	210.13 (104)	232.06 (117)	202.36 (105)	200.04 (107)
D07	Great Yarmouth and Waveney	322.59 (71)	258.04 (56)	281.98 (63)	200.08 (45)	244.45 (54)	196.33 (43)	227.42 (50)	231.75 (52)	173.28 (41)
D09	Huntingdon	383.65 (31)	348.68 (29)	203.39 (18)	265.15 (23)	292.61 (25)	244.91 (21)	229.29 (20)	177.86 (16)	111.72 (10)
D11	Suffolk	333.87 (169)	298.62 (151)	315.59 (161)	276.35 (141)	271.59 (138)	240.83 (120)	234.00 (119)	238.04 (124)	232.68 (123)
E01	North Bedfordshire	297.12 (52)	289.40 (53)	359.77 (66)	198.37 (37)	320.47 (59)	322.90 (59)	248.58 (46)	253.56 (48)	233.50 (45)
E02	South Bedfordshire	329.39 (60)	209.71 (41)	287.69 (56)	283.56 (54)	277.01 (52)	281.15 (51)	210.44 (39)	296.07 (55)	252.17 (48)
E05	North West Hertfordshire	345.77 (69)	239.56 (49)	307.42 (64)	296.75 (62)	233.89 (48)	177.38 (36)	221.80 (46)	104.50 (22)	192.86 (42)
E06	South West Hertfordshire	247.67 (55)	177.10 (40)	311.83 (70)	266.97 (60)	293.97 (64)	221.56 (47)	244.73 (52)	234.69 (50)	193.45 (43)
E07	Barnet	239.58 (70)	198.88 (57)	202.67 (57)	204.41 (57)	205.84 (53)	219.12 (55)	190.93 (47)	212.15 (52)	188.01 (46)
E09	Hillingdon	226.21 (47)	260.04 (52)	236.82 (48)	213.56 (43)	267.40 (52)	241.27 (46)	237.14 (45)	205.23 (38)	249.31 (48)
E18	East and North Hertfordshire	271.29 (97)	262.97 (98)	337.87 (129)	194.64 (74)	231.25 (87)	228.11 (85)	195.50 (74)	197.10 (76)	201.48 (80)
E19	Brent and Harrow	252.03 (98)	227.51 (89)	209.53 (79)	245.45 (89)	228.30 (78)	273.53 (89)	241.84 (77)	188.44 (60)	244.27 (76)
E20	Ealing, Hammersmith and Hounslow	299.21 (161)	271.85 (144)	273.77 (145)	268.17 (135)	255.05 (123)	262.51 (121)	272.32 (124)	293.39 (132)	218.57 (98)
E21	Kensington, Chelsea and Westminster	259.55 (71)	258.04 (69)	241.09 (64)	205.21 (54)	241.70 (61)	197.62 (48)	221.04 (54)	177.34 (43)	244.42 (60)
F31	North Essex	313.55 (240)	264.92 (208)	276.17 (218)	245.65 (193)	236.52 (183)	247.04 (188)	211.59 (164)	233.87 (184)	175.66 (141)
F32	South Essex	284.42 (163)	270.85 (160)	267.64 (161)	230.13 (139)	246.07 (147)	218.35 (129)	232.71 (140)	220.09 (135)	218.22 (136)

84

HON - A4

Mortality rates from stroke (ICD 430-438) in persons aged 65-74:
Age-standardised mortality rates per 100,000: 1984-92
(observed numbers of deaths in parentheses)
Persons

		1984	1985	1986	1987	1988	1989	1990	1991	1992
F33	Barking and Havering	299.20 (105)	233.77 (84)	277.73 (101)	230.26 (84)	214.07 (77)	215.55 (76)	247.99 (89)	243.94 (89)	196.19 (73)
F34	Redbridge and Waltham Forest	275.42 (114)	241.62 (103)	211.54 (88)	265.94 (108)	264.23 (101)	220.12 (80)	182.37 (66)	218.67 (77)	224.88 (81)
F35	East London and the City	366.12 (164)	335.77 (150)	276.32 (123)	305.07 (131)	297.76 (123)	236.72 (94)	261.26 (103)	289.46 (113)	300.39 (118)
F36	New River District	358.35 (145)	290.66 (114)	330.58 (126)	266.11 (100)	232.85 (82)	246.09 (82)	261.09 (87)	249.52 (83)	179.88 (60)
F37	Camden and Islington	257.04 (78)	253.52 (75)	237.00 (68)	285.19 (80)	229.25 (62)	215.50 (56)	276.18 (72)	211.92 (55)	247.66 (65)
G04	South East Kent	353.80 (98)	264.79 (74)	256.11 (74)	256.82 (73)	233.49 (65)	210.99 (58)	248.32 (69)	229.63 (66)	183.33 (53)
G05	Canterbury and Thanet	362.59 (127)	258.74 (93)	310.15 (110)	287.27 (102)	312.72 (110)	301.01 (103)	230.43 (80)	252.73 (88)	228.15 (83)
G06	Dartford and Gravesham	237.00 (40)	369.37 (64)	211.72 (37)	223.38 (39)	354.58 (61)	247.85 (43)	310.47 (54)	275.61 (49)	272.77 (50)
G07	Maidstone	284.06 (44)	321.68 (50)	251.66 (40)	332.17 (53)	218.87 (34)	242.43 (37)	288.97 (45)	178.29 (28)	177.76 (29)
G08	Medway	286.41 (72)	303.39 (77)	279.44 (72)	235.86 (60)	268.50 (68)	278.23 (70)	256.12 (65)	229.33 (58)	281.45 (73)
G09	Tunbridge Wells	260.16 (49)	320.19 (59)	282.31 (54)	220.39 (41)	193.17 (35)	238.05 (42)	233.94 (42)	262.26 (48)	230.30 (42)
G10	Bexley	257.96 (48)	259.33 (48)	296.06 (55)	233.10 (44)	246.27 (45)	297.27 (53)	177.69 (32)	245.12 (44)	208.25 (38)
G11	Greenwich	308.05 (59)	287.16 (56)	403.39 (78)	300.58 (57)	297.75 (55)	241.23 (43)	276.75 (50)	309.46 (56)	190.94 (35)
G12	Bromley	318.71 (88)	203.93 (57)	268.72 (77)	230.35 (65)	236.24 (65)	199.61 (54)	258.49 (70)	170.68 (47)	193.14 (53)
G21	East Sussex	275.59 (251)	309.68 (278)	257.91 (232)	250.18 (220)	245.01 (210)	234.25 (195)	236.89 (195)	212.90 (172)	196.27 (164)
G26	South East London	249.18 (160)	267.14 (164)	254.40 (157)	257.26 (154)	294.21 (167)	247.12 (134)	271.60 (145)	256.85 (136)	241.94 (127)
H04	Mid Surrey	282.41 (49)	304.84 (53)	300.22 (53)	225.91 (39)	240.61 (40)	215.09 (35)	203.94 (33)	135.80 (23)	224.22 (37)
H05	East Surrey	263.28 (47)	254.49 (45)	214.90 (38)	314.65 (55)	217.57 (37)	264.78 (44)	227.21 (38)	268.57 (45)	187.68 (32)
H06	Chichester	330.07 (78)	299.97 (72)	185.82 (47)	177.59 (42)	168.36 (40)	230.77 (53)	200.80 (46)	256.35 (58)	208.71 (49)
H07	Mid Downs	350.77 (75)	215.29 (47)	297.24 (65)	273.90 (61)	315.87 (70)	259.18 (57)	279.37 (63)	185.58 (43)	239.06 (57)
H08	Worthing	296.85 (102)	304.52 (105)	282.00 (95)	199.78 (67)	238.79 (79)	284.42 (90)	265.81 (83)	218.08 (68)	214.04 (67)
H09	Croydon	347.18 (86)	284.33 (72)	306.86 (78)	284.71 (71)	308.42 (74)	291.41 (68)	255.93 (60)	233.31 (55)	261.30 (62)

HON - A4
Mortality rates from stroke (ICD 430-438) in persons aged 65-74:
Age-standardised mortality rates per 100,000: 1984-92
(observed numbers of deaths in parentheses)
Persons

		1984	1985	1986	1987	1988	1989	1990	1991	1992
H12	Wandsworth	348.68 (57)	237.09 (39)	190.99 (30)	265.96 (39)	398.11 (55)	248.61 (32)	279.29 (35)	247.67 (30)	217.64 (27)
H13	Merton and Sutton	226.10 (73)	156.45 (50)	203.45 (63)	233.37 (71)	254.64 (74)	213.00 (60)	157.48 (44)	156.80 (44)	200.91 (56)
H14	North West Surrey	270.07 (82)	232.56 (71)	241.84 (77)	214.52 (67)	209.71 (64)	206.91 (62)	201.24 (61)	179.92 (55)	176.88 (56)
H15	South West Surrey	276.79 (60)	146.66 (33)	229.92 (51)	213.34 (47)	248.01 (53)	182.77 (38)	214.10 (45)	187.84 (39)	182.13 (39)
H16	Kingston and Richmond	219.28 (91)	265.23 (106)	230.39 (95)	222.07 (89)	247.87 (95)	178.30 (66)	241.07 (88)	187.50 (68)	208.56 (77)
J10	Dorset	258.59 (203)	227.83 (180)	248.65 (197)	238.25 (192)	212.17 (168)	243.74 (188)	208.53 (163)	197.49 (157)	204.23 (165)
J21	Portsmouth and South East Hampshire	281.78 (127)	249.12 (117)	245.90 (115)	209.96 (99)	271.35 (126)	286.99 (132)	225.12 (106)	273.46 (132)	260.77 (129)
J22	Southampton and South West Hampshire	228.72 (88)	233.67 (94)	263.70 (107)	249.05 (104)	254.69 (104)	232.33 (93)	235.93 (97)	251.20 (107)	217.13 (93)
J23	Winchester	199.62 (35)	217.98 (38)	255.55 (46)	314.62 (56)	232.33 (41)	231.38 (40)	224.73 (40)	206.45 (38)	187.27 (35)
J24	Basingstoke and North Hampshire	326.16 (74)	287.79 (67)	311.66 (73)	220.51 (52)	254.73 (60)	256.77 (60)	214.66 (51)	201.24 (49)	237.11 (59)
J31	Salisbury	270.38 (35)	329.99 (41)	285.45 (36)	281.24 (35)	210.16 (26)	122.07 (15)	289.15 (36)	195.71 (25)	206.14 (28)
J32	Swindon	261.86 (43)	367.26 (63)	321.65 (56)	185.37 (33)	305.33 (54)	280.36 (49)	241.70 (44)	257.55 (48)	277.38 (54)
J33	Bath	319.68 (120)	312.54 (117)	320.03 (122)	224.78 (86)	247.28 (93)	216.87 (80)	253.27 (95)	286.58 (110)	192.16 (74)
J41	Isle of Wight	220.55 (37)	204.33 (32)	241.28 (38)	199.37 (33)	271.80 (43)	277.77 (43)	210.73 (33)	268.96 (43)	225.88 (36)
K11	East Berkshire	253.26 (67)	262.56 (70)	233.97 (63)	272.18 (74)	220.79 (59)	232.99 (62)	212.31 (57)	262.69 (72)	247.06 (70)
K12	West Berkshire	286.75 (89)	324.08 (100)	308.60 (98)	227.47 (72)	206.40 (64)	272.19 (82)	192.74 (59)	190.81 (60)	201.76 (65)
K24	Buckinghamshire	301.28 (115)	311.06 (120)	261.64 (104)	250.30 (101)	246.12 (98)	238.98 (94)	267.42 (108)	238.21 (98)	241.60 (102)
K31	Kettering	255.63 (55)	291.01 (65)	285.14 (63)	253.80 (57)	368.50 (81)	336.08 (73)	251.64 (56)	235.87 (54)	223.43 (51)
K32	Northampton	250.49 (58)	333.21 (80)	330.28 (80)	312.74 (78)	309.13 (76)	238.43 (58)	280.68 (70)	204.33 (52)	267.21 (70)
K41	Oxfordshire	271.97 (109)	224.36 (90)	254.67 (104)	231.74 (94)	265.39 (106)	204.54 (80)	237.76 (95)	190.10 (77)	219.27 (92)
L10	Bristol and District	300.86 (222)	304.80 (232)	304.42 (230)	277.20 (209)	242.92 (180)	240.00 (174)	275.57 (203)	220.98 (166)	227.42 (173)
L21	Cornwall and Isles of Scilly	332.59 (162)	267.36 (137)	318.86 (163)	241.69 (122)	290.38 (145)	204.56 (101)	223.20 (113)	250.28 (130)	188.21 (101)

86

HON - A4
Mortality rates from stroke (ICD 430-438) in persons aged 65-74:
Age-standardised mortality rates per 100,000: 1984-92
(observed numbers of deaths in parentheses)
Persons

		1984	1985	1986	1987	1988	1989	1990	1991	1992
L35	Exeter and North Devon	287.43 (149)	312.99 (160)	263.84 (137)	262.45 (133)	268.95 (135)	202.86 (100)	249.51 (125)	220.72 (113)	196.23 (101)
L36	Plymouth and Torbay	253.50 (153)	268.58 (166)	292.02 (182)	254.04 (159)	255.22 (155)	275.28 (164)	226.71 (136)	226.88 (138)	202.66 (125)
L40	Gloucestershire	345.43 (168)	286.87 (141)	311.59 (156)	295.67 (148)	267.87 (133)	291.11 (143)	285.43 (144)	234.00 (122)	206.37 (109)
L51	Somerset	316.50 (137)	259.82 (114)	259.51 (113)	248.74 (107)	273.80 (118)	233.04 (99)	170.45 (74)	200.51 (88)	185.60 (85)
M02	Herefordshire	280.89 (45)	321.40 (51)	357.84 (57)	241.37 (39)	262.83 (42)	290.37 (46)	300.25 (49)	290.80 (49)	234.32 (41)
M04	Worcester and District	363.71 (77)	305.40 (69)	330.29 (75)	292.01 (67)	293.88 (67)	272.75 (62)	240.31 (56)	271.59 (66)	221.36 (56)
M05	Shropshire	369.55 (120)	400.14 (138)	349.17 (122)	273.37 (95)	354.76 (123)	287.06 (99)	295.78 (105)	264.51 (97)	220.27 (84)
M06	Mid Staffordshire	331.93 (74)	281.11 (64)	372.63 (87)	302.75 (72)	325.88 (77)	293.67 (70)	234.23 (57)	270.77 (68)	226.36 (59)
M07	North Staffordshire	366.56 (157)	375.55 (164)	330.67 (144)	315.39 (138)	346.58 (150)	344.63 (148)	272.31 (119)	276.01 (123)	282.42 (129)
M08	South East Staffordshire	397.15 (70)	431.50 (79)	309.40 (57)	326.12 (61)	256.27 (48)	377.34 (71)	229.09 (44)	292.89 (58)	267.58 (54)
M13	East Birmingham	362.99 (70)	391.18 (76)	388.09 (77)	299.70 (59)	320.18 (62)	279.09 (53)	218.62 (42)	273.65 (53)	286.29 (56)
M14	North Birmingham	373.84 (52)	324.87 (47)	362.33 (54)	312.67 (46)	360.72 (53)	272.86 (40)	290.12 (43)	285.10 (43)	187.48 (29)
M16	West Birmingham	459.07 (84)	403.75 (72)	341.68 (61)	431.31 (74)	424.12 (70)	332.59 (53)	289.49 (46)	280.71 (45)	250.40 (40)
M17	Coventry	370.15 (102)	384.92 (110)	336.69 (97)	369.70 (107)	397.77 (113)	312.28 (87)	334.01 (94)	317.35 (90)	296.44 (85)
M18	Dudley	523.28 (131)	360.07 (93)	486.96 (127)	434.71 (115)	349.14 (92)	305.12 (80)	335.93 (91)	296.16 (82)	300.13 (86)
M19	Sandwell	377.44 (106)	363.97 (104)	312.70 (90)	334.26 (97)	294.66 (84)	279.73 (79)	306.92 (88)	317.74 (93)	267.32 (79)
M20	Solihull	336.64 (50)	322.24 (50)	231.79 (37)	226.68 (37)	269.24 (44)	211.17 (34)	210.99 (35)	228.60 (39)	163.64 (29)
M21	Walsall	358.92 (77)	403.09 (89)	309.26 (69)	331.34 (74)	289.48 (64)	329.01 (72)	276.97 (62)	283.61 (65)	257.75 (59)
M22	Wolverhampton	324.62 (71)	441.32 (98)	287.18 (65)	415.77 (94)	335.73 (75)	317.75 (70)	339.47 (77)	261.50 (61)	329.03 (77)
M25	South Birmingham	448.65 (169)	323.65 (125)	371.93 (145)	349.02 (133)	350.42 (132)	322.60 (119)	354.69 (132)	235.96 (90)	282.42 (106)
M26	North Worcestershire	406.83 (81)	282.50 (59)	352.66 (75)	311.76 (67)	298.14 (64)	240.89 (51)	269.14 (59)	332.15 (75)	285.94 (66)
M28	Warwickshire	369.42 (147)	318.33 (130)	326.33 (137)	313.29 (132)	283.03 (119)	284.05 (119)	209.67 (90)	270.44 (120)	229.80 (104)

HON - A4
Mortality rates from stroke (ICD 430-438) in persons aged 65-74:
Age-standardised mortality rates per 100,000: 1984-92
(observed numbers of deaths in parentheses)
Persons

		1984	1985	1986	1987	1988	1989	1990	1991	1992
N11	Chester	379.11 (56)	358.45 (55)	279.41 (43)	259.90 (40)	224.44 (34)	271.38 (40)	236.29 (36)	236.90 (37)	186.83 (30)
N12	Crewe	359.26 (75)	388.20 (84)	364.14 (80)	426.70 (94)	348.78 (76)	280.73 (61)	231.52 (52)	335.39 (77)	279.94 (66)
N13	Halton	486.20 (51)	345.54 (37)	301.76 (33)	382.53 (42)	229.08 (25)	287.44 (31)	427.42 (47)	301.16 (34)	213.95 (25)
N14	Macclesfield	328.01 (52)	231.60 (37)	290.10 (47)	283.15 (45)	310.11 (49)	280.78 (44)	233.36 (37)	135.32 (22)	224.17 (37)
N15	Warrington	397.35 (56)	475.45 (70)	415.08 (62)	530.21 (78)	406.18 (59)	339.73 (49)	312.71 (46)	301.20 (45)	336.51 (52)
N21	Liverpool	379.37 (178)	339.37 (157)	401.28 (184)	294.23 (134)	375.51 (164)	368.85 (157)	324.89 (137)	383.19 (162)	271.57 (116)
N31	St Helens and Knowsley	440.42 (114)	434.67 (116)	350.08 (94)	326.40 (88)	297.62 (79)	230.41 (61)	374.85 (102)	327.62 (91)	316.54 (90)
N41	Southport and Formby	338.71 (41)	362.77 (45)	206.96 (26)	294.16 (38)	244.79 (31)	301.23 (38)	265.77 (34)	226.82 (29)	197.88 (26)
N42	South Sefton	311.24 (49)	290.81 (45)	310.83 (51)	297.73 (47)	267.74 (42)	317.38 (49)	269.03 (42)	294.71 (47)	265.02 (42)
N51	Wirral	350.21 (120)	289.99 (99)	300.23 (103)	276.44 (96)	310.07 (105)	321.53 (107)	241.55 (81)	221.98 (74)	273.65 (94)
P01	Lancaster	417.92 (60)	299.76 (43)	413.24 (59)	438.68 (59)	290.68 (39)	371.36 (48)	352.30 (46)	414.35 (55)	294.93 (40)
P02	Blackpool,Wyre and Fylde	391.84 (154)	410.79 (167)	399.09 (159)	318.81 (125)	307.61 (118)	286.03 (107)	270.07 (102)	283.32 (109)	252.48 (98)
P03	Preston	273.79 (33)	488.47 (57)	496.97 (57)	486.36 (56)	328.88 (37)	408.84 (45)	269.54 (30)	412.76 (46)	270.42 (31)
P04	Blackburn, Hyndburn and Ribble Valley	477.05 (117)	436.99 (110)	341.43 (84)	311.66 (76)	404.23 (95)	325.36 (75)	270.06 (62)	262.48 (61)	255.34 (60)
P05	Burnley, Pendle and Rossendale	482.68 (102)	446.36 (99)	365.60 (80)	271.27 (57)	294.82 (61)	356.83 (73)	334.46 (69)	317.03 (66)	227.11 (48)
P06	West Lancashire	389.16 (32)	474.23 (39)	295.44 (25)	283.69 (24)	310.50 (26)	217.27 (18)	293.28 (25)	208.53 (18)	168.79 (15)
P07	Chorley and South Ribble	306.29 (44)	348.82 (53)	343.02 (52)	366.40 (57)	286.84 (44)	221.58 (34)	299.35 (47)	222.87 (36)	207.11 (34)
P08	Bolton	344.56 (79)	433.10 (99)	476.64 (110)	368.45 (85)	332.29 (75)	359.46 (80)	284.05 (64)	322.42 (74)	286.22 (67)
P09	Bury	327.86 (52)	281.50 (44)	301.05 (45)	373.07 (57)	311.39 (46)	311.51 (45)	309.56 (45)	273.28 (40)	158.39 (24)
P10	North Manchester	481.79 (70)	402.09 (59)	339.22 (50)	348.54 (49)	467.88 (63)	423.77 (55)	301.31 (39)	301.75 (39)	210.67 (28)
P11	Central Manchester	420.79 (43)	348.01 (35)	392.77 (38)	384.41 (36)	460.92 (41)	345.61 (29)	239.76 (20)	443.57 (36)	408.19 (34)
P12	South Manchester	365.60 (61)	295.98 (52)	310.67 (52)	310.14 (52)	261.95 (43)	245.61 (39)	309.62 (49)	278.26 (44)	273.26 (44)

HON - A4

Mortality rates from stroke (ICD 430-438) in persons aged 65-74:
Age-standardised mortality rates per 100,000: 1984-92
(observed numbers of deaths in parentheses)
Persons

		1984	1985	1986	1987	1988	1989	1990	1991	1992
P13	Oldham	507.10	447.83	495.89	392.85	410.94	338.44	316.51	327.35	304.88
		(100)	(88)	(97)	(75)	(77)	(62)	(58)	(60)	(58)
P14	Rochdale	396.81	377.18	340.13	376.20	346.69	347.98	281.97	370.29	230.80
		(68)	(68)	(60)	(66)	(59)	(59)	(48)	(64)	(41)
P15	Salford	406.33	461.09	408.83	334.90	395.44	340.63	306.65	313.07	306.68
		(94)	(109)	(95)	(76)	(88)	(74)	(67)	(70)	(68)
P16	Stockport	327.89	292.85	364.61	335.85	269.14	312.81	297.74	261.46	291.31
		(83)	(77)	(93)	(86)	(67)	(77)	(74)	(66)	(76)
P17	Tameside and Glossop	385.56	394.14	429.80	475.17	411.03	317.34	382.22	265.88	327.57
		(85)	(89)	(95)	(105)	(89)	(68)	(82)	(58)	(73)
P18	Trafford	388.92	280.18	287.43	356.60	321.21	211.62	174.50	218.97	216.62
		(75)	(55)	(56)	(69)	(61)	(40)	(33)	(42)	(43)
P19	Wigan	467.56	463.41	396.64	443.11	418.53	386.97	401.26	345.16	326.36
		(119)	(119)	(104)	(115)	(107)	(98)	(103)	(90)	(87)

HON - B1
Mortality rates from breast cancer (ICD 174) in women aged 50-69:
Age-standardised mortality rates per 100,000: 1984-92
(observed numbers of deaths in parentheses)

		1984	1985	1986	1987	1988	1989	1990	1991	1992
	ENGLAND AND WALES	98.35	98.66	97.56	97.51	96.09	96.89	94.85	92.67	89.68
		(5541)	(5563)	(5451)	(5490)	(5443)	(5532)	(5331)	(5130)	(4898)
O00	ENGLAND	98.16	99.15	97.23	97.46	95.91	96.91	95.11	93.09	89.71
		(5204)	(5259)	(5109)	(5167)	(5104)	(5206)	(5016)	(4842)	(4602)
A00	NORTHERN RHA	95.55	86.34	88.63	87.74	87.01	97.82	89.94	90.15	86.81
		(345)	(323)	(321)	(322)	(314)	(358)	(320)	(318)	(304)
B00	YORKSHIRE RHA	104.46	84.13	94.89	83.45	82.73	92.13	90.06	78.32	87.73
		(422)	(345)	(380)	(335)	(337)	(375)	(366)	(316)	(348)
C00	TRENT RHA	105.45	96.78	94.82	103.36	106.39	97.77	97.51	92.11	92.45
		(546)	(498)	(486)	(543)	(555)	(524)	(512)	(481)	(482)
D00	EAST ANGLIAN RHA	100.83	95.45	96.93	87.31	93.24	89.62	100.76	92.94	78.87
		(215)	(210)	(218)	(192)	(212)	(210)	(236)	(212)	(180)
E00	NORTH WEST THAMES RHA	94.01	106.48	99.17	103.50	95.38	105.11	88.65	95.94	85.73
		(339)	(388)	(358)	(370)	(335)	(373)	(307)	(327)	(290)
F00	NORTH EAST THAMES RHA	99.66	99.55	108.80	104.86	101.64	101.41	90.18	100.88	87.95
		(405)	(404)	(429)	(418)	(404)	(401)	(359)	(394)	(333)
G00	SOUTH EAST THAMES RHA	95.96	102.70	94.77	105.71	93.73	98.21	92.40	96.93	101.66
		(407)	(429)	(390)	(439)	(391)	(412)	(378)	(383)	(397)
H00	SOUTH WEST THAMES RHA	95.33	101.37	105.49	102.80	97.70	101.06	96.35	95.36	92.67
		(333)	(345)	(356)	(347)	(325)	(337)	(316)	(308)	(291)
J00	WESSEX RHA	104.08	103.89	94.38	93.85	87.02	93.43	93.43	96.76	94.33
		(358)	(357)	(322)	(317)	(306)	(336)	(326)	(334)	(321)
K00	OXFORD RHA	100.48	106.88	103.20	93.15	96.47	101.27	105.26	95.15	86.16
		(235)	(250)	(242)	(227)	(239)	(250)	(258)	(231)	(209)
L00	SOUTH WESTERN RHA	84.14	100.14	90.27	91.91	98.93	93.21	92.38	96.69	87.40
		(317)	(374)	(345)	(355)	(386)	(364)	(361)	(365)	(324)
M00	WEST MIDLANDS RHA	101.40	109.02	101.98	100.41	97.80	99.02	97.97	95.49	94.47
		(586)	(636)	(585)	(583)	(576)	(588)	(567)	(553)	(536)
N00	MERSEY RHA	102.06	100.40	90.67	101.82	99.26	87.93	101.51	84.97	83.18
		(286)	(279)	(246)	(283)	(274)	(248)	(284)	(232)	(223)
P00	NORTH WESTERN RHA	90.25	94.60	95.65	96.71	99.72	94.53	99.42	91.32	86.41
		(410)	(421)	(431)	(436)	(450)	(430)	(426)	(388)	(364)
A01	Hartlepool	78.55	110.66	75.03	80.64	125.25	124.00	103.36	122.18	115.55
		(8)	(12)	(8)	(9)	(13)	(13)	(10)	(13)	(11)
A02	North Tees	72.59	57.27	70.92	95.61	89.12	111.97	79.09	112.46	96.71
		(13)	(11)	(13)	(18)	(16)	(20)	(15)	(22)	(18)
A03	South Tees	80.99	87.39	83.62	65.66	52.16	102.47	92.20	88.19	78.42
		(25)	(28)	(26)	(23)	(17)	(34)	(31)	(28)	(25)
A04	East Cumbria	77.27	97.82	51.96	99.75	86.63	77.00	134.17	77.59	82.29
		(17)	(21)	(12)	(21)	(19)	(16)	(29)	(17)	(18)
A05	South Cumbria	58.86	59.87	111.00	108.01	90.20	55.35	76.36	79.14	76.31
		(13)	(13)	(22)	(23)	(21)	(12)	(16)	(17)	(15)
A06	West Cumbria	80.62	83.68	96.53	96.44	86.75	72.61	66.87	87.70	74.98
		(13)	(14)	(14)	(16)	(14)	(12)	(11)	(14)	(12)

HON - B1
Mortality rates from breast cancer (ICD 174) in women aged 50-69:
Age-standardised mortality rates per 100,000: 1984-92
(observed numbers of deaths in parentheses)

		1984	1985	1986	1987	1988	1989	1990	1991	1992
A11	Northumberland	97.71	90.62	106.18	85.61	91.89	103.37	86.95	85.85	86.32
		(34)	(35)	(38)	(31)	(35)	(38)	(31)	(31)	(31)
A12	Gateshead	106.80	61.18	117.02	113.94	101.43	78.99	88.45	68.62	57.82
		(27)	(16)	(30)	(30)	(24)	(21)	(21)	(17)	(15)
A13	Newcastle	141.18	116.61	100.50	81.56	68.06	105.13	74.71	97.03	130.14
		(47)	(40)	(33)	(27)	(21)	(32)	(22)	(28)	(37)
A14	North Tyneside	156.65	112.05	111.15	92.93	98.64	140.65	78.29	99.70	103.46
		(37)	(32)	(28)	(22)	(24)	(35)	(19)	(24)	(23)
A15	South Tyneside	75.04	93.84	93.02	96.41	113.96	84.50	110.30	63.62	76.65
		(15)	(20)	(19)	(18)	(23)	(17)	(21)	(12)	(14)
A16	Sunderland	97.58	80.77	60.09	54.71	94.71	114.55	102.50	99.94	96.55
		(32)	(26)	(20)	(18)	(31)	(39)	(34)	(32)	(33)
A30	North Durham	94.70	64.97	84.11	86.43	80.15	95.81	85.00	103.00	83.11
		(36)	(25)	(31)	(31)	(31)	(38)	(31)	(37)	(32)
A31	South Durham	77.23	91.35	74.47	97.38	82.57	93.27	88.83	82.59	69.62
		(28)	(30)	(27)	(35)	(25)	(31)	(29)	(26)	(20)
B11	East Riding	105.13	70.19	98.90	98.38	83.42	113.71	100.97	79.98	88.07
		(63)	(40)	(57)	(55)	(48)	(67)	(58)	(47)	(51)
B16	Grimsby and Scunthorpe	90.85	134.78	104.58	120.87	133.15	98.10	118.05	91.61	81.84
		(37)	(54)	(42)	(47)	(53)	(39)	(47)	(37)	(31)
B21	North Yorkshire	106.91	67.12	79.23	71.50	86.55	87.67	75.40	98.89	95.14
		(87)	(56)	(67)	(60)	(73)	(74)	(63)	(81)	(80)
B31	Bradford	107.71	75.39	78.84	60.36	65.37	90.53	79.21	57.32	84.90
		(52)	(39)	(38)	(29)	(33)	(45)	(39)	(29)	(41)
B51	West Yorkshire	91.38	81.93	93.65	70.62	73.83	82.34	90.74	78.63	52.24
		(56)	(52)	(55)	(45)	(46)	(50)	(56)	(46)	(31)
B61	Leeds	112.69	96.64	107.54	84.24	73.52	95.29	72.62	57.89	98.92
		(88)	(78)	(84)	(65)	(58)	(75)	(58)	(46)	(76)
B71	Wakefield	112.54	77.39	109.93	97.24	75.82	72.48	127.93	84.39	116.68
		(39)	(26)	(37)	(34)	(26)	(25)	(45)	(30)	(38)
C01	North Derbyshire	87.21	118.33	112.13	92.09	105.79	80.13	91.41	121.25	78.72
		(37)	(52)	(48)	(40)	(47)	(36)	(39)	(51)	(36)
C02	Southern Derbyshire	95.26	111.85	89.48	105.11	109.02	79.70	94.65	121.28	92.29
		(59)	(63)	(53)	(62)	(67)	(50)	(57)	(76)	(54)
C03	Leicestershire	102.73	89.84	102.42	96.94	92.93	104.25	105.92	61.67	85.74
		(91)	(82)	(91)	(88)	(86)	(100)	(98)	(59)	(81)
C04	North Lincolnshire	123.09	76.29	82.09	90.70	139.65	103.43	77.81	91.36	121.23
		(36)	(26)	(26)	(30)	(43)	(34)	(27)	(31)	(39)
C05	South Lincolnshire	84.82	50.38	90.56	155.14	112.95	86.28	106.16	114.37	90.89
		(29)	(18)	(35)	(55)	(41)	(37)	(41)	(41)	(35)
C08	Nottingham	107.96	105.37	85.95	104.49	112.28	117.89	102.15	98.31	119.79
		(74)	(71)	(56)	(70)	(76)	(80)	(69)	(67)	(81)
C09	Barnsley	125.67	110.33	96.04	128.53	106.91	83.81	83.95	102.54	69.01
		(32)	(27)	(24)	(35)	(25)	(20)	(22)	(24)	(18)

HON - B1

Mortality rates from breast cancer (ICD 174) in women aged 50-69:
Age-standardised mortality rates per 100,000: 1984-92
(observed numbers of deaths in parentheses)

		1984	1985	1986	1987	1988	1989	1990	1991	1992
C10	Doncaster	122.50 (41)	99.76 (32)	81.90 (27)	84.02 (28)	104.86 (35)	115.77 (41)	73.56 (25)	67.03 (23)	81.69 (26)
C11	Rotherham	75.07 (21)	83.61 (22)	81.62 (22)	97.48 (25)	104.30 (30)	96.86 (28)	73.07 (20)	89.77 (25)	93.56 (25)
C12	Sheffield	134.13 (83)	90.56 (56)	106.17 (63)	99.96 (63)	80.34 (49)	99.32 (56)	120.81 (70)	87.78 (48)	79.38 (43)
C14	North Nottinghamshire	98.93 (43)	115.07 (49)	96.90 (41)	99.66 (47)	131.82 (56)	95.72 (42)	100.84 (44)	82.19 (36)	97.23 (44)
D01	Cambridge	101.26 (27)	93.57 (26)	79.14 (23)	79.65 (23)	126.70 (34)	69.46 (20)	119.41 (35)	113.31 (31)	88.07 (25)
D05	North West Anglia	66.82 (28)	99.82 (43)	114.85 (51)	103.77 (45)	103.90 (47)	101.60 (45)	110.62 (53)	92.51 (42)	71.06 (32)
D06	Norwich	113.25 (61)	96.64 (53)	106.51 (61)	85.03 (47)	86.02 (52)	74.02 (43)	72.05 (44)	93.63 (56)	61.05 (36)
D07	Great Yarmouth and Waveney	132.43 (30)	101.10 (24)	83.93 (19)	63.55 (17)	108.98 (27)	100.10 (28)	121.76 (32)	94.48 (24)	57.82 (14)
D09	Huntingdon	101.49 (10)	132.35 (14)	32.65 (4)	81.68 (9)	80.99 (9)	38.64 (4)	104.78 (12)	103.25 (12)	92.11 (12)
D11	Suffolk	100.71 (59)	83.41 (50)	101.39 (60)	91.97 (51)	71.77 (43)	109.44 (70)	102.24 (60)	79.93 (47)	104.60 (61)
E01	North Bedfordshire	111.88 (26)	84.49 (20)	163.39 (39)	79.21 (19)	94.76 (21)	117.78 (29)	83.31 (21)	105.33 (25)	110.23 (25)
E02	South Bedfordshire	117.00 (28)	125.28 (32)	113.06 (28)	58.52 (15)	102.08 (26)	114.76 (30)	101.59 (27)	99.83 (25)	66.59 (18)
E05	North West Hertfordshire	83.64 (24)	82.52 (24)	101.48 (29)	136.41 (38)	69.11 (20)	127.81 (37)	79.96 (23)	108.27 (30)	70.90 (19)
E06	South West Hertfordshire	104.15 (30)	113.50 (34)	113.14 (33)	75.75 (22)	47.54 (14)	94.69 (26)	89.58 (24)	119.83 (31)	60.64 (16)
E07	Barnet	84.93 (28)	91.74 (29)	96.19 (32)	104.09 (33)	96.03 (31)	104.02 (32)	78.52 (24)	103.76 (32)	95.76 (29)
E09	Hillingdon	65.51 (17)	110.51 (29)	72.76 (19)	118.78 (30)	119.60 (32)	130.19 (32)	77.76 (19)	80.12 (19)	109.18 (26)
E18	East and North Hertfordshire	116.45 (59)	123.22 (63)	97.63 (50)	107.69 (56)	113.40 (56)	102.48 (56)	106.58 (55)	97.55 (50)	70.06 (36)
E19	Brent and Harrow	79.92 (39)	110.33 (52)	94.57 (44)	109.24 (52)	72.10 (33)	97.44 (43)	96.06 (42)	84.35 (36)	97.56 (42)
E20	Ealing, Hammersmith and Hounslow	85.21 (56)	111.73 (74)	82.40 (54)	112.83 (71)	116.61 (71)	104.37 (63)	84.17 (48)	83.12 (49)	105.40 (59)
E21	Kensington, Chelsea and Westminster	95.77 (32)	93.33 (31)	89.87 (30)	107.66 (34)	95.03 (31)	75.61 (25)	77.54 (24)	94.70 (30)	64.66 (20)
F31	North Essex	95.86 (87)	98.02 (91)	113.34 (102)	102.95 (97)	108.18 (98)	87.11 (82)	103.68 (103)	92.19 (90)	87.19 (81)
F32	South Essex	111.96 (84)	108.99 (83)	121.80 (90)	116.42 (90)	114.87 (90)	115.24 (89)	88.87 (70)	105.93 (79)	93.22 (70)

HON - B1
Mortality rates from breast cancer (ICD 174) in women aged 50-69:
Age-standardised mortality rates per 100,000: 1984-92
(observed numbers of deaths in parentheses)

		1984	1985	1986	1987	1988	1989	1990	1991	1992
F33	Barking and Havering	95.97 (50)	107.23 (53)	86.15 (42)	109.90 (51)	106.39 (52)	98.24 (49)	80.28 (38)	92.88 (43)	75.65 (33)
F34	Redbridge and Waltham Forest	89.38 (42)	86.16 (44)	108.24 (52)	76.22 (37)	80.86 (39)	104.25 (49)	78.86 (35)	130.72 (59)	76.68 (34)
F35	East London and the City	92.51 (54)	92.54 (50)	95.08 (52)	115.09 (60)	90.74 (47)	112.44 (59)	107.33 (55)	90.16 (46)	88.28 (41)
F36	New River District	102.54 (48)	92.45 (44)	108.79 (50)	107.22 (49)	89.32 (40)	88.54 (39)	66.20 (30)	105.94 (46)	99.21 (43)
F37	Camden and Islington	110.84 (40)	110.88 (39)	121.37 (41)	94.22 (34)	109.65 (38)	109.37 (34)	89.07 (28)	94.60 (31)	94.37 (31)
G04	South East Kent	107.00 (34)	113.19 (35)	73.39 (23)	100.94 (33)	86.72 (27)	98.56 (34)	103.72 (34)	99.51 (30)	114.54 (34)
G05	Canterbury and Thanet	71.26 (27)	65.27 (24)	78.44 (28)	133.17 (51)	103.71 (38)	75.01 (31)	92.07 (36)	73.48 (26)	79.64 (29)
G06	Dartford and Gravesham	119.28 (29)	116.93 (28)	78.83 (19)	102.29 (25)	74.57 (18)	80.22 (20)	91.66 (22)	108.03 (26)	97.55 (24)
G07	Maidstone	99.93 (20)	93.53 (19)	105.54 (21)	102.16 (20)	43.49 (10)	118.05 (26)	92.47 (19)	66.24 (13)	102.46 (22)
G08	Medway	88.50 (28)	124.02 (39)	100.35 (33)	106.29 (34)	74.60 (26)	122.49 (40)	68.31 (22)	104.88 (34)	99.74 (31)
G09	Tunbridge Wells	97.33 (23)	92.51 (22)	101.32 (25)	93.35 (22)	69.38 (17)	143.60 (34)	96.45 (22)	103.27 (24)	93.49 (22)
G10	Bexley	110.59 (27)	100.51 (24)	76.37 (18)	109.24 (26)	103.83 (25)	108.29 (27)	92.51 (23)	98.10 (23)	136.43 (32)
G11	Greenwich	66.80 (16)	119.76 (29)	113.02 (27)	118.98 (27)	63.01 (16)	79.96 (17)	90.02 (20)	104.46 (23)	140.97 (28)
G12	Bromley	95.41 (35)	94.91 (36)	100.88 (37)	112.25 (41)	95.36 (34)	93.68 (33)	99.16 (35)	123.61 (41)	132.22 (43)
G21	East Sussex	86.41 (79)	112.95 (99)	102.36 (88)	92.94 (85)	94.00 (83)	99.28 (91)	110.90 (99)	102.76 (88)	75.67 (62)
G26	South East London	112.22 (89)	97.29 (74)	100.05 (71)	104.37 (75)	137.07 (97)	84.98 (59)	69.27 (46)	84.09 (55)	108.28 (70)
H04	Mid Surrey	105.67 (24)	112.39 (25)	118.08 (26)	98.52 (22)	88.90 (19)	115.76 (23)	90.76 (18)	62.85 (14)	84.83 (18)
H05	East Surrey	89.70 (20)	103.48 (22)	99.53 (23)	98.48 (22)	114.98 (26)	105.42 (24)	120.70 (26)	130.77 (27)	60.16 (12)
H06	Chichester	114.06 (31)	125.44 (28)	126.79 (29)	95.84 (22)	65.07 (16)	104.59 (28)	132.93 (32)	66.82 (16)	102.31 (23)
H07	Mid Downs	110.64 (34)	122.60 (35)	91.57 (29)	94.57 (28)	92.40 (29)	95.86 (30)	139.68 (42)	83.90 (27)	98.32 (30)
H08	Worthing	68.68 (22)	104.21 (35)	119.36 (37)	68.53 (26)	107.84 (38)	116.99 (36)	44.09 (18)	109.05 (34)	68.14 (20)
H09	Croydon	88.41 (30)	92.55 (31)	91.35 (30)	104.20 (35)	129.02 (41)	85.14 (27)	96.82 (32)	119.88 (39)	70.59 (22)

HON - B1
Mortality rates from breast cancer (ICD 174) in women aged 50-69:
Age-standardised mortality rates per 100,000: 1984-92
(observed numbers of deaths in parentheses)

		1984	1985	1986	1987	1988	1989	1990	1991	1992
H12	Wandsworth	78.35 (16)	72.66 (14)	93.05 (16)	118.98 (21)	71.42 (13)	81.75 (14)	102.48 (16)	71.53 (11)	171.41 (26)
H13	Merton and Sutton	122.59 (48)	81.77 (33)	113.58 (46)	131.10 (49)	111.27 (40)	107.56 (42)	104.11 (40)	103.14 (36)	73.49 (25)
H14	North West Surrey	100.97 (43)	94.63 (40)	105.37 (43)	98.06 (41)	85.43 (35)	114.79 (48)	93.24 (39)	85.83 (35)	78.28 (33)
H15	South West Surrey	82.81 (23)	98.84 (27)	104.37 (27)	105.40 (28)	71.86 (17)	85.96 (22)	69.85 (18)	90.14 (24)	83.12 (21)
H16	Kingston and Richmond	83.16 (42)	107.65 (55)	103.26 (50)	109.51 (53)	104.66 (51)	91.99 (43)	81.90 (35)	103.83 (45)	145.60 (61)
J10	Dorset	99.22 (83)	120.99 (100)	107.43 (88)	100.72 (78)	81.84 (71)	85.32 (78)	100.10 (86)	94.57 (77)	99.43 (78)
J21	Portsmouth and South East Hampshire	115.09 (65)	107.33 (60)	80.38 (48)	101.68 (56)	73.40 (42)	75.77 (44)	89.05 (52)	92.04 (52)	103.25 (60)
J22	Southampton and South West Hampshire	103.53 (50)	111.50 (54)	85.79 (42)	107.90 (48)	78.71 (37)	122.72 (59)	96.62 (46)	111.09 (54)	72.98 (32)
J23	Winchester	97.65 (22)	94.81 (22)	131.50 (28)	112.91 (26)	112.18 (26)	70.62 (18)	56.37 (13)	95.50 (22)	83.24 (19)
J24	Basingstoke and North Hampshire	122.26 (40)	65.69 (21)	86.69 (27)	107.01 (35)	90.16 (30)	86.75 (28)	106.33 (35)	88.71 (30)	101.40 (34)
J31	Salisbury	119.11 (18)	100.20 (16)	95.47 (14)	97.25 (16)	153.35 (23)	34.52 (5)	98.95 (15)	75.60 (13)	61.05 (8)
J32	Swindon	95.22 (22)	70.32 (16)	99.94 (22)	76.91 (18)	56.18 (14)	104.21 (25)	82.57 (21)	100.08 (24)	77.42 (18)
J33	Bath	93.36 (41)	109.27 (49)	83.30 (39)	57.32 (27)	95.54 (44)	120.98 (57)	109.34 (48)	109.03 (48)	104.15 (48)
J41	Isle of Wight	106.98 (17)	110.14 (19)	87.61 (14)	68.80 (13)	105.71 (19)	111.16 (22)	63.21 (10)	88.12 (14)	136.82 (24)
K11	East Berkshire	90.92 (33)	118.95 (42)	111.96 (40)	93.22 (35)	85.33 (32)	77.29 (29)	105.89 (39)	95.68 (34)	88.92 (32)
K12	West Berkshire	104.53 (43)	123.51 (52)	126.78 (52)	107.98 (45)	105.87 (45)	89.16 (37)	123.72 (52)	98.49 (42)	72.48 (31)
K24	Buckinghamshire	83.42 (43)	97.36 (51)	90.83 (48)	98.60 (53)	98.19 (55)	122.74 (71)	98.77 (56)	77.24 (44)	98.04 (55)
K31	Kettering	110.78 (28)	130.65 (34)	70.87 (19)	67.93 (20)	76.15 (22)	115.22 (31)	115.03 (31)	135.32 (35)	99.05 (27)
K32	Northampton	114.94 (33)	82.93 (25)	107.37 (32)	78.08 (25)	70.04 (23)	62.34 (20)	103.92 (32)	99.00 (32)	77.31 (23)
K41	Oxfordshire	109.21 (55)	95.16 (46)	104.03 (51)	94.56 (49)	119.79 (62)	121.21 (62)	92.61 (48)	89.63 (44)	80.70 (41)
L10	Bristol and District	92.35 (84)	92.20 (84)	87.36 (77)	102.93 (99)	98.06 (91)	78.49 (73)	89.32 (81)	79.66 (69)	88.91 (75)
L21	Cornwall and Isles of Scilly	49.40 (28)	122.66 (70)	121.36 (70)	96.56 (57)	105.49 (62)	77.79 (48)	74.99 (48)	94.36 (56)	81.12 (48)

94

HON - B1
Mortality rates from breast cancer (ICD 174) in women aged 50-69:
Age-standardised mortality rates per 100,000: 1984-92
(observed numbers of deaths in parentheses)

		1984	1985	1986	1987	1988	1989	1990	1991	1992
L35	Exeter and North Devon	66.77 (37)	87.51 (50)	80.13 (48)	80.34 (44)	86.35 (52)	93.97 (54)	109.20 (61)	87.42 (49)	101.10 (55)
L36	Plymouth and Torbay	96.24 (63)	105.52 (68)	66.15 (48)	92.08 (62)	93.57 (66)	98.75 (68)	106.56 (74)	109.53 (75)	82.99 (53)
L40	Gloucestershire	100.10 (59)	83.14 (47)	85.52 (53)	91.88 (53)	98.61 (61)	102.68 (62)	90.73 (55)	110.18 (65)	85.91 (52)
L51	Somerset	91.42 (46)	115.39 (55)	108.84 (49)	79.50 (40)	114.54 (54)	119.29 (59)	82.15 (42)	106.05 (51)	84.21 (41)
M02	Herefordshire	118.07 (23)	117.17 (22)	102.60 (21)	71.79 (14)	106.35 (20)	78.68 (17)	114.42 (20)	102.51 (21)	64.75 (13)
M04	Worcester and District	110.35 (29)	135.41 (38)	116.04 (31)	85.87 (24)	79.92 (25)	116.74 (33)	97.97 (28)	119.20 (34)	105.60 (30)
M05	Shropshire	134.60 (55)	103.86 (43)	91.31 (38)	86.18 (39)	89.15 (38)	110.64 (50)	100.07 (46)	101.31 (44)	86.72 (39)
M06	Mid Staffordshire	109.27 (33)	74.84 (24)	100.56 (32)	96.93 (31)	111.02 (38)	82.12 (29)	132.92 (44)	76.45 (26)	82.68 (28)
M07	North Staffordshire	89.32 (49)	112.98 (63)	120.39 (64)	99.12 (53)	85.95 (46)	115.42 (61)	100.25 (54)	92.09 (50)	95.10 (51)
M08	South East Staffordshire	113.61 (27)	121.13 (30)	71.25 (17)	103.43 (26)	111.38 (28)	105.02 (27)	86.98 (22)	89.16 (24)	87.10 (23)
M13	East Birmingham	109.49 (26)	73.97 (20)	104.39 (22)	74.34 (16)	79.71 (18)	86.18 (21)	76.47 (17)	123.23 (26)	90.77 (18)
M14	North Birmingham	98.93 (19)	159.15 (30)	84.18 (16)	121.34 (23)	104.87 (20)	106.78 (19)	84.91 (15)	115.87 (22)	103.93 (19)
M16	West Birmingham	100.37 (23)	92.09 (20)	83.84 (18)	116.91 (24)	75.95 (17)	93.61 (19)	60.98 (13)	108.13 (22)	82.88 (15)
M17	Coventry	116.41 (41)	93.29 (33)	108.43 (37)	64.51 (23)	83.65 (31)	101.39 (35)	84.77 (30)	82.84 (27)	99.40 (31)
M18	Dudley	99.56 (35)	121.91 (43)	93.34 (31)	106.36 (39)	71.76 (27)	96.55 (37)	104.33 (38)	92.56 (33)	102.11 (37)
M19	Sandwell	96.09 (36)	133.60 (48)	117.30 (44)	118.57 (41)	103.24 (36)	77.81 (30)	122.62 (40)	99.06 (32)	82.13 (27)
M20	Solihull	90.94 (20)	95.58 (22)	114.27 (26)	141.73 (31)	147.85 (35)	94.91 (22)	88.19 (21)	81.54 (19)	104.11 (24)
M21	Walsall	85.74 (26)	107.88 (32)	113.00 (34)	115.96 (35)	128.92 (39)	120.86 (36)	131.04 (40)	73.62 (22)	111.03 (34)
M22	Wolverhampton	68.92 (20)	91.17 (27)	91.31 (26)	123.24 (36)	107.96 (32)	112.93 (32)	94.99 (27)	103.82 (30)	100.50 (27)
M25	South Birmingham	84.76 (45)	99.63 (46)	105.56 (49)	95.74 (44)	107.15 (48)	105.91 (51)	87.08 (37)	112.39 (50)	76.66 (32)
M26	North Worcestershire	71.42 (18)	109.03 (28)	83.61 (23)	119.30 (33)	69.96 (20)	82.75 (24)	112.47 (33)	59.04 (17)	101.42 (29)
M28	Warwickshire	117.49 (61)	122.88 (67)	103.96 (56)	91.96 (51)	106.95 (58)	80.42 (45)	76.38 (42)	99.53 (54)	112.18 (59)

HON - B1
Mortality rates from breast cancer (ICD 174) in women aged 50-69:
Age-standardised mortality rates per 100,000: 1984-92
(observed numbers of deaths in parentheses)

		1984	1985	1986	1987	1988	1989	1990	1991	1992
N11	Chester	83.44 (17)	104.44 (20)	112.17 (23)	101.23 (21)	90.22 (19)	104.75 (21)	108.01 (23)	98.90 (21)	96.29 (20)
N12	Crewe	118.83 (34)	110.52 (32)	76.65 (21)	107.26 (30)	124.62 (36)	96.10 (28)	78.10 (23)	87.79 (25)	133.53 (36)
N13	Halton	97.33 (14)	110.92 (17)	59.64 (8)	130.21 (19)	133.91 (19)	125.37 (18)	100.67 (15)	133.49 (20)	67.53 (10)
N14	Macclesfield	126.45 (26)	101.94 (20)	116.38 (24)	96.52 (20)	120.41 (25)	114.73 (24)	120.13 (26)	60.01 (12)	95.68 (20)
N15	Warrington	120.64 (21)	123.26 (22)	97.33 (17)	122.22 (22)	78.34 (16)	106.98 (22)	150.10 (29)	94.24 (19)	95.29 (18)
N21	Liverpool	75.36 (47)	99.18 (59)	87.80 (51)	97.86 (56)	83.95 (49)	77.95 (42)	111.06 (59)	89.11 (48)	76.15 (40)
N31	St Helens and Knowsley	128.87 (48)	86.53 (33)	83.67 (31)	106.66 (41)	97.39 (36)	75.82 (30)	77.33 (29)	86.01 (33)	68.69 (28)
N41	Southport and Formby	71.83 (11)	124.43 (19)	77.24 (11)	95.26 (15)	69.43 (11)	84.69 (13)	85.20 (15)	60.80 (8)	69.81 (10)
N42	South Sefton	130.73 (28)	98.64 (21)	82.32 (17)	83.76 (18)	115.54 (23)	71.11 (16)	86.96 (18)	72.06 (15)	77.51 (16)
N51	Wirral	88.53 (40)	82.75 (36)	103.79 (43)	93.38 (41)	96.93 (40)	72.01 (34)	104.42 (47)	76.88 (31)	64.11 (25)
P01	Lancaster	61.20 (10)	76.79 (13)	97.21 (17)	90.25 (13)	85.92 (13)	96.04 (15)	118.67 (18)	42.37 (7)	55.37 (9)
P02	Blackpool, Wyre and Fylde	80.69 (35)	79.16 (37)	93.89 (40)	64.78 (32)	95.59 (45)	137.24 (62)	101.03 (44)	100.34 (39)	62.26 (26)
P03	Preston	79.59 (11)	112.05 (16)	84.65 (11)	132.41 (19)	98.41 (14)	137.57 (19)	90.39 (13)	110.03 (14)	67.54 (9)
P04	Blackburn, Hyndburn and Ribble Valley	56.71 (17)	79.54 (22)	61.41 (19)	82.06 (24)	110.63 (31)	117.57 (34)	107.00 (30)	74.92 (21)	130.73 (35)
P05	Burnley, Pendle and Rossendale	97.06 (27)	85.79 (23)	120.02 (30)	78.81 (20)	52.53 (14)	69.28 (22)	83.94 (22)	48.72 (12)	89.68 (22)
P06	West Lancashire	62.52 (7)	75.56 (9)	159.03 (17)	112.61 (13)	68.48 (8)	63.71 (7)	128.51 (15)	115.59 (13)	117.01 (14)
P07	Chorley and South Ribble	138.18 (26)	158.92 (30)	147.78 (30)	90.03 (19)	97.31 (20)	114.14 (23)	123.40 (24)	109.05 (23)	67.52 (13)
P08	Bolton	81.10 (23)	109.54 (29)	95.49 (27)	97.90 (29)	104.44 (28)	83.99 (27)	107.63 (29)	63.70 (18)	57.00 (16)
P09	Bury	104.81 (22)	107.31 (19)	119.93 (23)	132.77 (24)	129.23 (24)	87.42 (16)	95.85 (17)	98.67 (19)	77.85 (15)
P10	North Manchester	129.87 (21)	102.88 (18)	42.70 (7)	129.91 (21)	123.02 (19)	89.04 (13)	104.45 (16)	80.47 (12)	105.66 (16)
P11	Central Manchester	90.66 (11)	61.98 (8)	142.38 (16)	112.61 (13)	150.56 (17)	66.73 (8)	55.11 (6)	148.36 (15)	95.06 (9)
P12	South Manchester	76.92 (16)	68.27 (15)	72.29 (15)	85.04 (17)	106.86 (23)	64.93 (13)	106.38 (19)	53.57 (10)	54.77 (10)

HON - B1
Mortality rates from breast cancer (ICD 174) in women aged 50-69:
Age-standardised mortality rates per 100,000: 1984-92
(observed numbers of deaths in parentheses)

		1984	1985	1986	1987	1988	1989	1990	1991	1992
P13	Oldham	123.10	112.61	97.21	129.02	110.21	103.95	75.55	55.16	105.22
		(30)	(28)	(22)	(32)	(28)	(26)	(17)	(13)	(23)
P14	Rochdale	64.82	88.33	92.83	75.43	67.34	82.13	83.73	149.69	72.77
		(15)	(19)	(21)	(17)	(16)	(20)	(19)	(31)	(16)
P15	Salford	118.92	104.65	92.74	83.60	98.95	64.94	106.64	128.39	100.14
		(33)	(29)	(28)	(25)	(27)	(16)	(26)	(32)	(24)
P16	Stockport	91.61	106.06	88.65	109.21	99.15	81.92	72.59	106.05	93.33
		(29)	(34)	(30)	(34)	(35)	(28)	(24)	(34)	(30)
P17	Tameside and Glossop	91.07	96.91	80.03	85.69	85.12	107.87	117.79	108.23	76.76
		(27)	(27)	(22)	(22)	(22)	(28)	(29)	(28)	(20)
P18	Trafford	81.46	63.08	114.26	94.37	136.23	115.32	91.41	101.08	106.43
		(21)	(15)	(28)	(24)	(33)	(28)	(22)	(25)	(24)
P19	Wigan	89.84	95.34	79.53	113.85	97.02	69.62	114.16	71.27	104.74
		(29)	(30)	(28)	(38)	(33)	(25)	(36)	(22)	(33)

HON - B4,B5
Mortality rates from lung cancer (ICD 162) in men and women under 75:
Age-standardised mortality rates per 100,000: 1984-92
(observed numbers of deaths in parentheses)
Males

		1984	1985	1986	1987	1988	1989	1990	1991	1992
	ENGLAND AND WALES	71.79 (17871)	69.96 (17459)	67.38 (16886)	64.89 (16281)	64.63 (16106)	61.27 (15242)	60.13 (15035)	58.53 (14725)	55.90 (14269)
O00	ENGLAND	72.03 (16873)	70.21 (16494)	67.37 (15879)	65.06 (15356)	64.88 (15193)	61.26 (14312)	60.18 (14127)	58.62 (13840)	55.92 (13396)
A00	NORTHERN RHA	92.25 (1440)	91.66 (1430)	86.36 (1356)	87.71 (1382)	86.22 (1356)	82.95 (1304)	86.13 (1372)	75.53 (1209)	75.28 (1221)
B00	YORKSHIRE RHA	72.49 (1296)	79.62 (1413)	70.62 (1263)	67.11 (1205)	72.66 (1292)	64.67 (1147)	65.11 (1157)	62.98 (1134)	59.17 (1079)
C00	TRENT RHA	72.67 (1694)	73.53 (1735)	66.32 (1570)	66.03 (1574)	67.00 (1594)	62.37 (1493)	57.98 (1395)	56.90 (1387)	55.26 (1365)
D00	EAST ANGLIAN RHA	61.79 (630)	55.03 (563)	55.22 (572)	51.75 (545)	51.19 (540)	48.94 (514)	43.18 (464)	45.53 (497)	42.17 (473)
E00	NORTH WEST THAMES RHA	67.51 (1094)	60.29 (980)	61.01 (978)	55.14 (876)	59.02 (923)	56.57 (870)	55.51 (850)	50.23 (768)	48.46 (754)
F00	NORTH EAST THAMES RHA	73.61 (1339)	69.89 (1284)	71.63 (1300)	65.94 (1189)	64.55 (1142)	60.97 (1061)	61.09 (1066)	57.91 (1008)	57.52 (1017)
G00	SOUTH EAST THAMES RHA	69.91 (1304)	67.72 (1259)	64.91 (1213)	64.72 (1196)	62.73 (1149)	59.66 (1072)	57.72 (1041)	54.80 (990)	53.82 (984)
H00	SOUTH WEST THAMES RHA	61.57 (916)	58.36 (869)	57.81 (858)	55.18 (805)	52.34 (755)	47.78 (678)	49.43 (710)	48.08 (687)	43.64 (622)
J00	WESSEX RHA	58.64 (884)	57.30 (873)	54.60 (844)	52.65 (823)	51.45 (800)	53.31 (832)	48.73 (765)	51.09 (811)	47.04 (753)
K00	OXFORD RHA	64.30 (679)	61.26 (651)	54.99 (591)	57.47 (624)	53.86 (583)	53.45 (584)	50.47 (555)	48.88 (543)	46.25 (525)
L00	SOUTH WESTERN RHA	57.22 (969)	51.38 (886)	52.27 (907)	51.22 (893)	49.04 (853)	47.55 (824)	46.19 (803)	45.56 (802)	45.66 (831)
M00	WEST MIDLANDS RHA	78.81 (2014)	74.75 (1924)	71.60 (1861)	69.75 (1814)	67.67 (1752)	64.82 (1688)	65.22 (1709)	64.97 (1713)	61.32 (1636)
N00	MERSEY RHA	83.53 (976)	87.96 (1022)	84.82 (994)	81.23 (948)	78.43 (910)	73.83 (864)	75.09 (876)	79.43 (929)	69.48 (827)
P00	NORTH WESTERN RHA	83.11 (1638)	82.01 (1605)	80.95 (1572)	75.83 (1482)	80.52 (1544)	72.26 (1381)	70.99 (1364)	70.78 (1362)	67.42 (1309)
A01	Hartlepool	83.23 (37)	129.47 (58)	86.45 (38)	84.58 (38)	109.25 (50)	96.52 (45)	84.13 (38)	79.99 (37)	74.16 (35)
A02	North Tees	98.87 (73)	105.58 (81)	87.22 (67)	93.67 (74)	102.01 (82)	88.41 (70)	114.08 (93)	96.03 (80)	86.39 (72)
A03	South Tees	94.86 (128)	103.21 (140)	106.63 (145)	102.21 (142)	89.72 (125)	85.71 (117)	103.85 (147)	55.44 (79)	82.99 (119)
A04	East Cumbria	63.80 (59)	77.98 (73)	65.87 (65)	61.69 (59)	68.86 (66)	59.25 (58)	54.32 (52)	65.31 (62)	59.64 (57)
A05	South Cumbria	88.44 (81)	66.48 (62)	70.80 (67)	61.83 (60)	54.68 (52)	77.59 (73)	55.74 (53)	60.28 (57)	65.89 (64)
A06	West Cumbria	57.31 (41)	68.80 (47)	58.36 (41)	82.11 (58)	72.20 (49)	65.60 (46)	66.66 (48)	62.25 (46)	54.07 (40)

HON - B4,B5
Mortality rates from lung cancer (ICD 162) in men and women under 75:
Age-standardised mortality rates per 100,000: 1984-92
(observed numbers of deaths in parentheses)
Males

		1984	1985	1986	1987	1988	1989	1990	1991	1992
A11	Northumberland	81.43 (132)	66.52 (107)	70.07 (113)	75.94 (123)	77.76 (125)	67.96 (111)	67.45 (110)	62.03 (105)	59.39 (102)
A12	Gateshead	116.22 (126)	123.93 (134)	91.81 (100)	112.52 (122)	97.80 (106)	99.29 (109)	91.70 (100)	98.99 (107)	96.38 (109)
A13	Newcastle	91.50 (133)	93.71 (133)	106.07 (153)	108.96 (151)	105.58 (142)	103.96 (139)	90.46 (120)	105.00 (142)	86.32 (116)
A14	North Tyneside	89.93 (95)	109.48 (115)	91.02 (96)	99.99 (107)	82.89 (89)	83.76 (87)	104.93 (111)	69.88 (76)	69.95 (74)
A15	South Tyneside	128.97 (110)	125.76 (108)	127.16 (110)	108.34 (93)	120.23 (105)	119.00 (105)	103.80 (93)	99.12 (86)	104.47 (93)
A16	Sunderland	111.65 (156)	103.33 (144)	84.86 (119)	90.06 (125)	100.82 (142)	85.45 (120)	105.48 (151)	81.02 (114)	88.66 (128)
A30	North Durham	91.12 (146)	79.07 (128)	83.07 (135)	71.36 (118)	71.77 (116)	73.78 (119)	86.60 (145)	62.00 (103)	67.67 (115)
A31	South Durham	83.64 (123)	68.21 (100)	73.78 (107)	77.05 (112)	72.60 (107)	71.88 (105)	74.41 (111)	76.13 (115)	64.06 (97)
B11	East Riding	81.71 (209)	83.47 (211)	79.99 (205)	73.94 (194)	77.14 (198)	75.93 (196)	74.48 (190)	60.42 (160)	61.66 (167)
B16	Grimsby and Scunthorpe	71.98 (126)	94.97 (165)	67.97 (121)	69.65 (126)	68.75 (124)	62.14 (111)	74.51 (138)	61.22 (113)	52.53 (97)
B21	North Yorkshire	55.32 (202)	64.94 (233)	53.67 (196)	51.35 (191)	58.36 (214)	45.70 (170)	52.13 (193)	47.85 (182)	44.82 (174)
B31	Bradford	67.66 (143)	68.61 (146)	77.25 (165)	77.63 (163)	75.61 (160)	73.04 (153)	71.68 (149)	77.94 (165)	68.05 (145)
B51	West Yorkshire	70.98 (198)	78.00 (213)	67.94 (186)	65.49 (179)	76.48 (206)	63.77 (171)	54.00 (145)	67.94 (181)	61.53 (166)
B61	Leeds	84.98 (301)	89.34 (318)	73.92 (260)	69.86 (244)	79.95 (271)	71.69 (241)	70.65 (237)	65.51 (225)	62.83 (214)
B71	Wakefield	77.63 (117)	84.73 (127)	85.63 (130)	70.95 (108)	76.88 (119)	68.76 (105)	67.51 (105)	70.35 (108)	73.93 (116)
C01	North Derbyshire	65.30 (127)	67.02 (126)	56.39 (109)	58.27 (116)	62.97 (126)	51.89 (104)	54.28 (108)	57.79 (118)	56.82 (115)
C02	Southern Derbyshire	69.18 (187)	70.91 (196)	69.83 (191)	71.16 (196)	68.08 (189)	63.29 (174)	59.58 (166)	53.70 (151)	51.40 (144)
C03	Leicestershire	62.65 (251)	58.11 (236)	63.07 (260)	52.45 (217)	52.55 (217)	50.96 (211)	47.69 (200)	42.59 (181)	39.96 (174)
C04	North Lincolnshire	63.93 (91)	76.62 (109)	56.45 (84)	60.08 (91)	65.29 (100)	54.42 (85)	51.38 (84)	55.96 (89)	50.65 (84)
C05	South Lincolnshire	64.28 (107)	67.70 (111)	53.39 (90)	52.67 (93)	59.99 (105)	63.89 (110)	45.39 (79)	44.81 (80)	40.34 (78)
C08	Nottingham	76.28 (230)	75.68 (233)	69.70 (211)	67.96 (206)	77.52 (236)	71.35 (218)	56.31 (173)	58.22 (183)	53.75 (169)
C09	Barnsley	87.51 (101)	83.35 (97)	73.97 (85)	74.15 (87)	68.37 (76)	78.60 (91)	67.34 (76)	76.44 (90)	69.67 (84)

HON - B4,B5
Mortality rates from lung cancer (ICD 162) in men and women under 75:
Age-standardised mortality rates per 100,000: 1984-92
(observed numbers of deaths in parentheses)
Males

		1984	1985	1986	1987	1988	1989	1990	1991	1992
C10	Doncaster	76.40	98.14	75.21	84.73	69.02	65.36	61.26	57.51	64.80
		(108)	(143)	(110)	(125)	(101)	(95)	(92)	(88)	(99)
C11	Rotherham	80.59	58.70	74.38	72.04	77.89	82.10	67.73	65.50	69.73
		(96)	(71)	(91)	(88)	(95)	(102)	(83)	(83)	(88)
C12	Sheffield	85.88	94.67	74.79	79.60	79.34	69.46	70.99	67.33	67.90
		(247)	(274)	(218)	(221)	(219)	(194)	(195)	(183)	(185)
C14	North Nottinghamshire	77.78	70.56	61.99	66.96	64.68	52.47	68.61	68.99	69.36
		(149)	(139)	(121)	(134)	(130)	(109)	(139)	(141)	(145)
D01	Cambridge	49.84	56.87	52.78	49.71	44.08	51.49	42.37	41.00	40.68
		(63)	(70)	(67)	(62)	(55)	(65)	(56)	(54)	(55)
D05	North West Anglia	67.62	64.65	55.32	55.00	52.67	52.35	51.55	46.27	43.72
		(132)	(129)	(112)	(113)	(112)	(112)	(108)	(101)	(94)
D06	Norwich	54.67	46.97	56.33	45.31	47.15	44.30	38.36	46.27	38.53
		(143)	(123)	(150)	(127)	(130)	(119)	(105)	(128)	(115)
D07	Great Yarmouth and Waveney	75.79	64.44	55.96	55.16	68.58	55.45	47.26	48.51	45.51
		(90)	(66)	(64)	(63)	(79)	(65)	(56)	(58)	(57)
D09	Huntingdon	68.01	77.28	61.24	53.02	64.36	39.44	60.23	64.18	57.80
		(32)	(39)	(29)	(27)	(33)	(20)	(31)	(35)	(32)
D11	Suffolk	62.55	48.27	53.79	54.74	47.10	48.69	37.26	42.17	40.83
		(170)	(136)	(150)	(153)	(131)	(133)	(108)	(121)	(120)
E01	North Bedfordshire	73.51	51.10	59.38	52.50	55.92	52.31	68.38	43.39	64.52
		(77)	(56)	(65)	(58)	(61)	(57)	(75)	(49)	(75)
E02	South Bedfordshire	68.78	62.93	65.28	58.84	55.03	67.37	60.97	61.46	50.32
		(80)	(73)	(76)	(69)	(64)	(78)	(71)	(72)	(61)
E05	North West Hertfordshire	52.03	69.81	48.59	52.25	67.45	49.91	56.00	40.58	42.01
		(64)	(88)	(61)	(66)	(84)	(61)	(70)	(51)	(54)
E06	South West Hertfordshire	64.26	48.64	68.88	36.62	56.07	58.04	57.66	48.98	49.56
		(81)	(62)	(88)	(48)	(69)	(73)	(69)	(59)	(61)
E07	Barnet	48.23	60.29	44.11	53.81	52.39	43.86	59.01	50.29	26.96
		(72)	(88)	(63)	(78)	(73)	(59)	(80)	(65)	(37)
E09	Hillingdon	71.15	68.05	50.94	67.02	50.70	62.72	48.11	55.62	56.24
		(82)	(82)	(57)	(76)	(57)	(70)	(53)	(59)	(59)
E18	East and North Hertfordshire	73.80	52.36	58.47	56.34	57.50	54.43	45.22	45.99	44.27
		(162)	(118)	(132)	(128)	(130)	(122)	(103)	(106)	(105)
E19	Brent and Harrow	56.57	47.07	58.95	41.47	56.80	53.08	49.85	41.79	46.95
		(122)	(98)	(122)	(84)	(112)	(102)	(93)	(77)	(89)
E20	Ealing, Hammersmith and Hounslow	76.10	71.03	68.05	69.02	70.71	61.25	57.49	55.36	56.23
		(226)	(210)	(196)	(193)	(194)	(161)	(151)	(144)	(146)
E21	Kensington, Chelsea and Westminster	84.43	71.97	80.59	53.26	56.72	62.74	60.45	60.17	46.61
		(128)	(105)	(118)	(76)	(79)	(87)	(85)	(86)	(67)
F31	North Essex	62.52	56.02	60.62	53.87	52.75	44.10	47.08	51.81	45.14
		(262)	(238)	(257)	(235)	(227)	(185)	(206)	(223)	(202)
F32	South Essex	66.37	73.50	64.35	60.16	59.37	54.50	54.13	48.98	59.33
		(217)	(247)	(216)	(199)	(198)	(183)	(183)	(167)	(204)

HON - B4,B5
Mortality rates from lung cancer (ICD 162) in men and women under 75:
Age-standardised mortality rates per 100,000: 1984-92
(observed numbers of deaths in parentheses)
Males

		1984	1985	1986	1987	1988	1989	1990	1991	1992
F33	Barking and Havering	83.19 (172)	69.54 (145)	78.93 (166)	83.08 (172)	67.53 (139)	72.39 (146)	56.02 (110)	61.28 (124)	60.11 (122)
F34	Redbridge and Waltham Forest	75.66 (169)	66.22 (153)	68.08 (148)	64.70 (140)	54.63 (115)	62.50 (127)	62.15 (123)	48.23 (94)	49.56 (98)
F35	East London and the City	93.92 (245)	89.21 (234)	97.56 (250)	82.89 (209)	87.91 (213)	77.03 (183)	84.03 (198)	89.20 (204)	81.35 (190)
F36	New River District	67.69 (147)	55.40 (120)	65.20 (139)	58.49 (121)	57.20 (115)	63.60 (123)	59.65 (115)	52.12 (103)	45.72 (90)
F37	Camden and Islington	76.71 (127)	92.37 (147)	78.60 (124)	72.07 (113)	90.53 (135)	77.09 (114)	88.78 (131)	63.61 (93)	75.48 (111)
G04	South East Kent	67.13 (95)	58.00 (83)	58.29 (87)	64.54 (96)	62.68 (92)	58.75 (81)	51.71 (78)	40.81 (59)	58.89 (87)
G05	Canterbury and Thanet	76.90 (132)	66.82 (111)	63.64 (102)	60.09 (103)	68.46 (114)	59.89 (101)	58.72 (100)	60.18 (98)	38.55 (72)
G06	Dartford and Gravesham	65.12 (67)	68.88 (71)	58.79 (62)	60.90 (64)	70.34 (73)	52.52 (54)	60.16 (63)	61.67 (65)	56.10 (61)
G07	Maidstone	52.69 (46)	72.44 (65)	56.42 (51)	52.08 (47)	42.70 (39)	40.06 (37)	33.05 (30)	59.17 (55)	45.50 (43)
G08	Medway	62.47 (90)	69.26 (100)	64.88 (93)	62.80 (92)	62.63 (91)	57.82 (83)	65.00 (95)	56.79 (82)	47.28 (69)
G09	Tunbridge Wells	58.65 (58)	47.24 (48)	60.39 (61)	45.45 (45)	48.02 (49)	43.95 (44)	36.05 (37)	55.29 (57)	42.20 (44)
G10	Bexley	67.93 (71)	68.75 (72)	63.31 (68)	63.38 (66)	58.17 (60)	55.67 (57)	59.61 (61)	55.82 (58)	59.52 (62)
G11	Greenwich	92.32 (97)	99.41 (103)	79.58 (85)	93.69 (90)	74.83 (74)	71.17 (64)	71.38 (67)	70.13 (66)	73.15 (70)
G12	Bromley	50.73 (80)	51.47 (81)	56.48 (89)	67.12 (104)	46.10 (72)	65.67 (99)	49.11 (74)	46.76 (70)	53.18 (82)
G21	East Sussex	54.43 (226)	63.29 (251)	58.09 (230)	54.23 (225)	57.51 (225)	51.62 (208)	52.46 (206)	40.54 (164)	45.95 (180)
G26	South East London	99.05 (342)	79.97 (274)	84.67 (285)	82.29 (264)	82.22 (260)	80.38 (244)	77.29 (230)	73.21 (216)	72.22 (214)
H04	Mid Surrey	51.54 (48)	39.24 (37)	43.45 (43)	45.81 (44)	40.62 (37)	42.04 (38)	48.36 (44)	51.79 (48)	35.01 (33)
H05	East Surrey	57.48 (57)	62.63 (61)	44.32 (43)	52.82 (51)	51.60 (50)	58.51 (55)	38.21 (38)	36.01 (34)	45.24 (41)
H06	Chichester	42.13 (49)	49.12 (56)	56.75 (63)	50.62 (58)	44.11 (46)	43.76 (49)	44.46 (50)	42.34 (44)	51.28 (57)
H07	Mid Downs	55.63 (70)	53.56 (68)	63.25 (81)	55.24 (71)	61.71 (78)	47.89 (61)	52.45 (70)	53.19 (72)	36.02 (48)
H08	Worthing	53.78 (75)	58.32 (83)	60.03 (85)	52.69 (75)	52.07 (77)	31.79 (44)	33.10 (48)	42.03 (57)	43.68 (59)
H09	Croydon	84.80 (123)	60.53 (87)	51.07 (73)	68.47 (95)	54.66 (75)	51.57 (70)	51.67 (70)	48.29 (66)	46.63 (63)

101

HON - B4,B5

Mortality rates from lung cancer (ICD 162) in men and women under 75:
Age-standardised mortality rates per 100,000: 1984-92
(observed numbers of deaths in parentheses)
Males

		1984	1985	1986	1987	1988	1989	1990	1991	1992
H12	Wandsworth	98.69 (85)	89.05 (76)	96.54 (78)	76.35 (61)	60.12 (46)	65.31 (47)	92.08 (65)	71.94 (50)	70.22 (49)
H13	Merton and Sutton	69.76 (116)	62.76 (105)	63.81 (106)	63.02 (101)	62.41 (97)	57.05 (87)	60.75 (93)	66.20 (100)	43.87 (68)
H14	North West Surrey	55.04 (100)	56.24 (104)	56.62 (105)	51.77 (95)	50.78 (94)	46.90 (85)	43.58 (80)	43.45 (80)	45.13 (85)
H15	South West Surrey	54.01 (62)	58.53 (67)	51.52 (60)	35.71 (41)	44.22 (51)	37.00 (44)	47.41 (56)	39.66 (47)	29.06 (34)
H16	Kingston and Richmond	60.64 (131)	58.18 (125)	57.77 (121)	55.55 (113)	52.24 (104)	51.27 (98)	49.21 (96)	46.61 (89)	45.26 (85)
J10	Dorset	48.43 (174)	53.99 (199)	48.30 (183)	49.76 (197)	47.63 (188)	39.37 (153)	40.45 (159)	46.26 (180)	44.01 (170)
J21	Portsmouth and South East Hampshire	68.19 (166)	73.46 (179)	60.97 (151)	59.48 (150)	52.36 (130)	64.77 (163)	60.39 (155)	56.73 (144)	51.78 (133)
J22	Southampton and South West Hampshire	63.89 (138)	61.63 (137)	69.82 (155)	58.81 (132)	61.04 (133)	66.74 (146)	48.84 (107)	61.01 (133)	50.52 (115)
J23	Winchester	57.86 (56)	46.75 (46)	58.23 (58)	48.28 (48)	48.27 (48)	41.05 (41)	51.92 (53)	44.67 (46)	40.48 (42)
J24	Basingstoke and North Hampshire	67.98 (91)	58.49 (81)	46.87 (65)	62.40 (87)	51.97 (74)	52.41 (75)	49.63 (72)	58.79 (87)	55.33 (84)
J31	Salisbury	46.00 (31)	50.12 (33)	59.66 (41)	45.40 (30)	42.11 (28)	42.78 (29)	43.41 (28)	41.16 (28)	39.74 (27)
J32	Swindon	67.59 (68)	63.13 (64)	50.66 (53)	55.87 (58)	71.09 (75)	64.64 (69)	53.48 (58)	68.92 (76)	46.17 (53)
J33	Bath	58.58 (119)	44.63 (89)	46.35 (94)	42.38 (89)	42.76 (89)	55.36 (112)	44.28 (90)	37.34 (79)	43.42 (93)
J41	Isle of Wight	57.35 (41)	56.95 (45)	55.97 (44)	45.04 (32)	45.37 (35)	56.92 (44)	53.97 (43)	45.63 (38)	46.70 (36)
K11	East Berkshire	72.17 (117)	59.25 (95)	57.36 (92)	60.47 (99)	51.03 (82)	57.36 (93)	46.94 (76)	53.08 (87)	53.40 (89)
K12	West Berkshire	72.45 (128)	52.11 (95)	49.80 (92)	56.88 (105)	46.18 (85)	43.49 (80)	37.14 (69)	38.58 (73)	45.21 (87)
K24	Buckinghamshire	65.69 (152)	63.41 (147)	50.58 (120)	61.86 (150)	51.13 (123)	55.90 (137)	52.58 (131)	46.93 (119)	42.63 (110)
K31	Kettering	63.48 (78)	77.21 (95)	67.04 (84)	59.26 (74)	64.68 (80)	65.59 (83)	64.07 (82)	57.62 (74)	45.83 (59)
K32	Northampton	62.08 (83)	67.22 (90)	61.54 (86)	56.24 (77)	65.95 (92)	49.86 (70)	58.94 (85)	52.06 (75)	45.92 (67)
K41	Oxfordshire	53.82 (121)	56.17 (129)	50.64 (117)	51.94 (119)	52.05 (121)	51.93 (121)	47.76 (112)	48.93 (115)	47.21 (113)
L10	Bristol and District	62.84 (252)	55.95 (229)	56.45 (231)	52.86 (217)	55.77 (229)	45.62 (184)	51.02 (205)	56.28 (230)	50.21 (210)
L21	Cornwall and Isles of Scilly	53.83 (141)	53.01 (137)	45.63 (123)	46.27 (124)	48.79 (130)	57.14 (153)	47.95 (131)	43.24 (117)	39.03 (111)

102

HON - B4,B5
Mortality rates from lung cancer (ICD 162) in men and women under 75:
Age-standardised mortality rates per 100,000: 1984-92
(observed numbers of deaths in parentheses)
Males

		1984	1985	1986	1987	1988	1989	1990	1991	1992
L35	Exeter and North Devon	53.43	45.93	43.21	45.34	35.22	44.97	40.05	40.35	39.90
		(131)	(120)	(111)	(114)	(93)	(114)	(102)	(104)	(109)
L36	Plymouth and Torbay	59.75	48.99	55.15	53.73	52.44	47.87	51.49	45.67	50.45
		(182)	(152)	(166)	(169)	(159)	(149)	(157)	(146)	(159)
L40	Gloucestershire	58.27	49.77	59.98	53.85	51.46	49.07	43.57	40.36	46.29
		(154)	(133)	(163)	(146)	(140)	(134)	(121)	(109)	(135)
L51	Somerset	50.56	52.17	49.53	54.06	45.70	40.61	38.47	41.29	45.44
		(109)	(115)	(113)	(123)	(102)	(90)	(87)	(96)	(107)
M02	Herefordshire	55.15	54.85	34.98	50.10	51.26	59.13	37.37	41.99	47.34
		(46)	(48)	(31)	(47)	(44)	(54)	(35)	(41)	(44)
M04	Worcester and District	56.81	56.60	58.33	52.94	52.15	46.11	43.55	43.08	36.14
		(68)	(68)	(71)	(67)	(67)	(60)	(57)	(56)	(51)
M05	Shropshire	72.38	72.45	54.12	62.18	67.88	49.57	56.95	58.32	52.22
		(135)	(136)	(104)	(122)	(134)	(102)	(116)	(121)	(111)
M06	Mid Staffordshire	73.67	66.41	59.50	65.98	64.65	62.44	59.73	65.61	53.26
		(101)	(93)	(84)	(94)	(94)	(91)	(88)	(100)	(83)
M07	North Staffordshire	100.99	84.81	76.06	80.24	67.74	66.32	78.21	82.72	79.61
		(246)	(207)	(188)	(196)	(166)	(164)	(192)	(205)	(195)
M08	South East Staffordshire	73.76	92.42	84.95	75.79	62.38	75.82	67.94	47.90	47.59
		(79)	(100)	(93)	(85)	(71)	(87)	(80)	(58)	(58)
M13	East Birmingham	90.67	93.29	77.54	74.35	78.61	73.37	88.19	79.92	63.34
		(100)	(99)	(87)	(79)	(78)	(77)	(85)	(78)	(63)
M14	North Birmingham	63.18	81.14	77.07	53.60	76.85	68.73	67.15	62.11	53.85
		(51)	(67)	(64)	(44)	(63)	(57)	(55)	(51)	(46)
M16	West Birmingham	99.52	89.46	102.14	70.51	66.05	73.73	60.31	82.39	76.87
		(99)	(89)	(101)	(66)	(63)	(70)	(56)	(75)	(69)
M17	Coventry	90.29	77.57	63.58	62.66	82.03	66.68	78.96	72.56	62.96
		(145)	(125)	(105)	(99)	(128)	(100)	(124)	(107)	(96)
M18	Dudley	72.77	78.23	76.79	81.56	70.39	75.70	65.78	61.18	45.19
		(108)	(117)	(116)	(125)	(108)	(118)	(103)	(98)	(73)
M19	Sandwell	96.21	89.62	96.26	93.05	99.63	81.53	82.22	79.81	83.91
		(155)	(143)	(157)	(147)	(156)	(126)	(125)	(125)	(130)
M20	Solihull	58.71	58.51	61.59	52.26	43.37	51.53	53.74	55.52	44.68
		(55)	(56)	(59)	(51)	(43)	(51)	(54)	(56)	(46)
M21	Walsall	93.41	87.55	83.53	76.72	75.99	81.84	71.96	69.35	69.25
		(119)	(112)	(108)	(100)	(98)	(106)	(94)	(91)	(93)
M22	Wolverhampton	72.00	71.23	87.79	87.20	77.24	60.97	65.29	79.56	77.92
		(95)	(93)	(116)	(113)	(100)	(80)	(86)	(105)	(102)
M25	South Birmingham	79.61	72.84	71.72	74.07	65.87	71.47	71.30	67.80	74.72
		(168)	(153)	(151)	(157)	(133)	(144)	(143)	(134)	(152)
M26	North Worcestershire	67.57	58.32	50.22	63.07	54.33	49.70	54.19	70.92	56.84
		(79)	(70)	(60)	(78)	(67)	(62)	(69)	(93)	(74)
M28	Warwickshire	70.60	61.84	69.36	58.87	56.97	57.29	58.71	47.48	59.82
		(165)	(148)	(166)	(144)	(139)	(139)	(147)	(119)	(150)

103

HON - B4,B5
Mortality rates from lung cancer (ICD 162) in men and women under 75:
Age-standardised mortality rates per 100,000: 1984-92
(observed numbers of deaths in parentheses)
Males

		1984	1985	1986	1987	1988	1989	1990	1991	1992
N11	Chester	69.71 (60)	96.96 (82)	75.04 (65)	56.62 (50)	60.27 (54)	56.46 (50)	73.65 (65)	55.58 (50)	45.86 (42)
N12	Crewe	73.86 (91)	63.56 (77)	61.76 (77)	55.16 (68)	55.91 (69)	69.76 (89)	63.65 (81)	56.66 (74)	48.23 (65)
N13	Halton	86.55 (53)	61.97 (38)	88.56 (55)	76.25 (48)	77.93 (49)	77.00 (49)	77.58 (49)	84.35 (54)	71.08 (47)
N14	Macclesfield	51.26 (47)	61.83 (55)	72.94 (65)	50.16 (45)	42.85 (38)	48.91 (45)	45.53 (42)	75.08 (69)	40.99 (40)
N15	Warrington	80.33 (66)	73.67 (60)	65.35 (55)	70.05 (59)	66.14 (56)	66.10 (57)	71.71 (60)	54.59 (46)	68.86 (60)
N21	Liverpool	103.06 (251)	120.92 (291)	110.36 (263)	108.15 (256)	110.48 (251)	89.41 (204)	85.99 (194)	100.94 (226)	103.43 (232)
N31	St Helens and Knowsley	86.11 (136)	86.52 (135)	101.05 (157)	100.60 (157)	84.23 (132)	80.00 (125)	76.44 (122)	92.54 (147)	73.10 (118)
N41	Southport and Formby	73.83 (45)	62.16 (38)	47.07 (30)	55.85 (35)	69.25 (45)	60.71 (41)	66.54 (43)	61.59 (41)	47.65 (31)
N42	South Sefton	82.01 (70)	107.82 (94)	103.09 (89)	99.60 (84)	90.05 (76)	103.18 (88)	80.64 (70)	97.00 (84)	64.59 (57)
N51	Wirral	87.39 (157)	85.47 (152)	76.50 (138)	81.31 (146)	78.74 (140)	65.57 (116)	84.69 (150)	79.01 (138)	78.52 (135)
P01	Lancaster	61.86 (42)	64.64 (44)	59.52 (41)	52.49 (38)	61.05 (41)	75.63 (50)	63.62 (45)	45.98 (33)	63.26 (44)
P02	Blackpool, Wyre and Fylde	66.99 (133)	66.50 (130)	66.84 (132)	65.58 (127)	75.75 (144)	60.23 (116)	64.50 (125)	52.93 (104)	58.18 (114)
P03	Preston	76.99 (50)	72.04 (45)	68.13 (44)	64.00 (41)	74.55 (45)	61.21 (36)	73.72 (44)	76.23 (46)	69.17 (41)
P04	Blackburn, Hyndburn and Ribble Valley	70.25 (95)	81.94 (110)	70.18 (92)	58.01 (76)	77.27 (98)	62.00 (80)	68.60 (87)	60.35 (76)	58.73 (77)
P05	Burnley, Pendle and Rossendale	75.87 (86)	84.51 (94)	73.23 (82)	70.81 (78)	88.96 (98)	61.55 (69)	60.43 (68)	64.82 (71)	53.19 (61)
P06	West Lancashire	95.73 (45)	53.55 (25)	66.25 (31)	71.62 (35)	85.64 (41)	53.46 (26)	43.94 (22)	61.02 (31)	53.71 (28)
P07	Chorley and South Ribble	78.28 (67)	71.07 (63)	74.19 (64)	75.47 (68)	60.26 (54)	51.30 (46)	43.30 (40)	65.59 (61)	53.12 (50)
P08	Bolton	80.64 (99)	62.03 (76)	80.07 (98)	82.01 (100)	64.78 (80)	58.03 (71)	62.10 (76)	73.86 (90)	59.62 (75)
P09	Bury	65.54 (56)	72.02 (59)	70.87 (58)	64.65 (53)	72.22 (58)	74.64 (61)	68.25 (56)	45.92 (37)	40.42 (34)
P10	North Manchester	131.16 (98)	111.28 (82)	127.58 (95)	116.42 (83)	118.93 (80)	126.42 (86)	108.09 (71)	120.34 (78)	96.96 (63)
P11	Central Manchester	97.24 (56)	134.40 (71)	105.10 (56)	121.02 (63)	115.09 (58)	101.62 (51)	118.21 (57)	129.91 (61)	102.53 (46)
P12	South Manchester	101.28 (89)	96.63 (84)	89.09 (74)	74.92 (63)	107.75 (89)	111.32 (94)	73.33 (57)	86.51 (67)	91.41 (72)

HON - B4,B5
Mortality rates from lung cancer (ICD 162) in men and women under 75:
Age-standardised mortality rates per 100,000: 1984-92
(observed numbers of deaths in parentheses)
Males

		1984	1985	1986	1987	1988	1989	1990	1991	1992
P13	Oldham	83.66	86.13	92.61	81.05	62.08	72.32	76.25	75.00	66.61
		(88)	(92)	(96)	(83)	(63)	(71)	(77)	(75)	(67)
P14	Rochdale	86.42	87.87	66.36	76.25	72.68	72.42	64.54	79.93	74.73
		(84)	(85)	(63)	(75)	(70)	(68)	(63)	(79)	(73)
P15	Salford	109.84	105.57	112.70	107.79	114.20	93.93	103.61	84.76	113.56
		(134)	(131)	(134)	(130)	(134)	(107)	(120)	(98)	(129)
P16	Stockport	82.56	73.34	73.82	73.72	61.00	59.48	51.93	69.80	66.77
		(116)	(102)	(103)	(104)	(84)	(83)	(73)	(100)	(95)
P17	Tameside and Glossop	79.15	84.93	101.03	77.25	91.17	92.71	89.84	68.46	76.11
		(96)	(100)	(119)	(91)	(108)	(106)	(104)	(81)	(89)
P18	Trafford	74.22	82.05	83.93	67.40	64.67	67.40	66.78	71.23	56.18
		(80)	(89)	(88)	(73)	(69)	(70)	(69)	(75)	(61)
P19	Wigan	90.35	87.59	72.97	71.67	92.43	64.58	77.60	70.03	61.80
		(124)	(123)	(102)	(101)	(130)	(90)	(110)	(99)	(90)

HON - B4,B5
Mortality rates from lung cancer (ICD 162) in men and women under 75:
Age-standardised mortality rates per 100,000: 1984-92
(observed numbers of deaths in parentheses)

105

HON - B4,B5 (continued)
Mortality rates from lung cancer (ICD 162) in men and women under 75:
Age-standardised mortality rates per 100,000: 1984-92
(observed numbers of deaths in parentheses)
Females

		1984	1985	1986	1987	1988	1989	1990	1991	1992
	ENGLAND AND WALES	23.28 (6603)	23.11 (6621)	23.44 (6700)	23.53 (6712)	24.58 (6965)	24.14 (6847)	23.82 (6754)	24.06 (6846)	23.48 (6733)
O00	ENGLAND	23.55 (6288)	23.20 (6246)	23.64 (6357)	23.63 (6338)	24.73 (6589)	24.25 (6445)	23.79 (6340)	24.11 (6441)	23.48 (6317)
A00	NORTHERN RHA	32.42 (573)	31.24 (549)	32.74 (592)	36.68 (651)	38.34 (689)	37.29 (669)	35.62 (642)	37.89 (687)	34.30 (621)
B00	YORKSHIRE RHA	24.79 (509)	23.46 (478)	27.12 (549)	25.51 (526)	27.37 (552)	26.80 (542)	26.97 (548)	26.75 (549)	28.34 (577)
C00	TRENT RHA	22.29 (576)	23.02 (596)	22.37 (582)	23.67 (621)	23.37 (617)	22.68 (590)	22.49 (592)	24.07 (637)	22.93 (614)
D00	EAST ANGLIAN RHA	16.17 (187)	18.55 (216)	16.03 (186)	17.23 (201)	18.74 (218)	18.55 (218)	18.34 (212)	18.10 (216)	14.88 (183)
E00	NORTH WEST THAMES RHA	23.03 (424)	22.40 (414)	24.00 (439)	22.00 (401)	24.01 (421)	21.57 (377)	22.97 (393)	23.35 (393)	21.59 (377)
F00	NORTH EAST THAMES RHA	25.15 (514)	25.03 (511)	21.52 (445)	24.12 (490)	25.50 (505)	24.80 (483)	24.20 (475)	22.98 (451)	23.19 (461)
G00	SOUTH EAST THAMES RHA	22.51 (497)	23.38 (527)	24.88 (538)	23.07 (497)	23.10 (494)	25.00 (529)	22.43 (472)	24.28 (515)	21.71 (457)
H00	SOUTH WEST THAMES RHA	21.76 (388)	20.09 (357)	20.70 (369)	19.79 (347)	21.61 (370)	19.32 (330)	20.13 (336)	18.91 (320)	18.58 (309)
J00	WESSEX RHA	18.36 (321)	19.30 (341)	20.65 (361)	18.42 (329)	19.21 (340)	18.94 (348)	18.45 (341)	16.88 (310)	17.27 (321)
K00	OXFORD RHA	22.30 (257)	24.11 (289)	20.35 (245)	21.79 (258)	21.89 (265)	19.23 (229)	17.75 (219)	20.52 (245)	19.23 (235)
L00	SOUTH WESTERN RHA	18.10 (359)	16.38 (335)	17.49 (351)	17.11 (343)	16.65 (337)	17.71 (362)	17.34 (346)	17.65 (362)	18.13 (368)
M00	WEST MIDLANDS RHA	21.22 (599)	20.82 (601)	21.64 (625)	20.20 (588)	21.92 (633)	22.85 (659)	21.01 (618)	22.03 (647)	22.84 (681)
N00	MERSEY RHA	30.23 (407)	28.79 (402)	32.01 (433)	33.70 (457)	34.25 (468)	31.63 (435)	33.47 (456)	32.16 (437)	31.57 (436)
P00	NORTH WESTERN RHA	29.62 (677)	27.97 (630)	27.70 (642)	27.69 (629)	30.47 (680)	30.60 (674)	30.87 (690)	29.92 (672)	30.58 (677)
A01	Hartlepool	40.24 (19)	37.75 (19)	46.03 (24)	34.93 (17)	35.31 (17)	47.22 (26)	70.62 (37)	46.40 (23)	61.32 (33)
A02	North Tees	34.33 (29)	45.10 (37)	33.07 (29)	33.59 (30)	51.90 (47)	39.32 (37)	22.12 (20)	40.77 (39)	22.70 (22)
A03	South Tees	43.50 (65)	32.54 (50)	39.70 (62)	35.04 (54)	37.47 (57)	45.67 (70)	41.50 (65)	44.45 (70)	37.68 (60)
A04	East Cumbria	29.63 (29)	34.76 (33)	19.64 (20)	30.93 (30)	35.45 (39)	31.26 (34)	21.77 (25)	25.21 (28)	18.13 (22)
A05	South Cumbria	11.49 (12)	17.53 (19)	19.35 (21)	23.89 (27)	24.97 (29)	18.99 (21)	15.10 (17)	26.54 (29)	18.51 (20)
A06	West Cumbria	27.98 (21)	34.18 (27)	27.35 (21)	25.40 (21)	28.30 (22)	29.35 (24)	16.66 (14)	31.01 (26)	35.30 (28)

HON - B4,B5 (continued)
Mortality rates from lung cancer (ICD 162) in men and women under 75:
Age-standardised mortality rates per 100,000: 1984-92
(observed numbers of deaths in parentheses)
Females

		1984	1985	1986	1987	1988	1989	1990	1991	1992
A11	Northumberland	29.71 (53)	30.10 (54)	34.76 (63)	36.75 (64)	30.84 (57)	26.98 (49)	31.40 (57)	33.75 (63)	27.55 (48)
A12	Gateshead	49.68 (61)	35.84 (46)	24.01 (33)	38.98 (49)	44.08 (55)	40.26 (50)	41.57 (52)	45.84 (53)	46.50 (55)
A13	Newcastle	37.49 (67)	36.14 (60)	48.21 (83)	49.00 (78)	51.44 (83)	50.61 (78)	47.65 (76)	57.73 (92)	37.77 (59)
A14	North Tyneside	34.51 (44)	26.08 (34)	35.12 (43)	37.55 (48)	37.37 (48)	44.30 (55)	42.20 (52)	40.91 (52)	28.06 (37)
A15	South Tyneside	32.97 (33)	33.87 (33)	48.23 (48)	41.59 (42)	42.72 (43)	35.85 (36)	47.47 (45)	41.61 (41)	44.72 (44)
A16	Sunderland	35.84 (56)	28.45 (45)	26.50 (43)	48.92 (79)	43.11 (71)	34.46 (56)	42.49 (68)	32.29 (54)	44.81 (72)
A30	North Durham	26.42 (50)	34.11 (59)	27.75 (51)	31.88 (58)	35.30 (63)	41.47 (74)	35.07 (64)	34.46 (64)	32.84 (59)
A31	South Durham	20.99 (34)	19.77 (33)	31.24 (51)	34.05 (54)	34.92 (58)	35.70 (59)	29.47 (50)	31.80 (53)	34.17 (62)
B11	East Riding	28.00 (89)	23.89 (72)	23.97 (71)	24.19 (74)	30.53 (90)	26.78 (79)	31.95 (98)	32.04 (93)	33.02 (99)
B16	Grimsby and Scunthorpe	25.57 (49)	25.67 (49)	23.18 (44)	25.94 (51)	19.56 (38)	19.90 (41)	26.29 (53)	17.71 (36)	28.35 (54)
B21	North Yorkshire	18.75 (79)	17.71 (70)	22.99 (95)	21.97 (96)	20.89 (90)	19.68 (84)	23.25 (95)	16.91 (73)	19.26 (84)
B31	Bradford	25.29 (58)	27.00 (66)	30.02 (68)	29.19 (73)	25.03 (58)	32.85 (77)	23.99 (57)	30.38 (75)	33.15 (75)
B51	West Yorkshire	21.29 (68)	20.91 (68)	28.24 (92)	24.81 (77)	27.59 (87)	29.37 (90)	25.85 (77)	27.60 (85)	26.19 (82)
B61	Leeds	30.51 (126)	28.33 (112)	31.85 (129)	27.69 (109)	35.01 (135)	31.64 (123)	28.47 (114)	30.29 (121)	33.54 (132)
B71	Wakefield	24.37 (40)	22.69 (41)	29.73 (50)	27.08 (46)	32.11 (54)	27.93 (48)	31.12 (54)	38.10 (66)	27.57 (51)
C01	North Derbyshire	15.15 (33)	23.81 (51)	18.71 (40)	19.51 (43)	23.25 (51)	19.61 (42)	18.83 (43)	25.43 (55)	25.48 (56)
C02	Southern Derbyshire	21.25 (63)	24.06 (72)	22.82 (68)	22.60 (65)	25.22 (75)	19.43 (60)	20.94 (61)	22.37 (69)	19.81 (58)
C03	Leicestershire	18.41 (82)	18.77 (83)	17.56 (80)	17.39 (79)	16.04 (72)	19.32 (87)	17.67 (80)	18.77 (84)	16.87 (81)
C04	North Lincolnshire	22.08 (35)	18.72 (29)	20.05 (32)	21.21 (34)	22.05 (36)	21.36 (36)	16.92 (31)	21.18 (37)	21.47 (37)
C05	South Lincolnshire	17.52 (32)	16.73 (29)	23.74 (45)	21.56 (42)	16.44 (32)	21.68 (42)	20.26 (40)	24.75 (46)	19.86 (39)
C08	Nottingham	25.36 (86)	22.98 (80)	22.32 (73)	26.56 (90)	27.81 (97)	21.52 (72)	25.96 (87)	22.91 (77)	28.15 (97)
C09	Barnsley	20.66 (25)	30.21 (36)	22.15 (28)	26.84 (32)	30.07 (39)	24.87 (32)	21.33 (26)	27.59 (34)	25.15 (33)

HON - B4,B5 (continued)
Mortality rates from lung cancer (ICD 162) in men and women under 75:
Age-standardised mortality rates per 100,000: 1984-92
(observed numbers of deaths in parentheses)
Females

		1984	1985	1986	1987	1988	1989	1990	1991	1992
C10	Doncaster	24.21 (37)	24.44 (39)	22.01 (35)	29.32 (47)	27.61 (45)	35.77 (55)	34.01 (57)	28.11 (49)	27.46 (45)
C11	Rotherham	28.15 (36)	30.47 (42)	34.01 (45)	22.00 (30)	29.95 (39)	23.75 (34)	32.11 (44)	18.77 (25)	25.33 (34)
C12	Sheffield	28.49 (96)	27.70 (88)	25.25 (86)	33.04 (109)	26.02 (84)	28.80 (86)	25.02 (77)	34.14 (109)	24.19 (77)
C14	North Nottinghamshire	24.07 (51)	21.86 (47)	23.92 (50)	22.50 (50)	21.54 (47)	20.66 (44)	21.65 (46)	23.84 (52)	25.30 (57)
D01	Cambridge	15.49 (21)	12.63 (19)	17.89 (26)	14.96 (21)	20.42 (29)	18.46 (26)	17.50 (24)	8.95 (14)	13.65 (19)
D05	North West Anglia	19.81 (43)	22.13 (48)	17.09 (37)	18.09 (41)	24.24 (56)	20.23 (47)	18.21 (43)	23.66 (52)	13.68 (35)
D06	Norwich	12.53 (38)	17.28 (52)	12.71 (37)	14.24 (44)	13.22 (40)	15.18 (47)	15.20 (46)	16.32 (48)	13.18 (46)
D07	Great Yarmouth and Waveney	14.96 (21)	15.06 (19)	18.87 (26)	20.49 (25)	18.38 (23)	18.73 (27)	18.35 (23)	25.86 (36)	20.51 (26)
D09	Huntingdon	22.51 (12)	28.51 (15)	18.72 (10)	26.28 (15)	16.59 (9)	22.62 (13)	29.05 (16)	34.99 (21)	10.84 (6)
D11	Suffolk	16.69 (52)	19.64 (63)	16.01 (50)	17.50 (55)	19.76 (61)	19.53 (58)	19.85 (60)	13.70 (45)	16.38 (51)
E01	North Bedfordshire	21.21 (25)	24.41 (28)	16.83 (20)	21.48 (24)	15.80 (19)	22.45 (27)	24.18 (30)	19.11 (23)	18.65 (23)
E02	South Bedfordshire	24.72 (29)	21.31 (26)	21.12 (26)	19.57 (25)	23.61 (29)	21.91 (26)	27.26 (34)	26.13 (32)	21.38 (27)
E05	North West Hertfordshire	19.41 (26)	22.28 (31)	19.19 (26)	14.10 (21)	16.75 (23)	23.44 (33)	23.76 (32)	23.99 (31)	22.37 (31)
E06	South West Hertfordshire	19.06 (26)	20.50 (28)	24.95 (37)	23.46 (34)	26.32 (37)	19.30 (28)	12.75 (18)	8.38 (12)	15.95 (22)
E07	Barnet	18.94 (34)	25.21 (45)	22.43 (39)	20.41 (34)	21.56 (36)	22.83 (38)	24.25 (39)	18.19 (28)	19.93 (32)
E09	Hillingdon	22.03 (31)	20.94 (29)	15.96 (22)	21.20 (27)	28.05 (37)	19.83 (25)	20.84 (26)	28.62 (33)	19.46 (23)
E18	East and North Hertfordshire	18.43 (43)	19.55 (49)	24.77 (59)	22.15 (57)	20.27 (50)	18.18 (44)	21.82 (53)	22.69 (55)	22.40 (58)
E19	Brent and Harrow	20.01 (50)	20.45 (52)	24.28 (61)	16.14 (38)	19.11 (43)	16.81 (37)	18.88 (40)	21.08 (43)	19.32 (41)
E20	Ealing, Hammersmith and Hounslow	29.01 (100)	21.82 (71)	31.96 (106)	25.64 (86)	31.91 (95)	24.56 (75)	25.21 (72)	26.87 (81)	26.12 (77)
E21	Kensington, Chelsea and Westminster	31.14 (60)	29.90 (55)	24.11 (43)	33.51 (55)	31.31 (52)	26.23 (44)	29.71 (49)	35.35 (55)	24.70 (43)
F31	North Essex	15.95 (77)	19.44 (90)	18.74 (91)	22.27 (107)	21.84 (106)	18.66 (88)	18.63 (94)	15.61 (76)	20.25 (102)
F32	South Essex	24.47 (93)	24.78 (95)	18.86 (74)	23.15 (88)	20.53 (78)	22.69 (83)	25.13 (95)	21.22 (83)	16.39 (67)

HON - B4,B5 (continued)
Mortality rates from lung cancer (ICD 162) in men and women under 75:
Age-standardised mortality rates per 100,000: 1984-92
(observed numbers of deaths in parentheses)
Females

		1984	1985	1986	1987	1988	1989	1990	1991	1992
F33	Barking and Havering	27.66 (64)	21.09 (52)	20.88 (51)	21.22 (48)	26.50 (60)	27.28 (62)	22.26 (50)	23.68 (53)	26.07 (60)
F34	Redbridge and Waltham Forest	23.18 (56)	23.79 (61)	24.05 (59)	21.72 (54)	24.57 (57)	23.47 (56)	21.93 (51)	28.92 (65)	27.06 (60)
F35	East London and the City	35.51 (97)	36.10 (97)	23.68 (65)	27.52 (76)	34.89 (92)	30.14 (76)	32.10 (81)	33.59 (83)	29.90 (73)
F36	New River District	28.13 (70)	25.14 (62)	20.68 (51)	22.55 (55)	22.48 (50)	25.17 (56)	21.11 (45)	20.16 (46)	23.51 (52)
F37	Camden and Islington	29.43 (57)	29.65 (54)	29.87 (54)	35.40 (62)	36.29 (62)	36.91 (62)	36.01 (59)	27.76 (45)	28.18 (47)
G04	South East Kent	24.49 (39)	19.00 (33)	24.47 (43)	23.61 (41)	20.46 (37)	14.72 (27)	26.50 (45)	18.23 (34)	16.21 (28)
G05	Canterbury and Thanet	22.76 (45)	24.49 (53)	25.06 (53)	28.41 (55)	19.68 (40)	32.91 (63)	25.39 (48)	25.38 (55)	24.50 (45)
G06	Dartford and Gravesham	24.27 (28)	29.77 (34)	24.62 (29)	19.94 (22)	30.89 (37)	22.67 (27)	13.63 (15)	29.37 (33)	20.64 (25)
G07	Maidstone	19.66 (18)	25.78 (26)	11.47 (12)	14.14 (14)	14.88 (16)	24.69 (26)	15.23 (17)	14.57 (17)	24.71 (26)
G08	Medway	29.20 (49)	18.35 (30)	23.25 (41)	26.93 (45)	23.01 (38)	21.96 (36)	19.08 (32)	23.36 (39)	24.29 (40)
G09	Tunbridge Wells	13.08 (17)	11.36 (14)	19.67 (24)	9.15 (12)	15.46 (19)	21.21 (25)	12.17 (15)	23.16 (25)	13.29 (15)
G10	Bexley	21.43 (27)	22.36 (30)	29.23 (35)	31.31 (38)	27.80 (33)	28.42 (32)	26.82 (32)	23.30 (28)	25.82 (32)
G11	Greenwich	21.65 (26)	34.58 (42)	26.68 (31)	29.08 (35)	40.80 (45)	34.99 (40)	36.05 (42)	42.77 (48)	29.96 (34)
G12	Bromley	18.21 (34)	17.06 (34)	24.19 (40)	14.53 (26)	19.23 (34)	18.26 (33)	15.17 (27)	23.57 (39)	14.18 (25)
G21	East Sussex	17.76 (86)	20.65 (104)	21.23 (104)	19.77 (100)	17.04 (88)	18.53 (92)	18.53 (89)	17.17 (86)	16.54 (81)
G26	South East London	31.62 (128)	31.84 (127)	33.95 (126)	30.14 (109)	31.36 (107)	37.16 (128)	33.12 (110)	32.78 (111)	31.66 (106)
H04	Mid Surrey	17.29 (19)	18.01 (21)	15.46 (18)	15.09 (16)	13.62 (14)	12.53 (14)	14.60 (15)	18.33 (19)	10.12 (12)
H05	East Surrey	14.26 (16)	23.39 (27)	15.21 (17)	24.85 (29)	16.41 (19)	22.73 (26)	18.64 (20)	11.00 (13)	18.51 (20)
H06	Chichester	20.05 (26)	23.91 (32)	23.84 (33)	20.85 (25)	15.88 (22)	17.50 (25)	17.03 (23)	14.22 (19)	13.77 (19)
H07	Mid Downs	21.92 (34)	15.13 (22)	20.19 (30)	19.53 (28)	21.49 (32)	19.40 (28)	19.85 (32)	20.87 (32)	11.00 (18)
H08	Worthing	16.12 (34)	19.69 (33)	11.85 (27)	14.47 (30)	23.93 (42)	15.48 (33)	18.16 (33)	16.17 (26)	18.79 (32)
H09	Croydon	23.63 (40)	20.90 (37)	19.28 (33)	21.96 (37)	26.55 (42)	18.80 (30)	18.90 (29)	19.63 (33)	23.67 (36)

HON - B4,B5 (continued)
Mortality rates from lung cancer (ICD 162) in men and women under 75:
Age-standardised mortality rates per 100,000: 1984-92
(observed numbers of deaths in parentheses)
Females

		1984	1985	1986	1987	1988	1989	1990	1991	1992
H12	Wandsworth	31.36 (30)	32.13 (32)	28.64 (26)	23.52 (23)	32.62 (30)	26.46 (22)	32.80 (27)	29.67 (25)	33.67 (28)
H13	Merton and Sutton	22.07 (47)	14.32 (27)	25.81 (55)	23.05 (43)	28.36 (51)	21.98 (40)	26.15 (46)	23.58 (41)	20.27 (35)
H14	North West Surrey	27.45 (53)	21.58 (46)	18.55 (38)	20.41 (42)	15.92 (33)	21.73 (45)	20.74 (42)	19.65 (41)	18.38 (37)
H15	South West Surrey	16.42 (24)	18.95 (24)	19.25 (27)	12.41 (18)	16.85 (23)	13.63 (19)	13.69 (18)	12.31 (17)	12.98 (18)
H16	Kingston and Richmond	25.23 (65)	20.84 (56)	27.09 (65)	21.53 (56)	24.60 (62)	21.28 (48)	21.77 (51)	23.53 (54)	23.88 (54)
J10	Dorset	16.95 (75)	16.38 (78)	22.07 (91)	15.01 (69)	20.60 (86)	20.81 (95)	16.10 (83)	15.71 (75)	13.33 (64)
J21	Portsmouth and South East Hampshire	19.50 (55)	19.53 (55)	22.19 (66)	21.31 (63)	19.69 (56)	20.46 (61)	18.24 (52)	19.86 (57)	19.88 (62)
J22	Southampton and South West Hampshire	20.49 (49)	20.00 (49)	17.54 (47)	21.68 (55)	19.25 (50)	25.69 (64)	20.34 (50)	18.96 (49)	19.67 (48)
J23	Winchester	18.88 (22)	16.98 (20)	12.88 (15)	14.97 (19)	17.47 (20)	17.18 (21)	18.40 (23)	15.79 (19)	16.99 (21)
J24	Basingstoke and North Hampshire	19.22 (30)	23.17 (35)	22.56 (35)	16.73 (26)	15.29 (24)	15.31 (25)	21.36 (35)	14.66 (24)	25.30 (43)
J31	Salisbury	15.56 (11)	24.77 (18)	8.54 (7)	22.71 (17)	11.43 (9)	14.80 (11)	17.45 (13)	14.94 (12)	18.75 (14)
J32	Swindon	25.16 (27)	17.78 (19)	31.25 (35)	27.89 (32)	17.49 (21)	17.33 (20)	23.94 (29)	18.01 (21)	20.05 (24)
J33	Bath	16.78 (39)	19.80 (48)	18.38 (43)	14.81 (33)	18.22 (43)	13.16 (33)	17.46 (42)	16.08 (39)	11.14 (27)
J41	Isle of Wight	13.76 (13)	20.15 (19)	28.78 (22)	18.02 (15)	35.47 (31)	17.15 (18)	16.10 (14)	14.23 (14)	18.47 (18)
K11	East Berkshire	27.12 (49)	27.56 (49)	23.84 (42)	17.12 (31)	21.44 (39)	20.21 (33)	17.26 (32)	23.64 (43)	13.01 (24)
K12	West Berkshire	21.13 (41)	29.82 (63)	16.15 (34)	27.78 (57)	18.50 (41)	22.24 (47)	17.15 (36)	18.75 (37)	17.57 (36)
K24	Buckinghamshire	19.49 (49)	18.39 (49)	21.60 (57)	21.98 (58)	23.77 (63)	19.13 (52)	15.32 (43)	17.08 (46)	22.35 (63)
K31	Kettering	19.55 (25)	27.14 (35)	25.19 (34)	24.26 (34)	24.03 (33)	20.47 (28)	24.80 (34)	21.14 (30)	20.80 (27)
K32	Northampton	19.00 (27)	26.25 (40)	20.92 (33)	22.32 (31)	28.64 (44)	19.43 (32)	18.01 (30)	23.15 (35)	25.83 (40)
K41	Oxfordshire	26.23 (66)	20.28 (53)	17.02 (45)	18.64 (47)	17.98 (45)	15.47 (37)	17.06 (44)	21.74 (54)	16.87 (45)
L10	Bristol and District	18.21 (84)	12.65 (60)	18.80 (91)	17.52 (82)	15.08 (68)	18.79 (88)	19.76 (92)	20.98 (96)	17.55 (82)
L21	Cornwall and Isles of Scilly	16.31 (51)	18.00 (53)	12.67 (36)	19.87 (59)	17.33 (53)	17.98 (54)	16.65 (49)	15.20 (51)	14.40 (46)

HON - B4,B5 (continued)
Mortality rates from lung cancer (ICD 162) in men and women under 75:
Age-standardised mortality rates per 100,000: 1984-92
(observed numbers of deaths in parentheses)
Females

		1984	1985	1986	1987	1988	1989	1990	1991	1992
L35	Exeter and North Devon	17.88 (52)	16.87 (50)	17.53 (54)	14.24 (41)	14.80 (45)	12.03 (40)	18.53 (52)	15.92 (52)	19.56 (62)
L36	Plymouth and Torbay	19.32 (72)	20.20 (79)	25.84 (92)	19.82 (76)	20.54 (78)	18.70 (68)	18.31 (68)	21.26 (79)	22.12 (75)
L40	Gloucestershire	16.98 (51)	15.06 (47)	13.98 (44)	14.90 (45)	17.27 (54)	18.81 (60)	16.76 (53)	16.12 (50)	15.85 (50)
L51	Somerset	19.60 (49)	16.75 (46)	13.31 (34)	15.10 (40)	14.35 (39)	19.22 (52)	12.07 (32)	13.18 (34)	19.30 (53)
M02	Herefordshire	15.62 (16)	16.26 (14)	23.09 (20)	13.56 (13)	20.73 (21)	23.75 (22)	18.27 (17)	21.59 (21)	13.03 (13)
M04	Worcester and District	18.24 (25)	21.81 (29)	18.29 (27)	17.46 (26)	19.97 (29)	10.62 (17)	23.77 (34)	10.31 (15)	14.46 (22)
M05	Shropshire	16.11 (34)	16.89 (37)	20.93 (43)	17.41 (38)	26.53 (58)	20.91 (47)	13.96 (32)	17.45 (41)	22.52 (55)
M06	Mid Staffordshire	20.86 (31)	17.70 (28)	15.23 (23)	22.86 (36)	16.31 (27)	25.64 (41)	20.75 (33)	20.61 (35)	20.48 (34)
M07	North Staffordshire	20.10 (54)	25.32 (71)	19.70 (53)	28.20 (77)	16.53 (48)	23.50 (66)	25.59 (71)	19.87 (53)	27.23 (79)
M08	South East Staffordshire	23.07 (26)	9.42 (12)	18.83 (24)	24.27 (30)	15.57 (20)	17.30 (22)	20.54 (27)	13.98 (19)	18.21 (26)
M13	East Birmingham	36.74 (44)	24.10 (26)	29.17 (32)	20.30 (27)	34.31 (37)	29.79 (33)	24.66 (25)	29.97 (32)	23.90 (28)
M14	North Birmingham	19.84 (19)	5.80 (6)	13.19 (14)	17.07 (16)	22.23 (21)	23.53 (22)	12.44 (12)	26.80 (25)	21.65 (21)
M16	West Birmingham	20.34 (24)	34.23 (37)	21.55 (25)	21.54 (23)	36.11 (37)	29.70 (28)	17.07 (17)	24.74 (27)	31.84 (30)
M17	Coventry	26.23 (45)	28.48 (50)	30.80 (53)	16.31 (31)	32.67 (53)	24.95 (43)	22.62 (38)	28.22 (45)	31.90 (56)
M18	Dudley	15.81 (26)	19.78 (33)	13.33 (24)	17.44 (31)	18.06 (31)	18.99 (32)	15.56 (29)	15.86 (27)	14.89 (26)
M19	Sandwell	24.26 (43)	26.57 (50)	24.68 (43)	23.14 (42)	25.08 (43)	33.00 (55)	20.33 (39)	30.79 (54)	30.07 (51)
M20	Solihull	16.16 (17)	16.35 (18)	16.58 (18)	18.54 (20)	12.58 (14)	14.18 (16)	28.22 (32)	22.04 (26)	19.82 (22)
M21	Walsall	27.30 (37)	26.14 (38)	27.21 (40)	16.42 (22)	18.62 (27)	25.48 (37)	23.85 (34)	27.05 (40)	23.92 (35)
M22	Wolverhampton	20.98 (28)	24.89 (33)	30.97 (44)	22.64 (33)	22.94 (34)	25.54 (37)	23.28 (34)	23.97 (35)	26.13 (38)
M25	South Birmingham	25.67 (61)	20.98 (50)	27.58 (67)	22.88 (50)	26.77 (62)	26.34 (61)	23.84 (56)	30.04 (72)	25.04 (55)
M26	North Worcestershire	21.45 (28)	19.10 (27)	14.41 (19)	18.96 (27)	13.00 (18)	23.72 (34)	14.61 (22)	17.91 (25)	21.31 (32)
M28	Warwickshire	15.65 (41)	15.36 (42)	21.05 (56)	17.03 (46)	20.59 (53)	17.18 (46)	23.31 (66)	20.48 (55)	20.49 (58)

HON - B4,B5 (continued)
Mortality rates from lung cancer (ICD 162) in men and women under 75:
Age-standardised mortality rates per 100,000: 1984-92
(observed numbers of deaths in parentheses)
Females

		1984	1985	1986	1987	1988	1989	1990	1991	1992
N11	Chester	29.49 (28)	22.77 (22)	23.74 (24)	26.62 (26)	21.04 (21)	19.47 (20)	25.79 (26)	19.96 (20)	22.29 (23)
N12	Crewe	14.19 (19)	13.69 (20)	19.09 (27)	20.07 (28)	22.10 (32)	19.61 (27)	21.45 (31)	13.17 (19)	19.93 (28)
N13	Halton	37.82 (27)	20.68 (16)	18.98 (14)	35.57 (24)	41.40 (28)	33.01 (24)	35.35 (26)	35.06 (27)	32.64 (24)
N14	Macclesfield	17.86 (18)	11.70 (13)	15.96 (16)	20.98 (22)	22.43 (23)	23.19 (25)	13.35 (14)	16.41 (17)	21.51 (23)
N15	Warrington	32.90 (29)	29.09 (28)	21.72 (18)	29.88 (29)	33.26 (31)	26.22 (25)	25.60 (24)	32.34 (30)	24.13 (25)
N21	Liverpool	35.34 (102)	44.41 (133)	45.46 (128)	55.00 (153)	48.48 (134)	46.71 (124)	50.84 (134)	51.69 (133)	45.79 (121)
N31	St Helens and Knowsley	30.26 (54)	35.55 (63)	40.15 (72)	35.79 (65)	38.43 (68)	28.94 (54)	39.77 (72)	23.32 (44)	41.96 (76)
N41	Southport and Formby	15.40 (12)	23.41 (19)	28.76 (23)	18.05 (15)	21.81 (19)	25.63 (21)	32.19 (25)	27.11 (23)	31.06 (24)
N42	South Sefton	43.14 (46)	25.81 (27)	43.49 (46)	34.45 (36)	41.08 (43)	36.20 (41)	29.47 (32)	41.94 (44)	33.96 (35)
N51	Wirral	34.64 (72)	27.22 (61)	31.09 (65)	28.34 (59)	30.63 (69)	34.60 (74)	33.31 (72)	37.85 (80)	25.04 (57)
P01	Lancaster	28.36 (21)	31.46 (24)	21.35 (17)	32.04 (25)	15.10 (13)	32.72 (22)	21.94 (19)	32.16 (25)	18.91 (17)
P02	Blackpool, Wyre and Fylde	21.47 (53)	25.21 (57)	22.33 (56)	26.89 (60)	30.56 (71)	27.36 (63)	28.84 (65)	27.88 (66)	24.81 (56)
P03	Preston	31.61 (24)	27.54 (19)	25.50 (19)	27.16 (18)	28.76 (21)	24.13 (17)	39.22 (29)	35.78 (24)	29.24 (20)
P04	Blackburn, Hyndburn and Ribble Valley	32.46 (48)	28.62 (44)	23.80 (35)	28.72 (41)	23.23 (36)	25.18 (38)	18.70 (30)	25.51 (36)	24.44 (36)
P05	Burnley, Pendle and Rossendale	28.12 (38)	24.48 (34)	30.02 (43)	31.13 (41)	40.97 (53)	36.27 (43)	33.99 (45)	23.34 (30)	33.33 (44)
P06	West Lancashire	22.99 (12)	17.23 (10)	44.72 (24)	18.96 (11)	34.55 (18)	22.09 (12)	21.53 (12)	12.44 (8)	15.18 (9)
P07	Chorley and South Ribble	34.22 (32)	32.30 (32)	17.70 (20)	18.36 (19)	19.13 (19)	20.88 (21)	18.67 (19)	16.03 (17)	26.21 (27)
P08	Bolton	20.65 (31)	21.85 (32)	23.37 (33)	22.17 (32)	25.63 (38)	34.25 (46)	32.15 (44)	33.81 (48)	26.75 (38)
P09	Bury	22.65 (20)	24.38 (23)	30.72 (29)	19.05 (18)	29.33 (28)	19.78 (19)	27.17 (26)	26.40 (26)	35.35 (32)
P10	North Manchester	49.49 (40)	51.76 (41)	47.86 (38)	39.20 (32)	43.33 (31)	62.96 (47)	43.50 (34)	52.82 (40)	70.57 (51)
P11	Central Manchester	40.40 (23)	44.17 (26)	38.52 (21)	36.23 (22)	47.27 (25)	35.56 (19)	41.52 (21)	39.21 (19)	37.81 (20)
P12	South Manchester	33.73 (37)	35.58 (36)	42.85 (45)	38.79 (40)	26.40 (27)	38.59 (35)	35.26 (33)	35.73 (32)	40.74 (39)

HON - B4,B5 (continued)
Mortality rates from lung cancer (ICD 162) in men and women under 75:
Age-standardised mortality rates per 100,000: 1984-92
(observed numbers of deaths in parentheses)
Females

		1984	1985	1986	1987	1988	1989	1990	1991	1992
P13	Oldham	26.05 (32)	30.85 (38)	35.16 (40)	23.54 (30)	35.34 (41)	33.25 (41)	40.44 (44)	33.25 (41)	34.97 (40)
P14	Rochdale	34.47 (39)	29.55 (31)	32.43 (40)	25.55 (30)	29.31 (32)	28.90 (32)	38.82 (41)	24.22 (26)	30.06 (34)
P15	Salford	37.01 (53)	26.07 (39)	33.02 (48)	40.72 (56)	43.56 (61)	41.34 (58)	46.18 (61)	44.74 (59)	37.73 (50)
P16	Stockport	26.28 (43)	32.83 (52)	20.56 (35)	18.00 (29)	29.62 (46)	19.76 (32)	21.83 (38)	24.00 (41)	18.57 (32)
P17	Tameside and Glossop	36.15 (50)	17.92 (26)	23.26 (34)	27.08 (39)	28.43 (40)	32.92 (42)	34.83 (50)	25.14 (35)	38.86 (48)
P18	Trafford	25.90 (34)	21.51 (28)	23.19 (30)	30.49 (38)	32.06 (39)	32.89 (41)	30.08 (36)	34.62 (40)	33.23 (40)
P19	Wigan	27.54 (47)	24.86 (38)	20.77 (35)	29.45 (48)	24.44 (41)	26.38 (46)	24.72 (43)	33.09 (59)	25.55 (44)

HON - B4,B5 (continued)
Mortality rates from lung cancer (ICD 162) in men and women under 75:
Age-standardised mortality rates per 100,000: 1984-92
(observed numbers of deaths in parentheses)
Persons

		1984	1985	1986	1987	1988	1989	1990	1991	1992
	ENGLAND AND WALES	45.48	44.65	43.64	42.52	43.00	41.26	40.66	40.11	38.59
		(24474)	(24080)	(23586)	(22993)	(23071)	(22089)	(21789)	(21571)	(21002)
O00	ENGLAND	45.74	44.81	43.75	42.65	43.20	41.31	40.67	40.19	38.60
		(23161)	(22740)	(22236)	(21694)	(21782)	(20757)	(20467)	(20281)	(19713)
A00	NORTHERN RHA	59.71	58.90	57.39	59.94	60.27	58.17	58.83	55.24	53.24
		(2013)	(1979)	(1948)	(2033)	(2045)	(1973)	(2014)	(1896)	(1842)
B00	YORKSHIRE RHA	46.60	49.25	47.02	44.51	48.08	44.14	44.66	43.55	42.62
		(1805)	(1891)	(1812)	(1731)	(1844)	(1689)	(1705)	(1683)	(1656)
C00	TRENT RHA	45.80	46.63	42.91	43.43	43.76	41.28	39.16	39.56	38.22
		(2270)	(2331)	(2152)	(2195)	(2211)	(2083)	(1987)	(2024)	(1979)
D00	EAST ANGLIAN RHA	37.50	35.63	34.40	33.37	33.93	32.81	29.98	31.09	27.78
		(817)	(779)	(758)	(746)	(758)	(732)	(676)	(713)	(656)
E00	NORTH WEST THAMES RHA	43.49	39.94	41.20	37.43	40.11	37.76	38.17	35.91	34.23
		(1518)	(1394)	(1417)	(1277)	(1344)	(1247)	(1243)	(1161)	(1131)
F00	NORTH EAST THAMES RHA	47.43	45.56	44.70	43.36	43.43	41.52	41.38	39.35	39.26
		(1853)	(1795)	(1745)	(1679)	(1647)	(1544)	(1541)	(1459)	(1478)
G00	SOUTH EAST THAMES RHA	43.84	43.47	42.87	41.90	41.02	40.80	38.53	38.24	36.43
		(1801)	(1786)	(1751)	(1693)	(1643)	(1601)	(1513)	(1505)	(1441)
H00	SOUTH WEST THAMES RHA	39.65	37.25	37.41	35.79	35.44	32.19	33.38	32.21	30.11
		(1304)	(1226)	(1227)	(1152)	(1125)	(1008)	(1046)	(1007)	(931)
J00	WESSEX RHA	36.69	36.65	36.08	34.00	33.94	34.76	32.50	32.80	31.19
		(1205)	(1214)	(1205)	(1152)	(1140)	(1180)	(1106)	(1121)	(1074)
K00	OXFORD RHA	42.00	41.60	36.70	38.46	36.88	35.24	33.19	33.86	31.97
		(936)	(940)	(836)	(882)	(848)	(813)	(774)	(788)	(760)
L00	SOUTH WESTERN RHA	35.90	32.37	33.38	32.70	31.52	31.45	30.71	30.65	30.84
		(1328)	(1221)	(1258)	(1236)	(1190)	(1186)	(1149)	(1164)	(1199)
M00	WEST MIDLANDS RHA	48.00	45.99	44.85	43.26	43.27	42.36	41.72	42.22	40.96
		(2613)	(2525)	(2486)	(2402)	(2385)	(2347)	(2327)	(2360)	(2317)
N00	MERSEY RHA	54.00	55.63	55.73	55.13	54.35	50.70	52.61	53.96	48.98
		(1383)	(1424)	(1427)	(1405)	(1378)	(1299)	(1332)	(1366)	(1263)
P00	NORTH WESTERN RHA	53.66	52.47	52.01	49.54	53.35	49.63	49.32	48.91	47.70
		(2315)	(2235)	(2214)	(2111)	(2224)	(2055)	(2054)	(2034)	(1986)
A01	Hartlepool	60.09	81.18	64.75	58.01	69.39	70.52	76.82	61.16	66.80
		(56)	(77)	(62)	(55)	(67)	(71)	(75)	(60)	(68)
A02	North Tees	63.74	72.50	57.78	61.35	75.09	62.05	65.79	67.00	52.62
		(102)	(118)	(96)	(104)	(129)	(107)	(113)	(119)	(94)
A03	South Tees	67.30	65.42	71.33	66.24	61.45	64.17	70.25	49.44	58.97
		(193)	(190)	(207)	(196)	(182)	(187)	(212)	(149)	(179)
A04	East Cumbria	45.17	54.37	40.61	44.66	50.71	44.03	37.09	43.95	37.95
		(88)	(106)	(85)	(89)	(105)	(92)	(77)	(90)	(79)
A05	South Cumbria	46.37	39.58	42.58	40.80	38.44	45.39	33.72	42.06	40.27
		(93)	(81)	(88)	(87)	(81)	(94)	(70)	(86)	(84)
A06	West Cumbria	40.74	50.49	41.36	51.54	49.01	46.39	39.96	45.17	43.63
		(62)	(74)	(62)	(79)	(71)	(70)	(62)	(72)	(68)

HON - B4,B5 (continued)
Mortality rates from lung cancer (ICD 162) in men and women under 75:
Age-standardised mortality rates per 100,000: 1984-92
(observed numbers of deaths in parentheses)
Persons

		1984	1985	1986	1987	1988	1989	1990	1991	1992
A11	Northumberland	53.56 (185)	47.02 (161)	51.19 (176)	54.93 (187)	52.81 (182)	45.87 (160)	48.32 (167)	47.08 (168)	42.39 (150)
A12	Gateshead	79.14 (187)	75.61 (180)	54.87 (133)	72.61 (171)	68.06 (161)	66.89 (159)	64.37 (152)	69.36 (160)	68.52 (164)
A13	Newcastle	61.70 (200)	61.68 (193)	74.21 (236)	75.91 (229)	76.07 (225)	74.77 (217)	67.22 (196)	79.01 (234)	60.00 (175)
A14	North Tyneside	59.77 (139)	63.80 (149)	60.57 (139)	65.34 (155)	58.17 (137)	62.33 (142)	70.43 (163)	53.91 (128)	47.25 (111)
A15	South Tyneside	77.68 (143)	76.82 (141)	84.18 (158)	71.96 (135)	77.66 (148)	74.07 (141)	72.72 (138)	68.14 (127)	72.23 (137)
A16	Sunderland	69.91 (212)	62.50 (189)	53.62 (162)	67.78 (204)	69.52 (213)	57.89 (176)	70.97 (219)	55.19 (168)	64.88 (200)
A30	North Durham	56.36 (196)	54.48 (187)	53.48 (186)	49.53 (176)	51.99 (179)	55.61 (193)	58.65 (209)	47.19 (167)	48.93 (174)
A31	South Durham	49.53 (157)	41.94 (133)	50.84 (158)	53.62 (166)	52.19 (165)	52.33 (164)	50.07 (161)	52.21 (168)	48.17 (159)
B11	East Riding	52.77 (298)	51.47 (283)	49.76 (276)	46.86 (268)	51.83 (288)	49.38 (275)	51.89 (288)	44.93 (253)	46.19 (266)
B16	Grimsby and Scunthorpe	47.29 (175)	58.35 (214)	44.06 (165)	46.40 (177)	42.43 (162)	39.81 (152)	48.93 (191)	38.27 (149)	39.70 (151)
B21	North Yorkshire	35.29 (281)	39.15 (303)	36.83 (291)	35.19 (287)	37.98 (304)	31.49 (254)	36.55 (288)	31.24 (255)	31.04 (258)
B31	Bradford	44.59 (201)	46.23 (212)	51.50 (233)	51.73 (236)	48.29 (218)	51.10 (230)	46.08 (206)	52.80 (240)	49.24 (220)
B51	West Yorkshire	43.35 (266)	46.69 (281)	46.13 (278)	43.10 (256)	49.81 (293)	44.75 (261)	38.73 (222)	46.08 (266)	42.46 (248)
B61	Leeds	55.51 (427)	55.82 (430)	51.08 (389)	46.86 (353)	55.55 (406)	50.06 (364)	48.02 (351)	46.59 (346)	47.19 (346)
B71	Wakefield	49.23 (157)	52.22 (168)	55.96 (180)	47.49 (154)	52.47 (173)	46.72 (153)	48.07 (159)	53.00 (174)	49.32 (167)
C01	North Derbyshire	38.54 (160)	44.40 (177)	36.41 (149)	37.59 (159)	41.62 (177)	34.93 (146)	35.54 (151)	40.43 (173)	40.21 (171)
C02	Southern Derbyshire	43.80 (250)	46.02 (268)	45.06 (259)	45.26 (261)	45.34 (264)	40.33 (234)	39.07 (227)	37.15 (220)	34.81 (202)
C03	Leicestershire	39.19 (333)	37.17 (319)	38.95 (340)	33.93 (296)	33.08 (289)	34.34 (298)	31.93 (280)	30.11 (265)	27.95 (255)
C04	North Lincolnshire	41.52 (126)	45.93 (138)	37.04 (116)	39.44 (125)	42.48 (136)	36.90 (121)	33.05 (115)	37.88 (126)	35.35 (121)
C05	South Lincolnshire	39.58 (139)	40.92 (140)	37.79 (135)	36.14 (135)	37.02 (137)	41.72 (152)	32.27 (119)	34.32 (126)	29.53 (117)
C08	Nottingham	49.13 (316)	47.53 (313)	44.47 (284)	45.86 (296)	51.30 (333)	44.76 (290)	40.22 (260)	39.53 (260)	40.31 (266)
C09	Barnsley	51.93 (126)	55.11 (133)	46.33 (113)	48.58 (119)	48.13 (115)	49.88 (123)	42.72 (102)	50.56 (124)	46.22 (117)

HON - B4,B5 (continued)
Mortality rates from lung cancer (ICD 162) in men and women under 75:
Age-standardised mortality rates per 100,000: 1984-92
(observed numbers of deaths in parentheses)
Persons

		1984	1985	1986	1987	1988	1989	1990	1991	1992
C10	Doncaster	48.70 (145)	58.63 (182)	46.94 (145)	55.25 (172)	47.30 (146)	49.61 (150)	46.78 (149)	42.18 (137)	45.16 (144)
C11	Rotherham	52.18 (132)	43.61 (113)	52.51 (136)	45.29 (118)	52.08 (134)	50.97 (136)	48.58 (127)	40.60 (108)	46.01 (122)
C12	Sheffield	54.70 (343)	58.24 (362)	47.64 (304)	54.56 (330)	50.25 (303)	46.91 (280)	46.04 (272)	49.40 (292)	44.42 (262)
C14	North Nottinghamshire	49.44 (200)	44.93 (186)	42.06 (171)	43.40 (184)	41.77 (177)	35.79 (153)	43.98 (185)	45.52 (193)	46.25 (202)
D01	Cambridge	31.38 (84)	33.48 (89)	34.17 (93)	31.25 (83)	31.54 (84)	33.92 (91)	28.84 (80)	24.19 (68)	26.23 (74)
D05	North West Anglia	42.58 (175)	42.20 (177)	35.17 (149)	35.61 (154)	37.67 (168)	35.37 (159)	34.15 (151)	34.37 (153)	28.22 (129)
D06	Norwich	32.25 (181)	31.22 (175)	33.12 (187)	28.69 (171)	29.06 (170)	28.91 (166)	26.12 (151)	30.50 (176)	25.18 (161)
D07	Great Yarmouth and Waveney	42.86 (111)	38.50 (85)	36.14 (90)	36.57 (88)	41.65 (102)	35.91 (92)	31.81 (79)	36.63 (94)	32.20 (83)
D09	Huntingdon	44.44 (44)	51.25 (54)	39.33 (39)	38.88 (42)	39.31 (42)	30.63 (33)	43.96 (47)	48.93 (56)	32.80 (38)
D11	Suffolk	37.95 (222)	32.78 (199)	33.54 (200)	34.87 (208)	32.49 (192)	33.14 (191)	27.73 (168)	27.13 (166)	27.79 (171)
E01	North Bedfordshire	46.34 (102)	37.05 (84)	37.24 (85)	36.09 (82)	35.14 (80)	36.77 (84)	45.46 (105)	30.70 (72)	40.48 (98)
E02	South Bedfordshire	45.97 (109)	40.90 (99)	42.08 (102)	38.37 (94)	38.40 (93)	43.82 (104)	43.95 (105)	43.22 (104)	35.43 (88)
E05	North West Hertfordshire	34.28 (90)	44.53 (119)	33.05 (87)	32.46 (87)	40.55 (107)	35.68 (94)	38.98 (102)	31.46 (82)	31.52 (85)
E06	South West Hertfordshire	39.93 (107)	33.60 (90)	45.38 (125)	29.37 (82)	40.18 (106)	37.17 (101)	33.91 (87)	27.46 (71)	31.56 (83)
E07	Barnet	32.30 (106)	41.34 (133)	32.32 (102)	35.34 (112)	35.41 (109)	32.33 (97)	39.86 (119)	32.76 (93)	22.93 (69)
E09	Hillingdon	44.88 (113)	42.47 (111)	32.38 (79)	42.31 (103)	38.33 (94)	39.95 (95)	33.21 (79)	40.90 (92)	36.64 (82)
E18	East and North Hertfordshire	44.18 (205)	35.04 (167)	40.41 (191)	38.40 (185)	37.41 (180)	34.84 (166)	32.58 (156)	33.49 (161)	32.70 (163)
E19	Brent and Harrow	36.47 (172)	32.82 (150)	40.44 (183)	27.75 (122)	36.27 (155)	33.35 (139)	33.46 (133)	30.83 (120)	32.21 (130)
E20	Ealing, Hammersmith and Hounslow	50.32 (326)	44.14 (281)	48.64 (302)	45.93 (279)	49.50 (289)	41.32 (236)	39.83 (223)	40.43 (225)	40.43 (223)
E21	Kensington, Chelsea and Westminster	54.91 (188)	49.28 (160)	49.65 (161)	42.35 (131)	42.72 (131)	43.36 (131)	44.39 (134)	46.80 (141)	35.36 (110)
F31	North Essex	37.47 (339)	36.32 (328)	38.25 (348)	36.69 (342)	36.14 (333)	30.53 (273)	31.84 (300)	32.61 (299)	31.86 (304)
F32	South Essex	43.38 (310)	46.73 (342)	39.69 (290)	40.23 (287)	38.39 (276)	37.22 (266)	38.51 (278)	34.08 (250)	36.51 (271)

HON - B4,B5 (continued)
Mortality rates from lung cancer (ICD 162) in men and women under 75:
Age-standardised mortality rates per 100,000: 1984-92
(observed numbers of deaths in parentheses)
Persons

		1984	1985	1986	1987	1988	1989	1990	1991	1992
F33	Barking and Havering	53.51 (236)	43.71 (197)	47.74 (217)	49.61 (220)	45.16 (199)	47.85 (208)	37.94 (160)	40.92 (177)	41.61 (182)
F34	Redbridge and Waltham Forest	47.19 (225)	42.77 (214)	44.21 (207)	41.25 (194)	37.91 (172)	41.08 (183)	40.40 (174)	37.80 (159)	37.35 (158)
F35	East London and the City	62.94 (342)	60.74 (331)	58.91 (315)	54.00 (285)	59.94 (305)	52.67 (259)	57.03 (279)	60.88 (287)	54.89 (263)
F36	New River District	46.15 (217)	38.98 (182)	40.76 (190)	38.72 (176)	37.82 (165)	42.88 (179)	38.89 (160)	34.96 (149)	33.78 (142)
F37	Camden and Islington	50.81 (184)	58.03 (201)	52.19 (178)	51.96 (175)	61.39 (197)	55.52 (176)	60.71 (190)	44.33 (138)	50.48 (158)
G04	South East Kent	43.35 (134)	36.39 (116)	39.38 (130)	41.61 (137)	39.39 (129)	35.02 (108)	37.57 (123)	28.67 (93)	35.82 (115)
G05	Canterbury and Thanet	46.47 (177)	43.56 (164)	42.64 (155)	42.53 (158)	41.69 (154)	44.93 (164)	40.34 (148)	41.49 (153)	30.61 (117)
G06	Dartford and Gravesham	43.18 (95)	48.13 (105)	40.54 (91)	38.84 (86)	49.36 (110)	36.74 (81)	35.20 (78)	44.44 (98)	37.35 (86)
G07	Maidstone	35.15 (64)	47.36 (91)	32.31 (63)	31.60 (61)	27.51 (55)	32.01 (63)	23.73 (47)	35.82 (72)	34.65 (69)
G08	Medway	44.42 (139)	41.91 (130)	42.77 (134)	43.23 (137)	41.61 (129)	38.15 (119)	40.55 (127)	38.67 (121)	34.91 (109)
G09	Tunbridge Wells	34.12 (75)	27.49 (62)	38.06 (85)	25.90 (57)	30.21 (68)	31.62 (69)	22.97 (52)	37.34 (82)	26.42 (59)
G10	Bexley	42.68 (98)	44.14 (102)	44.14 (103)	45.83 (104)	41.53 (93)	40.45 (89)	42.20 (93)	38.39 (86)	41.78 (94)
G11	Greenwich	53.81 (123)	64.18 (145)	50.22 (116)	59.04 (125)	55.63 (119)	52.10 (104)	52.15 (109)	54.68 (114)	49.23 (104)
G12	Bromley	33.06 (114)	32.79 (115)	38.45 (129)	38.32 (130)	30.99 (106)	39.90 (132)	30.68 (101)	34.07 (109)	31.79 (107)
G21	East Sussex	33.36 (312)	39.11 (355)	37.21 (334)	34.69 (325)	34.95 (313)	33.14 (300)	33.56 (295)	27.57 (250)	29.79 (261)
G26	South East London	62.72 (470)	54.13 (401)	57.26 (411)	54.26 (373)	54.68 (367)	57.23 (372)	53.71 (340)	51.55 (327)	50.64 (320)
H04	Mid Surrey	33.30 (67)	27.78 (58)	28.16 (61)	29.01 (60)	26.19 (51)	26.23 (52)	30.41 (59)	33.95 (67)	21.75 (45)
H05	East Surrey	33.88 (73)	41.41 (88)	28.60 (60)	37.77 (80)	32.67 (69)	39.67 (81)	27.22 (58)	22.80 (47)	31.49 (61)
H06	Chichester	29.63 (75)	34.92 (88)	38.24 (96)	33.68 (83)	28.71 (68)	29.24 (74)	29.28 (73)	27.02 (63)	30.60 (76)
H07	Mid Downs	37.29 (104)	32.61 (90)	39.95 (111)	35.82 (99)	39.96 (110)	32.22 (89)	34.84 (102)	35.41 (104)	22.65 (66)
H08	Worthing	32.36 (109)	35.83 (116)	32.68 (112)	31.02 (105)	35.76 (119)	22.91 (77)	24.67 (81)	27.68 (83)	30.13 (91)
H09	Croydon	51.66 (163)	38.96 (124)	33.68 (106)	43.36 (132)	39.12 (117)	33.77 (100)	33.93 (99)	32.59 (99)	34.18 (99)

117

HON - B4,B5 (continued)
Mortality rates from lung cancer (ICD 162) in men and women under 75:
Age-standardised mortality rates per 100,000: 1984-92
(observed numbers of deaths in parentheses)
Persons

		1984	1985	1986	1987	1988	1989	1990	1991	1992
H12	Wandsworth	61.74 (115)	57.78 (108)	59.34 (104)	47.80 (84)	44.84 (76)	43.92 (69)	60.66 (92)	49.71 (75)	50.40 (77)
H13	Merton and Sutton	43.41 (163)	35.68 (132)	42.78 (161)	40.83 (144)	43.48 (148)	37.09 (127)	41.36 (139)	42.76 (141)	30.69 (103)
H14	North West Surrey	40.09 (153)	37.79 (150)	36.32 (143)	35.24 (137)	32.11 (127)	33.63 (130)	31.41 (122)	30.71 (121)	30.99 (122)
H15	South West Surrey	33.44 (86)	36.71 (91)	33.92 (87)	23.12 (59)	29.27 (74)	23.94 (63)	28.72 (74)	24.80 (64)	20.58 (52)
H16	Kingston and Richmond	40.77 (196)	37.56 (181)	40.55 (186)	36.80 (169)	36.79 (166)	34.55 (146)	33.95 (147)	33.88 (143)	33.56 (139)
J10	Dorset	31.07 (249)	33.36 (277)	33.72 (274)	30.60 (266)	32.60 (274)	29.26 (248)	27.35 (242)	29.85 (255)	27.56 (234)
J21	Portsmouth and South East Hampshire	41.36 (221)	44.04 (234)	39.78 (217)	38.49 (213)	34.50 (186)	40.61 (224)	37.43 (207)	36.88 (201)	34.78 (195)
J22	Southampton and South West Hampshire	40.66 (187)	39.18 (186)	41.87 (202)	38.82 (187)	38.83 (183)	44.78 (210)	33.57 (157)	38.78 (182)	33.96 (163)
J23	Winchester	36.80 (78)	30.69 (66)	33.54 (73)	30.45 (67)	31.65 (68)	28.15 (62)	33.81 (76)	29.34 (65)	28.11 (63)
J24	Basingstoke and North Hampshire	41.73 (121)	39.18 (116)	33.89 (100)	37.97 (113)	32.27 (98)	32.83 (100)	34.99 (107)	35.35 (111)	39.88 (127)
J31	Salisbury	29.08 (42)	36.21 (51)	31.66 (48)	32.93 (47)	25.36 (37)	27.57 (40)	29.55 (41)	26.97 (40)	28.39 (41)
J32	Swindon	44.75 (95)	38.82 (83)	40.09 (88)	41.19 (90)	42.71 (96)	39.43 (89)	38.01 (87)	42.08 (97)	32.14 (77)
J33	Bath	35.91 (158)	31.42 (137)	31.27 (137)	27.29 (122)	29.49 (132)	32.84 (145)	30.06 (132)	25.96 (118)	26.26 (120)
J41	Isle of Wight	33.29 (54)	36.37 (64)	40.31 (66)	29.97 (47)	39.59 (66)	34.86 (62)	32.98 (57)	28.31 (52)	31.45 (54)
K11	East Berkshire	48.08 (166)	42.47 (144)	39.85 (134)	37.29 (130)	35.18 (121)	37.53 (126)	31.44 (108)	37.34 (130)	31.91 (113)
K12	West Berkshire	44.79 (169)	40.03 (158)	31.80 (126)	40.95 (162)	31.60 (126)	32.08 (127)	26.46 (105)	28.03 (110)	30.35 (123)
K24	Buckinghamshire	41.21 (201)	39.78 (196)	35.33 (177)	40.60 (208)	36.53 (186)	36.50 (189)	33.18 (174)	31.19 (165)	32.02 (173)
K31	Kettering	40.07 (103)	50.46 (130)	44.79 (118)	40.76 (108)	43.16 (113)	41.34 (111)	42.89 (116)	38.43 (104)	32.36 (86)
K32	Northampton	39.45 (110)	45.85 (130)	40.30 (119)	38.39 (108)	46.28 (136)	34.12 (102)	37.39 (115)	36.69 (110)	35.23 (107)
K41	Oxfordshire	39.29 (187)	37.23 (182)	32.87 (162)	34.34 (166)	33.99 (166)	32.37 (158)	31.54 (156)	34.54 (169)	31.43 (158)
L10	Bristol and District	38.70 (336)	32.55 (289)	36.19 (322)	33.82 (299)	33.72 (297)	31.18 (272)	34.37 (297)	37.36 (326)	32.66 (292)
L21	Cornwall and Isles of Scilly	33.30 (192)	33.95 (190)	27.57 (159)	31.81 (183)	31.70 (183)	35.78 (207)	31.03 (180)	28.43 (168)	25.80 (157)

HON - B4,B5 (continued)
Mortality rates from lung cancer (ICD 162) in men and women under 75:
Age-standardised mortality rates per 100,000: 1984-92
(observed numbers of deaths in parentheses)
Persons

		1984	1985	1986	1987	1988	1989	1990	1991	1992
L35	Exeter and North Devon	34.04	29.94	29.21	28.45	24.04	27.32	28.38	27.33	28.93
		(183)	(170)	(165)	(155)	(138)	(154)	(154)	(156)	(171)
L36	Plymouth and Torbay	37.49	33.22	39.13	35.15	35.21	31.90	33.66	32.41	35.11
		(254)	(231)	(258)	(245)	(237)	(217)	(225)	(225)	(234)
L40	Gloucestershire	35.85	31.10	35.19	32.79	33.03	32.92	29.29	27.60	29.86
		(205)	(180)	(207)	(191)	(194)	(194)	(174)	(159)	(185)
L51	Somerset	33.67	33.03	29.77	33.00	28.92	29.14	24.29	26.16	31.44
		(158)	(161)	(147)	(163)	(141)	(142)	(119)	(130)	(160)
M02	Herefordshire	34.34	34.19	28.45	30.32	35.18	40.11	27.06	30.93	29.19
		(62)	(62)	(51)	(60)	(65)	(76)	(52)	(62)	(57)
M04	Worcester and District	36.27	38.04	37.08	33.84	34.76	27.16	32.87	25.71	24.47
		(93)	(97)	(98)	(93)	(96)	(77)	(91)	(71)	(73)
M05	Shropshire	42.30	43.06	36.28	38.14	45.64	34.04	34.03	36.62	36.35
		(169)	(173)	(147)	(160)	(192)	(149)	(148)	(162)	(166)
M06	Mid Staffordshire	45.81	40.49	36.14	43.27	38.94	42.87	39.10	41.96	35.92
		(132)	(121)	(107)	(130)	(121)	(132)	(121)	(135)	(117)
M07	North Staffordshire	57.02	52.70	45.63	52.10	40.52	43.25	50.43	49.32	51.96
		(300)	(278)	(241)	(273)	(214)	(230)	(263)	(258)	(274)
M08	South East Staffordshire	46.75	48.92	50.10	48.38	37.99	44.65	42.31	30.15	32.26
		(105)	(112)	(117)	(115)	(91)	(109)	(107)	(77)	(84)
M13	East Birmingham	61.58	56.54	51.00	45.66	54.81	49.47	54.60	53.25	42.27
		(144)	(125)	(119)	(106)	(115)	(110)	(110)	(110)	(91)
M14	North Birmingham	39.77	40.87	42.68	33.76	47.09	44.35	37.91	43.29	36.17
		(70)	(73)	(78)	(60)	(84)	(79)	(67)	(76)	(67)
M16	West Birmingham	57.76	60.24	59.23	45.04	50.02	50.05	37.89	53.30	54.03
		(123)	(126)	(126)	(89)	(100)	(98)	(73)	(102)	(99)
M17	Coventry	56.71	51.61	45.96	38.39	55.62	44.53	48.71	48.84	46.43
		(190)	(175)	(158)	(130)	(181)	(143)	(162)	(152)	(152)
M18	Dudley	42.01	46.78	42.87	47.27	42.60	45.15	39.22	36.94	29.03
		(134)	(150)	(140)	(156)	(139)	(150)	(132)	(125)	(99)
M19	Sandwell	56.89	55.78	57.06	55.16	59.14	55.40	49.60	53.61	55.41
		(198)	(193)	(200)	(189)	(199)	(181)	(164)	(179)	(181)
M20	Solihull	35.67	36.00	37.67	34.10	26.93	31.44	39.60	37.99	31.19
		(72)	(74)	(77)	(71)	(57)	(67)	(86)	(82)	(68)
M21	Walsall	57.82	54.28	53.07	44.21	45.80	52.05	46.20	46.80	45.23
		(156)	(150)	(148)	(122)	(125)	(143)	(128)	(131)	(128)
M22	Wolverhampton	44.37	46.51	57.50	53.47	48.40	42.19	43.33	49.92	50.70
		(123)	(126)	(160)	(146)	(134)	(117)	(120)	(140)	(140)
M25	South Birmingham	50.28	44.85	47.80	45.92	45.09	47.12	45.99	47.98	47.96
		(229)	(203)	(218)	(207)	(195)	(205)	(199)	(206)	(207)
M26	North Worcestershire	43.23	37.34	31.33	39.81	32.52	36.05	33.58	42.54	38.31
		(107)	(97)	(79)	(105)	(85)	(96)	(91)	(118)	(106)
M28	Warwickshire	41.78	37.49	43.97	36.69	37.57	36.16	39.97	33.35	39.40
		(206)	(190)	(222)	(190)	(192)	(185)	(213)	(174)	(208)

HON - B4,B5 (continued)
Mortality rates from lung cancer (ICD 162) in men and women under 75:
Age-standardised mortality rates per 100,000: 1984-92
(observed numbers of deaths in parentheses)
Persons

		1984	1985	1986	1987	1988	1989	1990	1991	1992
N11	Chester	47.81 (88)	57.56 (104)	47.59 (89)	40.39 (76)	39.06 (75)	36.63 (70)	47.98 (91)	36.58 (70)	33.28 (65)
N12	Crewe	41.39 (110)	37.26 (97)	38.85 (104)	36.38 (96)	37.91 (101)	42.77 (116)	41.32 (112)	33.57 (93)	33.06 (93)
N13	Halton	60.27 (80)	39.89 (54)	51.26 (69)	53.68 (72)	58.03 (77)	52.99 (73)	55.35 (75)	58.37 (81)	50.36 (71)
N14	Macclesfield	32.93 (65)	34.92 (68)	42.47 (81)	34.36 (67)	31.75 (61)	35.25 (70)	28.36 (56)	44.21 (86)	30.40 (63)
N15	Warrington	54.19 (95)	50.17 (88)	41.25 (73)	48.85 (88)	48.61 (87)	44.38 (82)	47.58 (84)	42.91 (76)	45.52 (85)
N21	Liverpool	65.21 (353)	78.75 (424)	74.16 (391)	78.28 (409)	76.56 (385)	65.77 (328)	66.83 (328)	73.81 (359)	71.93 (353)
N31	St Helens and Knowsley	55.21 (190)	58.06 (198)	66.91 (229)	65.14 (222)	59.10 (200)	51.98 (179)	56.47 (194)	55.64 (191)	55.50 (194)
N41	Southport and Formby	40.36 (57)	40.49 (57)	36.37 (53)	34.85 (50)	42.93 (64)	40.95 (62)	47.16 (68)	42.57 (64)	38.40 (55)
N42	South Sefton	60.73 (116)	61.77 (121)	69.79 (135)	63.71 (120)	62.42 (119)	66.62 (129)	52.45 (102)	66.78 (128)	47.70 (92)
N51	Wirral	57.82 (229)	53.26 (213)	51.20 (203)	51.90 (205)	52.47 (209)	48.24 (190)	56.86 (222)	56.58 (218)	50.04 (192)
P01	Lancaster	43.25 (63)	46.47 (68)	38.70 (58)	40.91 (63)	36.27 (54)	52.19 (72)	40.95 (64)	38.48 (58)	39.67 (61)
P02	Blackpool, Wyre and Fylde	41.46 (186)	43.32 (187)	42.16 (188)	44.08 (187)	50.92 (215)	42.01 (179)	45.11 (190)	39.37 (170)	40.16 (170)
P03	Preston	52.20 (74)	48.35 (64)	44.78 (63)	43.52 (59)	50.56 (66)	41.48 (53)	55.91 (73)	54.74 (70)	48.03 (61)
P04	Blackburn, Hyndburn and Ribble Valley	49.15 (143)	52.69 (154)	45.00 (127)	41.69 (117)	48.34 (134)	42.44 (118)	42.32 (117)	41.93 (112)	40.29 (113)
P05	Burnley, Pendle and Rossendale	49.73 (124)	51.99 (128)	49.82 (125)	49.25 (119)	62.81 (151)	47.29 (112)	45.97 (113)	42.75 (101)	42.37 (105)
P06	West Lancashire	55.97 (57)	34.35 (35)	54.37 (55)	43.09 (46)	57.72 (59)	36.36 (38)	31.84 (34)	35.48 (39)	33.39 (37)
P07	Chorley and South Ribble	53.88 (99)	49.44 (95)	44.27 (84)	44.52 (87)	37.80 (73)	34.54 (67)	30.06 (59)	39.07 (78)	38.91 (77)
P08	Bolton	47.85 (130)	39.98 (108)	48.72 (131)	49.80 (132)	43.62 (118)	44.84 (117)	45.78 (120)	52.49 (138)	41.85 (113)
P09	Bury	41.26 (76)	45.91 (82)	48.74 (87)	40.08 (71)	49.37 (86)	45.27 (80)	45.66 (82)	35.64 (63)	37.22 (66)
P10	North Manchester	86.21 (138)	78.62 (123)	83.99 (133)	74.94 (115)	78.50 (111)	92.07 (133)	74.30 (105)	85.35 (118)	83.21 (114)
P11	Central Manchester	66.88 (79)	88.36 (97)	70.05 (77)	77.01 (85)	79.10 (83)	67.61 (70)	79.03 (78)	83.30 (80)	69.86 (66)
P12	South Manchester	64.18 (126)	63.08 (120)	63.86 (119)	55.07 (103)	63.16 (116)	70.87 (129)	52.31 (90)	59.03 (99)	63.49 (111)

HON - B4,B5 (continued)
Mortality rates from lung cancer (ICD 162) in men and women under 75:
Age-standardised mortality rates per 100,000: 1984-92
(observed numbers of deaths in parentheses)
Persons

		1984	1985	1986	1987	1988	1989	1990	1991	1992
P13	Oldham	52.36	55.86	61.42	50.37	47.26	51.61	56.36	53.00	49.49
		(120)	(130)	(136)	(113)	(104)	(112)	(121)	(116)	(107)
P14	Rochdale	58.10	55.95	48.65	48.33	49.38	48.86	50.33	49.88	51.06
		(123)	(116)	(103)	(105)	(102)	(100)	(104)	(105)	(107)
P15	Salford	69.74	62.12	69.47	70.63	75.93	65.25	72.20	62.88	73.12
		(187)	(170)	(182)	(186)	(195)	(165)	(181)	(157)	(179)
P16	Stockport	51.47	51.03	44.71	42.92	43.73	37.66	35.65	45.05	41.17
		(159)	(154)	(138)	(133)	(130)	(115)	(111)	(141)	(127)
P17	Tameside and Glossop	54.99	49.07	58.92	49.98	56.68	59.88	59.93	44.75	55.86
		(146)	(126)	(153)	(130)	(148)	(148)	(154)	(116)	(137)
P18	Trafford	47.78	48.92	51.44	47.01	46.85	49.05	47.38	51.76	43.85
		(114)	(117)	(118)	(111)	(108)	(111)	(105)	(115)	(101)
P19	Wigan	56.13	52.54	44.44	48.08	55.28	44.16	48.80	50.26	42.18
		(171)	(161)	(137)	(149)	(171)	(136)	(153)	(158)	(134)

121

HON - C2
Suicide rates (ICD E950-E959, E980-E989):
Age-standardised mortality rates per 100,000: 1984-92
(observed numbers of deaths in parentheses)
Persons

		1984	1985	1986	1987	1988	1989	1990	1991	1992
	ENGLAND AND WALES	11.48 (5857)	11.93 (6153)	11.47 (6002)	11.30 (5904)	11.91 (6303)	10.75 (5677)	11.13 (5907)	11.16 (5904)	11.14 (5915)
O00	ENGLAND	11.50 (5544)	12.01 (5844)	11.45 (5660)	11.27 (5563)	11.93 (5955)	10.79 (5383)	11.17 (5594)	11.14 (5567)	11.05 (5541)
A00	NORTHERN RHA	9.93 (314)	11.40 (363)	11.33 (368)	11.05 (348)	11.75 (381)	10.73 (336)	10.72 (345)	10.77 (341)	11.42 (362)
B00	YORKSHIRE RHA	12.56 (458)	13.55 (495)	12.30 (462)	12.92 (482)	12.81 (494)	11.10 (420)	11.53 (432)	11.42 (428)	11.63 (437)
C00	TRENT RHA	10.66 (504)	11.40 (545)	10.34 (502)	10.23 (499)	11.01 (542)	10.15 (497)	10.49 (515)	10.60 (520)	10.67 (526)
D00	EAST ANGLIAN RHA	12.03 (234)	12.16 (249)	12.08 (249)	11.54 (244)	12.56 (260)	11.20 (241)	12.38 (261)	11.43 (251)	11.16 (245)
E00	NORTH WEST THAMES RHA	12.00 (430)	12.52 (438)	12.49 (451)	12.79 (464)	12.98 (468)	11.24 (405)	11.30 (410)	11.84 (436)	10.78 (395)
F00	NORTH EAST THAMES RHA	11.01 (410)	12.00 (460)	10.88 (417)	11.22 (430)	12.59 (486)	11.11 (435)	10.97 (430)	11.06 (443)	9.56 (379)
G00	SOUTH EAST THAMES RHA	13.32 (502)	13.43 (505)	12.59 (486)	12.45 (471)	12.68 (478)	12.51 (483)	12.62 (493)	12.22 (466)	12.37 (474)
H00	SOUTH WEST THAMES RHA	12.80 (387)	12.60 (393)	11.06 (349)	10.74 (334)	12.23 (390)	8.99 (289)	9.94 (320)	10.31 (317)	10.42 (337)
J00	WESSEX RHA	11.67 (360)	11.90 (372)	10.90 (344)	10.25 (333)	10.36 (346)	9.48 (316)	10.93 (360)	11.50 (376)	11.16 (368)
K00	OXFORD RHA	10.88 (259)	10.84 (263)	9.75 (239)	9.81 (248)	10.69 (276)	11.14 (288)	11.30 (293)	10.26 (264)	10.67 (284)
L00	SOUTH WESTERN RHA	12.16 (401)	11.13 (376)	11.80 (411)	11.93 (411)	12.17 (420)	11.10 (378)	11.81 (416)	11.31 (389)	12.11 (419)
M00	WEST MIDLANDS RHA	10.06 (528)	11.35 (602)	10.14 (546)	9.26 (496)	11.46 (622)	10.45 (569)	10.76 (584)	9.68 (533)	10.20 (555)
N00	MERSEY RHA	9.91 (242)	10.38 (252)	10.58 (262)	10.22 (257)	10.45 (261)	10.26 (253)	10.16 (250)	9.73 (244)	8.86 (216)
P00	NORTH WESTERN RHA	12.50 (515)	12.94 (531)	13.92 (574)	13.44 (546)	13.03 (531)	11.43 (473)	11.71 (485)	13.80 (559)	13.41 (544)
A01	Hartlepool	3.15 (3)	8.18 (8)	15.20 (14)	9.60 (9)	9.25 (8)	9.96 (9)	6.52 (6)	7.58 (7)	11.52 (10)
A02	North Tees	9.31 (16)	7.77 (14)	4.55 (7)	9.71 (17)	13.12 (23)	10.34 (18)	8.62 (16)	8.05 (15)	9.94 (17)
A03	South Tees	9.78 (28)	11.86 (33)	15.69 (45)	9.06 (27)	16.03 (46)	11.95 (35)	11.84 (33)	12.79 (38)	12.64 (35)
A04	East Cumbria	9.21 (18)	14.16 (26)	13.28 (25)	10.99 (20)	9.96 (19)	8.25 (15)	15.34 (28)	14.31 (26)	14.58 (27)
A05	South Cumbria	14.04 (27)	15.39 (29)	13.46 (25)	16.71 (30)	9.19 (18)	13.64 (25)	14.78 (28)	11.23 (19)	13.10 (23)
A06	West Cumbria	7.18 (10)	12.09 (17)	5.37 (8)	16.52 (23)	8.19 (13)	9.04 (13)	12.47 (18)	11.78 (18)	13.26 (19)

HON - C2
Suicide rates (ICD E950-E959, E980-E989):
Age-standardised mortality rates per 100,000: 1984-92
(observed numbers of deaths in parentheses)
Persons

		1984	1985	1986	1987	1988	1989	1990	1991	1992
A11	Northumberland	9.10 (27)	12.00 (39)	13.15 (41)	9.24 (28)	14.32 (45)	10.85 (35)	10.04 (32)	9.05 (28)	11.18 (37)
A12	Gateshead	10.15 (22)	8.39 (18)	10.88 (26)	11.50 (26)	11.55 (26)	9.50 (21)	9.40 (19)	7.29 (15)	8.42 (18)
A13	Newcastle	10.77 (31)	12.06 (35)	11.04 (34)	13.22 (40)	10.64 (28)	7.80 (21)	14.73 (44)	17.39 (47)	12.17 (34)
A14	North Tyneside	10.90 (22)	9.80 (22)	9.41 (21)	10.95 (22)	13.37 (29)	16.39 (32)	11.76 (24)	12.70 (27)	9.26 (19)
A15	South Tyneside	9.72 (16)	9.32 (16)	13.49 (23)	8.82 (13)	14.08 (24)	12.04 (18)	7.65 (12)	10.61 (16)	11.42 (19)
A16	Sunderland	9.53 (29)	11.27 (34)	8.34 (26)	9.03 (27)	10.79 (33)	9.98 (29)	8.83 (28)	10.67 (31)	8.83 (26)
A30	North Durham	11.75 (40)	9.52 (31)	11.90 (40)	11.63 (38)	11.59 (38)	12.35 (39)	9.97 (33)	7.27 (24)	12.89 (42)
A31	South Durham	9.30 (25)	14.60 (41)	11.13 (33)	9.90 (28)	9.77 (31)	8.89 (26)	8.13 (24)	10.03 (30)	11.96 (36)
B11	East Riding	11.15 (53)	14.06 (68)	12.12 (63)	12.28 (63)	15.27 (84)	8.73 (47)	10.73 (57)	10.19 (53)	7.62 (41)
B16	Grimsby and Scunthorpe	11.53 (41)	16.68 (59)	13.86 (49)	15.61 (54)	11.54 (43)	12.21 (45)	11.28 (40)	11.75 (42)	7.48 (26)
B21	North Yorkshire	11.89 (85)	12.93 (95)	12.29 (89)	11.47 (89)	11.53 (91)	11.70 (89)	10.78 (80)	8.98 (69)	14.60 (111)
B31	Bradford	13.92 (65)	12.72 (59)	10.11 (50)	14.52 (67)	14.93 (73)	7.77 (36)	11.34 (53)	13.89 (67)	12.10 (57)
B51	West Yorkshire	12.09 (70)	13.53 (79)	14.09 (83)	11.85 (70)	13.47 (83)	13.38 (79)	12.83 (78)	13.02 (75)	13.48 (80)
B61	Leeds	14.00 (102)	12.55 (92)	11.91 (89)	12.87 (95)	12.06 (87)	12.84 (95)	12.81 (94)	12.45 (91)	11.80 (88)
B71	Wakefield	12.91 (42)	14.02 (43)	11.43 (39)	13.76 (44)	10.37 (33)	8.85 (29)	9.42 (30)	9.85 (31)	10.36 (34)
C01	North Derbyshire	8.86 (33)	9.21 (35)	7.82 (31)	11.39 (42)	8.99 (36)	10.38 (39)	10.83 (43)	10.64 (43)	11.64 (44)
C02	Southern Derbyshire	10.79 (58)	10.05 (55)	9.34 (51)	9.73 (54)	10.78 (62)	10.71 (61)	9.55 (52)	11.45 (64)	7.93 (46)
C03	Leicestershire	11.54 (101)	11.60 (104)	10.57 (94)	8.99 (81)	9.85 (88)	10.81 (99)	9.69 (89)	9.51 (88)	10.88 (100)
C04	North Lincolnshire	11.49 (31)	9.11 (25)	9.77 (28)	11.50 (32)	12.57 (35)	8.81 (24)	12.67 (38)	9.16 (26)	7.82 (24)
C05	South Lincolnshire	10.93 (35)	10.74 (33)	7.45 (24)	11.32 (38)	12.18 (40)	11.12 (36)	10.43 (35)	12.49 (39)	8.13 (26)
C08	Nottingham	13.01 (79)	13.82 (85)	10.92 (70)	11.33 (73)	12.60 (81)	9.49 (61)	12.43 (79)	11.33 (75)	9.71 (63)
C09	Barnsley	9.06 (22)	14.47 (34)	18.16 (42)	10.86 (26)	14.31 (32)	10.10 (23)	9.28 (22)	10.54 (22)	9.92 (23)

123

HON - C2
Suicide rates (ICD E950-E959, E980-E989):
Age-standardised mortality rates per 100,000: 1984-92
(observed numbers of deaths in parentheses)
Persons

		1984	1985	1986	1987	1988	1989	1990	1991	1992
C10	Doncaster	10.97	13.54	17.37	8.43	10.96	10.63	14.00	9.82	14.24
		(31)	(40)	(51)	(25)	(33)	(32)	(42)	(31)	(42)
C11	Rotherham	11.00	10.91	7.51	9.43	11.50	8.92	6.84	13.34	12.62
		(29)	(27)	(20)	(24)	(30)	(23)	(18)	(35)	(32)
C12	Sheffield	8.37	10.48	11.72	9.76	9.43	10.31	9.53	7.48	12.00
		(46)	(61)	(65)	(58)	(56)	(58)	(53)	(41)	(67)
C14	North Nottinghamshire	9.65	11.63	5.69	11.21	11.34	9.67	10.83	13.67	13.95
		(39)	(46)	(26)	(46)	(49)	(41)	(44)	(56)	(59)
D01	Cambridge	12.75	10.53	11.80	10.06	14.80	14.25	13.69	8.64	13.50
		(35)	(29)	(32)	(29)	(43)	(42)	(38)	(26)	(43)
D05	North West Anglia	13.66	14.70	14.04	13.83	13.21	13.09	11.57	17.68	12.70
		(48)	(57)	(55)	(55)	(53)	(54)	(48)	(73)	(54)
D06	Norwich	11.68	12.35	11.76	9.70	12.29	10.76	13.30	9.56	10.65
		(58)	(62)	(58)	(50)	(61)	(55)	(65)	(51)	(55)
D07	Great Yarmouth and Waveney	11.77	10.24	12.92	15.34	14.52	10.33	7.38	10.82	12.89
		(23)	(21)	(25)	(31)	(28)	(22)	(15)	(22)	(27)
D09	Huntingdon	7.03	10.74	11.57	13.18	14.86	7.21	4.67	12.51	12.60
		(8)	(13)	(16)	(17)	(19)	(10)	(7)	(17)	(18)
D11	Suffolk	11.82	12.30	11.09	10.91	9.95	10.34	15.64	10.20	8.42
		(62)	(67)	(63)	(62)	(56)	(58)	(88)	(62)	(48)
E01	North Bedfordshire	8.77	7.48	9.13	10.83	10.49	11.90	13.53	13.24	10.60
		(20)	(16)	(22)	(28)	(26)	(29)	(35)	(33)	(28)
E02	South Bedfordshire	9.12	12.55	12.16	7.25	12.47	9.49	10.46	12.32	11.67
		(24)	(34)	(35)	(22)	(36)	(25)	(29)	(36)	(32)
E05	North West Hertfordshire	12.81	12.53	8.63	12.91	11.43	9.78	10.53	9.51	7.48
		(35)	(33)	(24)	(34)	(33)	(27)	(29)	(27)	(20)
E06	South West Hertfordshire	10.41	8.28	10.95	10.40	10.64	13.73	8.62	16.55	8.52
		(25)	(22)	(29)	(28)	(29)	(35)	(22)	(40)	(22)
E07	Barnet	13.28	9.59	12.22	8.52	9.62	8.57	9.00	10.93	8.83
		(40)	(29)	(39)	(27)	(30)	(29)	(26)	(34)	(29)
E09	Hillingdon	7.74	7.48	11.25	7.72	11.70	5.54	8.31	6.17	9.37
		(20)	(20)	(29)	(18)	(29)	(13)	(21)	(16)	(23)
E18	East and North Hertfordshire	8.72	9.90	15.05	12.06	8.96	10.53	8.92	7.46	7.59
		(43)	(47)	(73)	(60)	(45)	(50)	(44)	(38)	(39)
E19	Brent and Harrow	9.75	12.42	10.28	13.71	13.95	10.86	9.55	11.41	14.37
		(48)	(56)	(51)	(65)	(68)	(53)	(47)	(54)	(65)
E20	Ealing, Hammersmith and Hounslow	12.11	12.31	9.77	14.69	13.30	11.05	14.93	13.26	11.38
		(82)	(77)	(65)	(98)	(87)	(76)	(97)	(94)	(79)
E21	Kensington, Chelsea and Westminster	27.01	29.80	24.77	24.83	25.68	19.41	17.03	17.68	15.87
		(93)	(104)	(84)	(84)	(85)	(68)	(60)	(64)	(58)
F31	North Essex	9.55	12.22	9.69	8.59	12.21	7.87	9.49	10.83	8.32
		(78)	(106)	(84)	(77)	(106)	(73)	(85)	(95)	(76)
F32	South Essex	8.52	11.05	10.16	9.82	10.34	8.90	11.08	9.91	8.19
		(59)	(76)	(70)	(69)	(72)	(64)	(79)	(77)	(58)

124

HON - C2
Suicide rates (ICD E950-E959, E980-E989):
Age-standardised mortality rates per 100,000: 1984-92
(observed numbers of deaths in parentheses)
Persons

		1984	1985	1986	1987	1988	1989	1990	1991	1992
F33	Barking and Havering	6.09 (24)	8.37 (34)	9.07 (37)	10.14 (38)	5.97 (24)	8.54 (33)	11.78 (46)	10.25 (41)	7.69 (28)
F34	Redbridge and Waltham Forest	11.38 (53)	10.22 (49)	9.95 (46)	11.29 (52)	11.34 (52)	10.24 (46)	7.10 (34)	8.82 (43)	9.48 (46)
F35	East London and the City	14.83 (78)	12.74 (69)	12.66 (67)	12.14 (69)	15.09 (82)	15.30 (89)	12.68 (75)	13.35 (77)	9.83 (56)
F36	New River District	13.80 (65)	12.14 (58)	11.76 (57)	13.00 (63)	13.51 (69)	12.22 (59)	8.93 (43)	11.52 (56)	9.76 (52)
F37	Camden and Islington	14.83 (53)	18.30 (68)	14.07 (56)	17.23 (62)	22.13 (81)	19.80 (71)	17.14 (68)	13.56 (54)	17.28 (63)
G04	South East Kent	12.58 (33)	10.11 (32)	9.84 (26)	13.83 (37)	14.47 (41)	10.65 (30)	16.47 (46)	11.07 (32)	8.03 (23)
G05	Canterbury and Thanet	9.71 (31)	15.49 (46)	15.00 (46)	12.36 (38)	12.36 (37)	10.80 (35)	11.04 (36)	13.46 (39)	11.53 (38)
G06	Dartford and Gravesham	10.15 (22)	7.79 (18)	13.51 (31)	11.00 (25)	12.89 (28)	9.29 (21)	9.90 (23)	6.51 (15)	12.13 (28)
G07	Maidstone	11.16 (21)	8.35 (17)	7.20 (16)	7.17 (15)	9.81 (20)	9.65 (20)	9.16 (19)	10.38 (21)	10.47 (21)
G08	Medway	9.54 (33)	8.52 (29)	7.84 (25)	10.76 (33)	8.21 (26)	11.98 (40)	12.68 (45)	9.59 (33)	7.54 (25)
G09	Tunbridge Wells	9.22 (20)	13.04 (30)	7.94 (18)	8.88 (20)	10.63 (24)	10.17 (21)	11.79 (23)	9.68 (20)	7.45 (16)
G10	Bexley	4.75 (11)	12.01 (26)	7.92 (19)	6.06 (14)	6.56 (15)	11.30 (25)	9.44 (21)	8.00 (17)	6.70 (16)
G11	Greenwich	13.89 (30)	12.55 (25)	14.79 (34)	10.61 (25)	15.61 (34)	9.91 (21)	9.49 (20)	9.91 (21)	15.22 (32)
G12	Bromley	11.53 (37)	8.94 (27)	10.28 (34)	9.62 (29)	7.39 (25)	12.16 (42)	6.37 (21)	12.17 (36)	8.43 (26)
G21	East Sussex	15.79 (121)	15.35 (112)	14.77 (113)	11.85 (89)	13.49 (100)	11.88 (92)	13.28 (107)	14.49 (111)	16.57 (128)
G26	South East London	20.39 (143)	20.23 (143)	17.27 (124)	20.16 (146)	17.89 (128)	19.05 (136)	17.77 (132)	16.94 (121)	16.60 (121)
H04	Mid Surrey	8.55 (14)	15.12 (27)	7.56 (12)	7.98 (13)	7.99 (14)	10.26 (19)	6.68 (12)	10.61 (19)	9.82 (19)
H05	East Surrey	10.46 (21)	10.20 (20)	10.33 (20)	14.74 (27)	12.71 (27)	10.36 (19)	10.25 (21)	13.68 (27)	13.99 (28)
H06	Chichester	13.93 (23)	14.52 (29)	9.00 (20)	8.52 (16)	19.44 (39)	14.53 (30)	9.16 (16)	12.76 (20)	12.92 (24)
H07	Mid Downs	11.60 (31)	13.55 (40)	9.26 (27)	9.18 (26)	11.44 (34)	7.24 (21)	12.84 (39)	11.22 (33)	10.64 (32)
H08	Worthing	14.92 (43)	13.75 (40)	15.21 (39)	10.82 (31)	15.01 (39)	6.72 (21)	8.45 (26)	13.35 (33)	15.78 (43)
H09	Croydon	13.55 (46)	10.80 (36)	12.60 (43)	10.41 (35)	10.29 (33)	8.84 (29)	9.87 (31)	7.58 (24)	7.91 (27)

HON - C2
Suicide rates (ICD E950-E959, E980-E989):
Age-standardised mortality rates per 100,000: 1984-92
(observed numbers of deaths in parentheses)
Persons

		1984	1985	1986	1987	1988	1989	1990	1991	1992
H12	Wandsworth	19.75 (33)	12.70 (23)	8.99 (21)	14.77 (28)	19.89 (36)	9.28 (19)	11.25 (22)	14.76 (23)	13.23 (26)
H13	Merton and Sutton	11.59 (42)	14.00 (49)	12.75 (45)	9.62 (34)	9.96 (37)	6.92 (26)	13.69 (50)	10.69 (37)	7.58 (30)
H14	North West Surrey	13.89 (55)	11.84 (46)	11.18 (44)	11.34 (46)	10.78 (43)	10.56 (43)	8.01 (33)	10.21 (43)	8.89 (37)
H15	South West Surrey	9.46 (23)	10.01 (25)	8.49 (21)	9.54 (26)	10.19 (29)	7.81 (21)	9.50 (25)	6.54 (17)	9.28 (23)
H16	Kingston and Richmond	13.58 (56)	13.44 (58)	12.69 (57)	11.48 (52)	13.06 (59)	8.90 (41)	9.69 (45)	9.23 (41)	10.33 (48)
J10	Dorset	13.77 (96)	15.34 (106)	14.66 (100)	12.94 (92)	10.37 (77)	10.03 (75)	13.95 (100)	13.13 (88)	10.17 (75)
J21	Portsmouth and South East Hampshire	11.17 (56)	13.91 (75)	11.31 (58)	9.93 (57)	9.90 (55)	9.59 (51)	8.30 (46)	10.81 (62)	10.95 (61)
J22	Southampton and South West Hampshire	9.36 (41)	8.65 (38)	10.23 (46)	7.57 (35)	11.84 (54)	9.65 (44)	14.44 (66)	13.55 (61)	12.23 (56)
J23	Winchester	13.95 (31)	10.33 (22)	12.58 (29)	9.70 (22)	10.21 (23)	6.57 (16)	6.45 (15)	8.86 (21)	11.25 (26)
J24	Basingstoke and North Hampshire	10.79 (35)	12.39 (43)	8.02 (28)	9.20 (33)	9.83 (36)	10.39 (38)	8.42 (32)	10.68 (41)	12.52 (48)
J31	Salisbury	13.99 (17)	9.11 (12)	10.62 (16)	9.56 (13)	9.68 (12)	6.26 (8)	17.80 (23)	9.57 (13)	10.17 (12)
J32	Swindon	11.73 (26)	10.14 (22)	8.96 (21)	9.16 (21)	12.64 (31)	8.62 (21)	10.07 (25)	12.87 (32)	11.04 (27)
J33	Bath	10.78 (43)	11.36 (44)	8.29 (32)	10.48 (44)	10.01 (45)	10.39 (47)	7.94 (36)	10.51 (44)	12.31 (52)
J41	Isle of Wight	10.03 (15)	5.80 (10)	9.09 (14)	11.59 (16)	8.16 (13)	10.56 (16)	12.53 (17)	11.63 (14)	7.18 (11)
K11	East Berkshire	10.72 (39)	13.95 (50)	10.09 (36)	8.14 (31)	10.26 (38)	10.04 (38)	8.55 (31)	12.69 (47)	11.54 (43)
K12	West Berkshire	13.68 (55)	9.92 (44)	12.07 (52)	9.07 (42)	7.74 (36)	10.24 (48)	12.72 (59)	8.22 (39)	11.44 (53)
K24	Buckinghamshire	10.88 (59)	12.04 (67)	9.91 (55)	12.09 (71)	12.00 (69)	11.02 (66)	8.32 (51)	9.66 (55)	11.66 (75)
K31	Kettering	9.61 (25)	11.56 (28)	7.21 (19)	12.07 (31)	10.09 (28)	12.37 (34)	14.05 (38)	11.54 (31)	9.24 (26)
K32	Northampton	13.68 (40)	7.24 (21)	9.28 (28)	9.58 (29)	10.58 (34)	11.59 (35)	13.61 (43)	11.54 (37)	10.07 (33)
K41	Oxfordshire	7.74 (41)	9.88 (53)	8.91 (49)	8.34 (44)	12.19 (71)	11.82 (67)	12.82 (71)	9.58 (55)	9.62 (54)
L10	Bristol and District	10.88 (91)	10.79 (92)	12.39 (106)	14.01 (121)	13.40 (114)	9.04 (76)	11.26 (100)	11.52 (98)	10.64 (93)
L21	Cornwall and Isles of Scilly	14.76 (69)	14.06 (70)	10.61 (56)	12.46 (62)	13.99 (68)	12.77 (64)	12.83 (66)	11.93 (60)	14.59 (72)

HON - C2
Suicide rates (ICD E950-E959, E980-E989):
Age-standardised mortality rates per 100,000: 1984-92
(observed numbers of deaths in parentheses)
Persons

		1984	1985	1986	1987	1988	1989	1990	1991	1992
L35	Exeter and North Devon	14.40 (66)	11.35 (52)	15.90 (73)	12.85 (63)	13.26 (62)	14.66 (67)	10.00 (52)	10.61 (51)	10.09 (51)
L36	Plymouth and Torbay	15.25 (88)	10.76 (63)	11.37 (73)	9.84 (63)	10.77 (65)	12.07 (76)	10.20 (62)	12.30 (76)	13.34 (82)
L40	Gloucestershire	7.57 (40)	10.03 (56)	7.71 (45)	8.87 (49)	11.85 (70)	10.09 (55)	12.35 (71)	9.78 (55)	12.80 (73)
L51	Somerset	10.96 (47)	10.12 (43)	13.30 (58)	12.67 (53)	9.05 (41)	9.56 (40)	14.76 (65)	11.64 (49)	10.93 (48)
M02	Herefordshire	11.41 (19)	21.88 (37)	8.09 (13)	10.38 (17)	6.74 (11)	14.00 (26)	10.31 (18)	13.19 (23)	6.92 (13)
M04	Worcester and District	9.01 (21)	11.09 (26)	10.57 (26)	10.24 (26)	10.71 (28)	8.61 (22)	12.71 (32)	8.87 (23)	8.02 (21)
M05	Shropshire	7.46 (29)	11.69 (49)	10.82 (45)	8.93 (37)	11.47 (49)	7.73 (32)	7.89 (34)	8.31 (36)	7.40 (32)
M06	Mid Staffordshire	6.61 (20)	8.45 (26)	8.75 (27)	11.25 (37)	15.00 (49)	11.01 (37)	10.32 (35)	8.90 (30)	11.29 (37)
M07	North Staffordshire	11.32 (54)	13.14 (64)	10.54 (52)	10.06 (48)	11.85 (58)	10.20 (50)	14.77 (70)	8.54 (42)	10.33 (51)
M08	South East Staffordshire	8.41 (21)	10.75 (26)	5.31 (14)	6.85 (18)	10.96 (29)	11.21 (30)	9.71 (26)	7.08 (20)	8.21 (22)
M13	East Birmingham	12.10 (23)	6.59 (13)	7.29 (14)	5.18 (10)	9.96 (19)	12.55 (25)	10.23 (19)	10.93 (19)	11.04 (21)
M14	North Birmingham	7.14 (12)	9.27 (16)	8.43 (15)	7.75 (13)	12.15 (21)	8.93 (15)	9.40 (15)	7.24 (12)	12.31 (21)
M16	West Birmingham	15.18 (33)	15.23 (31)	10.67 (24)	12.93 (25)	15.54 (31)	16.78 (34)	18.01 (38)	16.93 (38)	12.54 (24)
M17	Coventry	11.01 (38)	12.01 (37)	9.70 (30)	10.53 (33)	13.54 (42)	8.01 (25)	10.73 (33)	14.08 (42)	13.98 (42)
M18	Dudley	12.52 (40)	9.02 (28)	14.01 (44)	5.69 (18)	9.69 (32)	8.20 (27)	11.63 (39)	7.17 (24)	7.50 (24)
M19	Sandwell	7.51 (22)	14.68 (45)	9.63 (31)	8.49 (25)	16.02 (50)	8.76 (26)	8.36 (24)	10.65 (32)	9.03 (26)
M20	Solihull	9.51 (18)	6.78 (14)	11.73 (24)	7.75 (16)	4.34 (9)	9.67 (21)	9.47 (21)	7.17 (15)	9.00 (19)
M21	Walsall	7.77 (20)	4.94 (14)	10.71 (28)	7.28 (20)	12.54 (34)	10.14 (27)	7.86 (21)	9.90 (26)	14.68 (41)
M22	Wolverhampton	12.89 (34)	10.82 (29)	9.52 (26)	12.83 (32)	10.96 (29)	14.56 (38)	12.72 (31)	15.63 (41)	9.96 (24)
M25	South Birmingham	12.32 (54)	13.55 (60)	11.08 (50)	8.17 (36)	14.84 (62)	12.41 (50)	12.57 (54)	10.24 (46)	12.99 (59)
M26	North Worcestershire	9.10 (24)	10.06 (27)	11.55 (31)	10.63 (29)	7.90 (22)	10.14 (29)	11.01 (31)	7.96 (23)	8.31 (23)
M28	Warwickshire	9.33 (46)	12.04 (60)	10.47 (52)	10.96 (56)	9.20 (47)	10.62 (55)	8.10 (43)	7.81 (41)	10.68 (55)

127

HON - C2
Suicide rates (ICD E950-E959, E980-E989):
Age-standardised mortality rates per 100,000: 1984-92
(observed numbers of deaths in parentheses)
Persons

		1984	1985	1986	1987	1988	1989	1990	1991	1992
N11	Chester	5.93 (11)	11.56 (22)	7.95 (15)	8.07 (15)	10.10 (18)	11.91 (21)	10.13 (18)	8.47 (15)	6.68 (13)
N12	Crewe	9.32 (24)	13.93 (34)	7.23 (21)	11.70 (32)	8.60 (22)	10.78 (28)	13.25 (34)	11.43 (30)	7.63 (21)
N13	Halton	10.63 (14)	10.31 (14)	12.07 (17)	7.06 (10)	9.13 (13)	10.06 (14)	7.90 (11)	12.86 (19)	8.27 (12)
N14	Macclesfield	9.60 (18)	12.87 (24)	7.76 (16)	14.76 (30)	10.35 (20)	6.89 (13)	10.20 (19)	7.48 (14)	6.41 (12)
N15	Warrington	9.79 (17)	11.46 (20)	14.18 (25)	9.60 (17)	10.87 (20)	10.01 (19)	12.36 (23)	10.12 (20)	12.31 (23)
N21	Liverpool	10.18 (50)	10.14 (48)	14.96 (68)	10.67 (53)	12.62 (62)	11.08 (54)	8.30 (43)	9.77 (47)	10.69 (49)
N31	St Helens and Knowsley	9.29 (31)	7.59 (26)	8.83 (30)	12.21 (43)	8.97 (31)	10.32 (36)	7.99 (28)	10.08 (35)	8.74 (29)
N41	Southport and Formby	9.32 (11)	5.88 (8)	14.28 (17)	9.34 (12)	8.08 (11)	10.22 (12)	10.67 (13)	9.98 (12)	6.00 (7)
N42	South Sefton	13.61 (25)	13.32 (24)	8.08 (15)	7.58 (14)	10.49 (20)	8.72 (16)	11.29 (22)	7.29 (14)	8.65 (16)
N51	Wirral	11.02 (41)	8.98 (32)	10.13 (38)	8.48 (31)	11.72 (44)	10.86 (40)	11.29 (39)	10.30 (38)	10.13 (34)
P01	Lancaster	13.29 (18)	10.64 (14)	7.02 (9)	13.99 (17)	10.30 (13)	12.06 (17)	14.93 (18)	14.34 (20)	9.43 (15)
P02	Blackpool, Wyre and Fylde	14.11 (51)	16.30 (56)	14.08 (51)	15.37 (53)	13.64 (51)	11.89 (43)	11.49 (42)	13.44 (46)	11.66 (39)
P03	Preston	14.05 (18)	13.12 (16)	16.57 (21)	9.80 (12)	12.19 (17)	9.78 (12)	13.55 (18)	18.15 (24)	14.05 (17)
P04	Blackburn, Hyndburn and Ribble Valley	13.63 (37)	12.99 (37)	14.02 (40)	13.70 (41)	13.75 (37)	11.70 (32)	13.33 (35)	8.78 (25)	16.43 (45)
P05	Burnley, Pendle and Rossendale	15.04 (35)	8.91 (22)	14.45 (34)	13.95 (33)	13.85 (31)	17.59 (43)	15.05 (37)	15.25 (37)	17.52 (42)
P06	West Lancashire	13.46 (14)	15.25 (16)	13.06 (15)	12.75 (14)	10.91 (12)	4.21 (5)	11.57 (13)	9.52 (10)	4.49 (5)
P07	Chorley and South Ribble	13.70 (26)	7.93 (15)	20.07 (38)	12.20 (24)	9.13 (19)	7.01 (13)	10.81 (22)	14.26 (30)	9.08 (19)
P08	Bolton	13.95 (38)	11.57 (31)	13.87 (35)	18.00 (47)	7.70 (21)	9.72 (26)	9.63 (27)	10.83 (28)	17.22 (47)
P09	Bury	9.76 (18)	13.39 (24)	8.65 (17)	10.79 (19)	7.28 (14)	7.30 (13)	5.46 (11)	19.41 (35)	10.52 (18)
P10	North Manchester	12.85 (17)	11.86 (17)	20.48 (29)	18.96 (26)	20.04 (26)	14.85 (20)	18.21 (23)	24.42 (32)	21.65 (28)
P11	Central Manchester	20.03 (23)	23.69 (27)	19.44 (22)	21.47 (22)	27.94 (32)	13.97 (15)	22.01 (22)	21.56 (26)	20.00 (24)
P12	South Manchester	12.76 (22)	15.12 (26)	21.18 (38)	14.64 (29)	18.91 (34)	17.75 (32)	9.55 (18)	18.97 (32)	18.55 (30)

HON - C2
Suicide rates (ICD E950-E959, E980-E989):
Age-standardised mortality rates per 100,000: 1984-92
(observed numbers of deaths in parentheses)
Persons

		1984	1985	1986	1987	1988	1989	1990	1991	1992
P13	Oldham	13.20	13.40	13.14	10.81	17.40	8.94	13.78	15.68	13.46
		(31)	(29)	(30)	(24)	(38)	(19)	(31)	(36)	(30)
P14	Rochdale	10.68	12.62	9.52	12.64	7.26	13.69	14.44	15.41	15.18
		(24)	(28)	(21)	(26)	(16)	(28)	(31)	(31)	(31)
P15	Salford	15.13	15.90	14.75	14.01	15.30	13.91	10.20	16.09	15.57
		(37)	(38)	(37)	(34)	(36)	(34)	(24)	(35)	(35)
P16	Stockport	10.19	11.03	10.19	15.13	10.26	10.41	10.86	9.04	10.68
		(30)	(31)	(30)	(44)	(30)	(32)	(32)	(26)	(32)
P17	Tameside and Glossop	8.90	12.85	9.76	8.26	10.13	10.44	8.72	11.63	7.73
		(22)	(32)	(26)	(21)	(25)	(26)	(23)	(30)	(20)
P18	Trafford	7.79	13.29	17.08	9.39	14.28	10.96	11.79	10.57	8.61
		(17)	(30)	(37)	(22)	(32)	(25)	(26)	(24)	(18)
P19	Wigan	11.13	13.41	13.34	12.16	14.75	11.52	9.58	10.17	15.17
		(37)	(42)	(44)	(38)	(47)	(38)	(32)	(32)	(49)

HON - E1
Mortality rates from accidents (ICD E800-E949) in children under 15:
Age-standardised mortality rates per 100,000: 1984-92
(observed numbers of deaths in parentheses)
Persons

		1984	1985	1986	1987	1988	1989	1990	1991	1992
	ENGLAND AND WALES	9.25 (880)	8.98 (853)	7.52 (703)	7.31 (681)	7.32 (686)	7.47 (705)	6.74 (642)	5.98 (579)	5.65 (553)
O00	ENGLAND	9.12 (818)	9.00 (807)	7.43 (655)	7.27 (639)	7.41 (655)	7.45 (663)	6.77 (608)	5.94 (543)	5.51 (509)
A00	NORTHERN RHA	8.81 (55)	10.37 (63)	8.11 (48)	5.89 (34)	9.21 (54)	9.42 (55)	9.11 (53)	8.48 (50)	5.55 (33)
B00	YORKSHIRE RHA	10.61 (76)	9.89 (71)	8.38 (58)	9.38 (65)	7.88 (54)	7.02 (49)	7.17 (50)	6.87 (49)	5.71 (41)
C00	TRENT RHA	10.01 (89)	9.40 (83)	8.91 (77)	7.05 (61)	7.05 (61)	7.08 (62)	6.41 (56)	4.63 (41)	4.80 (43)
D00	EAST ANGLIAN RHA	9.40 (35)	8.38 (31)	8.94 (33)	6.00 (22)	7.66 (29)	7.43 (28)	4.46 (17)	5.72 (22)	6.93 (27)
E00	NORTH WEST THAMES RHA	8.40 (52)	7.19 (45)	6.63 (41)	7.02 (43)	6.57 (41)	6.78 (42)	4.98 (32)	5.40 (35)	4.71 (31)
F00	NORTH EAST THAMES RHA	7.70 (54)	8.32 (58)	5.64 (39)	7.56 (52)	5.60 (39)	7.10 (50)	7.93 (57)	6.00 (44)	5.14 (38)
G00	SOUTH EAST THAMES RHA	9.53 (61)	8.05 (53)	6.25 (40)	5.81 (37)	6.53 (42)	5.65 (37)	6.56 (44)	4.49 (31)	5.75 (40)
H00	SOUTH WEST THAMES RHA	6.59 (33)	6.44 (33)	5.33 (27)	5.60 (28)	4.63 (23)	5.00 (25)	6.47 (33)	4.39 (23)	2.82 (15)
J00	WESSEX RHA	7.35 (41)	8.29 (45)	6.43 (35)	7.35 (40)	3.44 (19)	8.09 (45)	8.38 (47)	6.09 (35)	3.27 (19)
K00	OXFORD RHA	6.41 (31)	9.06 (44)	6.69 (32)	7.37 (36)	9.23 (45)	6.73 (33)	6.17 (31)	5.31 (27)	4.66 (24)
L00	SOUTH WESTERN RHA	8.64 (50)	6.79 (38)	6.50 (36)	6.44 (37)	7.91 (45)	7.88 (45)	2.77 (16)	3.57 (21)	5.04 (30)
M00	WEST MIDLANDS RHA	9.00 (92)	9.83 (101)	8.93 (89)	8.36 (84)	8.24 (83)	8.52 (86)	6.94 (70)	7.06 (72)	8.71 (90)
N00	MERSEY RHA	12.93 (62)	9.81 (48)	7.67 (37)	6.64 (31)	8.09 (38)	7.91 (37)	7.61 (36)	6.88 (33)	7.18 (35)
P00	NORTH WESTERN RHA	11.02 (87)	11.98 (94)	8.14 (63)	8.95 (69)	10.58 (82)	8.83 (69)	8.40 (66)	7.53 (60)	5.31 (43)
A01	Hartlepool	14.59 (3)	0.00 (0)	4.87 (1)	0.00 (0)	5.21 (1)	5.51 (1)	21.95 (4)	0.00 (0)	4.82 (1)
A02	North Tees	0.00 (0)	5.25 (2)	5.45 (2)	2.56 (1)	5.51 (2)	7.47 (3)	7.99 (3)	13.95 (5)	11.02 (4)
A03	South Tees	4.35 (3)	8.87 (6)	6.36 (4)	0.00 (0)	14.32 (9)	9.92 (6)	6.34 (4)	9.53 (6)	4.70 (3)
A04	East Cumbria	5.16 (2)	14.18 (5)	3.54 (1)	7.12 (2)	6.57 (2)	9.56 (3)	3.48 (1)	3.45 (1)	3.34 (1)
A05	South Cumbria	6.75 (2)	3.35 (1)	12.45 (4)	14.45 (4)	7.31 (2)	6.75 (2)	13.98 (4)	6.74 (2)	13.37 (4)
A06	West Cumbria	22.51 (6)	15.96 (4)	3.40 (1)	3.57 (1)	4.12 (1)	8.10 (2)	15.46 (4)	7.44 (2)	3.53 (1)

HON - E1
Mortality rates from accidents (ICD E800-E949) in children under 15:
Age-standardised mortality rates per 100,000: 1984-92
(observed numbers of deaths in parentheses)
Persons

		1984	1985	1986	1987	1988	1989	1990	1991	1992
A11	Northumberland	12.91 (7)	7.42 (4)	4.90 (3)	5.25 (3)	4.89 (3)	6.92 (4)	5.31 (3)	1.64 (1)	7.25 (4)
A12	Gateshead	7.61 (3)	8.25 (3)	10.68 (4)	2.90 (1)	0.00 (0)	19.32 (7)	5.30 (2)	2.83 (1)	5.52 (2)
A13	Newcastle	15.25 (8)	8.22 (4)	8.24 (4)	12.24 (6)	12.63 (6)	6.46 (3)	14.05 (7)	16.14 (8)	6.10 (3)
A14	North Tyneside	3.03 (1)	8.28 (3)	8.32 (3)	8.38 (3)	8.04 (3)	5.70 (2)	11.07 (4)	5.27 (2)	2.63 (1)
A15	South Tyneside	13.39 (4)	17.31 (5)	17.52 (5)	0.00 (0)	17.31 (5)	6.76 (2)	10.19 (3)	6.75 (2)	6.45 (2)
A16	Sunderland	7.11 (5)	11.03 (7)	14.39 (9)	9.98 (6)	11.71 (7)	6.85 (4)	13.03 (8)	5.05 (3)	3.37 (2)
A30	North Durham	5.34 (4)	19.44 (12)	6.93 (4)	4.95 (3)	14.70 (9)	16.89 (10)	3.46 (2)	12.91 (8)	3.06 (2)
A31	South Durham	13.23 (7)	11.92 (7)	5.26 (3)	7.91 (4)	7.61 (4)	11.06 (6)	7.71 (4)	17.13 (9)	5.60 (3)
B11	East Riding	15.94 (15)	9.31 (9)	4.39 (4)	11.50 (11)	7.45 (7)	9.35 (9)	3.00 (3)	6.15 (6)	8.11 (8)
B16	Grimsby and Scunthorpe	11.14 (8)	7.26 (5)	5.86 (4)	11.61 (9)	11.35 (8)	7.04 (5)	4.13 (3)	8.32 (6)	8.06 (6)
B21	North Yorkshire	9.99 (13)	8.31 (10)	9.31 (11)	3.30 (4)	8.20 (10)	3.95 (5)	6.62 (8)	1.52 (2)	2.23 (3)
B31	Bradford	10.96 (11)	13.19 (14)	8.75 (9)	12.88 (13)	5.84 (6)	4.81 (5)	15.64 (16)	7.58 (8)	5.74 (6)
B51	West Yorkshire	7.34 (9)	10.57 (13)	10.37 (12)	9.80 (11)	7.06 (8)	7.80 (9)	8.84 (10)	6.12 (7)	6.14 (7)
B61	Leeds	9.68 (13)	12.27 (16)	11.56 (15)	10.98 (14)	7.12 (9)	7.77 (10)	4.61 (6)	12.64 (17)	5.96 (8)
B71	Wakefield	10.18 (7)	5.94 (4)	4.88 (3)	5.15 (3)	10.09 (6)	10.20 (6)	6.65 (4)	5.00 (3)	4.69 (3)
C01	North Derbyshire	3.04 (2)	11.77 (8)	8.00 (5)	3.44 (2)	5.84 (4)	4.79 (3)	6.20 (4)	2.92 (2)	4.33 (3)
C02	Southern Derbyshire	10.27 (10)	14.43 (14)	8.64 (9)	2.96 (3)	7.16 (7)	6.90 (7)	6.01 (6)	4.92 (5)	1.93 (2)
C03	Leicestershire	11.57 (20)	7.36 (13)	10.15 (17)	8.68 (15)	6.36 (11)	5.57 (10)	4.57 (8)	5.13 (9)	6.21 (11)
C04	North Lincolnshire	9.56 (5)	4.02 (2)	5.87 (3)	9.84 (5)	4.42 (2)	4.04 (2)	6.20 (3)	5.69 (3)	3.97 (2)
C05	South Lincolnshire	10.73 (7)	9.89 (5)	10.76 (5)	11.85 (6)	16.96 (9)	7.20 (4)	5.65 (3)	3.67 (2)	5.04 (3)
C08	Nottingham	11.88 (13)	9.21 (11)	3.45 (4)	6.95 (8)	9.86 (11)	15.62 (18)	9.58 (11)	6.14 (7)	2.45 (3)
C09	Barnsley	12.15 (6)	4.74 (2)	2.39 (1)	9.48 (4)	2.32 (1)	6.99 (3)	9.29 (4)	0.00 (0)	4.62 (2)

HON - E1
Mortality rates from accidents (ICD E800-E949) in children under 15:
Age-standardised mortality rates per 100,000: 1984-92
(observed numbers of deaths in parentheses)
Persons

		1984	1985	1986	1987	1988	1989	1990	1991	1992
C10	Doncaster	11.90 (7)	7.51 (4)	8.64 (5)	3.60 (2)	5.22 (3)	7.15 (4)	8.65 (5)	8.40 (5)	5.08 (3)
C11	Rotherham	5.67 (3)	11.10 (6)	25.45 (13)	4.30 (2)	14.09 (7)	9.75 (5)	4.05 (2)	5.94 (3)	6.02 (3)
C12	Sheffield	8.25 (7)	8.96 (8)	7.82 (7)	9.17 (8)	2.31 (2)	4.54 (4)	4.50 (4)	1.12 (1)	8.78 (8)
C14	North Nottinghamshire	11.72 (9)	12.08 (10)	10.19 (8)	7.91 (6)	5.09 (4)	2.87 (2)	7.70 (6)	5.07 (4)	3.90 (3)
D01	Cambridge	6.31 (3)	14.27 (7)	10.15 (5)	6.23 (3)	8.21 (4)	0.00 (0)	4.03 (2)	9.73 (5)	7.66 (4)
D05	North West Anglia	11.67 (9)	13.65 (10)	7.80 (6)	9.32 (7)	5.12 (4)	10.30 (8)	2.64 (2)	7.66 (6)	11.61 (9)
D06	Norwich	11.80 (10)	7.26 (6)	10.84 (8)	8.08 (6)	7.61 (6)	6.06 (5)	3.66 (3)	8.86 (7)	4.52 (4)
D07	Great Yarmouth and Waveney	14.18 (5)	11.88 (4)	5.22 (2)	2.50 (1)	7.83 (3)	23.33 (8)	13.93 (5)	0.00 (0)	2.91 (1)
D09	Huntingdon	3.47 (1)	7.75 (2)	10.75 (3)	0.00 (0)	3.70 (1)	7.48 (2)	3.79 (1)	0.00 (0)	3.31 (1)
D11	Suffolk	7.16 (7)	1.85 (2)	8.75 (9)	4.73 (5)	10.18 (11)	4.61 (5)	3.59 (4)	3.66 (4)	7.27 (8)
E01	North Bedfordshire	11.58 (6)	10.49 (5)	6.04 (3)	8.38 (4)	5.97 (3)	12.35 (6)	2.17 (1)	6.10 (3)	10.47 (5)
E02	South Bedfordshire	11.85 (7)	6.51 (4)	6.76 (4)	8.35 (5)	9.66 (6)	8.21 (5)	6.41 (4)	7.87 (5)	0.00 (0)
E05	North West Hertfordshire	9.67 (5)	3.95 (2)	6.09 (3)	7.66 (4)	1.97 (1)	0.00 (0)	1.93 (1)	4.03 (2)	1.96 (1)
E06	South West Hertfordshire	4.84 (2)	12.04 (5)	4.59 (2)	9.33 (4)	15.92 (7)	4.45 (2)	9.00 (4)	8.69 (4)	2.10 (1)
E07	Barnet	11.24 (6)	1.95 (1)	9.65 (5)	1.79 (1)	11.46 (6)	5.43 (3)	1.75 (1)	1.81 (1)	7.08 (4)
E09	Hillingdon	2.50 (1)	9.65 (4)	7.41 (3)	4.90 (2)	7.17 (3)	7.14 (3)	4.32 (2)	0.00 (0)	8.84 (4)
E18	East and North Hertfordshire	8.92 (8)	2.16 (2)	6.68 (6)	5.62 (5)	6.55 (6)	2.18 (2)	3.28 (3)	3.23 (3)	5.31 (5)
E19	Brent and Harrow	5.99 (5)	7.14 (6)	5.87 (5)	4.86 (4)	2.45 (2)	1.16 (1)	4.65 (4)	6.82 (6)	2.34 (2)
E20	Ealing, Hammersmith and Hounslow	7.10 (8)	8.53 (10)	5.34 (6)	8.75 (10)	5.06 (6)	13.23 (15)	5.75 (7)	7.02 (8)	6.69 (8)
E21	Kensington, Chelsea and Westminster	12.42 (4)	20.94 (6)	10.43 (4)	13.77 (4)	2.71 (1)	13.35 (5)	10.18 (5)	6.20 (3)	2.33 (1)
F31	North Essex	5.53 (9)	6.62 (11)	3.35 (5)	4.97 (8)	4.53 (7)	6.22 (10)	8.91 (14)	2.47 (4)	6.24 (10)
F32	South Essex	5.75 (8)	5.34 (8)	8.46 (11)	8.42 (11)	4.58 (6)	2.99 (4)	10.53 (14)	9.17 (12)	3.81 (5)

132

HON - E1
Mortality rates from accidents (ICD E800-E949) in children under 15:
Age-standardised mortality rates per 100,000: 1984-92
(observed numbers of deaths in parentheses)
Persons

		1984	1985	1986	1987	1988	1989	1990	1991	1992
F33	Barking and Havering	5.26 (4)	8.25 (6)	6.09 (4)	9.86 (7)	6.80 (5)	2.85 (2)	8.31 (6)	9.75 (7)	6.91 (5)
F34	Redbridge and Waltham Forest	3.64 (3)	8.65 (7)	4.81 (4)	4.94 (4)	7.08 (6)	4.93 (4)	5.99 (5)	5.82 (5)	4.64 (4)
F35	East London and the City	12.18 (14)	12.41 (14)	7.78 (9)	9.73 (12)	9.20 (11)	11.42 (14)	7.31 (10)	5.79 (8)	3.45 (5)
F36	New River District	9.28 (8)	5.76 (5)	6.04 (5)	6.05 (5)	2.25 (2)	8.40 (7)	3.27 (3)	7.60 (7)	5.77 (5)
F37	Camden and Islington	16.69 (8)	13.98 (7)	1.78 (1)	9.57 (5)	3.44 (2)	15.35 (9)	8.99 (5)	1.95 (1)	6.76 (4)
G04	South East Kent	6.24 (3)	12.95 (7)	2.33 (1)	0.00 (0)	8.04 (4)	4.12 (2)	4.03 (2)	0.00 (0)	7.82 (4)
G05	Canterbury and Thanet	7.76 (4)	3.76 (2)	6.18 (3)	2.18 (1)	4.00 (2)	5.99 (3)	5.56 (3)	3.78 (2)	1.78 (1)
G06	Dartford and Gravesham	9.40 (4)	4.46 (2)	2.56 (1)	11.66 (5)	6.73 (3)	4.74 (2)	9.61 (4)	2.33 (1)	4.56 (2)
G07	Maidstone	12.69 (5)	8.67 (3)	15.18 (6)	5.36 (2)	4.99 (2)	8.10 (3)	7.91 (3)	10.09 (4)	12.82 (5)
G08	Medway	4.09 (3)	1.46 (1)	7.07 (5)	10.16 (7)	4.13 (3)	11.46 (8)	9.76 (7)	8.54 (6)	8.60 (6)
G09	Tunbridge Wells	18.38 (6)	15.01 (5)	8.14 (3)	0.00 (0)	6.54 (2)	8.13 (3)	13.90 (5)	2.75 (1)	2.49 (1)
G10	Bexley	9.48 (4)	7.30 (3)	4.83 (2)	2.30 (1)	4.97 (2)	2.50 (1)	4.84 (2)	0.00 (0)	7.19 (3)
G11	Greenwich	21.32 (9)	11.95 (5)	7.26 (3)	2.25 (1)	6.85 (3)	7.25 (3)	2.51 (1)	0.00 (0)	6.62 (3)
G12	Bromley	6.75 (3)	5.36 (3)	5.55 (3)	3.82 (2)	4.14 (2)	0.00 (0)	9.95 (5)	3.86 (2)	4.03 (2)
G21	East Sussex	7.08 (7)	4.85 (5)	5.84 (6)	4.82 (5)	8.30 (9)	1.78 (2)	2.63 (3)	5.09 (6)	3.29 (4)
G26	South East London	10.88 (13)	14.36 (17)	6.01 (7)	10.52 (13)	8.03 (10)	7.57 (10)	6.84 (9)	6.07 (9)	6.35 (9)
H04	Mid Surrey	8.16 (2)	0.00 (0)	0.00 (0)	3.24 (1)	0.00 (0)	7.08 (2)	6.53 (2)	0.00 (0)	6.74 (2)
H05	East Surrey	8.57 (3)	0.00 (0)	12.14 (4)	13.22 (4)	3.12 (1)	9.56 (3)	5.82 (2)	5.81 (2)	0.00 (0)
H06	Chichester	0.00 (0)	4.14 (1)	3.25 (1)	13.55 (4)	3.34 (1)	0.00 (0)	11.60 (3)	7.21 (2)	3.19 (1)
H07	Mid Downs	7.75 (4)	5.86 (3)	7.10 (4)	1.71 (1)	5.58 (3)	5.48 (3)	9.61 (5)	1.93 (1)	1.76 (1)
H08	Worthing	4.46 (2)	11.35 (4)	8.95 (3)	5.00 (2)	8.30 (3)	13.24 (5)	7.75 (3)	5.03 (2)	4.76 (2)
H09	Croydon	0.00 (0)	8.02 (5)	5.05 (3)	3.38 (2)	6.70 (4)	1.62 (1)	6.71 (4)	1.61 (1)	1.67 (1)

133

HON - E1
Mortality rates from accidents (ICD E800-E949) in children under 15:
Age-standardised mortality rates per 100,000: 1984-92
(observed numbers of deaths in parentheses)
Persons

		1984	1985	1986	1987	1988	1989	1990	1991	1992
H12	Wandsworth	9.07	9.60	6.44	9.49	6.66	5.90	6.57	7.16	7.02
		(3)	(3)	(2)	(3)	(2)	(2)	(2)	(2)	(2)
H13	Merton and Sutton	8.90	8.53	1.65	5.14	5.26	1.62	1.60	6.29	6.24
		(5)	(5)	(1)	(3)	(3)	(1)	(1)	(4)	(4)
H14	North West Surrey	4.35	8.58	5.74	4.30	3.22	6.02	8.85	2.84	1.41
		(3)	(6)	(4)	(3)	(2)	(4)	(6)	(2)	(1)
H15	South West Surrey	15.53	6.78	4.43	2.73	7.82	2.33	2.72	6.72	2.28
		(6)	(3)	(2)	(1)	(3)	(1)	(1)	(3)	(1)
H16	Kingston and Richmond	7.21	4.33	4.69	6.18	1.55	4.56	5.95	5.97	0.00
		(5)	(3)	(3)	(4)	(1)	(3)	(4)	(4)	(0)
J10	Dorset	7.68	3.82	2.86	4.98	2.94	5.43	6.78	7.20	1.74
		(8)	(4)	(3)	(5)	(3)	(6)	(7)	(8)	(2)
J21	Portsmouth and South East Hampshire	2.68	4.03	7.19	5.15	3.11	7.07	10.23	4.06	1.03
		(3)	(4)	(7)	(5)	(3)	(7)	(10)	(4)	(1)
J22	Southampton and South West Hampshire	5.09	10.77	5.19	1.29	0.00	9.14	5.00	7.63	0.00
		(4)	(8)	(4)	(1)	(0)	(7)	(4)	(6)	(0)
J23	Winchester	10.10	11.61	0.00	15.44	7.91	9.83	9.84	2.65	4.82
		(4)	(5)	(0)	(6)	(3)	(4)	(4)	(1)	(2)
J24	Basingstoke and North Hampshire	7.68	12.55	8.72	4.14	6.71	10.96	8.36	8.03	2.69
		(6)	(9)	(6)	(3)	(5)	(8)	(6)	(6)	(2)
J31	Salisbury	9.94	23.73	24.23	28.97	4.28	23.21	8.83	4.14	4.67
		(2)	(5)	(5)	(6)	(1)	(5)	(2)	(1)	(1)
J32	Swindon	17.78	10.75	8.60	10.32	2.14	8.45	12.60	6.17	8.26
		(8)	(5)	(4)	(5)	(1)	(4)	(6)	(3)	(4)
J33	Bath	6.54	7.18	6.88	7.25	4.25	4.25	5.46	6.73	7.83
		(5)	(5)	(5)	(5)	(3)	(3)	(4)	(5)	(6)
J41	Isle of Wight	5.06	0.00	4.79	20.33	0.00	4.31	18.31	4.34	4.36
		(1)	(0)	(1)	(4)	(0)	(1)	(4)	(1)	(1)
K11	East Berkshire	11.27	11.22	5.70	2.92	8.35	1.42	4.16	6.75	7.99
		(8)	(8)	(4)	(2)	(6)	(1)	(3)	(5)	(6)
K12	West Berkshire	10.65	4.85	5.86	5.85	11.76	3.50	3.38	9.08	5.67
		(9)	(4)	(5)	(5)	(10)	(3)	(3)	(8)	(5)
K24	Buckinghamshire	6.48	6.74	8.53	5.96	7.31	7.38	11.38	4.93	4.01
		(8)	(8)	(10)	(7)	(9)	(9)	(14)	(6)	(5)
K31	Kettering	1.96	17.17	2.18	15.06	7.68	5.83	7.62	9.18	5.51
		(1)	(9)	(1)	(8)	(4)	(3)	(4)	(5)	(3)
K32	Northampton	0.00	14.41	6.63	11.14	16.08	14.50	6.38	3.15	1.56
		(0)	(9)	(4)	(7)	(10)	(9)	(4)	(2)	(1)
K41	Oxfordshire	5.31	6.26	8.26	7.04	6.21	8.41	2.93	0.98	3.77
		(5)	(6)	(8)	(7)	(6)	(8)	(3)	(1)	(4)
L10	Bristol and District	9.57	5.08	6.16	7.39	4.00	6.59	3.32	3.96	8.49
		(14)	(7)	(9)	(11)	(6)	(10)	(5)	(6)	(13)
L21	Cornwall and Isles of Scilly	6.93	7.45	5.09	5.86	12.23	11.04	2.54	4.61	5.98
		(6)	(6)	(4)	(5)	(10)	(9)	(2)	(4)	(5)

HON - E1
Mortality rates from accidents (ICD E800-E949) in children under 15:
Age-standardised mortality rates per 100,000: 1984-92
(observed numbers of deaths in parentheses)
Persons

		1984	1985	1986	1987	1988	1989	1990	1991	1992
L35	Exeter and North Devon	9.66	14.15	8.05	5.07	6.70	12.04	3.98	4.03	6.57
		(7)	(10)	(6)	(4)	(5)	(9)	(3)	(3)	(5)
L36	Plymouth and Torbay	10.25	3.98	5.53	4.85	5.12	5.12	1.98	3.93	3.79
		(10)	(4)	(5)	(5)	(5)	(5)	(2)	(4)	(4)
L40	Gloucestershire	4.88	8.38	9.70	8.56	10.59	7.39	1.99	2.98	1.99
		(5)	(8)	(9)	(8)	(10)	(7)	(2)	(3)	(2)
L51	Somerset	10.34	3.65	4.12	6.04	13.04	6.94	2.90	1.42	1.23
		(8)	(3)	(3)	(4)	(9)	(5)	(2)	(1)	(1)
M02	Herefordshire	7.06	15.27	0.00	3.92	13.74	3.32	17.18	13.34	6.73
		(2)	(4)	(0)	(1)	(4)	(1)	(5)	(4)	(2)
M04	Worcester and District	1.91	9.84	12.18	11.64	11.61	6.81	8.81	0.00	2.32
		(1)	(4)	(5)	(5)	(5)	(3)	(4)	(0)	(1)
M05	Shropshire	4.04	6.85	5.17	11.95	10.61	6.50	10.06	4.01	13.78
		(3)	(5)	(4)	(9)	(8)	(5)	(8)	(3)	(11)
M06	Mid Staffordshire	6.84	14.09	8.17	8.66	5.24	13.02	6.65	10.22	9.87
		(4)	(8)	(5)	(5)	(3)	(8)	(4)	(6)	(6)
M07	North Staffordshire	9.43	9.56	4.47	6.94	4.72	11.40	3.54	9.28	6.72
		(8)	(9)	(4)	(6)	(4)	(10)	(3)	(8)	(6)
M08	South East Staffordshire	1.57	7.71	5.65	11.09	2.02	11.92	2.03	5.60	19.24
		(1)	(4)	(3)	(6)	(1)	(6)	(1)	(3)	(10)
M13	East Birmingham	16.77	14.88	9.83	11.79	15.81	18.04	17.71	8.66	10.30
		(7)	(6)	(4)	(5)	(7)	(8)	(8)	(4)	(5)
M14	North Birmingham	25.55	6.70	3.41	13.67	6.77	10.22	3.43	3.54	0.00
		(8)	(2)	(1)	(4)	(2)	(3)	(1)	(1)	(0)
M16	West Birmingham	20.09	9.79	12.18	13.85	17.90	8.54	6.43	2.02	9.61
		(10)	(5)	(6)	(7)	(9)	(4)	(3)	(1)	(5)
M17	Coventry	4.79	11.78	8.18	8.10	10.00	5.10	3.30	13.65	4.80
		(3)	(7)	(5)	(5)	(6)	(3)	(2)	(8)	(3)
M18	Dudley	9.35	3.47	8.87	6.68	8.94	1.88	7.20	8.75	5.17
		(5)	(2)	(5)	(4)	(5)	(1)	(4)	(5)	(3)
M19	Sandwell	13.61	18.11	12.26	1.63	12.21	7.06	6.94	8.30	8.30
		(8)	(12)	(7)	(1)	(7)	(4)	(4)	(5)	(5)
M20	Solihull	1.91	7.08	12.27	2.24	2.42	4.88	2.88	4.96	8.40
		(1)	(3)	(4)	(1)	(1)	(2)	(1)	(2)	(3)
M21	Walsall	15.96	3.58	10.12	11.91	6.04	13.71	5.55	3.71	5.40
		(9)	(2)	(5)	(6)	(3)	(7)	(3)	(2)	(3)
M22	Wolverhampton	8.69	3.38	20.82	6.31	2.18	10.17	6.12	8.07	9.88
		(4)	(2)	(10)	(3)	(1)	(5)	(3)	(4)	(5)
M25	South Birmingham	7.20	12.67	12.94	16.79	7.04	8.30	7.14	9.74	9.33
		(6)	(11)	(11)	(14)	(6)	(7)	(6)	(8)	(8)
M26	North Worcestershire	4.89	12.55	9.40	0.00	5.93	3.71	3.45	7.45	7.19
		(3)	(7)	(5)	(0)	(3)	(2)	(2)	(4)	(4)
M28	Warwickshire	9.72	8.76	5.38	2.03	8.65	8.00	8.96	4.55	11.02
		(9)	(8)	(5)	(2)	(8)	(7)	(8)	(4)	(10)

135

HON - E1
Mortality rates from accidents (ICD E800-E949) in children under 15:
Age-standardised mortality rates per 100,000: 1984-92
(observed numbers of deaths in parentheses)
Persons

		1984	1985	1986	1987	1988	1989	1990	1991	1992
N11	Chester	5.31 (2)	11.89 (4)	6.17 (2)	5.99 (2)	8.60 (3)	9.20 (3)	12.11 (4)	0.00 (0)	5.85 (2)
N12	Crewe	12.77 (6)	14.16 (7)	1.86 (1)	12.73 (6)	4.23 (2)	7.94 (4)	6.28 (3)	3.97 (2)	5.74 (3)
N13	Halton	11.73 (4)	9.18 (3)	3.03 (1)	0.00 (0)	6.12 (2)	6.18 (2)	6.06 (2)	9.65 (3)	6.05 (2)
N14	Macclesfield	8.17 (3)	11.31 (4)	5.79 (2)	6.41 (2)	2.97 (1)	9.44 (3)	6.58 (2)	6.37 (2)	5.91 (2)
N15	Warrington	3.06 (1)	12.95 (5)	2.53 (1)	16.53 (6)	2.72 (1)	2.73 (1)	2.58 (1)	2.71 (1)	2.73 (1)
N21	Liverpool	16.45 (15)	8.26 (8)	8.66 (8)	3.33 (3)	9.97 (9)	7.50 (7)	7.76 (7)	9.27 (9)	12.56 (12)
N31	St Helens and Knowsley	20.22 (16)	12.62 (9)	13.20 (10)	8.43 (6)	14.08 (10)	8.08 (6)	6.85 (5)	7.05 (5)	8.22 (6)
N41	Southport and Formby	10.18 (2)	4.07 (1)	4.27 (1)	5.94 (1)	0.00 (0)	5.75 (1)	21.06 (4)	0.00 (0)	0.00 (0)
N42	South Sefton	12.36 (4)	8.27 (3)	10.82 (4)	5.62 (2)	14.26 (5)	8.51 (3)	8.29 (3)	10.76 (4)	2.56 (1)
N51	Wirral	13.14 (9)	5.49 (4)	9.74 (7)	4.33 (3)	7.25 (5)	10.34 (7)	7.04 (5)	9.78 (7)	8.40 (6)
P01	Lancaster	0.00 (0)	18.68 (4)	4.90 (1)	9.31 (2)	4.29 (1)	0.00 (0)	0.00 (0)	0.00 (0)	8.73 (2)
P02	Blackpool,Wyre and Fylde	13.04 (7)	5.64 (3)	15.52 (8)	3.91 (2)	5.67 (3)	7.70 (4)	21.52 (11)	5.72 (3)	0.00 (0)
P03	Preston	3.28 (1)	0.00 (0)	0.00 (0)	4.13 (1)	15.57 (4)	22.85 (6)	3.63 (1)	11.39 (3)	0.00 (0)
P04	Blackburn, Hyndburn and Ribble Valley	13.61 (8)	9.81 (6)	3.32 (2)	17.81 (10)	8.58 (5)	3.69 (2)	1.77 (1)	1.64 (1)	1.81 (1)
P05	Burnley, Pendle and Rossendale	6.57 (3)	22.85 (11)	6.38 (3)	18.84 (9)	14.51 (7)	14.02 (7)	13.76 (7)	4.12 (2)	7.94 (4)
P06	West Lancashire	6.95 (2)	8.62 (2)	8.87 (2)	5.05 (1)	4.33 (1)	4.38 (1)	4.32 (1)	0.00 (0)	4.21 (1)
P07	Chorley and South Ribble	9.91 (4)	2.45 (1)	12.04 (5)	4.67 (2)	7.85 (3)	15.77 (6)	2.66 (1)	4.75 (2)	0.00 (0)
P08	Bolton	8.90 (5)	16.73 (10)	7.39 (4)	5.48 (3)	16.59 (9)	1.78 (1)	7.39 (4)	9.23 (5)	9.23 (5)
P09	Bury	2.96 (1)	18.61 (6)	11.79 (4)	2.79 (1)	17.78 (6)	11.46 (4)	5.87 (2)	11.36 (4)	2.65 (1)
P10	North Manchester	11.33 (3)	22.01 (6)	34.39 (10)	14.57 (4)	11.18 (3)	0.00 (0)	13.55 (4)	9.73 (3)	8.90 (3)
P11	Central Manchester	17.14 (5)	24.52 (6)	8.33 (2)	20.03 (5)	15.75 (4)	18.01 (4)	16.80 (4)	20.44 (5)	11.38 (3)
P12	South Manchester	12.56 (4)	16.41 (5)	6.48 (2)	10.47 (3)	9.60 (3)	2.82 (1)	8.53 (3)	11.48 (4)	14.61 (5)

HON - E1
Mortality rates from accidents (ICD E800-E949) in children under 15:
Age-standardised mortality rates per 100,000: 1984-92
(observed numbers of deaths in parentheses)
Persons

		1984	1985	1986	1987	1988	1989	1990	1991	1992
P13	Oldham	27.05	15.16	0.00	2.14	8.67	6.54	8.33	8.80	0.00
		(12)	(7)	(0)	(1)	(4)	(3)	(4)	(4)	(0)
P14	Rochdale	18.95	4.32	2.32	8.99	8.91	8.86	4.33	8.46	2.15
		(9)	(2)	(1)	(4)	(4)	(4)	(2)	(4)	(1)
P15	Salford	8.83	9.28	15.57	20.46	20.77	18.61	18.42	13.37	6.74
		(4)	(4)	(7)	(9)	(9)	(8)	(8)	(6)	(3)
P16	Stockport	9.94	5.05	5.64	3.54	9.48	3.85	9.44	7.19	5.38
		(5)	(3)	(3)	(2)	(5)	(2)	(5)	(4)	(3)
P17	Tameside and Glossop	10.97	10.54	10.63	14.72	0.00	10.19	2.00	9.74	8.02
		(5)	(5)	(5)	(7)	(0)	(5)	(1)	(5)	(4)
P18	Trafford	8.14	15.63	7.22	0.00	7.63	11.75	9.90	5.08	4.63
		(3)	(6)	(3)	(0)	(3)	(5)	(4)	(2)	(2)
P19	Wigan	9.10	11.97	1.65	4.64	13.75	9.55	4.94	4.90	8.06
		(6)	(7)	(1)	(3)	(8)	(6)	(3)	(3)	(5)

HON - E1
Mortality rates from accidents (ICD E800-E949) in children under 15:
Age-standardised mortality rates per 100,000: 1984-92
(observed numbers of deaths in parentheses)

137

HON - E2
Mortality rates from accidents (ICD E800-E949) in young persons aged 15-24:
Age-standardised mortality rates per 100,000: 1984-92
(observed numbers of deaths in parentheses)
Persons

		1984	1985	1986	1987	1988	1989	1990	1991	1992
	ENGLAND AND WALES	24.74	22.92	23.68	22.47	20.84	23.16	23.85	22.61	19.48
		(2011)	(1868)	(1924)	(1808)	(1650)	(1778)	(1782)	(1632)	(1363)
O00	ENGLAND	24.87	22.92	23.58	22.15	20.99	22.70	23.92	22.65	19.08
		(1910)	(1765)	(1812)	(1685)	(1572)	(1648)	(1690)	(1544)	(1261)
A00	NORTHERN RHA	23.52	20.59	20.15	22.29	16.98	22.37	21.22	20.48	19.74
		(117)	(101)	(97)	(106)	(78)	(101)	(93)	(88)	(81)
B00	YORKSHIRE RHA	24.91	31.61	24.12	23.52	22.20	22.86	26.41	23.54	21.85
		(148)	(187)	(142)	(137)	(128)	(129)	(146)	(126)	(113)
C00	TRENT RHA	26.38	21.61	23.56	23.99	21.24	22.09	25.16	27.33	20.79
		(198)	(162)	(176)	(177)	(155)	(156)	(177)	(184)	(138)
D00	EAST ANGLIAN RHA	29.82	32.12	30.25	29.30	29.23	25.33	26.98	28.07	27.57
		(92)	(100)	(95)	(92)	(91)	(76)	(80)	(82)	(79)
E00	NORTH WEST THAMES RHA	21.02	19.36	20.48	22.47	15.44	20.18	21.82	18.50	14.79
		(123)	(114)	(121)	(132)	(90)	(114)	(115)	(96)	(72)
F00	NORTH EAST THAMES RHA	19.45	15.78	17.73	20.29	19.70	19.55	21.60	22.73	14.47
		(117)	(95)	(109)	(126)	(121)	(114)	(124)	(123)	(77)
G00	SOUTH EAST THAMES RHA	25.30	22.20	29.18	19.27	21.15	18.74	26.70	17.08	14.38
		(148)	(131)	(173)	(113)	(123)	(105)	(142)	(88)	(71)
H00	SOUTH WEST THAMES RHA	27.72	25.46	21.56	21.37	18.72	23.89	22.52	21.15	16.04
		(126)	(117)	(99)	(97)	(84)	(102)	(95)	(85)	(60)
J00	WESSEX RHA	28.70	23.87	26.93	22.92	24.63	27.15	23.22	22.08	18.79
		(142)	(119)	(134)	(113)	(119)	(127)	(104)	(94)	(79)
K00	OXFORD RHA	23.98	28.22	23.78	21.52	24.90	28.55	28.00	19.97	22.50
		(101)	(120)	(102)	(91)	(104)	(116)	(111)	(75)	(84)
L00	SOUTH WESTERN RHA	30.53	26.61	27.02	25.74	26.61	26.37	30.66	28.37	20.54
		(150)	(131)	(134)	(127)	(130)	(125)	(140)	(126)	(90)
M00	WEST MIDLANDS RHA	26.13	24.00	25.33	21.15	21.61	25.07	22.56	21.12	19.21
		(222)	(204)	(214)	(177)	(178)	(202)	(176)	(162)	(142)
N00	MERSEY RHA	21.94	22.24	18.46	16.71	19.18	17.21	19.49	30.26	19.95
		(88)	(88)	(72)	(64)	(71)	(62)	(68)	(102)	(66)
P00	NORTH WESTERN RHA	21.36	14.88	22.53	21.15	16.17	19.90	20.00	19.57	19.97
		(138)	(96)	(144)	(133)	(100)	(119)	(119)	(113)	(109)
A01	Hartlepool	45.42	13.38	35.42	7.46	30.67	8.04	23.47	40.53	17.23
		(7)	(2)	(5)	(1)	(4)	(1)	(3)	(5)	(2)
A02	North Tees	38.88	35.86	29.93	16.04	24.19	36.81	8.77	21.87	8.85
		(11)	(10)	(8)	(4)	(6)	(9)	(2)	(5)	(2)
A03	South Tees	21.30	25.83	24.18	16.70	6.54	6.46	13.34	16.69	25.37
		(11)	(13)	(12)	(8)	(3)	(3)	(6)	(7)	(10)
A04	East Cumbria	46.38	59.14	19.97	32.31	32.62	37.55	37.85	25.64	26.98
		(12)	(15)	(5)	(8)	(8)	(9)	(9)	(6)	(6)
A05	South Cumbria	33.78	18.97	22.51	15.08	27.23	24.08	37.93	30.33	22.13
		(9)	(5)	(6)	(4)	(7)	(6)	(9)	(7)	(5)
A06	West Cumbria	18.59	4.72	25.16	25.16	36.40	30.91	32.42	32.97	51.52
		(4)	(1)	(5)	(5)	(7)	(6)	(6)	(6)	(9)

138

HON - E2
Mortality rates from accidents (ICD E800-E949) in young persons aged 15-24:
Age-standardised mortality rates per 100,000: 1984-92
(observed numbers of deaths in parentheses)
Persons

		1984	1985	1986	1987	1988	1989	1990	1991	1992
A11	Northumberland	30.10 (13)	30.88 (13)	24.16 (10)	34.18 (14)	24.88 (10)	32.75 (13)	25.48 (10)	31.38 (12)	18.62 (7)
A12	Gateshead	39.12 (13)	6.18 (2)	19.58 (6)	24.86 (8)	10.05 (3)	10.39 (3)	13.58 (4)	13.47 (4)	30.58 (8)
A13	Newcastle	9.94 (5)	11.09 (6)	11.24 (6)	17.92 (10)	6.05 (3)	19.25 (10)	8.46 (4)	10.17 (4)	7.54 (3)
A14	North Tyneside	10.26 (3)	17.60 (5)	10.84 (3)	14.72 (4)	3.58 (1)	7.60 (2)	8.01 (2)	16.36 (4)	12.41 (3)
A15	South Tyneside	15.67 (4)	20.30 (5)	8.33 (2)	13.71 (3)	8.96 (2)	27.39 (6)	19.29 (4)	10.00 (2)	10.40 (2)
A16	Sunderland	16.26 (8)	4.11 (2)	18.94 (9)	23.19 (11)	15.46 (7)	21.73 (10)	21.78 (10)	11.34 (5)	16.53 (7)
A30	North Durham	13.00 (7)	18.69 (10)	20.67 (11)	25.30 (13)	12.03 (6)	24.39 (12)	28.01 (13)	27.31 (13)	18.15 (8)
A31	South Durham	23.65 (10)	28.72 (12)	22.21 (9)	32.05 (13)	28.13 (11)	28.79 (11)	29.45 (11)	21.94 (8)	24.67 (9)
B11	East Riding	20.38 (17)	37.56 (31)	18.31 (15)	27.21 (22)	20.03 (16)	18.88 (15)	17.53 (14)	23.38 (18)	18.87 (14)
B16	Grimsby and Scunthorpe	30.08 (17)	39.67 (22)	36.89 (20)	34.30 (18)	36.77 (19)	30.92 (16)	34.14 (17)	37.24 (18)	23.38 (11)
B21	North Yorkshire	25.45 (29)	35.73 (40)	31.02 (34)	32.38 (35)	24.43 (26)	36.33 (38)	40.72 (41)	23.25 (23)	29.12 (27)
B31	Bradford	20.61 (16)	30.11 (23)	19.36 (15)	19.83 (15)	15.31 (12)	26.32 (19)	20.17 (15)	26.14 (18)	15.60 (11)
B51	West Yorkshire	32.33 (29)	32.43 (29)	29.12 (26)	18.88 (17)	23.65 (21)	16.53 (14)	15.24 (13)	8.23 (7)	17.26 (14)
B61	Leeds	20.88 (26)	23.77 (30)	18.26 (23)	14.38 (18)	17.17 (22)	13.60 (17)	27.09 (32)	24.97 (28)	23.76 (26)
B71	Wakefield	28.00 (14)	23.99 (12)	18.16 (9)	24.07 (12)	24.96 (12)	21.15 (10)	30.42 (14)	30.90 (14)	22.87 (10)
C01	North Derbyshire	29.74 (16)	30.09 (16)	26.60 (14)	30.85 (16)	23.59 (12)	20.26 (10)	26.55 (13)	23.03 (11)	25.73 (12)
C02	Southern Derbyshire	33.06 (27)	19.55 (16)	21.84 (18)	19.30 (16)	21.89 (18)	40.23 (32)	32.64 (26)	31.38 (24)	21.01 (16)
C03	Leicestershire	24.81 (36)	17.16 (25)	24.81 (36)	27.18 (39)	18.14 (26)	20.04 (28)	25.86 (36)	28.38 (38)	27.94 (37)
C04	North Lincolnshire	54.98 (22)	19.92 (8)	37.39 (15)	28.24 (11)	31.12 (12)	26.73 (10)	26.73 (10)	44.27 (16)	22.37 (8)
C05	South Lincolnshire	47.09 (20)	38.41 (16)	29.03 (12)	41.12 (17)	28.70 (12)	41.79 (17)	44.85 (18)	30.07 (12)	12.59 (5)
C08	Nottingham	17.34 (19)	22.93 (25)	22.86 (25)	19.64 (21)	22.71 (24)	11.07 (12)	15.86 (16)	29.27 (28)	17.07 (16)
C09	Barnsley	11.43 (4)	8.42 (3)	28.27 (10)	40.48 (14)	26.68 (9)	9.15 (3)	24.65 (8)	36.51 (11)	32.04 (10)

HON - E2
Mortality rates from accidents (ICD E800-E949) in young persons aged 15-24:
Age-standardised mortality rates per 100,000: 1984-92
(observed numbers of deaths in parentheses)
Persons

		1984	1985	1986	1987	1988	1989	1990	1991	1992
C10	Doncaster	29.71 (14)	23.87 (11)	17.68 (8)	29.25 (13)	17.81 (8)	12.35 (5)	21.72 (9)	26.69 (11)	15.19 (6)
C11	Rotherham	25.01 (10)	17.62 (7)	12.75 (5)	17.49 (7)	21.12 (8)	28.98 (11)	10.18 (4)	11.43 (4)	9.49 (3)
C12	Sheffield	13.55 (13)	15.52 (15)	7.23 (7)	15.73 (15)	8.52 (8)	11.77 (10)	11.93 (11)	11.35 (9)	12.81 (11)
C14	North Nottinghamshire	28.17 (17)	32.85 (20)	43.35 (26)	13.37 (8)	30.91 (18)	31.82 (18)	47.24 (26)	37.16 (20)	27.18 (14)
D01	Cambridge	15.75 (8)	11.75 (6)	22.74 (12)	20.87 (11)	22.78 (12)	22.85 (11)	27.07 (13)	41.98 (21)	30.40 (13)
D05	North West Anglia	24.85 (14)	38.52 (22)	43.17 (25)	32.53 (19)	30.78 (18)	21.57 (12)	32.28 (18)	27.73 (15)	31.28 (17)
D06	Norwich	38.75 (27)	34.11 (24)	33.81 (24)	32.61 (23)	34.42 (24)	33.71 (23)	28.84 (19)	27.53 (18)	37.87 (25)
D07	Great Yarmouth and Waveney	45.02 (12)	45.51 (12)	11.43 (3)	44.99 (12)	22.51 (6)	30.15 (8)	15.33 (4)	23.21 (6)	27.78 (7)
D09	Huntingdon	31.72 (6)	50.02 (10)	20.03 (4)	48.12 (10)	36.96 (7)	30.43 (6)	9.23 (2)	5.62 (1)	21.35 (4)
D11	Suffolk	29.36 (25)	30.37 (26)	31.94 (27)	19.98 (17)	28.84 (24)	20.00 (16)	30.28 (24)	26.83 (21)	17.12 (13)
E01	North Bedfordshire	12.88 (5)	15.12 (6)	33.63 (13)	32.99 (13)	18.55 (7)	27.50 (10)	32.62 (12)	10.76 (4)	25.99 (9)
E02	South Bedfordshire	34.28 (16)	24.44 (11)	39.76 (18)	37.35 (17)	11.00 (5)	22.77 (10)	37.67 (16)	24.19 (10)	17.96 (7)
E05	North West Hertfordshire	24.77 (10)	34.40 (14)	12.67 (5)	25.90 (10)	16.03 (6)	22.07 (8)	39.65 (14)	14.72 (5)	20.56 (7)
E06	South West Hertfordshire	29.62 (11)	23.87 (9)	21.59 (8)	16.50 (6)	8.41 (3)	14.51 (5)	24.77 (8)	15.61 (5)	6.28 (2)
E07	Barnet	21.75 (10)	14.64 (7)	18.60 (9)	23.15 (11)	14.93 (7)	10.68 (5)	2.71 (1)	20.46 (9)	15.62 (7)
E09	Hillingdon	7.82 (3)	12.55 (5)	21.42 (8)	17.61 (7)	24.14 (9)	20.56 (8)	8.15 (3)	18.61 (7)	24.89 (7)
E18	East and North Hertfordshire	20.17 (16)	21.28 (17)	11.44 (9)	24.51 (19)	19.97 (15)	19.23 (14)	24.14 (17)	26.51 (18)	30.82 (20)
E19	Brent and Harrow	15.36 (12)	21.44 (17)	18.97 (15)	18.85 (15)	21.46 (17)	23.49 (17)	12.97 (10)	15.34 (10)	9.13 (6)
E20	Ealing, Hammersmith and Hounslow	27.91 (30)	14.74 (17)	21.53 (25)	27.18 (30)	11.06 (13)	21.92 (26)	22.40 (21)	21.29 (23)	6.39 (6)
E21	Kensington, Chelsea and Westminster	14.53 (10)	13.72 (11)	14.41 (11)	5.37 (4)	11.66 (8)	17.76 (11)	27.15 (13)	12.31 (5)	1.31 (1)
F31	North Essex	21.38 (27)	23.58 (30)	19.72 (25)	26.92 (34)	24.07 (30)	28.90 (35)	26.65 (32)	28.43 (33)	19.55 (22)
F32	South Essex	17.47 (18)	17.50 (18)	21.21 (22)	15.41 (16)	13.11 (14)	15.63 (16)	18.57 (18)	23.14 (22)	11.61 (11)

HON - E2
Mortality rates from accidents (ICD E800-E949) in young persons aged 15-24:
Age-standardised mortality rates per 100,000: 1984-92
(observed numbers of deaths in parentheses)
Persons

		1984	1985	1986	1987	1988	1989	1990	1991	1992
F33	Barking and Havering	26.63 (16)	18.33 (11)	25.58 (15)	20.27 (12)	22.56 (13)	21.91 (12)	9.16 (5)	25.28 (13)	13.63 (7)
F34	Redbridge and Waltham Forest	19.43 (13)	7.09 (5)	7.01 (5)	22.58 (16)	21.22 (16)	14.93 (10)	27.30 (18)	13.48 (10)	13.02 (8)
F35	East London and the City	21.26 (21)	14.44 (14)	12.00 (12)	16.18 (18)	14.85 (15)	10.13 (10)	21.73 (21)	24.93 (21)	10.02 (9)
F36	New River District	15.01 (12)	9.31 (7)	20.78 (18)	16.12 (13)	19.41 (17)	21.34 (17)	12.73 (10)	18.24 (13)	16.22 (12)
F37	Camden and Islington	14.18 (10)	17.00 (10)	16.79 (12)	21.61 (17)	28.19 (16)	21.67 (14)	32.66 (20)	21.93 (11)	15.97 (8)
G04	South East Kent	17.40 (7)	35.52 (14)	35.22 (14)	22.92 (9)	28.31 (11)	21.63 (8)	42.17 (15)	27.94 (10)	22.01 (8)
G05	Canterbury and Thanet	40.44 (18)	21.08 (9)	23.56 (10)	23.03 (10)	29.71 (13)	26.17 (11)	31.70 (13)	26.59 (11)	12.20 (5)
G06	Dartford and Gravesham	32.91 (12)	10.89 (4)	21.97 (8)	5.50 (2)	22.64 (8)	20.76 (7)	33.73 (11)	18.95 (6)	27.24 (8)
G07	Maidstone	36.68 (11)	33.80 (10)	20.42 (6)	37.65 (11)	37.85 (11)	17.34 (5)	25.22 (7)	11.03 (3)	19.54 (5)
G08	Medway	24.66 (13)	26.02 (14)	40.66 (22)	19.28 (10)	18.03 (10)	14.52 (8)	30.15 (15)	18.66 (9)	17.20 (8)
G09	Tunbridge Wells	29.56 (10)	27.19 (9)	77.37 (25)	13.62 (4)	35.47 (11)	34.90 (10)	20.27 (6)	23.13 (6)	35.58 (9)
G10	Bexley	23.86 (8)	18.00 (6)	40.21 (13)	19.06 (6)	19.09 (6)	6.43 (2)	16.28 (5)	19.64 (6)	7.01 (2)
G11	Greenwich	22.34 (8)	24.13 (9)	34.24 (12)	22.03 (8)	16.56 (6)	13.91 (5)	24.64 (9)	20.55 (6)	2.83 (1)
G12	Bromley	31.14 (14)	17.91 (8)	17.94 (8)	27.54 (12)	14.05 (6)	9.33 (4)	20.32 (8)	12.55 (5)	10.64 (4)
G21	East Sussex	19.32 (19)	21.94 (22)	27.59 (28)	18.80 (19)	23.15 (24)	20.10 (20)	35.59 (34)	17.96 (16)	11.63 (11)
G26	South East London	20.73 (28)	19.56 (26)	18.19 (27)	14.49 (22)	11.75 (17)	19.78 (25)	15.83 (19)	8.90 (10)	12.56 (10)
H04	Mid Surrey	28.96 (6)	21.95 (5)	55.30 (12)	34.59 (7)	13.70 (3)	13.91 (3)	5.30 (1)	10.50 (2)	24.79 (5)
H05	East Surrey	20.20 (6)	32.06 (9)	21.66 (6)	26.13 (7)	27.46 (7)	23.23 (6)	16.40 (4)	29.42 (7)	17.72 (4)
H06	Chichester	37.65 (9)	42.70 (10)	20.19 (5)	50.12 (12)	25.66 (6)	30.83 (7)	37.06 (8)	13.89 (3)	0.00 (0)
H07	Mid Downs	28.55 (12)	23.32 (10)	18.39 (8)	18.49 (8)	23.69 (10)	31.75 (13)	40.28 (16)	29.01 (11)	15.90 (6)
H08	Worthing	36.02 (11)	19.27 (6)	21.97 (7)	28.67 (9)	13.09 (4)	36.68 (11)	10.29 (3)	49.35 (14)	26.57 (7)
H09	Croydon	24.74 (13)	30.47 (16)	20.33 (11)	20.09 (11)	13.27 (7)	20.97 (10)	16.77 (8)	27.32 (11)	17.71 (8)

HON - E2

Mortality rates from accidents (ICD E800-E949) in young persons aged 15-24:
Age-standardised mortality rates per 100,000: 1984-92
(observed numbers of deaths in parentheses)
Persons

		1984	1985	1986	1987	1988	1989	1990	1991	1992
H12	Wandsworth	8.75 (3)	17.20 (7)	3.92 (2)	3.79 (2)	15.25 (7)	5.83 (3)	15.15 (6)	14.41 (5)	0.00 (0)
H13	Merton and Sutton	13.66 (7)	24.08 (12)	19.57 (10)	22.61 (12)	24.07 (13)	26.46 (14)	12.04 (6)	24.53 (11)	9.46 (4)
H14	North West Surrey	35.71 (22)	24.44 (15)	26.41 (16)	20.47 (12)	14.08 (8)	34.53 (19)	18.38 (10)	12.49 (7)	13.25 (7)
H15	South West Surrey	38.46 (17)	35.58 (15)	13.29 (6)	27.75 (11)	13.73 (5)	21.98 (8)	35.74 (13)	14.18 (5)	23.45 (8)
H16	Kingston and Richmond	32.85 (20)	19.36 (12)	26.63 (16)	9.92 (6)	22.88 (14)	13.28 (8)	30.75 (20)	14.68 (9)	24.17 (11)
J10	Dorset	31.13 (28)	25.27 (23)	20.76 (19)	17.25 (16)	24.15 (22)	21.58 (19)	29.53 (25)	20.89 (17)	18.75 (15)
J21	Portsmouth and South East Hampshire	17.90 (17)	22.73 (22)	20.20 (19)	29.48 (28)	20.25 (18)	20.52 (18)	16.30 (14)	10.96 (8)	14.66 (11)
J22	Southampton and South West Hampshire	19.22 (13)	15.98 (11)	24.38 (17)	23.25 (16)	19.16 (13)	24.98 (16)	27.13 (17)	21.66 (13)	10.29 (6)
J23	Winchester	37.26 (13)	21.98 (8)	14.30 (5)	15.06 (5)	29.84 (10)	24.82 (8)	18.91 (6)	39.53 (12)	42.09 (13)
J24	Basingstoke and North Hampshire	35.52 (23)	22.90 (15)	36.77 (24)	31.92 (20)	29.93 (19)	36.95 (23)	32.57 (19)	21.76 (12)	14.83 (8)
J31	Salisbury	58.96 (12)	35.16 (7)	24.88 (5)	25.52 (5)	31.97 (6)	50.90 (9)	0.00 (0)	23.73 (4)	24.95 (4)
J32	Swindon	28.57 (11)	30.47 (12)	23.04 (9)	7.05 (3)	12.84 (5)	30.83 (11)	28.28 (10)	31.89 (11)	17.80 (6)
J33	Bath	37.05 (25)	25.38 (17)	51.82 (34)	24.23 (16)	29.20 (19)	30.24 (19)	18.32 (11)	18.99 (11)	29.10 (16)
J41	Isle of Wight	0.00 (0)	25.23 (4)	12.98 (2)	25.30 (4)	43.75 (7)	25.35 (4)	13.31 (2)	41.02 (6)	0.00 (0)
K11	East Berkshire	14.97 (9)	21.35 (13)	18.09 (11)	20.38 (12)	27.55 (16)	18.91 (11)	18.55 (10)	9.32 (5)	11.73 (6)
K12	West Berkshire	20.21 (16)	25.01 (20)	18.27 (15)	37.47 (30)	24.65 (19)	16.18 (12)	22.51 (16)	16.06 (11)	16.90 (12)
K24	Buckinghamshire	31.17 (28)	26.64 (24)	30.78 (28)	12.06 (11)	20.09 (18)	32.84 (29)	23.99 (21)	18.92 (16)	22.77 (19)
K31	Kettering	15.68 (6)	50.33 (20)	27.33 (11)	27.71 (11)	32.03 (13)	38.25 (15)	40.99 (16)	58.95 (22)	35.39 (13)
K32	Northampton	34.78 (16)	49.04 (23)	29.63 (14)	16.47 (8)	36.78 (18)	29.66 (14)	43.77 (20)	22.59 (10)	31.98 (14)
K41	Oxfordshire	25.06 (26)	18.30 (20)	21.37 (23)	18.07 (19)	19.63 (20)	34.82 (35)	28.93 (28)	11.52 (11)	22.33 (20)
L10	Bristol and District	25.46 (35)	25.11 (35)	26.83 (37)	23.24 (32)	22.03 (30)	25.87 (33)	25.62 (32)	24.42 (28)	15.47 (19)
L21	Cornwall and Isles of Scilly	27.98 (17)	31.51 (19)	38.64 (23)	43.72 (26)	33.43 (20)	22.25 (13)	48.35 (28)	19.59 (11)	26.79 (15)

142

HON - E2
Mortality rates from accidents (ICD E800-E949) in young persons aged 15-24:
Age-standardised mortality rates per 100,000: 1984-92
(observed numbers of deaths in parentheses)
Persons

		1984	1985	1986	1987	1988	1989	1990	1991	1992
L35	Exeter and North Devon	36.97 (24)	18.14 (12)	27.09 (18)	27.25 (18)	33.88 (22)	24.82 (16)	14.42 (9)	31.85 (19)	20.47 (12)
L36	Plymouth and Torbay	24.16 (21)	24.93 (22)	22.25 (20)	24.13 (22)	14.26 (13)	13.39 (12)	30.00 (24)	32.02 (26)	22.33 (17)
L40	Gloucestershire	47.39 (39)	30.51 (25)	20.70 (17)	17.10 (14)	24.83 (20)	29.55 (23)	41.31 (31)	34.01 (25)	11.48 (8)
L51	Somerset	23.70 (14)	30.34 (18)	32.79 (19)	25.96 (15)	43.42 (25)	49.10 (28)	29.04 (16)	32.18 (17)	35.95 (19)
M02	Herefordshire	41.88 (10)	13.21 (3)	17.80 (4)	35.17 (8)	40.72 (9)	41.61 (9)	43.18 (9)	19.89 (4)	41.07 (8)
M04	Worcester and District	33.76 (13)	45.46 (16)	25.64 (9)	38.52 (14)	30.64 (11)	11.50 (4)	35.27 (12)	24.36 (8)	27.92 (9)
M05	Shropshire	30.26 (19)	25.42 (16)	31.68 (20)	23.39 (15)	39.79 (25)	40.76 (25)	33.51 (20)	20.87 (12)	40.92 (23)
M06	Mid Staffordshire	23.27 (11)	27.80 (13)	30.44 (14)	21.65 (10)	26.60 (12)	28.73 (13)	45.35 (20)	36.31 (16)	26.23 (11)
M07	North Staffordshire	42.46 (31)	27.29 (20)	19.13 (14)	23.33 (17)	13.83 (10)	26.73 (19)	20.11 (14)	17.65 (12)	25.04 (16)
M08	South East Staffordshire	25.10 (10)	37.94 (15)	38.35 (15)	28.04 (11)	30.79 (12)	48.62 (19)	13.24 (5)	26.71 (10)	19.32 (7)
M13	East Birmingham	16.45 (6)	19.11 (7)	11.19 (4)	23.11 (8)	11.47 (4)	17.76 (6)	9.27 (3)	6.69 (2)	17.88 (5)
M14	North Birmingham	13.92 (4)	10.19 (3)	22.01 (6)	14.83 (4)	22.33 (6)	30.05 (8)	12.58 (3)	18.38 (4)	0.00 (0)
M16	West Birmingham	21.96 (9)	12.01 (5)	12.25 (5)	9.90 (4)	7.99 (3)	8.38 (3)	8.71 (3)	15.12 (6)	4.86 (2)
M17	Coventry	19.20 (11)	8.66 (5)	17.76 (10)	21.75 (12)	15.16 (8)	16.69 (9)	14.33 (8)	17.59 (8)	11.15 (5)
M18	Dudley	20.17 (9)	22.07 (10)	28.99 (13)	6.49 (3)	15.58 (7)	18.35 (8)	13.07 (6)	17.51 (7)	9.85 (4)
M19	Sandwell	12.29 (6)	26.39 (13)	20.60 (10)	22.81 (11)	19.39 (9)	20.53 (9)	23.64 (10)	12.61 (6)	21.07 (9)
M20	Solihull	13.26 (4)	32.17 (10)	12.93 (4)	16.13 (5)	6.42 (2)	13.80 (4)	17.84 (5)	29.50 (8)	22.78 (6)
M21	Walsall	20.98 (9)	14.08 (6)	35.81 (15)	16.87 (7)	29.44 (12)	12.37 (5)	12.07 (5)	26.05 (10)	10.34 (4)
M22	Wolverhampton	25.54 (11)	20.88 (9)	32.56 (14)	26.04 (11)	21.68 (9)	15.13 (6)	14.88 (6)	14.99 (6)	25.67 (9)
M25	South Birmingham	25.19 (19)	16.84 (13)	21.61 (17)	12.87 (10)	11.60 (9)	19.40 (15)	14.43 (10)	11.30 (9)	9.87 (7)
M26	North Worcestershire	31.06 (12)	20.15 (8)	35.48 (14)	34.95 (14)	38.18 (15)	31.16 (12)	29.19 (11)	38.43 (14)	22.00 (8)
M28	Warwickshire	36.56 (28)	41.86 (32)	34.41 (26)	17.37 (13)	20.46 (15)	39.79 (28)	38.13 (26)	30.31 (20)	13.73 (9)

HON - E2
Mortality rates from accidents (ICD E800-E949) in young persons aged 15-24:
Age-standardised mortality rates per 100,000: 1984-92
(observed numbers of deaths in parentheses)
Persons

		1984	1985	1986	1987	1988	1989	1990	1991	1992
N11	Chester	26.61 (8)	13.43 (4)	20.06 (6)	27.71 (8)	20.63 (6)	22.63 (6)	11.70 (3)	32.45 (8)	12.83 (3)
N12	Crewe	40.99 (15)	38.15 (14)	27.54 (10)	22.20 (8)	11.34 (4)	36.84 (13)	36.95 (13)	25.99 (9)	43.18 (15)
N13	Halton	8.68 (2)	21.74 (5)	4.39 (1)	21.87 (5)	17.77 (4)	18.27 (4)	37.55 (8)	33.91 (7)	9.97 (2)
N14	Macclesfield	22.07 (6)	27.23 (7)	23.44 (6)	16.15 (4)	20.18 (5)	21.71 (5)	17.88 (4)	9.23 (2)	14.17 (3)
N15	Warrington	24.38 (7)	38.79 (11)	16.97 (5)	13.97 (4)	43.68 (12)	22.45 (6)	15.56 (4)	35.43 (9)	31.48 (8)
N21	Liverpool	21.02 (20)	10.80 (10)	13.95 (13)	12.09 (11)	15.89 (14)	14.00 (12)	15.59 (13)	33.17 (25)	14.04 (10)
N31	St Helens and Knowsley	27.41 (17)	14.96 (9)	22.26 (13)	12.24 (7)	23.84 (13)	18.96 (10)	11.91 (6)	26.13 (13)	23.17 (11)
N41	Southport and Formby	0.00 (0)	57.71 (9)	32.39 (5)	27.05 (4)	7.00 (1)	13.98 (2)	7.22 (1)	42.19 (6)	7.47 (1)
N42	South Sefton	19.64 (6)	26.94 (8)	10.42 (3)	14.50 (4)	3.79 (1)	3.94 (1)	24.30 (6)	46.09 (11)	16.86 (4)
N51	Wirral	13.12 (7)	20.88 (11)	19.43 (10)	17.76 (9)	22.46 (11)	6.21 (3)	21.47 (10)	26.80 (12)	20.39 (9)
P01	Lancaster	9.32 (2)	13.89 (3)	22.88 (5)	19.02 (4)	24.44 (5)	20.60 (4)	10.99 (2)	10.34 (2)	5.91 (1)
P02	Blackpool,Wyre and Fylde	49.00 (22)	13.44 (6)	33.70 (15)	27.53 (12)	13.89 (6)	21.24 (9)	27.76 (11)	20.38 (8)	26.43 (10)
P03	Preston	32.92 (7)	14.24 (3)	22.63 (5)	4.32 (1)	8.67 (2)	8.81 (2)	9.03 (2)	67.74 (15)	29.53 (6)
P04	Blackburn, Hyndburn and Ribble Valley	11.67 (5)	16.46 (7)	40.48 (17)	24.24 (10)	22.67 (9)	22.95 (9)	15.61 (6)	24.10 (9)	5.52 (2)
P05	Burnley, Pendle and Rossendale	21.26 (7)	6.18 (2)	28.23 (9)	25.64 (8)	39.31 (12)	22.13 (7)	25.01 (8)	15.92 (5)	32.59 (10)
P06	West Lancashire	21.46 (4)	21.87 (4)	27.82 (5)	44.44 (8)	5.70 (1)	29.36 (5)	23.93 (4)	18.49 (3)	26.01 (4)
P07	Chorley and South Ribble	24.29 (7)	14.07 (4)	17.80 (5)	25.09 (7)	21.37 (6)	46.94 (13)	35.83 (10)	36.93 (10)	37.94 (10)
P08	Bolton	22.42 (9)	25.08 (10)	15.12 (6)	20.64 (8)	12.82 (5)	21.04 (8)	21.07 (8)	18.77 (7)	8.53 (3)
P09	Bury	15.20 (4)	15.23 (4)	27.04 (7)	19.24 (5)	31.78 (8)	12.23 (3)	21.01 (5)	12.64 (3)	13.25 (3)
P10	North Manchester	7.86 (2)	11.68 (3)	29.27 (7)	8.38 (2)	30.23 (6)	18.50 (4)	31.80 (7)	49.15 (10)	33.48 (7)
P11	Central Manchester	33.16 (11)	8.91 (3)	8.58 (3)	14.04 (5)	11.57 (4)	10.87 (4)	21.67 (7)	17.62 (4)	29.22 (9)
P12	South Manchester	15.58 (5)	0.00 (0)	8.83 (3)	13.51 (5)	5.10 (2)	24.49 (8)	22.75 (8)	9.66 (3)	17.96 (5)

HON - E2
Mortality rates from accidents (ICD E800-E949) in young persons aged 15-24:
Age-standardised mortality rates per 100,000: 1984-92
(observed numbers of deaths in parentheses)
Persons

		1984	1985	1986	1987	1988	1989	1990	1991	1992
P13	Oldham	20.76	6.00	18.16	6.15	21.19	22.10	6.17	13.46	17.05
		(7)	(2)	(6)	(2)	(7)	(7)	(2)	(4)	(5)
P14	Rochdale	20.83	26.98	21.51	31.04	9.65	9.89	10.11	16.87	14.67
		(7)	(9)	(7)	(10)	(3)	(3)	(3)	(5)	(4)
P15	Salford	13.81	18.69	28.66	16.93	12.27	33.78	16.27	9.60	27.69
		(6)	(8)	(12)	(7)	(5)	(12)	(6)	(4)	(9)
P16	Stockport	30.49	13.90	26.70	36.61	2.60	15.42	23.84	21.64	16.73
		(13)	(6)	(11)	(15)	(1)	(6)	(9)	(8)	(6)
P17	Tameside and Glossop	13.08	10.51	15.69	18.28	15.95	17.20	14.52	8.61	15.57
		(5)	(4)	(6)	(7)	(6)	(6)	(5)	(3)	(5)
P18	Trafford	14.35	20.12	30.18	21.53	15.25	10.02	22.97	20.98	15.05
		(5)	(7)	(10)	(7)	(5)	(3)	(7)	(6)	(4)
P19	Wigan	20.68	23.00	10.33	21.14	14.65	12.52	19.47	8.90	14.35
		(10)	(11)	(5)	(10)	(7)	(6)	(9)	(4)	(6)

145

HON - E3
Mortality rates from accidents (ICD E800-E949) in persons aged 65 and over:
Age-standardised mortality rates per 100,000: 1984-92
(observed numbers of deaths in parentheses)
Persons

		1984	1985	1986	1987	1988	1989	1990	1991	1992
	ENGLAND AND WALES	74.09	73.55	70.88	62.46	60.23	59.54	56.74	55.59	51.36
		(5762)	(5900)	(5795)	(5226)	(5131)	(5171)	(5015)	(5001)	(4709)
O00	ENGLAND	73.01	72.69	69.60	61.25	59.54	59.05	56.04	54.71	50.90
		(5347)	(5497)	(5361)	(4823)	(4777)	(4827)	(4660)	(4626)	(4392)
A00	NORTHERN RHA	90.40	94.30	79.62	78.43	72.57	77.89	73.25	70.97	61.13
		(399)	(425)	(373)	(378)	(353)	(388)	(372)	(370)	(324)
B00	YORKSHIRE RHA	81.92	79.92	72.60	65.66	58.16	57.81	50.37	54.22	48.87
		(466)	(463)	(425)	(398)	(357)	(362)	(318)	(350)	(322)
C00	TRENT RHA	74.30	69.76	70.16	66.93	59.98	61.13	55.71	57.84	51.66
		(506)	(481)	(492)	(486)	(453)	(466)	(437)	(470)	(431)
D00	EAST ANGLIAN RHA	70.07	70.86	69.09	59.59	68.69	64.87	60.88	61.07	58.65
		(222)	(237)	(233)	(209)	(249)	(245)	(236)	(241)	(234)
E00	NORTH WEST THAMES RHA	68.49	62.61	61.68	52.99	56.60	52.32	55.30	48.91	46.71
		(344)	(318)	(316)	(275)	(291)	(280)	(290)	(266)	(253)
F00	NORTH EAST THAMES RHA	70.91	77.57	72.46	59.88	58.61	49.73	50.57	49.40	51.15
		(394)	(444)	(425)	(357)	(350)	(303)	(306)	(306)	(324)
G00	SOUTH EAST THAMES RHA	65.57	63.26	62.43	56.43	46.98	49.60	46.47	44.23	45.20
		(435)	(432)	(423)	(389)	(323)	(348)	(330)	(306)	(331)
H00	SOUTH WEST THAMES RHA	53.73	55.57	57.02	46.74	43.58	45.81	44.25	43.69	40.91
		(282)	(298)	(315)	(260)	(241)	(258)	(253)	(252)	(235)
J00	WESSEX RHA	59.47	59.81	54.78	49.99	52.43	47.57	48.20	46.63	41.37
		(301)	(317)	(298)	(276)	(302)	(282)	(288)	(287)	(259)
K00	OXFORD RHA	76.15	76.00	76.18	60.82	57.77	68.34	58.60	58.43	48.63
		(225)	(247)	(249)	(207)	(200)	(242)	(216)	(220)	(186)
L00	SOUTH WESTERN RHA	53.34	59.72	58.06	50.18	57.86	54.09	51.63	51.02	46.33
		(311)	(363)	(355)	(321)	(381)	(354)	(356)	(356)	(333)
M00	WEST MIDLANDS RHA	88.48	84.55	80.99	65.56	71.57	74.13	70.49	65.54	59.93
		(620)	(616)	(602)	(502)	(560)	(600)	(587)	(557)	(522)
N00	MERSEY RHA	62.05	56.86	61.27	59.99	46.50	51.39	46.07	40.02	48.18
		(214)	(207)	(235)	(226)	(178)	(200)	(184)	(163)	(192)
P00	NORTH WESTERN RHA	102.41	103.70	96.02	82.40	79.99	73.75	69.94	70.56	62.97
		(628)	(649)	(620)	(539)	(539)	(499)	(487)	(482)	(446)
A01	Hartlepool	112.95	97.59	63.70	82.83	40.56	83.88	88.98	89.04	21.93
		(13)	(11)	(8)	(10)	(6)	(10)	(12)	(12)	(3)
A02	North Tees	79.70	54.70	103.05	100.30	116.60	67.36	92.09	80.74	63.10
		(14)	(9)	(19)	(20)	(23)	(15)	(21)	(18)	(15)
A03	South Tees	113.53	110.95	116.03	101.94	77.09	90.61	99.42	56.43	46.04
		(37)	(38)	(41)	(37)	(27)	(35)	(42)	(23)	(20)
A04	East Cumbria	48.37	43.27	45.28	67.70	45.13	65.91	43.57	52.00	32.03
		(14)	(14)	(15)	(20)	(16)	(20)	(14)	(18)	(12)
A05	South Cumbria	64.84	83.79	35.74	66.95	59.86	74.31	53.13	85.63	72.14
		(20)	(27)	(12)	(23)	(20)	(25)	(19)	(30)	(25)
A06	West Cumbria	102.90	153.25	104.87	77.23	69.21	87.43	151.21	92.38	66.71
		(18)	(27)	(20)	(16)	(14)	(18)	(32)	(21)	(15)

HON - E3
Mortality rates from accidents (ICD E800-E949) in persons aged 65 and over:
Age-standardised mortality rates per 100,000: 1984-92
(observed numbers of deaths in parentheses)
Persons

		1984	1985	1986	1987	1988	1989	1990	1991	1992
A11	Northumberland	100.85 (47)	99.90 (48)	97.50 (49)	88.10 (45)	93.87 (48)	82.90 (44)	89.76 (47)	75.15 (42)	74.78 (42)
A12	Gateshead	130.06 (40)	134.11 (41)	92.18 (28)	79.18 (28)	97.25 (31)	119.24 (40)	72.14 (25)	73.04 (25)	89.27 (30)
A13	Newcastle	76.96 (36)	114.15 (54)	93.62 (45)	77.32 (39)	59.58 (30)	70.68 (38)	58.57 (29)	64.84 (33)	41.54 (22)
A14	North Tyneside	64.21 (20)	91.66 (29)	61.16 (19)	75.70 (24)	97.61 (32)	56.07 (19)	56.93 (19)	60.45 (22)	61.23 (23)
A15	South Tyneside	109.04 (26)	49.71 (12)	66.34 (18)	73.62 (20)	66.73 (18)	108.85 (29)	67.87 (19)	85.41 (23)	57.96 (17)
A16	Sunderland	60.62 (21)	54.97 (21)	81.55 (33)	60.16 (25)	47.04 (20)	57.03 (23)	58.79 (24)	62.71 (27)	57.55 (26)
A30	North Durham	106.05 (46)	120.69 (57)	77.93 (36)	102.32 (48)	72.58 (36)	103.33 (51)	70.67 (36)	95.18 (50)	89.12 (47)
A31	South Durham	111.29 (47)	91.01 (37)	70.79 (30)	52.37 (23)	71.77 (32)	46.39 (21)	71.19 (33)	50.65 (26)	56.09 (27)
B11	East Riding	81.13 (64)	79.90 (65)	59.26 (48)	67.39 (57)	51.86 (45)	49.18 (43)	59.26 (52)	56.67 (52)	65.57 (64)
B16	Grimsby and Scunthorpe	63.17 (29)	35.56 (17)	57.04 (28)	47.26 (25)	38.63 (21)	40.35 (23)	22.97 (13)	36.29 (23)	43.28 (26)
B21	North Yorkshire	56.91 (71)	53.43 (69)	70.91 (93)	46.01 (61)	40.28 (57)	47.48 (67)	46.01 (69)	47.70 (67)	33.28 (50)
B31	Bradford	112.55 (79)	134.07 (94)	89.11 (63)	77.79 (56)	69.12 (51)	71.08 (53)	52.73 (39)	70.55 (53)	57.19 (43)
B51	West Yorkshire	96.01 (90)	97.07 (89)	95.86 (87)	88.62 (86)	83.47 (80)	67.38 (66)	63.51 (62)	67.06 (66)	51.11 (51)
B61	Leeds	92.93 (105)	92.84 (108)	75.99 (90)	73.15 (89)	75.72 (90)	76.20 (92)	50.20 (60)	56.45 (72)	54.88 (70)
B71	Wakefield	66.99 (28)	51.67 (21)	39.36 (16)	55.42 (24)	29.40 (13)	38.99 (18)	48.54 (23)	35.47 (17)	37.21 (18)
C01	North Derbyshire	162.87 (87)	171.88 (93)	175.64 (99)	166.49 (94)	104.78 (67)	94.56 (57)	100.64 (65)	121.67 (80)	104.75 (71)
C02	Southern Derbyshire	78.88 (64)	63.21 (50)	51.56 (40)	49.67 (41)	53.46 (49)	34.79 (32)	41.84 (38)	43.38 (40)	39.05 (37)
C03	Leicestershire	65.47 (81)	58.33 (72)	59.53 (78)	69.24 (89)	60.81 (79)	70.96 (96)	59.01 (83)	67.84 (100)	52.22 (79)
C04	North Lincolnshire	81.71 (33)	76.14 (32)	58.47 (24)	80.47 (36)	83.85 (37)	91.97 (42)	42.37 (21)	50.13 (26)	41.14 (23)
C05	South Lincolnshire	50.43 (26)	68.16 (35)	88.67 (43)	54.80 (31)	61.90 (35)	62.96 (37)	69.76 (41)	40.83 (25)	44.24 (27)
C08	Nottingham	63.82 (56)	52.92 (49)	69.95 (65)	57.42 (54)	40.33 (41)	53.46 (53)	50.57 (50)	49.66 (54)	50.95 (56)
C09	Barnsley	42.81 (14)	48.50 (16)	74.66 (24)	32.68 (11)	54.07 (19)	40.01 (14)	16.77 (6)	54.75 (20)	46.49 (17)

147

HON - E3
Mortality rates from accidents (ICD E800-E949) in persons aged 65 and over:
Age-standardised mortality rates per 100,000: 1984-92
(observed numbers of deaths in parentheses)
Persons

		1984	1985	1986	1987	1988	1989	1990	1991	1992
C10	Doncaster	62.51 (23)	44.39 (17)	40.07 (17)	39.29 (17)	65.67 (27)	43.69 (18)	31.46 (14)	53.41 (24)	62.28 (29)
C11	Rotherham	109.02 (34)	54.37 (19)	45.09 (14)	89.77 (32)	54.86 (18)	70.15 (26)	89.68 (34)	37.37 (15)	39.32 (16)
C12	Sheffield	55.80 (53)	66.20 (63)	47.31 (45)	54.04 (53)	47.97 (48)	59.72 (59)	48.68 (48)	38.03 (40)	39.29 (40)
C14	North Nottinghamshire	67.70 (35)	66.94 (35)	77.25 (43)	47.45 (28)	56.50 (33)	51.61 (32)	57.56 (37)	72.51 (46)	53.26 (36)
D01	Cambridge	91.12 (38)	87.73 (38)	100.28 (45)	77.91 (34)	64.30 (31)	78.85 (36)	87.93 (43)	108.97 (53)	73.66 (37)
D05	North West Anglia	97.64 (52)	82.93 (49)	102.38 (59)	86.23 (53)	103.65 (68)	122.99 (83)	76.95 (54)	60.05 (43)	72.81 (55)
D06	Norwich	45.80 (39)	50.66 (44)	49.65 (44)	40.76 (39)	53.71 (51)	40.41 (41)	50.39 (53)	55.23 (62)	63.58 (65)
D07	Great Yarmouth and Waveney	97.16 (35)	96.29 (35)	56.53 (23)	72.69 (29)	94.28 (41)	70.98 (31)	55.48 (26)	66.81 (28)	59.41 (27)
D09	Huntingdon	66.25 (9)	102.63 (14)	46.39 (6)	55.73 (9)	83.26 (12)	42.34 (7)	52.20 (9)	81.01 (14)	34.15 (6)
D11	Suffolk	56.92 (49)	60.71 (57)	62.01 (56)	48.65 (45)	49.38 (46)	46.16 (47)	51.74 (51)	40.60 (41)	41.32 (44)
E01	North Bedfordshire	69.21 (22)	44.38 (15)	52.42 (17)	58.33 (20)	44.26 (15)	44.51 (16)	57.62 (21)	48.78 (18)	33.98 (13)
E02	South Bedfordshire	99.13 (30)	56.66 (20)	39.66 (14)	51.71 (18)	72.36 (24)	30.44 (10)	103.52 (35)	27.79 (11)	74.18 (28)
E05	North West Hertfordshire	39.88 (14)	52.07 (19)	46.49 (17)	39.16 (16)	42.73 (17)	50.90 (19)	65.71 (27)	72.16 (29)	30.83 (12)
E06	South West Hertfordshire	52.66 (20)	74.22 (28)	87.31 (35)	65.05 (26)	56.16 (23)	61.09 (26)	47.15 (20)	56.87 (26)	59.39 (27)
E07	Barnet	61.85 (33)	65.82 (34)	52.31 (31)	43.65 (24)	50.88 (27)	38.44 (22)	54.71 (30)	38.28 (22)	35.79 (21)
E09	Hillingdon	84.67 (29)	50.65 (18)	80.63 (28)	34.66 (13)	32.76 (12)	65.69 (24)	28.92 (10)	32.50 (13)	44.30 (16)
E18	East and North Hertfordshire	48.77 (29)	44.98 (28)	54.60 (35)	39.91 (26)	43.83 (30)	52.99 (38)	42.96 (32)	67.42 (48)	42.14 (31)
E19	Brent and Harrow	61.72 (43)	39.32 (29)	56.23 (37)	47.31 (33)	49.74 (34)	41.51 (29)	44.73 (31)	37.06 (26)	35.44 (23)
E20	Ealing, Hammersmith and Hounslow	63.57 (62)	72.45 (68)	68.90 (65)	62.18 (59)	59.99 (53)	55.51 (54)	54.61 (47)	45.20 (42)	53.40 (50)
E21	Kensington, Chelsea and Westminster	119.59 (62)	115.60 (59)	74.73 (37)	83.97 (40)	109.75 (56)	81.42 (42)	73.91 (37)	61.01 (31)	62.92 (32)
F31	North Essex	72.01 (90)	72.83 (94)	75.09 (100)	57.46 (83)	60.51 (87)	44.04 (65)	46.05 (69)	47.62 (74)	40.86 (68)
F32	South Essex	69.74 (69)	66.99 (71)	74.54 (77)	66.14 (69)	50.96 (57)	48.14 (55)	48.36 (55)	32.45 (39)	30.73 (38)

148

HON - E3
Mortality rates from accidents (ICD E800-E949) in persons aged 65 and over:
Age-standardised mortality rates per 100,000: 1984-92
(observed numbers of deaths in parentheses)
Persons

		1984	1985	1986	1987	1988	1989	1990	1991	1992
F33	Barking and Havering	43.84	67.57	50.68	56.58	42.49	36.99	43.49	62.84	49.52
		(24)	(38)	(30)	(33)	(27)	(22)	(27)	(39)	(33)
F34	Redbridge and Waltham Forest	66.21	75.23	69.03	54.34	69.93	56.91	56.45	58.30	79.31
		(50)	(56)	(56)	(45)	(55)	(45)	(44)	(47)	(63)
F35	East London and the City	84.85	84.69	59.17	67.12	56.40	61.29	49.30	48.16	46.69
		(64)	(66)	(46)	(52)	(43)	(47)	(37)	(36)	(34)
F36	New River District	54.58	59.31	66.56	52.39	55.84	46.28	64.10	57.10	57.58
		(40)	(43)	(52)	(40)	(41)	(35)	(46)	(41)	(42)
F37	Camden and Islington	108.21	140.69	117.99	65.77	80.22	59.43	53.87	56.35	85.87
		(57)	(76)	(64)	(35)	(40)	(34)	(28)	(30)	(46)
G04	South East Kent	54.52	66.50	83.43	101.25	72.07	61.56	78.13	52.92	87.78
		(29)	(35)	(45)	(57)	(40)	(36)	(47)	(33)	(57)
G05	Canterbury and Thanet	82.01	57.03	81.06	60.31	54.44	47.31	43.93	46.11	39.39
		(52)	(40)	(57)	(45)	(40)	(36)	(33)	(33)	(30)
G06	Dartford and Gravesham	61.62	40.64	34.05	44.05	27.52	44.25	49.84	25.27	35.06
		(17)	(13)	(10)	(14)	(9)	(14)	(16)	(8)	(12)
G07	Maidstone	85.41	60.77	91.45	86.74	77.30	47.29	56.64	23.96	29.66
		(22)	(15)	(24)	(23)	(22)	(14)	(16)	(7)	(9)
G08	Medway	34.98	23.09	27.05	18.89	27.53	34.90	53.58	37.11	35.56
		(13)	(10)	(11)	(8)	(11)	(16)	(24)	(16)	(17)
G09	Tunbridge Wells	54.78	50.33	116.44	85.31	64.33	76.32	42.62	69.98	48.45
		(21)	(19)	(44)	(33)	(24)	(28)	(18)	(30)	(22)
G10	Bexley	35.78	37.04	32.81	64.19	49.81	43.46	45.60	27.47	29.25
		(11)	(12)	(10)	(21)	(16)	(16)	(16)	(9)	(10)
G11	Greenwich	53.35	45.89	66.83	40.99	39.94	61.00	28.91	36.69	56.88
		(18)	(15)	(21)	(14)	(13)	(21)	(9)	(12)	(20)
G12	Bromley	48.67	46.42	50.56	44.92	50.62	17.57	45.27	25.91	17.37
		(24)	(23)	(27)	(24)	(25)	(10)	(25)	(15)	(9)
G21	East Sussex	66.70	63.35	46.88	49.16	38.78	50.69	43.33	47.02	43.94
		(130)	(123)	(90)	(96)	(78)	(101)	(86)	(88)	(89)
G26	South East London	88.10	112.13	76.32	51.39	42.25	54.46	37.25	55.98	53.83
		(98)	(127)	(84)	(54)	(45)	(56)	(40)	(55)	(56)
H04	Mid Surrey	70.47	41.27	59.53	36.37	31.05	30.30	32.56	25.09	25.39
		(21)	(12)	(18)	(13)	(10)	(10)	(12)	(8)	(9)
H05	East Surrey	36.73	51.28	39.40	32.73	32.62	24.10	46.14	37.92	37.04
		(12)	(18)	(14)	(10)	(10)	(9)	(16)	(15)	(14)
H06	Chichester	51.31	47.51	40.42	48.04	29.38	40.20	37.04	55.17	39.37
		(24)	(19)	(20)	(23)	(14)	(20)	(20)	(29)	(23)
H07	Mid Downs	50.27	38.04	43.89	44.43	32.94	32.23	34.32	39.47	21.91
		(20)	(16)	(19)	(19)	(15)	(15)	(16)	(18)	(10)
H08	Worthing	35.50	23.03	36.64	28.97	35.01	42.88	43.29	31.80	38.95
		(26)	(18)	(28)	(23)	(26)	(35)	(32)	(28)	(28)
H09	Croydon	75.64	75.35	78.03	51.31	46.77	66.47	50.72	56.00	36.11
		(36)	(34)	(36)	(25)	(22)	(31)	(23)	(27)	(17)

HON - E3
Mortality rates from accidents (ICD E800-E949) in persons aged 65 and over:
Age-standardised mortality rates per 100,000: 1984-92
(observed numbers of deaths in parentheses)
Persons

		1984	1985	1986	1987	1988	1989	1990	1991	1992
H12	Wandsworth	47.11	57.07	76.73	42.23	52.72	74.40	34.33	55.59	49.24
		(14)	(19)	(23)	(12)	(16)	(21)	(9)	(15)	(14)
H13	Merton and Sutton	59.18	39.83	48.76	45.83	43.19	42.43	46.63	32.47	55.22
		(37)	(26)	(32)	(30)	(26)	(26)	(30)	(21)	(35)
H14	North West Surrey	71.60	93.14	81.38	55.25	60.19	61.87	60.15	59.46	54.27
		(34)	(50)	(44)	(31)	(35)	(36)	(37)	(38)	(35)
H15	South West Surrey	32.57	70.27	59.09	64.20	45.25	40.45	45.15	53.06	31.71
		(13)	(29)	(25)	(27)	(18)	(16)	(21)	(24)	(15)
H16	Kingston and Richmond	59.35	73.80	68.86	59.12	60.36	47.13	46.28	39.47	48.38
		(45)	(57)	(56)	(47)	(49)	(39)	(37)	(29)	(35)
J10	Dorset	58.12	62.28	63.34	57.16	53.55	65.17	52.75	53.33	47.92
		(85)	(91)	(99)	(87)	(89)	(111)	(93)	(93)	(88)
J21	Portsmouth and South East Hampshire	71.31	76.16	43.00	52.58	51.36	40.53	62.50	49.15	42.05
		(55)	(63)	(37)	(45)	(46)	(39)	(58)	(49)	(42)
J22	Southampton and South West Hampshire	64.77	58.31	46.66	28.66	41.08	36.65	49.17	30.31	37.58
		(44)	(42)	(34)	(22)	(32)	(30)	(41)	(26)	(32)
J23	Winchester	65.71	58.09	52.15	52.61	74.89	51.85	59.83	52.28	66.45
		(21)	(19)	(17)	(17)	(25)	(18)	(21)	(19)	(24)
J24	Basingstoke and North Hampshire	89.92	64.57	63.69	60.20	71.05	53.33	37.03	63.75	66.14
		(34)	(27)	(26)	(27)	(31)	(24)	(17)	(30)	(32)
J31	Salisbury	47.32	33.34	48.15	49.41	43.86	42.69	46.87	42.13	18.19
		(10)	(8)	(11)	(11)	(11)	(11)	(11)	(13)	(5)
J32	Swindon	22.14	34.47	39.56	50.77	56.46	55.65	51.14	45.61	30.99
		(7)	(11)	(12)	(16)	(18)	(18)	(16)	(15)	(11)
J33	Bath	46.05	51.73	49.46	40.51	41.63	34.19	32.65	40.21	28.47
		(30)	(37)	(35)	(30)	(30)	(25)	(24)	(30)	(22)
J41	Isle of Wight	47.35	67.22	86.34	64.13	56.34	17.10	16.79	34.13	9.29
		(15)	(19)	(27)	(21)	(20)	(6)	(7)	(12)	(3)
K11	East Berkshire	97.76	65.31	95.38	63.73	61.80	56.97	66.80	58.11	62.39
		(39)	(29)	(44)	(29)	(30)	(28)	(34)	(30)	(32)
K12	West Berkshire	74.13	96.73	86.06	61.48	95.05	104.92	81.81	68.60	47.60
		(39)	(56)	(47)	(36)	(56)	(64)	(52)	(46)	(31)
K24	Buckinghamshire	115.22	99.43	85.19	68.64	57.92	55.00	49.31	73.27	47.12
		(70)	(69)	(59)	(51)	(44)	(43)	(39)	(59)	(40)
K31	Kettering	75.61	67.77	82.93	78.46	38.14	88.68	63.57	53.73	40.69
		(27)	(26)	(32)	(31)	(16)	(37)	(28)	(24)	(19)
K32	Northampton	49.40	81.91	52.86	58.15	47.10	74.30	49.23	49.83	58.63
		(20)	(35)	(23)	(27)	(22)	(35)	(23)	(24)	(29)
K41	Oxfordshire	43.58	45.34	58.68	43.82	43.66	46.43	47.75	43.58	40.05
		(30)	(32)	(44)	(33)	(32)	(35)	(40)	(37)	(35)
L10	Bristol and District	37.81	42.94	38.12	43.00	45.01	43.09	36.96	29.85	37.60
		(49)	(60)	(52)	(61)	(65)	(60)	(57)	(44)	(59)
L21	Cornwall and Isles of Scilly	48.44	49.78	71.93	59.35	42.96	48.65	45.50	46.61	47.95
		(43)	(42)	(66)	(54)	(42)	(49)	(46)	(48)	(51)

HON - E3
Mortality rates from accidents (ICD E800-E949) in persons aged 65 and over:
Age-standardised mortality rates per 100,000: 1984-92
(observed numbers of deaths in parentheses)
Persons

		1984	1985	1986	1987	1988	1989	1990	1991	1992
L35	Exeter and North Devon	62.53 (60)	60.37 (58)	53.65 (53)	41.30 (44)	46.42 (49)	60.10 (62)	48.84 (54)	39.60 (46)	41.47 (48)
L36	Plymouth and Torbay	58.05 (66)	64.42 (78)	61.48 (73)	48.07 (63)	53.09 (72)	54.03 (72)	52.21 (71)	58.92 (81)	40.02 (57)
L40	Gloucestershire	68.33 (57)	82.28 (71)	62.63 (56)	61.64 (58)	108.77 (101)	52.48 (49)	59.25 (61)	68.37 (69)	57.48 (61)
L51	Somerset	50.18 (36)	66.90 (54)	70.49 (55)	52.30 (41)	61.30 (52)	73.07 (62)	77.34 (67)	73.91 (68)	61.17 (57)
M02	Herefordshire	45.71 (12)	37.37 (10)	43.13 (12)	63.78 (17)	24.44 (8)	46.22 (14)	41.99 (13)	27.77 (10)	27.74 (10)
M04	Worcester and District	47.82 (18)	84.23 (30)	68.94 (28)	44.08 (17)	69.85 (30)	37.16 (15)	52.10 (23)	52.65 (23)	58.46 (27)
M05	Shropshire	104.31 (60)	47.73 (29)	87.73 (50)	55.54 (34)	63.07 (39)	41.61 (26)	60.68 (39)	45.14 (31)	35.76 (24)
M06	Mid Staffordshire	77.70 (28)	37.33 (14)	77.62 (29)	38.38 (15)	39.84 (17)	59.22 (24)	95.30 (41)	36.50 (16)	75.74 (36)
M07	North Staffordshire	187.32 (118)	196.11 (133)	119.17 (83)	143.60 (102)	138.18 (99)	138.60 (104)	117.73 (89)	117.84 (92)	80.39 (64)
M08	South East Staffordshire	66.49 (18)	84.10 (25)	68.42 (21)	41.59 (14)	54.91 (18)	36.63 (12)	61.80 (22)	54.60 (20)	34.67 (13)
M13	East Birmingham	86.68 (24)	118.66 (34)	75.68 (22)	58.96 (18)	78.34 (23)	91.88 (29)	85.47 (27)	96.96 (31)	54.84 (18)
M14	North Birmingham	103.26 (23)	74.68 (18)	69.51 (17)	94.98 (25)	76.12 (20)	94.61 (26)	67.31 (19)	80.35 (25)	73.93 (21)
M16	West Birmingham	62.07 (21)	79.02 (22)	133.18 (37)	88.01 (26)	101.21 (29)	142.85 (42)	85.87 (26)	105.56 (31)	109.20 (34)
M17	Coventry	53.23 (21)	66.49 (31)	37.35 (17)	46.93 (21)	52.39 (25)	36.84 (19)	41.84 (20)	49.67 (23)	32.95 (16)
M18	Dudley	73.39 (31)	64.58 (28)	64.62 (28)	51.22 (22)	78.57 (35)	59.13 (27)	52.82 (27)	44.06 (22)	69.79 (35)
M19	Sandwell	90.76 (37)	61.55 (29)	70.23 (31)	73.56 (36)	75.81 (35)	72.86 (36)	49.47 (26)	82.30 (41)	61.96 (34)
M20	Solihull	119.69 (26)	85.26 (20)	63.02 (15)	41.60 (10)	64.13 (16)	59.84 (18)	74.78 (21)	71.83 (21)	77.11 (25)
M21	Walsall	67.33 (21)	32.96 (11)	65.03 (20)	49.79 (16)	34.79 (13)	96.51 (33)	56.70 (22)	45.55 (17)	51.35 (19)
M22	Wolverhampton	56.93 (20)	54.86 (20)	71.76 (27)	43.06 (17)	60.53 (24)	70.92 (26)	65.54 (26)	55.82 (24)	40.40 (17)
M25	South Birmingham	84.25 (55)	70.31 (47)	94.81 (65)	65.53 (44)	90.93 (61)	108.64 (79)	106.61 (74)	76.14 (55)	79.91 (56)
M26	North Worcestershire	99.19 (31)	128.88 (41)	100.75 (34)	66.64 (24)	60.88 (22)	82.14 (30)	79.35 (32)	78.12 (33)	76.13 (33)
M28	Warwickshire	84.54 (56)	112.43 (74)	93.93 (66)	62.09 (44)	61.53 (46)	50.79 (40)	49.25 (40)	53.32 (42)	47.67 (40)

HON - E3
Mortality rates from accidents (ICD E800-E949) in persons aged 65 and over:
Age-standardised mortality rates per 100,000: 1984-92
(observed numbers of deaths in parentheses)
Persons

		1984	1985	1986	1987	1988	1989	1990	1991	1992
N11	Chester	56.21 (14)	81.27 (18)	51.95 (15)	47.83 (12)	41.85 (11)	55.42 (15)	61.15 (17)	61.29 (18)	41.86 (12)
N12	Crewe	30.25 (9)	42.03 (14)	32.26 (12)	33.97 (12)	18.25 (7)	32.79 (13)	25.65 (10)	38.63 (16)	39.77 (15)
N13	Halton	37.92 (6)	59.69 (10)	50.75 (9)	42.80 (7)	50.40 (9)	65.28 (11)	33.78 (6)	16.55 (3)	47.14 (9)
N14	Macclesfield	69.61 (19)	58.38 (16)	48.77 (15)	88.76 (25)	55.06 (16)	50.10 (14)	60.82 (19)	14.66 (6)	46.86 (16)
N15	Warrington	25.92 (6)	19.59 (5)	35.16 (8)	26.51 (7)	29.73 (8)	26.32 (7)	38.18 (10)	39.71 (11)	51.49 (14)
N21	Liverpool	69.10 (55)	83.66 (68)	73.41 (61)	50.49 (43)	59.85 (48)	48.60 (39)	48.61 (40)	57.33 (43)	48.03 (37)
N31	St Helens and Knowsley	112.11 (42)	97.59 (39)	113.28 (48)	94.58 (40)	77.03 (34)	85.21 (39)	44.39 (21)	57.74 (27)	68.92 (31)
N41	Southport and Formby	52.36 (14)	40.24 (12)	75.90 (23)	73.17 (21)	42.52 (12)	61.86 (18)	62.01 (18)	31.81 (11)	38.99 (12)
N42	South Sefton	94.61 (22)	38.46 (10)	66.49 (18)	90.80 (24)	28.97 (8)	57.96 (16)	49.72 (16)	40.44 (13)	53.25 (17)
N51	Wirral	47.19 (27)	24.40 (15)	39.16 (26)	56.39 (35)	37.68 (25)	40.64 (28)	41.75 (27)	21.08 (15)	44.31 (29)
P01	Lancaster	67.25 (18)	77.31 (21)	55.36 (16)	33.41 (9)	37.57 (10)	55.00 (17)	78.62 (24)	79.48 (22)	53.00 (17)
P02	Blackpool, Wyre and Fylde	180.03 (129)	187.93 (142)	187.05 (148)	187.96 (147)	144.95 (120)	134.37 (109)	126.71 (107)	133.69 (111)	94.92 (84)
P03	Preston	231.39 (47)	243.72 (49)	239.62 (54)	136.61 (29)	156.80 (33)	128.22 (28)	132.36 (29)	130.18 (28)	68.34 (16)
P04	Blackburn, Hyndburn and Ribble Valley	88.46 (37)	58.05 (25)	89.69 (37)	49.41 (24)	72.58 (32)	69.30 (29)	63.34 (29)	69.99 (32)	49.36 (23)
P05	Burnley, Pendle and Rossendale	158.58 (57)	90.98 (34)	60.85 (24)	60.19 (24)	37.51 (16)	53.50 (21)	26.04 (11)	30.04 (13)	70.13 (29)
P06	West Lancashire	111.26 (13)	34.53 (4)	87.51 (12)	75.68 (10)	55.10 (7)	55.46 (8)	64.61 (10)	17.85 (3)	19.19 (3)
P07	Chorley and South Ribble	169.67 (40)	142.50 (34)	146.54 (35)	146.61 (39)	107.29 (29)	119.48 (33)	89.12 (27)	113.53 (33)	129.22 (40)
P08	Bolton	61.67 (24)	65.60 (26)	90.80 (37)	86.25 (34)	25.90 (11)	41.48 (17)	69.70 (29)	62.22 (27)	60.31 (26)
P09	Bury	60.62 (15)	87.01 (24)	70.86 (20)	37.25 (12)	67.21 (20)	34.52 (10)	45.74 (14)	70.27 (19)	71.76 (20)
P10	North Manchester	125.70 (30)	131.76 (33)	109.48 (26)	85.32 (23)	110.49 (26)	59.92 (15)	76.99 (18)	53.27 (12)	72.03 (16)
P11	Central Manchester	81.67 (15)	119.38 (22)	146.59 (25)	122.43 (21)	126.00 (21)	112.04 (19)	151.71 (25)	115.15 (19)	115.55 (17)
P12	South Manchester	128.45 (38)	132.67 (38)	48.29 (15)	41.74 (14)	82.99 (26)	85.28 (27)	78.31 (25)	73.23 (21)	88.46 (27)

HON - E3
Mortality rates from accidents (ICD E800-E949) in persons aged 65 and over:
Age-standardised mortality rates per 100,000: 1984-92
(observed numbers of deaths in parentheses)
Persons

		1984	1985	1986	1987	1988	1989	1990	1991	1992
P13	Oldham	40.73	94.91	73.99	80.53	94.45	76.74	58.90	72.07	27.02
		(14)	(29)	(24)	(26)	(35)	(26)	(22)	(25)	(10)
P14	Rochdale	65.53	70.26	36.76	46.92	86.36	37.74	43.87	34.89	42.95
		(19)	(22)	(11)	(14)	(26)	(12)	(15)	(11)	(15)
P15	Salford	95.21	156.43	110.12	95.47	72.98	61.12	63.82	65.12	73.98
		(36)	(57)	(43)	(38)	(30)	(26)	(26)	(27)	(31)
P16	Stockport	27.54	44.83	60.69	35.54	76.13	55.53	35.87	39.53	32.90
		(12)	(19)	(28)	(16)	(35)	(28)	(19)	(19)	(16)
P17	Tameside and Glossop	63.35	63.57	57.35	25.99	53.22	49.82	34.23	40.96	25.70
		(23)	(22)	(20)	(9)	(20)	(19)	(13)	(17)	(12)
P18	Trafford	92.64	55.66	52.74	66.87	57.10	57.00	39.85	39.57	39.41
		(31)	(20)	(17)	(22)	(21)	(21)	(15)	(15)	(16)
P19	Wigan	78.36	73.52	72.81	72.13	45.95	78.77	67.36	64.75	58.98
		(30)	(28)	(28)	(28)	(21)	(34)	(29)	(28)	(28)

PUBLIC HEALTH COMMON DATA SET

SELECTED INDICATORS

Public Health Common Data Set		CDS - B1 General fertility rate: 1992		CDS - B6 Percent of births under 2500g: 1992	
		Rate	Rank	Percent	Rank
	ENGLAND AND WALES	63.5		6.7	
O00	ENGLAND	63.5		6.7	
A00	NORTHERN RHA	61.8	5	6.8	9
B00	YORKSHIRE RHA	63.9	10	7.3	11
C00	TRENT RHA	62.6	7	7.3	11
D00	EAST ANGLIAN RHA	60.8	2	6.1	3
E00	NORTH WEST THAMES RHA	63.2	9	7.0	10
F00	NORTH EAST THAMES RHA	67.2	14	6.7	8
G00	SOUTH EAST THAMES RHA	64.2	11	6.0	2
H00	SOUTH WEST THAMES RHA	60.8	2	6.1	3
J00	WESSEX RHA	61.3	4	6.2	5
K00	OXFORD RHA	63.0	8	6.2	5
L00	SOUTH WESTERN RHA	60.6	1	5.9	1
M00	WEST MIDLANDS RHA	65.5	12	7.3	11
N00	MERSEY RHA	62.5	6	6.2	5
P00	NORTH WESTERN RHA	66.9	13	7.4	14
A01	Hartlepool	65.7	103	6.4	66
A02	North Tees	63.4	80	7.4	117
A03	South Tees	67.3	119	7.7	120
A04	East Cumbria	60.1	33	6.2	47
A05	South Cumbria	63.2	77	5.9	27
A06	West Cumbria	63.4	80	5.8	22
A11	Northumberland	57.7	15	6.2	47
A12	Gateshead	59.6	28	6.4	66
A13	Newcastle	56.3	6	7.7	120
A14	North Tyneside	60.8	42	6.7	89
A15	South Tyneside	63.6	84	8.1	132
A16	Sunderland	63.1	75	6.6	81
A30	North Durham	61.3	53	6.8	92
A31	South Durham	63.3	78	6.9	98
B11	East Riding	61.9	58	6.7	89
B16	Grimsby and Scunthorpe	65.8	104	6.6	81
B21	North Yorkshire	58.1	19	6.3	57
B31	Bradford	73.9	139	8.0	129
B51	West Yorkshire	66.6	113	7.7	120
B61	Leeds	60.7	39	7.9	128
B71	Wakefield	65.0	97	7.5	118
C01	North Derbyshire	61.2	50	6.3	57
C02	Southern Derbyshire	65.3	99	7.7	120
C03	Leicestershire	61.8	57	6.8	92
C04	North Lincolnshire	61.0	44	6.1	38
C05	South Lincolnshire	59.3	25	6.3	57

Public Health Common Data Set		CDS - B1 General fertility rate: 1992		CDS - B6 Percent of births under 2500g: 1992	
		Rate	Rank	Percent	Rank
C08	Nottingham	61.5	55	9.3	141
C09	Barnsley	67.2	117	7.0	104
C10	Doncaster	67.0	116	6.6	81
C11	Rotherham	66.2	110	6.6	81
C12	Sheffield	60.3	35	8.0	129
C14	North Nottinghamshire	61.9	58	6.8	92
D01	Cambridge	51.4	2	6.3	57
D05	North West Anglia	66.2	110	6.3	57
D06	Norwich	57.5	13	6.0	31
D07	Great Yarmouth and Waveney	66.9	115	5.7	13
D09	Huntingdon	63.5	83	6.9	98
D11	Suffolk	62.4	64	5.7	13
E01	North Bedfordshire	61.1	48	6.2	47
E02	South Bedfordshire	74.8	141	6.3	57
E05	North West Hertfordshire	64.3	92	6.1	38
E06	South West Hertfordshire	64.4	95	6.4	66
E07	Barnet	60.0	31	5.8	22
E09	Hillingdon	67.3	119	7.1	109
E18	East and North Hertfordshire	65.0	97	6.1	38
E19	Brent and Harrow	66.8	114	9.2	140
E20	Ealing, Hammersmith and Hounslow	63.4	80	7.7	120
E21	Kensington, Chelsea and Westminster	47.7	1	6.7	89
F31	North Essex	62.8	71	6.1	38
F32	South Essex	63.0	72	5.9	27
F33	Barking and Havering	66.0	108	6.0	31
F34	Redbridge and Waltham Forest	70.9	132	6.9	98
F35	East London and the City	82.3	143	8.5	136
F36	New River District	67.3	119	6.6	81
F37	Camden and Islington	56.0	5	6.4	66
G04	South East Kent	65.8	104	6.9	98
G05	Canterbury and Thanet	62.5	67	5.9	27
G06	Dartford and Gravesham	64.2	89	6.4	66
G07	Maidstone	63.6	84	6.2	47
G08	Medway	68.3	128	6.5	75
G09	Tunbridge Wells	61.0	44	4.6	1
G10	Bexley	64.2	89	5.8	22
G11	Greenwich	69.5	130	6.4	66
G12	Bromley	61.0	44	6.0	31
G21	East Sussex	58.2	21	5.4	5
G26	South East London	67.8	125	6.2	47

Public Health Common Data Set		CDS - B1 General fertility rate: 1992		CDS - B6 Percent of births under 2500g: 1992	
		Rate	Rank	Percent	Rank
H04	Mid Surrey	55.0	4	6.6	81
H05	East Surrey	59.0	22	5.7	13
H06	Chichester	56.8	8	6.0	31
H07	Mid Downs	60.7	39	5.7	13
H08	Worthing	63.3	78	5.2	3
H09	Croydon	65.9	106	7.2	113
H12	Wandsworth	59.4	26	5.5	8
H13	Merton and Sutton	65.5	100	6.9	98
H14	North West Surrey	62.6	68	6.0	31
H15	South West Surrey	57.8	16	5.5	8
H16	Kingston and Richmond	56.6	7	5.8	22
J10	Dorset	57.0	9	5.7	13
J21	Portsmouth and South East Hampshire	63.0	72	6.5	75
J22	Southampton and South West Hampshire	63.7	86	6.2	47
J23	Winchester	57.1	11	5.8	22
J24	Basingstoke and North Hampshire	62.7	70	6.2	47
J31	Salisbury	57.9	17	5.4	5
J32	Swindon	67.3	119	7.0	104
J33	Bath	61.1	48	6.2	47
J41	Isle of Wight	59.5	27	5.6	11
K11	East Berkshire	65.5	100	6.0	31
K12	West Berkshire	62.3	62	6.2	47
K24	Buckinghamshire	62.4	64	6.0	31
K31	Kettering	65.6	102	7.0	104
K32	Northampton	64.2	89	7.0	104
K41	Oxfordshire	60.7	39	5.9	27
L10	Bristol and District	61.2	50	5.7	13
L21	Cornwall and Isles of Scilly	61.0	44	6.2	47
L35	Exeter and North Devon	57.0	9	6.1	38
L36	Plymouth and Torbay	61.2	50	6.4	66
L40	Gloucestershire	61.3	53	5.5	8
L51	Somerset	60.6	38	5.6	11
M02	Herefordshire	62.6	68	5.7	13
M04	Worcester and District	60.5	37	6.5	75
M05	Shropshire	62.4	64	5.7	13
M06	Mid Staffordshire	58.0	18	6.1	38
M07	North Staffordshire	60.0	31	6.8	92
M08	South East Staffordshire	64.3	92	5.2	3
M13	East Birmingham	90.6	145	7.7	120
M14	North Birmingham	60.2	34	8.0	129
M16	West Birmingham	80.2	142	9.6	144
M17	Coventry	67.5	124	8.4	135

Public Health Common Data Set		CDS - B1 General fertility rate: 1992		CDS - B6 Percent of births under 2500g: 1992	
		Rate	Rank	Percent	Rank
M18	Dudley	64.3	92	7.7	120
M19	Sandwell	74.5	140	8.7	138
M20	Solihull	60.8	42	5.4	5
M21	Walsall	73.0	136	7.3	116
M22	Wolverhampton	70.8	131	8.3	134
M25	South Birmingham	67.3	119	9.0	139
M26	North Worcestershire	59.8	29	6.9	98
M28	Warwickshire	58.1	19	6.5	75
N11	Chester	62.3	62	6.1	38
N12	Crewe	62.0	60	5.7	13
N13	Halton	65.9	106	5.1	2
N14	Macclesfield	59.2	24	6.4	66
N15	Warrington	64.6	96	6.1	38
N21	Liverpool	61.5	55	6.3	57
N31	St Helens and Knowsley	66.1	109	6.6	81
N41	Southport and Formby	52.6	3	7.1	109
N42	South Sefton	63.0	72	6.8	92
N51	Wirral	62.2	61	6.3	57
P01	Lancaster	57.1	11	7.0	104
P02	Blackpool,Wyre and Fylde	59.8	29	6.5	75
P03	Preston	68.1	127	7.6	119
P04	Blackburn, Hyndburn and Ribble Valley	73.7	138	8.6	137
P05	Burnley, Pendle and Rossendale	71.7	133	7.2	113
P06	West Lancashire	57.6	14	6.1	38
P07	Chorley and South Ribble	59.1	23	6.4	66
P08	Bolton	67.2	117	7.7	120
P09	Bury	66.5	112	7.1	109
P10	North Manchester	83.9	144	9.6	144
P11	Central Manchester	68.7	129	9.4	142
P12	South Manchester	63.9	87	8.1	132
P13	Oldham	73.3	137	7.1	109
P14	Rochdale	72.9	135	9.5	143
P15	Salford	72.6	134	7.2	113
P16	Stockport	60.3	35	6.5	75
P17	Tameside and Glossop	67.9	126	6.6	81
P18	Trafford	63.1	75	6.3	57
P19	Wigan	63.9	87	6.8	92

CDS - B4, B9
Total birth rate (per 1000 females) by maternal age: 1992

		11-19		20-34		35+	
		Rate	Rank	Rate	Rank	Rate	Rank
	ENGLAND AND WALES	17.7		97.9		13.1	
O00	ENGLAND	17.4		97.6		13.2	
A00	NORTHERN RHA	22.2	13	96.5	4	9.9	1
B00	YORKSHIRE RHA	21.4	12	99.1	12	11.0	3
C00	TRENT RHA	19.8	10	98.0	6	10.4	2
D00	EAST ANGLIAN RHA	14.6	6	98.9	11	11.1	4
E00	NORTH WEST THAMES RHA	12.4	2	90.5	1	19.1	14
F00	NORTH EAST THAMES RHA	16.1	8	98.6	9	17.0	12
G00	SOUTH EAST THAMES RHA	15.8	7	96.0	3	15.0	11
H00	SOUTH WEST THAMES RHA	10.6	1	90.9	2	17.5	13
J00	WESSEX RHA	14.2	4	98.1	7	12.1	8
K00	OXFORD RHA	12.7	3	98.8	10	14.9	10
L00	SOUTH WESTERN RHA	14.2	4	98.5	8	11.5	5
M00	WEST MIDLANDS RHA	20.0	11	102.3	14	11.7	6
N00	MERSEY RHA	19.4	9	97.0	5	12.0	7
P00	NORTH WESTERN RHA	23.9	14	101.8	13	12.1	8
A01	Hartlepool	28.0	137	101.0	83	8.3	3
A02	North Tees	20.1	95	100.7	79	10.0	23
A03	South Tees	27.3	135	103.1	103	9.8	18
A04	East Cumbria	15.5	56	99.8	71	10.5	38
A05	South Cumbria	19.7	94	103.9	110	8.7	7
A06	West Cumbria	20.6	98	101.8	93	10.5	38
A11	Northumberland	14.1	45	98.3	56	10.3	32
A12	Gateshead	23.2	113	92.5	21	8.6	6
A13	Newcastle	23.0	111	78.2	5	12.1	81
A14	North Tyneside	19.0	93	97.1	48	10.8	48
A15	South Tyneside	23.8	114	97.8	55	10.0	23
A16	Sunderland	29.0	139	95.3	34	9.1	11
A30	North Durham	21.4	102	96.4	43	9.6	16
A31	South Durham	24.6	119	100.9	81	9.1	11
B11	East Riding	24.1	117	96.3	41	9.5	15
B16	Grimsby and Scunthorpe	22.8	109	105.5	122	9.2	13
B21	North Yorkshire	11.2	20	96.4	43	10.8	48
B31	Bradford	26.4	132	109.7	134	14.7	110
B51	West Yorkshire	22.7	107	104.6	114	11.3	65
B61	Leeds	22.2	104	88.7	16	11.9	76
B71	Wakefield	25.1	123	101.6	88	8.1	1
C01	North Derbyshire	17.1	74	100.7	79	9.9	20
C02	Southern Derbyshire	18.9	92	101.7	91	11.4	68
C03	Leicestershire	15.3	54	98.4	58	11.8	74
C04	North Lincolnshire	16.0	62	101.0	83	10.4	35
C05	South Lincolnshire	16.7	66	101.5	86	8.1	1

		11-19		20-34		35+	
		Rate	Rank	Rate	Rank	Rate	Rank
C08	Nottingham	23.8	114	90.3	18	11.7	72
C09	Barnsley	25.2	124	104.9	119	8.4	5
C10	Doncaster	26.3	131	104.7	116	9.0	10
C11	Rotherham	24.8	121	104.7	116	8.3	3
C12	Sheffield	20.4	97	87.9	14	11.5	69
C14	North Nottinghamshire	21.0	100	99.8	71	8.8	9
D01	Cambridge	8.4	7	77.5	4	15.8	118
D05	North West Anglia	18.6	87	108.2	130	10.0	23
D06	Norwich	12.2	30	95.0	29	10.9	51
D07	Great Yarmouth and Waveney	22.9	110	110.3	137	9.3	14
D09	Huntingdon	13.4	42	101.6	88	12.9	92
D11	Suffolk	14.3	47	103.7	108	9.9	20
E01	North Bedfordshire	12.1	29	96.6	45	14.2	104
E02	South Bedfordshire	18.3	84	111.8	139	15.6	115
E05	North West Hertfordshire	11.2	20	102.0	96	18.6	133
E06	South West Hertfordshire	9.2	11	101.3	85	16.0	122
E07	Barnet	7.0	2	86.6	11	21.6	137
E09	Hillingdon	12.6	32	99.4	67	16.6	124
E18	East and North Hertfordshire	11.3	23	103.3	105	13.8	100
E19	Brent and Harrow	12.0	28	95.5	36	20.9	136
E20	Ealing, Hammersmith and Hounslow	14.3	47	83.8	7	23.3	140
E21	Kensington, Chelsea and Westminster	14.3	47	54.7	1	25.6	143
F31	North Essex	11.2	20	104.4	112	11.8	74
F32	South Essex	13.9	44	102.5	98	10.9	51
F33	Barking and Havering	16.4	63	104.9	119	12.1	81
F34	Redbridge and Waltham Forest	15.3	54	102.9	101	19.1	134
F35	East London and the City	26.1	129	107.9	128	27.5	144
F36	New River District	15.5	56	92.5	21	21.7	138
F37	Camden and Islington	16.9	71	68.7	2	25.0	142
G04	South East Kent	18.2	82	108.4	131	10.3	32
G05	Canterbury and Thanet	18.8	88	101.6	88	10.9	51
G06	Dartford and Gravesham	13.2	36	104.6	114	10.6	41
G07	Maidstone	10.5	16	108.9	132	11.1	60
G08	Medway	17.5	77	109.1	133	9.9	20
G09	Tunbridge Wells	9.3	13	101.7	91	15.7	117
G10	Bexley	9.2	11	102.2	97	13.7	99
G11	Greenwich	22.7	107	99.1	64	16.9	127
G12	Bromley	10.5	16	96.0	40	15.3	114
G21	East Sussex	12.7	33	89.6	17	14.6	108
G26	South East London	23.0	111	84.3	8	24.7	141

CDS - B4, B9
Total birth rate (per 1000 females) by maternal age: 1992

		11-19		20-34		35+	
		Rate	Rank	Rate	Rank	Rate	Rank
H04	Mid Surrey	5.0	1	95.3	34	15.6	115
H05	East Surrey	7.8	5	96.9	47	16.2	123
H06	Chichester	10.3	14	94.3	28	13.3	96
H07	Mid Downs	8.5	8	98.4	58	14.4	107
H08	Worthing	13.2	36	105.9	123	10.9	51
H09	Croydon	16.7	66	95.5	36	17.2	130
H12	Wandsworth	20.1	95	68.9	3	28.5	145
H13	Merton and Sutton	14.6	52	93.5	24	18.5	132
H14	North West Surrey	7.6	4	98.3	56	16.7	125
H15	South West Surrey	7.3	3	93.2	23	16.9	127
H16	Kingston and Richmond	8.2	6	78.5	6	22.2	139
J10	Dorset	11.5	25	93.7	25	11.3	65
J21	Portsmouth and South East Hampshire	18.8	88	97.3	50	10.7	45
J22	Southampton and South West Hampshire	17.9	81	99.1	64	11.9	76
J23	Winchester	8.5	8	97.2	49	12.3	85
J24	Basingstoke and North Hampshire	11.4	24	99.6	69	13.9	101
J31	Salisbury	13.2	36	95.6	38	11.3	65
J32	Swindon	17.8	80	103.1	103	12.9	92
J33	Bath	12.2	30	99.1	64	13.4	97
J41	Isle of Wight	15.9	60	103.5	107	10.2	29
K11	East Berkshire	12.7	33	98.6	61	16.9	127
K12	West Berkshire	10.4	15	97.3	50	15.9	120
K24	Buckinghamshire	10.9	19	101.9	95	15.1	113
K31	Kettering	18.4	85	106.3	126	10.9	51
K32	Northampton	16.8	68	102.6	99	12.8	90
K41	Oxfordshire	11.5	25	91.7	19	15.8	118
L10	Bristol and District	13.7	43	95.0	29	12.7	89
L21	Cornwall and Isles of Scilly	15.9	60	104.8	118	11.0	58
L35	Exeter and North Devon	11.8	27	94.2	27	11.1	60
L36	Plymouth and Torbay	16.8	68	98.9	62	10.1	27
L40	Gloucestershire	13.3	39	99.0	63	12.4	86
L51	Somerset	13.3	39	104.3	111	10.7	45
M02	Herefordshire	14.4	51	106.7	127	10.4	35
M04	Worcester and District	14.2	46	99.5	68	12.9	92
M05	Shropshire	16.8	68	103.7	108	10.8	48
M06	Mid Staffordshire	13.3	39	96.8	46	10.0	23
M07	North Staffordshire	21.3	101	93.9	26	8.7	7
M08	South East Staffordshire	14.3	47	108.0	129	10.2	29
M13	East Birmingham	29.5	140	130.2	145	16.7	125
M14	North Birmingham	16.4	63	92.4	20	13.9	101
M16	West Birmingham	26.4	132	110.2	136	17.6	131
M17	Coventry	22.0	103	99.8	71	13.6	98

CDS - B4, B9
Total birth rate (per 1000 females) by maternal age: 1992

		11-19		20-34		35+	
		Rate	Rank	Rate	Rank	Rate	Rank
M18	Dudley	20.8	99	99.9	75	11.1	60
M19	Sandwell	30.0	141	110.0	135	10.9	51
M20	Solihull	15.6	58	102.8	100	11.2	64
M21	Walsall	28.4	138	111.3	138	11.1	60
M22	Wolverhampton	26.0	128	104.9	119	12.4	86
M25	South Birmingham	23.9	116	95.2	32	14.9	111
M26	North Worcestershire	15.7	59	100.9	81	11.6	71
M28	Warwickshire	12.9	35	96.3	41	11.0	58
N11	Chester	17.4	76	97.4	52	12.1	81
N12	Crewe	18.8	88	100.1	76	10.6	41
N13	Halton	25.5	127	106.1	124	10.1	27
N14	Macclesfield	9.1	10	99.6	69	14.9	111
N15	Warrington	18.4	85	102.9	101	10.3	32
N21	Liverpool	22.6	106	86.9	12	14.3	105
N31	St Helens and Knowsley	24.8	121	101.5	86	10.6	41
N41	Southport and Formby	10.6	18	88.5	15	10.4	35
N42	South Sefton	18.2	82	97.6	53	12.8	90
N51	Wirral	16.9	71	100.3	77	12.0	79
P01	Lancaster	18.8	88	87.7	13	10.5	38
P02	Blackpool, Wyre and Fylde	17.7	78	95.6	38	10.9	51
P03	Preston	24.5	118	100.3	77	11.9	76
P04	Blackburn, Hyndburn and Ribble Valley	26.9	134	115.3	144	12.1	81
P05	Burnley, Pendle and Rossendale	24.7	120	114.6	142	11.7	72
P06	West Lancashire	17.3	75	95.0	29	10.7	45
P07	Chorley and South Ribble	16.9	71	97.7	54	9.8	18
P08	Bolton	25.3	125	104.4	112	10.6	41
P09	Bury	17.7	78	106.1	124	11.5	69
P10	North Manchester	45.1	145	115.0	143	12.0	79
P11	Central Manchester	34.7	144	84.4	9	20.4	135
P12	South Manchester	30.7	142	84.4	9	15.9	120
P13	Oldham	26.2	130	112.5	140	13.1	95
P14	Rochdale	27.3	135	112.5	140	12.5	88
P15	Salford	31.6	143	101.8	93	14.6	108
P16	Stockport	14.6	52	95.2	32	14.0	103
P17	Tameside and Glossop	25.3	125	103.3	105	10.2	29
P18	Trafford	16.5	65	98.4	58	14.3	105
P19	Wigan	22.5	105	99.8	71	9.7	17

Public Health Common Data Set		CDS - B10 Abortion rate (maternal ages 11 years and over): 1992			CDS - B13 Percent of abortions in the NHS: 1992	
		Observed	Rate	Rank	Percent	Rank
	ENGLAND AND WALES	160456	11.66		49.6	
O00	ENGLAND	153601	11.80		49.0	
A00	NORTHERN RHA	6818	8.30	1	85.2	11
B00	YORKSHIRE RHA	9671	9.81	5	53.0	6
C00	TRENT RHA	12217	9.68	4	70.1	8
D00	EAST ANGLIAN RHA	4785	8.69	3	82.6	10
E00	NORTH WEST THAMES RHA	-	-	-	-	-
F00	NORTH EAST THAMES RHA	19831	18.76	11	55.7	7
G00	SOUTH EAST THAMES RHA	15392	15.34	10	43.2	2
H00	SOUTH WEST THAMES RHA	-	-	-	-	-
J00	WESSEX RHA	-	-	-	-	-
K00	OXFORD RHA	7494	10.30	6	48.7	4
L00	SOUTH WESTERN RHA	7368	8.64	2	77.0	9
M00	WEST MIDLANDS RHA	16687	11.90	9	17.1	1
N00	MERSEY RHA	7027	10.90	7	49.5	5
P00	NORTH WESTERN RHA	11644	10.90	7	44.3	3
A01	Hartlepool	185	7.59	4	87.0	123
A02	North Tees	376	7.72	9	82.7	119
A03	South Tees	677	8.62	26	90.8	131
A04	East Cumbria	414	9.01	37	93.5	135
A05	South Cumbria	309	7.05	1	68.6	96
A06	West Cumbria	311	8.67	29	90.7	130
A11	Northumberland	616	7.65	5	90.1	128
A12	Gateshead	410	7.71	7	79.8	110
A13	Newcastle	774	10.06	70	90.2	129
A14	North Tyneside	442	8.63	27	93.4	134
A15	South Tyneside	328	8.15	14	82.3	118
A16	Sunderland	731	9.02	38	73.2	105
A30	North Durham	644	7.33	3	84.0	121
A31	South Durham	601	8.20	17	84.0	121
B11	East Riding	1346	9.83	62	63.5	93
B16	Grimsby and Scunthorpe	1053	11.04	96	87.6	126
B21	North Yorkshire	-	-	-	-	-
B31	Bradford	-	-	-	-	-
B51	West Yorkshire	1522	9.72	60	16.4	19
B61	Leeds	2130	10.91	92	54.0	70
B71	Wakefield	821	9.57	56	50.7	64
C01	North Derbyshire	876	9.06	41	58.6	78
C02	Southern Derbyshire	1362	9.40	50	71.3	102
C03	Leicestershire	2400	9.71	58	61.7	85
C04	North Lincolnshire	583	8.16	15	80.8	116
C05	South Lincolnshire	677	8.36	19	75.5	108

Public Health Common Data Set		CDS - B10 Abortion rate (maternal ages 11 years and over): 1992			CDS - B13 Percent of abortions in the NHS: 1992	
		Observed	Rate	Rank	Percent	Rank
C08	Nottingham	1863	10.88	90	78.9	109
C09	Barnsley	591	9.91	64	62.1	88
C10	Doncaster	936	12.06	109	87.2	124
C11	Rotherham	599	8.70	31	69.6	99
C12	Sheffield	1391	10.00	66	62.6	90
C14	North Nottinghamshire	939	8.92	36	72.6	104
D01	Cambridge	866	10.51	81	88.7	127
D05	North West Anglia	910	8.58	25	68.9	98
D06	Norwich	1049	8.38	20	91.3	132
D07	Great Yarmouth and Waveney	406	8.03	13	80.0	111
D09	Huntingdon	352	8.85	33	83.5	120
D11	Suffolk	1202	8.19	16	81.5	117
E01	North Bedfordshire	644	9.24	44	80.1	112
E02	South Bedfordshire	912	11.30	103	61.4	84
E05	North West Hertfordshire	657	9.13	42	42.9	46
E06	South West Hertfordshire	747	11.16	100	48.6	61
E07	Barnet	1476	17.32	128	44.3	53
E09	Hillingdon	886	13.59	114	43.5	50
E18	East and North Hertfordshire	1141	8.63	27	44.4	54
E19	Brent and Harrow	-	-	-	-	-
E20	Ealing, Hammersmith and Hounslow	-	-	-	-	-
E21	Kensington, Chelsea and Westminster	-	-	-	-	-
F31	North Essex	2385	10.38	78	61.8	86
F32	South Essex	-	-	-	-	-
F33	Barking and Havering	-	-	-	-	-
F34	Redbridge and Waltham Forest	2489	19.64	130	35.0	39
F35	East London and the City	5087	30.40	134	68.6	96
F36	New River District	3356	24.58	132	51.9	66
F37	Camden and Islington	3050	27.93	133	53.5	68
G04	South East Kent	609	8.67	29	60.1	83
G05	Canterbury and Thanet	734	9.80	61	27.7	29
G06	Dartford and Gravesham	515	8.46	23	31.5	33
G07	Maidstone	467	8.44	22	21.8	22
G08	Medway	990	10.56	82	37.9	41
G09	Tunbridge Wells	484	9.02	38	25.6	26
G10	Bexley	703	11.75	108	46.9	58
G11	Greenwich	1009	16.64	127	60.0	82
G12	Bromley	951	12.08	110	54.6	72
G21	East Sussex	2265	12.67	112	43.3	48
G26	South East London	6665	30.72	135	43.2	47

		CDS - B10 Abortion rate (maternal ages 11 years and over): 1992			CDS - B13 Percent of abortions in the NHS: 1992	
		Observed	Rate	Rank	Percent	Rank
H04	Mid Surrey	452	10.40	79	56.2	75
H05	East Surrey	482	9.48	51	44.0	51
H06	Chichester	395	9.38	49	59.7	81
H07	Mid Downs	810	10.25	74	16.2	18
H08	Worthing	628	10.94	93	49.2	62
H09	Croydon	1411	15.42	123	27.5	28
H12	Wandsworth	1461	23.20	131	44.4	54
H13	Merton and Sutton	1418	14.74	121	34.3	37
H14	North West Surrey	-	-	-	-	-
H15	South West Surrey	-	-	-	-	-
H16	Kingston and Richmond	1617	13.61	115	44.0	51
J10	Dorset	1534	9.54	53	29.8	32
J21	Portsmouth and South East Hampshire	1489	10.56	82	66.6	95
J22	Southampton and South West Hampshire	1275	11.18	101	39.8	44
J23	Winchester	459	7.71	7	22.4	24
J24	Basingstoke and North Hampshire	-	-	-	-	-
J31	Salisbury	261	7.91	11	24.1	25
J32	Swindon	676	10.00	66	15.8	17
J33	Bath	912	8.31	18	39.9	45
J41	Isle of Wight	235	7.96	12	51.1	65
K11	East Berkshire	1157	11.04	96	10.4	10
K12	West Berkshire	1391	10.80	88	38.2	42
K24	Buckinghamshire	1785	10.19	72	33.0	34
K31	Kettering	697	9.48	51	72.0	103
K32	Northampton	865	9.55	55	59.2	79
K41	Oxfordshire	1599	10.31	75	87.2	124
L10	Bristol and District	2075	9.19	43	80.1	112
L21	Cornwall and Isles of Scilly	909	7.67	6	62.7	91
L35	Exeter and North Devon	959	8.40	21	91.6	133
L36	Plymouth and Torbay	1260	8.52	24	80.3	115
L40	Gloucestershire	1413	9.92	65	69.9	100
L51	Somerset	752	7.21	2	75.3	107
M02	Herefordshire	368	9.02	38	14.7	16
M04	Worcester and District	617	9.37	47	46.0	56
M05	Shropshire	1064	9.71	58	13.2	14
M06	Mid Staffordshire	811	9.37	47	20.2	21
M07	North Staffordshire	1215	9.84	63	64.2	94
M08	South East Staffordshire	647	8.89	35	33.7	35
M13	East Birmingham	753	14.69	120	12.3	12
M14	North Birmingham	595	14.01	117	2.7	5
M16	West Birmingham	1071	18.36	129	1.7	3
M17	Coventry	1267	15.72	124	1.4	2

Public Health Common Data Set		CDS - B10 Abortion rate (maternal ages 11 years and over): 1992			CDS - B13 Percent of abortions in the NHS: 1992	
		Observed	Rate	Rank	Percent	Rank
M18	Dudley	958	11.72	107	0.9	1
M19	Sandwell	1045	13.81	116	3.4	7
M20	Solihull	660	12.15	111	21.8	22
M21	Walsall	780	11.35	105	55.6	73
M22	Wolverhampton	952	14.68	119	2.3	4
M25	South Birmingham	1677	14.27	118	2.7	5
M26	North Worcestershire	708	9.26	45	43.4	49
M28	Warwickshire	1499	11.38	106	4.7	8
N11	Chester	555	11.34	104	26.1	27
N12	Crewe	622	8.85	33	50.5	63
N13	Halton	423	10.60	84	17.5	20
N14	Macclesfield	405	8.72	32	39.0	43
N15	Warrington	505	10.05	69	13.3	15
N21	Liverpool	1742	13.42	113	62.5	89
N31	St Helens and Knowsley	941	10.34	76	59.5	80
N41	Southport and Formby	298	10.45	80	54.4	71
N42	South Sefton	516	11.05	98	53.5	68
N51	Wirral	1020	11.02	95	62.0	87
P01	Lancaster	330	9.70	57	70.9	101
P02	Blackpool,Wyre and Fylde	846	10.75	87	12.4	13
P03	Preston	373	10.63	85	7.0	9
P04	Blackburn, Hyndburn and Ribble Valley	774	10.99	94	74.2	106
P05	Burnley, Pendle and Rossendale	631	10.01	68	80.2	114
P06	West Lancashire	308	10.19	72	63.0	92
P07	Chorley and South Ribble	428	7.80	10	11.7	11
P08	Bolton	710	10.06	70	29.3	31
P09	Bury	532	10.90	91	48.1	59
P10	North Manchester	586	16.17	125	57.5	76
P11	Central Manchester	577	16.50	126	53.0	67
P12	South Manchester	711	15.04	122	48.1	59
P13	Oldham	555	9.33	46	46.5	57
P14	Rochdale	620	10.71	86	57.6	77
P15	Salford	610	10.34	76	28.7	30
P16	Stockport	854	11.14	99	35.1	40
P17	Tameside and Glossop	761	11.22	102	34.0	36
P18	Trafford	625	10.86	89	34.9	38
P19	Wigan	813	9.54	53	55.6	73

CDS - C3A
SMRs for selected causes of death in the period 1988-92:
Motor vehicle traffic accidents (ICD E810-E819)

		Males			Females			Persons		
		Observed	SMR	Rank	Observed	SMR	Rank	Observed	SMR	Rank
	ENGLAND AND WALES	15654	100		6550	100		22204	100	
O00	ENGLAND	14870	101		6240	101		21110	101	
A00	NORTHERN RHA	960	103	8	442	112	12	1402	106	9
B00	YORKSHIRE RHA	1250	111	12	480	102	9	1730	108	10
C00	TRENT RHA	1607	110	11	658	110	11	2265	110	12
D00	EAST ANGLIAN RHA	837	130	14	314	118	14	1151	126	14
E00	NORTH WEST THAMES RHA	913	85	1	391	91	2	1304	87	1
F00	NORTH EAST THAMES RHA	1046	90	3	428	90	1	1474	90	3
G00	SOUTH EAST THAMES RHA	1022	90	3	456	92	3	1478	91	4
H00	SOUTH WEST THAMES RHA	773	85	1	374	94	4	1147	88	2
J00	WESSEX RHA	1061	108	10	446	109	10	1507	109	11
K00	OXFORD RHA	892	113	13	344	113	13	1236	113	13
L00	SOUTH WESTERN RHA	1081	106	9	430	97	5	1511	103	8
M00	WEST MIDLANDS RHA	1635	101	7	662	101	7	2297	101	7
N00	MERSEY RHA	669	93	5	313	101	7	982	95	6
P00	NORTH WESTERN RHA	1124	93	5	502	97	5	1626	94	5
A01	Hartlepool	27	101	82	13	115	113	40	106	92
A02	North Tees	46	90	47	21	101	76	67	93	57
A03	South Tees	84	96	67	45	126	128	129	105	89
A04	East Cumbria	68	126	128	38	161	142	106	136	137
A05	South Cumbria	53	100	77	32	135	134	85	111	108
A06	West Cumbria	66	159	144	34	199	145	100	171	145
A11	Northumberland	101	111	104	45	115	113	146	112	110
A12	Gateshead	51	83	37	25	94	54	76	87	39
A13	Newcastle	73	81	32	35	93	50	108	85	36
A14	North Tyneside	43A	75	20	27	104	87	70	84	32
A15	South Tyneside	43	93	55	19	94	54	62	93	57
A16	Sunderland	83	94	59	30	82	23	113	90	44
A30	North Durham	113	114	109	38	93	50	151	108	99
A31	South Durham	109	131	132	40	112	107	149	125	131
B11	East Riding	150	95	64	63	94	54	213	95	63
B16	Grimsby and Scunthorpe	146	136	137	38	85	33	184	121	125
B21	North Yorkshire	297	134	135	103	108	101	400	126	132
B31	Bradford	165	115	112	61	103	83	226	111	108
B51	West Yorkshire	162	94	59	72	97	66	234	95	63
B61	Leeds	240	106	94	102	110	104	342	107	96
B71	Wakefield	90	94	59	41	106	97	131	98	74
C01	North Derbyshire	111	99	74	45	96	64	156	98	74
C02	Southern Derbyshire	203	121	120	74	108	101	277	117	120
C03	Leicestershire	320	115	112	121	110	104	441	114	114
C04	North Lincolnshire	104	124	125	36	101	76	140	117	120
C05	South Lincolnshire	149	157	143	64	158	141	213	157	143

CDS - C3A
SMRs for selected causes of death in the period 1988-92:
Motor vehicle traffic accidents (ICD E810-E819)

		Males			Females			Persons		
		Observed	SMR	Rank	Observed	SMR	Rank	Observed	SMR	Rank
C08	Nottingham	214	109	100	95	120	122	309	112	110
C09	Barnsley	77	112	107	23	82	23	100	104	85
C10	Doncaster	97	109	100	40	112	107	137	110	105
C11	Rotherham	60	78	25	35	112	107	95	88	41
C12	Sheffield	122	71	13	66	93	50	188	77	18
C14	North Nottinghamshire	150	125	126	59	121	124	209	124	130
D01	Cambridge	125	131	132	37	103	83	162	123	127
D05	North West Anglia	197	160	145	76	150	139	273	157	143
D06	Norwich	217	143	139	74	113	111	291	134	136
D07	Great Yarmouth and Waveney	56	92	51	40	144	137	96	108	99
D09	Huntingdon	45	109	100	14	93	50	59	105	89
D11	Suffolk	197	114	109	73	103	83	270	110	105
E01	North Bedfordshire	84	110	103	35	119	120	119	112	110
E02	South Bedfordshire	95	111	104	29	90	44	124	105	89
E05	North West Hertfordshire	78	99	74	15	47	2	93	84	32
E06	South West Hertfordshire	54	74	15	27	87	39	81	78	19
E07	Barnet	55	60	2	40	101	76	95	72	13
E09	Hillingdon	59	79	28	23	78	18	82	79	20
E18	East and North Hertfordshire	135	91	48	49	84	30	184	89	42
E19	Brent and Harrow	114	81	32	46	82	23	160	81	24
E20	Ealing, Hammersmith and Hounslow	173	86	41	90	113	111	263	94	62
E21	Kensington, Chelsea and Westminster	66	62	4	37	88	41	103	69	4
F31	North Essex	298	113	108	107	97	66	405	109	102
F32	South Essex	165	79	28	78	89	43	243	82	27
F33	Barking and Havering	106	92	51	45	92	47	151	92	53
F34	Redbridge and Waltham Forest	114	83	37	62	107	99	176	90	44
F35	East London and the City	137	76	22	39	58	3	176	71	9
F36	New River District	136	93	55	61	104	87	197	96	67
F37	Camden and Islington	90	81	32	36	81	21	126	81	24
G04	South East Kent	85	102	85	32	86	36	117	97	71
G05	Canterbury and Thanet	96	104	92	46	104	87	142	104	85
G06	Dartford and Gravesham	72	106	94	20	74	14	92	97	71
G07	Maidstone	69	114	109	17	70	11	86	101	80
G08	Medway	72	70	11	40	100	74	112	79	20
G09	Tunbridge Wells	74	122	124	23	84	30	97	110	105
G10	Bexley	40	60	2	23	84	30	63	67	1
G11	Greenwich	53	82	35	23	85	33	76	83	31
G12	Bromley	61	68	9	28	71	13	89	69	4
G21	East Sussex	211	96	67	115	104	87	326	98	74
G26	South East London	189	84	39	89	100	74	278	89	42

CDS - C3A
SMRs for selected causes of death in the period 1988-92:
Motor vehicle traffic accidents (ICD E810-E819)

		Males			Females			Persons		
		Observed	SMR	Rank	Observed	SMR	Rank	Observed	SMR	Rank
H04	Mid Surrey	27	53	1	22	96	64	49	67	1
H05	East Surrey	57	100	77	17	68	8	74	90	44
H06	Chichester	55	100	77	17	61	5	72	87	39
H07	Mid Downs	86	100	77	45	128	130	131	108	99
H08	Worthing	77	102	85	43	105	93	120	103	83
H09	Croydon	75	78	25	32	81	21	107	79	20
H12	Wandsworth	42	66	5	20	82	23	62	70	7
H13	Merton and Sutton	75	72	14	48	106	97	123	82	27
H14	North West Surrey	114	97	70	35	74	14	149	90	44
H15	South West Surrey	71	94	59	39	122	126	110	103	83
H16	Kingston and Richmond	94	74	15	56	101	76	150	82	27
J10	Dorset	211	103	89	112	115	113	323	107	96
J21	Portsmouth and South East Hampshire	133	78	25	59	86	36	192	80	23
J22	Southampton and South West Hampshire	137	101	82	53	94	54	190	99	78
J23	Winchester	80	118	117	39	144	137	119	126	132
J24	Basingstoke and North Hampshire	142	120	119	56	132	132	198	123	127
J31	Salisbury	60	153	142	23	135	134	83	147	141
J32	Swindon	97	130	131	49	172	144	146	142	138
J33	Bath	170	133	134	47	88	41	217	120	124
J41	Isle of Wight	31	80	30	8	42	1	39	68	3
K11	East Berkshire	97	86	41	38	87	39	135	86	37
K12	West Berkshire	137	95	64	46	86	36	183	93	57
K24	Buckinghamshire	196	108	98	77	110	104	273	109	102
K31	Kettering	118	146	140	50	152	140	168	147	141
K32	Northampton	129	135	136	65	169	143	194	145	140
K41	Oxfordshire	215	121	120	68	104	87	283	116	118
L10	Bristol and District	253	97	70	99	92	47	352	96	67
L21	Cornwall and Isles of Scilly	133	94	59	54	83	28	187	91	50
L35	Exeter and North Devon	141	100	77	60	92	47	201	97	71
L36	Plymouth and Torbay	136	74	15	61	75	17	197	74	16
L40	Gloucestershire	243	148	141	91	130	131	334	142	138
L51	Somerset	175	138	138	65	116	117	240	131	135
M02	Herefordshire	60	121	120	21	99	72	81	115	117
M04	Worcester and District	81	108	98	29	90	44	110	102	81
M05	Shropshire	163	129	130	65	127	129	228	129	134
M06	Mid Staffordshire	106	111	104	45	121	124	151	114	114
M07	North Staffordshire	128	88	44	61	103	83	189	92	53
M08	South East Staffordshire	98	125	126	32	104	87	130	119	123
M13	East Birmingham	60	97	70	29	115	113	89	102	81
M14	North Birmingham	34	67	7	20	94	54	54	75	17
M16	West Birmingham	51	77	23	25	97	66	76	82	27
M17	Coventry	91	93	55	31	80	20	122	90	44

CDS - C3A
SMRs for selected causes of death in the period 1988-92:
Motor vehicle traffic accidents (ICD E810-E819)

		Males			Females			Persons		
		Observed	SMR	Rank	Observed	SMR	Rank	Observed	SMR	Rank
M18	Dudley	69	74	15	26	68	8	95	72	13
M19	Sandwell	79	88	44	36	94	54	115	90	44
M20	Solihull	61	101	82	17	69	10	78	92	53
M21	Walsall	73	92	51	29	90	44	102	91	50
M22	Wolverhampton	70	91	48	33	105	93	103	95	63
M25	South Birmingham	138	102	85	64	116	117	202	106	92
M26	North Worcestershire	99	121	120	37	112	107	136	118	122
M28	Warwickshire	174	117	115	62	102	81	236	112	110
N11	Chester	48	89	46	22	97	66	70	92	53
N12	Crewe	70	91	48	45	142	136	115	106	92
N13	Halton	44	104	92	21	123	127	65	109	102
N14	Macclesfield	51	97	70	18	78	18	69	91	50
N15	Warrington	57	102	85	27	120	122	84	107	96
N21	Liverpool	158	106	94	68	108	101	226	106	92
N31	St Helens and Knowsley	93	92	51	39	94	54	132	93	57
N41	Southport and Formby	24	70	11	13	74	14	37	71	9
N42	South Sefton	39	74	15	15	65	6	54	72	13
N51	Wirral	85	82	35	45	94	54	130	86	37
P01	Lancaster	30	75	20	11	59	4	41	70	7
P02	Blackpool, Wyre and Fylde	93	95	64	47	98	71	140	96	67
P03	Preston	48	116	114	20	118	119	68	116	118
P04	Blackburn, Hyndburn and Ribble Valley	95	119	118	46	134	133	141	123	127
P05	Burnley, Pendle and Rossendale	88	128	129	32	105	93	120	121	125
P06	West Lancashire	28	87	43	9	66	7	37	81	24
P07	Chorley and South Ribble	55	93	55	23	95	62	78	93	57
P08	Bolton	83	106	94	33	99	72	116	104	85
P09	Bury	45	85	40	27	119	120	72	95	63
P10	North Manchester	49	117	115	19	105	93	68	114	114
P11	Central Manchester	46	103	89	13	85	33	59	98	74
P12	South Manchester	58	103	89	25	107	99	83	104	85
P13	Oldham	62	96	67	27	97	66	89	96	67
P14	Rochdale	50	80	30	25	95	62	75	84	32
P15	Salford	72	99	74	31	101	76	103	99	78
P16	Stockport	58	68	9	26	70	11	84	69	4
P17	Tameside and Glossop	49	66	5	26	83	28	75	71	9
P18	Trafford	43	67	7	23	82	23	66	71	9
P19	Wigan	72	77	23	39	102	81	111	84	32

CDS - C3A
SMRs for selected causes of death in the period 1988-92:
All causes (ICD 001-999) (ages 0-14)

		Males			Females			Persons		
		Observed	SMR	Rank	Observed	SMR	Rank	Observed	SMR	Rank
	ENGLAND AND WALES	21762	100		15740	100		37502	100	
O00	ENGLAND	20609	100		14923	100		35532	100	
A00	NORTHERN RHA	1306	102	9	991	107	11	2297	104	11
B00	YORKSHIRE RHA	1739	110	12	1238	108	12	2977	109	12
C00	TRENT RHA	2037	104	11	1410	99	8	3447	102	10
D00	EAST ANGLIAN RHA	699	83	1	503	83	1	1202	83	1
E00	NORTH WEST THAMES RHA	1406	92	3	1020	92	4	2426	92	4
F00	NORTH EAST THAMES RHA	1657	96	7	1220	98	7	2877	97	8
G00	SOUTH EAST THAMES RHA	1606	102	9	1134	99	8	2740	100	9
H00	SOUTH WEST THAMES RHA	1054	88	2	765	88	2	1819	88	2
J00	WESSEX RHA	1173	93	4	841	92	4	2014	93	5
K00	OXFORD RHA	1057	93	4	810	99	8	1867	96	6
L00	SOUTH WESTERN RHA	1205	93	4	827	89	3	2032	91	3
M00	WEST MIDLANDS RHA	2674	116	14	1964	118	14	4638	117	14
N00	MERSEY RHA	1015	97	8	713	94	6	1728	96	6
P00	NORTH WESTERN RHA	1981	110	12	1487	114	13	3468	112	13
A01	Hartlepool	51	123	131	36	118	119	87	121	132
A02	North Tees	83	102	83	73	123	126	156	111	112
A03	South Tees	161	120	128	120	121	124	281	120	131
A04	East Cumbria	61	90	39	49	99	70	110	94	50
A05	South Cumbria	67	101	76	45	97	63	112	99	67
A06	West Cumbria	45	78	12	45	109	103	90	91	38
A11	Northumberland	106	91	43	82	98	65	188	94	50
A12	Gateshead	96	116	118	58	99	70	154	109	107
A13	Newcastle	131	115	117	86	104	85	217	110	109
A14	North Tyneside	76	98	67	51	90	45	127	95	56
A15	South Tyneside	48	72	4	43	92	49	91	80	12
A16	Sunderland	133	101	76	119	126	134	252	111	112
A30	North Durham	133	103	86	100	106	92	233	104	86
A31	South Durham	115	100	73	84	101	77	199	100	73
B11	East Riding	226	104	93	173	110	106	399	107	97
B16	Grimsby and Scunthorpe	149	93	49	105	92	49	254	92	44
B21	North Yorkshire	242	90	39	166	85	26	408	87	29
B31	Bradford	316	134	139	239	140	140	555	136	140
B51	West Yorkshire	316	123	131	220	118	119	536	121	132
B61	Leeds	345	114	115	236	107	100	581	111	112
B71	Wakefield	145	105	94	99	98	65	244	102	79
C01	North Derbyshire	138	96	61	81	79	15	219	89	33
C02	Southern Derbyshire	250	108	101	150	91	46	400	101	77
C03	Leicestershire	432	110	107	298	106	92	730	108	100
C04	North Lincolnshire	115	105	94	93	119	123	208	111	112
C05	South Lincolnshire	109	94	53	86	101	77	195	97	62

172

CDS - C3A
SMRs for selected causes of death in the period 1988-92:
All causes (ICD 001-999) (ages 0-14)

		Males			Females			Persons		
		Observed	SMR	Rank	Observed	SMR	Rank	Observed	SMR	Rank
C08	Nottingham	302	114	115	177	91	46	479	104	86
C09	Barnsley	97	103	86	69	100	74	166	102	79
C10	Doncaster	130	100	73	99	104	85	229	102	79
C11	Rotherham	120	105	94	88	108	101	208	106	93
C12	Sheffield	190	91	43	162	108	101	352	99	67
C14	North Nottinghamshire	154	94	53	107	91	46	261	93	48
D01	Cambridge	86	78	12	53	67	3	139	73	4
D05	North West Anglia	152	89	36	126	101	77	278	94	50
D06	Norwich	148	85	26	106	83	21	254	84	22
D07	Great Yarmouth and Waveney	90	113	112	44	78	12	134	98	66
D09	Huntingdon	39	63	2	28	61	1	67	62	1
D11	Suffolk	184	76	11	146	84	22	330	80	12
E01	North Bedfordshire	101	93	49	69	89	41	170	91	38
E02	South Bedfordshire	147	99	68	99	93	53	246	96	61
E05	North West Hertfordshire	82	75	8	70	89	41	152	81	17
E06	South West Hertfordshire	77	74	5	71	95	59	148	83	19
E07	Barnet	106	83	21	63	69	6	169	77	8
E09	Hillingdon	109	103	86	66	85	26	175	95	56
E18	East and North Hertfordshire	156	75	8	101	68	5	257	72	3
E19	Brent and Harrow	199	96	61	158	106	92	357	100	73
E20	Ealing, Hammersmith and Hounslow	316	109	102	220	104	85	536	107	97
E21	Kensington, Chelsea and Westminster	113	94	53	103	118	119	216	104	86
F31	North Essex	262	74	5	218	85	26	480	79	11
F32	South Essex	267	91	43	158	74	8	425	84	22
F33	Barking and Havering	143	87	30	116	98	65	259	92	44
F34	Redbridge and Waltham Forest	218	105	94	177	117	117	395	110	109
F35	East London and the City	375	112	111	288	117	117	663	114	123
F36	New River District	225	103	86	141	89	41	366	97	62
F37	Camden and Islington	167	113	112	122	112	107	289	113	122
G04	South East Kent	122	109	102	61	75	9	183	95	56
G05	Canterbury and Thanet	106	93	49	90	109	103	196	100	73
G06	Dartford and Gravesham	88	90	39	58	82	18	146	86	27
G07	Maidstone	106	124	134	57	92	49	163	111	112
G08	Medway	162	99	68	133	112	107	295	105	90
G09	Tunbridge Wells	64	83	21	43	77	11	107	80	12
G10	Bexley	84	87	30	46	65	2	130	78	9
G11	Greenwich	117	110	107	87	114	112	204	111	112
G12	Bromley	90	78	12	65	78	12	155	78	9
G21	East Sussex	256	99	68	186	98	65	442	99	67
G26	South East London	411	117	119	308	118	119	719	117	128

173

CDS - C3A
SMRs for selected causes of death in the period 1988-92:
All causes (ICD 001-999) (ages 0-14)

		Males			Females			Persons		
		Observed	SMR	Rank	Observed	SMR	Rank	Observed	SMR	Rank
H04	Mid Surrey	46	75	8	30	69	6	76	73	4
H05	East Surrey	59	81	16	43	80	16	102	80	12
H06	Chichester	34	57	1	37	85	26	71	69	2
H07	Mid Downs	99	82	19	65	76	10	164	80	12
H08	Worthing	83	95	57	54	85	26	137	91	38
H09	Croydon	161	110	107	101	94	55	262	103	82
H12	Wandsworth	90	105	94	71	112	107	161	108	100
H13	Merton and Sutton	129	85	26	106	98	65	235	91	38
H14	North West Surrey	128	82	19	94	82	18	222	82	18
H15	South West Surrey	90	99	68	65	99	70	155	99	67
H16	Kingston and Richmond	135	84	24	99	84	22	234	84	22
J10	Dorset	198	85	26	134	80	16	332	83	19
J21	Portsmouth and South East Hampshire	225	100	73	154	94	55	379	97	62
J22	Southampton and South West Hampshire	167	93	49	109	84	22	276	89	33
J23	Winchester	55	64	3	52	84	22	107	73	4
J24	Basingstoke and North Hampshire	146	88	33	116	96	62	262	92	44
J31	Salisbury	57	119	127	40	115	115	97	117	128
J32	Swindon	124	109	102	81	100	74	205	105	90
J33	Bath	148	90	39	119	100	74	267	94	50
J41	Isle of Wight	53	118	125	36	113	110	89	116	126
K11	East Berkshire	135	80	15	124	102	82	259	89	33
K12	West Berkshire	163	83	21	126	88	39	289	85	25
K24	Buckinghamshire	275	101	76	193	99	70	468	100	73
K31	Kettering	114	96	61	106	125	129	220	108	100
K32	Northampton	171	117	119	113	109	103	284	114	123
K41	Oxfordshire	199	84	24	148	87	32	347	85	25
L10	Bristol and District	329	96	61	232	94	55	561	95	56
L21	Cornwall and Isles of Scilly	169	94	53	113	87	32	282	91	38
L35	Exeter and North Devon	196	118	125	112	93	53	308	108	100
L36	Plymouth and Torbay	205	91	43	141	88	39	346	90	36
L40	Gloucestershire	177	81	16	151	97	63	328	88	30
L51	Somerset	129	81	16	78	67	3	207	75	7
M02	Herefordshire	65	101	76	41	87	32	106	95	56
M04	Worcester and District	109	113	112	72	103	83	181	109	107
M05	Shropshire	172	101	76	140	114	112	312	107	97
M06	Mid Staffordshire	153	117	119	80	85	26	233	103	82
M07	North Staffordshire	246	126	136	143	101	77	389	115	125
M08	South East Staffordshire	108	92	48	105	125	129	213	106	93
M13	East Birmingham	145	132	138	121	153	143	266	141	142
M14	North Birmingham	62	95	57	60	125	129	122	108	100
M16	West Birmingham	165	136	141	127	146	142	292	140	141
M17	Coventry	195	139	142	133	129	138	328	134	138

CDS - C3A
SMRs for selected causes of death in the period 1988-92:
All causes (ICD 001-999) (ages 0-14)

		Males			Females			Persons		
		Observed	SMR	Rank	Observed	SMR	Rank	Observed	SMR	Rank
M18	Dudley	150	117	119	95	104	85	245	112	120
M19	Sandwell	166	122	129	133	137	139	299	128	136
M20	Solihull	75	91	43	73	123	126	148	105	90
M21	Walsall	128	109	102	107	126	134	235	116	126
M22	Wolverhampton	139	122	129	96	116	116	235	119	130
M25	South Birmingham	285	139	142	213	144	141	498	141	142
M26	North Worcestershire	102	88	33	76	92	49	178	90	36
M28	Warwickshire	209	106	99	149	106	92	358	106	93
N11	Chester	57	74	5	52	95	59	109	83	19
N12	Crewe	96	88	33	68	87	32	164	88	30
N13	Halton	65	95	57	43	87	32	108	91	38
N14	Macclesfield	66	99	68	42	87	32	108	94	50
N15	Warrington	80	97	66	63	105	89	143	101	77
N21	Liverpool	226	103	86	141	89	41	367	97	62
N31	St Helens and Knowsley	158	102	83	107	95	59	265	99	67
N41	Southport and Formby	41	102	83	27	94	55	68	99	67
N42	South Sefton	81	101	76	45	78	12	126	92	44
N51	Wirral	145	95	57	125	114	112	270	103	82
P01	Lancaster	52	103	86	44	122	125	96	111	112
P02	Blackpool,Wyre and Fylde	106	89	36	71	82	18	177	86	27
P03	Preston	76	123	131	56	124	128	132	124	134
P04	Blackburn, Hyndburn and Ribble Valley	140	109	102	104	113	110	244	111	112
P05	Burnley, Pendle and Rossendale	151	134	139	133	165	144	284	147	144
P06	West Lancashire	48	103	86	35	105	89	83	104	86
P07	Chorley and South Ribble	95	110	107	66	106	92	161	108	100
P08	Bolton	159	131	137	112	128	137	271	130	137
P09	Bury	86	107	100	61	106	92	147	106	93
P10	North Manchester	85	117	119	53	101	77	138	110	109
P11	Central Manchester	97	156	145	75	167	145	172	161	145
P12	South Manchester	114	142	144	73	125	129	187	135	139
P13	Oldham	132	124	134	95	126	134	227	125	135
P14	Rochdale	122	117	119	80	106	92	202	112	120
P15	Salford	107	101	76	81	106	92	188	103	82
P16	Stockport	105	87	30	91	103	83	196	94	50
P17	Tameside and Glossop	98	85	26	89	105	89	187	93	48
P18	Trafford	88	96	61	83	125	129	171	108	100
P19	Wigan	120	89	36	85	87	32	205	88	30

CDS - C3A
SMRs for selected causes of death in the period 1988-92:
All causes (ICD 001-999) (ages 15-64)

		Males Observed	SMR	Rank	Females Observed	SMR	Rank	Persons Observed	SMR	Rank
	ENGLAND AND WALES	308887	100		185591	100		494478	100	
O00	ENGLAND	290251	100		174358	100		464609	100	
A00	NORTHERN RHA	22623	116	13	14036	119	14	36659	117	13
B00	YORKSHIRE RHA	23494	106	11	14096	105	11	37590	106	11
C00	TRENT RHA	29425	101	8	17743	103	9	47168	102	9
D00	EAST ANGLIAN RHA	10506	84	1	6329	84	1	16835	84	1
E00	NORTH WEST THAMES RHA	19780	96	6	11269	93	6	31049	95	6
F00	NORTH EAST THAMES RHA	22385	101	8	12908	98	8	35293	100	8
G00	SOUTH EAST THAMES RHA	21279	99	7	12879	97	7	34158	98	7
H00	SOUTH WEST THAMES RHA	15076	85	2	9449	87	3	24525	86	2
J00	WESSEX RHA	16242	87	4	9792	86	2	26034	86	2
K00	OXFORD RHA	12636	85	2	7732	89	4	20368	86	2
L00	SOUTH WESTERN RHA	18128	90	5	10984	89	4	29112	89	5
M00	WEST MIDLANDS RHA	33430	102	10	19944	104	10	53374	103	10
N00	MERSEY RHA	16831	113	12	10450	115	12	27281	114	12
P00	NORTH WESTERN RHA	28416	119	14	16747	116	13	45163	118	14
A01	Hartlepool	682	118	117	450	129	140	1132	122	127
A02	North Tees	1279	118	117	758	116	113	2037	117	118
A03	South Tees	2176	122	128	1384	129	140	3560	125	133
A04	East Cumbria	1174	101	81	742	105	87	1916	102	79
A05	South Cumbria	1104	101	81	697	103	79	1801	102	79
A06	West Cumbria	1080	122	128	625	118	120	1705	121	125
A11	Northumberland	2007	102	85	1318	111	103	3325	105	90
A12	Gateshead	1672	126	132	978	122	131	2650	124	132
A13	Newcastle	2074	128	135	1272	128	139	3346	128	136
A14	North Tyneside	1394	112	100	882	113	105	2276	113	103
A15	South Tyneside	1310	129	136	777	124	136	2087	127	135
A16	Sunderland	2281	125	131	1359	122	131	3640	123	130
A30	North Durham	2319	112	100	1491	120	124	3810	115	112
A31	South Durham	2071	117	113	1303	121	127	3374	119	121
B11	East Riding	3150	100	78	1983	103	79	5133	101	76
B16	Grimsby and Scunthorpe	2513	112	100	1473	110	100	3986	111	99
B21	North Yorkshire	4123	92	50	2504	91	43	6627	92	49
B31	Bradford	3178	118	117	1827	113	105	5005	116	115
B51	West Yorkshire	3770	112	100	2228	109	98	5998	111	99
B61	Leeds	4709	110	96	2720	106	90	7429	109	94
B71	Wakefield	2051	107	93	1361	118	120	3412	111	99
C01	North Derbyshire	2458	104	89	1420	100	72	3878	102	79
C02	Southern Derbyshire	3425	102	85	2020	103	79	5445	102	79
C03	Leicestershire	4945	93	52	2934	94	54	7879	93	54
C04	North Lincolnshire	1716	96	68	1079	101	75	2795	98	73
C05	South Lincolnshire	1936	95	62	1237	100	72	3173	97	70

176

Public Health Common Data Set

CDS - C3A
SMRs for selected causes of death in the period 1988-92:
All causes (ICD 001-999) (ages 15-64)

		Males Observed	SMR	Rank	Females Observed	SMR	Rank	Persons Observed	SMR	Rank
C08	Nottingham	3867	102	85	2302	103	79	6169	103	86
C09	Barnsley	1561	113	106	990	117	117	2551	114	108
C10	Doncaster	1933	105	90	1281	116	113	3214	110	96
C11	Rotherham	1701	109	95	1029	111	103	2730	110	96
C12	Sheffield	3327	105	90	1955	103	79	5282	104	88
C14	North Nottinghamshire	2556	102	85	1496	102	77	4052	102	79
D01	Cambridge	1313	79	9	799	83	10	2112	80	9
D05	North West Anglia	2330	94	58	1397	94	54	3727	94	58
D06	Norwich	2424	80	12	1462	79	2	3886	79	7
D07	Great Yarmouth and Waveney	1191	95	62	705	90	38	1896	93	54
D09	Huntingdon	548	74	2	320	75	1	868	74	1
D11	Suffolk	2700	81	14	1646	83	10	4346	82	14
E01	North Bedfordshire	1283	86	31	810	94	54	2093	89	37
E02	South Bedfordshire	1574	95	62	929	101	75	2503	97	70
E05	North West Hertfordshire	1253	76	4	803	83	10	2056	78	3
E06	South West Hertfordshire	1243	84	24	769	86	??	2012	85	23
E07	Barnet	1400	84	24	929	89	33	2329	86	26
E09	Hillingdon	1302	91	47	820	97	67	2122	93	54
E18	East and North Hertfordshire	2516	83	20	1536	86	22	4052	84	20
E19	Brent and Harrow	2571	98	74	1364	88	29	3935	94	58
E20	Ealing, Hammersmith and Hounslow	4277	118	117	2218	105	87	6495	113	103
E21	Kensington, Chelsea and Westminster	2361	121	124	1091	96	64	3452	112	102
F31	North Essex	4362	83	20	2822	90	38	7184	86	26
F32	South Essex	3747	89	43	2405	95	63	6152	91	44
F33	Barking and Havering	2301	96	68	1357	92	47	3658	95	63
F34	Redbridge and Waltham Forest	2371	94	58	1451	96	64	3822	94	58
F35	East London and the City	4223	134	139	2120	120	124	6343	129	138
F36	New River District	2533	95	62	1466	94	54	3999	94	58
F37	Camden and Islington	2848	144	143	1287	110	100	4135	131	141
G04	South East Kent	1460	90	46	928	92	47	2388	90	40
G05	Canterbury and Thanet	1727	100	78	1162	103	79	2889	101	76
G06	Dartford and Gravesham	1337	95	62	781	94	54	2118	95	63
G07	Maidstone	1063	86	31	635	87	25	1698	87	32
G08	Medway	1798	93	52	1135	100	72	2933	96	67
G09	Tunbridge Wells	980	77	5	625	79	2	1605	78	3
G10	Bexley	1090	81	14	759	94	54	1849	86	26
G11	Greenwich	1253	108	94	741	104	85	1994	107	92
G12	Bromley	1454	78	8	976	84	14	2430	80	9
G21	East Sussex	3809	93	52	2356	88	29	6165	91	44
G26	South East London	5308	136	140	2781	120	124	8089	130	140

CDS - C3A
SMRs for selected causes of death in the period 1988-92:
All causes (ICD 001-999) (ages 15-64)

		Males Observed	SMR	Rank	Females Observed	SMR	Rank	Persons Observed	SMR	Rank
H04	Mid Surrey	860	77	5	549	81	7	1409	79	7
H05	East Surrey	990	82	17	635	87	25	1625	84	20
H06	Chichester	929	85	28	583	80	6	1512	83	15
H07	Mid Downs	1383	81	14	902	86	22	2285	83	15
H08	Worthing	1261	88	35	805	84	14	2066	87	32
H09	Croydon	1638	88	35	1015	90	38	2653	89	37
H12	Wandsworth	1233	121	124	637	108	96	1870	116	115
H13	Merton and Sutton	1734	88	35	1131	93	50	2865	90	40
H14	North West Surrey	1809	73	1	1136	79	2	2945	75	2
H15	South West Surrey	1112	75	3	737	82	9	1849	78	3
H16	Kingston and Richmond	2127	88	35	1319	89	33	3446	89	37
J10	Dorset	3334	83	20	2155	84	14	5489	83	15
J21	Portsmouth and South East Hampshire	2902	91	47	1738	91	43	4640	91	44
J22	Southampton and South West Hampshire	2516	97	71	1417	91	43	3933	95	63
J23	Winchester	1042	77	5	624	79	2	1666	78	3
J24	Basingstoke and North Hampshire	1771	82	17	1065	87	25	2836	84	20
J31	Salisbury	643	82	17	403	84	14	1046	83	15
J32	Swindon	1216	87	34	730	89	33	1946	88	34
J33	Bath	2079	84	24	1203	81	7	3282	83	15
J41	Isle of Wight	739	94	58	457	89	33	1196	92	49
K11	East Berkshire	1966	89	43	1202	94	54	3168	91	44
K12	West Berkshire	2146	80	12	1263	83	10	3409	81	11
K24	Buckinghamshire	2784	79	9	1749	85	19	4533	81	11
K31	Kettering	1582	101	81	992	106	90	2574	103	86
K32	Northampton	1676	93	52	1018	96	64	2694	94	58
K41	Oxfordshire	2482	79	9	1508	84	14	3990	81	11
L10	Bristol and District	4618	92	50	2659	89	33	7277	91	44
L21	Cornwall and Isles of Scilly	2674	88	35	1649	88	29	4323	88	34
L35	Exeter and North Devon	2409	86	31	1535	87	25	3944	86	26
L36	Plymouth and Torbay	3263	93	52	1956	90	38	5219	92	49
L40	Gloucestershire	2922	88	35	1839	92	47	4761	90	40
L51	Somerset	2242	88	35	1346	85	19	3588	86	26
M02	Herefordshire	857	83	20	559	90	38	1416	86	26
M04	Worcester and District	1336	85	28	803	85	19	2139	85	23
M05	Shropshire	2364	93	52	1366	91	43	3730	92	49
M06	Mid Staffordshire	1831	91	47	1132	97	67	2963	93	54
M07	North Staffordshire	3401	114	108	2012	113	105	5413	113	103
M08	South East Staffordshire	1577	98	74	917	99	71	2494	99	75
M13	East Birmingham	1395	121	124	818	123	133	2213	121	125
M14	North Birmingham	992	94	58	657	105	87	1649	98	73
M16	West Birmingham	1539	130	137	836	126	137	2375	128	136
M17	Coventry	2050	113	106	1228	115	110	3278	114	108

CDS - C3A
SMRs for selected causes of death in the period 1988-92:
All causes (ICD 001-999) (ages 15-64)

		Males			Females			Persons		
		Observed	SMR	Rank	Observed	SMR	Rank	Observed	SMR	Rank
M18	Dudley	1958	97	71	1111	94	54	3069	96	67
M19	Sandwell	2263	121	124	1271	116	113	3534	119	121
M20	Solihull	1103	84	24	702	88	29	1805	85	23
M21	Walsall	1954	114	108	1187	119	122	3141	116	115
M22	Wolverhampton	1764	112	100	1059	115	110	2823	113	103
M25	South Birmingham	2855	116	111	1591	110	100	4446	114	108
M26	North Worcestershire	1427	85	28	917	93	50	2344	88	34
M28	Warwickshire	2764	89	43	1778	97	67	4542	92	49
N11	Chester	1116	99	76	784	114	109	1900	104	88
N12	Crewe	1551	97	71	1018	106	90	2569	101	76
N13	Halton	946	112	100	545	108	96	1491	110	96
N14	Macclesfield	1040	88	35	659	93	50	1699	90	40
N15	Warrington	1247	110	96	777	117	117	2024	113	103
N21	Liverpool	3933	138	141	2391	137	142	6324	138	142
N31	St Helens and Knowsley	2550	122	128	1579	123	133	4129	122	127
N41	Southport and Formby	720	96	68	451	94	54	1171	95	63
N42	South Sefton	1312	117	113	788	113	105	2100	115	112
N51	Wirral	2416	111	99	1458	107	95	3874	109	94
P01	Lancaster	861	110	96	495	102	77	1356	107	92
P02	Blackpool,Wyre and Fylde	2491	117	113	1481	109	98	3972	114	108
P03	Preston	985	127	134	545	121	127	1530	125	133
P04	Blackburn, Hyndburn and Ribble Valley	1902	119	121	1130	119	122	3032	119	121
P05	Burnley, Pendle and Rossendale	1609	116	111	1027	123	133	2636	118	119
P06	West Lancashire	669	99	76	430	106	90	1099	102	79
P07	Chorley and South Ribble	1144	95	62	697	97	67	1841	96	67
P08	Bolton	1832	119	121	1079	117	117	2911	118	119
P09	Bury	1115	105	90	685	106	90	1800	105	90
P10	North Manchester	1392	173	145	686	146	144	2078	163	145
P11	Central Manchester	1023	155	144	547	154	145	1570	155	144
P12	South Manchester	1272	133	138	720	121	127	1992	129	138
P13	Oldham	1610	126	132	891	116	113	2501	122	127
P14	Rochdale	1502	120	123	955	127	138	2457	123	130
P15	Salford	2010	143	142	1178	141	143	3188	143	143
P16	Stockport	1793	100	78	1020	93	50	2813	97	70
P17	Tameside and Glossop	1723	117	113	1065	121	127	2788	119	121
P18	Trafford	1343	101	81	842	104	85	2185	102	79
P19	Wigan	2140	115	110	1274	115	110	3414	115	112

CDS - C3A
SMRs for selected causes of death in the period 1988-92:
All causes (ICD 001-999) (ages 65-74)

		Males			Females			Persons		
		Observed	SMR	Rank	Observed	SMR	Rank	Observed	SMR	Rank
	ENGLAND AND WALES	389631	100		272983	100		662614	100	
O00	ENGLAND	363915	100		255154	100		619069	100	
A00	NORTHERN RHA	28766	117	14	20893	121	14	49659	119	14
B00	YORKSHIRE RHA	29622	106	10	20671	106	11	50293	106	10
C00	TRENT RHA	38630	102	9	26193	103	9	64823	103	9
D00	EAST ANGLIAN RHA	14673	85	1	9928	87	2	24601	86	1
E00	NORTH WEST THAMES RHA	21091	92	6	14727	93	6	35818	93	6
F00	NORTH EAST THAMES RHA	26390	99	8	17975	97	8	44365	98	8
G00	SOUTH EAST THAMES RHA	26966	94	7	19250	93	6	46216	94	7
H00	SOUTH WEST THAMES RHA	19064	86	2	14012	87	2	33076	87	2
J00	WESSEX RHA	22098	88	3	15137	86	1	37235	87	2
K00	OXFORD RHA	14701	90	5	10069	91	5	24770	90	5
L00	SOUTH WESTERN RHA	24993	88	3	17299	87	2	42292	88	4
M00	WEST MIDLANDS RHA	42743	107	11	28854	104	10	71597	106	10
N00	MERSEY RHA	19929	112	12	14795	114	12	34724	113	12
P00	NORTH WESTERN RHA	34249	114	13	25351	117	13	59600	115	13
A01	Hartlepool	874	128	142	620	130	139	1494	129	141
A02	North Tees	1410	119	130	1038	126	134	2448	122	132
A03	South Tees	2566	121	134	1885	127	135	4451	124	135
A04	East Cumbria	1572	104	82	1158	110	96	2730	107	94
A05	South Cumbria	1514	100	70	1052	96	59	2566	99	67
A06	West Cumbria	1291	118	122	939	122	129	2230	120	127
A11	Northumberland	2769	107	92	1943	112	105	4712	109	97
A12	Gateshead	2149	130	143	1541	128	136	3690	129	141
A13	Newcastle	2595	119	130	1947	122	129	4542	121	128
A14	North Tyneside	1962	116	114	1463	118	120	3425	117	118
A15	South Tyneside	1715	125	137	1213	123	131	2928	124	135
A16	Sunderland	2677	127	140	1954	130	139	4631	128	139
A30	North Durham	2942	118	122	2210	128	136	5152	122	132
A31	South Durham	2730	118	122	1930	119	121	4660	119	125
B11	East Riding	4195	103	78	2963	104	82	7158	104	81
B16	Grimsby and Scunthorpe	3067	109	97	1982	105	85	5049	107	94
B21	North Yorkshire	5461	93	51	3767	92	44	9228	93	49
B31	Bradford	3657	113	106	2640	115	112	6297	114	109
B51	West Yorkshire	4708	113	106	3372	111	99	8080	112	103
B61	Leeds	5753	108	95	4004	106	90	9757	107	94
B71	Wakefield	2781	118	122	1943	119	121	4724	119	125
C01	North Derbyshire	3144	100	70	2113	100	70	5257	100	71
C02	Southern Derbyshire	4623	106	90	3044	105	85	7667	106	93
C03	Leicestershire	5924	92	45	3968	93	48	9892	93	49
C04	North Lincolnshire	2480	97	64	1635	98	66	4115	98	65
C05	South Lincolnshire	2686	93	51	1851	98	66	4537	95	56

CDS - C3A
SMRs for selected causes of death in the period 1988-92:
All causes (ICD 001-999) (ages 65-74)

		Males			Females			Persons		
		Observed	SMR	Rank	Observed	SMR	Rank	Observed	SMR	Rank
C08	Nottingham	4930	103	78	3254	102	77	8184	103	80
C09	Barnsley	2124	118	122	1415	116	116	3539	117	118
C10	Doncaster	2492	109	97	1745	115	112	4237	111	98
C11	Rotherham	2178	114	110	1484	113	107	3662	114	109
C12	Sheffield	4886	111	101	3506	110	96	8392	111	98
C14	North Nottinghamshire	3163	101	73	2178	105	85	5341	102	76
D01	Cambridge	1604	81	4	1151	85	15	2755	82	5
D05	North West Anglia	3079	90	35	2061	93	48	5140	91	41
D06	Norwich	3659	81	4	2405	81	5	6064	81	3
D07	Great Yarmouth and Waveney	1742	88	27	1189	91	37	2931	89	29
D09	Huntingdon	678	87	19	477	93	48	1155	90	35
D11	Suffolk	3911	87	19	2645	87	22	6556	87	19
E01	North Bedfordshire	1521	91	41	1044	96	59	2565	93	49
E02	South Bedfordshire	1615	97	64	1143	105	85	2758	100	71
E05	North West Hertfordshire	1649	89	30	1106	90	34	2755	90	35
E06	South West Hertfordshire	1709	92	45	1160	91	37	2869	91	41
E07	Barnet	1765	85	11	1352	89	30	3117	87	19
E09	Hillingdon	1473	90	35	1045	91	37	2518	91	41
E18	East and North Hertfordshire	2931	87	19	1975	87	22	4906	87	19
E19	Brent and Harrow	2403	87	19	1713	88	26	4116	87	19
E20	Ealing, Hammersmith and Hounslow	4055	104	82	2770	100	70	6825	102	76
E21	Kensington, Chelsea and Westminster	1970	95	56	1419	95	56	3389	95	56
F31	North Essex	5890	87	19	4073	88	26	9963	87	19
F32	South Essex	4972	96	59	3401	93	48	8373	95	56
F33	Barking and Havering	3168	101	73	2180	100	70	5348	101	74
F34	Redbridge and Waltham Forest	2990	98	68	2115	96	59	5105	97	62
F35	East London and the City	4196	118	122	2672	115	112	6868	117	118
F36	New River District	2757	96	59	1933	95	56	4690	96	61
F37	Camden and Islington	2417	108	95	1601	101	75	4018	105	87
G04	South East Kent	2088	89	30	1529	90	34	3617	89	29
G05	Canterbury and Thanet	2695	91	41	1933	92	44	4628	91	41
G06	Dartford and Gravesham	1496	97	64	1110	106	90	2606	101	74
G07	Maidstone	1207	89	30	882	94	55	2089	91	41
G08	Medway	2215	103	78	1549	102	77	3764	102	76
G09	Tunbridge Wells	1315	86	17	899	82	6	2214	84	11
G10	Bexley	1417	92	45	1047	96	59	2464	93	49
G11	Greenwich	1605	107	92	1130	101	75	2735	105	87
G12	Bromley	2023	87	19	1370	83	10	3393	85	15
G21	East Sussex	5762	85	11	4213	82	6	9975	84	11
G26	South East London	5143	110	100	3588	111	99	8731	111	98

CDS - C3A
SMRs for selected causes of death in the period 1988-92:
All causes (ICD 001-999) (ages 65-74)

		Males			Females			Persons		
		Observed	SMR	Rank	Observed	SMR	Rank	Observed	SMR	Rank
H04	Mid Surrey	1209	85	11	774	78	2	1983	82	5
H05	East Surrey	1198	83	8	925	91	37	2123	86	17
H06	Chichester	1516	79	2	1165	83	10	2681	81	3
H07	Mid Downs	1682	86	17	1226	89	30	2908	87	19
H08	Worthing	2091	83	8	1643	83	10	3734	83	8
H09	Croydon	1866	94	55	1380	96	59	3246	95	56
H12	Wandsworth	1189	112	102	902	116	116	2091	113	106
H13	Merton and Sutton	2079	90	35	1568	90	34	3647	90	35
H14	North West Surrey	2277	85	11	1476	82	6	3753	84	11
H15	South West Surrey	1333	75	1	973	76	1	2306	75	1
H16	Kingston and Richmond	2624	87	19	1980	86	19	4604	87	19
J10	Dorset	5336	79	2	3785	80	4	9121	80	2
J21	Portsmouth and South East Hampshire	3813	96	59	2559	89	30	6372	93	49
J22	Southampton and South West Hampshire	3217	90	35	2117	86	19	5334	88	27
J23	Winchester	1382	91	41	968	88	26	2350	90	35
J24	Basingstoke and North Hampshire	1823	88	27	1216	85	15	3039	87	19
J31	Salisbury	911	85	11	592	78	2	1503	82	5
J32	Swindon	1606	99	69	1068	99	69	2674	99	67
J33	Bath	2787	85	11	1959	87	22	4746	86	17
J41	Isle of Wight	1223	93	51	873	92	44	2096	92	48
K11	East Berkshire	2199	93	51	1504	93	48	3703	93	49
K12	West Berkshire	2318	87	19	1545	83	10	3863	85	15
K24	Buckinghamshire	3220	90	35	2191	91	37	5411	91	41
K31	Kettering	1979	101	73	1282	97	64	3261	99	67
K32	Northampton	2095	95	56	1474	100	70	3569	97	62
K41	Oxfordshire	2890	82	6	2073	87	22	4963	84	11
L10	Bristol and District	5840	92	45	4054	91	37	9894	91	41
L21	Cornwall and Isles of Scilly	3890	89	30	2674	88	26	6564	88	27
L35	Exeter and North Devon	3630	84	10	2472	82	6	6102	83	8
L36	Plymouth and Torbay	4523	88	27	3263	89	30	7786	89	29
L40	Gloucestershire	4019	92	45	2602	85	15	6621	89	29
L51	Somerset	3091	82	6	2234	85	15	5325	83	8
M02	Herefordshire	1349	92	45	807	84	14	2156	89	29
M04	Worcester and District	1807	89	30	1292	92	44	3099	90	35
M05	Shropshire	2972	96	59	2027	95	56	4999	95	56
M06	Mid Staffordshire	2267	104	82	1545	106	90	3812	105	87
M07	North Staffordshire	4471	118	122	3006	114	109	7477	116	116
M08	South East Staffordshire	1778	105	87	1208	105	85	2986	105	87
M13	East Birmingham	1867	114	110	1295	111	99	3162	113	106
M14	North Birmingham	1248	100	70	903	98	66	2151	100	71
M16	West Birmingham	1669	118	122	1168	124	132	2837	121	128
M17	Coventry	2872	117	117	1882	112	105	4754	115	113

CDS - C3A
SMRs for selected causes of death in the period 1988-92:
All causes (ICD 001-999) (ages 65-74)

		Males			Females			Persons		
		Observed	SMR	Rank	Observed	SMR	Rank	Observed	SMR	Rank
M18	Dudley	2513	107	92	1638	100	70	4151	104	81
M19	Sandwell	2908	119	130	1946	111	99	4854	116	116
M20	Solihull	1322	91	41	868	86	19	2190	89	29
M21	Walsall	2229	115	113	1509	111	99	3738	114	109
M22	Wolverhampton	2282	114	110	1494	111	99	3776	112	103
M25	South Birmingham	3547	112	102	2558	113	107	6105	112	103
M26	North Worcestershire	1963	102	77	1221	93	48	3184	98	65
M28	Warwickshire	3679	97	64	2487	97	64	6166	97	62
N11	Chester	1354	101	73	943	102	77	2297	102	76
N12	Crewe	2039	104	82	1422	106	90	3461	105	87
N13	Halton	1100	116	114	813	121	126	1913	118	122
N14	Macclesfield	1243	90	35	869	91	37	2112	90	35
N15	Warrington	1420	112	102	1046	117	119	2466	114	109
N21	Liverpool	4426	127	140	3434	130	139	7860	128	139
N31	St Helens and Knowsley	2771	121	134	2093	124	132	4864	122	132
N41	Southport and Formby	988	95	56	749	93	48	1737	94	55
N42	South Sefton	1493	116	114	1120	114	109	2613	115	113
N51	Wirral	3095	112	102	2306	110	96	5401	111	98
P01	Lancaster	1177	105	87	810	102	77	1987	104	81
P02	Blackpool,Wyre and Fylde	3374	105	87	2471	106	90	5845	105	87
P03	Preston	1067	113	106	777	114	109	1844	113	106
P04	Blackburn, Hyndburn and Ribble Valley	2307	117	117	1668	119	121	3975	117	118
P05	Burnley, Pendle and Rossendale	2030	117	117	1527	120	125	3557	118	122
P06	West Lancashire	754	103	78	551	107	95	1305	104	81
P07	Chorley and South Ribble	1410	104	82	991	104	82	2401	104	81
P08	Bolton	2156	113	106	1622	116	116	3778	115	113
P09	Bury	1344	109	97	1033	115	112	2377	111	98
P10	North Manchester	1523	138	145	1069	136	145	2592	137	145
P11	Central Manchester	998	133	144	650	132	142	1648	132	144
P12	South Manchester	1586	120	133	1198	121	126	2784	121	128
P13	Oldham	1820	117	117	1500	132	142	3320	124	135
P14	Rochdale	1725	117	117	1235	119	121	2960	118	122
P15	Salford	2314	126	138	1737	128	136	4051	127	138
P16	Stockport	2237	106	90	1572	103	81	3809	104	81
P17	Tameside and Glossop	2182	121	134	1611	121	126	3793	121	128
P18	Trafford	1569	96	59	1191	104	82	2760	99	67
P19	Wigan	2676	126	138	2138	133	144	4814	129	141

CDS - C3A
SMRs for selected causes of death in the period 1988-92:
All causes (ICD 001-999) (all ages)

		Males			Females			Persons		
		Observed	SMR	Rank	Observed	SMR	Rank	Observed	SMR	Rank
	ENGLAND AND WALES	1382951	100		1448956	100		2831907	100	
O00	ENGLAND	1299069	100		1361832	100		2660901	100	
A00	NORTHERN RHA	92687	114	14	96032	113	14	188719	114	14
B00	YORKSHIRE RHA	102109	105	10	107697	103	10	209806	104	10
C00	TRENT RHA	132054	103	9	131282	102	9	263336	102	9
D00	EAST ANGLIAN RHA	55665	90	1	55999	93	2	111664	91	1
E00	NORTH WEST THAMES RHA	81685	95	6	83787	95	5	165472	95	6
F00	NORTH EAST THAMES RHA	95528	99	8	98523	97	8	194051	98	8
G00	SOUTH EAST THAMES RHA	101804	96	7	111547	96	6	213351	96	7
H00	SOUTH WEST THAMES RHA	76360	90	1	88263	93	2	164623	91	1
J00	WESSEX RHA	83308	90	1	88607	92	1	171915	91	1
K00	OXFORD RHA	56063	92	5	57585	96	6	113648	94	5
L00	SOUTH WESTERN RHA	94557	91	4	100547	93	2	195104	92	4
M00	WEST MIDLANDS RHA	142811	105	10	141931	104	11	284742	104	10
N00	MERSEY RHA	67475	110	12	73111	109	12	140586	109	12
P00	NORTH WESTERN RHA	116963	113	13	126921	111	13	243884	112	13
A01	Hartlepool	2672	120	138	2671	116	135	5343	118	136
A02	North Tees	4440	114	118	4355	113	121	8795	114	123
A03	South Tees	8076	118	132	8029	117	139	16105	118	136
A04	East Cumbria	5375	101	73	5931	108	105	11306	105	91
A05	South Cumbria	5255	98	64	5739	101	68	10994	99	63
A06	West Cumbria	4183	118	132	4149	115	131	8332	117	134
A11	Northumberland	9424	108	98	9893	113	121	19317	111	111
A12	Gateshead	6534	122	140	6636	115	131	13170	119	139
A13	Newcastle	8608	116	127	9476	112	117	18084	114	123
A14	North Tyneside	6053	113	111	6628	113	121	12681	113	119
A15	South Tyneside	5176	123	142	5245	116	135	10421	119	139
A16	Sunderland	8464	121	139	8570	117	139	17034	119	139
A30	North Durham	9600	115	122	9650	114	129	19250	115	127
A31	South Durham	8827	115	122	9060	115	131	17887	115	127
B11	East Riding	14463	103	81	15170	102	75	29633	102	75
B16	Grimsby and Scunthorpe	10095	107	94	9559	102	75	19654	104	86
B21	North Yorkshire	20597	95	48	22496	98	55	43093	97	54
B31	Bradford	12667	112	109	14029	109	109	26696	110	109
B51	West Yorkshire	16165	111	105	17605	108	105	33770	109	105
B61	Leeds	19439	104	88	20350	100	63	39789	102	75
B71	Wakefield	8683	113	111	8488	110	113	17171	111	111
C01	North Derbyshire	10961	103	81	10800	104	85	21761	104	86
C02	Southern Derbyshire	15630	105	91	15504	105	93	31134	105	91
C03	Leicestershire	22011	95	48	22158	96	45	44169	96	48
C04	North Lincolnshire	8375	101	73	8143	102	75	16518	101	72
C05	South Lincolnshire	9425	96	52	9061	97	49	18486	96	48

184

CDS - C3A
SMRs for selected causes of death in the period 1988-92:
All causes (ICD 001-999) (all ages)

		Males			Females			Persons		
		Observed	SMR	Rank	Observed	SMR	Rank	Observed	SMR	Rank
C08	Nottingham	16638	101	73	17253	103	83	33891	102	75
C09	Barnsley	6755	113	111	6375	109	109	13130	111	111
C10	Doncaster	8132	108	98	7814	109	109	15946	108	101
C11	Rotherham	7023	112	109	6592	106	97	13615	109	105
C12	Sheffield	16214	107	94	17189	104	85	33403	105	91
C14	North Nottinghamshire	10890	102	79	10393	102	75	21283	102	75
D01	Cambridge	6596	86	3	6796	89	4	13392	87	3
D05	North West Anglia	11187	95	48	10579	97	49	21766	96	48
D06	Norwich	14209	87	5	14624	92	16	28833	89	5
D07	Great Yarmouth and Waveney	6341	93	38	6420	95	38	12761	94	40
D09	Huntingdon	2686	91	30	2521	91	12	5207	91	17
D11	Suffolk	14646	90	23	15059	94	28	29705	92	25
E01	North Bedfordshire	5845	96	52	5901	100	63	11746	98	58
E02	South Bedfordshire	6105	99	65	5941	102	75	12046	100	67
E05	North West Hertfordshire	5849	89	15	6201	93	22	12050	91	17
E06	South West Hertfordshire	6171	93	38	6678	97	49	12849	95	44
E07	Barnet	7218	87	5	8667	94	28	15885	91	17
E09	Hillingdon	5676	93	38	5852	95	38	11528	94	40
E18	East and North Hertfordshire	10730	90	23	10994	94	28	21724	92	25
E19	Brent and Harrow	10315	92	34	10209	89	4	20524	91	17
E20	Ealing, Hammersmith and Hounslow	15787	104	88	15439	98	55	31226	101	72
E21	Kensington, Chelsea and Westminster	7989	99	65	7905	90	10	15894	94	40
F31	North Essex	21802	89	15	23129	94	28	44931	92	25
F32	South Essex	17470	96	52	18747	99	62	36217	98	58
F33	Barking and Havering	10162	100	70	10229	98	55	20391	99	63
F34	Redbridge and Waltham Forest	11270	96	52	12355	95	38	23625	95	44
F35	East London and the City	14636	116	127	13416	105	93	28052	111	111
F36	New River District	10914	97	58	11728	94	28	22642	96	48
F37	Camden and Islington	9274	111	105	8919	97	49	18193	104	86
G04	South East Kent	7910	92	34	8794	94	28	16704	93	34
G05	Canterbury and Thanet	10281	97	58	11811	98	55	22092	97	54
G06	Dartford and Gravesham	5483	102	79	5683	105	93	11166	103	81
G07	Maidstone	4643	94	45	4899	97	49	9542	96	48
G08	Medway	7599	100	70	7704	101	68	15303	101	72
G09	Tunbridge Wells	5183	89	15	6218	93	22	11401	91	17
G10	Bexley	5080	90	23	5338	92	16	10418	91	17
G11	Greenwich	5653	107	94	5699	100	63	11352	103	81
G12	Bromley	7323	88	11	7967	88	3	15290	88	4
G21	East Sussex	23860	89	15	29194	91	12	53054	90	11
G26	South East London	18789	114	118	18240	103	83	37029	108	101

CDS - C3A
SMRs for selected causes of death in the period 1988-92:
All causes (ICD 001-999) (all ages)

		Males			Females			Persons		
		Observed	SMR	Rank	Observed	SMR	Rank	Observed	SMR	Rank
H04	Mid Surrey	4809	88	11	5477	95	38	10286	92	25
H05	East Surrey	4807	86	3	5778	96	45	10585	92	25
H06	Chichester	6352	87	5	7491	93	22	13843	90	11
H07	Mid Downs	6303	87	5	7090	93	22	13393	90	11
H08	Worthing	8988	88	11	11465	89	4	20453	89	5
H09	Croydon	7214	95	48	8411	101	68	15625	98	58
H12	Wandsworth	4854	114	118	5363	109	109	10217	111	111
H13	Merton and Sutton	8265	91	30	9451	89	4	17716	90	11
H14	North West Surrey	8698	87	5	9407	92	16	18105	90	11
H15	South West Surrey	5712	82	1	6329	84	1	12041	83	1
H16	Kingston and Richmond	10358	89	15	12001	91	12	22359	90	11
J10	Dorset	20963	84	2	23337	87	2	44300	86	2
J21	Portsmouth and South East Hampshire	13750	96	52	14649	95	38	28399	95	44
J22	Southampton and South West Hampshire	12002	93	38	12126	93	22	24128	93	34
J23	Winchester	5142	89	15	5603	96	45	10745	92	25
J24	Basingstoke and North Hampshire	7041	89	15	7264	92	16	14305	91	17
J31	Salisbury	3613	90	23	3715	89	4	7328	89	5
J32	Swindon	5548	97	58	5455	98	55	11003	98	58
J33	Bath	10727	90	23	11564	94	28	22291	92	25
J41	Isle of Wight	4522	92	34	4894	94	28	9416	93	34
K11	East Berkshire	8036	94	45	8528	100	63	16564	97	54
K12	West Berkshire	9280	90	23	9706	94	28	18986	92	25
K24	Buckinghamshire	12356	91	30	12662	95	38	25018	93	34
K31	Kettering	7153	101	73	6826	98	55	13979	100	67
K32	Northampton	7646	97	58	7934	101	68	15580	99	63
K41	Oxfordshire	11592	87	5	11929	91	12	23521	89	5
L10	Bristol and District	21650	94	45	23063	94	28	44713	94	40
L21	Cornwall and Isles of Scilly	14367	91	30	15245	95	38	29612	93	34
L35	Exeter and North Devon	14488	89	15	15254	90	10	29742	89	5
L36	Plymouth and Torbay	17578	92	34	19225	92	16	36803	92	25
L40	Gloucestershire	14438	93	38	14836	92	16	29274	93	34
L51	Somerset	12036	88	11	12924	93	22	24960	91	17
M02	Herefordshire	4891	93	38	4789	96	45	9680	95	44
M04	Worcester and District	6631	93	38	7182	98	55	13813	96	48
M05	Shropshire	10720	97	58	10603	97	49	21323	97	54
M06	Mid Staffordshire	7801	103	81	7734	106	97	15535	104	86
M07	North Staffordshire	13924	113	111	13653	108	105	27577	111	111
M08	South East Staffordshire	6292	105	91	6344	108	105	12636	107	97
M13	East Birmingham	5772	111	105	5553	107	102	11325	109	105
M14	North Birmingham	4428	101	73	4929	104	85	9357	103	81
M16	West Birmingham	5828	118	132	5595	113	121	11423	115	127
M17	Coventry	9063	110	102	8273	106	97	17336	108	101

CDS - C3A
SMRs for selected causes of death in the period 1988-92:
All causes (ICD 001-999) (all ages)

		Males			Females			Persons		
		Observed	SMR	Rank	Observed	SMR	Rank	Observed	SMR	Rank
M18	Dudley	8060	103	81	8152	101	68	16212	102	75
M19	Sandwell	9130	116	127	8640	105	93	17770	110	109
M20	Solihull	4484	90	23	4342	89	4	8826	89	5
M21	Walsall	7219	113	111	6982	110	113	14201	111	111
M22	Wolverhampton	7203	110	102	6984	107	102	14187	108	101
M25	South Birmingham	11969	110	102	12359	104	85	24328	107	97
M26	North Worcestershire	6592	99	65	6778	102	75	13370	100	67
M28	Warwickshire	12804	97	58	13039	102	75	25843	99	63
N11	Chester	4642	100	70	4943	104	85	9585	102	75
N12	Crewe	6750	101	73	6987	106	97	13737	103	81
N13	Halton	3589	114	118	3492	112	117	7081	113	119
N14	Macclesfield	4757	96	52	5306	100	63	10063	98	58
N15	Warrington	4841	111	105	5181	115	131	10022	113	119
N21	Liverpool	14665	122	140	15862	116	135	30527	119	139
N31	St Helens and Knowsley	8933	118	132	8953	113	121	17886	115	127
N41	Southport and Formby	3792	99	65	5076	101	68	8868	100	67
N42	South Sefton	4851	109	101	5172	104	85	10023	106	96
N51	Wirral	10655	108	98	12139	106	97	22794	107	97
P01	Lancaster	4262	103	81	4845	102	75	9107	103	81
P02	Blackpool, Wyre and Fylde	11996	106	93	13540	104	85	25536	105	91
P03	Preston	3870	117	130	4146	113	121	8016	115	127
P04	Blackburn, Hyndburn and Ribble Valley	7864	115	122	8608	114	129	16472	114	123
P05	Burnley, Pendle and Rossendale	6998	113	111	7740	113	121	14738	113	119
P06	West Lancashire	2615	103	81	2892	110	113	5507	107	97
P07	Chorley and South Ribble	4794	103	81	5194	107	102	9988	105	91
P08	Bolton	7352	113	111	8007	112	117	15359	112	118
P09	Bury	4769	107	94	5515	111	116	10284	109	105
P10	North Manchester	4927	138	145	4723	118	142	9650	127	145
P11	Central Manchester	3450	132	144	3250	119	145	6700	126	144
P12	South Manchester	5291	118	132	5716	112	117	11007	115	127
P13	Oldham	6351	117	130	6953	118	142	13304	117	134
P14	Rochdale	5805	115	122	6399	117	139	12204	116	133
P15	Salford	7655	125	143	8020	116	135	15675	120	143
P16	Stockport	7799	104	88	8634	104	85	16433	104	86
P17	Tameside and Glossop	7045	115	122	7485	113	121	14530	114	123
P18	Trafford	5663	99	65	6366	101	68	12029	100	67
P19	Wigan	8457	119	137	8888	118	142	17345	118	136

CDS - C5
SMRs for "avoidable" and other potentially reducible causes of death
in the period 1988-92:
Hypertensive and cerebrovascular disease (ICD 401-405, 430-438) (ages 35-64)

		Males			Females			Persons		
		Observed	SMR	Rank	Observed	SMR	Rank	Observed	SMR	Rank
	ENGLAND AND WALES	15718	100		11891	100		27609	100	
O00	ENGLAND	14709	99		11112	99		25821	99	
A00	NORTHERN RHA	1226	123	13	969	127	14	2195	124	13
B00	YORKSHIRE RHA	1222	109	12	931	108	10	2153	109	11
C00	TRENT RHA	1555	104	9	1112	100	8	2667	103	9
D00	EAST ANGLIAN RHA	472	74	1	409	85	5	881	79	1
E00	NORTH WEST THAMES RHA	969	94	6	662	87	6	1631	91	6
F00	NORTH EAST THAMES RHA	1112	100	8	832	100	8	1944	100	8
G00	SOUTH EAST THAMES RHA	1062	97	7	814	96	7	1876	97	7
H00	SOUTH WEST THAMES RHA	724	80	4	531	76	1	1255	79	1
J00	WESSEX RHA	734	77	3	594	81	3	1328	79	1
K00	OXFORD RHA	569	76	2	443	81	3	1012	79	1
L00	SOUTH WESTERN RHA	874	84	5	626	78	2	1500	81	5
M00	WEST MIDLANDS RHA	1816	108	11	1388	112	12	3204	110	12
N00	MERSEY RHA	808	106	10	649	111	11	1457	108	10
P00	NORTH WESTERN RHA	1566	128	14	1152	124	13	2718	127	14
A01	Hartlepool	46	154	137	34	151	141	80	152	142
A02	North Tees	48	86	47	50	120	110	98	101	80
A03	South Tees	131	144	134	101	147	140	232	145	138
A04	East Cumbria	72	119	105	43	94	62	115	108	91
A05	South Cumbria	60	106	87	60	136	130	120	119	105
A06	West Cumbria	43	94	66	38	111	96	81	102	82
A11	Northumberland	119	117	103	106	137	133	225	126	118
A12	Gateshead	92	133	121	67	129	125	159	132	128
A13	Newcastle	88	109	90	80	126	124	168	117	102
A14	North Tyneside	71	110	91	56	111	96	127	110	93
A15	South Tyneside	66	124	116	45	110	93	111	118	104
A16	Sunderland	144	154	137	72	100	79	216	130	125
A30	North Durham	127	119	105	116	145	137	243	130	125
A31	South Durham	119	130	119	101	145	137	220	137	133
B11	East Riding	158	98	75	130	105	86	288	101	80
B16	Grimsby and Scunthorpe	112	97	73	84	98	75	196	97	70
B21	North Yorkshire	192	84	40	179	101	82	371	91	52
B31	Bradford	181	134	124	118	114	101	299	126	118
B51	West Yorkshire	204	120	110	159	122	116	363	121	110
B61	Leeds	256	119	105	180	109	92	436	115	101
B71	Wakefield	119	122	114	81	110	93	200	117	102
C01	North Derbyshire	127	104	84	83	90	51	210	98	71
C02	Southern Derbyshire	190	110	91	124	98	75	314	105	88
C03	Leicestershire	265	98	75	175	88	47	440	94	62
C04	North Lincolnshire	88	95	68	68	98	75	156	96	67
C05	South Lincolnshire	111	104	84	84	104	84	195	104	86

CDS - C5

SMRs for "avoidable" and other potentially reducible causes of death in the period 1988-92:

Hypertensive and cerebrovascular disease (ICD 401-405, 430-438) (ages 35-64)

		Males			Females			Persons		
		Observed	SMR	Rank	Observed	SMR	Rank	Observed	SMR	Rank
C08	Nottingham	211	110	91	163	114	101	374	112	97
C09	Barnsley	79	111	96	64	118	106	143	114	100
C10	Doncaster	83	88	55	66	93	59	149	90	51
C11	Rotherham	96	121	112	71	119	108	167	120	109
C12	Sheffield	185	116	100	112	92	56	297	106	90
C14	North Nottinghamshire	120	93	65	102	108	88	222	99	76
D01	Cambridge	58	71	19	49	80	29	107	75	20
D05	North West Anglia	112	88	55	92	95	63	204	91	52
D06	Norwich	104	66	12	93	77	20	197	71	14
D07	Great Yarmouth and Waveney	59	90	59	62	122	116	121	104	86
D09	Huntingdon	15	41	1	13	49	2	28	44	1
D11	Suffolk	124	73	24	100	79	26	224	76	23
E01	North Bedfordshire	44	59	5	51	93	59	95	73	18
E02	South Bedfordshire	69	83	39	60	105	86	129	92	59
E05	North West Hertfordshire	53	63	7	50	80	29	103	70	11
E06	South West Hertfordshire	77	101	79	56	98	75	133	100	78
E07	Barnet	63	75	27	43	65	7	106	71	14
E09	Hillingdon	71	99	77	46	86	40	117	93	61
E18	East and North Hertfordshire	134	87	49	89	78	23	223	83	39
E19	Brent and Harrow	135	103	81	93	96	66	228	100	78
E20	Ealing, Hammersmith and Hounslow	202	114	99	114	87	44	316	102	82
E21	Kensington, Chelsea and Westminster	121	127	117	60	86	40	181	110	93
F31	North Essex	216	81	34	186	92	56	402	85	42
F32	South Essex	161	75	27	157	96	66	318	84	41
F33	Barking and Havering	85	69	17	71	74	16	156	71	14
F34	Redbridge and Waltham Forest	148	117	103	116	121	113	264	119	105
F35	East London and the City	245	159	141	134	124	120	379	144	136
F36	New River District	128	97	73	88	90	51	216	94	62
F37	Camden and Islington	129	133	121	80	111	96	209	124	114
G04	South East Kent	57	68	15	50	76	19	107	72	17
G05	Canterbury and Thanet	104	116	100	90	122	116	194	119	105
G06	Dartford and Gravesham	64	89	57	59	111	96	123	99	76
G07	Maidstone	49	78	30	39	84	35	88	81	35
G08	Medway	77	81	34	65	91	53	142	85	42
G09	Tunbridge Wells	39	60	6	24	47	1	63	54	3
G10	Bexley	43	63	7	49	96	66	92	77	24
G11	Greenwich	71	123	115	43	96	66	114	111	95
G12	Bromley	82	85	44	54	72	13	136	79	29
G21	East Sussex	177	84	40	139	80	29	316	82	36
G26	South East London	299	157	140	202	141	135	501	150	141

CDS - C5
SMRs for "avoidable" and other potentially reducible causes of death in the period 1988-92:
Hypertensive and cerebrovascular disease (ICD 401-405, 430-438) (ages 35-64)

		Males			Females			Persons		
		Observed	SMR	Rank	Observed	SMR	Rank	Observed	SMR	Rank
H04	Mid Surrey	42	72	21	35	79	26	77	75	20
H05	East Surrey	45	72	21	28	60	5	73	67	6
H06	Chichester	38	66	12	34	71	12	72	68	7
H07	Mid Downs	59	68	15	46	68	10	105	68	7
H08	Worthing	67	90	59	42	67	9	109	79	29
H09	Croydon	105	113	97	68	96	66	173	105	88
H12	Wandsworth	64	134	124	39	110	93	103	124	114
H13	Merton and Sutton	88	89	57	77	100	79	165	94	62
H14	North West Surrey	71	57	3	50	54	3	121	56	4
H15	South West Surrey	31	41	1	37	64	6	68	51	2
H16	Kingston and Richmond	114	95	68	75	80	29	189	88	48
J10	Dorset	148	71	19	142	84	35	290	77	24
J21	Portsmouth and South East Hampshire	129	81	34	103	84	35	232	82	36
J22	Southampton and South West Hampshire	120	91	62	91	91	53	211	91	52
J23	Winchester	39	57	3	39	77	20	78	66	5
J24	Basingstoke and North Hampshire	66	63	7	57	75	17	123	68	7
J31	Salisbury	41	101	79	27	87	44	68	95	65
J32	Swindon	48	69	17	43	83	34	91	75	20
J33	Bath	99	79	32	62	65	7	161	73	18
J41	Isle of Wight	44	107	88	30	88	47	74	98	71
K11	East Berkshire	91	82	38	66	81	33	157	82	36
K12	West Berkshire	98	74	25	82	86	40	180	79	29
K24	Buckinghamshire	113	64	10	123	95	63	236	77	24
K31	Kettering	69	87	49	53	89	50	122	88	48
K32	Northampton	79	87	49	52	78	23	131	83	39
K41	Oxfordshire	119	77	29	67	59	4	186	70	11
L10	Bristol and District	222	87	49	160	84	35	382	86	45
L21	Cornwall and Isles of Scilly	135	85	44	92	75	17	227	80	33
L35	Exeter and North Devon	106	72	21	100	87	44	206	79	29
L36	Plymouth and Torbay	145	81	34	103	73	14	248	78	27
L40	Gloucestershire	154	91	62	99	77	20	253	85	42
L51	Somerset	112	84	40	72	69	11	184	78	27
M02	Herefordshire	43	80	33	32	79	26	75	80	33
M04	Worcester and District	68	84	40	61	100	79	129	91	52
M05	Shropshire	125	96	70	93	96	66	218	96	67
M06	Mid Staffordshire	89	87	49	69	92	56	158	89	50
M07	North Staffordshire	178	116	100	156	136	130	334	124	114
M08	South East Staffordshire	69	85	44	65	111	96	134	96	67
M13	East Birmingham	96	164	143	66	155	143	162	160	143
M14	North Birmingham	52	96	70	38	95	63	90	95	65
M16	West Birmingham	102	172	144	83	200	145	185	184	145
M17	Coventry	110	120	110	85	125	122	195	122	111

CDS - C5
SMRs for "avoidable" and other potentially reducible causes of death in the period 1988-92:
Hypertensive and cerebrovascular disease (ICD 401-405, 430-438) (ages 35-64)

		Males			Females			Persons		
		Observed	SMR	Rank	Observed	SMR	Rank	Observed	SMR	Rank
M18	Dudley	117	113	97	69	91	53	186	103	84
M19	Sandwell	141	146	135	87	122	116	228	136	132
M20	Solihull	45	66	12	38	73	14	83	69	10
M21	Walsall	97	110	91	90	140	134	187	122	111
M22	Wolverhampton	110	136	127	71	120	110	181	129	123
M25	South Birmingham	161	130	119	123	134	128	284	132	128
M26	North Worcestershire	75	87	49	61	97	73	136	91	52
M28	Warwickshire	138	86	47	101	86	40	239	86	45
N11	Chester	43	74	25	46	104	84	89	87	47
N12	Crewe	90	110	91	70	114	101	160	112	97
N13	Halton	39	91	62	30	93	59	69	92	59
N14	Macclesfield	39	64	10	36	78	23	75	70	11
N15	Warrington	68	119	105	50	118	106	118	119	105
N21	Liverpool	202	140	132	135	121	113	337	132	128
N31	St Helens and Knowsley	128	119	105	107	130	126	235	124	114
N41	Southport and Formby	38	96	70	27	85	39	65	91	52
N42	South Sefton	60	103	81	52	115	104	112	108	91
N51	Wirral	101	90	59	96	108	88	197	98	71
P01	Lancaster	40	99	77	30	96	66	70	98	71
P02	Blackpool,Wyre and Fylde	154	137	129	106	119	108	260	129	123
P03	Preston	55	141	133	31	108	88	86	127	121
P04	Blackburn, Hyndburn and Ribble Valley	99	121	112	83	136	130	182	128	122
P05	Burnley, Pendle and Rossendale	96	135	126	83	154	142	179	143	135
P06	West Lancashire	27	78	30	28	108	88	55	91	52
P07	Chorley and South Ribble	63	103	81	55	120	110	118	111	95
P08	Bolton	108	138	130	71	121	113	179	131	127
P09	Bury	58	107	88	40	97	73	98	103	84
P10	North Manchester	80	196	145	43	143	136	123	173	144
P11	Central Manchester	51	163	142	25	116	105	76	144	136
P12	South Manchester	73	155	139	47	125	122	120	142	134
P13	Oldham	90	139	131	50	102	83	140	123	113
P14	Rochdale	81	127	117	60	124	120	141	126	118
P15	Salford	104	146	135	78	146	139	182	146	139
P16	Stockport	97	105	86	62	88	47	159	98	71
P17	Tameside and Glossop	101	136	127	75	133	127	176	135	131
P18	Trafford	64	94	66	70	134	128	134	112	97
P19	Wigan	125	133	121	115	163	144	240	146	139

CDS - C5
SMRs for "avoidable" and other potentially reducible causes of death
in the period 1988-92:
Tuberculosis (ICD 010-018) (ages 5-64)

		Males			Females			Persons		
		Observed	SMR	Rank	Observed	SMR	Rank	Observed	SMR	Rank
	ENGLAND AND WALES	396	100		166	100		562	100	
O00	ENGLAND	374	100		157	100		531	100	
A00	NORTHERN RHA	18	72	6	7	67	4	25	71	6
B00	YORKSHIRE RHA	23	81	7	14	117	10	37	92	8
C00	TRENT RHA	26	70	5	11	71	5	37	70	4
D00	EAST ANGLIAN RHA	6	37	3	4	60	3	10	44	3
E00	NORTH WEST THAMES RHA	42	159	12	19	172	14	61	163	14
F00	NORTH EAST THAMES RHA	47	166	13	14	117	10	61	151	12
G00	SOUTH EAST THAMES RHA	35	127	10	11	92	7	46	116	10
H00	SOUTH WEST THAMES RHA	19	83	8	13	133	12	32	98	9
J00	WESSEX RHA	8	33	1	4	40	1	12	35	1
K00	OXFORD RHA	10	52	4	9	115	9	19	70	4
L00	SOUTH WESTERN RHA	9	35	2	6	55	2	15	41	2
M00	WEST MIDLANDS RHA	63	150	11	27	157	13	90	152	13
N00	MERSEY RHA	17	89	9	6	74	6	23	85	7
P00	NORTH WESTERN RHA	51	166	13	12	93	8	63	144	11

(Not presented for DHAs because of the low observed numbers)

CDS - C5
SMRs for "avoidable" and other potentially reducible causes of death
in the period 1988-92:
Hodgkin's disease (ICD 201) (ages 5-64)

		Males			Females			Persons		
		Observed	SMR	Rank	Observed	SMR	Rank	Observed	SMR	Rank
	ENGLAND AND WALES	762	100		437	100		1199	100	
O00	ENGLAND	715	99		410	99		1125	99	
A00	NORTHERN RHA	42	91	3	17	64	2	59	81	3
B00	YORKSHIRE RHA	64	118	12	37	119	11	101	118	13
C00	TRENT RHA	76	107	10	54	134	13	130	117	12
D00	EAST ANGLIAN RHA	30	98	7	21	121	12	51	106	9
E00	NORTH WEST THAMES RHA	41	76	2	27	87	5	68	80	2
F00	NORTH EAST THAMES RHA	54	95	6	35	106	9	89	99	7
G00	SOUTH EAST THAMES RHA	65	120	13	27	85	3	92	107	11
H00	SOUTH WEST THAMES RHA	28	63	1	22	85	3	50	71	1
J00	WESSEX RHA	47	101	9	12	46	1	59	81	3
K00	OXFORD RHA	48	123	14	31	141	14	79	129	14
L00	SOUTH WESTERN RHA	44	91	3	24	87	5	68	90	5
M00	WEST MIDLANDS RHA	85	107	10	47	105	8	132	106	9
N00	MERSEY RHA	33	92	5	19	91	7	52	92	6
P00	NORTH WESTERN RHA	58	98	7	37	109	10	95	102	8

(Not presented for DHAs because of the low observed numbers)

CDS - C5
SMRs for "avoidable" and other potentially reducible causes of death
in the period 1988-92:
Asthma (ICD 493) (ages 5-44)

		Males			Females			Persons		
		Observed	SMR	Rank	Observed	SMR	Rank	Observed	SMR	Rank
	ENGLAND AND WALES	659	100		541	100		1200	100	
O00	ENGLAND	628	101		514	101		1142	101	
A00	NORTHERN RHA	38	97	4	31	96	7	69	96	4
B00	YORKSHIRE RHA	37	78	2	46	119	12	83	96	4
C00	TRENT RHA	61	100	6	44	89	5	105	95	2
D00	EAST ANGLIAN RHA	27	102	7	23	107	10	50	104	11
E00	NORTH WEST THAMES RHA	67	142	14	40	102	8	107	124	14
F00	NORTH EAST THAMES RHA	45	90	3	44	106	9	89	97	6
G00	SOUTH EAST THAMES RHA	51	108	10	31	79	1	82	95	2
H00	SOUTH WEST THAMES RHA	37	97	4	35	110	11	72	103	10
J00	WESSEX RHA	44	109	11	41	127	13	85	117	12
K00	OXFORD RHA	39	111	12	25	88	4	64	100	9
L00	SOUTH WESTERN RHA	42	103	8	31	93	6	73	98	7
M00	WEST MIDLANDS RHA	51	75	1	46	83	3	97	79	1
N00	MERSEY RHA	34	112	13	21	82	2	55	98	7
P00	NORTH WESTERN RHA	55	107	9	56	133	14	111	119	13

(Not presented for DHAs because of the low observed numbers)

		CDS - C8 Perinatal mortality rate: average for the years 1990-92			CDS - C10 Mortality rates in infancy: average for the years 1990-92		
					Under 1 year		
		Observed	Rate	Rank	Observed	Rate	Rank
	ENGLAND AND WALES	16587	7.9		15095	7.2	
O00	ENGLAND	15733	7.9		14352	7.3	
A00	NORTHERN RHA	1014	8.3	8	959	7.9	8
B00	YORKSHIRE RHA	1180	7.7	5	1229	8.1	9
C00	TRENT RHA	1619	8.5	9	1430	7.6	7
D00	EAST ANGLIAN RHA	495	6.2	1	463	5.9	1
E00	NORTH WEST THAMES RHA	-	-	-	-	-	-
F00	NORTH EAST THAMES RHA	1408	8.1	7	1190	6.9	4
G00	SOUTH EAST THAMES RHA	1221	7.9	6	1128	7.3	6
H00	SOUTH WEST THAMES RHA	-	-	-	-	-	-
J00	WESSEX RHA	-	-	-	-	-	-
K00	OXFORD RHA	801	7.3	4	747	6.9	4
L00	SOUTH WESTERN RHA	845	6.9	2	766	6.3	2
M00	WEST MIDLANDS RHA	2170	9.8	11	1978	8.9	11
N00	MERSEY RHA	715	7.2	3	660	6.7	3
P00	NORTH WESTERN RHA	1518	8.7	10	1403	8.1	9
A01	Hartlepool	23	5.9	11	40	10.2	131
A02	North Tees	48	6.2	15	65	8.5	107
A03	South Tees	116	9.2	108	118	9.4	122
A04	East Cumbria	77	11.6	131	49	7.4	74
A05	South Cumbria	45	7.1	42	44	6.9	51
A06	West Cumbria	41	7.5	55	40	7.3	69
A11	Northumberland	82	7.6	64	77	7.2	65
A12	Gateshead	84	10.7	126	63	8.1	102
A13	Newcastle	106	9.5	116	95	8.6	108
A14	North Tyneside	59	8.0	76	44	6.0	25
A15	South Tyneside	49	7.9	72	37	6.0	25
A16	Sunderland	101	8.1	80	108	8.7	110
A30	North Durham	108	8.5	94	98	7.8	87
A31	South Durham	75	6.8	33	81	7.3	69
B11	East Riding	158	7.6	64	156	7.5	79
B16	Grimsby and Scunthorpe	124	8.3	84	103	6.9	51
B21	North Yorkshire	-	-	-	-	-	-
B31	Bradford	-	-	-	-	-	-
B51	West Yorkshire	214	8.5	94	222	8.9	116
B61	Leeds	237	8.1	80	252	8.6	108
B71	Wakefield	106	7.9	72	99	7.4	74
C01	North Derbyshire	95	6.9	38	83	6.1	27
C02	Southern Derbyshire	164	7.2	44	158	7.0	57
C03	Leicestershire	349	9.4	114	291	7.9	94
C04	North Lincolnshire	104	10.3	122	92	9.1	119
C05	South Lincolnshire	102	9.3	110	78	7.1	59

		CDS - C8 Perinatal mortality rate: average for the years 1990-92			CDS - C10 Mortality rates in infancy: average for the years 1990-92		
					Under 1 year		
		Observed	Rate	Rank	Observed	Rate	Rank
C08	Nottingham	222	8.6	96	210	8.1	102
C09	Barnsley	88	9.3	110	72	7.7	83
C10	Doncaster	110	8.7	100	100	8.0	99
C11	Rotherham	96	8.7	100	86	7.9	94
C12	Sheffield	176	8.6	96	161	7.9	94
C14	North Nottinghamshire	113	7.3	49	99	6.4	33
D01	Cambridge	52	5.0	1	48	4.6	5
D05	North West Anglia	123	7.5	55	106	6.5	36
D06	Norwich	93	5.6	6	98	5.9	23
D07	Great Yarmouth and Waveney	45	6.0	12	52	6.9	51
D09	Huntingdon	36	6.0	12	30	5.0	13
D11	Suffolk	146	6.6	27	129	5.8	21
E01	North Bedfordshire	74	7.4	54	73	7.3	69
E02	South Bedfordshire	99	6.8	33	90	6.2	29
E05	North West Hertfordshire	76	7.2	44	55	5.2	16
E06	South West Hertfordshire	64	6.3	17	43	4.2	2
E07	Barnet	63	5.1	2	59	4.8	8
E09	Hillingdon	92	8.6	96	75	7.0	57
E18	East and North Hertfordshire	128	6.4	21	88	4.4	4
E19	Brent and Harrow	-	-	-	-	-	-
E20	Ealing, Hammersmith and Hounslow	-	-	-	-	-	-
E21	Kensington, Chelsea and Westminster	-	-	-	-	-	-
F31	North Essex	227	6.7	30	166	4.9	9
F32	South Essex	-	-	-	-	-	-
F33	Barking and Havering	-	-	-	-	-	-
F34	Redbridge and Waltham Forest	205	9.5	116	178	8.3	105
F35	East London and the City	314	9.0	107	267	7.7	83
F36	New River District	175	7.8	70	178	7.9	94
F37	Camden and Islington	149	9.2	108	142	8.8	114
G04	South East Kent	82	7.6	64	84	7.8	87
G05	Canterbury and Thanet	74	6.7	30	71	6.5	36
G06	Dartford and Gravesham	82	8.7	100	66	7.1	59
G07	Maidstone	64	7.9	72	61	7.6	82
G08	Medway	124	8.0	76	116	7.5	79
G09	Tunbridge Wells	47	6.2	15	38	5.0	13
G10	Bexley	53	5.6	6	46	4.9	9
G11	Greenwich	79	7.5	55	83	7.9	94
G12	Bromley	69	6.3	17	63	5.7	20
G21	East Sussex	187	7.6	64	174	7.1	59
G26	South East London	360	9.6	118	326	8.7	110

Public Health Common Data Set		CDS - C8 Perinatal mortality rate: average for the years 1990-92			CDS - C10 Mortality rates in infancy: average for the years 1990-92		
					Under 1 year		
		Observed	Rate	Rank	Observed	Rate	Rank
H04	Mid Surrey	30	5.4	4	23	4.1	1
H05	East Surrey	46	6.5	25	30	4.3	3
H06	Chichester	30	5.3	3	26	4.6	5
H07	Mid Downs	78	6.9	38	56	4.9	9
H08	Worthing	63	7.5	55	57	6.9	51
H09	Croydon	124	8.4	90	107	7.2	65
H12	Wandsworth	77	8.1	80	70	7.4	74
H13	Merton and Sutton	114	7.5	55	102	6.7	42
H14	North West Surrey	-	-	-	-	-	-
H15	South West Surrey	-	-	-	-	-	-
H16	Kingston and Richmond	92	5.7	8	94	5.8	21
J10	Dorset	125	5.7	8	119	5.4	17
J21	Portsmouth and South East Hampshire	174	8.1	80	152	7.1	59
J22	Southampton and South West Hampshire	115	6.6	27	115	6.7	42
J23	Winchester	50	6.3	17	40	5.1	15
J24	Basingstoke and North Hampshire	-	-	-	-	-	.
J31	Salisbury	40	8.9	104	35	7.8	87
J32	Swindon	60	5.5	5	74	6.8	46
J33	Bath	109	6.9	38	101	6.5	36
J41	Isle of Wight	32	7.9	72	26	6.4	33
K11	East Berkshire	112	6.8	33	91	5.5	18
K12	West Berkshire	138	7.3	49	130	6.9	51
K24	Buckinghamshire	185	7.1	42	189	7.3	69
K31	Kettering	90	8.0	76	77	6.8	46
K32	Northampton	111	8.0	76	122	8.9	116
K41	Oxfordshire	165	7.2	44	138	6.1	27
L10	Bristol and District	224	6.8	33	195	5.9	23
L21	Cornwall and Isles of Scilly	128	7.7	68	113	6.8	46
L35	Exeter and North Devon	112	7.2	44	113	7.3	69
L36	Plymouth and Torbay	139	6.5	25	140	6.6	40
L40	Gloucestershire	149	7.2	44	135	6.5	36
L51	Somerset	93	6.3	17	70	4.7	7
M02	Herefordshire	52	8.4	90	39	6.3	31
M04	Worcester and District	77	8.4	90	84	9.2	120
M05	Shropshire	135	8.3	84	117	7.2	65
M06	Mid Staffordshire	104	8.6	96	94	7.8	87
M07	North Staffordshire	202	10.9	127	177	9.6	124
M08	South East Staffordshire	86	7.7	68	89	8.0	99
M13	East Birmingham	144	12.8	135	112	10.0	129
M14	North Birmingham	69	11.0	129	60	9.6	124
M16	West Birmingham	151	12.6	134	138	11.6	135
M17	Coventry	139	10.2	121	132	9.7	126

		CDS - C8 Perinatal mortality rate: average for the years 1990-92			CDS - C10 Mortality rates in infancy: average for the years 1990-92		
					Under 1 year		
		Observed	Rate	Rank	Observed	Rate	Rank
M18	Dudley	103	8.3	84	101	8.2	104
M19	Sandwell	154	11.4	130	133	9.9	128
M20	Solihull	56	7.3	49	59	7.7	83
M21	Walsall	108	9.3	110	96	8.3	105
M22	Wolverhampton	123	10.9	127	99	8.8	114
M25	South Birmingham	212	10.5	124	222	11.0	134
M26	North Worcestershire	72	6.7	30	79	7.4	74
M28	Warwickshire	183	9.9	120	147	8.0	99
N11	Chester	42	5.8	10	35	4.9	9
N12	Crewe	76	7.3	49	73	7.1	59
N13	Halton	47	7.5	55	42	6.7	42
N14	Macclesfield	52	8.3	84	45	7.2	65
N15	Warrington	54	6.8	33	62	7.8	87
N21	Liverpool	162	7.8	70	132	6.4	33
N31	St Helens and Knowsley	111	7.5	55	97	6.6	40
N41	Southport and Formby	22	6.1	14	27	7.5	79
N42	South Sefton	55	7.3	49	51	6.8	46
N51	Wirral	94	6.6	27	96	6.8	46
P01	Lancaster	44	9.3	110	41	8.7	110
P02	Blackpool, Wyre and Fylde	85	7.5	55	76	6.7	42
P03	Preston	39	6.4	21	58	9.5	123
P04	Blackburn, Hyndburn and Ribble Valley	108	8.7	100	123	10.0	129
P05	Burnley, Pendle and Rossendale	113	10.4	123	113	10.4	133
P06	West Lancashire	41	9.4	114	34	7.8	87
P07	Chorley and South Ribble	52	6.4	21	50	6.2	29
P08	Bolton	135	11.6	131	113	9.8	127
P09	Bury	76	9.8	119	60	7.8	87
P10	North Manchester	90	12.0	133	55	7.4	74
P11	Central Manchester	53	8.4	90	64	10.2	131
P12	South Manchester	55	7.0	41	70	8.9	116
P13	Oldham	108	10.5	124	94	9.2	120
P14	Rochdale	85	8.3	84	88	8.7	110
P15	Salford	86	8.3	84	71	6.9	51
P16	Stockport	101	8.9	104	87	7.7	83
P17	Tameside and Glossop	72	6.4	21	71	6.3	31
P18	Trafford	78	8.9	104	62	7.1	59
P19	Wigan	97	7.5	55	73	5.6	19

CDS - D1
SRRs for selected cancers in the period 1984-88:
Malignant neoplasm of stomach (ICD 151)

		Males			Females			Persons		
		Observed	SRR	Rank	Observed	SRR	Rank	Observed	SRR	Rank
	ENGLAND AND WALES	35064	100		22556	100		57620	100	
O00	ENGLAND	32624	99		20863	98		53487	99	
A00	NORTHERN RHA	2307	110	12	1594	119	13	3901	113	12
B00	YORKSHIRE RHA	2536	102	8	1721	105	10	4257	103	8
C00	TRENT RHA	3401	104	9	1988	100	8	5389	103	8
D00	EAST ANGLIAN RHA	1220	81	2	679	75	1	1899	79	1
E00	NORTH WEST THAMES RHA	1944	87	5	1242	88	6	3186	87	5
F00	NORTH EAST THAMES RHA	2604	104	9	1629	101	9	4233	103	8
G00	SOUTH EAST THAMES RHA	2564	95	6	1531	83	4	4095	90	6
H00	SOUTH WEST THAMES RHA	1716	79	1	1224	83	4	2940	81	2
J00	WESSEX RHA	1953	86	4	1158	80	2	3111	84	4
K00	OXFORD RHA	1456	97	7	860	95	7	2316	97	7
L00	SOUTH WESTERN RHA	2087	82	3	1343	82	3	3430	82	3
M00	WEST MIDLANDS RHA	4082	118	14	2444	115	12	6526	117	13
N00	MERSEY RHA	1716	108	11	1214	114	11	2930	111	11
P00	NORTH WESTERN RHA	3038	113	13	2236	122	14	5274	117	13
A01	Hartlepool	90	153	144	51	139	133	141	148	143
A02	North Tees	102	104	81	85	141	136	187	118	115
A03	South Tees	220	124	126	139	129	124	359	126	127
A04	East Cumbria	113	85	39	85	100	72	198	91	50
A05	South Cumbria	96	71	7	81	91	52	177	79	20
A06	West Cumbria	107	117	112	62	109	89	169	114	102
A11	Northumberland	208	94	57	138	101	74	346	97	70
A12	Gateshead	149	105	83	124	133	128	273	116	108
A13	Newcastle	237	121	122	154	112	98	391	117	112
A14	North Tyneside	149	107	87	110	118	110	259	111	97
A15	South Tyneside	143	126	132	74	101	74	217	117	112
A16	Sunderland	214	117	112	152	130	125	366	122	121
A30	North Durham	263	120	120	204	152	142	467	132	135
A31	South Durham	216	109	95	135	109	89	351	109	90
B11	East Riding	408	114	104	254	110	95	662	113	101
B16	Grimsby and Scunthorpe	228	96	65	147	103	80	375	98	74
B21	North Yorkshire	406	76	14	280	80	26	686	78	17
B31	Bradford	313	107	87	237	117	109	550	111	97
B51	West Yorkshire	414	110	98	286	110	95	700	110	95
B61	Leeds	551	113	101	348	107	88	899	111	97
B71	Wakefield	216	108	92	169	139	133	385	120	118
C01	North Derbyshire	270	100	75	166	103	80	436	101	79
C02	Southern Derbyshire	356	94	57	225	98	68	581	95	62
C03	Leicestershire	598	104	81	290	82	31	888	96	68
C04	North Lincolnshire	173	86	42	78	65	1	251	78	17
C05	South Lincolnshire	206	85	39	127	91	52	333	88	45

CDS - D1
SRRs for selected cancers in the period 1984-88:
Malignant neoplasm of stomach (ICD 151)

		Males			Females			Persons		
		Observed	SRR	Rank	Observed	SRR	Rank	Observed	SRR	Rank
C08	Nottingham	451	108	92	272	104	82	723	107	88
C09	Barnsley	179	115	105	114	125	119	293	119	116
C10	Doncaster	206	107	87	125	112	98	331	109	90
C11	Rotherham	190	118	117	108	112	98	298	116	108
C12	Sheffield	495	123	123	317	120	116	812	122	121
C14	North Nottinghamshire	277	103	80	166	106	86	443	104	83
D01	Cambridge	138	74	11	84	73	9	222	74	7
D05	North West Anglia	263	92	54	132	81	29	395	88	45
D06	Norwich	296	75	12	163	68	6	459	72	5
D07	Great Yarmouth and Waveney	148	88	48	78	76	21	226	84	36
D09	Huntingdon	46	67	4	33	83	35	79	73	6
D11	Suffolk	329	82	28	189	78	23	518	80	25
E01	North Bedfordshire	141	93	56	76	86	44	217	90	48
E02	South Bedfordshire	179	115	105	82	91	52	261	106	85
E05	North West Hertfordshire	108	65	2	94	91	52	202	75	10
E06	South West Hertfordshire	148	86	42	94	88	47	242	87	42
E07	Barnet	167	78	17	115	79	25	282	79	20
E09	Hillingdon	128	81	23	115	118	110	243	95	62
E18	East and North Hertfordshire	281	94	57	140	78	23	421	88	45
E19	Brent and Harrow	243	81	23	160	84	39	403	82	31
E20	Ealing, Hammersmith and Hounslow	393	96	65	239	91	52	632	94	60
E21	Kensington, Chelsea and Westminster	156	75	12	127	87	45	283	80	25
F31	North Essex	518	86	42	304	82	31	822	84	36
F32	South Essex	478	105	83	275	94	61	753	101	79
F33	Barking and Havering	324	119	119	183	109	89	507	115	105
F34	Redbridge and Waltham Forest	309	99	72	215	101	74	524	100	78
F35	East London and the City	443	128	134	288	133	128	731	130	132
F36	New River District	290	97	70	198	97	67	488	97	70
F37	Camden and Islington	242	110	98	166	109	89	408	110	95
G04	South East Kent	172	81	23	96	67	4	268	75	10
G05	Canterbury and Thanet	245	94	57	159	87	45	404	91	50
G06	Dartford and Gravesham	140	101	78	76	90	51	216	97	70
G07	Maidstone	117	95	62	56	73	9	173	86	41
G08	Medway	198	102	79	88	73	9	286	91	50
G09	Tunbridge Wells	120	82	28	76	75	18	196	79	20
G10	Bexley	162	112	100	97	106	86	259	109	90
G11	Greenwich	164	117	112	102	110	95	266	114	102
G12	Bromley	174	81	23	119	84	39	293	82	31
G21	East Sussex	545	82	28	321	65	1	866	75	10
G26	South East London	527	115	105	341	112	98	868	114	102

CDS - D1
SRRs for selected cancers in the period 1984-88:
Malignant neoplasm of stomach (ICD 151)

		Males			Females			Persons		
		Observed	SRR	Rank	Observed	SRR	Rank	Observed	SRR	Rank
H04	Mid Surrey	90	66	3	66	74	13	156	69	2
H05	East Surrey	112	80	21	62	67	4	174	75	10
H06	Chichester	104	59	1	89	74	13	193	65	1
H07	Mid Downs	135	76	14	94	82	31	229	78	17
H08	Worthing	207	83	33	148	75	18	355	79	20
H09	Croydon	182	91	52	87	66	3	269	81	27
H12	Wandsworth	117	100	75	102	122	118	219	109	90
H13	Merton and Sutton	199	83	33	178	105	84	377	92	54
H14	North West Surrey	178	71	7	124	80	26	302	74	7
H15	South West Surrey	145	84	37	87	76	21	232	81	27
H16	Kingston and Richmond	247	82	28	187	88	47	434	84	36
J10	Dorset	473	79	18	300	74	13	773	77	14
J21	Portsmouth and South East Hampshire	373	105	83	174	74	13	547	93	57
J22	Southampton and South West Hampshire	266	84	37	164	83	35	430	83	35
J23	Winchester	122	87	46	93	105	84	215	94	60
J24	Basingstoke and North Hampshire	158	82	28	96	82	31	254	82	31
J31	Salisbury	68	69	5	44	71	8	112	70	3
J32	Swindon	153	108	92	79	94	61	232	103	81
J33	Bath	244	83	33	150	80	26	394	82	31
J41	Isle of Wight	96	80	21	58	73	9	154	77	14
K11	East Berkshire	166	77	16	108	83	35	274	79	20
K12	West Berkshire	243	95	62	130	83	35	373	90	48
K24	Buckinghamshire	326	99	72	181	92	57	507	96	68
K31	Kettering	176	100	75	122	116	107	298	106	85
K32	Northampton	249	129	135	133	113	103	382	123	124
K41	Oxfordshire	296	90	51	186	94	61	482	92	54
L10	Bristol and District	557	96	65	355	94	61	912	95	62
L21	Cornwall and Isles of Scilly	268	70	6	211	88	47	479	77	14
L35	Exeter and North Devon	288	73	9	191	75	18	479	74	7
L36	Plymouth and Torbay	415	88	48	267	85	42	682	87	42
L40	Gloucestershire	280	73	9	165	68	6	445	71	4
L51	Somerset	279	85	39	154	74	13	433	81	27
M02	Herefordshire	102	81	23	69	92	57	171	85	40
M04	Worcester and District	145	83	33	92	85	42	237	84	36
M05	Shropshire	287	107	87	132	81	29	419	97	70
M06	Mid Staffordshire	215	115	105	130	119	114	345	116	108
M07	North Staffordshire	525	164	145	293	146	139	818	157	145
M08	South East Staffordshire	166	113	101	86	99	70	252	108	89
M13	East Birmingham	184	133	139	107	125	119	291	130	132
M14	North Birmingham	106	95	62	86	119	114	192	105	84
M16	West Birmingham	163	123	123	95	116	107	258	120	118
M17	Coventry	268	124	126	127	102	79	395	116	108

CDS - D1
SRRs for selected cancers in the period 1984-88:
Malignant neoplasm of stomach (ICD 151)

		Males Observed	SRR	Rank	Females Observed	SRR	Rank	Persons Observed	SRR	Rank
M18	Dudley	243	123	123	172	139	133	415	129	130
M19	Sandwell	319	152	143	174	131	126	493	144	142
M20	Solihull	113	91	52	81	109	89	194	98	74
M21	Walsall	224	135	140	134	135	131	358	135	137
M22	Wolverhampton	202	118	117	130	125	119	332	120	118
M25	South Birmingham	355	125	129	239	126	123	594	125	126
M26	North Worcestershire	140	87	46	107	109	89	247	95	62
M28	Warwickshire	325	99	72	190	98	68	515	99	77
N11	Chester	101	86	42	76	104	82	177	93	57
N12	Crewe	131	79	18	103	101	74	234	87	42
N13	Halton	105	130	136	55	113	103	160	124	125
N14	Macclesfield	99	79	18	68	84	39	167	81	27
N15	Warrington	137	124	126	82	118	110	219	122	121
N21	Liverpool	408	125	129	314	136	132	722	130	132
N31	St Helens and Knowsley	281	141	142	186	146	139	467	143	141
N41	Southport and Formby	88	94	57	66	88	47	154	92	54
N42	South Sefton	123	107	87	87	112	98	210	109	90
N51	Wirral	243	96	65	177	100	72	420	98	74
P01	Lancaster	115	109	95	76	101	74	191	106	85
P02	Blackpool,Wyre and Fylde	276	96	65	194	95	65	470	95	62
P03	Preston	109	125	129	78	131	126	187	127	129
P04	Blackburn, Hyndburn and Ribble Valley	205	113	101	146	120	116	351	115	105
P05	Burnley, Pendle and Rossendale	186	116	110	124	114	105	310	115	105
P06	West Lancashire	58	92	54	37	93	59	95	93	57
P07	Chorley and South Ribble	133	115	105	92	125	119	225	119	116
P08	Bolton	195	117	112	134	118	110	329	117	112
P09	Bury	119	105	83	77	99	70	196	103	81
P10	North Manchester	119	120	120	107	156	143	226	135	137
P11	Central Manchester	85	116	110	67	142	138	152	126	127
P12	South Manchester	131	109	95	96	114	105	227	111	97
P13	Oldham	187	132	138	126	133	128	313	132	135
P14	Rochdale	179	137	141	124	141	136	303	139	139
P15	Salford	206	126	132	178	158	144	384	139	139
P16	Stockport	169	88	48	125	96	66	294	91	50
P17	Tameside and Glossop	208	131	137	184	173	145	392	148	143
P18	Trafford	142	97	70	91	93	59	233	95	62
P19	Wigan	216	117	112	180	147	141	396	129	130

CDS - D1
SRRs for selected cancers in the period 1984-88:
Malignant neoplasm of small intestine, colon, rectum, rectosigmoid junction
and anus (ICD 152-154)

		Males			Females			Persons		
		Observed	SRR	Rank	Observed	SRR	Rank	Observed	SRR	Rank
	ENGLAND AND WALES	65698	100		68688	100		134386	100	
O00	ENGLAND	61334	99		64350	100		125684	99	
A00	NORTHERN RHA	4316	109	13	3956	96	3	8272	102	8
B00	YORKSHIRE RHA	4789	103	11	5038	101	8	9827	102	8
C00	TRENT RHA	6215	102	9	5889	97	5	12104	99	6
D00	EAST ANGLIAN RHA	2838	101	7	2865	104	11	5703	103	11
E00	NORTH WEST THAMES RHA	3642	87	2	4090	95	2	7732	91	2
F00	NORTH EAST THAMES RHA	4031	86	1	4523	92	1	8554	89	1
G00	SOUTH EAST THAMES RHA	4451	89	3	5268	96	3	9719	92	3
H00	SOUTH WEST THAMES RHA	3598	89	3	4353	98	6	7951	94	4
J00	WESSEX RHA	4275	101	7	4725	108	14	9000	105	12
K00	OXFORD RHA	2758	98	6	2881	104	11	5639	101	7
L00	SOUTH WESTERN RHA	4505	95	5	4935	100	7	9440	98	5
M00	WEST MIDLANDS RHA	7554	116	14	6841	104	11	14395	110	14
N00	MERSEY RHA	3230	108	12	3325	102	9	6555	105	12
P00	NORTH WESTERN RHA	5132	102	9	5661	102	9	10793	102	8
A01	Hartlepool	137	124	139	100	88	15	237	106	101
A02	North Tees	182	97	59	165	87	13	347	92	29
A03	South Tees	414	124	139	371	110	123	785	117	139
A04	East Cumbria	217	87	20	242	93	32	459	90	22
A05	South Cumbria	226	89	30	251	93	32	477	91	24
A06	West Cumbria	203	117	128	195	111	128	398	114	130
A11	Northumberland	381	92	38	396	95	42	777	93	34
A12	Gateshead	331	124	139	297	103	89	628	113	128
A13	Newcastle	441	120	133	386	93	32	827	106	101
A14	North Tyneside	255	97	59	263	92	26	518	95	41
A15	South Tyneside	232	109	104	223	99	64	455	104	95
A16	Sunderland	406	118	131	302	83	5	708	100	68
A30	North Durham	475	116	125	380	92	26	855	104	95
A31	South Durham	416	112	113	385	101	78	801	107	110
B11	East Riding	681	102	81	703	100	70	1384	101	76
B16	Grimsby and Scunthorpe	478	107	99	438	99	64	916	103	91
B21	North Yorkshire	999	100	74	1088	103	89	2087	102	85
B31	Bradford	536	98	66	611	100	70	1147	99	61
B51	West Yorkshire	685	97	59	723	92	26	1408	94	37
B61	Leeds	1032	113	116	1112	112	130	2144	113	128
B71	Wakefield	378	100	74	363	96	48	741	98	52
C01	North Derbyshire	539	106	98	450	91	22	989	99	61
C02	Southern Derbyshire	652	92	38	636	91	22	1288	91	24
C03	Leicestershire	944	87	20	920	85	9	1864	86	9
C04	North Lincolnshire	386	102	81	414	113	132	800	108	116
C05	South Lincolnshire	425	94	46	443	104	98	868	99	61

203

CDS - D1
SRRs for selected cancers in the period 1984-88:
Malignant neoplasm of small intestine, colon, rectum, rectosigmoid junction
and anus (ICD 152-154)

		Males			Females			Persons		
		Observed	SRR	Rank	Observed	SRR	Rank	Observed	SRR	Rank
C08	Nottingham	882	113	116	837	105	104	1719	109	119
C09	Barnsley	315	108	100	266	94	38	581	101	76
C10	Doncaster	418	115	123	341	98	58	759	107	110
C11	Rotherham	308	102	81	285	95	42	593	98	52
C12	Sheffield	826	110	108	825	103	89	1651	106	101
C14	North Nottinghamshire	520	102	81	472	97	53	992	100	68
D01	Cambridge	389	111	110	372	106	111	761	109	119
D05	North West Anglia	537	100	74	526	105	104	1063	103	91
D06	Norwich	708	96	54	707	98	58	1415	97	50
D07	Great Yarmouth and Waveney	321	103	87	302	98	58	623	100	68
D09	Huntingdon	110	84	14	123	100	70	233	92	29
D11	Suffolk	773	103	87	835	113	132	1608	108	116
E01	North Bedfordshire	278	97	59	277	101	78	555	99	61
E02	South Bedfordshire	302	102	81	330	118	140	632	110	124
E05	North West Hertfordshire	249	79	5	300	94	38	549	87	12
E06	South West Hertfordshire	293	91	34	320	98	58	613	94	37
E07	Barnet	364	91	34	436	100	70	800	96	45
E09	Hillingdon	260	88	25	252	84	8	512	86	9
E18	East and North Hertfordshire	489	86	17	511	92	26	1000	89	21
E19	Brent and Harrow	464	83	11	561	97	53	1025	90	22
E20	Ealing, Hammersmith and Hounslow	622	81	6	691	86	10	1313	84	7
E21	Kensington, Chelsea and Westminster	321	82	7	412	94	38	733	88	17
F31	North Essex	1051	93	43	1191	105	104	2242	99	61
F32	South Essex	739	87	20	848	95	42	1587	91	24
F33	Barking and Havering	387	76	2	451	87	13	838	81	3
F34	Redbridge and Waltham Forest	478	82	7	598	94	38	1076	88	17
F35	East London and the City	568	88	25	567	86	10	1135	87	12
F36	New River District	408	72	1	455	74	1	863	73	1
F37	Camden and Islington	400	97	59	413	90	20	813	93	34
G04	South East Kent	341	86	17	410	95	42	751	91	24
G05	Canterbury and Thanet	461	95	49	562	104	98	1023	100	68
G06	Dartford and Gravesham	216	82	7	242	92	26	458	87	12
G07	Maidstone	210	90	32	236	100	70	446	95	41
G08	Medway	316	87	20	326	88	15	642	87	12
G09	Tunbridge Wells	227	83	11	255	83	5	482	83	5
G10	Bexley	245	90	32	289	103	89	534	96	45
G11	Greenwich	249	95	49	283	100	70	532	98	52
G12	Bromley	334	83	11	339	78	2	673	80	2
G21	East Sussex	1186	97	59	1515	105	104	2701	101	76
G26	South East London	666	78	4	811	88	15	1477	83	5

CDS - D1
SRRs for selected cancers in the period 1984-88:
Malignant neoplasm of small intestine, colon, rectum, rectosigmoid junction
and anus (ICD 152-154)

		Males			Females			Persons		
		Observed	SRR	Rank	Observed	SRR	Rank	Observed	SRR	Rank
H04	Mid Surrey	255	99	72	248	92	26	503	96	45
H05	East Surrey	239	91	34	292	104	98	531	98	52
H06	Chichester	324	99	72	371	104	98	695	102	85
H07	Mid Downs	306	91	34	369	105	104	675	98	52
H08	Worthing	423	92	38	629	109	122	1052	102	85
H09	Croydon	316	84	14	360	89	18	676	87	12
H12	Wandsworth	189	86	17	241	96	48	430	91	24
H13	Merton and Sutton	339	76	2	462	91	22	801	84	7
H14	North West Surrey	411	87	20	482	101	78	893	94	37
H15	South West Surrey	297	92	38	371	107	116	668	100	68
H16	Kingston and Richmond	499	88	25	528	83	5	1027	86	9
J10	Dorset	1048	94	46	1289	108	120	2337	101	76
J21	Portsmouth and South East Hampshire	753	114	120	781	110	123	1534	112	126
J22	Southampton and South West Hampshire	625	105	93	634	106	111	1259	106	101
J23	Winchester	286	108	100	338	125	144	624	117	139
J24	Basingstoke and North Hampshire	363	100	74	369	102	88	732	101	76
J31	Salisbury	192	105	93	178	95	42	370	100	68
J32	Swindon	302	113	116	305	118	140	607	115	134
J33	Bath	488	89	30	571	101	78	1059	95	41
J41	Isle of Wight	218	98	66	260	110	123	478	104	95
K11	East Berkshire	339	84	14	376	93	32	715	88	17
K12	West Berkshire	455	94	46	480	99	64	935	97	50
K24	Buckinghamshire	621	100	74	634	104	98	1255	102	85
K31	Kettering	307	93	43	316	98	58	623	96	45
K32	Northampton	405	112	113	403	112	130	808	112	126
K41	Oxfordshire	631	103	87	672	111	128	1303	107	110
L10	Bristol and District	1009	93	43	1174	103	89	2183	98	52
L21	Cornwall and Isles of Scilly	657	92	38	697	96	48	1354	94	37
L35	Exeter and North Devon	704	96	54	811	107	116	1515	102	85
L36	Plymouth and Torbay	837	95	49	954	101	78	1791	99	61
L40	Gloucestershire	714	100	74	730	99	64	1444	99	61
L51	Somerset	584	95	49	569	91	22	1153	93	34
M02	Herefordshire	269	114	120	247	108	120	516	111	125
M04	Worcester and District	354	109	104	344	104	98	698	106	101
M05	Shropshire	559	111	110	534	107	116	1093	109	119
M06	Mid Staffordshire	410	116	125	332	97	53	742	106	101
M07	North Staffordshire	741	123	137	665	107	116	1406	115	134
M08	South East Staffordshire	291	105	93	307	113	132	598	109	119
M13	East Birmingham	296	114	120	257	97	53	553	106	101
M14	North Birmingham	242	116	125	252	113	132	494	114	130
M16	West Birmingham	315	127	144	295	118	140	610	122	143
M17	Coventry	474	117	128	358	93	32	832	106	101

205

CDS - D1
SRRs for selected cancers in the period 1984-88:
Malignant neoplasm of small intestine, colon, rectum, rectosigmoid junction
and anus (ICD 152-154)

		Males			Females			Persons		
		Observed	SRR	Rank	Observed	SRR	Rank	Observed	SRR	Rank
M18	Dudley	455	122	136	407	106	111	862	114	130
M19	Sandwell	505	128	145	429	105	104	934	116	138
M20	Solihull	229	98	66	241	103	89	470	101	76
M21	Walsall	354	113	116	314	101	78	668	107	110
M22	Wolverhampton	379	117	128	308	96	48	687	106	101
M25	South Birmingham	666	125	143	609	106	111	1275	115	134
M26	North Worcestershire	332	109	104	322	106	111	654	107	110
M28	Warwickshire	683	111	110	620	103	89	1303	107	110
N11	Chester	238	108	100	229	101	78	467	104	95
N12	Crewe	257	82	7	258	82	4	515	82	4
N13	Halton	184	121	135	176	115	138	360	118	141
N14	Macclesfield	240	102	81	235	95	42	475	98	52
N15	Warrington	248	119	132	236	110	123	484	115	134
N21	Liverpool	752	123	137	800	114	137	1552	118	141
N31	St Helens and Knowsley	423	112	113	397	99	64	820	105	100
N41	Southport and Formby	168	96	54	179	81	3	347	88	17
N42	South Sefton	249	115	123	272	113	132	521	114	130
N51	Wirral	471	100	74	543	101	78	1014	101	76
P01	Lancaster	203	104	91	199	89	18	402	96	45
P02	Blackpool, Wyre and Fylde	516	96	54	604	99	64	1120	98	52
P03	Preston	179	109	104	174	97	53	353	103	91
P04	Blackburn, Hyndburn and Ribble Valley	356	104	91	369	100	70	725	102	85
P05	Burnley, Pendle and Rossendale	263	88	25	332	101	78	595	95	41
P06	West Lancashire	114	96	54	124	100	70	238	98	52
P07	Chorley and South Ribble	208	95	49	205	90	20	413	92	29
P08	Bolton	278	88	25	332	96	48	610	92	29
P09	Bury	229	108	100	221	93	32	450	100	68
P10	North Manchester	221	120	133	281	136	145	502	128	145
P11	Central Manchester	144	105	93	144	101	78	288	103	91
P12	South Manchester	231	103	87	293	115	138	524	109	119
P13	Oldham	293	110	108	283	98	58	576	104	95
P14	Rochdale	239	97	59	277	103	89	516	100	68
P15	Salford	381	124	139	418	122	143	799	123	144
P16	Stockport	353	98	66	340	86	10	693	92	29
P17	Tameside and Glossop	313	105	93	360	110	123	673	108	116
P18	Trafford	270	98	66	310	103	89	580	101	76
P19	Wigan	341	98	66	395	105	104	736	101	76

PUBLIC HEALTH COMMON DATA SET

TREND DATA FOR SELECTED INDICATORS

CDS - B5A
Trends in percent of live births in NHS hospitals in the period 1984-92

		1984	1985	1986	1987	1988	1989	1990	1991	1992
	ENGLAND AND WALES	94.9	95.4	95.6	95.5	95.7	96.4	96.3	96.5	96.5
O00	ENGLAND	94.9	95.3	95.6	95.5	95.6	96.3	96.2	96.5	96.5
A00	NORTHERN RHA	95.3	95.6	95.8	96.1	96.2	96.5	96.5	98.0	97.9
B00	YORKSHIRE RHA	95.0	95.0	95.7	96.5	97.1	98.6	96.4	97.6	97.6
C00	TRENT RHA	95.0	95.3	95.6	95.7	96.2	97.6	97.3	97.5	97.6
D00	EAST ANGLIAN RHA	89.0	90.4	90.0	90.3	91.2	93.0	93.6	95.3	95.4
E00	NORTH WEST THAMES RHA	96.7	96.8	96.6	96.5	96.3	96.0	95.9	95.8	95.6
F00	NORTH EAST THAMES RHA	95.5	95.8	96.0	96.0	95.8	95.4	95.4	95.3	95.1
G00	SOUTH EAST THAMES RHA	97.9	98.3	98.3	98.3	98.0	98.1	97.8	97.7	97.5
H00	SOUTH WEST THAMES RHA	92.6	92.6	93.1	93.5	93.1	93.3	93.9	94.2	95.1
J00	WESSEX RHA	90.4	90.8	90.8	90.6	90.9	91.1	91.1	90.7	91.8
K00	OXFORD RHA	91.2	92.1	93.2	93.4	94.4	94.9	95.7	96.0	95.9
L00	SOUTH WESTERN RHA	91.6	93.6	94.1	89.8	89.7	95.1	94.9	94.6	94.2
M00	WEST MIDLANDS RHA	95.8	96.2	96.5	97.1	97.4	97.4	97.5	97.8	97.6
N00	MERSEY RHA	98.9	99.3	99.2	99.4	99.3	99.3	99.4	99.1	99.1
P00	NORTH WESTERN RHA	97.2	97.4	97.7	97.8	98.2	98.1	98.3	98.5	98.4

CDS - C3C
Trends in selected causes of death in the period 1984-92:
Motor vehicle traffic accidents (ICD E810-E819):
SMRs (observed numbers of deaths in parentheses)
Persons

		1984	1985	1986	1987	1988	1989	1990	1991	1992
	ENGLAND AND WALES	126 (4921)	120 (4733)	121 (4775)	118 (4681)	110 (4392)	119 (4717)	121 (4815)	108 (4309)	100 (3971)
O00	ENGLAND	127 (4688)	120 (4468)	121 (4527)	118 (4437)	112 (4207)	119 (4484)	122 (4591)	109 (4077)	100 (3751)
A00	NORTHERN RHA	110 (264)	110 (264)	102 (243)	122 (292)	100 (237)	120 (286)	137 (327)	127 (302)	106 (250)
B00	YORKSHIRE RHA	134 (378)	140 (397)	129 (367)	132 (376)	124 (353)	131 (374)	130 (374)	114 (328)	105 (301)
C00	TRENT RHA	139 (502)	124 (450)	133 (486)	125 (458)	114 (419)	121 (444)	132 (488)	133 (491)	115 (423)
D00	EAST ANGLIAN RHA	150 (232)	144 (225)	143 (227)	145 (233)	153 (247)	147 (239)	135 (221)	134 (220)	136 (224)
E00	NORTH WEST THAMES RHA	136 (368)	108 (293)	116 (318)	122 (333)	96 (259)	100 (272)	104 (283)	92 (248)	90 (242)
F00	NORTH EAST THAMES RHA	118 (339)	109 (316)	118 (346)	105 (307)	97 (284)	106 (312)	122 (358)	94 (276)	83 (244)
G00	SOUTH EAST THAMES RHA	126 (363)	125 (362)	124 (361)	108 (316)	111 (324)	108 (316)	114 (333)	96 (280)	78 (225)
H00	SOUTH WEST THAMES RHA	125 (289)	119 (279)	109 (256)	110 (258)	101 (237)	110 (258)	105 (247)	95 (222)	79 (183)
J00	WESSEX RHA	121 (290)	119 (290)	120 (296)	122 (303)	121 (301)	138 (343)	131 (325)	116 (287)	101 (251)
K00	OXFORD RHA	131 (246)	130 (249)	132 (257)	133 (260)	134 (263)	135 (264)	140 (275)	103 (203)	117 (231)
L00	SOUTH WESTERN RHA	126 (316)	119 (303)	119 (307)	116 (302)	112 (292)	131 (345)	122 (320)	117 (306)	94 (248)
M00	WEST MIDLANDS RHA	134 (539)	127 (511)	120 (487)	115 (468)	105 (427)	127 (515)	120 (489)	103 (420)	110 (446)
N00	MERSEY RHA	119 (224)	104 (196)	114 (214)	100 (186)	118 (220)	108 (200)	106 (196)	95 (176)	103 (190)
P00	NORTH WESTERN RHA	109 (338)	107 (333)	116 (362)	111 (345)	111 (344)	102 (316)	114 (355)	103 (318)	95 (293)
A01	Hartlepool	141 (10)	57 (4)	115 (8)	117 (8)	178 (12)	59 (4)	176 (12)	117 (8)	59 (4)
A02	North Tees	93 (12)	84 (11)	131 (17)	155 (20)	100 (13)	132 (17)	70 (9)	133 (17)	86 (11)
A03	South Tees	106 (24)	138 (31)	112 (25)	117 (26)	108 (24)	99 (22)	136 (30)	100 (22)	142 (31)
A04	East Cumbria	147 (20)	176 (24)	117 (16)	109 (15)	138 (19)	187 (26)	143 (20)	150 (21)	143 (20)
A05	South Cumbria	161 (22)	123 (17)	101 (14)	137 (19)	123 (17)	101 (14)	109 (15)	132 (18)	155 (21)
A06	West Cumbria	170 (18)	105 (11)	105 (11)	133 (14)	124 (13)	114 (12)	323 (34)	210 (22)	182 (19)

CDS - C3C
Trends in selected causes of death in the period 1984-92:
Motor vehicle traffic accidents (ICD E810-E819):
SMRs (observed numbers of deaths in parentheses)
Persons

		1984	1985	1986	1987	1988	1989	1990	1991	1992
A11	Northumberland	125 (29)	104 (24)	104 (24)	125 (29)	112 (26)	137 (32)	124 (29)	149 (35)	103 (24)
A12	Gateshead	155 (25)	93 (15)	87 (14)	131 (21)	63 (10)	158 (25)	108 (17)	51 (8)	103 (16)
A13	Newcastle	95 (22)	103 (24)	86 (20)	145 (34)	65 (15)	87 (20)	123 (28)	115 (26)	84 (19)
A14	North Tyneside	60 (9)	67 (10)	60 (9)	127 (19)	93 (14)	60 (9)	107 (16)	101 (15)	108 (16)
A15	South Tyneside	105 (13)	73 (9)	74 (9)	91 (11)	58 (7)	159 (19)	101 (12)	143 (17)	59 (7)
A16	Sunderland	79 (18)	62 (14)	106 (24)	97 (22)	71 (16)	111 (25)	133 (30)	107 (24)	81 (18)
A30	North Durham	75 (19)	147 (37)	127 (32)	103 (26)	92 (23)	128 (32)	143 (36)	135 (34)	104 (26)
A31	South Durham	107 (23)	154 (33)	93 (20)	131 (28)	131 (28)	136 (29)	183 (39)	164 (35)	85 (18)
B11	East Riding	97 (38)	142 (56)	83 (33)	131 (52)	116 (46)	122 (49)	99 (40)	91 (37)	101 (41)
B16	Grimsby and Scunthorpe	114 (31)	122 (33)	159 (43)	144 (39)	151 (41)	135 (37)	132 (36)	124 (34)	132 (36)
B21	North Yorkshire	135 (75)	159 (89)	148 (83)	140 (79)	131 (74)	172 (98)	165 (94)	123 (70)	112 (64)
B31	Bradford	139 (50)	128 (46)	138 (50)	153 (55)	100 (36)	143 (52)	143 (52)	123 (45)	113 (41)
B51	West Yorkshire	157 (69)	154 (68)	122 (54)	113 (50)	149 (66)	108 (48)	115 (51)	79 (35)	77 (34)
B61	Leeds	136 (77)	137 (78)	141 (81)	119 (68)	115 (66)	115 (66)	116 (66)	145 (83)	107 (61)
B71	Wakefield	160 (38)	114 (27)	97 (23)	139 (33)	101 (24)	100 (24)	145 (35)	100 (24)	100 (24)
C01	North Derbyshire	125 (35)	146 (41)	145 (41)	127 (36)	106 (30)	77 (22)	116 (33)	144 (41)	105 (30)
C02	Southern Derbyshire	157 (64)	112 (46)	128 (53)	89 (37)	140 (59)	163 (69)	144 (61)	106 (45)	101 (43)
C03	Leicestershire	148 (100)	107 (73)	146 (100)	143 (98)	96 (66)	127 (88)	140 (97)	139 (97)	133 (93)
C04	North Lincolnshire	157 (32)	97 (20)	163 (34)	157 (33)	118 (25)	117 (25)	121 (26)	185 (40)	110 (24)
C05	South Lincolnshire	201 (46)	183 (42)	184 (43)	178 (42)	162 (39)	208 (50)	198 (48)	172 (42)	138 (34)
C08	Nottingham	140 (68)	132 (65)	124 (61)	105 (52)	124 (61)	122 (60)	130 (64)	158 (78)	93 (46)
C09	Barnsley	64 (11)	75 (13)	104 (18)	179 (31)	133 (23)	92 (16)	104 (18)	127 (22)	122 (21)

210

CDS - C3C
Trends in selected causes of death in the period 1984-92:
Motor vehicle traffic accidents (ICD E810-E819):
SMRs (observed numbers of deaths in parentheses)
Persons

		1984	1985	1986	1987	1988	1989	1990	1991	1992
C10	Doncaster	122	140	108	148	116	80	121	153	144
		(27)	(31)	(24)	(33)	(26)	(18)	(27)	(34)	(32)
C11	Rotherham	115	120	57	120	78	165	62	103	83
		(22)	(23)	(11)	(23)	(15)	(32)	(12)	(20)	(16)
C12	Sheffield	106	101	81	95	71	96	108	67	90
		(47)	(45)	(36)	(42)	(31)	(42)	(47)	(29)	(39)
C14	North Nottinghamshire	167	169	215	103	145	72	181	142	149
		(50)	(51)	(65)	(31)	(44)	(22)	(55)	(43)	(45)
D01	Cambridge	98	102	126	135	138	142	128	164	117
		(22)	(23)	(29)	(31)	(32)	(33)	(30)	(39)	(28)
D05	North West Anglia	139	181	212	188	172	187	164	167	187
		(40)	(53)	(63)	(57)	(53)	(58)	(51)	(52)	(59)
D06	Norwich	161	137	121	136	156	139	138	142	170
		(59)	(51)	(46)	(52)	(60)	(54)	(54)	(56)	(67)
D07	Great Yarmouth and Waveney	147	147	92	155	134	177	120	75	100
		(22)	(22)	(14)	(24)	(21)	(28)	(19)	(12)	(16)
D09	Huntingdon	188	191	156	192	110	159	129	99	87
		(17)	(18)	(15)	(19)	(11)	(16)	(13)	(10)	(9)
D11	Suffolk	170	135	139	115	161	114	123	115	103
		(72)	(58)	(60)	(50)	(70)	(50)	(54)	(51)	(45)
E01	North Bedfordshire	125	114	123	142	100	127	147	110	141
		(23)	(21)	(23)	(27)	(19)	(24)	(28)	(21)	(27)
E02	South Bedfordshire	188	149	153	167	118	109	146	118	94
		(39)	(31)	(32)	(35)	(25)	(23)	(31)	(25)	(20)
E05	North West Hertfordshire	136	140	90	166	65	91	126	116	71
		(27)	(28)	(18)	(33)	(13)	(18)	(25)	(23)	(14)
E06	South West Hertfordshire	101	122	117	112	54	102	97	86	95
		(19)	(23)	(22)	(21)	(10)	(19)	(18)	(16)	(18)
E07	Barnet	150	93	122	97	108	72	55	89	80
		(35)	(22)	(29)	(23)	(25)	(17)	(13)	(21)	(19)
E09	Hillingdon	108	91	86	102	91	144	53	81	70
		(20)	(17)	(16)	(19)	(17)	(27)	(10)	(15)	(13)
E18	East and North Hertfordshire	107	84	124	108	111	68	100	108	111
		(39)	(31)	(46)	(40)	(41)	(25)	(37)	(40)	(41)
E19	Brent and Harrow	114	108	107	110	114	87	102	80	69
		(41)	(39)	(39)	(40)	(41)	(31)	(36)	(28)	(24)
E20	Ealing, Hammersmith and Hounslow	172	98	140	146	90	136	116	79	98
		(87)	(50)	(72)	(75)	(46)	(69)	(59)	(40)	(49)
E21	Kensington, Chelsea and Westminster	137	111	75	73	83	70	95	70	63
		(38)	(31)	(21)	(20)	(22)	(19)	(26)	(19)	(17)
F31	North Essex	120	118	134	97	115	133	153	111	94
		(77)	(77)	(88)	(64)	(77)	(89)	(102)	(74)	(63)
F32	South Essex	113	108	128	114	83	85	140	83	68
		(58)	(56)	(67)	(60)	(44)	(45)	(74)	(44)	(36)

211

CDS - C3C
Trends in selected causes of death in the period 1984-92:
Motor vehicle traffic accidents (ICD E810-E819):
SMRs (observed numbers of deaths in parentheses)
Persons

		1984	1985	1986	1987	1988	1989	1990	1991	1992
F33	Barking and Havering	97 (29)	124 (37)	117 (35)	104 (31)	114 (34)	99 (29)	116 (34)	103 (30)	83 (24)
F34	Redbridge and Waltham Forest	110 (38)	103 (36)	74 (26)	100 (35)	94 (33)	103 (36)	122 (43)	88 (31)	94 (33)
F35	East London and the City	140 (60)	116 (50)	113 (49)	110 (48)	75 (33)	93 (41)	92 (41)	86 (38)	52 (23)
F36	New River District	141 (52)	83 (31)	120 (45)	119 (44)	106 (39)	98 (36)	111 (41)	105 (39)	115 (42)
F37	Camden and Islington	88 (25)	101 (29)	125 (36)	87 (25)	85 (24)	129 (36)	82 (23)	71 (20)	83 (23)
G04	South East Kent	99 (21)	156 (33)	98 (21)	107 (23)	88 (19)	134 (29)	102 (22)	107 (23)	111 (24)
G05	Canterbury and Thanet	178 (42)	135 (32)	101 (24)	142 (34)	136 (33)	128 (31)	133 (32)	118 (29)	69 (17)
G06	Dartford and Gravesham	122 (21)	128 (22)	98 (17)	81 (14)	140 (24)	106 (18)	106 (18)	100 (17)	88 (15)
G07	Maidstone	149 (22)	135 (20)	107 (16)	126 (19)	190 (29)	85 (13)	111 (17)	105 (16)	73 (11)
G08	Medway	108 (27)	111 (28)	142 (36)	94 (24)	86 (22)	74 (19)	123 (32)	71 (18)	83 (21)
G09	Tunbridge Wells	145 (23)	151 (24)	220 (35)	125 (20)	144 (23)	101 (16)	107 (17)	127 (20)	134 (21)
G10	Bexley	96 (16)	78 (13)	118 (20)	100 (17)	89 (15)	83 (14)	89 (15)	53 (9)	60 (10)
G11	Greenwich	136 (23)	154 (26)	158 (27)	83 (14)	102 (17)	128 (21)	73 (12)	98 (16)	61 (10)
G12	Bromley	125 (29)	99 (23)	86 (20)	124 (29)	77 (18)	73 (17)	129 (30)	57 (13)	48 (11)
G21	East Sussex	117 (67)	115 (66)	125 (73)	114 (67)	124 (74)	98 (58)	127 (75)	125 (74)	76 (45)
G26	South East London	127 (72)	131 (75)	125 (72)	96 (55)	88 (50)	142 (80)	112 (63)	80 (45)	72 (40)
H04	Mid Surrey	107 (14)	114 (15)	136 (18)	145 (19)	77 (10)	106 (14)	83 (11)	38 (5)	68 (9)
H05	East Surrey	114 (17)	187 (28)	140 (21)	129 (19)	122 (18)	88 (13)	88 (13)	115 (17)	88 (13)
H06	Chichester	148 (21)	111 (16)	109 (16)	169 (25)	94 (14)	114 (17)	95 (14)	122 (18)	61 (9)
H07	Mid Downs	137 (29)	99 (21)	102 (22)	143 (31)	101 (22)	124 (27)	179 (39)	106 (23)	92 (20)
H08	Worthing	123 (25)	98 (20)	101 (21)	134 (28)	120 (25)	139 (29)	101 (21)	130 (27)	87 (18)
H09	Croydon	117 (29)	109 (27)	117 (29)	105 (26)	77 (19)	82 (20)	110 (27)	90 (22)	78 (19)

CDS - C3C
Trends in selected causes of death in the period 1984-92:
Motor vehicle traffic accidents (ICD E810-E819):
SMRs (observed numbers of deaths in parentheses)
Persons

		1984	1985	1986	1987	1988	1989	1990	1991	1992
H12	Wandsworth	89 (14)	119 (19)	118 (19)	93 (15)	99 (16)	81 (13)	57 (9)	89 (14)	64 (10)
H13	Merton and Sutton	102 (27)	134 (36)	100 (27)	93 (25)	97 (26)	119 (32)	71 (19)	97 (26)	75 (20)
H14	North West Surrey	149 (44)	125 (37)	108 (32)	85 (25)	98 (29)	129 (38)	101 (30)	74 (22)	101 (30)
H15	South West Surrey	143 (28)	148 (29)	116 (23)	103 (20)	103 (20)	125 (24)	145 (28)	114 (22)	84 (16)
H16	Kingston and Richmond	127 (41)	95 (31)	86 (28)	77 (25)	117 (38)	95 (31)	109 (36)	79 (26)	58 (19)
J10	Dorset	112 (57)	108 (56)	102 (54)	112 (60)	116 (63)	151 (82)	124 (67)	99 (54)	105 (57)
J21	Portsmouth and South East Hampshire	86 (37)	97 (42)	78 (34)	89 (39)	88 (38)	100 (43)	112 (48)	75 (32)	73 (31)
J22	Southampton and South West Hampshire	88 (29)	137 (46)	112 (38)	94 (32)	126 (43)	105 (36)	151 (52)	87 (30)	84 (29)
J23	Winchester	149 (25)	124 (21)	107 (18)	159 (27)	152 (26)	124 (21)	112 (19)	165 (28)	147 (25)
J24	Basingstoke and North Hampshire	151 (42)	155 (44)	152 (43)	158 (45)	132 (38)	163 (47)	191 (55)	129 (37)	73 (21)
J31	Salisbury	210 (21)	188 (19)	203 (21)	148 (15)	178 (18)	220 (22)	109 (11)	179 (18)	138 (14)
J32	Swindon	139 (24)	108 (19)	135 (24)	133 (24)	109 (20)	175 (32)	167 (31)	204 (38)	134 (25)
J33	Bath	157 (50)	109 (35)	177 (57)	163 (53)	134 (44)	153 (50)	111 (36)	130 (42)	139 (45)
J41	Isle of Wight	51 (5)	81 (8)	70 (7)	79 (8)	106 (11)	96 (10)	58 (6)	78 (8)	39 (4)
K11	East Berkshire	93 (26)	125 (35)	114 (32)	108 (30)	136 (38)	89 (25)	99 (28)	64 (18)	93 (26)
K12	West Berkshire	106 (36)	115 (40)	135 (48)	150 (54)	120 (43)	131 (46)	102 (36)	85 (30)	80 (28)
K24	Buckinghamshire	155 (65)	141 (60)	117 (51)	120 (53)	128 (57)	123 (55)	137 (62)	93 (42)	125 (57)
K31	Kettering	114 (22)	190 (37)	172 (34)	150 (30)	148 (30)	186 (38)	185 (38)	166 (34)	137 (28)
K32	Northampton	171 (38)	172 (39)	165 (38)	153 (36)	172 (41)	171 (41)	191 (46)	124 (30)	149 (36)
K41	Oxfordshire	137 (59)	87 (38)	122 (54)	129 (57)	123 (54)	135 (59)	149 (65)	113 (49)	128 (56)
L10	Bristol and District	114 (74)	120 (78)	120 (79)	94 (62)	107 (71)	127 (84)	100 (66)	112 (74)	87 (57)
L21	Cornwall and Isles of Scilly	101 (35)	125 (44)	132 (47)	142 (51)	88 (32)	128 (47)	127 (47)	83 (31)	81 (30)

213

CDS - C3C
Trends in selected causes of death in the period 1984-92:
Motor vehicle traffic accidents (ICD E810-E819):
SMRs (observed numbers of deaths in parentheses)
Persons

		1984	1985	1986	1987	1988	1989	1990	1991	1992
L35	Exeter and North Devon	120 (42)	82 (29)	103 (37)	105 (38)	123 (45)	146 (54)	92 (34)	100 (37)	83 (31)
L36	Plymouth and Torbay	116 (53)	87 (40)	89 (42)	104 (49)	71 (34)	63 (30)	131 (62)	98 (46)	53 (25)
L40	Gloucestershire	169 (68)	182 (74)	126 (52)	139 (58)	162 (68)	164 (69)	176 (74)	164 (69)	129 (54)
L51	Somerset	141 (44)	120 (38)	157 (50)	137 (44)	130 (42)	186 (61)	112 (37)	149 (49)	154 (51)
M02	Herefordshire	207 (25)	131 (16)	81 (10)	152 (19)	103 (13)	142 (18)	174 (22)	103 (13)	118 (15)
M04	Worcester and District	137 (25)	174 (32)	108 (20)	148 (28)	115 (22)	109 (21)	130 (25)	93 (18)	123 (24)
M05	Shropshire	151 (46)	123 (38)	122 (38)	150 (47)	158 (50)	135 (43)	163 (52)	91 (29)	170 (54)
M06	Mid Staffordshire	109 (25)	143 (33)	112 (26)	94 (22)	102 (24)	156 (37)	172 (41)	113 (27)	92 (22)
M07	North Staffordshire	191 (69)	110 (40)	102 (37)	126 (46)	68 (25)	128 (47)	87 (32)	93 (34)	140 (51)
M08	South East Staffordshire	143 (27)	201 (38)	142 (27)	161 (31)	149 (29)	189 (37)	86 (17)	132 (26)	107 (21)
M13	East Birmingham	136 (22)	150 (24)	101 (16)	121 (19)	102 (16)	154 (24)	135 (21)	97 (15)	85 (13)
M14	North Birmingham	116 (15)	107 (14)	114 (15)	107 (14)	99 (13)	100 (13)	78 (10)	86 (11)	55 (7)
M16	West Birmingham	124 (21)	118 (20)	148 (25)	137 (23)	79 (13)	122 (20)	79 (13)	115 (19)	67 (11)
M17	Coventry	104 (26)	120 (30)	116 (29)	133 (33)	110 (27)	106 (26)	110 (27)	82 (20)	92 (22)
M18	Dudley	87 (20)	95 (22)	104 (24)	90 (21)	81 (19)	80 (19)	76 (18)	67 (16)	97 (23)
M19	Sandwell	114 (27)	140 (33)	111 (26)	90 (21)	78 (18)	113 (26)	100 (23)	105 (24)	105 (24)
M20	Solihull	134 (20)	126 (19)	106 (16)	98 (15)	65 (10)	92 (14)	79 (12)	158 (24)	119 (18)
M21	Walsall	120 (24)	75 (15)	95 (19)	80 (16)	85 (17)	110 (22)	90 (18)	134 (27)	90 (18)
M22	Wolverhampton	132 (26)	91 (18)	153 (30)	102 (20)	82 (16)	150 (29)	104 (20)	98 (19)	99 (19)
M25	South Birmingham	124 (42)	88 (30)	143 (49)	76 (26)	123 (42)	111 (38)	126 (43)	112 (38)	121 (41)
M26	North Worcestershire	118 (23)	116 (23)	140 (28)	133 (27)	132 (27)	122 (25)	160 (33)	111 (23)	135 (28)
M28	Warwickshire	151 (56)	177 (66)	139 (52)	106 (40)	122 (46)	149 (56)	165 (62)	98 (37)	93 (35)

CDS - C3C
Trends in selected causes of death in the period 1984-92:
Motor vehicle traffic accidents (ICD E810-E819):
SMRs (observed numbers of deaths in parentheses)
Persons

		1984	1985	1986	1987	1988	1989	1990	1991	1992
N11	Chester	123 (17)	101 (14)	100 (14)	108 (15)	101 (14)	110 (15)	96 (13)	102 (14)	102 (14)
N12	Crewe	139 (26)	155 (29)	117 (22)	116 (22)	74 (14)	125 (24)	154 (30)	107 (21)	132 (26)
N13	Halton	123 (13)	57 (6)	56 (6)	112 (12)	103 (11)	112 (12)	178 (19)	132 (14)	86 (9)
N14	Macclesfield	141 (19)	88 (12)	146 (20)	80 (11)	102 (14)	124 (17)	110 (15)	66 (9)	104 (14)
N15	Warrington	82 (11)	96 (13)	145 (20)	78 (11)	156 (22)	106 (15)	99 (14)	113 (16)	122 (17)
N21	Liverpool	128 (52)	124 (50)	133 (53)	100 (39)	145 (56)	105 (40)	129 (49)	109 (41)	107 (40)
N31	St Helens and Knowsley	134 (36)	72 (19)	141 (37)	85 (22)	136 (35)	121 (31)	67 (17)	83 (21)	111 (28)
N41	Southport and Formby	44 (4)	184 (17)	98 (9)	109 (10)	97 (9)	86 (8)	64 (6)	75 (7)	75 (7)
N42	South Sefton	129 (18)	72 (10)	80 (11)	131 (18)	74 (10)	52 (7)	104 (14)	82 (11)	90 (12)
N51	Wirral	102 (28)	95 (26)	81 (22)	95 (26)	128 (35)	113 (31)	70 (19)	81 (22)	85 (23)
P01	Lancaster	85 (9)	113 (12)	140 (15)	113 (12)	66 (7)	67 (7)	57 (6)	114 (12)	85 (9)
P02	Blackpool,Wyre and Fylde	143 (37)	135 (35)	138 (36)	145 (38)	84 (22)	115 (30)	151 (39)	115 (30)	72 (19)
P03	Preston	170 (17)	90 (9)	157 (16)	96 (10)	114 (12)	124 (13)	95 (10)	211 (22)	106 (11)
P04	Blackburn, Hyndburn and Ribble Valley	104 (22)	133 (28)	124 (26)	144 (30)	141 (29)	155 (32)	166 (34)	142 (29)	84 (17)
P05	Burnley, Pendle and Rossendale	85 (15)	80 (14)	149 (26)	151 (26)	157 (27)	124 (22)	172 (31)	94 (17)	128 (23)
P06	West Lancashire	123 (10)	85 (7)	134 (11)	121 (10)	97 (8)	73 (6)	134 (11)	73 (6)	73 (6)
P07	Chorley and South Ribble	126 (18)	97 (14)	138 (20)	103 (15)	115 (17)	101 (15)	93 (14)	73 (11)	140 (21)
P08	Bolton	131 (26)	121 (24)	96 (19)	136 (27)	116 (23)	130 (26)	130 (26)	100 (20)	105 (21)
P09	Bury	98 (13)	90 (12)	128 (17)	67 (9)	186 (25)	89 (12)	110 (15)	66 (9)	81 (11)
P10	North Manchester	117 (14)	161 (19)	182 (21)	107 (12)	148 (16)	96 (10)	139 (15)	149 (16)	104 (11)
P11	Central Manchester	124 (14)	170 (19)	115 (13)	168 (19)	152 (17)	99 (11)	153 (16)	38 (4)	108 (11)
P12	South Manchester	111 (16)	118 (17)	62 (9)	97 (14)	83 (12)	98 (14)	145 (21)	134 (19)	123 (17)

CDS - C3C
Trends in selected causes of death in the period 1984-92:
Motor vehicle traffic accidents (ICD E810-E819):
SMRs (observed numbers of deaths in parentheses)
Persons

		1984	1985	1986	1987	1988	1989	1990	1991	1992
P13	Oldham	102	84	108	79	103	85	126	114	109
		(17)	(14)	(18)	(13)	(17)	(14)	(21)	(19)	(18)
P14	Rochdale	155	106	75	137	138	75	94	88	75
		(25)	(17)	(12)	(22)	(22)	(12)	(15)	(14)	(12)
P15	Salford	77	125	145	131	122	96	75	136	126
		(15)	(24)	(28)	(25)	(23)	(18)	(14)	(25)	(23)
P16	Stockport	77	68	149	90	68	104	78	68	64
		(17)	(15)	(33)	(20)	(15)	(23)	(17)	(15)	(14)
P17	Tameside and Glossop	80	85	101	53	90	79	53	79	95
		(15)	(16)	(19)	(10)	(17)	(15)	(10)	(15)	(18)
P18	Trafford	101	119	78	60	78	78	85	91	67
		(17)	(20)	(13)	(10)	(13)	(13)	(14)	(15)	(11)
P19	Wigan	91	73	43	98	94	97	110	84	84
		(21)	(17)	(10)	(23)	(22)	(23)	(26)	(20)	(20)

CDS - C3C
Trends in selected causes of death in the period 1984-92:
All causes (ICD 001-999) (ages 0-14):
SMRs (observed numbers of deaths in parentheses)
Persons

		1984	1985	1986	1987	1988	1989	1990	1991	1992
	ENGLAND AND WALES	145 (8380)	143 (8522)	142 (8470)	139 (8391)	137 (8467)	129 (7934)	122 (7587)	113 (7188)	100 (6326)
O00	ENGLAND	145 (7920)	143 (8009)	141 (7982)	139 (7915)	138 (8060)	129 (7486)	122 (7191)	114 (6814)	100 (5981)
A00	NORTHERN RHA	142 (515)	139 (512)	142 (526)	126 (460)	130 (480)	128 (465)	122 (445)	137 (511)	105 (396)
B00	YORKSHIRE RHA	158 (680)	165 (716)	162 (709)	160 (705)	144 (651)	141 (631)	138 (622)	132 (610)	100 (463)
C00	TRENT RHA	140 (741)	134 (725)	147 (797)	137 (745)	139 (772)	126 (700)	124 (694)	121 (693)	102 (588)
D00	EAST ANGLIAN RHA	136 (296)	141 (321)	122 (281)	119 (279)	115 (276)	101 (241)	104 (248)	97 (239)	82 (198)
E00	NORTH WEST THAMES RHA	133 (542)	137 (573)	128 (537)	126 (534)	127 (548)	125 (541)	108 (472)	103 (460)	91 (405)
F00	NORTH EAST THAMES RHA	142 (639)	133 (612)	139 (643)	149 (703)	129 (624)	125 (608)	116 (574)	105 (530)	107 (541)
G00	SOUTH EAST THAMES RHA	151 (608)	149 (619)	131 (555)	142 (617)	148 (658)	126 (568)	120 (545)	111 (513)	99 (456)
H00	SOUTH WEST THAMES RHA	133 (415)	140 (447)	128 (412)	134 (436)	130 (439)	119 (398)	109 (370)	90 (316)	84 (296)
J00	WESSEX RHA	140 (460)	132 (449)	131 (447)	133 (465)	130 (465)	127 (456)	114 (413)	98 (359)	89 (321)
K00	OXFORD RHA	129 (377)	128 (387)	131 (401)	134 (416)	130 (416)	126 (404)	116 (373)	107 (353)	96 (321)
L00	SOUTH WESTERN RHA	130 (437)	129 (444)	135 (474)	131 (467)	143 (528)	115 (422)	106 (392)	101 (377)	84 (313)
M00	WEST MIDLANDS RHA	170 (1059)	157 (1008)	153 (974)	148 (956)	156 (1023)	148 (965)	147 (973)	130 (876)	120 (801)
N00	MERSEY RHA	137 (398)	138 (411)	141 (420)	134 (395)	125 (378)	123 (367)	124 (372)	105 (321)	97 (290)
P00	NORTH WESTERN RHA	154 (753)	157 (785)	161 (806)	147 (737)	157 (802)	142 (720)	135 (698)	125 (656)	113 (592)
A01	Hartlepool	204 (24)	140 (17)	134 (16)	182 (22)	140 (17)	176 (21)	189 (22)	116 (14)	108 (13)
A02	North Tees	149 (35)	153 (37)	147 (35)	112 (26)	113 (27)	162 (37)	150 (35)	135 (32)	105 (25)
A03	South Tees	157 (63)	137 (55)	141 (57)	122 (49)	167 (67)	141 (55)	116 (44)	148 (57)	148 (58)
A04	East Cumbria	117 (22)	167 (32)	166 (31)	196 (36)	150 (28)	106 (20)	92 (18)	124 (25)	93 (19)
A05	South Cumbria	157 (27)	127 (23)	121 (22)	223 (40)	101 (19)	103 (19)	104 (19)	131 (25)	155 (30)
A06	West Cumbria	180 (29)	188 (31)	142 (23)	126 (20)	127 (21)	79 (13)	167 (27)	128 (21)	47 (8)

217

CDS - C3C
Trends in selected causes of death in the period 1984-92:
All causes (ICD 001-999) (ages 0-14):
SMRs (observed numbers of deaths in parentheses)
Persons

		1984	1985	1986	1987	1988	1989	1990	1991	1992
A11	Northumberland	117 (39)	131 (45)	119 (40)	121 (40)	102 (34)	115 (38)	111 (37)	109 (37)	123 (42)
A12	Gateshead	121 (29)	170 (39)	169 (41)	98 (23)	148 (35)	181 (43)	108 (25)	132 (31)	84 (20)
A13	Newcastle	162 (51)	102 (33)	127 (43)	122 (41)	133 (44)	119 (38)	120 (39)	175 (58)	113 (38)
A14	North Tyneside	123 (26)	118 (26)	141 (31)	139 (31)	98 (22)	132 (29)	154 (34)	102 (23)	84 (19)
A15	South Tyneside	134 (23)	133 (25)	174 (34)	47 (9)	116 (22)	80 (15)	96 (18)	93 (18)	96 (18)
A16	Sunderland	156 (60)	135 (53)	133 (51)	118 (45)	137 (52)	131 (49)	138 (51)	159 (61)	102 (39)
A30	North Durham	110 (41)	164 (61)	147 (54)	114 (42)	149 (55)	124 (44)	112 (41)	135 (52)	106 (41)
A31	South Durham	144 (46)	109 (35)	148 (48)	113 (36)	112 (37)	136 (44)	106 (35)	169 (57)	77 (26)
B11	East Riding	160 (93)	142 (83)	135 (81)	165 (98)	141 (87)	159 (96)	127 (78)	114 (73)	103 (65)
B16	Grimsby and Scunthorpe	138 (61)	149 (66)	127 (57)	126 (56)	125 (58)	120 (55)	104 (47)	112 (52)	92 (42)
B21	North Yorkshire	146 (103)	140 (102)	122 (89)	121 (90)	142 (107)	108 (83)	112 (88)	99 (78)	66 (52)
B31	Bradford	200 (133)	184 (123)	236 (156)	203 (135)	155 (104)	175 (117)	188 (126)	178 (123)	123 (85)
B51	West Yorkshire	153 (110)	187 (135)	181 (130)	181 (132)	151 (112)	161 (115)	153 (112)	149 (112)	114 (85)
B61	Leeds	149 (122)	171 (140)	172 (144)	163 (137)	140 (121)	134 (116)	138 (119)	148 (132)	105 (93)
B71	Wakefield	157 (58)	175 (67)	135 (52)	151 (57)	155 (62)	127 (49)	132 (52)	100 (40)	100 (41)
C01	North Derbyshire	117 (45)	132 (53)	142 (55)	116 (46)	118 (48)	128 (51)	125 (50)	94 (40)	71 (30)
C02	Southern Derbyshire	136 (83)	143 (88)	138 (87)	127 (79)	164 (105)	131 (84)	109 (72)	109 (74)	96 (65)
C03	Leicestershire	128 (136)	128 (139)	164 (177)	150 (164)	157 (174)	139 (153)	123 (139)	110 (126)	123 (138)
C04	North Lincolnshire	172 (50)	126 (37)	99 (30)	134 (41)	144 (45)	125 (39)	142 (45)	143 (44)	112 (35)
C05	South Lincolnshire	163 (51)	154 (48)	136 (43)	127 (40)	149 (50)	108 (36)	102 (34)	130 (44)	91 (31)
C08	Nottingham	152 (106)	128 (93)	132 (94)	123 (90)	125 (94)	132 (100)	137 (103)	136 (106)	97 (76)
C09	Barnsley	161 (43)	148 (39)	161 (42)	177 (47)	115 (31)	134 (35)	147 (39)	115 (32)	103 (29)

218

CDS - C3C
Trends in selected causes of death in the period 1984-92:
All causes (ICD 001-999) (ages 0-14):
SMRs (observed numbers of deaths in parentheses)
Persons

		1984	1985	1986	1987	1988	1989	1990	1991	1992
C10	Doncaster	120 (43)	118 (43)	132 (49)	118 (44)	138 (52)	109 (40)	131 (49)	123 (47)	108 (41)
C11	Rotherham	156 (48)	144 (46)	192 (61)	132 (41)	130 (42)	151 (48)	104 (34)	158 (52)	97 (32)
C12	Sheffield	123 (69)	138 (78)	146 (84)	147 (85)	109 (64)	116 (68)	121 (71)	133 (81)	111 (68)
C14	North Nottinghamshire	150 (67)	132 (61)	162 (75)	149 (68)	145 (67)	100 (46)	124 (58)	99 (47)	89 (43)
D01	Cambridge	96 (28)	137 (41)	111 (34)	109 (33)	100 (31)	76 (24)	95 (30)	89 (29)	78 (25)
D05	North West Anglia	146 (64)	120 (55)	128 (60)	148 (70)	141 (69)	91 (45)	115 (56)	110 (55)	108 (53)
D06	Norwich	142 (66)	142 (68)	127 (61)	112 (55)	120 (60)	98 (48)	107 (54)	112 (57)	68 (35)
D07	Great Yarmouth and Waveney	164 (35)	180 (39)	105 (?3)	107 (24)	114 (26)	150 (34)	151 (34)	93 (21)	83 (19)
D09	Huntingdon	110 (17)	144 (24)	87 (15)	90 (16)	79 (14)	79 (14)	86 (15)	59 (11)	71 (13)
D11	Suffolk	138 (86)	144 (94)	134 (88)	119 (81)	109 (76)	111 (76)	87 (59)	93 (66)	77 (53)
E01	North Bedfordshire	161 (48)	191 (59)	117 (36)	121 (37)	112 (36)	110 (34)	137 (42)	107 (33)	81 (25)
E02	South Bedfordshire	152 (59)	129 (52)	155 (63)	122 (50)	144 (60)	132 (56)	104 (44)	115 (50)	85 (36)
E05	North West Hertfordshire	93 (28)	129 (38)	120 (36)	151 (46)	112 (35)	115 (35)	84 (26)	109 (35)	65 (21)
E06	South West Hertfordshire	120 (32)	113 (30)	130 (35)	120 (33)	155 (45)	99 (29)	88 (26)	85 (26)	72 (22)
E07	Barnet	101 (34)	133 (45)	124 (44)	114 (41)	131 (46)	100 (36)	86 (31)	70 (26)	80 (30)
E09	Hillingdon	101 (27)	125 (35)	107 (30)	81 (23)	115 (34)	135 (41)	138 (42)	87 (27)	99 (31)
E18	East and North Hertfordshire	153 (84)	99 (55)	114 (64)	98 (56)	117 (69)	100 (58)	79 (47)	69 (42)	68 (41)
E19	Brent and Harrow	121 (68)	154 (89)	150 (88)	150 (88)	131 (78)	121 (71)	113 (67)	122 (73)	114 (68)
E20	Ealing, Hammersmith and Hounslow	140 (110)	150 (124)	118 (96)	144 (117)	138 (112)	161 (131)	120 (100)	119 (101)	106 (92)
E21	Kensington, Chelsea and Westminster	165 (52)	142 (46)	136 (45)	134 (43)	102 (33)	151 (50)	137 (47)	126 (47)	112 (39)
F31	North Essex	127 (121)	114 (109)	111 (106)	135 (134)	105 (106)	112 (113)	99 (100)	70 (72)	87 (89)
F32	South Essex	127 (101)	121 (96)	134 (110)	123 (101)	117 (99)	110 (92)	103 (87)	95 (81)	78 (66)

219

CDS - C3C
Trends in selected causes of death in the period 1984-92:
All causes (ICD 001-999) (ages 0-14):
SMRs (observed numbers of deaths in parentheses)
Persons

		1984	1985	1986	1987	1988	1989	1990	1991	1992
F33	Barking and Havering	133 (58)	124 (55)	160 (72)	140 (62)	121 (57)	103 (49)	100 (47)	116 (55)	108 (51)
F34	Redbridge and Waltham Forest	136 (73)	156 (85)	154 (84)	156 (87)	157 (90)	133 (77)	130 (77)	110 (68)	134 (83)
F35	East London and the City	170 (144)	147 (128)	159 (138)	182 (165)	165 (152)	154 (146)	118 (115)	134 (132)	119 (118)
F36	New River District	142 (79)	146 (86)	120 (70)	151 (89)	115 (69)	119 (73)	129 (80)	103 (66)	120 (78)
F37	Camden and Islington	167 (63)	133 (53)	159 (63)	162 (65)	126 (51)	139 (58)	159 (68)	127 (56)	127 (56)
G04	South East Kent	152 (43)	160 (46)	125 (38)	103 (32)	133 (42)	107 (34)	126 (40)	119 (39)	86 (28)
G05	Canterbury and Thanet	157 (46)	140 (42)	128 (40)	167 (53)	154 (50)	139 (45)	120 (38)	107 (36)	80 (27)
G06	Dartford and Gravesham	131 (34)	156 (42)	124 (34)	157 (43)	115 (32)	93 (26)	118 (33)	106 (30)	88 (25)
G07	Maidstone	146 (32)	115 (26)	182 (41)	138 (32)	157 (38)	174 (42)	133 (33)	118 (29)	85 (21)
G08	Medway	118 (52)	117 (53)	122 (55)	178 (81)	142 (67)	142 (68)	133 (63)	123 (57)	87 (40)
G09	Tunbridge Wells	152 (30)	139 (28)	120 (24)	96 (20)	111 (24)	116 (25)	110 (24)	80 (18)	69 (16)
G10	Bexley	147 (37)	119 (31)	62 (16)	96 (26)	125 (34)	115 (32)	97 (27)	59 (17)	73 (20)
G11	Greenwich	199 (54)	181 (51)	152 (45)	143 (41)	160 (48)	157 (47)	109 (33)	116 (36)	128 (40)
G12	Bromley	92 (27)	107 (33)	99 (31)	124 (39)	114 (38)	67 (22)	106 (35)	107 (35)	75 (25)
G21	East Sussex	151 (97)	175 (116)	116 (77)	133 (94)	152 (112)	126 (93)	108 (80)	113 (85)	95 (72)
G26	South East London	178 (156)	166 (151)	166 (154)	164 (156)	180 (173)	134 (134)	136 (139)	125 (131)	135 (142)
H04	Mid Surrey	121 (19)	85 (14)	102 (16)	130 (21)	98 (17)	117 (20)	133 (23)	62 (11)	28 (5)
H05	East Surrey	123 (23)	142 (28)	135 (26)	149 (30)	128 (27)	120 (25)	95 (20)	38 (8)	102 (22)
H06	Chichester	123 (19)	113 (18)	133 (22)	131 (21)	98 (17)	84 (14)	105 (18)	62 (11)	64 (11)
H07	Mid Downs	117 (38)	156 (50)	138 (45)	92 (30)	131 (45)	95 (32)	80 (27)	107 (37)	65 (23)
H08	Worthing	147 (32)	139 (30)	122 (27)	151 (35)	147 (37)	102 (25)	100 (25)	90 (23)	105 (27)
H09	Croydon	125 (48)	166 (66)	147 (59)	145 (59)	152 (62)	126 (52)	133 (57)	115 (50)	96 (41)

CDS - C3C
Trends in selected causes of death in the period 1984-92:
All causes (ICD 001-999) (ages 0-14):
SMRs (observed numbers of deaths in parentheses)
Persons

		1984	1985	1986	1987	1988	1989	1990	1991	1992
H12	Wandsworth	158 (38)	119 (29)	126 (31)	167 (40)	155 (36)	153 (37)	113 (28)	119 (30)	113 (30)
H13	Merton and Sutton	138 (52)	150 (59)	121 (48)	119 (48)	130 (55)	113 (48)	135 (57)	80 (35)	89 (40)
H14	North West Surrey	150 (61)	132 (55)	132 (55)	150 (63)	123 (55)	109 (48)	118 (53)	80 (37)	63 (29)
H15	South West Surrey	124 (30)	123 (31)	136 (34)	123 (30)	141 (37)	133 (34)	87 (22)	112 (30)	119 (32)
H16	Kingston and Richmond	131 (55)	154 (67)	110 (49)	133 (59)	113 (51)	138 (63)	87 (40)	92 (44)	76 (36)
J10	Dorset	121 (71)	107 (66)	135 (85)	108 (70)	119 (78)	114 (75)	96 (65)	87 (59)	82 (55)
J21	Portsmouth and South East Hampshire	129 (79)	142 (89)	142 (91)	151 (97)	131 (86)	124 (81)	125 (81)	103 (66)	100 (65)
J22	Southampton and South West Hampshire	141 (65)	124 (60)	118 (56)	146 (71)	98 (50)	140 (71)	114 (59)	119 (62)	66 (34)
J23	Winchester	139 (31)	107 (25)	109 (25)	182 (43)	107 (26)	65 (16)	106 (26)	81 (20)	77 (19)
J24	Basingstoke and North Hampshire	128 (57)	162 (73)	130 (59)	119 (55)	149 (69)	125 (59)	106 (51)	92 (45)	79 (38)
J31	Salisbury	167 (22)	141 (19)	188 (25)	183 (25)	141 (19)	177 (24)	148 (21)	120 (17)	117 (16)
J32	Swindon	201 (58)	154 (47)	150 (45)	114 (36)	146 (48)	143 (46)	128 (41)	106 (35)	109 (35)
J33	Bath	146 (62)	108 (47)	102 (44)	104 (47)	135 (62)	132 (62)	102 (49)	89 (42)	110 (52)
J41	Isle of Wight	131 (15)	190 (23)	139 (17)	166 (21)	206 (27)	172 (22)	158 (20)	100 (13)	56 (7)
K11	East Berkshire	133 (59)	137 (62)	117 (53)	125 (57)	136 (64)	125 (60)	92 (44)	86 (43)	98 (48)
K12	West Berkshire	120 (61)	117 (62)	154 (84)	116 (65)	110 (63)	93 (52)	95 (53)	117 (66)	96 (55)
K24	Buckinghamshire	127 (89)	144 (105)	106 (78)	146 (108)	142 (107)	128 (99)	133 (102)	117 (93)	83 (67)
K31	Kettering	152 (45)	153 (48)	164 (51)	200 (64)	160 (53)	136 (46)	113 (38)	134 (46)	106 (37)
K32	Northampton	94 (34)	136 (51)	169 (64)	140 (55)	152 (62)	166 (68)	146 (61)	102 (43)	120 (50)
K41	Oxfordshire	147 (89)	95 (59)	111 (71)	106 (67)	100 (67)	121 (79)	112 (75)	89 (62)	91 (64)
L10	Bristol and District	143 (128)	143 (132)	145 (138)	142 (136)	152 (149)	124 (122)	100 (97)	101 (101)	92 (92)
L21	Cornwall and Isles of Scilly	125 (59)	146 (71)	131 (64)	121 (60)	133 (71)	102 (53)	119 (62)	107 (55)	81 (41)

221

CDS - C3C
Trends in selected causes of death in the period 1984-92:
All causes (ICD 001-999) (ages 0-14):
SMRs (observed numbers of deaths in parentheses)
Persons

		1984	1985	1986	1987	1988	1989	1990	1991	1992
L35	Exeter and North Devon	131 (56)	122 (53)	171 (77)	131 (60)	192 (91)	125 (59)	119 (58)	118 (56)	93 (44)
L36	Plymouth and Torbay	123 (72)	138 (83)	121 (75)	122 (76)	121 (77)	124 (79)	112 (72)	94 (61)	88 (57)
L40	Gloucestershire	116 (65)	115 (67)	136 (79)	147 (87)	129 (79)	110 (68)	107 (67)	105 (67)	74 (47)
L51	Somerset	140 (57)	91 (38)	98 (41)	112 (48)	135 (61)	90 (41)	78 (36)	81 (37)	68 (32)
M02	Herefordshire	191 (31)	173 (29)	125 (21)	103 (18)	153 (28)	99 (18)	136 (25)	125 (24)	58 (11)
M04	Worcester and District	134 (33)	130 (33)	148 (38)	145 (38)	130 (35)	110 (30)	143 (40)	132 (37)	137 (39)
M05	Shropshire	146 (65)	148 (68)	129 (60)	155 (72)	162 (77)	140 (67)	120 (59)	118 (59)	101 (50)
M06	Mid Staffordshire	123 (44)	165 (61)	113 (42)	83 (31)	128 (49)	142 (53)	142 (53)	112 (43)	96 (35)
M07	North Staffordshire	217 (114)	171 (94)	136 (73)	166 (91)	165 (94)	122 (69)	149 (83)	135 (77)	119 (66)
M08	South East Staffordshire	165 (54)	173 (56)	118 (37)	182 (58)	118 (39)	153 (50)	117 (40)	115 (39)	133 (45)
M13	East Birmingham	238 (68)	175 (51)	167 (50)	177 (52)	185 (55)	162 (50)	216 (69)	154 (50)	130 (42)
M14	North Birmingham	177 (31)	163 (29)	136 (25)	143 (27)	149 (28)	129 (24)	139 (26)	115 (22)	114 (22)
M16	West Birmingham	189 (64)	171 (61)	164 (56)	162 (55)	192 (65)	162 (55)	188 (65)	163 (58)	139 (49)
M17	Coventry	197 (78)	145 (59)	173 (71)	149 (61)	184 (75)	165 (67)	143 (59)	179 (73)	135 (54)
M18	Dudley	126 (43)	139 (49)	177 (62)	150 (53)	157 (56)	144 (52)	152 (55)	105 (39)	114 (43)
M19	Sandwell	229 (86)	208 (80)	177 (68)	136 (52)	201 (78)	128 (49)	156 (60)	161 (64)	122 (48)
M20	Solihull	127 (28)	133 (30)	107 (24)	112 (26)	134 (32)	180 (42)	124 (29)	87 (21)	104 (24)
M21	Walsall	191 (61)	138 (46)	192 (63)	150 (50)	172 (57)	162 (53)	127 (43)	128 (44)	109 (38)
M22	Wolverhampton	161 (50)	153 (48)	182 (57)	190 (59)	122 (39)	186 (60)	166 (54)	150 (50)	95 (32)
M25	South Birmingham	190 (105)	182 (106)	188 (108)	166 (95)	187 (108)	188 (107)	170 (99)	152 (91)	154 (93)
M26	North Worcestershire	112 (37)	125 (41)	158 (51)	133 (44)	126 (41)	108 (36)	99 (33)	82 (27)	124 (41)
M28	Warwickshire	127 (67)	124 (67)	126 (68)	133 (74)	121 (67)	148 (83)	143 (81)	101 (58)	123 (69)

CDS - C3C
Trends in selected causes of death in the period 1984-92:
All causes (ICD 001-999) (ages 0-14):
SMRs (observed numbers of deaths in parentheses)
Persons

		1984	1985	1986	1987	1988	1989	1990	1991	1992
N11	Chester	139 (28)	163 (35)	162 (34)	123 (26)	149 (33)	102 (22)	88 (19)	60 (13)	97 (22)
N12	Crewe	149 (43)	153 (45)	104 (31)	160 (46)	93 (28)	105 (32)	128 (40)	119 (38)	82 (26)
N13	Halton	113 (22)	123 (24)	120 (24)	136 (27)	111 (23)	134 (27)	115 (22)	103 (20)	84 (16)
N14	Macclesfield	180 (33)	154 (29)	150 (28)	110 (21)	109 (21)	152 (29)	110 (21)	109 (21)	83 (16)
N15	Warrington	90 (19)	139 (31)	121 (27)	149 (34)	130 (31)	132 (31)	139 (32)	112 (27)	92 (22)
N21	Liverpool	125 (77)	134 (85)	165 (104)	130 (81)	117 (75)	127 (79)	119 (74)	122 (78)	99 (61)
N31	St Helens and Knowsley	137 (64)	126 (59)	120 (55)	121 (55)	156 (70)	118 (52)	132 (59)	85 (39)	101 (45)
N41	Southport and Formby	184 (19)	133 (15)	166 (19)	83 (9)	98 (11)	102 (12)	189 (22)	86 (10)	119 (13)
N42	South Sefton	139 (31)	112 (25)	114 (26)	139 (31)	125 (28)	88 (20)	125 (29)	80 (19)	132 (30)
N51	Wirral	149 (62)	146 (63)	167 (72)	151 (65)	132 (58)	145 (63)	123 (54)	127 (56)	91 (39)
P01	Lancaster	146 (20)	141 (20)	163 (22)	193 (28)	209 (30)	120 (17)	141 (20)	110 (16)	88 (13)
P02	Blackpool, Wyre and Fylde	180 (53)	144 (44)	152 (48)	118 (38)	69 (24)	124 (42)	155 (52)	88 (31)	82 (28)
P03	Preston	142 (23)	153 (25)	192 (31)	165 (28)	169 (29)	143 (25)	104 (19)	201 (36)	127 (23)
P04	Blackburn, Hyndburn and Ribble Valley	184 (66)	168 (61)	166 (60)	145 (52)	160 (58)	116 (43)	129 (47)	127 (47)	133 (49)
P05	Burnley, Pendle and Rossendale	202 (62)	190 (59)	184 (58)	180 (56)	210 (66)	196 (62)	193 (62)	141 (46)	146 (48)
P06	West Lancashire	125 (17)	87 (12)	150 (20)	180 (24)	175 (23)	122 (16)	135 (18)	66 (9)	128 (17)
P07	Chorley and South Ribble	150 (36)	125 (30)	131 (31)	103 (25)	199 (50)	166 (40)	68 (17)	106 (27)	111 (27)
P08	Bolton	148 (51)	176 (61)	173 (60)	165 (55)	187 (65)	138 (47)	119 (42)	141 (50)	195 (67)
P09	Bury	130 (27)	188 (41)	168 (36)	175 (38)	156 (35)	156 (36)	107 (25)	134 (31)	86 (20)
P10	North Manchester	175 (33)	224 (43)	139 (28)	141 (28)	126 (25)	152 (30)	141 (29)	138 (30)	109 (24)
P11	Central Manchester	190 (34)	160 (29)	232 (42)	183 (33)	188 (33)	211 (37)	204 (36)	223 (41)	141 (25)
P12	South Manchester	155 (32)	154 (34)	192 (42)	92 (21)	162 (37)	176 (40)	145 (34)	131 (31)	197 (45)

CDS - C3C
Trends in selected causes of death in the period 1984-92:
All causes (ICD 001-999) (ages 0-14):
SMRs (observed numbers of deaths in parentheses)
Persons

		1984	1985	1986	1987	1988	1989	1990	1991	1992
P13	Oldham	141	158	148	138	194	133	183	132	108
		(41)	(47)	(44)	(40)	(58)	(40)	(55)	(41)	(33)
P14	Rochdale	172	156	180	201	141	157	146	127	106
		(49)	(46)	(53)	(59)	(42)	(45)	(44)	(39)	(32)
P15	Salford	175	177	184	129	145	136	137	101	105
		(50)	(52)	(55)	(38)	(43)	(41)	(41)	(31)	(32)
P16	Stockport	99	137	158	110	137	105	121	115	86
		(33)	(47)	(54)	(38)	(49)	(36)	(41)	(40)	(30)
P17	Tameside and Glossop	133	147	140	178	135	119	123	98	87
		(40)	(46)	(44)	(57)	(44)	(39)	(41)	(33)	(30)
P18	Trafford	148	142	139	142	154	148	124	130	94
		(37)	(37)	(36)	(36)	(41)	(38)	(32)	(35)	(25)
P19	Wigan	129	132	111	112	132	120	111	106	60
		(49)	(51)	(42)	(43)	(50)	(46)	(43)	(42)	(24)

CDS - C3C
Trends in selected causes of death in the period 1984-92:
All causes (ICD 001-999) (ages 15-64):
SMRs (observed numbers of deaths in parentheses)
Persons

		1984	1985	1986	1987	1988	1989	1990	1991	1992
	ENGLAND AND WALES	120 (116449)	120 (114714)	117 (110366)	114 (106903)	111 (104296)	108 (101092)	106 (99251)	103 (96206)	100 (93633)
O00	ENGLAND	120 (109411)	119 (107516)	116 (103479)	113 (100290)	111 (97970)	108 (94967)	106 (93223)	103 (90487)	100 (87962)
A00	NORTHERN RHA	141 (8837)	141 (8698)	135 (8186)	134 (8057)	130 (7740)	129 (7635)	124 (7322)	120 (7072)	117 (6890)
B00	YORKSHIRE RHA	129 (9007)	130 (8935)	123 (8355)	120 (8091)	121 (8111)	114 (7688)	112 (7546)	107 (7201)	105 (7044)
C00	TRENT RHA	121 (11061)	122 (10990)	119 (10570)	115 (10167)	114 (10044)	111 (9768)	106 (9327)	105 (9183)	101 (8846)
D00	EAST ANGLIAN RHA	104 (3859)	99 (3653)	100 (3661)	99 (3661)	95 (3543)	90 (3361)	91 (3422)	88 (3342)	82 (3167)
E00	NORTH WEST THAMES RHA	109 (7164)	108 (6977)	110 (6981)	106 (6658)	104 (6495)	102 (6301)	101 (6265)	100 (6166)	94 (5822)
F00	NORTH EAST THAMES RHA	116 (8322)	115 (8048)	113 (7811)	112 (7647)	109 (7364)	108 (7248)	108 (7191)	104 (6896)	99 (6594)
G00	SOUTH EAST THAMES RHA	112 (7777)	115 (7850)	110 (7386)	112 (7486)	107 (7068)	105 (6934)	107 (7014)	102 (6692)	98 (6450)
H00	SOUTH WEST THAMES RHA	105 (5998)	104 (5850)	99 (5476)	100 (5456)	95 (5152)	93 (5043)	89 (4801)	89 (4817)	87 (4712)
J00	WESSEX RHA	105 (5958)	105 (5947)	102 (5750)	98 (5488)	95 (5386)	92 (5236)	92 (5249)	90 (5121)	88 (5042)
K00	OXFORD RHA	104 (4534)	104 (4509)	101 (4404)	98 (4271)	95 (4173)	94 (4172)	89 (3966)	89 (4008)	89 (4049)
L00	SOUTH WESTERN RHA	110 (6790)	107 (6528)	107 (6497)	100 (6092)	99 (6061)	96 (5926)	96 (5899)	92 (5669)	90 (5557)
M00	WEST MIDLANDS RHA	124 (12784)	123 (12454)	120 (12002)	117 (11555)	115 (11328)	112 (11003)	109 (10750)	104 (10229)	103 (10064)
N00	MERSEY RHA	136 (6496)	137 (6420)	134 (6213)	131 (5975)	128 (5840)	123 (5589)	119 (5389)	118 (5353)	113 (5110)
P00	NORTH WESTERN RHA	140 (10824)	140 (10657)	136 (10187)	131 (9686)	132 (9665)	124 (9063)	125 (9082)	121 (8738)	119 (8615)
A01	Hartlepool	150 (282)	151 (279)	156 (284)	159 (285)	143 (251)	124 (218)	129 (227)	125 (219)	123 (217)
A02	North Tees	134 (450)	134 (447)	119 (393)	139 (457)	131 (433)	122 (403)	119 (390)	125 (409)	122 (402)
A03	South Tees	149 (858)	148 (836)	146 (814)	143 (785)	136 (740)	129 (698)	140 (757)	131 (703)	124 (662)
A04	East Cumbria	129 (462)	130 (463)	120 (422)	115 (400)	115 (404)	117 (414)	109 (388)	102 (362)	98 (348)
A05	South Cumbria	125 (432)	113 (383)	117 (394)	107 (358)	107 (358)	112 (375)	113 (378)	108 (363)	98 (327)
A06	West Cumbria	134 (381)	144 (398)	128 (350)	135 (366)	134 (359)	131 (350)	130 (348)	121 (323)	122 (325)

CDS - C3C
Trends in selected causes of death in the period 1984-92:
All causes (ICD 001-999) (ages 15-64):
SMRs (observed numbers of deaths in parentheses)
Persons

		1984	1985	1986	1987	1988	1989	1990	1991	1992
A11	Northumberland	128	137	123	126	123	115	111	108	100
		(785)	(830)	(739)	(748)	(731)	(688)	(665)	(645)	(596)
A12	Gateshead	155	144	139	147	148	135	128	121	125
		(680)	(618)	(585)	(609)	(607)	(549)	(514)	(484)	(496)
A13	Newcastle	136	149	140	141	144	140	138	130	125
		(760)	(808)	(742)	(733)	(731)	(698)	(681)	(629)	(607)
A14	North Tyneside	136	140	138	130	124	123	116	116	117
		(575)	(575)	(556)	(513)	(484)	(474)	(444)	(438)	(436)
A15	South Tyneside	155	152	147	147	140	150	121	130	130
		(542)	(517)	(488)	(478)	(445)	(472)	(377)	(399)	(394)
A16	Sunderland	153	145	133	136	132	137	127	130	127
		(891)	(834)	(757)	(767)	(738)	(766)	(710)	(723)	(703)
A30	North Durham	143	144	145	130	120	129	125	116	118
		(939)	(930)	(926)	(824)	(756)	(807)	(781)	(728)	(738)
A31	South Durham	139	139	133	134	130	134	123	121	120
		(800)	(780)	(736)	(734)	(703)	(723)	(662)	(647)	(639)
B11	East Riding	122	125	114	119	116	111	105	100	104
		(1198)	(1212)	(1095)	(1132)	(1106)	(1058)	(1009)	(957)	(1003)
B16	Grimsby and Scunthorpe	131	131	123	125	124	115	121	123	104
		(916)	(902)	(839)	(850)	(839)	(784)	(823)	(832)	(708)
B21	North Yorkshire	111	114	107	104	103	101	100	90	92
		(1505)	(1529)	(1428)	(1387)	(1388)	(1366)	(1362)	(1233)	(1278)
B31	Bradford	138	147	134	134	139	122	122	117	113
		(1199)	(1254)	(1128)	(1112)	(1147)	(1003)	(994)	(950)	(911)
B51	West Yorkshire	133	135	135	124	127	121	115	113	110
		(1434)	(1428)	(1410)	(1281)	(1305)	(1244)	(1177)	(1153)	(1119)
B61	Leeds	138	133	128	119	125	118	116	108	106
		(1917)	(1817)	(1718)	(1567)	(1633)	(1538)	(1502)	(1385)	(1371)
B71	Wakefield	137	132	125	130	119	119	117	119	113
		(838)	(793)	(737)	(762)	(693)	(695)	(679)	(691)	(654)
C01	North Derbyshire	118	122	119	108	106	112	109	111	103
		(889)	(898)	(867)	(778)	(761)	(802)	(782)	(796)	(737)
C02	Southern Derbyshire	126	122	121	117	112	115	108	105	100
		(1327)	(1264)	(1241)	(1186)	(1133)	(1159)	(1088)	(1052)	(1013)
C03	Leicestershire	109	112	108	105	105	103	99	99	87
		(1770)	(1803)	(1730)	(1681)	(1669)	(1642)	(1584)	(1579)	(1405)
C04	North Lincolnshire	114	115	108	110	110	104	98	102	105
		(600)	(600)	(567)	(579)	(586)	(555)	(526)	(552)	(576)
C05	South Lincolnshire	111	112	98	107	109	108	100	102	94
		(664)	(667)	(587)	(647)	(667)	(664)	(616)	(632)	(594)
C08	Nottingham	125	122	121	115	120	113	105	102	101
		(1500)	(1444)	(1409)	(1326)	(1369)	(1294)	(1198)	(1161)	(1147)
C09	Barnsley	129	135	138	128	128	123	121	118	114
		(581)	(599)	(600)	(551)	(547)	(523)	(509)	(494)	(478)

226

CDS - C3C
Trends in selected causes of death in the period 1984-92:
All causes (ICD 001-999) (ages 15-64):
SMRs (observed numbers of deaths in parentheses)
Persons

		1984	1985	1986	1987	1988	1989	1990	1991	1992
C10	Doncaster	131 (762)	133 (763)	139 (792)	127 (715)	123 (689)	121 (678)	116 (646)	102 (563)	116 (638)
C11	Rotherham	127 (628)	133 (647)	120 (577)	119 (569)	123 (584)	123 (583)	112 (529)	114 (534)	107 (500)
C12	Sheffield	128 (1389)	124 (1306)	127 (1294)	129 (1292)	119 (1164)	113 (1091)	110 (1049)	106 (1001)	103 (977)
C14	North Nottinghamshire	122 (951)	130 (999)	119 (906)	111 (843)	116 (875)	103 (777)	106 (800)	109 (819)	104 (781)
D01	Cambridge	93 (451)	87 (417)	90 (436)	96 (465)	98 (479)	85 (415)	82 (410)	82 (415)	77 (393)
D05	North West Anglia	117 (850)	113 (816)	115 (833)	109 (797)	101 (749)	100 (750)	101 (762)	100 (756)	93 (710)
D06	Norwich	96 (862)	102 (922)	94 (845)	93 (839)	88 (802)	83 (762)	87 (809)	83 (773)	79 (740)
D07	Great Yarmouth and Waveney	113 (440)	100 (380)	103 (392)	100 (379)	103 (394)	101 (388)	101 (388)	102 (391)	87 (335)
D09	Huntingdon	101 (197)	104 (209)	97 (198)	107 (223)	98 (208)	74 (160)	79 (174)	73 (165)	69 (161)
D11	Suffolk	106 (1059)	92 (909)	97 (957)	97 (958)	92 (911)	89 (886)	88 (879)	83 (842)	81 (828)
E01	North Bedfordshire	109 (482)	104 (454)	112 (491)	100 (439)	95 (418)	95 (421)	93 (412)	97 (433)	90 (409)
E02	South Bedfordshire	107 (528)	111 (541)	116 (563)	108 (520)	106 (513)	100 (483)	106 (516)	107 (525)	94 (466)
E05	North West Hertfordshire	96 (505)	100 (518)	93 (474)	94 (473)	91 (453)	90 (447)	90 (447)	74 (363)	70 (346)
E06	South West Hertfordshire	106 (532)	96 (467)	96 (458)	96 (448)	94 (428)	96 (433)	90 (402)	86 (386)	81 (363)
E07	Barnet	98 (552)	98 (540)	98 (528)	90 (475)	95 (490)	90 (469)	95 (490)	89 (455)	83 (425)
E09	Hillingdon	108 (501)	103 (468)	96 (429)	96 (425)	104 (457)	104 (455)	90 (386)	98 (415)	96 (409)
E18	East and North Hertfordshire	100 (936)	98 (910)	100 (919)	99 (906)	97 (880)	92 (831)	86 (783)	86 (784)	85 (774)
E19	Brent and Harrow	98 (836)	99 (829)	108 (889)	100 (808)	103 (826)	98 (770)	102 (804)	104 (819)	90 (716)
E20	Ealing, Hammersmith and Hounslow	125 (1497)	127 (1484)	125 (1434)	126 (1417)	124 (1371)	119 (1302)	119 (1295)	118 (1270)	116 (1257)
E21	Kensington, Chelsea and Westminster	130 (795)	128 (766)	135 (796)	129 (747)	116 (659)	120 (690)	124 (730)	121 (716)	110 (657)
F31	North Essex	100 (1582)	104 (1631)	102 (1590)	98 (1532)	98 (1536)	89 (1402)	94 (1497)	87 (1390)	84 (1359)
F32	South Essex	111 (1462)	108 (1399)	103 (1331)	107 (1369)	101 (1286)	99 (1255)	99 (1259)	94 (1190)	91 (1162)

227

Public Health Common Data Set

CDS - C3C
Trends in selected causes of death in the period 1984-92:
All causes (ICD 001-999) (ages 15-64):
SMRs (observed numbers of deaths in parentheses)
Persons

		1984	1985	1986	1987	1988	1989	1990	1991	1992
F33	Barking and Havering	109 (913)	111 (902)	113 (902)	111 (860)	106 (807)	102 (758)	100 (730)	102 (729)	90 (634)
F34	Redbridge and Waltham Forest	116 (990)	104 (865)	103 (837)	99 (791)	102 (796)	100 (766)	101 (771)	102 (773)	94 (716)
F35	East London and the City	146 (1518)	139 (1399)	140 (1377)	142 (1374)	136 (1297)	143 (1340)	138 (1280)	140 (1278)	126 (1148)
F36	New River District	113 (987)	109 (933)	108 (903)	108 (887)	98 (792)	105 (837)	101 (806)	99 (797)	95 (767)
F37	Camden and Islington	134 (870)	144 (919)	139 (871)	135 (834)	140 (850)	149 (890)	142 (848)	124 (739)	136 (808)
G04	South East Kent	116 (591)	109 (548)	105 (523)	120 (592)	102 (504)	99 (492)	96 (481)	95 (475)	87 (436)
G05	Canterbury and Thanet	119 (648)	115 (622)	118 (625)	118 (627)	120 (644)	102 (547)	114 (608)	102 (557)	98 (533)
G06	Dartford and Gravesham	120 (523)	114 (490)	108 (460)	106 (451)	109 (459)	98 (412)	106 (447)	95 (402)	93 (398)
G07	Maidstone	116 (423)	110 (396)	96 (345)	113 (409)	98 (359)	94 (346)	95 (351)	89 (332)	82 (310)
G08	Medway	105 (615)	114 (659)	112 (645)	108 (618)	99 (572)	108 (624)	100 (582)	103 (591)	97 (564)
G09	Tunbridge Wells	86 (340)	101 (393)	98 (377)	86 (331)	82 (317)	83 (321)	80 (310)	84 (327)	84 (330)
G10	Bexley	97 (415)	98 (411)	91 (378)	99 (406)	91 (373)	97 (394)	99 (402)	85 (343)	83 (337)
G11	Greenwich	114 (467)	126 (499)	127 (490)	131 (493)	114 (417)	117 (418)	115 (407)	117 (406)	99 (346)
G12	Bromley	96 (602)	93 (566)	88 (528)	91 (537)	90 (522)	83 (477)	85 (490)	88 (499)	78 (442)
G21	East Sussex	102 (1331)	116 (1484)	105 (1326)	102 (1299)	97 (1233)	94 (1206)	98 (1247)	98 (1260)	95 (1219)
G26	South East London	134 (1822)	135 (1782)	131 (1689)	138 (1723)	137 (1668)	142 (1697)	144 (1689)	129 (1500)	133 (1535)
H04	Mid Surrey	108 (392)	97 (344)	87 (302)	95 (326)	88 (298)	87 (294)	80 (269)	83 (279)	79 (269)
H05	East Surrey	102 (394)	110 (416)	100 (375)	94 (347)	103 (375)	89 (327)	86 (314)	82 (302)	83 (307)
H06	Chichester	106 (364)	107 (364)	93 (316)	93 (319)	92 (319)	94 (324)	88 (302)	83 (286)	82 (281)
H07	Mid Downs	95 (499)	101 (528)	89 (467)	97 (507)	94 (492)	88 (460)	88 (460)	86 (451)	80 (422)
H08	Worthing	99 (452)	105 (472)	102 (454)	97 (432)	95 (424)	99 (444)	82 (369)	95 (427)	89 (402)
H09	Croydon	116 (708)	112 (667)	108 (634)	100 (581)	103 (585)	90 (510)	86 (489)	101 (566)	89 (503)

228

CDS - C3C
Trends in selected causes of death in the period 1984-92:
All causes (ICD 001-999) (ages 15-64):
SMRs (observed numbers of deaths in parentheses)
Persons

		1984	1985	1986	1987	1988	1989	1990	1991	1992
H12	Wandsworth	137 (467)	129 (431)	127 (412)	134 (428)	111 (347)	123 (381)	128 (392)	113 (343)	134 (407)
H13	Merton and Sutton	103 (674)	97 (622)	97 (612)	110 (683)	97 (595)	97 (590)	95 (575)	95 (570)	89 (535)
H14	North West Surrey	97 (740)	92 (693)	92 (688)	94 (692)	75 (554)	89 (650)	81 (595)	78 (574)	77 (572)
H15	South West Surrey	92 (428)	98 (448)	89 (403)	86 (386)	95 (423)	82 (367)	82 (371)	76 (347)	75 (341)
H16	Kingston and Richmond	108 (880)	109 (865)	105 (813)	100 (755)	100 (740)	94 (696)	90 (665)	92 (672)	92 (673)
J10	Dorset	105 (1297)	105 (1298)	104 (1283)	94 (1165)	91 (1130)	88 (1091)	90 (1126)	84 (1051)	87 (1091)
J21	Portsmouth and South East Hampshire	111 (1085)	114 (1099)	108 (1038)	107 (1027)	96 (918)	97 (928)	99 (955)	96 (932)	93 (907)
J22	Southampton and South West Hampshire	102 (820)	107 (854)	97 (770)	96 (760)	104 (821)	97 (766)	102 (805)	99 (778)	97 (763)
J23	Winchester	105 (413)	94 (369)	106 (413)	97 (380)	93 (368)	87 (346)	76 (308)	75 (308)	81 (336)
J24	Basingstoke and North Hampshire	107 (648)	103 (625)	97 (587)	95 (584)	89 (554)	91 (575)	87 (552)	88 (570)	89 (585)
J31	Salisbury	101 (242)	103 (245)	89 (211)	96 (226)	92 (218)	83 (197)	88 (210)	85 (205)	89 (216)
J32	Swindon	110 (454)	113 (465)	113 (467)	107 (444)	100 (417)	94 (394)	89 (376)	97 (410)	82 (349)
J33	Bath	97 (736)	98 (729)	97 (718)	90 (670)	93 (695)	94 (704)	90 (668)	84 (629)	77 (586)
J41	Isle of Wight	107 (263)	108 (263)	109 (263)	95 (232)	107 (265)	95 (235)	102 (249)	98 (238)	86 (209)
K11	East Berkshire	108 (741)	114 (772)	100 (667)	98 (648)	102 (666)	100 (657)	92 (608)	92 (612)	93 (625)
K12	West Berkshire	102 (782)	94 (728)	101 (786)	99 (774)	89 (701)	87 (681)	84 (665)	88 (708)	80 (654)
K24	Buckinghamshire	98 (986)	98 (983)	98 (989)	89 (911)	93 (953)	90 (941)	81 (856)	80 (858)	85 (925)
K31	Kettering	110 (516)	119 (551)	124 (577)	107 (497)	118 (550)	116 (546)	104 (492)	108 (514)	99 (472)
K32	Northampton	113 (596)	112 (584)	106 (557)	106 (561)	100 (532)	100 (539)	101 (549)	97 (532)	98 (542)
K41	Oxfordshire	99 (913)	97 (891)	90 (828)	96 (880)	84 (771)	88 (808)	85 (796)	83 (784)	87 (831)
L10	Bristol and District	109 (1725)	109 (1691)	107 (1649)	101 (1540)	102 (1545)	97 (1474)	100 (1511)	94 (1425)	87 (1322)
L21	Cornwall and Isles of Scilly	108 (967)	108 (968)	106 (953)	97 (875)	101 (923)	94 (873)	92 (856)	87 (816)	91 (855)

CDS - C3C
Trends in selected causes of death in the period 1984-92:
All causes (ICD 001-999) (ages 15-64):
SMRs (observed numbers of deaths in parentheses)
Persons

		1984	1985	1986	1987	1988	1989	1990	1991	1992
L35	Exeter and North Devon	110 (927)	99 (832)	103 (866)	98 (823)	94 (802)	95 (815)	89 (776)	88 (769)	89 (782)
L36	Plymouth and Torbay	115 (1239)	109 (1166)	114 (1211)	111 (1179)	103 (1097)	98 (1044)	97 (1037)	99 (1060)	91 (981)
L40	Gloucestershire	110 (1113)	105 (1055)	103 (1028)	94 (935)	98 (981)	98 (984)	97 (974)	89 (891)	92 (931)
L51	Somerset	106 (819)	106 (816)	103 (790)	96 (740)	92 (713)	94 (736)	95 (745)	90 (708)	86 (686)
M02	Herefordshire	106 (326)	104 (317)	112 (340)	98 (302)	100 (309)	96 (300)	90 (282)	80 (252)	86 (273)
M04	Worcester and District	105 (487)	109 (502)	102 (471)	105 (489)	98 (458)	86 (407)	91 (433)	85 (406)	90 (435)
M05	Shropshire	114 (831)	119 (869)	110 (805)	107 (793)	107 (806)	96 (729)	97 (743)	93 (718)	94 (734)
M06	Mid Staffordshire	114 (671)	115 (672)	107 (627)	105 (616)	102 (606)	101 (603)	103 (618)	95 (579)	91 (557)
M07	North Staffordshire	142 (1373)	134 (1270)	134 (1253)	137 (1258)	127 (1155)	115 (1042)	126 (1137)	119 (1064)	114 (1015)
M08	South East Staffordshire	113 (515)	121 (551)	115 (525)	106 (491)	110 (514)	115 (545)	103 (495)	102 (493)	91 (447)
M13	East Birmingham	148 (615)	143 (573)	131 (502)	121 (449)	130 (470)	136 (478)	137 (472)	125 (417)	114 (376)
M14	North Birmingham	107 (360)	122 (404)	100 (326)	109 (353)	109 (349)	106 (340)	103 (326)	103 (326)	98 (308)
M16	West Birmingham	151 (591)	144 (550)	137 (510)	149 (542)	143 (509)	141 (494)	126 (441)	136 (472)	134 (459)
M17	Coventry	141 (882)	131 (795)	122 (722)	121 (698)	128 (723)	131 (721)	117 (638)	111 (593)	114 (603)
M18	Dudley	119 (738)	123 (747)	112 (676)	113 (677)	110 (663)	106 (638)	102 (615)	96 (582)	94 (571)
M19	Sandwell	138 (873)	140 (862)	134 (803)	132 (774)	132 (761)	135 (765)	124 (693)	119 (659)	120 (656)
M20	Solihull	99 (398)	96 (387)	96 (383)	100 (398)	94 (378)	93 (374)	91 (365)	90 (362)	81 (326)
M21	Walsall	135 (726)	125 (658)	140 (728)	127 (653)	122 (624)	135 (690)	130 (664)	117 (599)	110 (564)
M22	Wolverhampton	125 (652)	128 (655)	135 (672)	122 (596)	124 (598)	122 (582)	120 (562)	120 (556)	114 (525)
M25	South Birmingham	131 (1089)	129 (1044)	133 (1049)	126 (970)	125 (944)	120 (894)	123 (910)	114 (835)	118 (863)
M26	North Worcestershire	112 (542)	106 (514)	105 (510)	98 (481)	106 (523)	99 (493)	93 (469)	86 (439)	81 (420)
M28	Warwickshire	117 (1115)	115 (1084)	117 (1100)	108 (1015)	100 (938)	97 (908)	95 (887)	94 (877)	99 (932)

CDS - C3C
Trends in selected causes of death in the period 1984-92:
All causes (ICD 001-999) (ages 15-64):
SMRs (observed numbers of deaths in parentheses)
Persons

		1984	1985	1986	1987	1988	1989	1990	1991	1992
N11	Chester	122 (427)	128 (447)	116 (404)	117 (403)	123 (423)	112 (382)	106 (363)	110 (379)	102 (353)
N12	Crewe	121 (595)	113 (546)	118 (565)	107 (513)	113 (537)	116 (558)	101 (489)	103 (498)	100 (487)
N13	Halton	137 (359)	137 (356)	129 (332)	131 (335)	126 (323)	115 (296)	119 (305)	126 (322)	96 (245)
N14	Macclesfield	104 (375)	107 (383)	113 (402)	98 (346)	104 (368)	96 (340)	91 (324)	96 (344)	90 (323)
N15	Warrington	134 (450)	135 (448)	130 (429)	136 (455)	125 (421)	114 (386)	123 (419)	116 (397)	117 (401)
N21	Liverpool	151 (1481)	161 (1538)	157 (1456)	158 (1428)	153 (1357)	153 (1338)	140 (1215)	139 (1196)	143 (1218)
N31	St Helens and Knowsley	158 (1083)	152 (1018)	153 (1012)	148 (962)	140 (902)	136 (875)	135 (863)	120 (760)	115 (729)
N41	Southport and Formby	118 (274)	125 (291)	125 (286)	109 (250)	114 (262)	108 (251)	93 (217)	98 (228)	91 (213)
N42	South Sefton	138 (504)	146 (523)	133 (471)	135 (472)	130 (451)	121 (419)	118 (406)	127 (435)	114 (389)
N51	Wirral	135 (948)	126 (870)	126 (856)	120 (811)	119 (796)	111 (744)	118 (788)	119 (794)	113 (752)
P01	Lancaster	129 (318)	146 (356)	126 (305)	110 (264)	119 (286)	121 (289)	121 (289)	109 (261)	97 (231)
P02	Blackpool,Wyre and Fylde	127 (866)	132 (890)	129 (859)	125 (826)	123 (814)	130 (859)	127 (834)	114 (751)	108 (714)
P03	Preston	139 (345)	149 (361)	146 (349)	142 (337)	132 (311)	119 (278)	132 (308)	140 (321)	136 (312)
P04	Blackburn, Hyndburn and Ribble Valley	141 (737)	141 (723)	133 (669)	141 (696)	142 (692)	126 (612)	122 (588)	121 (577)	118 (563)
P05	Burnley, Pendle and Rossendale	145 (642)	135 (584)	131 (561)	133 (558)	135 (563)	121 (513)	132 (559)	121 (510)	117 (491)
P06	West Lancashire	115 (228)	129 (255)	120 (238)	118 (236)	121 (243)	109 (220)	110 (225)	100 (206)	99 (205)
P07	Chorley and South Ribble	123 (435)	134 (473)	123 (435)	114 (404)	111 (397)	110 (396)	98 (359)	91 (333)	97 (356)
P08	Bolton	148 (735)	152 (738)	141 (675)	131 (622)	129 (607)	126 (589)	124 (578)	124 (575)	121 (562)
P09	Bury	127 (418)	132 (429)	124 (397)	114 (366)	116 (371)	112 (361)	115 (372)	115 (373)	99 (323)
P10	North Manchester	187 (539)	188 (521)	166 (444)	168 (436)	187 (467)	167 (405)	169 (407)	160 (380)	180 (419)
P11	Central Manchester	158 (359)	188 (408)	168 (355)	158 (326)	166 (332)	156 (305)	166 (317)	162 (306)	169 (310)
P12	South Manchester	152 (524)	128 (426)	151 (493)	133 (420)	148 (455)	137 (412)	132 (388)	129 (368)	133 (369)

CDS - C3C
Trends in selected causes of death in the period 1984-92:
All causes (ICD 001-999) (ages 15-64):
SMRs (observed numbers of deaths in parentheses)
Persons

		1984	1985	1986	1987	1988	1989	1990	1991	1992
P13	Oldham	139	147	146	141	139	123	123	130	132
		(579)	(599)	(585)	(556)	(542)	(477)	(474)	(498)	(510)
P14	Rochdale	157	141	138	135	136	120	128	132	132
		(629)	(554)	(539)	(520)	(519)	(457)	(487)	(497)	(497)
P15	Salford	164	149	154	142	161	147	150	144	153
		(798)	(705)	(708)	(636)	(703)	(630)	(632)	(594)	(629)
P16	Stockport	118	123	113	113	109	101	99	100	104
		(671)	(688)	(626)	(623)	(599)	(555)	(541)	(546)	(572)
P17	Tameside and Glossop	132	141	137	139	131	127	136	120	113
		(629)	(656)	(627)	(628)	(588)	(567)	(603)	(530)	(500)
P18	Trafford	120	108	132	111	111	109	115	107	99
		(521)	(462)	(553)	(460)	(454)	(443)	(464)	(428)	(396)
P19	Wigan	146	145	136	138	129	124	117	122	115
		(851)	(829)	(769)	(772)	(722)	(695)	(657)	(684)	(656)

CDS - C3C
Trends in selected causes of death in the period 1984-92:
All causes (ICD 001-999) (ages 65-74):
SMRs (observed numbers of deaths in parentheses)
Persons

		1984	1985	1986	1987	1988	1989	1990	1991	1992
	ENGLAND AND WALES	114 (141087)	115 (144516)	112 (142329)	109 (138416)	109 (136973)	108 (134478)	104 (130918)	103 (130959)	100 (129286)
O00	ENGLAND	114 (132151)	114 (135409)	112 (133320)	109 (129613)	109 (128176)	108 (125544)	104 (122301)	102 (122294)	100 (120754)
A00	NORTHERN RHA	135 (10162)	132 (10183)	130 (10118)	128 (10070)	129 (10088)	128 (9988)	123 (9791)	123 (9947)	119 (9845)
B00	YORKSHIRE RHA	121 (10748)	122 (11044)	120 (10873)	117 (10592)	116 (10434)	114 (10180)	112 (10078)	110 (10000)	103 (9601)
C00	TRENT RHA	116 (13197)	119 (13805)	113 (13313)	113 (13384)	112 (13260)	112 (13180)	105 (12625)	105 (12870)	104 (12888)
D00	EAST ANGLIAN RHA	102 (5255)	101 (5299)	99 (5254)	95 (5098)	94 (5046)	93 (4980)	89 (4808)	88 (4878)	87 (4889)
E00	NORTH WEST THAMES RHA	104 (8109)	107 (8411)	103 (8087)	100 (7773)	102 (7701)	99 (7253)	97 (7097)	93 (6846)	94 (6921)
F00	NORTH EAST THAMES RHA	110 (9825)	113 (10201)	109 (9845)	108 (9698)	106 (9277)	105 (8992)	102 (8791)	101 (8696)	98 (8609)
G00	SOUTH EAST THAMES RHA	107 (10413)	108 (10561)	107 (10535)	103 (10018)	101 (9669)	100 (9335)	98 (9205)	96 (9006)	95 (9001)
H00	SOUTH WEST THAMES RHA	101 (7672)	101 (7760)	100 (7655)	93 (7050)	94 (7012)	92 (6682)	92 (6651)	89 (6428)	86 (6303)
J00	WESSEX RHA	98 (7620)	98 (7835)	96 (7793)	93 (7552)	93 (7554)	95 (7617)	89 (7254)	91 (7508)	87 (7302)
K00	OXFORD RHA	105 (5143)	105 (5314)	101 (5211)	98 (5087)	99 (5106)	98 (5001)	93 (4852)	94 (4939)	90 (4872)
L00	SOUTH WESTERN RHA	102 (9077)	99 (8915)	100 (9114)	97 (8891)	96 (8737)	95 (8576)	92 (8394)	90 (8316)	87 (8269)
M00	WEST MIDLANDS RHA	121 (14611)	121 (15101)	120 (15210)	115 (14644)	115 (14705)	115 (14639)	110 (14162)	109 (14234)	104 (13857)
N00	MERSEY RHA	128 (7363)	131 (7635)	125 (7367)	123 (7236)	120 (7023)	123 (7109)	117 (6838)	117 (6954)	113 (6800)
P00	NORTH WESTERN RHA	130 (12956)	132 (13345)	128 (12945)	125 (12520)	127 (12564)	123 (12012)	120 (11755)	118 (11672)	115 (11597)
A01	Hartlepool	140 (286)	148 (308)	137 (289)	138 (293)	150 (317)	136 (289)	141 (309)	125 (283)	127 (296)
A02	North Tees	128 (423)	132 (453)	116 (411)	130 (471)	128 (470)	130 (481)	121 (463)	131 (517)	127 (517)
A03	South Tees	134 (823)	136 (866)	131 (854)	132 (875)	139 (926)	127 (851)	135 (924)	125 (877)	122 (873)
A04	East Cumbria	121 (568)	120 (574)	119 (576)	113 (549)	120 (580)	117 (557)	108 (524)	108 (534)	106 (535)
A05	South Cumbria	117 (574)	116 (578)	112 (568)	108 (543)	104 (518)	111 (548)	95 (471)	104 (519)	102 (510)
A06	West Cumbria	136 (444)	132 (445)	117 (401)	135 (468)	130 (449)	129 (448)	127 (449)	127 (460)	115 (424)

CDS - C3C
Trends in selected causes of death in the period 1984-92:
All causes (ICD 001-999) (ages 65-74):
SMRs (observed numbers of deaths in parentheses)
Persons

		1984	1985	1986	1987	1988	1989	1990	1991	1992
A11	Northumberland	140 (1090)	129 (1030)	132 (1062)	130 (1048)	125 (1002)	116 (930)	107 (885)	112 (948)	110 (947)
A12	Gateshead	150 (789)	135 (721)	136 (737)	138 (750)	138 (747)	147 (788)	124 (674)	136 (748)	131 (733)
A13	Newcastle	133 (984)	136 (1016)	134 (1005)	123 (911)	123 (895)	133 (950)	125 (895)	130 (935)	120 (867)
A14	North Tyneside	138 (706)	140 (738)	124 (668)	129 (699)	124 (677)	125 (682)	128 (710)	122 (698)	114 (658)
A15	South Tyneside	135 (545)	133 (556)	143 (609)	135 (580)	142 (616)	140 (608)	121 (542)	122 (565)	126 (597)
A16	Sunderland	144 (931)	142 (938)	127 (848)	130 (879)	135 (908)	133 (897)	142 (970)	130 (909)	131 (947)
A30	North Durham	131 (1019)	132 (1040)	141 (1122)	134 (1067)	131 (1033)	133 (1046)	129 (1028)	124 (1019)	122 (1026)
A31	South Durham	140 (980)	128 (920)	133 (968)	128 (937)	129 (950)	125 (913)	127 (947)	123 (935)	118 (915)
B11	East Riding	116 (1497)	116 (1515)	117 (1541)	114 (1502)	114 (1490)	115 (1489)	113 (1470)	105 (1388)	97 (1321)
B16	Grimsby and Scunthorpe	126 (1040)	125 (1067)	112 (974)	122 (1065)	114 (999)	115 (1008)	116 (1037)	112 (1026)	105 (979)
B21	North Yorkshire	108 (2010)	109 (2051)	106 (2004)	104 (1968)	101 (1892)	99 (1847)	99 (1863)	96 (1850)	90 (1776)
B31	Bradford	121 (1261)	131 (1382)	129 (1364)	123 (1294)	122 (1278)	124 (1292)	117 (1225)	121 (1288)	111 (1214)
B51	West Yorkshire	134 (1848)	126 (1763)	129 (1814)	124 (1742)	125 (1727)	126 (1712)	115 (1577)	112 (1552)	108 (1512)
B61	Leeds	120 (2120)	128 (2287)	121 (2172)	116 (2070)	117 (2051)	114 (1950)	114 (1959)	112 (1945)	105 (1852)
B71	Wakefield	136 (972)	133 (979)	135 (1004)	127 (951)	134 (997)	118 (882)	125 (947)	123 (951)	121 (947)
C01	North Derbyshire	112 (1043)	117 (1124)	112 (1091)	113 (1113)	114 (1117)	102 (999)	103 (1033)	100 (1024)	104 (1084)
C02	Southern Derbyshire	121 (1594)	122 (1633)	116 (1575)	114 (1556)	116 (1588)	114 (1552)	112 (1535)	108 (1521)	104 (1471)
C03	Leicestershire	107 (2070)	105 (2080)	103 (2053)	105 (2114)	101 (2010)	105 (2099)	92 (1868)	94 (1951)	93 (1964)
C04	North Lincolnshire	117 (814)	119 (859)	103 (763)	105 (801)	109 (842)	106 (821)	100 (800)	98 (815)	99 (837)
C05	South Lincolnshire	106 (879)	110 (928)	103 (887)	108 (943)	102 (898)	102 (900)	100 (907)	98 (919)	95 (913)
C08	Nottingham	118 (1718)	122 (1821)	114 (1710)	112 (1692)	117 (1745)	110 (1642)	104 (1571)	105 (1621)	102 (1605)
C09	Barnsley	125 (690)	128 (718)	131 (745)	123 (704)	121 (686)	124 (704)	122 (701)	121 (710)	125 (738)

234

CDS - C3C
Trends in selected causes of death in the period 1984-92:
All causes (ICD 001-999) (ages 65-74):
SMRs (observed numbers of deaths in parentheses)
Persons

		1984	1985	1986	1987	1988	1989	1990	1991	1992
C10	Doncaster	122 (798)	132 (885)	120 (825)	117 (818)	122 (853)	121 (854)	111 (803)	115 (851)	114 (876)
C11	Rotherham	121 (678)	125 (723)	129 (761)	127 (760)	124 (743)	129 (775)	117 (716)	117 (732)	109 (696)
C12	Sheffield	117 (1762)	127 (1932)	120 (1829)	117 (1764)	117 (1730)	122 (1765)	110 (1581)	117 (1694)	113 (1622)
C14	North Nottinghamshire	126 (1151)	117 (1102)	112 (1074)	116 (1119)	108 (1048)	110 (1069)	112 (1110)	102 (1032)	105 (1082)
D01	Cambridge	95 (592)	90 (572)	95 (608)	96 (616)	96 (604)	86 (536)	86 (544)	82 (529)	82 (542)
D05	North West Anglia	108 (1040)	111 (1095)	106 (1070)	105 (1081)	99 (1036)	104 (1089)	90 (965)	92 (1018)	91 (1032)
D06	Norwich	97 (1310)	97 (1335)	91 (1278)	90 (1265)	89 (1247)	85 (1190)	83 (1181)	83 (1205)	84 (1241)
D07	Great Yarmouth and Waveney	101 (607)	99 (601)	99 (605)	92 (569)	94 (580)	94 (579)	95 (594)	92 (580)	92 (598)
D09	Huntingdon	112 (248)	105 (243)	110 (262)	103 (249)	105 (253)	94 (227)	90 (220)	99 (248)	81 (207)
D11	Suffolk	107 (1458)	104 (1453)	101 (1431)	92 (1318)	93 (1326)	96 (1359)	92 (1304)	90 (1298)	86 (1269)
E01	North Bedfordshire	105 (516)	108 (548)	107 (554)	92 (481)	103 (535)	103 (532)	96 (503)	94 (495)	93 (500)
E02	South Bedfordshire	110 (568)	112 (594)	106 (567)	113 (603)	112 (594)	99 (516)	106 (553)	103 (543)	103 (552)
E05	North West Hertfordshire	101 (554)	103 (584)	97 (558)	99 (579)	100 (581)	98 (564)	101 (586)	84 (498)	87 (526)
E06	South West Hertfordshire	99 (601)	102 (629)	100 (625)	95 (591)	97 (589)	99 (589)	99 (587)	94 (559)	90 (545)
E07	Barnet	91 (710)	102 (787)	93 (711)	90 (670)	95 (676)	93 (649)	92 (630)	89 (596)	84 (566)
E09	Hillingdon	107 (596)	101 (569)	100 (562)	101 (559)	101 (546)	92 (492)	95 (505)	90 (469)	96 (506)
E18	East and North Hertfordshire	100 (993)	107 (1102)	99 (1045)	98 (1043)	100 (1054)	94 (984)	89 (947)	86 (929)	90 (992)
E19	Brent and Harrow	103 (1092)	100 (1055)	100 (1035)	95 (951)	99 (938)	94 (853)	92 (816)	83 (725)	90 (784)
E20	Ealing, Hammersmith and Hounslow	113 (1656)	117 (1696)	114 (1630)	111 (1546)	106 (1425)	107 (1377)	105 (1332)	113 (1413)	102 (1278)
E21	Kensington, Chelsea and Westminster	110 (823)	113 (847)	108 (800)	104 (750)	110 (763)	103 (697)	95 (638)	91 (619)	99 (672)
F31	North Essex	101 (2108)	101 (2150)	101 (2184)	100 (2175)	97 (2108)	93 (1996)	93 (2009)	89 (1954)	85 (1896)
F32	South Essex	109 (1709)	113 (1820)	105 (1732)	105 (1748)	102 (1700)	99 (1639)	102 (1709)	97 (1659)	96 (1666)

CDS - C3C
Trends in selected causes of death in the period 1984-92:
All causes (ICD 001-999) (ages 65-74):
SMRs (observed numbers of deaths in parentheses)
Persons

		1984	1985	1986	1987	1988	1989	1990	1991	1992
F33	Barking and Havering	108 (1047)	112 (1120)	110 (1111)	106 (1078)	104 (1050)	115 (1142)	100 (1011)	104 (1063)	105 (1082)
F34	Redbridge and Waltham Forest	105 (1206)	111 (1279)	104 (1175)	101 (1105)	102 (1075)	101 (1018)	104 (1031)	102 (1004)	100 (977)
F35	East London and the City	127 (1595)	131 (1634)	124 (1525)	132 (1588)	128 (1482)	124 (1394)	119 (1327)	121 (1328)	120 (1337)
F36	New River District	113 (1230)	112 (1208)	111 (1170)	108 (1092)	103 (994)	106 (986)	100 (929)	97 (903)	94 (878)
F37	Camden and Islington	115 (930)	123 (990)	119 (948)	117 (912)	116 (868)	112 (817)	107 (775)	108 (785)	106 (773)
G04	South East Kent	104 (790)	105 (814)	110 (855)	96 (749)	97 (751)	95 (728)	93 (717)	89 (691)	93 (730)
G05	Canterbury and Thanet	112 (1064)	103 (1002)	109 (1061)	107 (1039)	104 (1009)	95 (907)	94 (903)	93 (916)	91 (893)
G06	Dartford and Gravesham	113 (530)	126 (603)	121 (587)	109 (532)	111 (539)	110 (530)	107 (524)	98 (487)	103 (526)
G07	Maidstone	111 (470)	115 (495)	108 (471)	106 (463)	101 (438)	97 (417)	95 (415)	97 (428)	87 (391)
G08	Medway	118 (809)	115 (806)	115 (814)	114 (813)	108 (765)	107 (749)	110 (778)	103 (720)	107 (752)
G09	Tunbridge Wells	93 (469)	95 (481)	104 (529)	93 (471)	94 (470)	88 (434)	85 (421)	88 (445)	87 (444)
G10	Bexley	108 (545)	106 (546)	104 (540)	103 (534)	98 (498)	98 (487)	95 (474)	101 (508)	97 (497)
G11	Greenwich	118 (618)	120 (636)	121 (643)	117 (616)	111 (567)	106 (528)	113 (562)	109 (538)	109 (540)
G12	Bromley	103 (781)	94 (724)	100 (780)	89 (695)	95 (729)	94 (708)	93 (698)	81 (618)	83 (640)
G21	East Sussex	98 (2371)	101 (2463)	95 (2297)	94 (2248)	90 (2099)	90 (2045)	87 (1970)	87 (1956)	84 (1905)
G26	South East London	114 (1966)	116 (1991)	116 (1958)	113 (1858)	114 (1804)	119 (1802)	117 (1743)	115 (1699)	114 (1683)
H04	Mid Surrey	101 (482)	107 (512)	103 (491)	95 (449)	91 (420)	87 (396)	87 (396)	84 (388)	82 (383)
H05	East Surrey	96 (465)	96 (469)	97 (473)	94 (454)	90 (428)	100 (464)	93 (432)	87 (406)	83 (393)
H06	Chichester	92 (593)	95 (620)	88 (578)	77 (502)	84 (539)	92 (582)	84 (526)	79 (495)	85 (539)
H07	Mid Downs	108 (625)	100 (596)	98 (600)	96 (594)	97 (601)	91 (565)	93 (588)	89 (575)	87 (579)
H08	Worthing	92 (840)	96 (877)	92 (845)	90 (819)	92 (810)	88 (759)	90 (771)	86 (726)	78 (668)
H09	Croydon	115 (790)	113 (778)	106 (730)	100 (683)	102 (676)	99 (642)	97 (634)	104 (677)	94 (617)

236

CDS - C3C
Trends in selected causes of death in the period 1984-92:
All causes (ICD 001-999) (ages 65-74):
SMRs (observed numbers of deaths in parentheses)
Persons

		1984	1985	1986	1987	1988	1989	1990	1991	1992
H12	Wandsworth	122 (541)	121 (523)	123 (513)	111 (442)	128 (485)	116 (416)	118 (410)	112 (381)	119 (399)
H13	Merton and Sutton	101 (862)	95 (807)	101 (853)	100 (825)	99 (791)	94 (730)	94 (726)	91 (699)	91 (701)
H14	North West Surrey	100 (831)	99 (846)	105 (906)	87 (748)	91 (777)	92 (779)	91 (775)	84 (720)	80 (702)
H15	South West Surrey	89 (526)	91 (546)	94 (567)	85 (505)	81 (477)	86 (496)	80 (464)	77 (449)	71 (420)
H16	Kingston and Richmond	99 (1117)	105 (1186)	98 (1099)	94 (1029)	96 (1008)	84 (853)	92 (929)	92 (912)	91 (902)
J10	Dorset	90 (1929)	89 (1946)	88 (1933)	89 (1962)	84 (1820)	88 (1887)	83 (1807)	83 (1824)	80 (1783)
J21	Portsmouth and South East Hampshire	105 (1282)	102 (1284)	101 (1294)	93 (1201)	99 (1278)	100 (1281)	96 (1244)	97 (1284)	96 (1285)
J22	Southampton and South West Hampshire	101 (1103)	98 (1100)	100 (1144)	96 (1101)	97 (1107)	94 (1071)	92 (1053)	92 (1080)	86 (1023)
J23	Winchester	107 (497)	104 (500)	96 (467)	97 (480)	98 (482)	97 (474)	91 (450)	96 (483)	89 (461)
J24	Basingstoke and North Hampshire	105 (646)	108 (690)	101 (655)	94 (614)	90 (595)	95 (621)	91 (603)	89 (603)	89 (617)
J31	Salisbury	83 (279)	96 (329)	91 (316)	94 (327)	96 (332)	82 (280)	90 (314)	81 (288)	80 (289)
J32	Swindon	99 (456)	110 (521)	103 (504)	96 (474)	105 (524)	114 (572)	98 (500)	108 (567)	94 (511)
J33	Bath	99 (1012)	99 (1025)	99 (1036)	93 (980)	92 (963)	95 (988)	89 (929)	89 (948)	85 (918)
J41	Isle of Wight	95 (416)	99 (440)	100 (444)	94 (413)	104 (453)	103 (443)	82 (354)	99 (431)	95 (415)
K11	East Berkshire	113 (808)	108 (801)	100 (752)	104 (785)	99 (742)	99 (741)	94 (706)	102 (782)	93 (732)
K12	West Berkshire	104 (861)	104 (891)	104 (899)	92 (801)	95 (823)	96 (818)	89 (758)	83 (716)	84 (748)
K24	Buckinghamshire	107 (1118)	109 (1173)	96 (1058)	97 (1087)	98 (1092)	98 (1097)	94 (1070)	90 (1040)	94 (1112)
K31	Kettering	105 (622)	117 (705)	113 (692)	105 (650)	107 (657)	113 (695)	98 (613)	111 (706)	91 (590)
K32	Northampton	103 (663)	104 (690)	113 (769)	106 (732)	107 (742)	96 (664)	102 (716)	103 (731)	99 (716)
K41	Oxfordshire	98 (1071)	95 (1054)	93 (1041)	91 (1032)	94 (1050)	89 (986)	88 (989)	85 (964)	83 (974)
L10	Bristol and District	102 (2043)	102 (2097)	102 (2125)	99 (2057)	98 (2024)	99 (2016)	96 (1978)	93 (1932)	92 (1944)
L21	Cornwall and Isles of Scilly	105 (1423)	103 (1418)	102 (1423)	98 (1368)	98 (1362)	93 (1294)	90 (1275)	94 (1353)	87 (1280)

CDS - C3C
Trends in selected causes of death in the period 1984-92:
All causes (ICD 001-999) (ages 65-74):
SMRs (observed numbers of deaths in parentheses)
Persons

		1984	1985	1986	1987	1988	1989	1990	1991	1992
L35	Exeter and North Devon	97 (1330)	95 (1318)	94 (1312)	92 (1293)	92 (1275)	88 (1216)	86 (1193)	86 (1209)	84 (1209)
L36	Plymouth and Torbay	101 (1678)	97 (1644)	97 (1660)	99 (1694)	95 (1591)	96 (1586)	95 (1576)	89 (1504)	90 (1529)
L40	Gloucestershire	109 (1430)	97 (1307)	103 (1412)	97 (1338)	97 (1348)	98 (1360)	96 (1351)	88 (1274)	87 (1288)
L51	Somerset	102 (1173)	96 (1131)	99 (1182)	95 (1141)	95 (1137)	93 (1104)	84 (1021)	85 (1044)	81 (1019)
M02	Herefordshire	104 (440)	103 (448)	97 (430)	97 (437)	97 (435)	99 (446)	87 (399)	96 (453)	88 (423)
M04	Worcester and District	111 (656)	107 (652)	103 (641)	100 (636)	107 (683)	97 (618)	93 (608)	93 (621)	82 (569)
M05	Shropshire	114 (1044)	114 (1070)	114 (1090)	105 (1017)	107 (1039)	101 (985)	101 (1002)	98 (999)	93 (974)
M06	Mid Staffordshire	110 (676)	119 (756)	120 (781)	105 (696)	115 (769)	117 (784)	109 (752)	108 (765)	101 (742)
M07	North Staffordshire	136 (1581)	134 (1594)	129 (1554)	126 (1535)	124 (1494)	128 (1545)	119 (1457)	122 (1521)	115 (1460)
M08	South East Staffordshire	124 (596)	120 (597)	128 (653)	113 (586)	108 (569)	125 (661)	109 (589)	110 (609)	98 (558)
M13	East Birmingham	125 (660)	121 (658)	130 (716)	111 (611)	117 (633)	127 (678)	115 (617)	117 (627)	114 (607)
M14	North Birmingham	112 (428)	117 (467)	122 (497)	116 (475)	108 (441)	103 (421)	112 (462)	105 (435)	93 (392)
M16	West Birmingham	138 (678)	134 (660)	130 (634)	129 (616)	136 (627)	130 (579)	120 (534)	130 (580)	115 (517)
M17	Coventry	115 (889)	123 (973)	117 (941)	111 (899)	134 (1069)	122 (960)	119 (939)	112 (889)	113 (897)
M18	Dudley	122 (840)	122 (868)	131 (953)	118 (869)	113 (833)	117 (868)	111 (843)	106 (822)	99 (785)
M19	Sandwell	133 (1026)	126 (989)	132 (1058)	128 (1022)	125 (993)	123 (969)	119 (953)	119 (968)	120 (971)
M20	Solihull	105 (436)	106 (459)	97 (435)	94 (431)	93 (428)	91 (417)	100 (470)	92 (438)	89 (437)
M21	Walsall	127 (747)	132 (796)	122 (751)	125 (776)	123 (758)	123 (761)	119 (742)	119 (757)	111 (720)
M22	Wolverhampton	112 (671)	126 (780)	121 (763)	127 (806)	120 (756)	123 (775)	119 (758)	110 (719)	116 (768)
M25	South Birmingham	132 (1378)	123 (1305)	125 (1336)	127 (1351)	116 (1215)	123 (1265)	120 (1245)	116 (1210)	112 (1170)
M26	North Worcestershire	111 (611)	114 (656)	111 (650)	105 (628)	107 (644)	110 (666)	102 (624)	95 (599)	102 (651)
M28	Warwickshire	114 (1254)	121 (1373)	115 (1327)	107 (1253)	112 (1319)	105 (1241)	97 (1168)	99 (1222)	97 (1216)

CDS - C3C
Trends in selected causes of death in the period 1984-92:
All causes (ICD 001-999) (ages 65-74):
SMRs (observed numbers of deaths in parentheses)
Persons

		1984	1985	1986	1987	1988	1989	1990	1991	1992
N11	Chester	114 (458)	124 (513)	113 (472)	113 (477)	108 (456)	111 (466)	109 (464)	103 (449)	102 (462)
N12	Crewe	119 (686)	127 (758)	123 (746)	116 (709)	117 (713)	109 (672)	114 (717)	106 (687)	102 (672)
N13	Halton	134 (387)	131 (389)	128 (389)	139 (424)	122 (371)	129 (393)	126 (388)	125 (389)	117 (372)
N14	Macclesfield	119 (501)	108 (469)	95 (418)	97 (430)	99 (436)	101 (441)	95 (422)	89 (402)	90 (411)
N15	Warrington	130 (507)	143 (572)	135 (548)	133 (545)	130 (529)	123 (497)	120 (494)	112 (468)	113 (478)
N21	Liverpool	138 (1744)	141 (1794)	140 (1757)	135 (1673)	133 (1601)	142 (1665)	130 (1516)	136 (1580)	128 (1498)
N31	St Helens and Knowsley	144 (1028)	140 (1022)	136 (1005)	132 (984)	130 (962)	129 (958)	125 (943)	130 (1003)	126 (998)
N41	Southport and Formby	114 (376)	112 (381)	103 (356)	104 (362)	97 (337)	105 (364)	101 (353)	97 (343)	95 (340)
N42	South Sefton	130 (554)	133 (574)	132 (575)	124 (538)	124 (535)	134 (573)	107 (463)	118 (515)	119 (527)
N51	Wirral	121 (1122)	124 (1163)	116 (1101)	116 (1094)	116 (1083)	117 (1080)	117 (1078)	120 (1118)	111 (1042)
P01	Lancaster	116 (446)	112 (428)	109 (417)	110 (417)	103 (382)	104 (377)	113 (411)	115 (422)	106 (395)
P02	Blackpool, Wyre and Fylde	119 (1277)	123 (1331)	117 (1261)	119 (1277)	122 (1285)	112 (1164)	109 (1136)	105 (1114)	105 (1146)
P03	Preston	132 (422)	134 (430)	137 (438)	130 (412)	119 (372)	122 (375)	112 (348)	126 (391)	114 (358)
P04	Blackburn, Hyndburn and Ribble Valley	136 (921)	136 (926)	132 (887)	122 (811)	128 (836)	132 (846)	118 (755)	118 (761)	119 (777)
P05	Burnley, Pendle and Rossendale	133 (789)	134 (791)	121 (710)	120 (695)	133 (758)	124 (703)	125 (717)	120 (690)	117 (689)
P06	West Lancashire	127 (282)	131 (299)	132 (307)	112 (263)	122 (286)	117 (274)	109 (258)	104 (252)	95 (235)
P07	Chorley and South Ribble	129 (525)	124 (516)	117 (494)	119 (509)	117 (500)	110 (472)	109 (480)	110 (495)	99 (454)
P08	Bolton	129 (790)	137 (856)	134 (843)	119 (749)	129 (804)	119 (734)	120 (750)	117 (747)	115 (743)
P09	Bury	127 (537)	126 (532)	133 (561)	115 (480)	121 (494)	117 (471)	119 (481)	112 (455)	115 (476)
P10	North Manchester	147 (591)	161 (648)	148 (587)	156 (604)	143 (535)	155 (558)	136 (486)	147 (522)	138 (491)
P11	Central Manchester	135 (372)	139 (380)	135 (360)	146 (380)	139 (346)	136 (326)	140 (329)	146 (337)	132 (310)
P12	South Manchester	129 (592)	122 (565)	128 (593)	115 (532)	136 (613)	129 (567)	122 (536)	121 (529)	124 (539)

239

CDS - C3C
Trends in selected causes of death in the period 1984-92:
All causes (ICD 001-999) (ages 65-74):
SMRs (observed numbers of deaths in parentheses)
Persons

		1984	1985	1986	1987	1988	1989	1990	1991	1992
P13	Oldham	139	145	131	126	133	136	123	129	126
		(744)	(776)	(701)	(666)	(688)	(692)	(627)	(661)	(652)
P14	Rochdale	133	139	134	136	126	122	121	123	124
		(627)	(663)	(640)	(650)	(599)	(573)	(576)	(596)	(616)
P15	Salford	135	148	146	143	140	132	138	128	126
		(853)	(939)	(929)	(895)	(859)	(799)	(835)	(785)	(773)
P16	Stockport	115	118	122	113	111	114	106	105	111
		(781)	(818)	(848)	(790)	(765)	(778)	(734)	(738)	(794)
P17	Tameside and Glossop	136	136	135	132	133	128	131	120	121
		(821)	(831)	(824)	(798)	(794)	(757)	(781)	(724)	(737)
P18	Trafford	115	119	107	114	115	102	103	102	97
		(607)	(634)	(576)	(612)	(605)	(534)	(546)	(545)	(530)
P19	Wigan	142	139	136	137	147	144	137	126	120
		(979)	(982)	(969)	(980)	(1043)	(1012)	(969)	(908)	(882)

CDS - C3C
Trends in selected causes of death in the period 1984-92:
All causes (ICD 001-999) (all ages):
SMRs (observed numbers of deaths in parentheses)
Persons

		1984	1985	1986	1987	1988	1989	1990	1991	1992
	ENGLAND AND WALES	114 (564966)	117 (588686)	113 (579257)	109 (565069)	108 (569534)	108 (574938)	104 (562879)	103 (568108)	100 (556448)
O00	ENGLAND	114 (531314)	116 (553150)	113 (544545)	109 (531150)	108 (535553)	107 (539804)	104 (528916)	103 (533972)	100 (522656)
A00	NORTHERN RHA	130 (37900)	132 (39149)	126 (38038)	123 (37431)	123 (37890)	122 (38307)	118 (37480)	118 (37970)	114 (37072)
B00	YORKSHIRE RHA	121 (43192)	122 (44146)	118 (43348)	114 (42249)	113 (42406)	113 (42920)	109 (41955)	107 (42044)	102 (40481)
C00	TRENT RHA	117 (51646)	119 (53805)	115 (52876)	111 (51969)	111 (52714)	112 (53907)	105 (51717)	106 (52827)	103 (52171)
D00	EAST ANGLIAN RHA	105 (21263)	107 (22303)	103 (22029)	100 (21872)	99 (22155)	98 (22306)	95 (22296)	95 (22700)	91 (22207)
E00	NORTH WEST THAMES RHA	106 (33597)	109 (35117)	106 (34571)	103 (33737)	103 (34015)	102 (33665)	99 (32897)	98 (33078)	94 (31817)
F00	NORTH EAST THAMES RHA	111 (39854)	114 (41517)	109 (40252)	108 (40007)	105 (39359)	104 (39115)	102 (38574)	102 (38997)	99 (38006)
G00	SOUTH EAST THAMES RHA	109 (43942)	112 (45666)	109 (44855)	105 (43716)	103 (43241)	102 (43166)	100 (42353)	99 (42589)	97 (42002)
H00	SOUTH WEST THAMES RHA	104 (33662)	107 (35297)	103 (34335)	99 (33187)	98 (33315)	98 (33421)	94 (32630)	95 (33108)	91 (32149)
J00	WESSEX RHA	102 (32491)	106 (34736)	103 (34425)	98 (33429)	97 (33909)	97 (34558)	95 (34497)	94 (34756)	92 (34195)
K00	OXFORD RHA	106 (21448)	109 (22646)	107 (22756)	102 (22234)	103 (22778)	101 (22809)	97 (22320)	97 (22935)	95 (22806)
L00	SOUTH WESTERN RHA	105 (37881)	106 (38947)	105 (39589)	99 (37891)	99 (38810)	99 (39513)	96 (38937)	95 (39234)	92 (38610)
M00	WEST MIDLANDS RHA	120 (55970)	122 (57971)	119 (57725)	114 (56153)	113 (57133)	113 (57775)	108 (56762)	107 (56980)	104 (56092)
N00	MERSEY RHA	125 (28243)	128 (29526)	122 (28458)	118 (28094)	117 (28126)	118 (28864)	113 (27906)	113 (28230)	109 (27460)
P00	NORTH WESTERN RHA	128 (50225)	132 (52324)	128 (51288)	121 (49181)	122 (49702)	120 (49478)	116 (48592)	115 (48524)	112 (47588)
A01	Hartlepool	134 (1083)	141 (1155)	142 (1167)	138 (1140)	131 (1096)	126 (1064)	125 (1080)	119 (1053)	118 (1050)
A02	North Tees	125 (1618)	129 (1714)	121 (1652)	126 (1754)	120 (1704)	118 (1719)	117 (1732)	120 (1817)	119 (1823)
A03	South Tees	136 (3225)	138 (3317)	132 (3237)	131 (3238)	129 (3238)	121 (3099)	128 (3350)	121 (3218)	119 (3200)
A04	East Cumbria	120 (2219)	124 (2358)	115 (2221)	114 (2226)	116 (2307)	113 (2297)	109 (2257)	109 (2290)	101 (2155)
A05	South Cumbria	112 (2169)	113 (2229)	114 (2292)	107 (2183)	106 (2193)	109 (2290)	103 (2171)	103 (2203)	98 (2137)
A06	West Cumbria	130 (1611)	134 (1683)	121 (1544)	126 (1638)	120 (1591)	124 (1675)	124 (1700)	125 (1725)	117 (1641)

241

CDS - C3C
Trends in selected causes of death in the period 1984-92:
All causes (ICD 001-999) (all ages):
SMRs (observed numbers of deaths in parentheses)
Persons

		1984	1985	1986	1987	1988	1989	1990	1991	1992
A11	Northumberland	131 (3916)	130 (3969)	125 (3887)	121 (3848)	122 (3943)	121 (3975)	112 (3749)	113 (3864)	110 (3786)
A12	Gateshead	135 (2683)	132 (2660)	129 (2646)	130 (2690)	131 (2719)	131 (2767)	119 (2518)	125 (2686)	115 (2480)
A13	Newcastle	126 (3696)	131 (3893)	124 (3718)	115 (3474)	120 (3634)	123 (3735)	119 (3609)	117 (3558)	116 (3548)
A14	North Tyneside	131 (2545)	135 (2680)	125 (2524)	122 (2509)	120 (2504)	120 (2534)	120 (2572)	118 (2581)	113 (2490)
A15	South Tyneside	134 (2130)	136 (2185)	137 (2223)	125 (2036)	132 (2173)	133 (2193)	120 (1988)	119 (2012)	121 (2055)
A16	Sunderland	142 (3594)	139 (3560)	127 (3302)	128 (3356)	126 (3350)	129 (3473)	122 (3351)	125 (3473)	121 (3387)
A30	North Durham	129 (3792)	136 (4089)	132 (4012)	121 (3740)	123 (3834)	123 (3888)	118 (3794)	119 (3888)	117 (3846)
A31	South Durham	134 (3619)	133 (3657)	129 (3613)	127 (3599)	126 (3604)	123 (3598)	122 (3609)	119 (3602)	114 (3474)
B11	East Riding	120 (6013)	118 (6034)	116 (6005)	114 (5982)	110 (5901)	111 (6057)	107 (5930)	105 (5907)	102 (5838)
B16	Grimsby and Scunthorpe	120 (3804)	124 (4010)	117 (3854)	115 (3869)	108 (3733)	113 (3994)	112 (4046)	109 (4034)	103 (3847)
B21	North Yorkshire	108 (8298)	112 (8743)	108 (8630)	105 (8515)	105 (8653)	104 (8751)	101 (8630)	101 (8753)	94 (8306)
B31	Bradford	126 (5519)	130 (5745)	127 (5641)	122 (5499)	123 (5552)	117 (5358)	115 (5292)	116 (5430)	107 (5064)
B51	West Yorkshire	132 (7325)	130 (7293)	125 (7109)	120 (6869)	121 (7018)	119 (6971)	113 (6653)	112 (6677)	107 (6451)
B61	Leeds	121 (8615)	121 (8664)	117 (8491)	110 (8021)	110 (8091)	112 (8297)	108 (8027)	104 (7809)	99 (7565)
B71	Wakefield	135 (3618)	134 (3657)	131 (3618)	125 (3494)	122 (3458)	121 (3492)	115 (3377)	115 (3434)	112 (3410)
C01	North Derbyshire	116 (4166)	122 (4500)	119 (4426)	110 (4176)	110 (4281)	112 (4431)	108 (4348)	105 (4298)	106 (4403)
C02	Southern Derbyshire	120 (6141)	121 (6343)	119 (6292)	112 (6048)	112 (6169)	115 (6429)	106 (6049)	110 (6365)	105 (6122)
C03	Leicestershire	108 (8532)	111 (8971)	108 (8878)	106 (8874)	104 (8864)	105 (9109)	98 (8614)	100 (8942)	94 (8640)
C04	North Lincolnshire	120 (3184)	121 (3267)	114 (3166)	114 (3266)	112 (3283)	110 (3335)	105 (3278)	101 (3266)	102 (3356)
C05	South Lincolnshire	109 (3414)	112 (3580)	102 (3360)	105 (3561)	105 (3653)	104 (3727)	100 (3657)	99 (3716)	97 (3733)
C08	Nottingham	117 (6693)	118 (6954)	116 (6921)	110 (6638)	114 (6984)	111 (6907)	104 (6587)	103 (6687)	103 (6726)
C09	Barnsley	126 (2590)	133 (2763)	126 (2664)	120 (2578)	116 (2529)	121 (2690)	114 (2567)	116 (2657)	115 (2687)

242

CDS - C3C
Trends in selected causes of death in the period 1984-92:
All causes (ICD 001-999) (all ages):
SMRs (observed numbers of deaths in parentheses)
Persons

		1984	1985	1986	1987	1988	1989	1990	1991	1992
C10	Doncaster	123 (3092)	130 (3335)	123 (3215)	116 (3098)	120 (3265)	119 (3268)	109 (3072)	109 (3135)	110 (3206)
C11	Rotherham	123 (2613)	128 (2771)	121 (2669)	119 (2683)	117 (2671)	120 (2802)	113 (2689)	114 (2773)	109 (2680)
C12	Sheffield	121 (6983)	120 (7034)	119 (7043)	114 (6804)	114 (6833)	115 (6959)	109 (6606)	110 (6703)	102 (6302)
C14	North Nottinghamshire	120 (4238)	118 (4287)	115 (4242)	113 (4243)	109 (4182)	109 (4250)	107 (4250)	106 (4285)	105 (4316)
D01	Cambridge	97 (2541)	101 (2690)	98 (2683)	98 (2718)	98 (2766)	90 (2601)	89 (2628)	89 (2677)	89 (2720)
D05	North West Anglia	110 (4058)	112 (4263)	111 (4323)	107 (4285)	106 (4363)	107 (4509)	98 (4254)	96 (4274)	96 (4366)
D06	Norwich	102 (5448)	106 (5843)	99 (5617)	97 (5599)	93 (5530)	95 (5759)	95 (5864)	95 (5975)	89 (5705)
D07	Great Yarmouth and Waveney	107 (2421)	108 (2482)	104 (2459)	97 (2359)	101 (2518)	99 (2534)	99 (2585)	96 (2568)	94 (2556)
D09	Huntingdon	113 (999)	111 (1035)	107 (1029)	107 (1070)	103 (1066)	93 (988)	94 (1039)	97 (1096)	88 (1018)
D11	Suffolk	105 (5796)	106 (5990)	103 (5918)	100 (5841)	99 (5912)	97 (5915)	95 (5926)	96 (6110)	91 (5842)
E01	North Bedfordshire	108 (2181)	112 (2319)	113 (2382)	106 (2295)	102 (2259)	110 (2461)	102 (2329)	99 (2311)	100 (2386)
E02	South Bedfordshire	110 (2247)	113 (2381)	110 (2348)	108 (2350)	108 (2403)	105 (2375)	108 (2462)	107 (2490)	98 (2316)
E05	North West Hertfordshire	103 (2354)	111 (2594)	104 (2466)	102 (2457)	102 (2484)	99 (2463)	97 (2442)	91 (2323)	90 (2338)
E06	South West Hertfordshire	106 (2518)	112 (2709)	105 (2585)	103 (2565)	103 (2597)	103 (2627)	98 (2528)	101 (2637)	93 (2460)
E07	Barnet	101 (3256)	107 (3470)	101 (3289)	97 (3204)	101 (3316)	97 (3227)	94 (3150)	93 (3169)	89 (3023)
E09	Hillingdon	107 (2332)	108 (2410)	103 (2325)	98 (2244)	104 (2381)	101 (2364)	97 (2271)	96 (2264)	94 (2248)
E18	East and North Hertfordshire	105 (4170)	105 (4296)	104 (4352)	102 (4347)	99 (4329)	97 (4328)	96 (4369)	95 (4376)	92 (4322)
E19	Brent and Harrow	98 (4279)	102 (4484)	103 (4520)	97 (4272)	100 (4380)	96 (4176)	92 (4005)	95 (4086)	89 (3877)
E20	Ealing, Hammersmith and Hounslow	112 (6799)	115 (6960)	113 (6872)	110 (6669)	110 (6575)	107 (6347)	105 (6203)	106 (6248)	99 (5853)
E21	Kensington, Chelsea and Westminster	106 (3461)	107 (3494)	105 (3432)	103 (3334)	102 (3291)	102 (3297)	97 (3138)	98 (3174)	92 (2994)
F31	North Essex	105 (8597)	108 (9084)	103 (8907)	103 (9112)	100 (9035)	96 (8841)	97 (9106)	95 (9062)	91 (8887)
F32	South Essex	112 (7106)	114 (7426)	111 (7367)	109 (7333)	107 (7301)	102 (7128)	101 (7189)	102 (7349)	99 (7250)

CDS - C3C
Trends in selected causes of death in the period 1984-92:
All causes (ICD 001-999) (all ages):
SMRs (observed numbers of deaths in parentheses)
Persons

		1984	1985	1986	1987	1988	1989	1990	1991	1992
F33	Barking and Havering	112 (4143)	115 (4330)	113 (4309)	108 (4157)	106 (4103)	107 (4165)	100 (3972)	104 (4147)	100 (4004)
F34	Redbridge and Waltham Forest	103 (4870)	107 (5104)	101 (4823)	100 (4787)	100 (4778)	100 (4740)	100 (4755)	100 (4730)	98 (4622)
F35	East London and the City	123 (6148)	127 (6371)	120 (5990)	122 (6060)	118 (5828)	120 (5858)	114 (5510)	117 (5566)	111 (5290)
F36	New River District	112 (5171)	112 (5213)	108 (5008)	105 (4821)	101 (4573)	104 (4699)	98 (4450)	100 (4531)	97 (4389)
F37	Camden and Islington	113 (3819)	118 (3989)	113 (3848)	110 (3737)	111 (3741)	110 (3684)	107 (3592)	108 (3612)	107 (3564)
G04	South East Kent	105 (3298)	110 (3496)	108 (3507)	104 (3415)	100 (3318)	101 (3403)	97 (3336)	96 (3333)	94 (3314)
G05	Canterbury and Thanet	113 (4525)	113 (4581)	114 (4661)	107 (4452)	109 (4583)	105 (4461)	103 (4417)	97 (4318)	96 (4313)
G06	Dartford and Gravesham	122 (2293)	124 (2378)	120 (2330)	114 (2253)	115 (2299)	111 (2246)	104 (2140)	107 (2244)	105 (2237)
G07	Maidstone	117 (1959)	112 (1916)	110 (1925)	113 (2026)	103 (1880)	106 (1981)	100 (1911)	99 (1933)	92 (1837)
G08	Medway	108 (2864)	115 (3127)	113 (3112)	110 (3074)	105 (2990)	105 (3047)	104 (3043)	107 (3108)	106 (3115)
G09	Tunbridge Wells	102 (2247)	108 (2408)	107 (2421)	97 (2234)	98 (2274)	98 (2313)	93 (2229)	95 (2296)	93 (2289)
G10	Bexley	102 (2062)	104 (2144)	104 (2158)	102 (2155)	98 (2079)	97 (2084)	96 (2106)	94 (2087)	92 (2062)
G11	Greenwich	115 (2362)	122 (2525)	118 (2466)	114 (2375)	109 (2272)	111 (2316)	106 (2224)	108 (2281)	107 (2259)
G12	Bromley	104 (3232)	101 (3193)	104 (3294)	98 (3146)	95 (3105)	96 (3136)	92 (3070)	90 (3035)	86 (2944)
G21	East Sussex	102 (10979)	108 (11709)	102 (11098)	98 (10848)	96 (10713)	94 (10590)	93 (10475)	94 (10708)	92 (10568)
G26	South East London	118 (8121)	119 (8189)	115 (7883)	114 (7738)	115 (7728)	115 (7589)	113 (7402)	112 (7246)	110 (7064)
H04	Mid Surrey	111 (2185)	113 (2242)	113 (2268)	104 (2115)	100 (2074)	100 (2115)	94 (2038)	95 (2084)	89 (1975)
H05	East Surrey	102 (2047)	106 (2174)	101 (2106)	102 (2152)	100 (2139)	99 (2149)	96 (2120)	94 (2128)	90 (2049)
H06	Chichester	101 (2633)	107 (2842)	101 (2742)	93 (2592)	95 (2719)	97 (2810)	95 (2795)	92 (2749)	91 (2770)
H07	Mid Downs	100 (2526)	109 (2798)	102 (2659)	100 (2666)	99 (2690)	95 (2632)	96 (2714)	93 (2699)	91 (2658)
H08	Worthing	97 (4086)	104 (4462)	96 (4137)	94 (4092)	96 (4192)	95 (4189)	89 (3944)	94 (4192)	88 (3936)
H09	Croydon	115 (3415)	118 (3511)	112 (3348)	106 (3200)	107 (3215)	106 (3198)	97 (2960)	106 (3240)	98 (3012)

CDS - C3C
Trends in selected causes of death in the period 1984-92:
All causes (ICD 001-999) (all ages):
SMRs (observed numbers of deaths in parentheses)
Persons

		1984	1985	1986	1987	1988	1989	1990	1991	1992
H12	Wandsworth	122 (2316)	128 (2405)	123 (2273)	115 (2114)	114 (2071)	118 (2108)	116 (2048)	115 (1989)	116 (2001)
H13	Merton and Sutton	100 (3712)	100 (3750)	100 (3754)	102 (3840)	97 (3637)	96 (3635)	94 (3571)	92 (3483)	89 (3390)
H14	North West Surrey	103 (3533)	105 (3685)	105 (3748)	96 (3478)	93 (3461)	99 (3757)	92 (3562)	93 (3684)	91 (3641)
H15	South West Surrey	98 (2475)	100 (2560)	97 (2525)	90 (2381)	93 (2495)	87 (2370)	86 (2380)	85 (2408)	83 (2388)
H16	Kingston and Richmond	103 (4734)	104 (4868)	102 (4775)	97 (4557)	98 (4622)	94 (4458)	95 (4498)	94 (4452)	90 (4329)
J10	Dorset	96 (8398)	99 (8914)	97 (8918)	92 (8653)	90 (8662)	91 (8822)	90 (8899)	89 (9023)	87 (8894)
J21	Portsmouth and South East Hampshire	105 (5350)	111 (5797)	105 (5575)	103 (5546)	101 (5569)	101 (5650)	101 (5786)	97 (5658)	97 (5736)
J22	Southampton and South West Hampshire	103 (4520)	107 (4832)	105 (4812)	99 (4622)	100 (4808)	99 (4845)	98 (4852)	97 (4891)	92 (4732)
J23	Winchester	108 (2109)	110 (2205)	108 (2198)	102 (2126)	103 (2205)	100 (2176)	95 (2113)	93 (2123)	92 (2128)
J24	Basingstoke and North Hampshire	105 (2734)	111 (2974)	104 (2838)	100 (2800)	97 (2798)	98 (2895)	94 (2837)	94 (2913)	90 (2862)
J31	Salisbury	98 (1360)	108 (1525)	103 (1486)	99 (1447)	98 (1460)	92 (1418)	96 (1505)	92 (1483)	90 (1462)
J32	Swindon	106 (2015)	113 (2201)	108 (2154)	105 (2129)	103 (2144)	110 (2329)	99 (2121)	104 (2281)	96 (2128)
J33	Bath	103 (4290)	105 (4474)	105 (4544)	98 (4313)	97 (4352)	100 (4561)	98 (4525)	94 (4431)	93 (4422)
J41	Isle of Wight	99 (1715)	102 (1814)	105 (1900)	97 (1793)	101 (1911)	97 (1862)	95 (1859)	99 (1953)	92 (1831)
K11	East Berkshire	112 (3248)	114 (3398)	110 (3325)	107 (3283)	108 (3372)	105 (3365)	100 (3249)	100 (3323)	97 (3255)
K12	West Berkshire	107 (3744)	107 (3873)	110 (4034)	99 (3720)	102 (3870)	99 (3812)	96 (3770)	96 (3851)	90 (3683)
K24	Buckinghamshire	105 (4616)	109 (4922)	102 (4726)	100 (4782)	103 (5032)	99 (4954)	96 (4909)	95 (4970)	96 (5153)
K31	Kettering	103 (2445)	113 (2734)	111 (2766)	106 (2683)	107 (2770)	108 (2856)	100 (2683)	105 (2873)	101 (2797)
K32	Northampton	107 (2821)	112 (3037)	113 (3148)	109 (3085)	104 (3027)	105 (3105)	104 (3147)	104 (3194)	100 (3107)
K41	Oxfordshire	102 (4574)	102 (4682)	102 (4757)	98 (4681)	97 (4707)	95 (4717)	90 (4562)	92 (4724)	91 (4811)
L10	Bristol and District	105 (8714)	107 (9059)	106 (9120)	101 (8797)	103 (9063)	101 (9046)	98 (8892)	97 (8930)	94 (8782)
L21	Cornwall and Isles of Scilly	106 (5568)	109 (5920)	108 (5966)	98 (5588)	101 (5896)	99 (5895)	95 (5815)	98 (6132)	93 (5874)

CDS - C3C
Trends in selected causes of death in the period 1984-92:
All causes (ICD 001-999) (all ages):
SMRs (observed numbers of deaths in parentheses)
Persons

		1984	1985	1986	1987	1988	1989	1990	1991	1992
L35	Exeter and North Devon	101 (5712)	100 (5815)	103 (6041)	95 (5700)	96 (5885)	95 (5992)	92 (5902)	92 (5982)	91 (5981)
L36	Plymouth and Torbay	105 (7246)	103 (7269)	104 (7513)	99 (7229)	97 (7196)	99 (7477)	97 (7450)	95 (7396)	93 (7284)
L40	Gloucestershire	108 (5731)	106 (5783)	105 (5828)	100 (5657)	100 (5815)	100 (5936)	98 (5946)	94 (5804)	92 (5773)
L51	Somerset	107 (4910)	109 (5101)	107 (5121)	100 (4920)	99 (4955)	100 (5167)	93 (4932)	92 (4990)	89 (4916)
M02	Herefordshire	102 (1717)	106 (1846)	101 (1791)	96 (1759)	102 (1912)	105 (2017)	94 (1849)	97 (1942)	97 (1960)
M04	Worcester and District	114 (2691)	110 (2677)	110 (2722)	106 (2723)	107 (2809)	103 (2771)	100 (2758)	98 (2771)	93 (2704)
M05	Shropshire	115 (4147)	118 (4356)	115 (4338)	107 (4159)	107 (4276)	104 (4258)	102 (4271)	100 (4293)	96 (4225)
M06	Mid Staffordshire	112 (2683)	118 (2934)	117 (2987)	108 (2849)	108 (2925)	116 (3211)	111 (3156)	108 (3156)	104 (3087)
M07	North Staffordshire	131 (5710)	131 (5797)	125 (5614)	122 (5562)	122 (5637)	116 (5464)	118 (5595)	115 (5544)	109 (5337)
M08	South East Staffordshire	121 (2321)	129 (2526)	124 (2503)	120 (2486)	116 (2476)	121 (2672)	107 (2439)	110 (2579)	104 (2470)
M13	East Birmingham	129 (2447)	130 (2494)	125 (2404)	117 (2264)	118 (2297)	117 (2311)	117 (2322)	112 (2242)	106 (2153)
M14	North Birmingham	112 (1725)	122 (1923)	119 (1917)	114 (1867)	111 (1858)	109 (1867)	106 (1851)	108 (1920)	103 (1861)
M16	West Birmingham	137 (2529)	137 (2560)	132 (2454)	131 (2456)	131 (2440)	128 (2397)	115 (2170)	120 (2299)	111 (2117)
M17	Coventry	119 (3363)	119 (3425)	117 (3423)	112 (3336)	123 (3671)	118 (3567)	111 (3390)	108 (3345)	107 (3363)
M18	Dudley	118 (3115)	121 (3287)	121 (3351)	113 (3210)	111 (3204)	110 (3266)	107 (3253)	106 (3279)	101 (3210)
M19	Sandwell	128 (3665)	123 (3593)	123 (3650)	121 (3622)	119 (3595)	116 (3552)	115 (3559)	113 (3521)	113 (3543)
M20	Solihull	105 (1653)	104 (1701)	101 (1694)	96 (1673)	95 (1693)	96 (1766)	98 (1840)	91 (1766)	88 (1761)
M21	Walsall	132 (2818)	127 (2776)	126 (2816)	123 (2809)	119 (2772)	123 (2935)	118 (2866)	114 (2839)	110 (2789)
M22	Wolverhampton	119 (2742)	126 (2966)	124 (2957)	117 (2834)	117 (2860)	117 (2891)	115 (2871)	110 (2805)	108 (2760)
M25	South Birmingham	124 (5100)	123 (5166)	121 (5127)	118 (5026)	115 (4918)	115 (4971)	112 (4862)	111 (4881)	107 (4696)
M26	North Worcestershire	117 (2459)	120 (2616)	120 (2688)	110 (2553)	107 (2552)	108 (2679)	106 (2719)	100 (2638)	104 (2782)
M28	Warwickshire	118 (5085)	120 (5328)	117 (5289)	107 (4965)	110 (5238)	107 (5180)	100 (4991)	101 (5160)	102 (5274)

CDS - C3C
Trends in selected causes of death in the period 1984-92:
All causes (ICD 001-999) (all ages):
SMRs (observed numbers of deaths in parentheses)
Persons

		1984	1985	1986	1987	1988	1989	1990	1991	1992
N11	Chester	115 (1829)	121 (1976)	113 (1878)	110 (1872)	110 (1911)	111 (1949)	107 (1912)	103 (1896)	102 (1917)
N12	Crewe	117 (2608)	125 (2838)	119 (2764)	113 (2675)	116 (2802)	110 (2741)	107 (2726)	106 (2762)	102 (2706)
N13	Halton	136 (1429)	130 (1400)	127 (1402)	127 (1443)	122 (1418)	120 (1419)	119 (1427)	121 (1474)	109 (1343)
N14	Macclesfield	119 (2074)	114 (2043)	108 (1965)	101 (1874)	106 (2014)	103 (1997)	102 (2012)	100 (2006)	100 (2034)
N15	Warrington	127 (1890)	135 (2064)	128 (1986)	127 (2024)	127 (2064)	121 (2008)	119 (2019)	113 (1965)	112 (1966)
N21	Liverpool	130 (6464)	137 (6839)	131 (6527)	128 (6335)	127 (6260)	130 (6399)	121 (5949)	123 (6042)	120 (5877)
N31	St Helens and Knowsley	138 (3775)	140 (3896)	132 (3702)	131 (3735)	124 (3581)	126 (3674)	120 (3563)	120 (3606)	114 (3462)
N41	Southport and Formby	112 (1703)	114 (1759)	111 (1762)	110 (1772)	106 (1738)	112 (1884)	104 (1770)	102 (1775)	97 (1701)
N42	South Sefton	122 (1997)	130 (2164)	120 (2034)	118 (2023)	111 (1936)	118 (2107)	107 (1924)	110 (2019)	109 (2037)
N51	Wirral	120 (4474)	120 (4547)	115 (4438)	111 (4341)	111 (4402)	116 (4686)	113 (4604)	113 (4685)	106 (4417)
P01	Lancaster	117 (1928)	124 (2046)	114 (1895)	109 (1817)	106 (1786)	107 (1815)	113 (1919)	106 (1819)	103 (1768)
P02	Blackpool, Wyre and Fylde	118 (5122)	124 (5489)	118 (5237)	113 (5124)	113 (5149)	113 (5207)	112 (5211)	109 (5113)	102 (4856)
P03	Preston	126 (1622)	136 (1761)	125 (1638)	126 (1665)	120 (1598)	118 (1578)	119 (1593)	124 (1657)	119 (1590)
P04	Blackburn, Hyndburn and Ribble Valley	133 (3527)	135 (3624)	136 (3662)	129 (3481)	125 (3380)	126 (3463)	117 (3208)	118 (3263)	113 (3158)
P05	Burnley, Pendle and Rossendale	135 (3193)	135 (3200)	129 (3076)	123 (2960)	127 (3064)	119 (2945)	116 (2930)	114 (2901)	113 (2898)
P06	West Lancashire	127 (1066)	133 (1145)	126 (1112)	118 (1071)	123 (1141)	122 (1154)	108 (1061)	105 (1071)	103 (1080)
P07	Chorley and South Ribble	125 (1955)	125 (2017)	121 (1987)	118 (1995)	117 (2034)	117 (2073)	105 (1911)	108 (2019)	103 (1951)
P08	Bolton	129 (3128)	133 (3293)	133 (3309)	119 (2992)	123 (3132)	118 (3057)	119 (3121)	115 (3048)	112 (3001)
P09	Bury	126 (2085)	132 (2225)	132 (2243)	117 (2014)	115 (2020)	115 (2059)	117 (2114)	116 (2116)	107 (1975)
P10	North Manchester	141 (2096)	156 (2308)	143 (2113)	144 (2120)	140 (2028)	139 (2001)	129 (1875)	130 (1906)	127 (1840)
P11	Central Manchester	127 (1394)	140 (1536)	138 (1498)	130 (1396)	131 (1385)	136 (1403)	129 (1315)	139 (1377)	123 (1220)
P12	South Manchester	130 (2352)	129 (2354)	128 (2339)	117 (2142)	127 (2339)	120 (2212)	117 (2146)	116 (2132)	120 (2178)

CDS - C3C
Trends in selected causes of death in the period 1984-92:
All causes (ICD 001-999) (all ages):
SMRs (observed numbers of deaths in parentheses)
Persons

		1984	1985	1986	1987	1988	1989	1990	1991	1992
P13	Oldham	135 (2735)	138 (2845)	133 (2769)	125 (2624)	123 (2619)	126 (2715)	122 (2656)	121 (2647)	121 (2667)
P14	Rochdale	134 (2533)	134 (2553)	130 (2520)	123 (2400)	125 (2464)	119 (2367)	119 (2408)	123 (2503)	120 (2462)
P15	Salford	136 (3232)	141 (3400)	136 (3308)	129 (3167)	130 (3214)	125 (3101)	126 (3148)	124 (3112)	123 (3100)
P16	Stockport	116 (3212)	119 (3365)	123 (3510)	115 (3326)	114 (3341)	113 (3364)	107 (3215)	104 (3201)	106 (3312)
P17	Tameside and Glossop	130 (2921)	130 (2971)	129 (2992)	124 (2933)	125 (2967)	124 (2973)	121 (2960)	115 (2822)	112 (2808)
P18	Trafford	115 (2413)	118 (2533)	118 (2570)	109 (2397)	110 (2454)	106 (2399)	104 (2391)	103 (2406)	101 (2379)
P19	Wigan	142 (3711)	139 (3659)	131 (3510)	132 (3557)	131 (3587)	130 (3592)	122 (3410)	120 (3411)	116 (3345)

CDS - C5A
Trends in avoidable causes of death in the period 1984-92:
Asthma (ages 5-44) (ICD 493):
SMRs (observed numbers of deaths in parentheses)
Persons

		1984	1985	1986	1987	1988	1989	1990	1991	1992
	ENGLAND AND WALES	149 (265)	165 (297)	161 (294)	165 (304)	157 (291)	136 (252)	125 (231)	131 (243)	100 (183)
O00	ENGLAND	150 (252)	164 (279)	163 (281)	164 (286)	159 (278)	136 (238)	124 (218)	133 (233)	101 (175)
A00	NORTHERN RHA	212 (23)	119 (13)	146 (16)	191 (21)	163 (18)	109 (12)	100 (11)	190 (21)	64 (7)
B00	YORKSHIRE RHA	142 (18)	164 (21)	154 (20)	191 (25)	160 (21)	151 (20)	120 (16)	127 (17)	68 (9)
C00	TRENT RHA	121 (20)	198 (33)	190 (32)	141 (24)	182 (31)	193 (33)	105 (18)	88 (15)	47 (8)
D00	EAST ANGLIAN RHA	203 (14)	128 (9)	250 (18)	164 (12)	203 (15)	149 (11)	94 (7)	121 (9)	109 (8)
E00	NORTH WEST THAMES RHA	155 (20)	107 (14)	136 (18)	158 (21)	211 (28)	120 (16)	179 (24)	163 (22)	127 (17)
F00	NORTH EAST THAMES RHA	158 (21)	185 (25)	109 (15)	208 (29)	128 (18)	156 (22)	99 (14)	175 (25)	71 (10)
G00	SOUTH EAST THAMES RHA	143 (18)	148 (19)	191 (25)	128 (17)	202 (27)	112 (15)	97 (13)	112 (15)	91 (12)
H00	SOUTH WEST THAMES RHA	68 (7)	267 (28)	94 (10)	186 (20)	139 (15)	138 (15)	101 (11)	128 (14)	157 (17)
J00	WESSEX RHA	103 (11)	138 (15)	154 (17)	151 (17)	159 (18)	186 (21)	151 (17)	134 (15)	127 (14)
K00	OXFORD RHA	131 (12)	139 (13)	177 (17)	246 (24)	132 (13)	92 (9)	122 (12)	163 (16)	144 (14)
L00	SOUTH WESTERN RHA	223 (24)	173 (19)	161 (18)	132 (15)	78 (9)	104 (12)	201 (23)	140 (16)	115 (13)
M00	WEST MIDLANDS RHA	140 (26)	160 (30)	169 (32)	136 (26)	131 (25)	110 (21)	95 (18)	101 (19)	75 (14)
N00	MERSEY RHA	140 (12)	151 (13)	185 (16)	219 (19)	162 (14)	116 (10)	139 (12)	116 (10)	107 (9)
P00	NORTH WESTERN RHA	185 (26)	191 (27)	190 (27)	112 (16)	181 (26)	146 (21)	153 (22)	132 (19)	162 (23)

(Not presented for DHAs because of the low observed numbers)

CDS - C8A
Trends in perinatal mortality in the period 1984-92
(observed numbers of deaths in parentheses)

		1984	1985	1986	1987	1988	1989	1990	1991	1992
	ENGLAND AND WALES	10.1	9.8	9.6	8.9	8.7	8.3	8.1	8.0	7.5
		(6445)	(6478)	(6361)	(6093)	(6065)	(5742)	(5740)	(5633)	(5214)
O00	ENGLAND	10.0	9.8	9.5	8.9	8.7	8.3	8.1	8.0	7.6
		(6065)	(6100)	(5977)	(5742)	(5731)	(5424)	(5450)	(5332)	(4951)
A00	NORTHERN RHA	11.0	9.8	10.1	8.5	9.0	9.2	7.9	9.4	7.6
		(434)	(403)	(408)	(344)	(362)	(362)	(322)	(388)	(304)
B00	YORKSHIRE RHA	11.6	10.6	10.3	9.5	9.2	8.5	8.0	8.1	7.2
		(545)	(513)	(499)	(469)	(460)	(423)	(410)	(412)	(358)
C00	TRENT RHA	9.8	9.5	10.2	9.3	9.2	8.5	8.4	8.6	8.5
		(568)	(563)	(606)	(572)	(567)	(524)	(538)	(548)	(533)
D00	EAST ANGLIAN RHA	8.9	9.8	7.7	7.9	6.7	6.7	5.9	6.7	6.2
		(213)	(241)	(191)	(206)	(180)	(174)	(157)	(176)	(162)
E00	NORTH WEST THAMES RHA	9.0	9.1	8.6	8.6	8.1	8.3	7.4	7.6	7.0
		(420)	(435)	(416)	(430)	(410)	(414)	(380)	(395)	(364)
F00	NORTH EAST THAMES RHA	9.7	9.3	9.6	9.4	9.1	8.3	8.6	8.2	7.6
		(499)	(488)	(513)	(525)	(516)	(468)	(503)	(470)	(435)
G00	SOUTH EAST THAMES RHA	10.5	9.5	8.5	8.5	9.1	8.4	8.2	7.4	7.9
		(473)	(450)	(407)	(428)	(468)	(433)	(430)	(384)	(407)
H00	SOUTH WEST THAMES RHA	8.6	9.3	8.2	7.5	7.9	7.0	7.0	7.3	6.3
		(302)	(340)	(302)	(288)	(310)	(274)	(282)	(293)	(255)
J00	WESSEX RHA	8.6	9.2	8.8	8.9	8.7	8.3	7.0	7.0	6.6
		(293)	(323)	(317)	(331)	(331)	(317)	(271)	(261)	(246)
K00	OXFORD RHA	8.7	8.5	8.9	8.0	6.9	7.2	8.2	7.5	6.3
		(277)	(284)	(297)	(279)	(247)	(258)	(299)	(273)	(229)
L00	SOUTH WESTERN RHA	9.3	9.1	9.5	7.5	7.9	6.7	7.1	6.9	6.8
		(340)	(343)	(363)	(302)	(324)	(273)	(292)	(281)	(272)
M00	WEST MIDLANDS RHA	12.3	11.7	11.0	9.9	10.3	9.7	10.2	9.9	9.2
		(852)	(825)	(776)	(725)	(752)	(712)	(771)	(735)	(664)
N00	MERSEY RHA	9.0	10.2	9.2	9.0	7.4	8.2	7.9	7.1	6.6
		(286)	(338)	(302)	(296)	(249)	(270)	(268)	(238)	(209)
P00	NORTH WESTERN RHA	10.3	9.9	10.4	9.6	9.6	9.2	8.9	8.2	9.1
		(563)	(554)	(580)	(547)	(555)	(522)	(527)	(478)	(513)

CDS - C10A
Trends in mortality rates in infancy (ages under 1 year) in the period 1984-92
(observed numbers of deaths in parentheses)

		1984	1985	1986	1987	1988	1989	1990	1991	1992
	ENGLAND AND WALES	9.4 (5986)	9.3 (6078)	9.5 (6269)	9.1 (6203)	9.0 (6217)	8.4 (5756)	7.8 (5506)	7.3 (5105)	6.5 (4484)
O00	ENGLAND	9.4 (5672)	9.2 (5716)	9.5 (5917)	9.1 (5844)	9.1 (5923)	8.4 (5452)	7.9 (5238)	7.3 (4855)	6.5 (4259)
A00	NORTHERN RHA	9.4 (370)	8.4 (343)	9.8 (394)	8.7 (352)	8.4 (337)	8.4 (330)	7.9 (322)	8.5 (351)	7.1 (286)
B00	YORKSHIRE RHA	10.7 (499)	10.7 (513)	10.6 (513)	10.1 (498)	9.6 (481)	9.1 (450)	9.1 (467)	8.5 (433)	6.6 (329)
C00	TRENT RHA	9.1 (524)	8.6 (505)	9.9 (585)	9.1 (553)	9.5 (586)	8.1 (499)	7.8 (496)	8.0 (508)	6.9 (426)
D00	EAST ANGLIAN RHA	8.2 (195)	9.4 (231)	8.1 (198)	7.8 (201)	6.9 (183)	6.4 (166)	6.9 (183)	6.0 (159)	4.6 (121)
E00	NORTH WEST THAMES RHA	8.6 (397)	9.0 (429)	8.6 (412)	8.3 (411)	8.2 (416)	8.2 (406)	6.9 (349)	6.3 (324)	5.5 (286)
F00	NORTH EAST THAMES RHA	9.3 (474)	8.5 (441)	9.3 (491)	9.9 (549)	8.3 (471)	8.4 (470)	6.9 (403)	6.7 (384)	7.1 (403)
G00	SOUTH EAST THAMES RHA	9.9 (442)	9.5 (445)	8.6 (408)	9.3 (463)	9.5 (487)	8.4 (431)	8.1 (423)	7.4 (378)	6.4 (327)
H00	SOUTH WEST THAMES RHA	8.5 (298)	9.1 (332)	8.8 (323)	8.4 (323)	8.6 (339)	7.7 (297)	6.9 (275)	5.6 (222)	5.7 (231)
J00	WESSEX RHA	9.7 (329)	9.0 (316)	9.1 (326)	9.5 (352)	9.0 (340)	8.8 (332)	7.1 (272)	6.3 (234)	5.5 (206)
K00	OXFORD RHA	8.5 (270)	8.2 (271)	9.0 (299)	8.6 (299)	8.4 (301)	7.9 (282)	7.2 (264)	7.3 (265)	6.0 (218)
L00	SOUTH WESTERN RHA	8.5 (309)	8.5 (320)	9.5 (361)	8.6 (342)	9.6 (395)	7.3 (298)	6.8 (281)	6.5 (263)	5.5 (222)
M00	WEST MIDLANDS RHA	11.2 (771)	10.5 (741)	10.0 (706)	9.5 (687)	10.2 (745)	9.9 (724)	9.9 (744)	8.7 (647)	8.2 (587)
N00	MERSEY RHA	8.0 (252)	8.9 (293)	9.4 (307)	8.5 (279)	7.7 (257)	7.6 (251)	7.6 (256)	6.7 (222)	5.7 (182)
P00	NORTH WESTERN RHA	10.0 (542)	9.6 (536)	10.7 (594)	9.4 (535)	10.2 (585)	9.1 (516)	8.5 (503)	8.0 (465)	7.7 (435)

1991 CENSUS SUPPLEMENT

SELECTED INDICATORS

CEN - B2
Population with limiting long-term illness (all ages):
Age-standardised illness ratios

		Males			Females			Persons		
		Number	Ratio	Rank	Number	Ratio	Rank	Number	Ratio	Rank
	ENGLAND AND WALES	2955964	100		3558236	100		6514200	100	
O00	ENGLAND	2725584	98		3302621	99		6028205	98	
A00	NORTHERN RHA	227036	126	14	251064	116	14	478100	121	14
B00	YORKSHIRE RHA	217643	104	10	261576	102	9	479219	103	10
C00	TRENT RHA	299655	108	11	344147	106	11	643802	107	11
D00	EAST ANGLIAN RHA	106993	84	5	129528	88	4	236521	86	4
E00	NORTH WEST THAMES RHA	157380	83	3	200102	89	5	357482	86	4
F00	NORTH EAST THAMES RHA	200860	96	8	248903	99	8	449763	98	8
G00	SOUTH EAST THAMES RHA	197115	92	7	252498	93	7	449613	93	7
H00	SOUTH WEST THAMES RHA	134182	77	1	183336	83	1	317518	81	1
J00	WESSEX RHA	156010	83	3	197868	87	3	353878	85	3
K00	OXFORD RHA	106118	77	1	131866	84	2	237984	81	1
L00	SOUTH WESTERN RHA	186783	91	6	228058	90	6	414841	91	6
M00	WEST MIDLANDS RHA	307740	101	9	364104	103	10	671844	102	9
N00	MERSEY RHA	160732	118	12	187010	111	12	347742	114	12
P00	NORTH WESTERN RHA	267337	118	12	322561	115	13	589898	117	13
A01	Hartlepool	7143	138	137	7747	127	137	14890	132	137
A02	North Tees	11915	125	123	12613	116	116	24528	120	119
A03	South Tees	22067	138	137	23440	125	132	45507	131	135
A04	East Cumbria	10458	94	66	12268	92	53	22726	93	62
A05	South Cumbria	9993	92	61	12710	95	64	22703	94	65
A06	West Cumbria	8569	106	94	9522	101	84	18091	103	87
A11	Northumberland	20718	110	101	22643	102	86	43361	106	95
A12	Gateshead	16289	135	134	18155	124	129	34444	129	132
A13	Newcastle	19139	124	121	22685	115	114	41824	119	117
A14	North Tyneside	13912	119	114	16639	114	111	30551	116	112
A15	South Tyneside	12476	133	131	13618	119	121	26094	125	128
A16	Sunderland	24298	149	141	25963	134	142	50261	141	141
A30	North Durham	28531	151	142	29227	132	141	57758	141	141
A31	South Durham	21528	129	128	23834	119	121	45362	123	124
B11	East Riding	31176	104	90	37539	103	89	68715	103	87
B16	Grimsby and Scunthorpe	21397	101	86	25178	103	89	46575	102	86
B21	North Yorkshire	39110	89	52	48562	90	44	87672	89	48
B31	Bradford	27743	110	101	33658	108	100	61401	109	99
B51	West Yorkshire	33170	104	90	40828	103	89	73998	103	87
B61	Leeds	42070	105	93	51138	104	92	93208	105	94
B71	Wakefield	22977	129	128	24673	120	124	47650	124	127
C01	North Derbyshire	24655	108	96	28065	106	97	52720	107	96
C02	Southern Derbyshire	31306	97	76	37987	102	86	69293	100	84
C03	Leicestershire	43669	87	47	53044	91	48	96713	89	48
C04	North Lincolnshire	17571	100	83	20169	99	78	37740	99	82
C05	South Lincolnshire	18568	91	59	21371	92	53	39939	92	55

CEN - B2
Population with limiting long-term illness (all ages):
Age-standardised illness ratios

		Males			Females			Persons		
		Number	Ratio	Rank	Number	Ratio	Rank	Number	Ratio	Rank
C08	Nottingham	36857	103	89	42913	102	86	79770	103	87
C09	Barnsley	20022	152	143	20809	136	143	40831	144	143
C10	Doncaster	23240	137	136	24059	125	132	47299	130	134
C11	Rotherham	19299	134	132	21301	128	138	40600	131	135
C12	Sheffield	36083	117	112	44791	116	116	80874	116	112
C14	North Nottinghamshire	28385	121	117	29638	111	107	58023	116	112
D01	Cambridge	12287	76	14	15762	84	20	28049	80	16
D05	North West Anglia	22425	91	59	26321	94	59	48746	92	55
D06	Norwich	27707	87	47	32916	88	38	60623	87	39
D07	Great Yarmouth and Waveney	12569	94	66	14860	93	57	27429	93	62
D09	Huntingdon	5216	74	9	6359	83	15	11575	79	11
D11	Suffolk	26789	80	26	33310	85	23	60099	83	25
E01	North Bedfordshire	10714	78	22	13443	87	31	24157	83	25
E02	South Bedfordshire	12630	85	37	14871	92	53	27501	89	48
E05	North West Hertfordshire	11296	76	14	14169	83	15	25465	79	11
E06	South West Hertfordshire	10761	76	14	14235	85	23	24996	81	20
E07	Barnet	12972	77	18	18467	86	28	31439	82	23
E09	Hillingdon	10492	79	25	13578	87	31	24070	84	27
E18	East and North Hertfordshire	19868	73	7	25308	81	9	45176	77	6
E19	Brent and Harrow	21226	88	50	27388	96	70	48614	92	55
E20	Ealing, Hammersmith and Hounslow	32180	96	72	39511	99	78	71691	98	78
E21	Kensington, Chelsea and Westminster	15241	86	43	19132	88	38	34373	87	39
F31	North Essex	42040	82	30	52400	86	28	94440	84	27
F32	South Essex	35621	90	55	44485	94	59	80106	92	55
F33	Barking and Havering	20583	92	61	25504	95	64	46087	94	65
F34	Redbridge and Waltham Forest	23263	95	71	30430	100	81	53693	97	73
F35	East London and the City	36035	125	123	41133	125	132	77168	125	128
F36	New River District	23144	94	66	30232	100	81	53376	97	73
F37	Camden and Islington	20174	110	101	24719	110	104	44893	110	104
G04	South East Kent	15651	93	64	19522	92	53	35173	92	55
G05	Canterbury and Thanet	19157	97	76	24609	95	64	43766	96	70
G06	Dartford and Gravesham	10564	85	37	12792	89	42	23356	87	39
G07	Maidstone	8861	78	22	10944	83	15	19805	81	20
G08	Medway	15804	90	55	18973	94	59	34777	92	55
G09	Tunbridge Wells	8831	73	7	12156	79	5	20987	77	6
G10	Bexley	10208	82	30	12806	87	31	23014	85	31
G11	Greenwich	11809	104	90	14800	105	93	26609	104	92
G12	Bromley	13498	77	18	18087	82	12	31585	80	16
G21	East Sussex	42143	90	55	58731	90	44	100874	90	51
G26	South East London	40589	111	104	49078	110	104	89667	111	106

CEN - B2
Population with limiting long-term illness (all ages):
Age-standardised illness ratios

		Males			Females			Persons		
		Number	Ratio	Rank	Number	Ratio	Rank	Number	Ratio	Rank
H04	Mid Surrey	8071	74	9	10713	80	6	18784	77	6
H05	East Surrey	8394	72	6	11288	80	6	19682	77	6
H06	Chichester	10297	81	28	14054	83	15	24351	82	23
H07	Mid Downs	11392	71	4	15058	78	3	26450	75	4
H08	Worthing	14419	84	36	21270	85	23	35689	85	31
H09	Croydon	14112	83	34	18723	90	44	32835	87	39
H12	Wandsworth	9463	100	83	12352	105	93	21815	103	87
H13	Merton and Sutton	15234	80	26	21254	87	31	36488	84	27
H14	North West Surrey	14975	67	1	20049	77	1	35024	73	1
H15	South West Surrey	9965	70	2	13750	78	3	23715	74	2
H16	Kingston and Richmond	17860	75	13	24825	81	9	42685	79	11
J10	Dorset	38599	86	43	50536	87	31	89135	87	39
J21	Portsmouth and South East Hampshire	27287	89	52	35048	94	59	62335	92	55
J22	Southampton and South West Hampshire	22459	86	43	27202	87	31	49661	86	36
J23	Winchester	9349	74	9	11917	81	9	21266	78	10
J24	Basingstoke and North Hampshire	13728	71	4	17233	80	6	30961	76	5
J31	Salisbury	6091	76	14	8013	82	12	14104	79	11
J32	Swindon	11182	85	37	13457	91	48	24639	88	44
J33	Bath	18888	77	18	24134	82	12	43022	80	16
J41	Isle of Wight	8427	96	72	10328	91	48	18755	93	62
K11	East Berkshire	15466	77	18	19233	84	20	34699	81	20
K12	West Berkshire	16793	70	2	20920	77	1	37713	74	2
K24	Buckinghamshire	23734	74	9	30144	84	20	53878	79	11
K31	Kettering	13036	85	37	16146	91	48	29182	88	44
K32	Northampton	14312	81	28	17885	89	42	32197	85	31
K41	Oxfordshire	22777	78	22	27538	83	15	50315	80	16
L10	Bristol and District	43198	90	55	53390	91	48	96588	90	51
L21	Cornwall and Isles of Scilly	31265	101	86	36312	96	70	67577	98	78
L35	Exeter and North Devon	26784	89	52	33343	88	38	60127	88	44
L36	Plymouth and Torbay	36116	99	80	44056	95	64	80172	97	73
L40	Gloucestershire	26655	82	30	33177	85	23	59832	84	27
L51	Somerset	22765	85	37	27780	85	23	50545	85	31
M02	Herefordshire	9022	86	43	10449	86	28	19471	86	36
M04	Worcester and District	12460	82	30	15642	87	31	28102	85	31
M05	Shropshire	23164	96	72	26735	95	64	49899	95	68
M06	Mid Staffordshire	16863	94	66	19465	97	73	36328	96	70
M07	North Staffordshire	33583	122	118	39080	121	126	72663	121	122
M08	South East Staffordshire	13394	93	64	15686	97	73	29080	95	68
M13	East Birmingham	13419	120	115	15413	117	118	28832	119	117
M14	North Birmingham	9032	94	66	11340	97	73	20372	96	70
M16	West Birmingham	13435	122	118	15115	119	121	28550	121	122
M17	Coventry	17801	102	88	21213	105	93	39014	104	92

CEN - B2
Population with limiting long-term illness (all ages):
Age-standardised illness ratios

		Males			Females			Persons		
		Number	Ratio	Rank	Number	Ratio	Rank	Number	Ratio	Rank
M18	Dudley	17736	98	78	20973	100	81	38709	99	82
M19	Sandwell	19855	114	109	23858	115	114	43713	114	108
M20	Solihull	9652	83	34	11872	88	38	21524	86	36
M21	Walsall	17085	114	109	19489	113	109	36574	113	107
M22	Wolverhampton	16414	113	105	19089	114	111	35503	114	108
M25	South Birmingham	25516	109	98	31073	109	103	56589	109	99
M26	North Worcestershire	13472	87	47	16692	94	59	30164	90	51
M28	Warwickshire	25837	88	50	30920	93	57	56757	91	54
N11	Chester	10147	98	78	11912	97	73	22059	97	73
N12	Crewe	14847	99	80	16961	98	77	31808	98	78
N13	Halton	9634	126	125	10504	120	124	20138	123	124
N14	Macclesfield	9185	85	37	11867	90	44	21052	88	44
N15	Warrington	11041	107	95	12711	106	97	23752	107	96
N21	Liverpool	36713	142	140	41722	126	135	78435	133	139
N31	St Helens and Knowsley	25635	141	139	28295	130	140	53930	135	140
N41	Southport and Formby	7387	99	80	10214	96	70	17601	97	73
N42	South Sefton	12590	126	125	14132	112	108	26722	118	116
N51	Wirral	23553	113	105	28692	107	99	52245	109	99
P01	Lancaster	8640	109	98	10844	105	93	19484	107	96
P02	Blackpool, Wyre and Fylde	24449	113	105	30807	108	100	55256	110	104
P03	Preston	8554	118	113	9921	113	109	18475	115	111
P04	Blackburn, Hyndburn and Ribble Valley	18747	124	121	22501	122	128	41248	123	124
P05	Burnley, Pendle and Rossendale	16937	126	125	20800	124	129	37737	125	128
P06	West Lancashire	6595	109	98	7719	108	100	14314	109	99
P07	Chorley and South Ribble	11108	100	83	13024	101	84	24132	101	85
P08	Bolton	17722	122	118	21041	118	120	38763	120	119
P09	Bury	10736	108	96	13502	110	104	24238	109	99
P10	North Manchester	11809	154	145	13167	138	144	24976	145	144
P11	Central Manchester	8735	153	144	9261	141	145	17996	147	145
P12	South Manchester	12070	130	130	14903	124	129	26973	126	131
P13	Oldham	13861	115	111	17380	117	118	31241	116	112
P14	Rochdale	13872	120	115	16984	121	126	30856	120	119
P15	Salford	17560	134	132	20752	126	135	38312	129	132
P16	Stockport	15272	92	61	19428	95	64	34700	94	65
P17	Tameside and Glossop	15634	113	105	19284	114	111	34918	114	108
P18	Trafford	11992	96	72	15251	99	78	27243	98	78
P19	Wigan	23044	136	135	25992	129	139	49036	132	137

		Males			Females			Persons		
		Number	Ratio	Rank	Number	Ratio	Rank	Number	Ratio	Rank
	ENGLAND AND WALES	914016	100		660002	100		1574018	100	
O00	ENGLAND	817741	95		595625	96		1413366	95	
A00	NORTHERN RHA	92043	162	14	56221	138	12	148264	152	14
B00	YORKSHIRE RHA	66589	102	10	44936	95	9	111525	99	10
C00	TRENT RHA	93557	109	11	60100	99	11	153657	104	11
D00	EAST ANGLIAN RHA	25578	68	5	19172	72	4	44750	69	4
E00	NORTH WEST THAMES RHA	41092	67	4	36078	82	6	77170	73	5
F00	NORTH EAST THAMES RHA	56292	86	8	44485	93	8	100777	89	8
G00	SOUTH EAST THAMES RHA	50232	78	6	41074	85	7	91306	81	7
H00	SOUTH WEST THAMES RHA	29715	56	2	28317	71	3	58032	62	2
J00	WESSEX RHA	35566	63	3	28266	69	2	63832	66	3
K00	OXFORD RHA	23424	53	1	19668	62	1	43092	57	1
L00	SOUTH WESTERN RHA	47650	79	7	33754	77	5	81404	78	6
M00	WEST MIDLANDS RHA	93525	97	9	65323	97	10	158848	97	9
N00	MERSEY RHA	63640	147	13	45405	143	14	109045	145	13
P00	NORTH WESTERN RHA	98838	140	12	72826	142	13	171664	141	12
A01	Hartlepool	3183	188	138	1976	165	135	5159	179	137
A02	North Tees	4826	152	124	2930	131	116	7756	144	124
A03	South Tees	9417	181	135	5702	155	130	15119	170	134
A04	East Cumbria	3021	87	71	2101	86	67	5122	87	70
A05	South Cumbria	2757	84	66	2079	88	71	4836	86	68
A06	West Cumbria	2979	115	98	2031	112	97	5010	113	96
A11	Northumberland	7833	134	115	4807	115	102	12640	126	109
A12	Gateshead	7145	185	137	4180	153	129	11325	171	135
A13	Newcastle	7512	161	127	4865	141	122	12377	152	125
A14	North Tyneside	5317	146	122	3250	123	108	8567	136	117
A15	South Tyneside	5318	179	134	2949	141	122	8267	163	131
A16	Sunderland	11241	212	143	6417	169	138	17658	194	141
A30	North Durham	13031	215	144	7653	178	140	20684	200	142
A31	South Durham	8463	162	129	5281	142	124	13744	154	126
B11	East Riding	9657	104	91	6050	90	76	15707	98	84
B16	Grimsby and Scunthorpe	6276	94	80	4074	87	70	10350	91	77
B21	North Yorkshire	10335	78	56	7382	76	41	17717	77	51
B31	Bradford	9029	115	98	6328	110	96	15357	113	96
B51	West Yorkshire	10087	101	87	7142	98	85	17229	100	87
B61	Leeds	13033	106	93	9146	101	88	22179	104	93
B71	Wakefield	8172	144	121	4814	119	105	12986	133	114
C01	North Derbyshire	7368	104	91	4486	90	76	11854	99	86
C02	Southern Derbyshire	8564	86	68	5847	84	61	14411	85	65
C03	Leicestershire	11780	75	50	9134	82	57	20914	78	54
C04	North Lincolnshire	5241	99	85	3337	89	73	8578	95	81
C05	South Lincolnshire	5228	85	67	3444	81	56	8672	83	61

CEN - B3

Population prevented from working by permanent sickness (ages 16 and over):
Age-standardised permanent sickness ratios

		Males			Females			Persons		
		Number	Ratio	Rank	Number	Ratio	Rank	Number	Ratio	Rank
C08	Nottingham	10747	97	83	7359	93	81	18106	95	81
C09	Barnsley	8201	199	140	4712	161	132	12913	183	138
C10	Doncaster	9138	170	131	5165	137	119	14303	156	127
C11	Rotherham	6943	151	123	4028	123	108	10971	139	120
C12	Sheffield	10986	119	102	7304	108	94	18290	114	100
C14	North Nottinghamshire	9361	126	107	5284	102	90	14645	116	102
D01	Cambridge	2638	53	12	2233	63	14	4871	57	13
D05	North West Anglia	5942	80	60	4367	84	61	10309	81	59
D06	Norwich	6713	73	47	4697	71	29	11410	72	42
D07	Great Yarmouth and Waveney	3399	90	75	2293	84	61	5692	87	70
D09	Huntingdon	1002	44	4	934	58	7	1936	50	4
D11	Suffolk	5884	58	22	4648	65	17	10532	61	18
E01	North Bedfordshire	2708	61	27	2345	76	41	5053	67	30
E02	South Bedfordshire	3260	66	36	2430	72	31	5690	69	36
E05	North West Hertfordshire	3063	63	29	2398	70	24	5461	66	28
E06	South West Hertfordshire	2629	60	25	2481	78	51	5110	68	34
E07	Barnet	2965	59	24	2989	77	46	5954	67	30
E09	Hillingdon	2378	57	20	2234	74	35	4612	64	22
E18	East and North Hertfordshire	4454	50	10	3788	60	10	8242	54	10
E19	Brent and Harrow	5740	74	49	5354	94	82	11094	83	61
E20	Ealing, Hammersmith and Hounslow	9337	87	71	8122	102	90	17459	94	80
E21	Kensington, Chelsea and Westminster	4558	79	59	3937	91	78	8495	84	63
F31	North Essex	9877	63	29	7693	68	21	17570	65	24
F32	South Essex	9283	75	50	6957	77	46	16240	76	48
F33	Barking and Havering	5629	81	62	4200	84	61	9829	82	60
F34	Redbridge and Waltham Forest	6264	83	63	5324	95	83	11588	88	74
F35	East London and the City	12194	133	112	9153	142	124	21347	137	118
F36	New River District	6582	83	63	5727	97	84	12309	89	75
F37	Camden and Islington	6463	111	97	5431	124	111	11894	117	103
G04	South East Kent	3837	78	56	2851	79	54	6688	78	54
G05	Canterbury and Thanet	4858	91	79	3711	91	78	8569	91	77
G06	Dartford and Gravesham	2699	66	36	2111	73	33	4810	68	34
G07	Maidstone	2092	57	20	1719	65	17	3811	60	17
G08	Medway	3888	68	40	2832	70	24	6720	69	36
G09	Tunbridge Wells	1788	48	8	1507	54	2	3295	50	4
G10	Bexley	2372	60	25	1867	65	17	4239	62	19
G11	Greenwich	3294	96	81	2739	106	93	6033	100	87
G12	Bromley	3045	56	15	2622	64	15	5667	59	16
G21	East Sussex	10009	80	60	8670	88	71	18679	84	63
G26	South East London	12350	107	94	10445	121	106	22795	113	96

		Males			Females			Persons		
		Number	Ratio	Rank	Number	Ratio	Rank	Number	Ratio	Rank
H04	Mid Surrey	1858	56	15	1836	76	41	3694	65	24
H05	East Surrey	2002	56	15	1936	74	35	3938	63	21
H06	Chichester	2033	61	27	1772	68	21	3805	64	22
H07	Mid Downs	2351	46	6	2095	56	5	4446	50	4
H08	Worthing	2859	64	34	2488	70	24	5347	67	30
H09	Croydon	3542	65	35	3354	82	57	6896	72	42
H12	Wandsworth	2701	89	74	2651	114	101	5352	100	87
H13	Merton and Sutton	3415	58	22	3317	74	35	6732	65	24
H14	North West Surrey	3125	43	2	3180	62	12	6305	51	7
H15	South West Surrey	1767	40	1	1827	56	5	3594	47	1
H16	Kingston and Richmond	4062	56	15	3861	70	24	7923	62	19
J10	Dorset	8516	70	42	6592	72	31	15108	70	40
J21	Portsmouth and South East Hampshire	6608	70	42	5682	83	60	12290	76	48
J22	Southampton and South West Hampshire	5633	72	45	3942	71	29	9575	72	42
J23	Winchester	1896	48	8	1553	55	3	3449	51	7
J24	Basingstoke and North Hampshire	2768	43	2	2504	55	3	5272	48	2
J31	Salisbury	1210	51	11	1026	60	10	2236	55	11
J32	Swindon	2795	66	36	2166	74	35	4961	69	36
J33	Bath	4102	56	15	3295	62	12	7397	58	14
J41	Isle of Wight	2038	86	68	1506	84	61	3544	85	65
K11	East Berkshire	3522	53	12	2981	64	15	6503	58	14
K12	West Berkshire	3509	44	4	2977	53	1	6486	48	2
K24	Buckinghamshire	4926	47	7	4441	59	8	9367	52	9
K31	Kettering	3149	67	39	2567	76	41	5716	71	41
K32	Northampton	3454	63	29	2872	73	33	6326	67	30
K41	Oxfordshire	4864	53	12	3830	59	8	8694	55	11
L10	Bristol and District	11452	77	53	8368	78	51	19820	78	54
L21	Cornwall and Isles of Scilly	8719	96	81	5682	86	67	14401	92	79
L35	Exeter and North Devon	6504	77	53	4659	74	35	11163	76	48
L36	Plymouth and Torbay	9433	90	75	6418	82	57	15851	87	70
L40	Gloucestershire	6213	63	29	4785	67	20	10998	65	24
L51	Somerset	5329	69	41	3842	69	23	9171	69	36
M02	Herefordshire	2267	73	47	1653	76	41	3920	74	46
M04	Worcester and District	2931	63	29	2321	70	24	5252	66	28
M05	Shropshire	6680	88	73	4507	84	61	11187	86	68
M06	Mid Staffordshire	4937	83	63	3171	77	46	8108	80	57
M07	North Staffordshire	11661	133	112	8758	144	127	20419	137	118
M08	South East Staffordshire	3692	78	56	2554	77	46	6246	77	51
M13	East Birmingham	4276	129	111	2688	116	104	6964	123	106
M14	North Birmingham	2611	86	68	1924	89	73	4535	87	70
M16	West Birmingham	4570	134	115	3161	134	118	7731	134	116
M17	Coventry	5654	107	94	4318	115	102	9972	111	94

CEN - B3

Population prevented from working by permanent sickness (ages 16 and over):
Age-standardised permanent sickness ratios

		Males			Females			Persons		
		Number	Ratio	Rank	Number	Ratio	Rank	Number	Ratio	Rank
M18	Dudley	5362	90	75	3161	77	46	8523	85	65
M19	Sandwell	6269	115	98	4124	109	95	10393	113	96
M20	Solihull	2696	70	42	2040	75	40	4736	72	42
M21	Walsall	6108	123	105	3826	112	97	9934	118	104
M22	Wolverhampton	5303	117	101	3507	113	100	8810	115	101
M25	South Birmingham	7839	110	96	5746	112	97	13585	111	94
M26	North Worcestershire	3613	72	45	2838	80	55	6451	75	47
M28	Warwickshire	7056	76	52	5026	78	51	12082	77	51
N11	Chester	3326	100	86	2397	100	87	5723	100	87
N12	Crewe	4806	101	87	3115	92	80	7921	97	83
N13	Halton	4098	164	130	2766	155	130	6864	160	128
N14	Macclesfield	2668	77	53	2141	86	67	4809	80	57
N15	Warrington	4299	127	109	3086	129	113	7385	128	111
N21	Liverpool	16289	201	141	11967	200	144	28256	201	143
N31	St Helens and Knowsley	11681	194	139	8173	188	141	19854	191	140
N41	Southport and Formby	2223	101	87	1739	102	90	3962	101	91
N42	South Sefton	5648	175	132	3817	161	132	9465	169	133
N51	Wirral	8602	135	117	6204	129	113	14806	133	114
P01	Lancaster	2804	121	103	2078	121	106	4882	121	105
P02	Blackpool, Wyre and Fylde	8392	133	112	5791	123	108	14183	129	112
P03	Preston	3184	141	120	2265	142	124	5449	142	122
P04	Blackburn, Hyndburn and Ribble Valley	7239	154	125	5684	168	137	12923	160	128
P05	Burnley, Pendle and Rossendale	6473	156	126	5008	166	136	11481	160	128
P06	West Lancashire	2499	126	107	1861	129	113	4360	127	110
P07	Chorley and South Ribble	3671	102	90	2595	101	88	6266	102	92
P08	Bolton	6418	140	119	4577	138	120	10995	139	120
P09	Bury	3836	121	103	3068	131	116	6904	125	108
P10	North Manchester	5100	219	145	3477	210	145	8577	215	145
P11	Central Manchester	3754	208	142	2440	198	143	6194	204	144
P12	South Manchester	4436	161	127	3395	164	134	7831	163	131
P13	Oldham	4811	127	109	3861	139	121	8672	132	113
P14	Rochdale	5081	138	118	4007	151	128	9088	143	123
P15	Salford	7151	178	133	5029	173	139	12180	176	136
P16	Stockport	4768	90	75	3438	89	73	8206	90	76
P17	Tameside and Glossop	5436	124	106	3942	124	111	9378	124	107
P18	Trafford	3795	97	83	2802	98	85	6597	98	84
P19	Wigan	9990	181	135	7508	189	142	17498	184	139

CEN - B5
Ethnic group:
Percent of resident population that is

		Non-white			Black			Asian (excluding Chinese)		
		Number	Percent	Rank	Number	Percent	Rank	Number	Percent	Rank
	ENGLAND AND WALES	2952416	5.9		884374	1.8		1640199	3.3	
O00	ENGLAND	2910865	6.2		874882	1.9		1620601	3.4	
A00	NORTHERN RHA	38547	1.3	1	4507	0.1	1	23778	0.8	4
B00	YORKSHIRE RHA	177869	5.0	7	26714	0.7	5	131887	3.7	10
C00	TRENT RHA	203580	4.4	6	41301	0.9	7	137075	3.0	7
D00	EAST ANGLIAN RHA	43403	2.1	5	14489	0.7	5	17680	0.9	5
E00	NORTH WEST THAMES RHA	558967	16.4	14	145303	4.3	12	334155	9.8	14
F00	NORTH EAST THAMES RHA	513469	13.9	13	204272	5.5	14	245900	6.7	13
G00	SOUTH EAST THAMES RHA	278518	7.7	11	156570	4.3	12	77503	2.1	6
H00	SOUTH WEST THAMES RHA	206128	7.1	10	70547	2.4	11	97365	3.3	9
J00	WESSEX RHA	48611	1.6	4	11577	0.4	2	21664	0.7	3
K00	OXFORD RHA	127775	5.1	8	33510	1.3	9	73654	3.0	7
L00	SOUTH WESTERN RHA	44778	1.4	2	16799	0.5	3	15227	0.5	2
M00	WEST MIDLANDS RHA	424359	8.2	12	102206	2.0	10	288237	5.6	12
N00	MERSEY RHA	35281	1.5	3	11349	0.5	3	9472	0.4	1
P00	NORTH WESTERN RHA	209580	5.4	9	35738	0.9	7	147004	3.8	11
A01	Hartlepool	644	0.7	10	78	0.1	1	392	0.4	33
A02	North Tees	2803	1.6	55	207	0.1	1	1967	1.1	70
A03	South Tees	7197	2.5	73	713	0.2	16	5318	1.9	84
A04	East Cumbria	821	0.5	2	165	0.1	1	293	0.2	5
A05	South Cumbria	797	0.5	2	173	0.1	1	221	0.1	1
A06	West Cumbria	493	0.4	1	112	0.1	1	157	0.1	1
A11	Northumberland	1547	0.5	2	180	0.1	1	804	0.3	14
A12	Gateshead	1630	0.8	19	192	0.1	1	866	0.4	33
A13	Newcastle	10551	4.1	94	950	0.4	64	7397	2.9	100
A14	North Tyneside	2072	1.1	37	320	0.2	16	1014	0.5	38
A15	South Tyneside	2403	1.6	55	391	0.3	51	1148	0.7	51
A16	Sunderland	3220	1.1	37	304	0.1	1	1920	0.7	51
A30	North Durham	2161	0.7	10	265	0.1	1	1171	0.4	33
A31	South Durham	2208	0.8	19	457	0.2	16	1110	0.4	33
B11	East Riding	4585	0.9	28	1145	0.2	16	1627	0.3	14
B16	Grimsby and Scunthorpe	4119	1.2	44	648	0.2	16	2438	0.7	51
B21	North Yorkshire	5034	0.7	10	1020	0.1	1	1852	0.3	14
B31	Bradford	71319	15.6	129	5336	1.2	101	62243	13.6	139
B51	West Yorkshire	48489	8.6	115	7221	1.3	104	38002	6.7	119
B61	Leeds	39725	5.8	104	10815	1.6	113	22536	3.3	106
B71	Wakefield	4598	1.5	52	529	0.2	16	3189	1.0	66
C01	North Derbyshire	2615	0.7	10	739	0.2	16	913	0.3	14
C02	Southern Derbyshire	24641	4.6	97	5517	1.0	94	16629	3.1	104
C03	Leicestershire	96350	11.1	122	8528	1.0	94	81090	9.3	132
C04	North Lincolnshire	2154	0.8	19	591	0.2	16	730	0.3	14
C05	South Lincolnshire	2299	0.7	10	594	0.2	16	759	0.2	5

CEN - B5
Ethnic group:
Percent of resident population that is

		Non-white			Black			Asian (excluding Chinese)		
		Number	Percent	Rank	Number	Percent	Rank	Number	Percent	Rank
C08	Nottingham	35887	5.9	106	14246	2.4	123	16321	2.7	99
C09	Barnsley	1296	0.6	6	266	0.1	1	606	0.3	14
C10	Doncaster	4631	1.6	55	1288	0.4	64	2447	0.8	60
C11	Rotherham	5000	2.0	64	394	0.2	16	3913	1.6	79
C12	Sheffield	25225	5.0	100	7972	1.6	113	12325	2.5	94
C14	North Nottinghamshire	3482	0.9	28	1166	0.3	51	1342	0.3	14
D01	Cambridge	7534	2.8	76	1598	0.6	81	3234	1.2	72
D05	North West Anglia	13391	3.4	83	2678	0.7	88	8801	2.2	88
D06	Norwich	4109	0.9	28	984	0.2	16	1345	0.3	14
D07	Great Yarmouth and Waveney	1491	0.7	10	378	0.2	16	509	0.3	14
D09	Huntingdon	3170	2.4	71	1414	1.1	96	991	0.7	51
D11	Suffolk	13708	2.5	73	7437	1.4	106	2800	0.5	38
E01	North Bedfordshire	15766	6.5	109	4441	1.8	120	9559	3.9	108
E02	South Bedfordshire	36174	12.9	127	8889	3.2	126	24435	8.7	129
E05	North West Hertfordshire	9926	3.8	91	1940	0.8	90	5666	2.2	88
E06	South West Hertfordshire	14592	6.1	107	2592	1.1	96	8986	3.8	107
E07	Barnet	54015	18.4	132	10472	3.6	128	33658	11.5	137
E09	Hillingdon	28453	12.3	125	3810	1.6	113	20876	9.0	130
E18	East and North Hertfordshire	14906	3.1	80	3790	0.8	90	7639	1.6	79
E19	Brent and Harrow	161300	36.4	143	47594	10.7	140	98068	22.1	144
E20	Ealing, Hammersmith and Hounslow	164793	26.2	142	40218	6.4	134	104715	16.7	141
E21	Kensington, Chelsea and Westminster	59042	18.9	135	21557	6.9	135	20553	6.6	118
F31	North Essex	15265	1.8	60	3299	0.4	64	6611	0.8	60
F32	South Essex	13772	2.0	64	2866	0.4	64	6630	1.0	66
F33	Barking and Havering	17102	4.6	97	5513	1.5	110	8629	2.3	92
F34	Redbridge and Waltham Forest	102630	23.4	138	33528	7.7	137	60064	13.7	140
F35	East London and the City	208215	37.3	144	81794	14.6	144	110256	19.7	143
F36	New River District	94982	20.7	136	50432	11.0	141	32081	7.0	121
F37	Camden and Islington	61503	18.4	132	26840	8.0	138	21629	6.5	117
G04	South East Kent	3121	1.2	44	799	0.3	51	1306	0.5	38
G05	Canterbury and Thanet	3718	1.3	47	815	0.3	51	1394	0.5	38
G06	Dartford and Gravesham	11656	5.3	101	1141	0.5	74	9137	4.2	112
G07	Maidstone	2981	1.5	52	546	0.3	51	1506	0.8	60
G08	Medway	11062	3.3	82	1837	0.6	81	7343	2.2	88
G09	Tunbridge Wells	2202	1.1	37	385	0.2	16	896	0.5	38
G10	Bexley	12498	5.8	104	3012	1.4	106	6932	3.2	105
G11	Greenwich	26457	12.7	126	11119	5.4	133	11084	5.3	114
G12	Bromley	13581	4.7	99	4548	1.6	113	5586	1.9	84
G21	East Sussex	13028	1.9	62	2611	0.4	64	5146	0.7	51
G26	South East London	178214	25.7	141	129757	18.7	145	27173	3.9	108

CEN - B5
Ethnic group:
Percent of resident population that is

		Non-white			Black			Asian (excluding Chinese)		
		Number	Percent	Rank	Number	Percent	Rank	Number	Percent	Rank
H04	Mid Surrey	5898	3.5	86	953	0.6	81	3317	2.0	86
H05	East Surrey	3869	2.1	67	582	0.3	51	2063	1.1	70
H06	Chichester	1661	0.9	28	376	0.2	16	590	0.3	14
H07	Mid Downs	9506	3.4	83	927	0.3	51	6731	2.4	93
H08	Worthing	2796	1.1	37	483	0.2	16	1159	0.5	38
H09	Croydon	55114	17.6	131	23712	7.6	136	23631	7.5	124
H12	Wandsworth	43080	23.1	137	23735	12.7	142	14587	7.8	125
H13	Merton and Sutton	37355	11.1	122	11978	3.6	128	18848	5.6	115
H14	North West Surrey	13312	3.5	86	1447	0.4	64	8459	2.2	88
H15	South West Surrey	3781	1.6	55	560	0.2	16	1711	0.7	51
H16	Kingston and Richmond	29756	7.3	111	5794	1.4	106	16269	4.0	110
J10	Dorset	5771	0.9	28	1172	0.2	16	1979	0.3	14
J21	Portsmouth and South East Hampshire	7733	1.5	52	1593	0.3	51	3260	0.6	46
J22	Southampton and South West Hampshire	11701	2.8	76	2119	0.5	74	6860	1.6	79
J23	Winchester	2725	1.3	47	493	0.2	16	1313	0.6	46
J24	Basingstoke and North Hampshire	7626	2.1	67	2100	0.6	81	3432	0.9	63
J31	Salisbury	1017	0.8	19	235	0.2	16	371	0.3	14
J32	Swindon	5885	2.5	73	1449	0.6	81	2883	1.2	72
J33	Bath	5243	1.3	47	2138	0.5	74	1284	0.3	14
J41	Isle of Wight	910	0.7	10	278	0.2	16	282	0.2	5
K11	East Berkshire	38086	10.4	121	5222	1.4	106	29315	8.0	127
K12	West Berkshire	19481	4.4	95	6888	1.6	113	9027	2.1	87
K24	Buckinghamshire	32073	5.4	102	8816	1.5	110	17732	3.0	103
K31	Kettering	8094	3.1	80	2438	0.9	93	4431	1.7	82
K32	Northampton	12222	3.9	93	4688	1.5	110	5386	1.7	82
K41	Oxfordshire	17819	3.5	86	5458	1.1	96	7763	1.5	78
L10	Bristol and District	23412	2.9	78	10026	1.2	101	8222	1.0	66
L21	Cornwall and Isles of Scilly	2536	0.5	2	834	0.2	16	524	0.1	1
L35	Exeter and North Devon	2843	0.6	6	599	0.1	1	844	0.2	5
L36	Plymouth and Torbay	4003	0.7	10	1065	0.2	16	1097	0.2	5
L40	Gloucestershire	9730	1.8	60	3738	0.7	88	3936	0.7	51
L51	Somerset	2254	0.6	6	537	0.1	1	604	0.1	1
M02	Herefordshire	895	0.6	6	227	0.1	1	241	0.2	5
M04	Worcester and District	2639	1.1	37	450	0.2	16	1497	0.6	46
M05	Shropshire	6673	1.6	55	1354	0.3	51	3840	0.9	63
M06	Mid Staffordshire	3901	1.2	44	1117	0.4	64	1845	0.6	46
M07	North Staffordshire	9324	2.0	64	1640	0.4	64	6168	1.3	74
M08	South East Staffordshire	5807	2.2	69	1246	0.5	74	3715	1.4	77
M13	East Birmingham	46115	23.9	139	7747	4.0	130	35847	18.6	142
M14	North Birmingham	9701	6.1	107	4536	2.9	125	3894	2.5	94
M16	West Birmingham	81730	40.2	145	27105	13.3	143	50789	25.0	145
M17	Coventry	34874	11.8	124	4822	1.6	113	27623	9.4	133

264

CEN - B5
Ethnic group:
Percent of resident population that is

		Non-white			Black			Asian (excluding Chinese)		
		Number	Percent	Rank	Number	Percent	Rank	Number	Percent	Rank
M18	Dudley	13662	4.5	96	3293	1.1	96	8872	2.9	100
M19	Sandwell	42605	14.7	128	9596	3.3	127	31103	10.7	135
M20	Solihull	5805	2.9	78	2112	1.1	96	2609	1.3	74
M21	Walsall	24794	9.6	118	3383	1.3	104	20173	7.8	125
M22	Wolverhampton	45015	18.6	134	12433	5.1	132	30621	12.6	138
M25	South Birmingham	69221	17.0	130	16988	4.2	131	45022	11.1	136
M26	North Worcestershire	5057	1.9	62	1657	0.6	81	2379	0.9	63
M28	Warwickshire	16541	3.4	83	2500	0.5	74	11999	2.5	94
N11	Chester	1617	0.9	28	310	0.2	16	662	0.4	33
N12	Crewe	2253	0.9	28	650	0.3	51	797	0.3	14
N13	Halton	1087	0.8	19	294	0.2	16	343	0.2	5
N14	Macclesfield	1923	1.1	37	344	0.2	16	832	0.5	38
N15	Warrington	2411	1.3	47	362	0.2	16	1289	0.7	51
N21	Liverpool	17046	3.8	91	7247	1.6	113	3021	0.7	51
N31	St Helens and Knowsley	2737	0.8	19	831	0.3	51	763	0.2	5
N41	Southport and Formby	1257	1.1	37	273	0.2	16	369	0.3	14
N42	South Sefton	1456	0.8	19	383	0.2	16	369	0.2	5
N51	Wirral	3494	1.0	35	649	0.2	16	1027	0.3	14
P01	Lancaster	1564	1.3	47	239	0.2	16	774	0.6	46
P02	Blackpool,Wyre and Fylde	2233	0.7	10	471	0.1	1	887	0.3	14
P03	Preston	12873	10.2	120	1529	1.2	101	10508	8.3	128
P04	Blackburn, Hyndburn and Ribble Valley	26196	9.9	119	756	0.3	51	23919	9.0	130
P05	Burnley, Pendle and Rossendale	15386	6.5	109	447	0.2	16	14119	6.0	116
P06	West Lancashire	828	0.8	19	212	0.2	16	283	0.3	14
P07	Chorley and South Ribble	1989	1.0	35	477	0.2	16	921	0.5	38
P08	Bolton	21388	8.3	114	1546	0.6	81	18404	7.1	122
P09	Bury	6455	3.7	89	928	0.5	74	4337	2.5	94
P10	North Manchester	10327	7.7	113	3125	2.3	122	5386	4.0	110
P11	Central Manchester	25649	24.0	140	11148	10.4	139	10932	10.2	134
P12	South Manchester	15207	9.2	117	4585	2.8	124	7382	4.5	113
P13	Oldham	18830	8.7	116	1796	0.8	90	15888	7.3	123
P14	Rochdale	15948	7.6	112	932	0.4	64	14007	6.7	119
P15	Salford	4810	2.2	69	1022	0.5	74	2129	1.0	66
P16	Stockport	6747	2.4	71	1122	0.4	64	3589	1.3	74
P17	Tameside and Glossop	9181	3.7	89	846	0.3	51	7089	2.9	100
P18	Trafford	11560	5.4	102	4062	1.9	121	5467	2.6	98
P19	Wigan	2409	0.8	19	495	0.2	16	983	0.3	14

CEN - D2
Social class as defined by occupation of head of household
Percentage distribution

		I	II	IIIN	IIIM	IV	V	Other	Manual group (IIIM, IV & V) Percent	Rank
	ENGLAND AND WALES	6.8	30.6	12.0	28.4	13.5	4.4	4.3	46.3	
O00	ENGLAND	6.8	30.7	12.1	28.3	13.4	4.4	4.3	46.1	
A00	NORTHERN RHA	5.5	24.9	11.2	32.1	15.6	5.8	4.9	53.5	14
B00	YORKSHIRE RHA	5.5	28.5	11.2	30.5	14.9	5.2	4.2	50.5	11
C00	TRENT RHA	5.9	27.2	10.3	32.6	15.2	4.7	4.2	52.5	13
D00	EAST ANGLIAN RHA	6.7	30.3	10.8	28.1	14.2	4.2	5.8	46.5	8
E00	NORTH WEST THAMES RHA	9.0	35.7	14.0	23.3	10.6	3.6	3.8	37.5	2
F00	NORTH EAST THAMES RHA	6.1	30.8	14.3	26.6	12.9	4.5	4.7	44.0	6
G00	SOUTH EAST THAMES RHA	6.7	32.9	14.2	26.1	11.7	4.5	4.0	42.2	4
H00	SOUTH WEST THAMES RHA	10.1	39.6	14.2	21.4	9.0	3.2	2.4	33.6	1
J00	WESSEX RHA	7.7	32.0	11.7	26.2	12.7	3.9	5.8	42.8	5
K00	OXFORD RHA	8.8	35.8	11.2	25.6	11.6	3.6	3.4	40.8	3
L00	SOUTH WESTERN RHA	6.8	31.3	11.8	27.9	13.2	4.3	4.7	45.4	7
M00	WEST MIDLANDS RHA	5.8	27.4	10.5	32.2	15.4	4.2	4.5	51.8	12
N00	MERSEY RHA	6.6	28.4	11.6	28.6	14.8	4.7	5.3	48.1	9
P00	NORTH WESTERN RHA	6.0	27.9	12.5	30.2	14.8	4.9	3.7	49.9	10
A01	Hartlepool	4.1	21.0	7.4	35.0	18.7	6.9	6.9	60.6	141
A02	North Tees	7.2	25.1	12.0	30.3	14.4	5.5	5.5	50.3	94
A03	South Tees	5.5	22.7	10.5	31.2	17.0	7.2	5.9	55.4	120
A04	East Cumbria	4.9	30.8	11.0	32.4	13.5	4.7	2.7	50.6	96
A05	South Cumbria	5.6	28.3	11.5	34.8	13.2	4.8	1.7	52.8	108
A06	West Cumbria	5.7	22.6	8.2	32.6	20.2	6.8	3.9	59.7	140
A11	Northumberland	6.5	29.5	11.0	28.3	15.4	5.2	4.1	48.9	85
A12	Gateshead	4.2	22.4	11.7	34.4	15.4	6.5	5.5	56.2	126
A13	Newcastle	8.2	24.7	13.3	27.9	12.8	6.3	6.7	47.0	73
A14	North Tyneside	5.7	26.9	13.5	30.4	13.8	6.0	3.7	50.2	92
A15	South Tyneside	4.4	21.0	11.5	36.8	15.4	5.1	5.8	57.3	128
A16	Sunderland	4.0	20.9	12.2	34.3	16.0	5.3	7.3	55.6	122
A30	North Durham	5.5	24.1	10.5	33.4	16.3	5.7	4.4	55.5	121
A31	South Durham	4.8	25.5	9.7	32.9	17.3	5.4	4.3	55.6	122
B11	East Riding	5.4	26.6	11.4	30.7	15.7	5.8	4.4	52.2	104
B16	Grimsby and Scunthorpe	3.9	23.6	9.6	35.7	17.1	6.8	3.4	59.5	139
B21	North Yorkshire	6.4	34.7	11.3	25.2	13.0	4.1	5.3	42.3	42
B31	Bradford	5.1	27.6	11.7	28.7	16.0	5.5	5.3	50.3	94
B51	West Yorkshire	5.4	28.8	10.2	31.9	15.0	4.8	3.9	51.7	103
B61	Leeds	6.3	28.8	12.9	30.1	13.6	4.9	3.5	48.6	83
B71	Wakefield	4.3	23.5	10.4	36.9	16.5	5.5	3.0	58.9	137
C01	North Derbyshire	5.8	28.5	10.0	33.9	14.4	5.0	2.4	53.3	111
C02	Southern Derbyshire	6.9	27.1	10.1	33.8	14.1	4.8	3.1	52.7	106
C03	Leicestershire	6.8	29.8	10.8	30.7	14.7	3.8	3.4	49.2	86
C04	North Lincolnshire	5.7	29.0	10.5	29.5	14.2	4.2	6.9	47.9	79
C05	South Lincolnshire	4.6	28.8	9.2	30.5	16.4	4.5	6.0	51.4	101

CEN - D2
Social class as defined by occupation of head of household
Percentage distribution

		I	II	IIIN	IIIM	IV	V	Other	Manual group (IIIM, IV & V)	
									Percent	Rank
C08	Nottingham	6.6	29.1	11.3	29.7	14.5	4.6	4.2	48.8	84
C09	Barnsley	3.9	21.0	9.1	37.1	17.8	6.7	4.4	61.6	143
C10	Doncaster	3.5	23.1	9.9	35.2	17.0	5.5	5.8	57.7	129
C11	Rotherham	4.1	22.5	9.9	37.3	15.8	6.1	4.3	59.2	138
C12	Sheffield	7.2	25.7	10.8	31.0	14.9	5.2	5.3	51.0	99
C14	North Nottinghamshire	4.3	25.5	9.0	37.1	16.4	4.6	3.1	58.1	131
D01	Cambridge	12.7	35.8	10.6	22.6	11.6	3.4	3.2	37.7	23
D05	North West Anglia	4.2	27.0	10.7	30.4	17.1	4.1	6.5	51.6	102
D06	Norwich	6.1	30.7	12.0	28.4	14.1	4.2	4.5	46.7	69
D07	Great Yarmouth and Waveney	4.4	26.6	10.8	34.5	15.2	5.4	3.1	55.1	119
D09	Huntingdon	7.2	35.0	9.5	23.8	12.0	2.7	9.8	38.5	28
D11	Suffolk	6.5	29.4	10.4	27.9	13.9	4.5	7.4	46.3	63
E01	North Bedfordshire	9.2	35.9	10.9	25.6	11.1	3.5	3.9	40.2	35
E02	South Bedfordshire	6.1	28.2	12.0	31.2	15.7	3.7	3.1	50.6	96
E05	North West Hertfordshire	11.2	42.3	12.0	20.7	9.2	2.9	1.7	32.8	9
E06	South West Hertfordshire	9.3	37.2	14.4	23.5	9.7	2.9	3.1	36.0	17
E07	Barnet	12.2	41.4	15.4	17.3	7.3	2.1	4.2	26.8	4
E09	Hillingdon	7.1	30.4	14.7	28.6	10.5	4.4	4.3	43.6	47
E18	East and North Hertfordshire	8.8	35.9	13.2	25.9	11.7	3.0	1.5	40.7	36
E19	Brent and Harrow	8.6	33.1	16.2	24.8	9.3	3.3	4.8	37.3	19
E20	Ealing, Hammersmith and Hounslow	7.9	33.8	15.9	21.4	11.5	5.0	4.5	37.9	25
E21	Kensington, Chelsea and Westminster	11.6	42.5	13.1	12.5	8.7	4.3	7.3	25.5	3
F31	North Essex	7.4	34.8	13.0	27.0	11.6	3.8	2.4	42.4	44
F32	South Essex	5.3	32.3	14.6	29.8	11.9	4.0	2.0	45.7	59
F33	Barking and Havering	3.2	25.5	16.6	33.6	13.8	4.9	2.3	52.3	105
F34	Redbridge and Waltham Forest	5.7	31.8	17.1	25.3	12.0	3.5	4.5	40.8	39
F35	East London and the City	4.2	21.4	12.5	24.3	18.6	6.9	12.1	49.8	89
F36	New River District	7.1	31.6	14.5	25.1	12.1	4.0	5.7	41.1	40
F37	Camden and Islington	10.5	34.4	13.5	16.4	11.3	5.8	7.9	33.6	11
G04	South East Kent	5.5	30.5	11.7	29.2	14.8	4.4	4.0	48.3	82
G05	Canterbury and Thanet	6.2	30.8	12.6	29.0	13.0	5.1	3.4	47.0	73
G06	Dartford and Gravesham	5.4	30.8	13.8	31.9	11.6	4.2	2.3	47.7	77
G07	Maidstone	7.3	37.2	12.6	26.4	10.6	3.7	2.1	40.7	36
G08	Medway	4.9	26.4	12.3	34.6	13.8	4.7	3.2	53.1	109
G09	Tunbridge Wells	9.3	43.3	11.9	20.9	9.8	3.4	1.5	34.1	13
G10	Bexley	5.1	30.1	18.5	30.2	9.9	3.6	2.6	43.7	48
G11	Greenwich	5.1	26.9	14.9	26.1	14.1	6.1	6.8	46.4	65
G12	Bromley	9.0	41.4	17.1	20.4	7.0	2.6	2.5	30.0	5
G21	East Sussex	7.5	36.5	14.1	24.6	10.9	4.1	2.4	39.6	32
G26	South East London	6.9	29.5	15.6	20.4	12.8	6.0	8.9	39.1	30

267

CEN - D2
Social class as defined by occupation of head of household
Percentage distribution

		I	II	IIIN	IIIM	IV	V	Other	Manual group (IIIM, IV & V)	
									Percent	Rank
H04	Mid Surrey	13.4	47.3	13.3	16.7	6.1	1.7	1.6	24.4	1
H05	East Surrey	10.2	41.8	13.1	21.6	8.4	3.0	1.9	33.0	10
H06	Chichester	7.0	36.0	11.3	25.7	13.1	3.7	3.3	42.5	45
H07	Mid Downs	8.7	38.7	13.6	23.2	10.5	4.0	1.5	37.6	22
H08	Worthing	7.9	35.2	14.0	25.4	11.5	3.8	2.2	40.7	36
H09	Croydon	7.8	36.1	17.0	23.8	9.0	3.1	3.1	35.9	16
H12	Wandsworth	9.7	37.7	16.4	16.8	9.8	4.5	5.0	31.2	6
H13	Merton and Sutton	8.8	34.9	16.8	24.8	9.2	3.3	2.2	37.3	19
H14	North West Surrey	10.5	39.9	13.4	22.3	8.6	3.0	2.3	33.9	12
H15	South West Surrey	12.9	41.9	11.5	19.7	8.7	2.9	2.4	31.3	7
H16	Kingston and Richmond	12.9	45.7	14.2	15.6	6.8	2.5	2.3	24.9	2
J10	Dorset	7.1	31.9	12.3	27.0	13.3	3.6	4.9	43.9	50
J21	Portsmouth and South East Hampshire	7.4	29.4	11.4	26.0	12.1	4.2	9.5	42.3	42
J22	Southampton and South West Hampshire	7.3	31.4	12.8	27.6	13.6	4.6	2.7	45.9	60
J23	Winchester	9.8	35.9	11.3	23.7	10.9	3.1	5.3	37.7	23
J24	Basingstoke and North Hampshire	10.0	36.0	11.1	23.5	10.5	3.0	5.8	37.0	18
J31	Salisbury	7.4	31.0	12.0	23.2	11.8	4.1	10.4	39.1	30
J32	Swindon	5.7	29.9	12.6	25.5	15.4	4.2	6.6	45.1	53
J33	Bath	7.4	32.3	10.2	29.1	12.1	4.0	4.9	45.2	55
J41	Isle of Wight	6.0	29.2	11.5	28.3	16.5	5.3	3.1	50.1	90
K11	East Berkshire	9.3	37.1	11.6	24.1	11.4	3.2	3.2	38.8	29
K12	West Berkshire	11.5	39.9	11.1	22.2	9.3	3.4	2.7	34.9	15
K24	Buckinghamshire	8.7	39.3	11.6	24.3	10.1	3.0	3.1	37.4	21
K31	Kettering	4.5	27.8	10.6	35.2	15.4	4.2	2.3	54.8	115
K32	Northampton	6.2	32.7	11.8	28.9	13.5	4.1	2.9	46.4	65
K41	Oxfordshire	9.9	33.0	10.3	24.3	12.5	4.3	5.7	41.1	40
L10	Bristol and District	8.2	31.8	13.2	27.7	12.4	3.8	3.0	43.9	50
L21	Cornwall and Isles of Scilly	4.9	29.1	10.7	29.5	13.4	5.0	7.3	48.0	81
L35	Exeter and North Devon	6.1	33.2	11.4	28.1	12.9	4.5	3.7	45.5	56
L36	Plymouth and Torbay	5.7	28.1	11.9	27.8	13.6	4.7	8.2	46.1	62
L40	Gloucestershire	8.1	33.0	11.8	25.9	13.9	4.1	3.3	43.8	49
L51	Somerset	6.5	32.2	10.7	28.7	13.6	4.4	3.9	46.7	69
M02	Herefordshire	5.3	33.5	9.5	28.4	15.0	3.6	4.6	47.1	75
M04	Worcester and District	7.8	35.6	11.1	26.1	13.4	3.6	2.3	43.2	46
M05	Shropshire	5.6	31.5	10.2	28.8	15.9	4.6	3.5	49.3	87
M06	Mid Staffordshire	6.2	33.1	11.8	31.0	12.4	3.2	2.4	46.6	68
M07	North Staffordshire	3.9	22.9	9.5	40.6	14.8	5.5	2.8	60.9	142
M08	South East Staffordshire	5.7	31.1	9.7	32.9	14.1	4.0	2.3	51.1	100
M13	East Birmingham	2.1	14.4	10.7	35.8	21.1	5.6	10.3	62.6	144
M14	North Birmingham	8.6	33.8	13.3	25.3	11.9	2.9	4.1	40.1	34
M16	West Birmingham	3.4	15.9	9.9	33.1	19.8	5.3	12.7	58.2	134
M17	Coventry	6.9	22.6	10.7	31.3	19.2	4.2	5.1	54.8	115

268

CEN - D2
Social class as defined by occupation of head of household
Percentage distribution

		I	II	IIIN	IIIM	IV	V	Other	Manual group (IIIM, IV & V) Percent	Rank
M18	Dudley	5.0	26.3	10.6	36.5	13.9	3.8	4.0	54.2	113
M19	Sandwell	2.8	15.8	9.3	40.3	19.5	5.3	7.0	65.1	145
M20	Solihull	9.3	37.3	12.3	24.7	10.9	2.5	3.0	38.1	26
M21	Walsall	3.8	22.3	9.9	38.7	14.9	4.4	6.0	58.1	131
M22	Wolverhampton	4.0	21.5	9.0	37.7	16.4	4.4	7.0	58.5	136
M25	South Birmingham	7.6	23.9	10.9	27.9	17.5	4.8	7.3	50.2	92
M26	North Worcestershire	6.6	33.4	10.0	29.4	14.6	3.5	2.5	47.4	76
M28	Warwickshire	8.0	32.4	10.9	28.6	14.3	3.4	2.4	46.3	63
N11	Chester	8.3	29.3	12.1	26.5	15.9	4.4	3.5	46.8	71
N12	Crewe	7.2	33.0	10.0	28.4	15.3	4.1	2.0	47.8	78
N13	Halton	5.3	23.0	8.8	33.7	19.4	5.1	4.7	58.1	131
N14	Macclesfield	12.2	44.2	10.2	20.2	9.0	2.9	1.4	32.0	8
N15	Warrington	8.3	30.1	12.4	29.9	13.4	3.5	2.5	46.8	71
N21	Liverpool	4.2	19.5	12.1	28.4	17.6	7.2	11.0	53.2	110
N31	St Helens and Knowsley	3.2	21.4	10.1	35.6	16.6	5.4	7.6	57.7	129
N41	Southport and Formby	7.5	41.6	14.0	22.5	9.6	2.2	2.6	34.3	14
N42	South Sefton	4.0	25.8	15.0	30.6	13.3	5.4	5.9	49.3	87
N51	Wirral	8.1	29.9	12.5	26.6	13.8	4.2	5.0	44.5	52
P01	Lancaster	7.1	28.4	13.3	28.4	14.1	5.4	3.2	47.9	79
P02	Blackpool,Wyre and Fylde	6.1	30.3	14.5	27.8	13.7	4.6	3.2	46.0	61
P03	Preston	6.6	26.3	13.1	27.2	16.1	6.8	3.9	50.1	90
P04	Blackburn, Hyndburn and Ribble Valley	5.1	27.3	9.5	33.3	16.0	4.5	4.4	53.7	112
P05	Burnley, Pendle and Rossendale	4.5	26.2	11.3	33.7	16.5	4.4	3.4	54.6	114
P06	West Lancashire	7.4	33.1	10.6	28.2	14.0	3.4	3.4	45.6	57
P07	Chorley and South Ribble	6.9	32.4	13.1	28.4	13.5	3.7	2.1	45.6	57
P08	Bolton	5.7	27.0	12.5	31.0	14.5	5.4	4.0	50.8	98
P09	Bury	6.8	31.7	12.9	30.1	12.6	3.7	2.2	46.4	65
P10	North Manchester	2.0	17.5	13.2	28.4	21.4	8.4	9.1	58.2	134
P11	Central Manchester	4.1	18.2	10.6	27.8	20.0	8.2	10.9	56.1	125
P12	South Manchester	8.6	27.3	12.5	23.4	15.0	6.7	6.5	45.1	53
P13	Oldham	4.3	24.7	11.6	34.0	16.7	4.9	3.7	55.7	124
P14	Rochdale	4.7	26.4	12.5	31.3	16.2	5.2	3.8	52.7	106
P15	Salford	4.7	24.2	12.0	30.8	17.9	6.2	4.1	55.0	118
P16	Stockport	10.1	35.7	13.9	24.9	10.3	2.9	2.2	38.1	26
P17	Tameside and Glossop	4.2	25.6	12.2	34.8	15.1	4.9	3.1	54.8	115
P18	Trafford	9.5	33.1	15.2	25.2	10.8	3.6	2.7	39.6	32
P19	Wigan	4.7	24.1	11.8	36.3	15.3	5.1	2.6	56.8	127